▸▸ Wizards and Visual De

Visual FoxPro's Wizards let you creat
(Chapter 4), Reports (Chapter 6), Mailing Labels (Chapter 7), and other files by filling out a series of forms, each with explanations in plain English. Visual Designers let you design these files yourself or customize those you've created using the Wizards (Chapter 17).

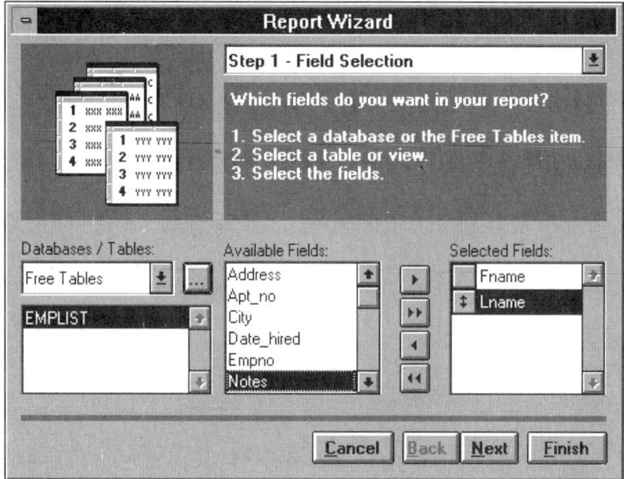

The Report Wizard

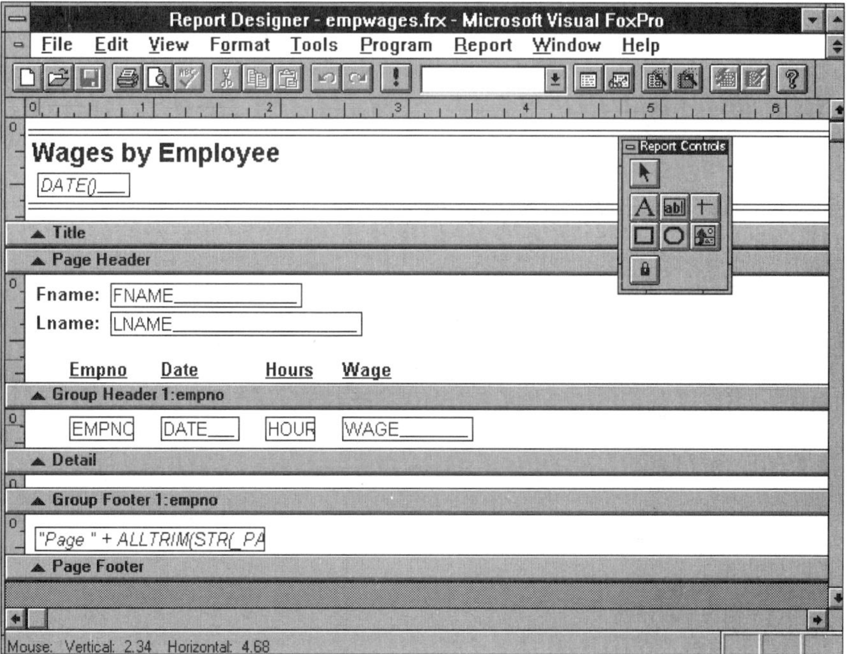

The Report Designer

Mastering Visual FoxPro® 3 Special Edition

Third Edition

Charles Siegel

SanFrancisco ▲ Paris ▼ Düsseldorf ▲ Soest

Acquisitions Manager: Kristine Plachy
Developmental Editor: Melanie Spiller
Editor: James A. Compton
Technical Editors: David Goyne, Tom Palke
Book Designer: Suzanne Albertson
Chapter Artist: Helen Bruno
Desktop Publisher: Deborah A. Bevilacqua
Proofreader/Production Assistant: Taris Duffié
Indexer: Matthew Spence
Cover Designer: DesignSite
Cover Illustrator/Photographer: Mark Johann

Screen reproductions produced with Collage Plus.

Library of Congress Card Number: 95-67725

ISBN: 0-7821-1647-7

Manufactured in the United States of America

10 9 8 7 6 5 4 3 2

▸▸ Acknowledgements

I would like to thank all the people at SYBEX who have helped take this book through its various editions: Dianne King, David Clark, Doug Robert, David Peal, Michelle Nance, Dusty Bernard, Maurice Frank, Jim Compton, and many others. Special thanks to Stephen Wheeler.

Contents at a Glance

Table of Contents

▶▶ Introduction

Whether you are a beginner at using computer database programs or a seasoned DBMS user, this book will give you a solid understanding of Visual FoxPro 3.0 for Windows and will teach you everything you need to know in managing your own data. Starting with the very basics, you will quickly progress, through step-by-step tutorials, to creating a sample database and using all of Visual FoxPro's major features.

▶▶ Is This Book for You?

This book is designed for a wide variety of readers.

It is meant for beginners who want a quick but thorough introduction to Visual FoxPro, for power users who want to work with its more advanced features, and for people who want to learn enough Visual FoxPro programming to customize the interface and to manipulate data in any way they want. It is not meant for developers, and it does not cover advanced programming techniques that ordinary Visual FoxPro users will never need.

This book is based on actual experience as a consultant helping end users work with FoxPro to manage their own businesses. You can use it to get started using Visual FoxPro in the quickest and easiest way possible. Or you can go on to learn all the features of Visual FoxPro that most users call on consultants to help them with.

▶▶ How This Book Is Organized

This book includes many step-by-step exercises. Because the work you do in these exercises typically builds upon work you did in earlier chapters, it is best to start at the beginning of Part I and actually work through its examples.

Part One of the book—the first eight chapters—is a tutorial on the features of Visual FoxPro that are essential for ordinary business users. It is called "Up and Running" because it is meant to get you started with the program as quickly as possible. If you just want to learn the fundamentals of Visual FoxPro, you can just read this section and get down to work. Use the later sections for reference.

Part Two of this book teaches you to tap the power of Visual FoxPro by working with the Command window. While you can do many things by making menu selections and using Wizards, you can do much more—and do some things more easily—if you take the extra time to learn the basics of the FoxPro language.

Part Three covers relational databases. Earlier parts of the book deal only with simple databases that can be kept in a single table. However, most business applications involve more complex data, which must be stored in multiple tables. Chapter 12, at the beginning of Part Three, covers the basics of relational database theory, and teaches you common-sense methods of recognizing when data should be stored in multiple tables rather than in a single table. Everyone should read this chapter to avoid the problems that arise if you try to store complex data in a single table. The rest of Part Three covers the different methods that Visual FoxPro offers for working with multiple-table databases.

Part Four teaches you to use Visual FoxPro power tools, such as the Report and Label Designers and the Macro Recorder. Learn these features of Visual FoxPro to customize the reports and labels that you create using the Wizards, which were covered in Part I, and to add more ease and power to your work.

Part Five is an introduction to programming and developing simple applications. It begins with a thorough tutorial on the sort of procedural programming that ordinary users need to manipulate their data; once you have read this tutorial, you should be able to create the sort of utility programs that most users must find consultants to program for them. It also covers the Menu Designer, which you can use to create custom menu systems, and the Project Manager, which makes it easier to manage complex applications that include many files and also lets you compile these applications into a single APP or EXE file.

This book does not cover features of the Visual FoxPro interface or language that are of interest only to developers who are creating complete turnkey systems or commercial programs. Instead, it is aimed at people who use Visual FoxPro to manage their own businesses, and who want to use all of its power to work with their own data—without being distracted by the advanced features intended solely for professional developers. It does give you a thorough grounding in the basics of programming, enough background to let you go on to more advanced books that teach object-oriented development in Visual FoxPro.

The Visual FoxPro language is so extensive that it is hard for anyone to learn it all. It includes all of the Xbase language, as it grew over the years, plus much more. Even experienced programmers can browse through the reference manual and suddenly be surprised to learn a new command or function that gives them an easier way of doing things they have done for years. The basic features of the Visual FoxPro interface and language that you need to know, on the other hand, are not difficult to use: You can never finish learning Visual FoxPro, but with this book, you will find it easy to begin.

►► Conventions Used in This Book

►► **NOTE**

The Note icon points out additional information or reiterates the importance of a point made in the text.

►► **TIP**

The Tip icon flags a different, faster, or easier way of doing something.

►► **WARNING**

The Warning icon warns you of potential problems.

The text itself uses boldface type in procedures to denote commands and other words you are instructed to type at the keyboard. Command keywords (words that are part of the Visual FoxPro language) are all uppercase. Descriptions of information that should appear in a command are shown enclosed by angle brackets (less-than and greater-than signs); these words, and the brackets themselves, should be replaced by actual values when you use the command. For example, if a command includes <file name>, you must type the name of an actual file.

This book also uses a special notation to indicate selections from menus. For example, to indicate that you should choose Cut from the Edit menu, this book says, "Choose Edit ➤ Cut," and to indicate that you should choose Paste from the Edit menu, this book says, "Choose Edit ➤ Paste."

PART ONE

Up and Running

CHAPTER 1

Getting Started

▸▸ *Visual FoxPro 3.0* is the latest version of FoxPro, which many people consider the most important database product to appear in many years. This chapter first gives you some background in database theory and a brief history of FoxPro, so that you can understand what the program is designed to do. The second half of the chapter presents a general overview of the FoxPro interface.

▸▸ Database Fundamentals

When businesses began to computerize their record keeping during the 1960s, computer scientists developed theories about how to redesign the data that used to be kept in paper files so it could be managed more efficiently on computer. In many cases, they simply used new terms in order to speak more precisely about the same sorts of things people had always used when they worked with paper files. In other cases, though, they developed entirely new ways of handling data that had not been possible before computers were used.

▸ Simple Databases

A simple database is organized in much the same way that data has always been organized on paper.

A typical file in an old-fashioned office was made up of a collection of identical forms, each with blank spaces where information was supposed to be filled in. A common example is a list of names kept on a collection of index cards, each of which is printed to show you where to fill out the name, address, city, state, ZIP code, and telephone number. Most data was kept on larger forms that went into file folders, but the basic principle was the same: A standard form would be preprinted to indicate the type of data that was needed, and there were blank spaces where you had to fill in the actual data.

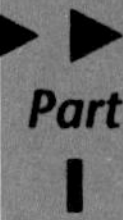

Simple databases are organized in the same way. All you need to learn are the new terms that describe them once they have been computerized:

- **Field:** Each blank space is called a *field*. In the index card database mentioned above, there is one field for the name, one field for the address, and so on.
- **Record:** All the data that would appear on a single form is called a *record*. In our example, the name, address, and phone number of one person makes up one record.
- **File or table:** A collection of similar records that are used together is called a *file* or *table*. In our example, the whole box of index cards holding all the names and addresses you use together make up a file. Of course, you could also have another file with similar records—just as you could have another box of index cards where you keep another list of names and addresses.

These are the three basic terms you will hear repeatedly when people are talking about databases. They are illustrated in Figure 1.1, which shows how database terminology would be used to describe the old-fashioned index card file.

FIGURE 1.1

Database terminology

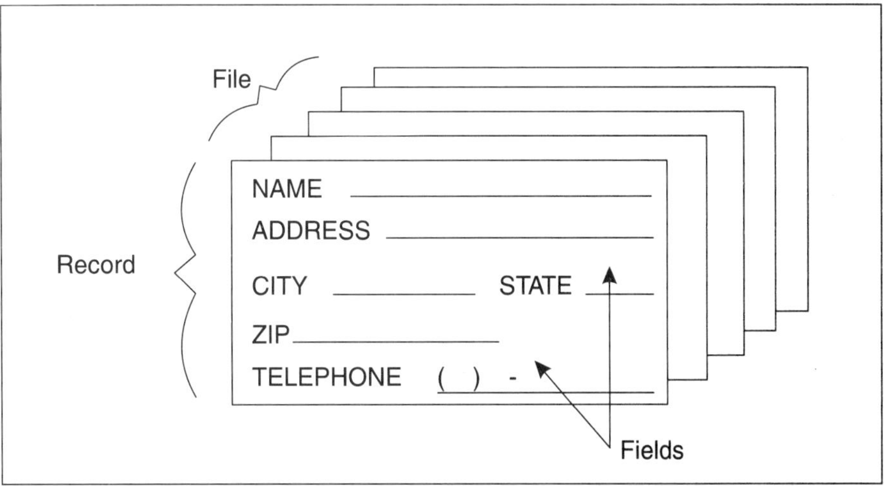

A computer lets you display your data either as *data entry forms* showing one record at a time, with one form for each person, or as a *table* showing many records at once, with a column for the name, a column for the address, and so on, so that the data for each person can be listed on one line. When the data is arranged as a table, each column represents a field, each line represents a record, and the table as a whole represents the file.

Because it is so common to arrange data in tabular form, database files are generally called *tables*.

► Relational Databases

Some of the advantages of computerizing data are obvious:

- A computer can instantly look up the data you want—for example, the telephone number of a certain person.
- It can print the data in different forms, saving you the trouble of copying it from the list in the form you need—for example, as a list of names and phone numbers when you want to call people and as labels when you want to do a mailing.
- It can instantly select specific records from the file—for example, it can list the names and phone numbers of only the people who live in New York, or it can print mailing labels for only the people who live in New Jersey.
- It lets you use the data in different orders—for example, you can effortlessly print your mailing labels in ZIP-code order and print your list of names and phone numbers in alphabetical order.
- It can merge the name and address from each record into a form letter and print copies of the letter addressed to all the people in the table—or all the people who meet some criterion that you specify, such as accounts more than 30 days overdue.

In addition to these obvious advantages of computerizing data, early computer scientists found a more subtle advantage: They found that computers made it possible to avoid repetitive data.

In the days of the paper office, for example, a typical large business had dozens of different forms that included the name and address of each employee. The Payroll department used a form with the name, address, and wages of each employee; the Benefits department used a form with the name, address, and eligibility for benefits of each employee; the Human Resources Development department used a form with the name, address, and training courses taken by each employee; and so on.

This repetition was obviously inefficient. The same name and address—and, of course, other basic information such as social security number and telephone number—had to be filled out over and over. If an employee moved, a dozen different people in a dozen different departments had to change the address on a dozen different forms.

Repetition could not be avoided in a paper office, but computer scientists quickly devised ways to let a business enter the names and addresses only once and let each department use those names and addresses in combination with the specific data that it needed about wages, benefits, training courses, or whatever.

Early methods used for tying together all this data were very complex and unwieldy. There were hierarchically organized databases and databases organized as networks that were held together using pointers, both of which were so complicated they could only be understood and used by programmers with training in database theory. Companies needed teams of programmers just to retrieve information or produce reports.

Relational Basics

In 1970, E. F. Codd invented a new way of tying together this sort of data, which was called the *relational* database. His idea was to break down the data into separate files that could be related by using a common key field.

In the example you have been looking at, the business would probably use an employee number as a key field. Each employee would be given a unique number, and there would be one file with general information on each employee, such as the employee number, name, address, and other basic data. There would be another file with each employee's employee number and wages, another file with each employee's employee number and eligibility for benefits, and so on. Basic information such as the name and address would have to appear only once. Each department would have a program that used the employee number to relate the data it needed on wages or benefits to the basic data that everyone needed.

With relational databases, most of the work of relating the data was built into the database management program. You did not need programmers to create pointers to relate one record to another. You just had to enter the right employee number and wage in one file, and the database management system would do the work of relating that record to the record that had the name and address for that employee number.

Codd analyzed the relational database using mathematical set theory and discovered ways to minimize repetition by breaking down the data. Because they were both powerful and simple to visualize and use, relational databases quickly became the preferred method of handling complex data.

In simple databases—for example, the simple list of names and addresses that could be kept on index cards—there is no distinction between the database and the table; a simple database consists of only one table. Relational databases, though, consist of more than one table. Thus, we can add one more term to our list of definitions. A *database* consists of all the data used together in an application, whether it is kept in one table or many.

►► dBASE versus Visual FoxPro

When the IBM PC and compatibles became popular during the 1980s, dBASE II, developed by Ashton-Tate, quickly emerged as the leading database management program. A couple of simpler programs had some brief popularity because they were so easy to use, but none of them let you manage more than a simple database, like the basic list of names and addresses you could keep on index cards. dBASE II let you work with either a simple or a relational database.

dBASE's interactive commands let business users create, edit, and print reports on databases. dBASE also included a programming language that was relatively easy to learn and use, and programmers used it to create menu-driven custom applications for their clients. Business

users who did not want to bother learning about dBASE could have programmers set up their applications for them so they could just make choices from menus and edit data or print exactly the reports they needed. It was quicker and easier to do this programming in dBASE than in other computer languages because dBASE was specifically designed for this sort of task.

Because of its power, dBASE was by far the most popular database management system for microcomputers. At the high point of its popularity, it was estimated that 80 to 85 percent of all database applications on IBM PC and compatible microcomputers used dBASE. dBASE became an industry standard. Even unrelated database programs were designed so they could use dBASE tables.

dBASE II was followed by dBASE III and dBASE III+, both of which added power without overcoming some basic limitations of the product.

In response to users' complaints, a couple of companies that were not related to Ashton-Tate came up with improved versions of the dBASE language. One of these was Fox Software, which developed FoxBASE, a dBASE-compatible development system. The next stage was FoxPro, a program designed for database users as well as developers. FoxPro was a major advance over FoxBASE, both because it added a modern interface based on windows, drop-down menus, and dialog boxes and because it added many extensions to the programming language.

You can see that different dialects of dBASE were emerging, as several new programs emerged that enhanced the original dBASE language and differed from it in minor ways. As more enhancements appeared, the dBASE standard became diffuse. Ashton-Tate (eventually acquired by Borland) could no longer define what was the standard dBASE language. Programmers now use the term Xbase to refer generally to all of the dBASE-compatible programming languages.

Because of the failings of dBASE IV and dBASE for Windows, FoxPro has become the most important dialect of the Xbase language. It became even better established when Fox Software was acquired by Microsoft, which decided to make Xbase one of the three major languages it will continue to support, along with C/C++ and BASIC.

When the first version of FoxPro came out, users appreciated how easy its interface was to use, and developers appreciated the many extensions that it added to the Xbase language.

Version 2 of FoxPro added Fox's *Rushmore* technology, which tests have shown can make some queries run hundreds of times faster than in competing products. For programmers, version 2 of FoxPro added many features—most impressively, a menu and screen builder that make it easy to create drop-down menus and dialog boxes; even intermediate-level programmers could create an impressive user interface with mouse support.

Beginning with version 2.5, FoxPro began to provide virtually identical programs for four major operating environments: Windows, DOS, UNIX, and the Macintosh. Because of differences among these operating environments, there had to be some differences among these four versions of FoxPro, but these are relatively minor. All of these versions have many advantages of Windows—a graphical interface and common features shared with many other applications, making the program easy to use. But FoxPro for Windows has other advantages that are not available in the other environments, such as the ability to share data easily with other applications by using simple cut-and-paste techniques or the more sophisticated techniques of Object Linking and Embedding. Users can now move among these platforms without much training, and developers can easily create applications that run on all of these platforms.

This book focuses on Visual FoxPro 3.0, the newest version of the software.

Version 3.0 is the first completely new version of FoxPro released since Microsoft acquired Fox Software. It includes Wizards, like those in other Microsoft products, which make it easy to create tables, queries, reports, mailing labels, and other types of files. It also adds advanced features such as object-oriented programming and database schemas, making it a more powerful tool for application developers.

As you can see, FoxPro has evolved in two directions: toward greater ease of use for beginners and toward more sophisticated features for developers. Early versions of dBASE required users to enter the same commands used by developers; you had to learn the language before you could begin to use the product, and a user just needed to learn a few extra commands to begin programming. Now, Visual FoxPro 3.0 has drop-down menus and Wizards that even a beginner can use, its language includes object-oriented commands that are meant for advanced developers, and it has a range of features in between that let you use it on many different levels of sophistication.

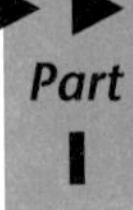

▶▶ A Quick Tour of Visual FoxPro

Since Part I of this book is meant to get you started using Visual Fox-Pro in the easiest way possible, you should begin with a quick tour of the FoxPro interface. We'll look at both the basic features that you must understand to use the program and some of the advanced features that you should avoid at first.

▶▶ NOTE

If you do not know how to make menu selections, use dialog boxes, and use the basic features of the Windows interface, such as the Notepad text editor, see one of the many excellent introductory Windows books before you go on with the rest of this chapter. Some hands-on practice using Windows will also be helpful. This book assumes only that you know the Windows basics; and if you have used other Windows applications you should have no trouble learning to use Visual FoxPro.

▶ The Menu System

The menu system that is displayed when you start Visual FoxPro, shown in Figure 1.2, is similar to that of other Windows applications, and is easy to understand.

The File menu is used, as in other Windows applications, to create, open, close, save, and print files. As in other applications, choosing File ➤ Exit lets you quit Visual FoxPro. The File menu also includes an Import and Export command, which let you share data with other applications.

Likewise, the Edit menu is used for the same editing functions as in other Windows applications, such as Cut or Copy and Paste, and includes the special Edit options for working with OLE objects that are also common in many Windows applications (and are covered in Chapter 22 of this book). It also includes Find and Replace and Goto, which let you move through a file.

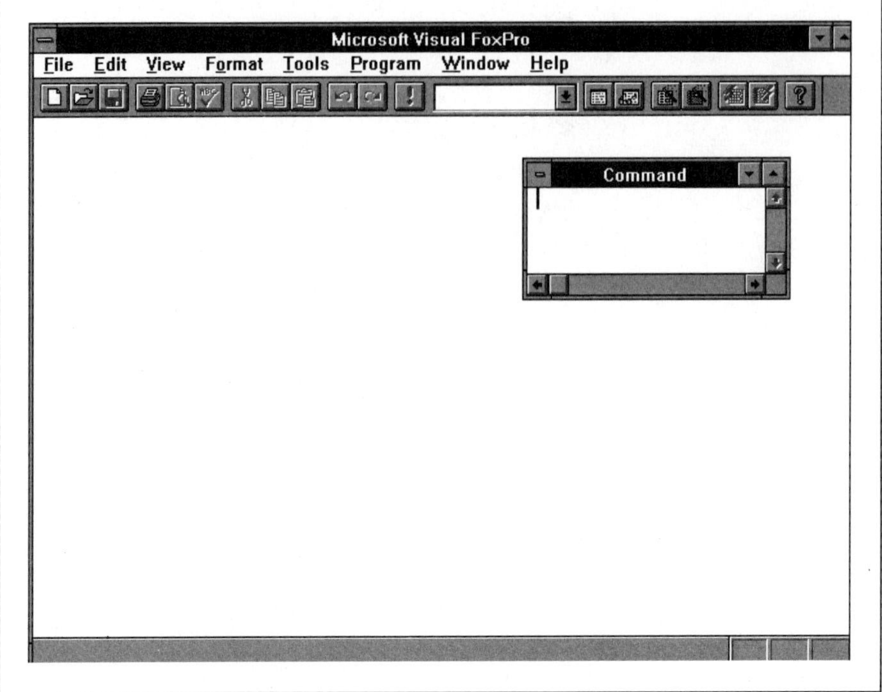

FIGURE 1.2

The initial Visual FoxPro screen

If no files are open, the View menu includes only the command Toolbars, which lets you customize toolbars. However, after you open a table, it contains an option that lets you view the data in the table, and after you have begun viewing the data, it also includes options that let you work with the data. Thus, you will find this menu very important in your work.

A Table menu is also added when you view data, and it gives you other options for working with data.

The Format menu let you format text—for example, to determine its font and spacing.

The Tools menu includes a few tools that everyone can use; it lets you use the Wizards (we'll look at them a little later in this chapter), the Spelling tool (discussed in Chapter 22), and the Macro Recorder (discussed in Chapter 21). It also includes a few tools that are meant only for programmers: the Trace window and Debug window, both of which are used for debugging programs. Finally, the Tools ➤ Options command displays the Options dialog box, which lets you customize many features of Visual FoxPro.

The Program menu lets you run programs, stop programs that are running, and compile programs.

The Window menu lets you switch among document windows, as it does in all Windows applications.

The Help menu lets you use the Help system, as it does in other Windows applications. It's an important tool for getting oriented as you learn to use the program; we'll take a quick look at it in the next section.

In summary, then:

- The File, Edit, Window, and Help menus are used as they are in other Windows applications.
- The Tools, Program, and Format menus let you use utilities.
- The View menu is used for viewing the data in a table that you have already opened using the File menu and for working with that data.
- The Table menu that is added when you open a table is also used for working with data.
- Other menus, such as a Report menu and Query menu, are also added when you are designing other types of files.

If you keep this overview in mind, it should be easy for you to navigate Visual FoxPro's menus.

Getting Help

The Visual FoxPro for Windows Help system gives you several ways of getting help, which are also available in other Windows applications:

- Context-sensitive help: gives you help on the feature you are currently using.
- Contents: lets you start with general topics and search for more specific topics.
- Search: lets you search for keywords alphabetically to find the topic you want.

In addition to these features of its conventional Windows Help system, Visual FoxPro has a second, entirely different Help facility, called DBF Help, which is meant for more advanced users and is covered in Chapter 19.

You can get context-sensitive information on the current window or dialog box at any time by pressing F1. If you want help on a menu option, first press Shift+F1 and then select the option.

If you select Help ➤ Contents, Visual FoxPro displays the initial table of contents for the Help system, which lists very general topics, such as *Language Reference*. Select from this table to display more specific topics, such as *Commands and Functions by Category*. Keep making these selections to narrow down the topic until you reach the specific topic you want. You can select underlined topics in this way, or select topics with a dotted underline to display a definition of those topics.

You can return to the previous list by selecting the Back pushbutton, return to the initial table of contents by selecting the Contents pushbutton, select from a history of all the options you chose by selecting the History pushbutton, or search for topics by selecting the Search pushbutton. This displays the same Search dialog box you can display by selecting Help ➤ Search for Help.

In the Search dialog box, you search through an alphabetical list of help topics (rather than searching from more general to more specific, as you do using the Help table of contents). Scroll through this list, or type in the text box to automatically move the highlight to the topic you type. Typing searches cumulatively; if you type **D**, the list scrolls to the first *D* entry, and if you then type **E**, the list scrolls to the first topic beginning with *DE* (or the nearest thing to it on the list).

You can also print the help on a topic by selecting File ➤ Print, copy selected help text to the Clipboard by selecting Edit ➤ Copy, add your own notes on a topic by selecting Edit ➤ Annotate, and create a bookmark that lets you jump quickly to a frequently used topic by selecting Bookmark ➤ Define.

▸ File Types

You create and open files in Visual FoxPro as you do in other applications.

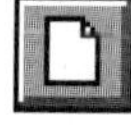

To create a new file, choose File ➤ New or click the New tool to display the New dialog box, shown in Figure 1.3.

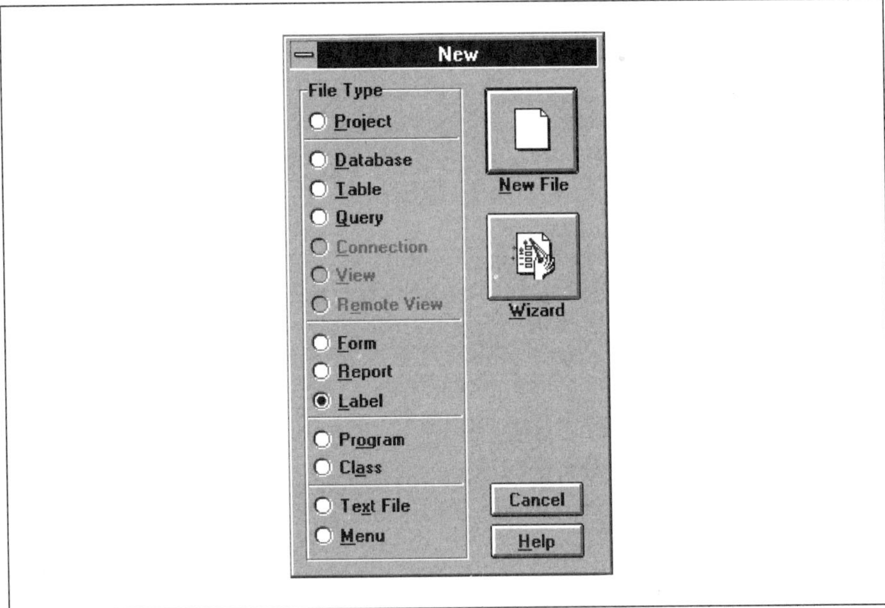

FIGURE 1.3

The New dialog box

As you can see, this dialog box includes radio buttons that let you create many different types of files, by selecting the radio button and clicking either the New File or the Wizard button.

When you create the basic types of files that are needed by every Visual FoxPro user and that are covered in Part I of this book, the Wizard button is enabled. You can design the file using either the Wizards or the Visual Designer for that file type. Wizards and Visual Designers are available for the following file types:

- **Table**: the file that is used to hold data. Chapter 2 shows how to create tables, and Chapter 3 shows how to work with data in them.
- **Query:** a file that is used to control which records and fields of a table are displayed, and the order in which records are displayed. A query lets you pull data out of a table in a form that is convenient to use. You'll begin working with queries in Chapter 4.
- **Form:** a file that contains a custom data-entry screen that makes it easy to view and work with data, as discussed in Chapter 5.

- **Report:** a file that contains the design of a printed report, as discussed in Chapters 6 and 17.
- **Label:** a file that contains specifications for mailing labels, as discussed in Chapters 7 and 17.

The following file types cannot be created using Wizards, and are not needed by beginners:

- **Project:** a file used to hold all of the other files used in an application. A project can be used to organize files to make them easier to work with. It is also used by developers to compile all these files into a stand-alone application. Chapter 25 discusses using the Project window.
- **Database:** a type of file that lets you create a database schema to define persistent relationships among the tables of a relational database. Chapter 16 discusses databases.
- **Connection**, **View**, and **Remote View:** files that you can create only when using a FoxPro database. A Connection file lets you name and save the specifications used to connect to a server on a network. View and Remote View files let you create updatable queries based on local and remote tables.
- **Program:** a plain text file used to hold Visual FoxPro programming code. Chapters 23–25 discuss programming.
- **Class:** in object-oriented programming, a file used to hold a class.
- **Text File:** a plain text file.
- **Menu:** a file used to hold the specifications of the menu system for a custom application. Chapter 24 discusses the Menu Designer.

As you can see, many of these file types, such as Class and Menu, are meant for advanced users and developers. Other types, such as Project and Database, are not essential to getting started with Visual FoxPro, but intermediate users may find it convenient to use them to organize their files and tables.

The Toolbars

In addition to its main toolbar, which is always displayed, Visual FoxPro includes a number of floating toolbars, which are displayed only at certain times.

The Main Toolbar

The main Visual FoxPro toolbar, shown in Figure 1.4, is also easy to understand. Only two of its features need explanation:

- The Run button is used to run programs. It is also used to work with some features of Visual FoxPro, such as Queries, that are actually programs.
- The Database drop-down list is used to select a Visual FoxPro database file. As noted earlier, the database file type is an advanced feature of Visual FoxPro, which is most useful when you work with relational databases and is covered in Chapter 16.

FIGURE 1.4

The main toolbar

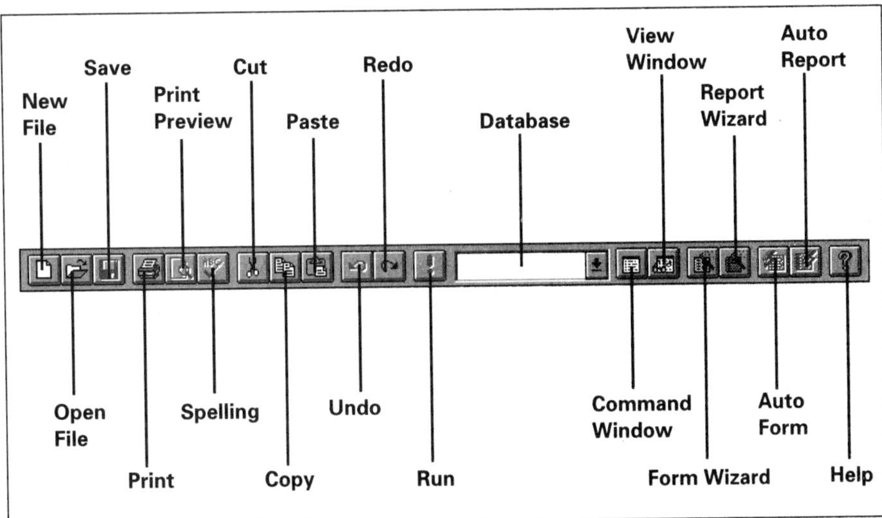

►► **NOTE**

All tables in Visual FoxPro are either part of a FoxPro database or are free tables. If a table is part of a FoxPro database, that database must be open and its name must be displayed in the Database drop-down list box before you can open the table. You can use free tables at any time. To get you started as quickly as possible, this book begins by using only free tables.

Of the remaining tools on the main toolbar, the Form Wizard, Report Wizard, AutoForm, and AutoReport tools give you access to features of the Visual Fox Pro interface that you'll be working with in Part I. The Command Window tool displays a window that lets you work with FoxPro by typing commands, and the View Window tool displays a window that lets you control properties of the table; both of these windows are discussed in Part II.

Floating Toolbars

Visual FoxPro also includes a number of floating toolbars, which are displayed only when you need them. For example, Figure 1.5 shows the Query Designer and the special toolbar that is displayed when you use it.

These toolbars always remain on top of other windows. You can move these toolbars by clicking and dragging and can close them by clicking the Close (–) button in the upper-left corner. They will be covered in later chapters of this book, which discuss the files they are used to design.

► Visual Designers and Wizards

You can create all of the basic files covered in Part I of this book by using either a Visual Designer or a Wizard.

Visual Designers are named for the type of file they are used to design—for example, the Table Designer, the Query Designer, and so on. Many Visual Designers have multiple panels, which you can display by clicking labeled tabs. For example, the Query Designer, shown in Figure 1.5, includes Selection Criteria, Fields, Order By, and Group By tabs, each used to define a different feature of the query.

FIGURE 1.5

The Query Designer and its toolbar

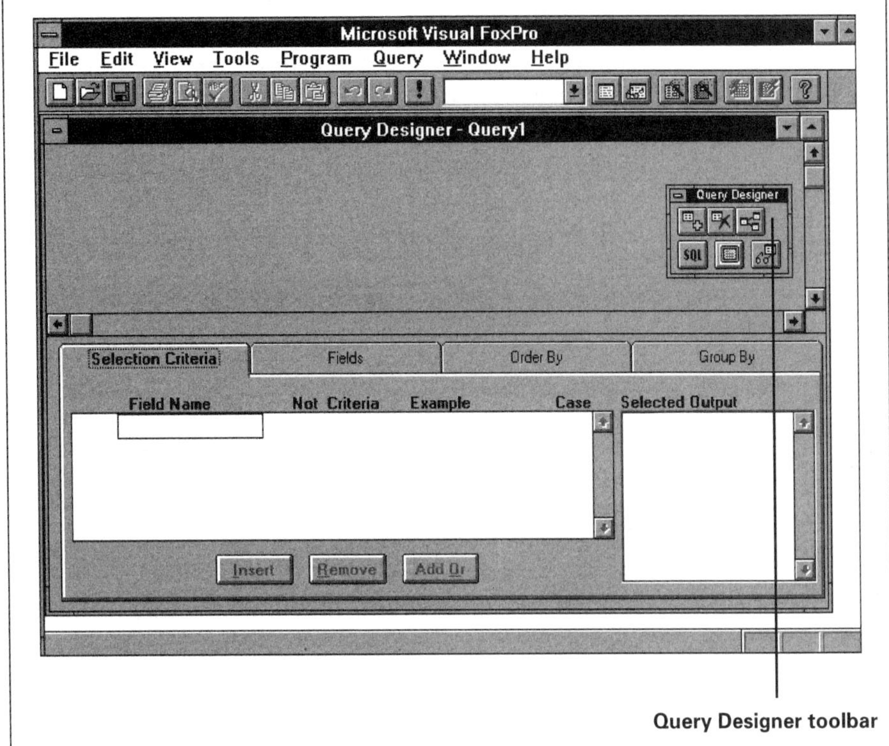

Using Wizards

Visual FoxPro Designers can be complex and difficult to understand. Wizards make it easy to create files by responding to a series of dialog boxes, with instructions in simple English. Visual FoxPro generates the design of the file on the basis of the selections you make. You can then use this file as-is or use the Visual Designer to modify it.

There are two ways of starting a Wizard: Either choose File ➤ New and click the Wizard button of the New dialog box, as described above, or choose Tools ➤ Wizards to display the submenu that lets you select among all available Wizards.

Some of the Wizards on this submenu do not create Visual FoxPro files, and so they are not available through the New dialog box. For example, you can select Tools ➤ Wizards ➤ Mail Merge to create Mail Merge files that can be used by word processing programs to create form letters based on data from Visual FoxPro.

If you select an object that can be created by several different Wizards, Visual FoxPro displays a dialog box that lets you select which of the available Wizards you want to use, as shown in Figure 1.6. After you make this selection, Visual FoxPro displays the Wizard itself.

FIGURE 1.6

Selecting a Wizard

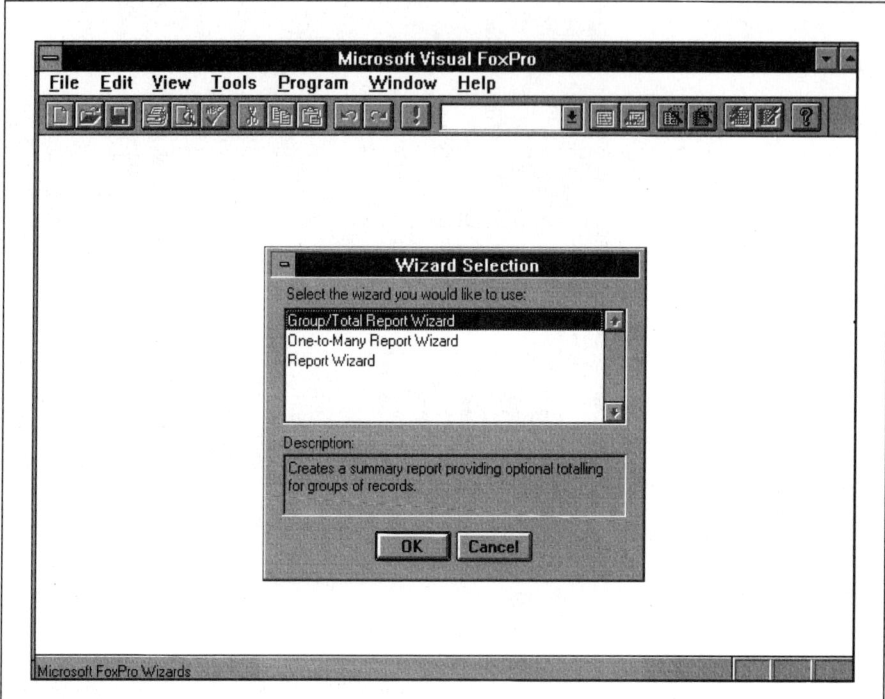

Navigating through a Wizard

A Wizard presents you with a series of numbered steps, each displayed in its own dialog box. Figure 1.7 shows a typical Wizard step. As you can see, Wizards include instructions in plain English.

You can use the Step drop-down list to move directly to any of the dialog boxes of the Wizard. The easiest way to get an overview of a wizard is to display this list, so you can look at the names of all its steps.

FIGURE 1.7

One dialog box of a Wizard

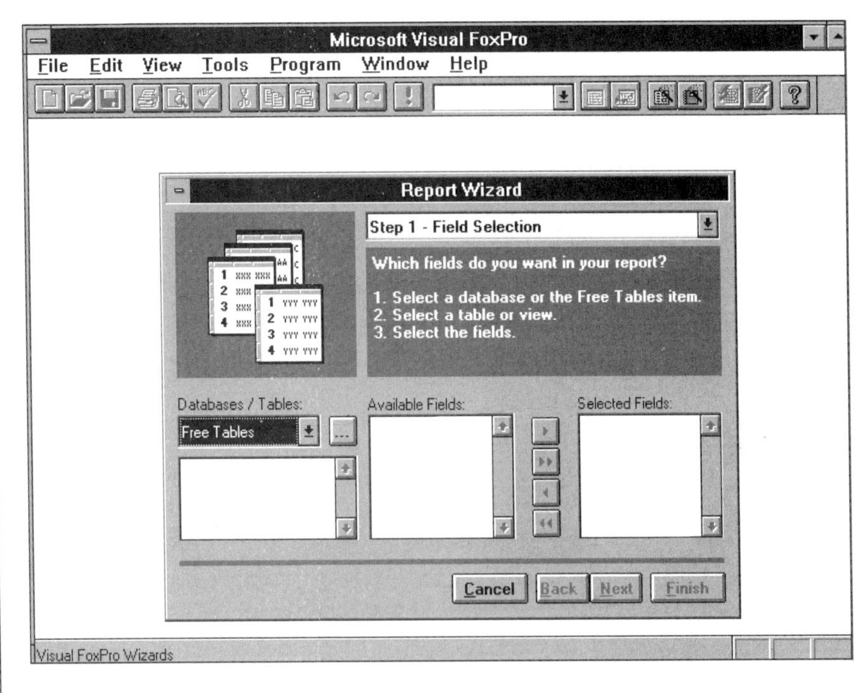

You can also use three of the pushbuttons at the bottom of the dialog box to navigate through all the steps of a Wizard:

- **Back** and **Next:** Select the Back or Next button to display the previous or next dialog box of the Wizard.
- **Finish:** Select the Finish button to display the final dialog box of the Wizard. When the final dialog box is already displayed, clicking Finish generates the file whose specifications you have entered in the Wizard.

You can also select the Cancel button or press Esc to close the Wizard and abandon changes without creating the object.

All Wizards have the basic features just described. Of course, the specific questions asked in each dialog box are different depending on the type of file you are creating; and the following chapters discuss each Wizard in detail.

► The Command Window and the View Window

Visual FoxPro's interface is based on a powerful combination that includes both menus and dialog boxes, like other Windows applications, and a Command window in which you can enter the sort of procedural commands that used to be entered at the dBASE dot prompt. Often, Visual FoxPro automatically generates commands in the Command window when you make the equivalent choices from the menu system, as shown in Figure 1.8. These generated commands make it easier to learn about the FoxPro language as you use the program, but you should ignore them as you read Part I of this book; Part II introduces the language.

FIGURE 1.8 ►

Commands are generated automatically in the Command window.

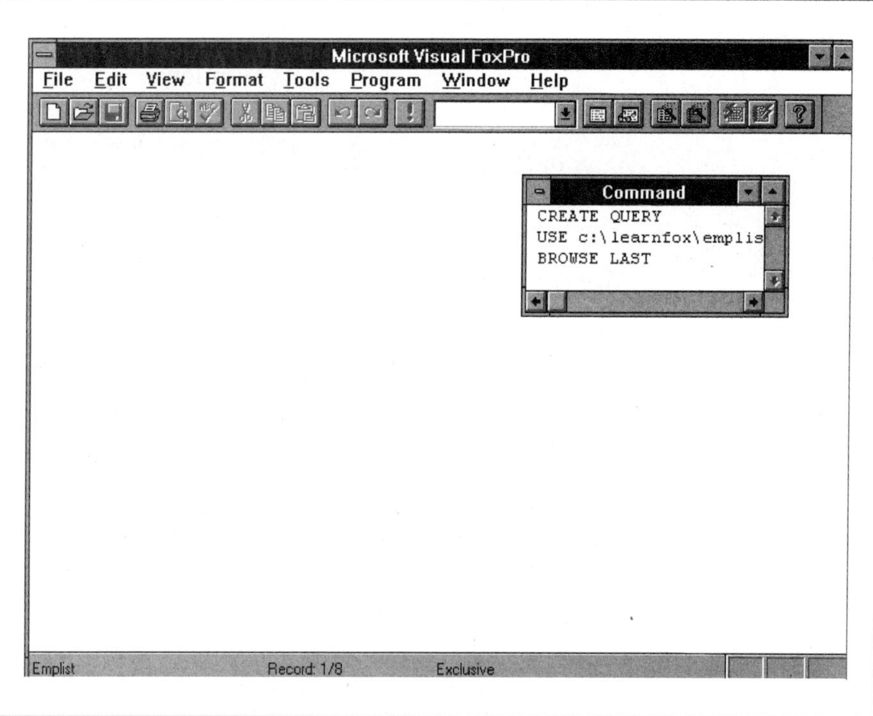

Because it is so fundamental to Visual FoxPro, the Command window behaves a bit differently from most Visual FoxPro windows. You cannot

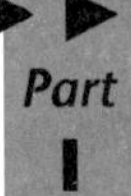

close it by pressing Esc. The only way to remove it is through the menu system. To hide the Command window, select Window ➤ Hide or choose Close from its Control menu when it is the current window. To unhide it, simply select Window ➤ Command or click the Command Window button of the main toolbar.

The View window is also important to using Visual FoxPro. It gives you a quick way of opening, setting up, and displaying the data in tables; it also lets you control table properties, and open multiple tables at the same time, and relate them.

Because the Command window and the View window are so important, both are always included on the Window menu—unlike other windows, which are added to this window only if they are open—and both have their own tools on the toolbar. To use these Windows at any time:

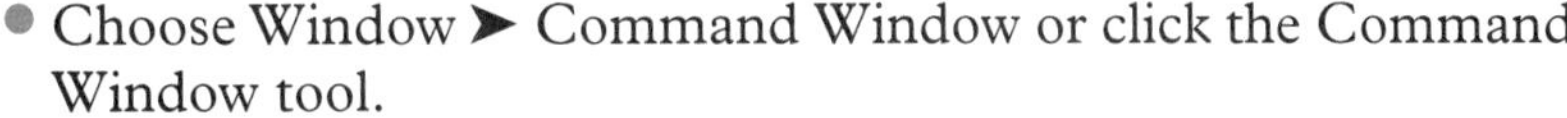

- Choose Window ➤ Command Window or click the Command Window tool.

- Choose Window ➤ View Window or click the View Window tool.

However, it is not necessary for beginners to use either of these windows, and neither will be covered until Part II of this book.

Other Features of the Visual FoxPro Interface

There are a couple of other features of the Visual FoxPro interface that you should know about before you begin, so they do not cause confusion. Some will be familiar from other Windows applications; others may be new to you:

- **Esc:** The Esc key is used to back out of menus and close dialog boxes in Visual FoxPro, as it is in other Windows applications. It also closes most windows within Visual FoxPro, with the exception of the Command window. In addition, pressing Esc may interrupt Visual FoxPro commands or programs. If you interrupt a command or program by pressing Esc, Visual FoxPro displays a dialog box with the choices Cancel, Suspend, and Ignore, which let you completely stop execution of the command or program, pause execution (until you select Program ➤ Resume or enter

RESUME in the Command window), or immediately continue to execute the command or program.

- **Alerts:** An alert, such as the one shown in Figure 1.9, may appear on the screen if you tell Visual FoxPro to do something that is impossible or that will destroy data. Its message is generally self-explanatory. After you understand the reason for the alert, to make it disappear, click the mouse button or press any key except a function key, Shift, Ctrl, or Alt.

FIGURE 1.9

An alert

- **System messages:** Like an alert, a system message is a box that gives you information about an action you have performed. Unlike an alert, it is not a warning or an error message. Alerts actually interrupt what you are doing, since it could be destructive, and you must remove them explicitly by clicking the mouse or pressing a key, as you just saw. A system message does not interrupt you. If you go on with what you were doing, it disappears.

- **Status bar:** The status bar at the bottom of the screen tells you if Insert mode, Caps Lock, or Num Lock is on. It also includes help lines as you make menu selections and use various Visual FoxPro windows, as well as other information. If a database file is open, for example, the status bar tells you its name, which record number you are on, and the total number of records in the file.

- **"Talk":** When you make certain menu choices or use certain commands, Visual FoxPro displays what is called *talk* in the status bar. For example, if you create an index, it tells you how many records were indexed.

▶▶ To Sum Up

In this chapter, you first looked at some basic database theory and at a bit of the history of Visual FoxPro. Then you looked at the menu system, Wizards, and other major features of the Visual FoxPro interface that you must know before you can use it—and some features of the interface that it's best to avoid as a beginner. Now that you have a general overview of Visual FoxPro, you can begin working with it.

CHAPTER 2

Creating a Table

▸▸ Fast Track

▶▶ **B***efore* you can work with a table, you must define its *structure*. Every record in a table has the same set of fields, and defining a table's structure means deciding exactly what fields you want the records to contain—in other words, it means deciding what information you want the table to hold.

Defining the structure of a table is a bit like designing a preprinted form you would use if you were working with paper files. You would have to decide, for example, that your index cards would have blank spaces for name, address, phone number, and so on.

With a computerized database table you don't need to worry about the physical arrangement of the fields, as you do with paper forms, because the computer lets you look at the same data in different ways. For example, you can view the same data as a form, with one record displayed at a time, or as a table, with many records displayed. But in exchange for this flexibility, you need to define in advance various characteristics of the table's fields much more precisely than when working with paper files. You must define what sort of data can be entered in each field, since some fields can hold only certain types of data, such as numbers, logical values, or dates. You must also define the maximum size for some data types.

In this chapter, you will define the structure of a table that is used as an example throughout this book and that illustrates most of the data types that are available in Visual FoxPro.

▶▶ Creating a New Table

You create a new table as you do other types of Visual FoxPro files. Choose File ➤ New, select the Table radio button of the New dialog box, and then click one of its buttons to use the Table Wizard or to create a New Table from scratch.

The Table Wizard is often a useful shortcut, and you will look at it briefly below. For many applications, however, you will need to create a new table from scratch: because this is more difficult than using the Wizard, the exercise in this chapter will concentrate on it.

Even if you do use the Wizard to create that table, you will often want to use the Table Designer to modify its structure so that it is exactly what you need. Once you have experience creating a table from scratch, it will be easy for you to use the Table Designer to modify the structure of an existing table.

The Table Wizard

The Table Wizard lets you create new tables based on any of a group of typical tables that are distributed with Visual FoxPro.

NOTE

The basic features of this Wizard—the Step drop-down list and the Cancel, Back, Next, and Finish buttons—are used in the same way as in other Wizards. If you want to review how they are used, go back to the section on Wizards in Chapter 1.

Selecting Fields

As you can see in Figure 2.1, the Table Wizard's first dialog box includes a list of standard tables designed to record Accounts, Book Collections, Classes, Contacts, Customers, and many other types of data.

Whichever of these standard tables is selected has its fields displayed in the Available Fields list. You select the fields to include in your new table by using the Field Picker to move them from the Available Fields list to the Selected Fields list.

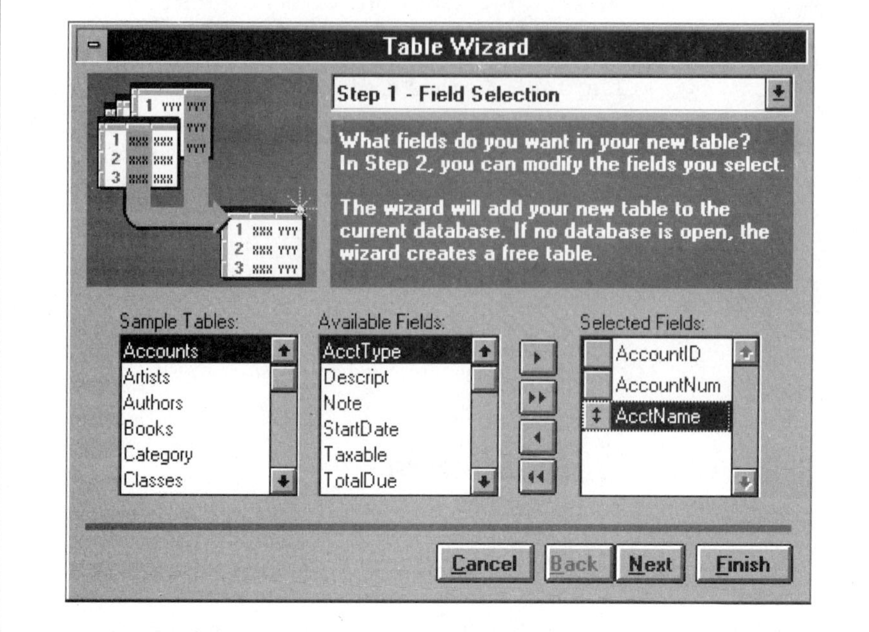

FIGURE 2.1

Step 1 of the Table Wizard—selecting fields from a standard table

Using The Field Picker Many Wizard dialog boxes offer a Field Picker like this one, which lets you move fields from one list to another; and they all work similarly:

- Select a field in the Available Fields list and click the > button (or simply double-click the field) to add it to the Selected Fields list.
- Click the >> button to add all the fields to the Selected Fields list.
- Select a field in the Selected Fields list, and click the < button (or double-click the field name) to remove it from the Selected Fields list.
- Click the << button to remove all the fields from the Selected Fields list and start over.

Changing Field Order You can also change the order of fields in the table simply by clicking and dragging the move box (which is to the left of the field's name in the Selected Field list) up or down.

Modifying Field Settings

Once you have added all the fields you want to the Selected Fields list, you can go on to Step 2—Field Settings, which lets you modify the definition of these fields. Figure 2.2 shows the Step 2 window.

FIGURE 2.2

Step 2 of the Table Wizard—altering field settings

This dialog box makes it easy to change the Name, Data Type, and other features of the field. Before you use it, however, you must understand how to define these properties of a field. These settings are used in the same way when you create a table from scratch, and so they are covered in the section on the Table Designer later in this chapter.

Creating Indexes

The Step 3 dialog box, shown in Figure 2.3, lets you select fields that you've included to be used as the basis of an index, which can be used to determine the sort order in which the table's records are displayed.

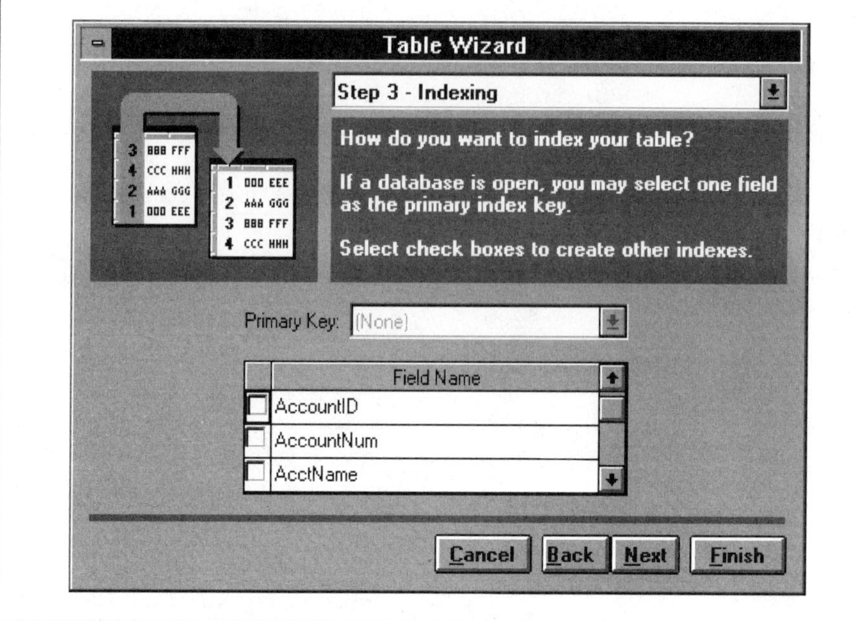

FIGURE 2.3

Step 3 of the Table Wizard—indexing the table

If a FoxPro database is open when you begin creating this table, you should use the drop-down to select one field that is used as a primary key index. A primary key index contains a value such as an employee number that is used to identify each record, and it must be different in each record of the table. You can only create primary indexes for tables that are part of a FoxPro database, however, and so they are covered in Chapter 16.

You can also select the check box to the left of any other field to create an *Index Tag* for the table based on that field, which lets you control the order in which records are displayed.

Although the Wizard seems to make it easy to create indexes, you should read the discussion of indexing in Chapter 10 before creating indexes. There are two major limitations to the indexes you can create using the Wizard:

- You can only create index tags based on a single field in ascending order using the Wizard, and for most tables you will also want to create some indexes based on multiple fields, and perhaps also some in descending order.

- Indexes arrange records in ASCII order rather than alphabetical order by default, and you should usually change this default before creating the index.

Chapter 10, which introduces indexes, discusses these issues and also covers using the View window to specify which index should be used to determine the order in which a table's records are displayed.

The Final Dialog Box

The final dialog box, shown in Figure 2.4, includes radio buttons that give you several ways to display the newly created table. You can simply save it; save it and display it in a Browse window, where you can add data to it immediately; or save it and display it immediately in the Table Designer, which you can use to modify the structure that the Wizard generated.

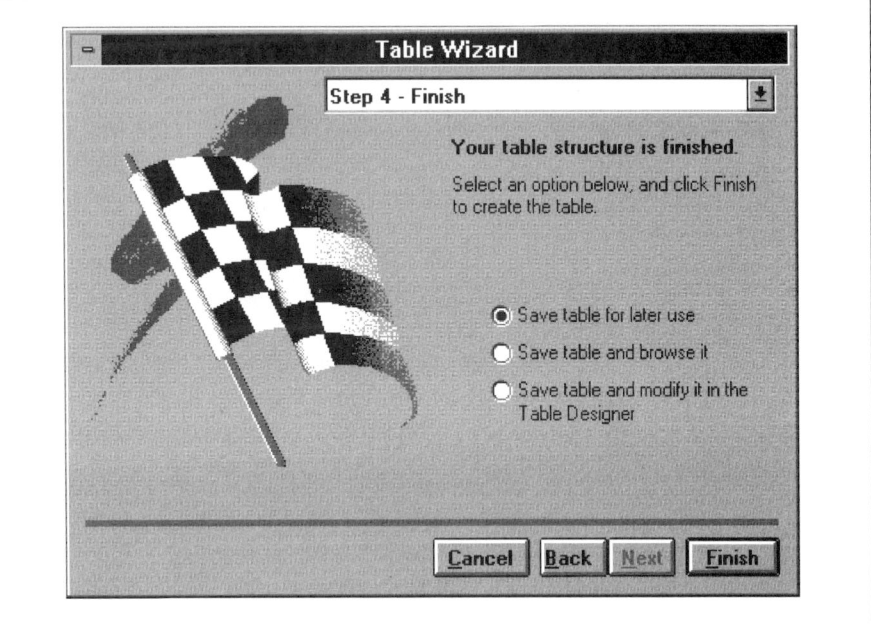

FIGURE 2.4

Step 4—the final dialog box of the Table Wizard

Most Wizards have an option like this final one, to make it easy to create an object using the Wizard and then customize it using the usual Visual FoxPro Designers.

►► **TIP**

When you are creating a new table, it is generally easiest to begin by using the Wizard to create a table that's approximately what you want, and then use the Structure dialog box to add fields that were not available in the Wizard. To do this, you must understand the Structure dialog box, which is covered in detail below.

Naming the Table

When you select the Finish button to create the table, Visual FoxPro displays the Save As dialog box, which you are probably familiar with from other Windows applications.

Choose a directory in which to save the table, and enter a name for it in the Name text box. Table names are discussed below under the heading "The Table Name and Extension."

► Using the Table Designer

You can also create a table from scratch, by using the Table Designer. To start this tool, click the New Table button of the Create Table dialog box.

The Table Name and Extension

Before you use the Table Designer to define the new table's structure, Visual FoxPro displays the Create dialog box to let you name the table. This dialog box is identical to the Save As dialog box, and is used in the same way to specify the directory and name of the table.

Tables, like other files, may have names up to eight characters long. If you do not include an extension, the table is automatically given the extension DBF, which stands for *d*ata*b*ase *f*ile. For example, in this chapter, you will create a sample employee list file and name it EMPLIST, and it will be stored with the name EMPLIST.DBF.

As you will see, Visual FoxPro tables can have memo fields, which are kept in a separate file from the rest of the table. Visual FoxPro memo files are given the extension FPT, which stands for *F*ox*P*ro *t*ext. Thus, when you create your EMPLIST table later in this chapter, it will actually be stored in two files: EMPLIST.DBF and EMPLIST.FPT.

WARNING

Because a Memo field is not kept in the same file as the rest of the table, there is a danger of losing your memo data when you are copying a table—for example, to transfer it to another computer. You must be sure to copy the memo file as well as the table. The easiest way to do this is by using the DOS * (asterisk) wildcard character. For instance, to copy a table named SAMPLE, use the DOS command COPY SAMPLE.*, which will copy SAMPLE.DBF and also SAMPLE.FPT and SAMPLE.DBT.

Features of the Table Designer

After you have named the table in the Create dialog box, Visual FoxPro displays the Table Designer, shown in Figure 2.5.

FIGURE 2.5

The Table Designer

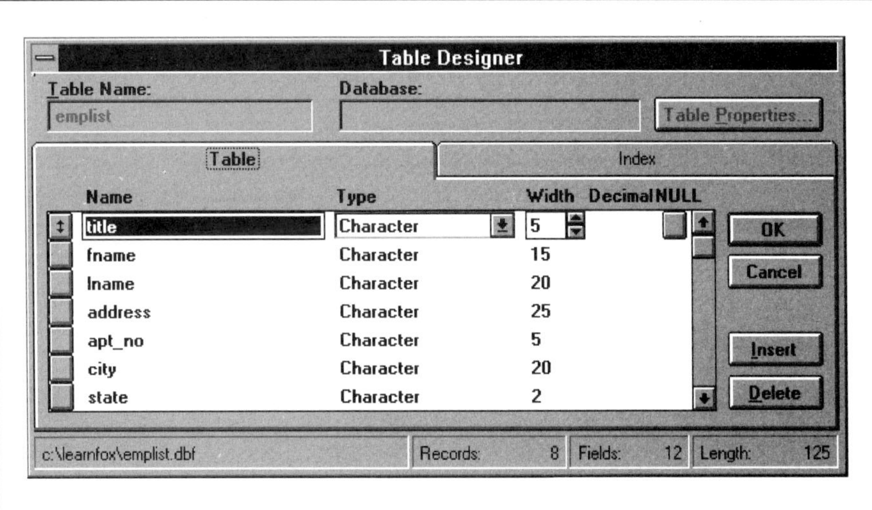

The table's name is displayed in the upper-left corner. If the table is part of a FoxPro database, the database name is displayed at the upper right; FoxPro databases are used primarily for working with relational databases and are discussed in Chapter 16.

As you can see, this dialog box has a Table and an Index tab, which you can click to display the Table or Index panel. The Index panel will be covered in Chapter 10. Here, we will look at the Table panel.

To define the structure of the table, simply list its fields. The first line describes the first field in each record, the second line the second field, and so on.

You must fill in the Name and Type columns for each field. Some data types also require that you fill in the Width and Decimal columns.

Type the name in the Name column, and select a data type from the drop-down control that appears in the Type column. If the type requires you to specify a Width and a number of Decimal places, those columns will be enabled and a spinner control will be displayed to their right. If a number is entered in the Width column but no spinner control is displayed, that number is the required width for the data type. The next section, "Working with the Field List," describes the process of defining fields in more detail.

The NULL column determines whether you can enter a NULL value in a field, an advanced feature that is covered in Chapter 8.

Working with the Field List

Normally, you simply fill out the field definitions in sequence, from the first in each record to the last, but it is possible to move among the fields—to make changes in a definition before saving it or to modify the structure of a table you created earlier. To navigate the field list using the keyboard:

- Press Tab to move one column to the right (or if you are in the last column, to the first column of the next line).
- Press Shift+Tab to move one column to the left (or the last column of the previous line).
- Press ↑ and ↓ to move up and down the list one line at a time.
- Press PgUp and PgDn to move up and down the list one window at a time.

Of course, you can also use the mouse to click the location where you want to place the cursor or click the field list's scroll bar to scroll through it.

You can use the Insert button in the dialog box to insert a new field above the current field: Visual FoxPro initially gives it the name New-Field, and you can edit its name and specifications.

Click the Delete pushbutton to remove the currently selected field from the list.

Click and drag the buttons to the left of the field names up or down to change the order of the fields.

Field Names A field name may have up to ten characters, including the letters from *A* to *Z*, whole numbers, and the underscore character (_). The field must begin with a letter. Field names do not distinguish between uppercase and lowercase letters.

Of course, you cannot use two fields with the same name in the same table.

Table 2.1 gives examples of a few valid and invalid field names to illustrate these rules. Note that a field name's validity alone is not sufficient to ensure its usefulness. A useful field name will also tell you about the contents of that field.

TABLE 2.1: *Examples of Valid and Invalid Field Names*

FIELD NAME(S)	VALID OR INVALID?
Z	Valid
2	Invalid: It begins with a number.
UP_DOWN	Valid
_NAME	Invalid: It begins with an underscore.
CITY_STATE_ZIP	Invalid: It has more than ten characters.
ADDRESS_1 and ADDRESS_2	Both are valid and may be used in same file.
NOTES and notes	Both are valid but they may not be used in same file, as both have the same name (capitalization differences are ignored).

▶▶ TIP

A field name cannot include any spaces. For this reason, if you have a field name made up of more than one word, it is a good idea to use the underscore character (_) to separate words to make them easier to read.

You can use longer and more flexible field names if you include the table in a database, as discussed in Chapter 16.

Data Types When you begin to enter a field name, *Character* and *10* automatically appear in the Type and Width columns, respectively. You can use the drop-down list to change the type from this default, as shown in Figure 2.6; the width changes automatically depending on the type you select. The data types, their default widths, and the sort of data that each is used to store are summarized in Table 2.2.

FIGURE 2.6

Selecting a field's data type

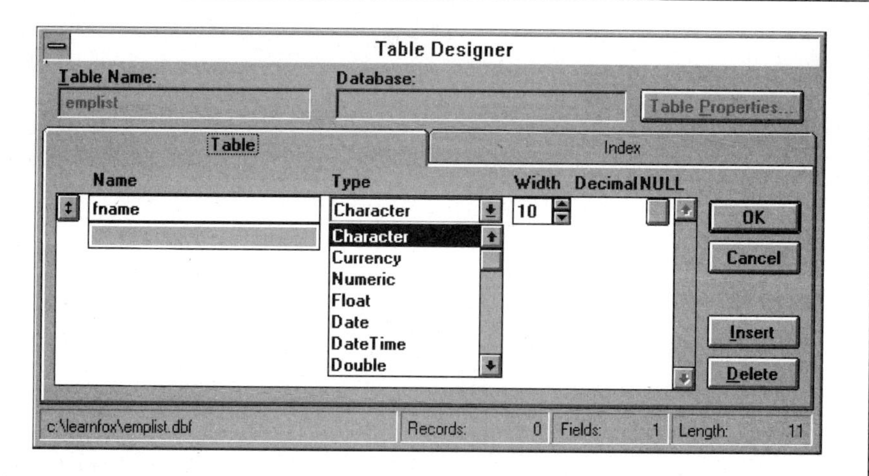

▶▶ NOTE

An additional data type, Picture, is listed on the Type drop-down for compatibility with the Macintosh version of FoxPro, but it is always dimmed since this data type is not implemented in the Windows version.

TABLE 2.2: *Data Types and Their Defaults*

DATA TYPE	DEFAULT WIDTH	DEFAULT DECIMAL PLACES	CHANGE DEFAULTS?	USED TO STORE
Character	8	N/A	Yes	from 1 to 254 characters
Currency	8	N/A	No	monetary amounts
Numeric	8	0	Yes	numbers used in calculations
Float	8	0	Yes	numbers used in calculations
Date	8	N/A	No	dates
DateTime	14	N/A	No	dates and times
Double	8	0	Yes	numeric values where extremely accurate calculation is needed
Logical	1	N/A	No	.T. (true) or .F. (false)
Memo	10	N/A	No	text of any length
General	10	N/A	No	OLE objects
Character (binary)	8	N/A	Yes	text or binary data up to 254 characters
Memo (binary)	10	N/A	No	text or binary data of any length

The data type you choose determines what you can enter into the field.

- **Character** and **Binary Character:** The Character data type may contain any of the characters on the keyboard, including letters, numbers, and special characters (such as & and *). Visual FoxPro's Binary Character data may include any 8-bit value, including the null character (ASCII character 0); thus, experienced users can use Binary Character fields to store virtually any data, including binary data. The maximum width of a Character field is 254 characters.

- **Currency:** The currency data type is used for money values. It holds amounts from over 900 trillion to less than –900 trillion. It is accurate to four decimal places, which allows it to do fast calculations with the accuracy needed for money amounts. As you will see in later chapters, it displays four decimal places when you view data, but automatically changes the format to two decimal places when you create reports.
- **Numeric:** The Numeric data type may contain numbers and a decimal point and may also begin with a + or – sign. The maximum width of a Numeric field is 20 characters. The decimal point and + or – sign each take up one place, so you must take them into account when you define the field width. If you want a field to hold amounts that are less than 1000 with two decimal places, for example, it must be six places wide: three for the unit digits, one for the decimal point, and two for the decimal digits. Add an extra place if you want to indicate + or – amounts.
- **Float:** The Float data type is identical to the numeric data type and is included for compatibility with other software.
- **Double:** The Double data type holds numeric data, but it does calculations with more accuracy than the Numeric data type.

►► NOTE

Visual FoxPro's Numeric and Float fields use only 16 significant digits internally and round off any numeric data wider than this. Although this is more than enough precision for most business uses, there are many scientific and statistical calculations in which rounding might create errors. When in doubt about potential rounding errors, use the Double type.

- **Date:** The Date data type includes date numbers and the slash character to separate them—for example, 10/02/96. Dates can be displayed with a four-character year—for example, as 10/02/1996 instead of a two-character year, with different separators, and with other variations from the usual format, covered in Chapter 19.

- **DateTime:** The DateTime data type can hold either a date such as **10/02/96**, a time such as **11:59:59PM**, or a date and time such as **10/02/96 11:59:59PM**.
- **Logical:** The Logical data type may contain only the value T or F, to indicate true or false. However, when you are entering data you may enter Y (for yes) or N (for no) as well as T or F, and the entry will be read as a logical true or false. Any of these characters may be entered as upper- or lowercase letters. Thus, this type makes it easy to enter true/false and yes/no responses.
- **Memo:** The memo data type may contain any amount and type of data. The only limit to the length of a Memo field is the amount of disk space you have. Like a Binary Character field, a Binary Memo field may include the null character and binary data. Thus, you can use Visual FoxPro Binary Memo fields to hold types of data that could never before be manipulated with database management programs, such as scanned images and digitized sound. In ordinary use, Memo fields act as variable-length character fields, and you can manipulate them using any of the functions that manipulate Character fields.
- **General:** The General data type contains OLE objects, a feature of Windows that lets you embed objects created in one application within another application. For example, you can use a General field to include spreadsheets, graphics, or sound created in another Windows application within your Visual FoxPro table. Object linking and embedding is discussed in Chapter 22.

Every field you define takes up disk space for the entire width that is specified, even if there is little or no data in the field. Certain fields have unalterable widths: the Logical type is always one character wide, the Date type is always eight characters wide, and the DateTime type is always fourteen characters wide.

Memo Fields You probably noticed in Figure 2.2 that Memo fields, although they can hold any amount of data, are automatically defined as ten characters wide. The ten spaces reserved for a Memo field in the table are just used to point to the location in a separate, variable-length file where the actual data for that field is kept.

When you are entering data, the Memo field at first appears to be only ten spaces wide, but if you press Ctrl+PgDn when the cursor is on that field, you open a special Memo window, as illustrated in Figure 2.7, where you can enter any amount of text (or other data); closing the memo window returns you to ordinary data entry. Likewise, General fields in Visual FoxPro for Windows are automatically defined as ten characters wide, but the OLE object that the field contains is obviously not stored in the table.

FIGURE 2.7

A Memo window

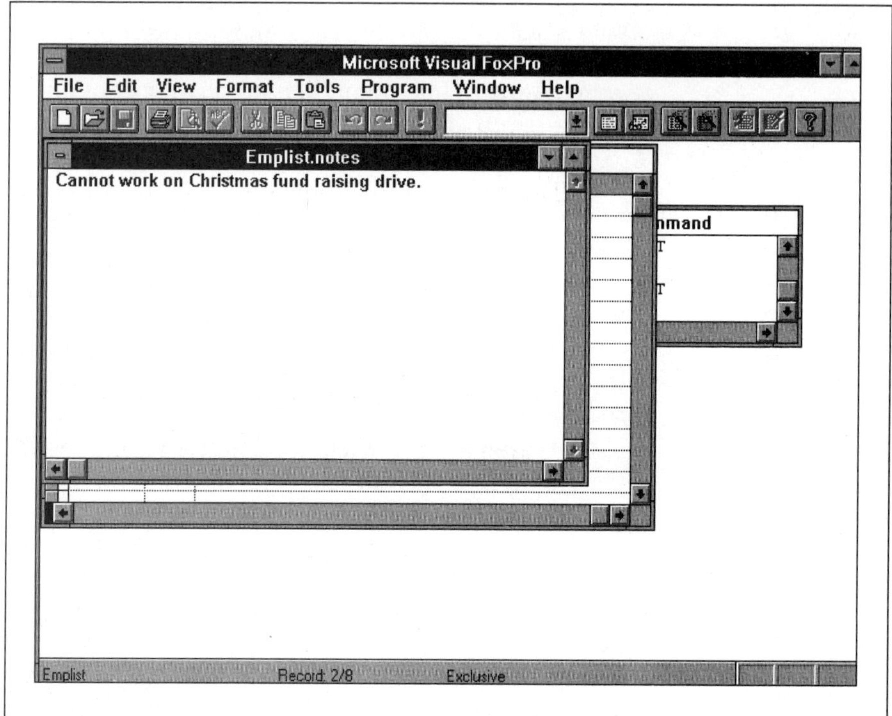

Choosing a Data Type

No doubt you have noticed that some kinds of real-world information might fit into several different field types. For example, numbers can go into Character, Numeric, Float, or Double fields, and dates can go into Date, DateTime, or Character fields.

The data type you should choose depends on how the data will be used.

You can perform numeric calculations, for example, only on Numeric, Currency, Float, or Double fields—not on numbers that are stored in Character fields. You can also use indexes to arrange the values in these fields in numeric order, regardless of their length, and you cannot do this if the numbers are in character fields (which are sorted on the basis of the first character in the field, so that 100 would come before 9).

Date and DateTime fields provide similar advantages. In the earliest versions of dBASE, dates were stored as characters, and there was no Date type. As a result, it was hard to arrange records in order of date. Now that there are special Date and DateTime types, though, you can not only sort records in order of date, you can also perform calculations with dates and times—to find the number of days between two dates, for example.

Beginners are often tempted to define the ZIP code field as Numeric because it has numbers in it. Postal codes from foreign countries, however, contain letters as well as numbers, and extended ZIP codes include a hyphen after the first five digits. Neither of these could be entered in a Numeric field. In addition, ZIP codes are always the same length and include leading zeroes; it is difficult to display leading zeroes in number fields, and because they are all the same length and include leading zeroes, ZIP codes can be sorted in proper order when they are in a Character field.

There is no advantage, then, to using a numeric field except for the ability to perform calculations and to sort in numeric order. When you are designing a table, it is generally best to use one of the number types only for fields that will actually have calculations performed on them.

To save disk space and improve performance, you should choose the field type that stores data with only as much precision as you need. For example, you should use a Double field only for numbers used in calculations that require extra precision, and you should use a DateTime field only if you may need to use the field to store times as well as dates.

▶▶ Creating a Sample Table

The sample table you will work with in this book is a list of employees. It is similar to the single-table database that a small business might actually use, but it is simplified to save you data entry; for example, it will not include social security numbers. The fields that are in the table will be chosen to illustrate Visual FoxPro's capabilities, rather than as an example of an actual business application.

▸ Breaking Down the Data

It's best to think about how much you need to break down the data for the uses you are going to make of it *before* you create the structure of your table. This is one of the most important things to think about when you are planning the design of a table.

When even a very small business computerizes, entering names and addresses in its mailing list usually takes a week or more of full-time work for a data entry person (or for an overworked owner). There have been cases where users decided to print out the names on their mailing list in alphabetical order after the data entry was done—and only then realized that you cannot alphabetize by last name if the first, middle and last name are all in a single field. Sometimes these people have managed to get by without the alphabetical listings they wanted; in other cases they have gone back, redefined the table, and spent an extra week reentering all their data.

The sample application in this book is a simple list of employees. As with most lists of names and addresses, it is best to break down the name into fields for first and last name so you can alphabetize records. We should also have separate fields for city, state, and ZIP, rather than a single field for all three. In this sort of application, you may well want to see a list of only the people who live in a certain city or a certain state or to print mailing labels by ZIP code. You can do these things if you have a separate field for each.

Keep in mind, however, that there are costs to creating fields for which you rarely have data—fields that, in many records, will be empty. For one thing, it takes data-entry time to skip that field and leave it empty. In addition, a field takes up space on your disk regardless of whether there is any data in it. To save disk space, it is best not to create unnecessary fields and not to make fields wider than necessary.

In many cases, for example, it is best not to create a separate field for middle initial, which will be left empty in most records: instead, you can record the middle initial in the same field as the first name where one is needed. If you plan to use the first name in form letters, however, you will not want the middle initial in the same field; you will want the letter to begin "Dear John" rather than "Dear John Q." If you have already entered the middle initial in the first name field, and then decide that you want to create a mail merge that uses the first name, you will have to redo much of your initial data entry.

On the other hand, if you plan to create form letters that will use salutations such as "Dear Mr. Smith," you will want to include a field for a title, such as Mr., Ms., or Dr. It is generally easier to include these from the beginning. We'll use this method in the sample application, so that the table will include a field for title but not a separate field for middle initial, since middle initials can be entered in the First Name field if necessary.

The essential point here is that you can save extra work in the long run if you think through how your data is going to be used when you are first creating the table. When in doubt, it is generally safest to break down the data into more fields, rather than fewer.

One-to-One Relationships

In addition, as you learned in Chapter 1, when you create a table, you should make sure that there is a one-to-one relationship between each field in the table and the entire record.

In the sample table, each record represents an employee. You can keep the name and address in the table, because each employee has only one name and one address. However, you cannot keep the number of hours that the employee works each week in the same table, because each employee works many weeks.

If you find that the data you are working with includes this sort of one-to-many relationship, you must use a relational database and store the data in multiple tables. Chapter 12 discusses how to break up data into multiple tables, and the chapters that follow it in Part III discuss the different ways that Visual FoxPro lets you work with relational databases.

Creating a Directory

Before you create any sample files, you should create a directory to hold all the work from this book. You can work through the following exercise to create a directory named \LEARNFOX on your C: drive. If you have some reason to use a different drive, substitute it for C in the following exercise and in all the later exercises in this book.

This exercise uses the DOS prompt to create the new directory. Of course, you can also create the directory using Windows, if you prefer:

1. Double-click the MS-DOS icon to display the DOS prompt.
2. Enter **C:** to make the C drive the current drive.
3. Enter **MD \LEARNFOX** to create a new directory with that name.
4. Enter **EXIT** to return to Windows.

Be sure to use this directory to hold all the files you create in this book. Then it will be easy to delete them all when you are done with them.

▸ Creating the Table

Now that you have a directory to hold the sample table, you are ready to start Visual FoxPro and use the Table Designer to create the table. (If you have not yet installed Visual FoxPro, see Appendix A.)

1. If necessary, start Visual FoxPro by double-clicking its icon in the Program Manager. Choose File ➤ New to display the New dialog box, select the Table radio button, and click the New File button.
2. Visual FoxPro displays the Create dialog box, to let you name the table. Enter **EMPLIST** in the Enter Table Name text box. Use the Directories list (and the Drives drop-down list if necessary) to select the LEARNFOX directory that you just created; its folder should be displayed as opened. Click the Create button.
3. Type **title** in the Name column. As soon as you begin typing, *Character* appears in the Type column, and *10* appears in the Width column. These are the default assignments for these items. A double-headed arrow also appears in the move box, to the left of the name, as shown in Figure 2.8. Edit the width so it is **5**, which is enough to hold titles such as Mr., Ms., or Prof.
4. Click the second row of the Name column, where there is an empty text box. Type **fname** in the Name column. Click the Width column to edit it, and change the width to **15**.

FIGURE 2.8

The default data type and width appear as soon as you start typing.

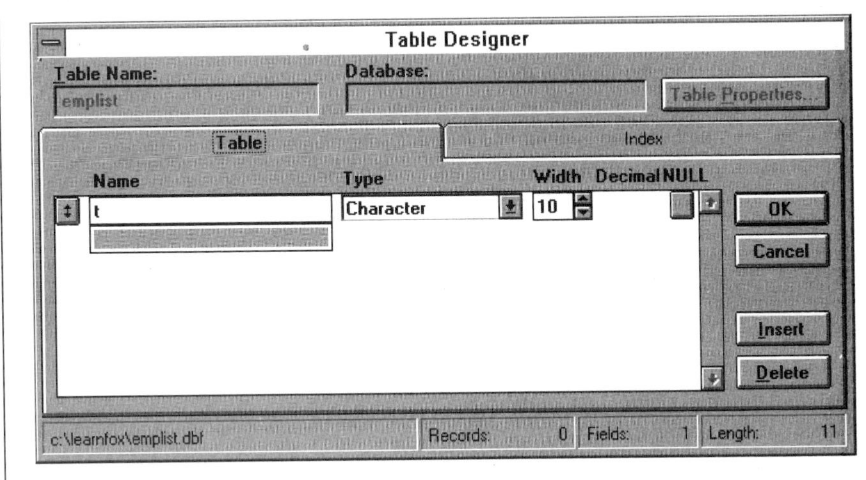

5. Press Tab twice to move to the Name column of the next line. Type **lname**. Press Tab twice to move to the Width column, and type **20** to replace the value in it.

6. Now that you have created new fields using both the mouse and the keyboard, continue by using whichever method you find most convenient. On the next five lines, enter the following field names and widths:

Name	Width
address	25
apt_no	5
city	20
state	2
zip	5

7. Now, you must enter some fields of other data types. On the next line, type **date_hired** as the field Name. Select Date from the Type drop-down list; notice that the width automatically becomes 8 and cannot be changed.

8. On the next line, type **wage** as the field name, and select Currency as its type.

9. On the next line, type **probation** as the field Name. This is a Logical field in which you can record whether the employee is on probation. Press Tab to move to the Type column and type **L** to make it a Logical field. Notice that the width is automatically 1.

10. Press Tab. Because you cannot change the width of a Logical field, the cursor moves to the next line. Type **notes**. Press Tab to move to the Type column and type **M** to choose the Memo type. The width of a Memo field is listed as 10, even when it is holding much more than that, as you will see. There is no need to change it. You now have all the fields you need for this sample table. Your Table Designer should look like Figure 2.9 (not all the fields are visible in the illustration).

FIGURE 2.9

The definition of the new table

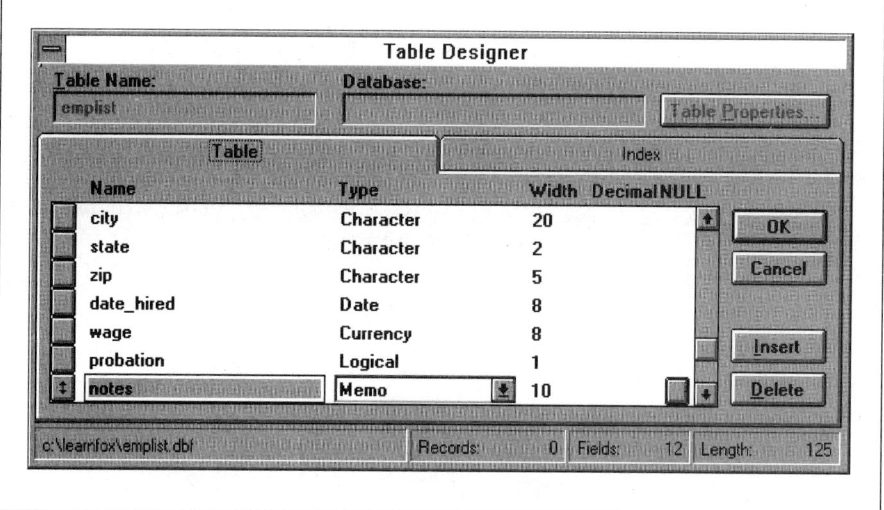

11. Scroll to the top of the list of fields you entered in order to see if they are all correct. If you made any typographical errors, correct them in the same way you changed the default values. When you have confirmed that the definition is right, click OK to create the table. Visual FoxPro displays a dialog box asking if you want to enter records now, as shown in Figure 2.10. Select No.

In practice, you would usually want to enter records immediately after creating a table. You will add records to this sample table in Chapter 3.

FIGURE 2.10

You can enter records immediately.

Opening and Working with a Table

Once you have created a table, you can open it at any time by choosing File ➤ Open to display the Open dialog box, which is similar to the Open dialog box in other Windows applications. If necessary, select Table from the List Fields of Type drop-down list, and use the dialog box in the usual way to select the directory and name of the table.

When you first create a table, it is automatically opened. Notice that the name of the Emplist table, which you just created, is displayed at the left of the status bar. The status bar also indicates that it has no records, and that it is opened exclusively, so it is not accessible to other users on a network.

WARNING

There is an Exclusive check box in the Open dialog box which you can deselect to open the table for shared use on a network, but this can lead to loss of data. Consult with your network administrator before using this option.

When a table is open, the option Browse <table name> is added to the View menu, and you can choose this option to display the table in a Browse window, shown in Figure 2.11. When you are using a Browse window, the View menu contains other options, which you can use to work with the table. Chapter 3 discusses the Browse window and most of these options: the one option that we should look at in this chapter is View ➤ Table Designer, which you can use at any time to call up the Table Designer to modify the structure of that table.

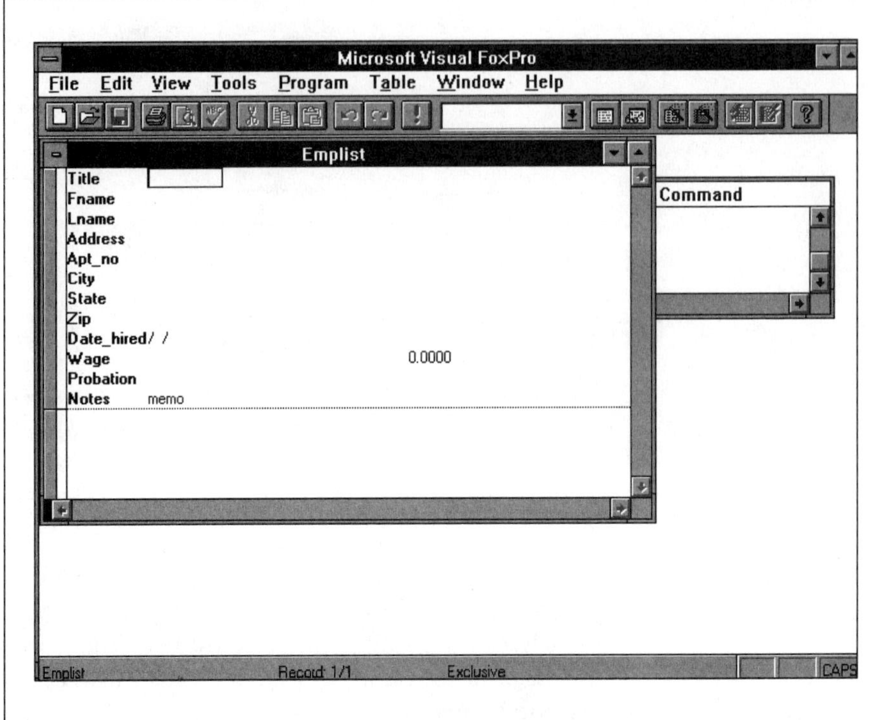

FIGURE 2.11

Displaying the table in a Browse window

▸▸ Modifying the Structure of a Table

There are several common reasons for modifying the structure of a table you have already created.

▸ Modifying a Table Created with the Wizard

If you created a new table using the Wizard, you might want to modify its structure to add new fields that were not available in the Wizard.

To do this, you must select the "Save Table and Modify It ..." radio button in the final step of the Table Wizard, and then click the Finish button. Visual FoxPro displays the Table Designer with the definition of the table as you created it using the Wizard. You can then make whatever changes you need.

▶ Modifying a Table That Already Holds Data

You may also want to modify the structure of a table you have already used to store data, because the requirements of your application have changed. For example, if you have been entering five-digit ZIP codes, you might want to begin using extended ZIP codes instead.

In fact, you will need to modify the structure of EMPLIST in Chapter 12 to add an employee number, so you can use it in a relational database.

To do this, open the table, choose View ➤ Browse to display it in a Browse window, and then choose View ➤ Table Designer.

▶▶ WARNING

You can lose data when you modify a table's structure—for example, if you mistakenly shorten a field so it is no longer large enough to hold some of the data in it or if you mistakenly delete a field with data in it.

Using Backup Tables

Because of this risk of data loss, Visual FoxPro automatically backs up a table when you modify its structure. It backs up the data in the DBF (table) and FPT (memo text) files by creating new files with the same name and with the extensions .BAK and .TBK.

If you ever lose data and want to use the backup files as your table, you can do so in several ways. One easy way is to use the DOS commands

```
COPY <filename>.BAK <filename>.DBF
```

and

```
COPY <filename>.TBK <filename>.FPT
```

if there is a memo field. These commands will overwrite the files that have lost data with the backup files.

Modifying the Sample Table

Since you may well need to modify the structure of a table in your actual work, you should try doing so with your sample table as the last exercise of this chapter.

1. The table should already be open, because you just created it: look for its name in the status bar to make sure. If necessary, choose File ➤ Open and open it.

2. Choose View ➤ Browse Emplist to display the table in a Browse window. Then choose View ➤ Table Designer to display the Table Designer with its specifications.

3. Try moving the Fname field below the Lname field. Click and drag the Move button at the far left of the Fname row; hold down the mouse button, drag the field below the Lname field, and release the mouse button.

4. Try inserting a middle-initial field. Place the cursor in the Address field and select the Insert button. A field called NewField with the Character data type and the default width of 10 is inserted above the address field, where the cursor was, as shown in Figure 2.12. Edit this field: Type **mi** (for middle initial) to change its name, and type **1** in the Width column to change its width.

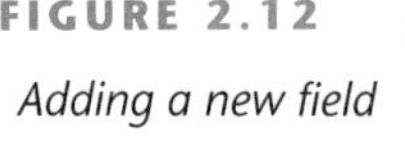

FIGURE 2.12

Adding a new field

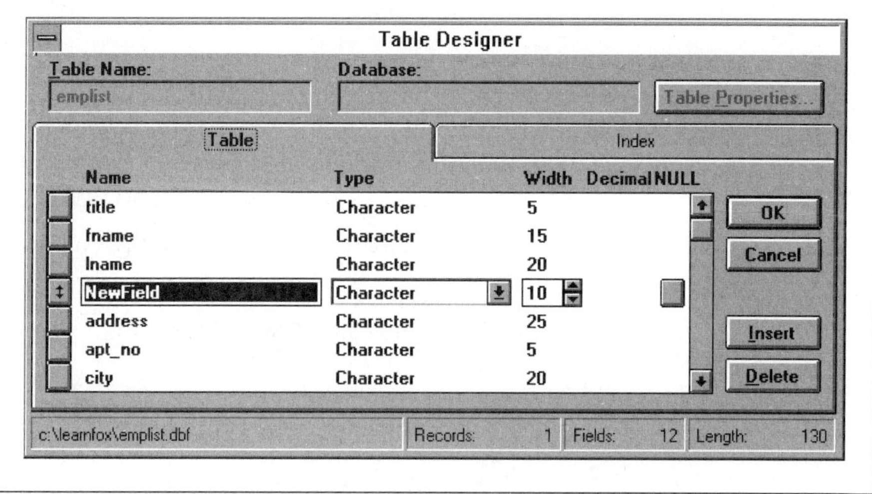

5. Finally, delete the Probation field. Move the highlight to this field using the mouse or ↓. Then select the Delete push button. The Probation field disappears.

6. In an actual application, you would click the OK button to save these changes. Since this is just an exercise, however, you should click the Cancel button, and select Yes in the Visual FoxPro Alert to discard the changes and retain the original definition of the table.

By doing this exercise, you've tried all the methods that you would need to use to modify the structure of a table in a real application. If you'd like to take a break before going on to the next chapter, choose File ➤ Exit.

▶▶ To Sum Up

In this chapter, you learned how to create a new table or modify the structure of an existing one. You looked at how to analyze the requirements of your application to decide how to break down data into separate fields and determine which data type to use for each, and you created a sample table that will be used in the rest of this book. Now you can go on to add and edit data.

CHAPTER 3

Adding, Editing, and Viewing Data

▶▶ FAST TRACK

▶ ***To switch the Browse window between Browse and Edit display of data,*** **61**

choose View ➤ Browse or View ➤ Edit.

▶ ***To display or edit the text in a Memo field,*** **64**

double-click the field or move the cursor to it and press Ctrl+PageDn to open a Memo window with its contents.

▶ ***To add a single record to the table,*** **64**

choose Table ➤ Append New Record.

▶ ***To add a series of records to the table,*** **64**

choose View ➤ Append Mode.

▶ ***To find a value in the table,*** **76**

choose Edit ➤ Find and enter the value you are searching for in the Look For box.

▶ *To mark or unmark a record for deletion,* 77

move the cursor to that record and choose Table ➤ Toggle Deletion Mark or double-click the deletion box to the left of the record.

▶ *To finalize deletions you've marked,* 77

choose Table ➤ Remove Deleted Records. Once deleted, records cannot be recovered.

▶ *To resize a field in the Browse window,* 79

click and drag the grid line to the right of the field's name.

▶ *To move a field in the Browse window,* 79

click and drag the field's name.

▶ *To partition the Browse window,* 80

click and drag the partition separator on the bottom edge of the window.

▶▶ *In* this chapter, you will learn how to use Visual FoxPro to add data to a table and to view and edit data. In general, adding, viewing, and editing data is straightforward and easy to understand, but there are also a few special features of Visual FoxPro that you must learn about to work effectively with the program. For example, FoxPro uses a two-step process of deleting records, and you should learn how to deal with records that are marked for deletion but not yet removed from the table. This chapter also covers some special techniques that add extra power to your work—for example, how to partition the data-entry window.

▶▶ Working with Data

To view the data in a table, first choose File ➤ Open and use the Open dialog box to open the table. Its name is displayed in the status bar. Then the option Browse <table name> is added to the View menu, and you can choose it to display the table in a *Browse window*.

When you are using a Browse window, a Table menu is added to the main menu bar and additional options (which you'll learn about in this chapter) are added to the View menu to let you work with the table.

▶ Switching from Browse to Edit Display

Visual FoxPro lets you look at the table in two fundamentally different ways when you add, edit, or view data—the Browse display and the Edit display.

The default Browse display, shown in Figure 3.1, is designed to let you look quickly through the entire table. It displays the table in tabular form so that each record takes just one line. In the Browse display, you can see many records at a time, but you usually cannot see all the fields of each record.

FIGURE 3.1

Using the Browse display

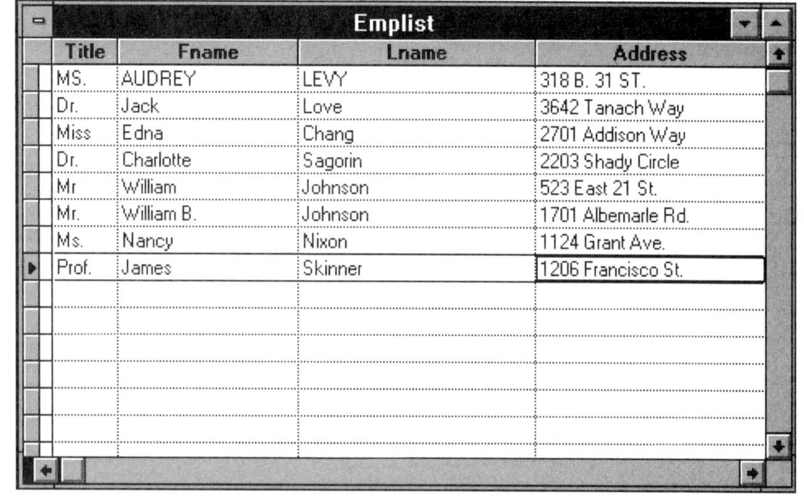

Emplist

Title	Fname	Lname	Address
MS.	AUDREY	LEVY	318 B. 31 ST.
Dr.	Jack	Love	3642 Tanach Way
Miss	Edna	Chang	2701 Addison Way
Dr.	Charlotte	Sagorin	2203 Shady Circle
Mr	William	Johnson	523 East 21 St.
Mr.	William B.	Johnson	1701 Albemarle Rd.
Ms.	Nancy	Nixon	1124 Grant Ave.
Prof.	James	Skinner	1206 Francisco St.

The Edit display, shown in Figure 3.2, is designed to let you work on the table one record at a time. The fields of the record are arranged one above another, so you can see the entire record—or at least as much of it as can fit onto the screen. The Edit display is essentially record-oriented, and its vertical field arrangement comes as close as possible to letting you see an entire record. Figure 3.2 shows a complete record and, because there is still room in the window, the beginning of the next record in the table.

When you are using a Browse window, the first two options on the View menu are Browse and Edit, which let you switch between these two displays. These options simply alter the way the table is displayed, without closing the Browse window or interrupting your work.

FIGURE 3.2

Using the Edit display

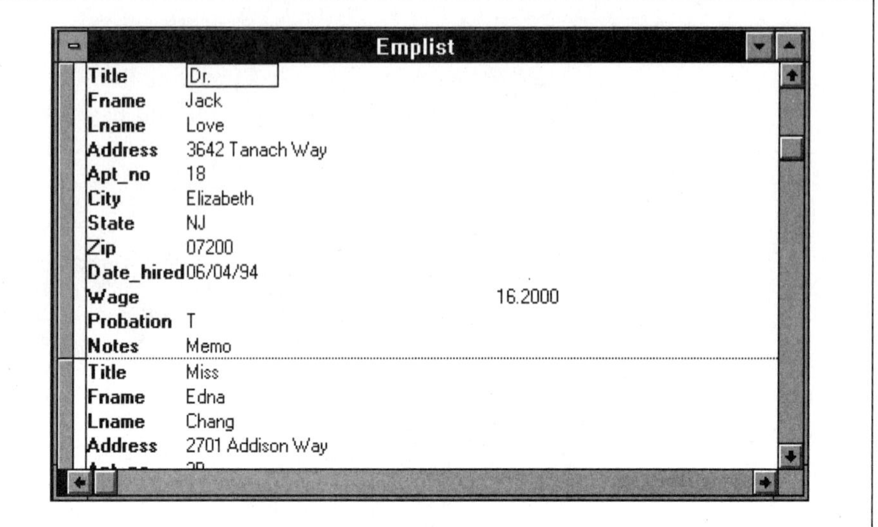

►► **NOTE**

Do not let the names of these menu options mislead you. You can work with the tables in the same ways using Browse or Edit displays. You can edit the table in Browse display and browse through its records in Edit display. These options just change the way that you view the table; use the display that you find most convenient.

► Entering and Editing Data

In general, to enter and edit data you use conventional editing techniques that are common to many other Windows programs. For example, click to place the cursor, double-click to highlight a word, and click and drag to highlight text.

Visual FoxPro will not accept invalid data in any field. If you try to enter a letter in the Wage field or the Date_hired field, for example, the program will beep and will not accept the input.

Navigating through a Table

To move through a table:

- Press Tab or Enter to move to the next field.
- Press Shift+Tab to move to the previous field.
- Press ↑ or ↓ to move up or down a line.
- Press PgUp or PgDn to scroll up or down a window.

Or use the scroll bars to scroll through the Browse window.

In addition, if you fill the entire length of a field when you are entering data, Visual FoxPro beeps and goes on to the next field. This saves a bit of time when you are entering fields of a fixed length, such as date fields.

Closing the Browse Window

When you are finished editing the table's records you may close the Browse window and either save or discard the changes you've just made:

- To close the window and save all changes, press Ctrl+End or Ctrl+W, choose File ➤ Close, or click the Control-menu box and choose Close.
- To close the window and discard changes to the current field, press Esc or Ctrl+Q.

Note that the last option only discards changes to the current field of the current record. Changes that you made to other fields and records are automatically saved.

WARNING

If you press Esc or Ctrl+Q to close the Browse window while appending, editing, or browsing records, remember that Visual FoxPro does not give you any notice before closing the window and discarding any changes you have made to the current field.

Using Memo Fields

Memo fields of a table display the word *memo* in the Browse window. If there is any text in the memo, this word will begin with an uppercase *M*, as in Figure 3.2; if not, it will begin with a lowercase *m*.

To view or edit the contents of a Memo field, double-click it with the mouse or press Ctrl+PgDn. A Memo window is opened, with the name of the table and field in its title bar. Enter or change the memo contents using the conventional editing keys.

To close the Memo window and save the changes you made, press Ctrl+W or select File ➤ Close. (Ctrl+End does not close a Memo window; it moves the cursor to the end of the document.)

To close the Memo window and discard changes, press Esc or Ctrl+Q. When you are editing a Memo field, Visual FoxPro warns you before discarding changes if you press these keys.

▸ Appending Data

You can append new records to the table either by adding records individually or by using Append mode to add a series of records.

Appending a Single Record

To add a single record, choose Table ➤ Append New Record. Visual FoxPro creates a new blank record at the end of the table, and makes it the current record so you can type data into it using the editing techniques described above. You can choose this menu option again to add more records.

Using Append Mode

Choose View ➤ Append Mode to add a series of records to the table. When you select this option, a new blank record is added to the end of the table, so you can add data to it, using the editing methods described above. As soon as you add any data to this record, Visual FoxPro adds another blank record to the end of the table, as shown in Figure 3.3, so you can continue to add data as long as you remain in Append mode.

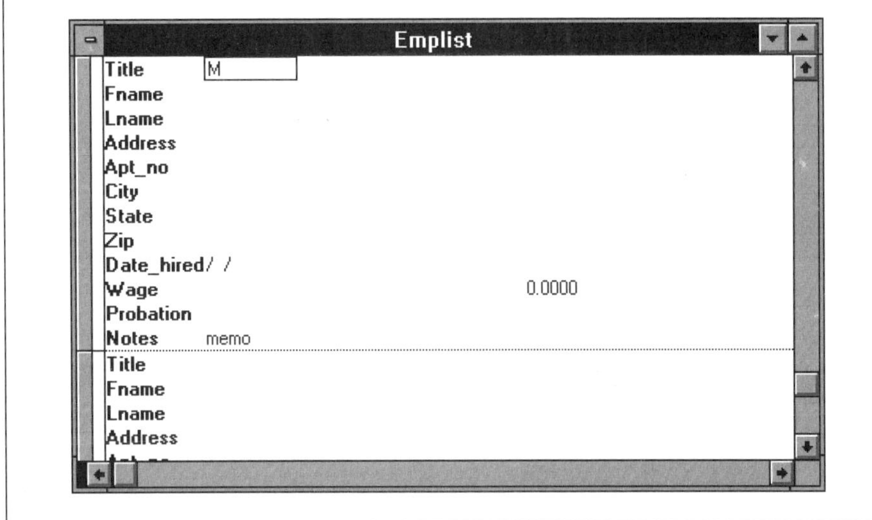

FIGURE 3.3 *As soon as you enter data, a new blank record is appended.*

TIP

It is a common error for users of dBASE-compatible programs to enter blank records. If you make any entry in a record—even a blank space—the record will be saved. One way to avoid this problem is to see whether a new record has been added below the current record in Append mode. If it has been, the current record will be saved, even if appears to be blank.

A check mark is added to the left of the Append Mode option in the View menu when you are in Append mode. Choose View ➤ Append Mode again to toggle out of Append mode.

When you are appending data, you can use the View menu to switch from Browse to Edit display, just as you do when you are editing data. Use whichever display you find most convenient.

▸▸ Adding Sample Data

In the Chapter 2 exercises, you defined the structure of a sample database table. To become comfortable using the Browse window (and so that you will have sample data for later exercises), you can try adding a few records to this table. You'll use both the Edit and Browse displays.

In general, it is easiest to work with your data if you enter it with the same capitalization you want to use in reports, mailing labels, and the like. This usually means that the first letter of each word should be capitalized and the rest in lowercase letters, though there are exceptions, such as state abbreviations, which are generally displayed as two capital letters. You will learn in Chapter 9 how to control capitalization by using FoxPro *expressions*, and in Chapter 17 you will see how to control capitalization in reports and mailing labels; but it is obviously easier to have the data capitalized properly from the start, so you do not have to worry about capitalization and can simply use the Wizards to create reports, labels, and the like.

In large tables, though, it is also common to have some names that were inadvertently entered with all capital letters or with some other nonstandard form of capitalization. For the purposes of this exercise, you will enter the first record in all capital letters and the rest of the records in mixed uppercase and lowercase. In later chapters you will see what difficulties this inconsistency causes and how to get around them.

The sample records you'll add in this exercise also have other inconsistencies that commonly arise in data entry. For example, *Christmas* and *fund raising* are each spelled in more than one way. There are also two people with the same name, as there often are in a large database. Although this is a small sample, it should give you an idea of some of the difficulties you usually come across in actual practice.

▸ Appending Data using Edit Display

First, try adding a series of records in Edit display, which most people find easiest for entering new data. You must begin by choosing Table ➤ Append New Record. After you have created the first record, you can enter Append mode to add new records continuously.

1. If necessary, choose File ➤ Open and open the Emplist table you created in the last chapter. Choose View ➤ Browse "Emplist" to display the table in a Browse window. Choose Table ➤ Append New record to add a blank record to the table. Choose View ➤ Edit to use Edit display.

2. Press Caps Lock, so that the first record is entered in all uppercase. Type **MS.** in the Title field and press Tab. Type **AUDREY** in the Fname field and press Tab. Type **LEVY** in the Lname field and press Tab. Type **318 B. 31 ST.** in the Address field and press Tab. Press Tab again to skip the Apt_no field. Type **FAR ROCKAWAY** in the City field and press Tab.

3. Type **NY** in the State field. Because the data fills the entire field, the cursor automatically moves to the next field. Type **11600** in the Zip field. Again, the cursor moves to the next field.

4. Type **071686** in the Date_hired field. Visual FoxPro automatically adds the / marks used to separate the day, month, and year, so that the date appears as 07/16/86, and then moves to the next field.

5. You want to enter 8.00 in the Wage field. Simply type **8**, and then press Tab to move to the next field. The decimal point and zeros are entered automatically.

6. Type **N** for no in the Probation field. The letter *n* appears for an instant and is then replaced by an *F*, as Visual FoxPro translates yes and no answers into true or false logic statements. Visual FoxPro beeps to tell you the field is full, and the cursor moves to the next field. (If you enter anything but an uppercase or lowercase *T*, *F*, *Y*, or *N* in a Logical field, Visual FoxPro beeps to show that you have made an invalid entry, and the cursor stays in the field.)

7. Since the Notes field is a Memo field, press Ctrl+PgDn (or double-click it) to use the Memo window. You can see that it is titled **Emplist.notes** to show that it is the Notes field of the EMPLIST table. Try entering a note that is longer than one line, so you can see the word-wrap feature: Type **VACATION TIME NOW TOTALS MORE THAN THREE WEEKS PER YEAR. WORKS ON ANNUAL CHRISTMAS FUND-RAISING DRIVE,** as

shown in Figure 3.4. When you have finished typing, press Ctrl+W or select Control ➤ Close to close the Memo window and return to the Browse window. Notice that the word *Memo* now has a capital *M*.

FIGURE 3.4

Entering data in a Memo field

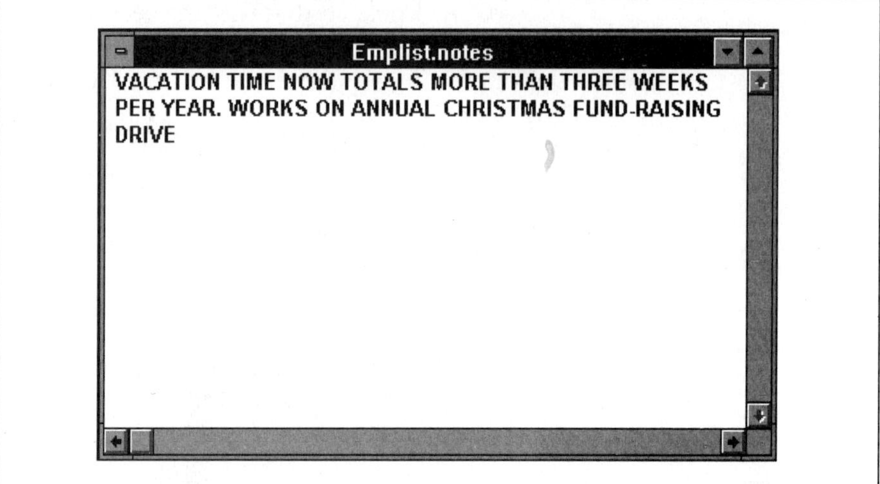

8. Try pressing Tab to move to the next record; you'll see that Visual FoxPro does not respond. Now, choose View ➤ Append Mode, and Visual FoxPro automatically adds the new record. Press the Caps Lock key again, so that the rest of your data will be properly capitalized.

9. Enter the following additional names to get used to the way the Append mode works and to give yourself some sample data to work with in the rest of the book. Leave blank any field marked (None).

Title:	Dr.
Fname:	Jack
Lname:	Love
Address:	3642 Tanach Way
Apt_no:	18
City:	Elizabeth
State:	NJ

Zip:	07200
Date_hired:	06/04/94
Wage:	16.20
Probation:	T
Notes:	Cannot work on Christmas fund raising drive.

Title:	Miss
Fname:	Edna
Lname:	Chang
Address:	2701 Addison Way
Apt_no:	2B
City:	Berkeley
State:	CA
Zip:	94706
Date_hired:	09/07/93
Wage:	9.75
Probation:	T
Notes:	(None)

Title:	Dr.
Fname:	Charlotte
Lname:	Sagorin
Address:	2203 Shady Circle
Apt_no:	(None)
City:	East Orange
State:	NJ
Zip:	07000
Date_hired:	06/06/86

Wage:	22.75
Probation:	F
Notes:	On Xmas fundraising committee.

Title:	Mr.
Fname:	William
Lname:	Johnson
Address:	523 East 21 St.
Apt_no:	F-23
City:	New York
State:	NY
Zip:	10022
Date_hired:	04/23/85
Wage:	6.25
Probation:	F
Notes:	Long term and loyal employee.

Title:	Mr.
Fname:	William B.
Lname:	Johnson
Address:	1701 Albemarle Rd.
Apt_no:	D-14
City:	Brooklyn
State:	NY
Zip:	11226
Date_hired:	12/15/93
Wage:	19.70
Probation:	T
Notes:	(None)

Figure 3.5 shows some of this data entered into the Browse window. Now that you've had some practice appending data with the Edit display, we'll try working with the Browse display.

FIGURE 3.5

Entering data with the Edit display

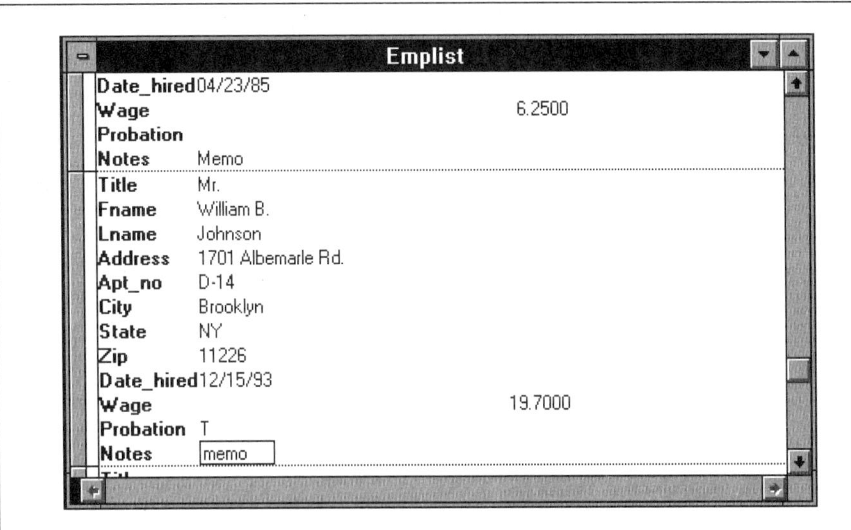

▶ Appending Data with the Browse Display

In this exercise, you will continue creating your sample database by appending another record with the Browse display. You will use the menu system to toggle the screen to this display, and then go on adding records in much the same way as you did before.

1. If the cursor isn't already in the first field of the blank record, move it there now. Then choose View ➤ Browse to toggle the window to the Browse display. The Browse window is now large enough to show only a few fields of each record, and the cursor is right where it was before you toggled to the Browse display.

2. To enter the next record, type **Ms.** in the Title field and press Tab. Type **Nancy** in the Fname field and press Tab. Type **Nixon** in the Lname field and press Tab. Type **1124 Grant Ave** in the Address Field and press Tab. Then press Tab again to skip the Apt_no field. Type **Palo Alto** in the City field and press Tab. Type **CA** in the

State field, **94300** in the Zip field, **02/01/89** in the Date_hired field, **18.25** in the Wage field, and **N** in the Probation field. There is no entry in the Notes field.

3. In the Title field of the next record, type **Prof.** For Fname, type **James**. For Lname, type **Skinner**. For address, type **1206 Francisco St.** Skip the Apt_no field. For City, type **Menlo Park**. For State, type **CA**. For Zip, type **94025**. For Date_hired, type **12/01/92**. For Wage, type **8.2**. For Probation, type **Y**. Type nothing in the Memo field. The table at this point is shown in Figure 3.6.

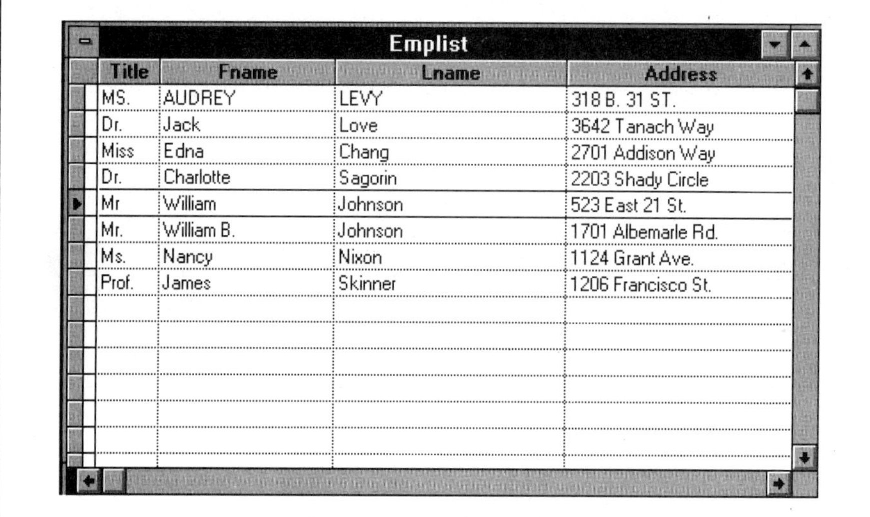

Emplist

Title	Fname	Lname	Address
MS.	AUDREY	LEVY	318 B. 31 ST.
Dr.	Jack	Love	3642 Tanach Way
Miss	Edna	Chang	2701 Addison Way
Dr.	Charlotte	Sagorin	2203 Shady Circle
Mr	William	Johnson	523 East 21 St.
Mr.	William B.	Johnson	1701 Albemarle Rd.
Ms.	Nancy	Nixon	1124 Grant Ave.
Prof.	James	Skinner	1206 Francisco St.

FIGURE 3.6

Entering data with the Browse display

4. Close the window to save your changes: Press Ctrl+End or Ctrl+W, select File ➤ Close, or click the Control-menu box and choose Close.

Remember that the EMPLIST table is still in use. Even if you selected File ➤ Close, you closed only the current window and not the table file itself.

▶▶ Editing Data

At this point, you should find it very easy to edit data, since it is so similar to appending data. If you want some practice, you can do the following exercise, where you open the sample table, move the cursor through it, and edit it, but do not save changes.

1. Choose View ➤ Browse Emplist to display the data, and choose View ➤ Edit to toggle to Edit mode. The last record you entered is still the current record, as shown in Figure 3.7.

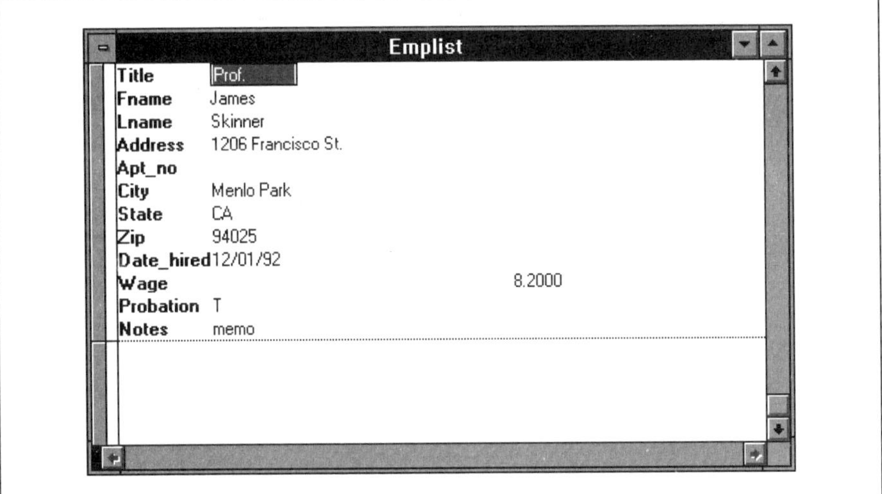

FIGURE 3.7 ▶

The Browse window with the last record you entered still current

2. Try moving up and down through the table. After moving up, use the scroll bar or press PgDn repeatedly to try to move beyond the last record. You will see that you cannot. Try again by using the ↓ key to move to the final field of the last record. When you try to go farther, you will see that you cannot go beyond the last record to add a new record, as you could in Append mode.

3. Let's say you find that Shady Circle is supposed to be Shady Lane. To correct it, double-click the word *Circle* to highlight it and type **Lane** to replace it. To prevent this change from being saved, do not move the cursor to another field.

4. That's all there is to editing fields. Close the window and discard the changes by pressing Esc or Ctrl+Q.

To edit a Memo field, just double-click the field or move the cursor to the field and press Ctrl+PgDn to access the Memo window; then edit the field just as you did when you were first entering it, using the conventional editing keys. If you delete the entire contents of a Memo field, the word *memo* in the table will begin with a lowercase *m* again, to show that the field is empty.

►► Moving through a Table

It can take a long time to scroll through a large table using the mouse or the cursor keys. Visual FoxPro lets you use a couple of shortcuts to move through the table more quickly.

► The GoTo Record Command

Choose Table ➤ Goto Record to display the submenu shown in Figure 3.8.

FIGURE 3.8 ►

The Goto submenu

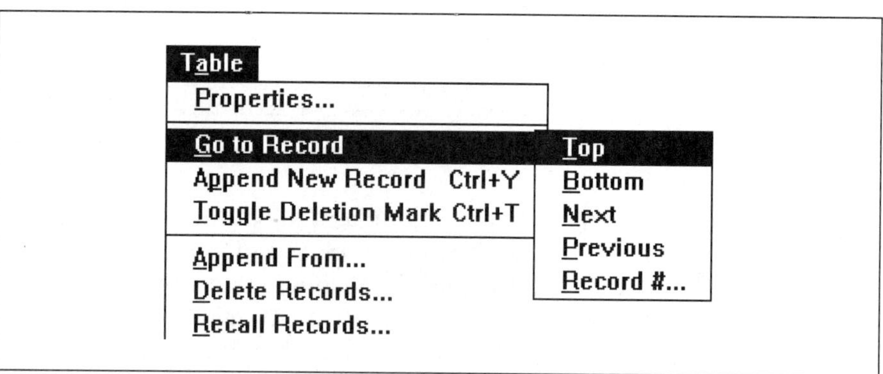

As you can see, this dialog box gives you five choices of where to move in the table:

- **Top:** Moves to the first record of the table.

- **Bottom:** Moves to the last record of the table.
- **Next:** Moves to the record after the current record.
- **Previous:** Moves to the record preceding the current record.
- **Record #:** Displays the Go to Record dialog box, shown in Figure 3.9 to let you move to a specific record.

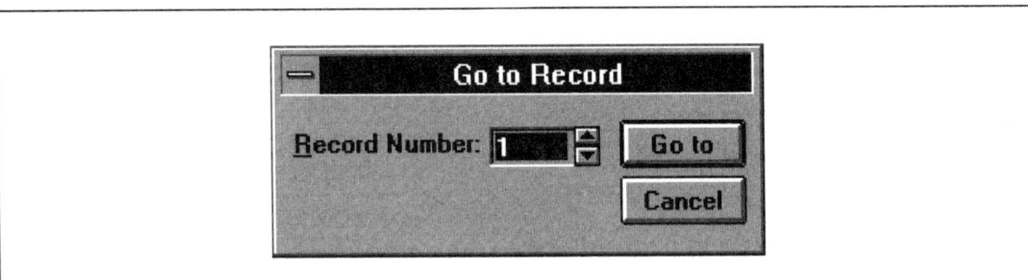

FIGURE 3.9

The Go to Record dialog box

If you select Record, you can either enter the number of the record you want in the text box or select the number using the spin arrows. Although you will not usually know the exact number of the record you want, if you have an approximate idea, this option is generally the fastest method for moving the pointer to the place you want in a long table. If you have ten thousand records in the table, for example, and you know that the record you want was entered recently (say among the last hundred), you can use this command to GOTO record 9900 and then scroll through the Browse window beginning at that point.

NOTE

The record number used in this dialog box is based on the order in which the records were entered. If you are not using an index, records are displayed in this order.

Find and Replace

To let you search for and change specific data, Visual FoxPro includes both a Find and a Find-and-Replace utility, similar to those used in many other types of programs, such as word processors.

►► TIP

This search can be slow if you are working with a large table. Chapter 11 covers more advanced methods that let you use indexes to do faster searches.

Find Command

If you choose Edit ➤ Find, Visual FoxPro displays the Find dialog box, shown in Figure 3.10.

FIGURE 3.10

The Find dialog box

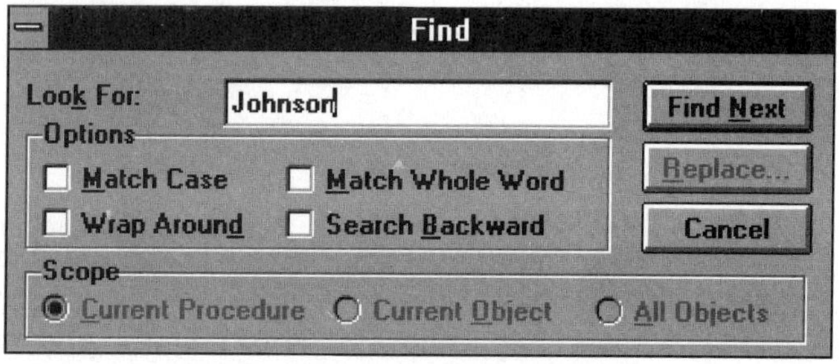

Enter the data you are searching for in the Look For text box, and use the check boxes to select the following options:

- **Match Case:** By default, Visual FoxPro ignores capitalization in looking for a match. Select the Match Case check box to find a match only if capitalization is identical.
- **Wrap Around:** By default, the search looks only from the current record to the end of the table. Select the Wrap Around check box to keep searching at the beginning of the table after reaching the end, until the entire table has been searched.
- **Match Whole Word:** By default, the search finds a match even if the value you are looking for is not in a separate word. For example, if you enter **Smith** in the Look For box, it will find a match

with **Smithson** or **Smithers** as well as with Smith. Select the Match Whole Word check box to find a match only if the value you have entered appears as a separate word.

- **Search Backward:** By default, the search begins at the current record and proceeds toward the end of the table. Select the Search Backward check box to have the search proceed toward the beginning of the table. (If you also have selected Wrap Around, the search will continue at the end after reaching the beginning, until the entire table has been searched.)

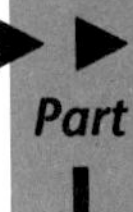

If the first value you find is not the one you want, click the Find Next button repeatedly to continue searching for other occurrences of that value. When you are done, select Cancel to close the Find dialog box.

Click the Replace button to enter a value that will replace the found value.

►► Deleting a Record

Visual FoxPro uses a two-step process to delete records. First, you must mark a record for deletion. Records that are marked for deletion are not actually removed from the table until you *pack* the file by choosing Table ➤ Remove Deleted Records.

When you "pack" the file, the program finalizes the deletion by copying all of the records that are not marked for deletion to a new file, and then using that file as a replacement for the original file. The process is called *packing* because it compresses the file into a smaller amount of space by removing the deleted records. Because it takes time to copy the records to a new file, this process occurs only when you select Pack. If you were working with a long file, there would be an annoying delay if the file were packed every time you deleted a record.

To mark a record for deletion, choose Table ➤ Toggle Deletion Mark. When a record is marked for deletion, the deletion box to its left is darkened, as shown in Figure 3.11; this is the deletion mark.

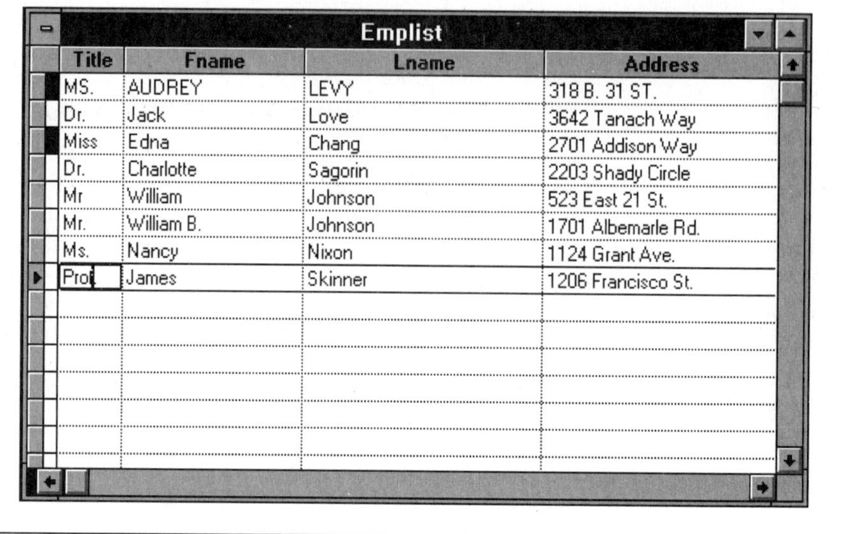
Emplist

Title	Fname	Lname	Address
MS.	AUDREY	LEVY	318 B. 31 ST.
Dr.	Jack	Love	3642 Tanach Way
Miss	Edna	Chang	2701 Addison Way
Dr.	Charlotte	Sagorin	2203 Shady Circle
Mr	William	Johnson	523 East 21 St.
Mr.	William B.	Johnson	1701 Albemarle Rd.
Ms.	Nancy	Nixon	1124 Grant Ave.
Prof	James	Skinner	1206 Francisco St.

FIGURE 3.11 ► *The dark marks at their left show that the first and third records are marked for deletion.*

If a record is already marked for deletion, selecting Table ➤ Toggle Deletion Mark unmarks it. Thus, you can easily recover records marked for deletion until the table is finally packed.

►► **TIP**

As a shortcut, rather than choosing Table ➤ Toggle Deletion Mark, you can toggle the deletion mark on and off simply by clicking the deletion box.

After you choose Table ➤ Remove Deleted Records, marked records can no longer be recovered. If records are marked for deletion but have not yet been removed permanently in this way, they are still included in reports, mailing labels, and any other output based on the table. Remember to use this option before producing mailing labels or other output in which you do not want to include records marked for deletion.

More advanced methods for marking and unmarking multiple records are covered in Chapter 11, where you will also learn how to hide records that are marked for deletion without removing them from the table.

►► Altering the Display of the Browse Window

There are a number of ways you can alter the display of the Browse window. You can change the size or order of fields in the display, divide the window into partitions, or toggle grid lines on and off. (Most of these options are available whether you are using Browse or Edit display, but they are more useful when you are using Browse display and cannot see the entire record.) Experiment with these options as you read their descriptions below. Experiment also to see how they work when you toggle back and forth between Edit and Browse.

► Changing the Size and Order of Fields

The most common alteration you will want to make in the Browse window is to change the order and size of the fields so you can see the data you want. If you move the fields that you need to the left and make some of the fields smaller, you can generally see all of the data you need within the Browse window. (Of course, if this is a problem, you should begin by maximizing this window to see more data.)

Changing the size or order of fields in this way affects only their display in the Browse window; it does not affect the way they are actually stored in the database, so there is no danger of losing data.

Altering Field Size and Order Using a Mouse

By manipulating the header above the records, you can easily change field size or order using a mouse. First make sure you can see the grid lines to the right of each field name. If you cannot, select View ➤ Grid Lines.

- **Size:** To change the size of a field, move the pointer to the grid line to the right of the field's name. Hold down the mouse button and drag left or right to make the field smaller or larger.
- **Order:** To change the order of a field, move the pointer to the field's name. Then, hold down the mouse button and drag left or right to reposition the column where you want it.

Altering Field Size and Order Using the Keyboard

Use the Table menu to change the size or order of fields with the keyboard:

- **Size:** Select Browse ➤ Size Field, and then select the field whose size will be changed. The name of the current field is highlighted. If it is not the field you want, use Tab or Shift+Tab to move to that field. Then press ← to shorten the field or → to lengthen the field. When it is the size you want, press Enter.
- **Order:** Select Browse ➤ Move Field, and then select a field to be moved. The name of the current field is underlined. If it is not the field you want, use Tab or Shift+Tab to move to that field. Then press ← or → to move the field. When it is in the location you want, press Enter.

▸ Partitioning the Window

You can divide the window into two partitions. This is a bit like having separate windows that let you look at two parts of the table at once, or at the same part of the table in two different ways.

By default, the two partitions are linked. That is, when you scroll through the records in one partition, records scroll through the other partition automatically, so the same record is visible in both. However, you can unlink partitions in order to view records independently. Choose Table ➤ Link Partitions or Table ➤ Unlink Partitions to toggle between linked and unlinked partitions. There is a check mark to the left of this option if the partitions are linked. After you have unlinked partitions, you would choose Link to tie them together again. Figure 3.12 shows linked partitions, and Figure 3.13 shows unlinked partitions.

After you have partitioned the window, only one partition is active and available for editing. You can move around this partition in the same way you move around any Browse window, by using the scroll bar or the Tab, arrow, PgUp, and PgDn keys.

As you can see from the illustrations, the partitioned window is very versatile. All the options of the View menu are available in either partition. In Figure 3.12, we've used the Browse display in the right partition to select a record and the Edit display on the left to view all of the fields in that record; in Figure 3.13 we're using the Edit display in both partitions to

FIGURE 3.12

Browse window with linked partitions

Emplist

Title Prof.
Fname James
Lname Skinner
Address 1206 Francisco St.
Apt_no
City Menlo Park
State CA
Zip 94025
Date_hired 12/01/92
Wage
Probation T
Notes memo

Title	Fname	Lname
MS.	AUDREY	LEVY
Dr.	Jack	Love
Miss	Edna	Chang
Dr.	Charlotte	Sagorin
Mr	William	Johnson
Mr.	William B.	Johnson
Ms.	Nancy	Nixon
Prof.	James	Skinner

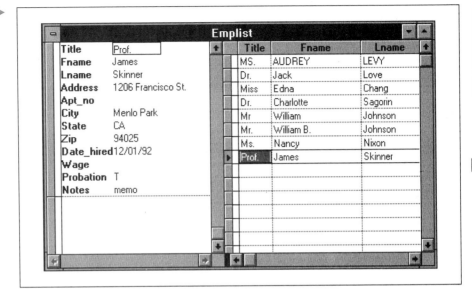

look at the contents of two records. Experiment with these and other possibilities as you try out the following techniques for working with partitioned windows, using either a mouse or the keyboard.

FIGURE 3.13

Browse window with unlinked partitions

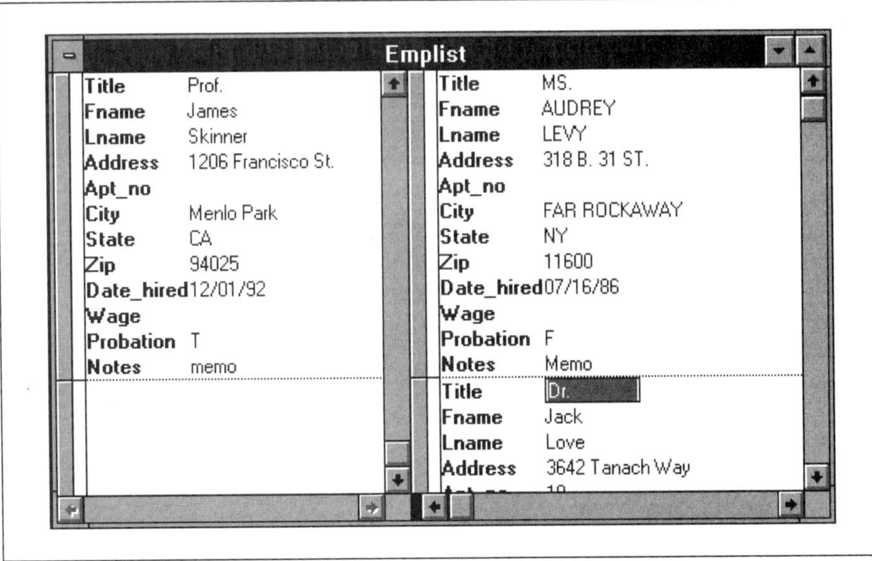

Using a Mouse in Partitioned Windows

It is very simple to work with partitions using the mouse.

- **Create, resize, or remove:** Move the pointer to the window splitter, a small black area that is initially located in the lower-left corner of the Browse window, immediately to the left of the horizontal scroll bar; after partitions have been created, it appears at the bottom of the bar separating the two partitions. The pointer becomes a two-headed arrow with a vertical line in its center when you put it on the window splitter, as shown in Figure 3.14. From its initial position, drag the splitter to the right to divide the window into two partitions. To resize the partitions, drag the partition splitter in the same way until the partitions are the sizes you want. To remove the partitions, drag the splitter until one partition is closed.
- **Change:** To move the cursor from one partition to another, just click the partition you want to make active.

FIGURE 3.14

Using the window splitter

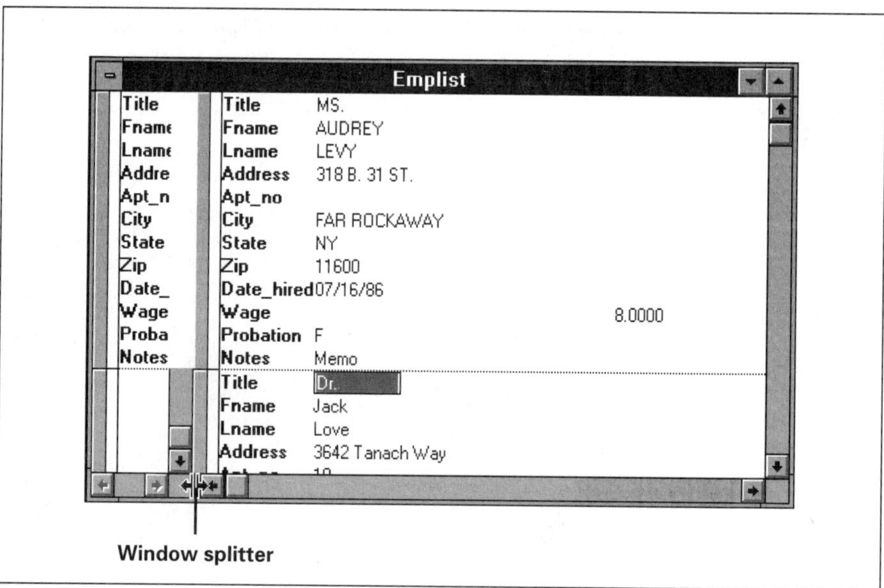

Using the Keyboard in Partitioned Windows

Again, to work with partitions using the keyboard, you make selections from the Table menu.

- **Create, resize, or remove:** Select Table ➤ Resize Partitions. Then press →. The window splitter moves right, dividing the window into two partitions. As you press →, the partition on the left becomes larger and the one on the right becomes smaller. Keep pressing → and ← until the partitions are the sizes you want. Resize existing partitions in the same way. To remove the partitions, press ← until one partition is closed.
- **Change:** To move the cursor from one partition to another, select Table ➤ Change Partitions.

Removing Grid Lines

You can also change the appearance of the Browse window by choosing View ➤ Grid Lines to remove the lines separating fields and records in the Browse display or the lines separating records in the Edit display, as shown in Figure 3.15. This option is a toggle; the check mark to its left disappears and reappears as you select it repeatedly to indicate whether the grid is off or on.

FIGURE 3.15

The Browse window without grid lines

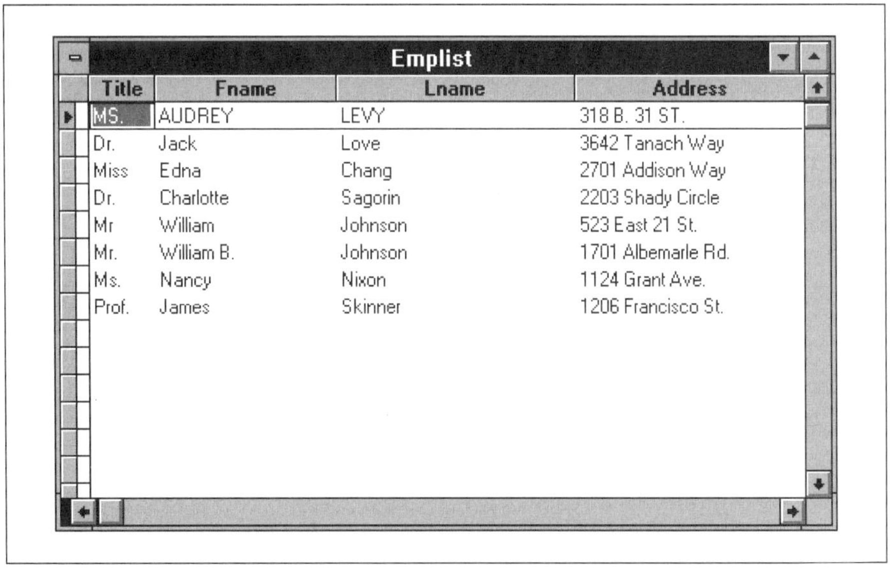

Emplist

Title	Fname	Lname	Address
MS.	AUDREY	LEVY	318 B. 31 ST.
Dr.	Jack	Love	3642 Tanach Way
Miss	Edna	Chang	2701 Addison Way
Dr.	Charlotte	Sagorin	2203 Shady Circle
Mr	William	Johnson	523 East 21 St.
Mr.	William B.	Johnson	1701 Albemarle Rd.
Ms.	Nancy	Nixon	1124 Grant Ave.
Prof.	James	Skinner	1206 Francisco St.

►► To Sum Up

In this chapter, you learned the basic techniques for working with data in a table. In the chapters that follow, you will learn to work with data in other ways. In the next chapter, you will learn to use queries to control which records are displayed. Then you will go on to display your data using forms, reports, and mailing labels.

CHAPTER 4

Working with Queries

FAST TRACK

▶ *To create a query,* 91

choose File ➤ New and select the Query button of the New dialog box. Then click the Wizard button to use the Query Wizard or click the New button to create the query using the Query Designer.

▶ *To define the query using the Query Wizard,* 91

use the first step to select the table and the fields to be included. Use the next step to specify the sort order. Use the next step to filter the data.

▶ *To create a simple data filter using the Filtering step of the Query Wizard,* 94

use only the top set of controls of this dialog box. Select a field name from the Field drop-down list. Select an operator from the Operator list. Enter a value in the Value text box if one is needed with the operator you selected. Only records with a value in the field that matches the value you entered will be included in the result of the query.

▶ *To create a more complex data filter using the Filtering step of the Query Wizard,* 95

use both sets of controls in the same way you use the top set of controls for a simple filter. Select the And radio button to include records in the result only if they match both of your criteria. Select the Or radio button to include records in the result if they match either criterion.

► ***To define the query using the Query Designer,*** **98**

use the Selection Criteria panel to specify the records to be included in the result. Use the Fields panel to specify the felds to be included in the result. Use the Order By panel to specify the sort order.

► ***To modify a query,*** **98**

choose File ➤ Open and open the query. It will be displayed in the Query Designer.

► ***To create a data filter using the Selection Criteria panel of the Query Designer,*** **100**

use the Field Name drop-down list to choose a field name, use the Criteria list to choose an operator, and enter the value you want to match in the Example text box. To create a more complex filter, add additional criteria on following lines in the same way. All criteria must match for records to be included in the result, unless you click the OR button to add an OR before a criterion.

► ***To run a query,*** **107**

click the Run button when it is displayed in the Query Designer, or choose File ➤ Do and select it from the Do dialog box.

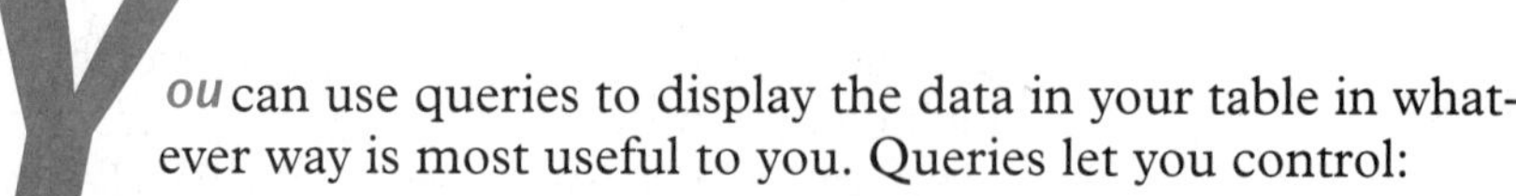

You can use queries to display the data in your table in whatever way is most useful to you. Queries let you control:

- which fields of a table are displayed
- which records of a table are displayed
- the order in which records are displayed

They also let you join two or more tables and display a result with fields from them all, but to do this, you must understand relational databases, which are covered in Part III of this book.

Despite their power, queries are very easy to create and use. This chapter begins by discussing the Query Wizard, which can create most queries that you will need. Then it goes on to look at the Query Designer, which lets you use somewhat more sophisticated selection criteria, as you may need to do for some queries.

The Query Designer is similar to the Query Wizard and almost as easy to use. You may find that you prefer to use it rather than the Wizard to create queries, as well as using it to modify queries you created using the Wizard.

Because Part I of this book is meant to get you up and running as quickly as possible, this chapter simply introduces the basic techniques for using the Query Designer with a single table. Chapter 15 shows how to use the Query Designer to work with relational databases and covers other advanced features of the Designer, such as the programming code that it generates.

▶▶ Creating a Query

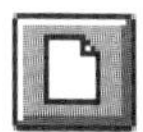

Create a query as you do other types of files, by choosing File ➤ New or clicking the New tool, and using the New dialog box to display either the Query Wizard or the Query Designer.

▶ The Query Wizard

If you use the Wizard, Visual FoxPro displays the Wizard Selection dialog box, which lets you use Wizards to create several special-purpose queries as well as ordinary Visual FoxPro queries. Select Query Wizard to display the Wizard that is covered in this chapter, which is fundamental to working with your data.

Selecting the Table

The first dialog box of the Query Wizard, shown in Figure 4.1, lets you select one or more tables to base the query on and select the fields of that table to include in the result.

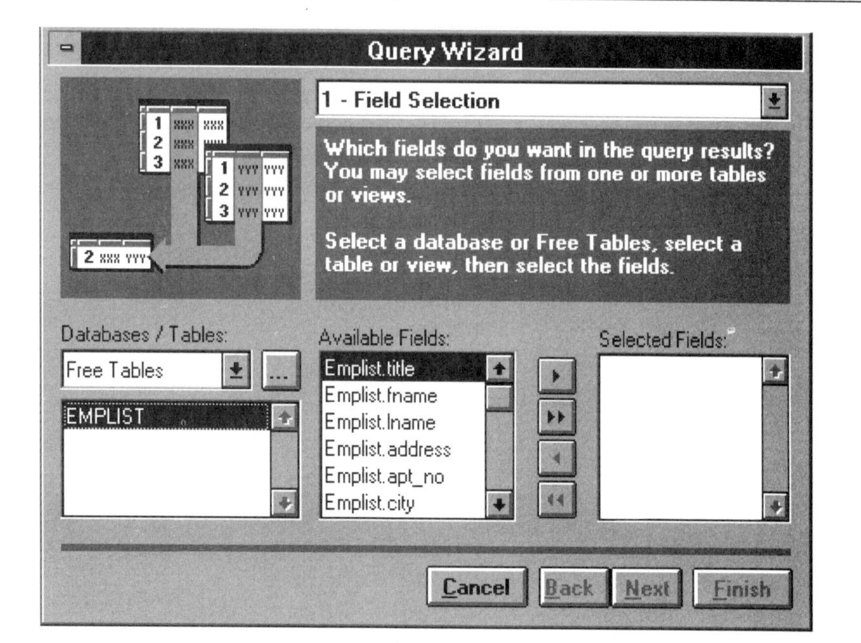

FIGURE 4.1 ▶

Selecting the table and fields

►► **WARNING**

To work with more than one table, you must understand a bit about relational database theory, which is covered in Chapter 12. Until you have learned about relational databases, you should always select just one table.

This dialog box also includes a Field Picker, which you work with in the same way as in the Table Wizard, described in Chapter 2. Use the buttons to move field names from the Available Fields list to the Selected Fields list. Only the Selected Fields are included in the result.

After you've added fields to the Selected Fields list, you can click and drag the mover boxes to their left to control the order in which they appear in the result, as you do when you are using the Field Picker in the Table Wizard.

This dialog box also includes a Databases/Tables drop-down list, which lets you use tables from FoxPro databases, as covered in Chapter 16. For now, you will only use free tables.

►► **NOTE**

If you open the table you want before creating the query, it will be included in this list. If the table you want is not included in the list, click the ... button to its right to display the Open dialog box, which you can use in the usual way to select the table.

Relating the Tables and Grouping Records

If you selected more than one table, the next two dialog boxes let you specify the relationship among the tables and how the tables are grouped. These dialog boxes are covered in Chapter 13, which discusses how to work with relational databases using the Wizards. As long as you are working with a single table, you cannot use these dialog boxes.

Specifying Sort Order

The next dialog box, shown in Figure 4.2, lets you select fields that will be used as the basis for sorting records in the query's result. If you do not specify any sort order, the records will be listed in the order in which they were entered in the table.

FIGURE 4.2

Specifying sort order

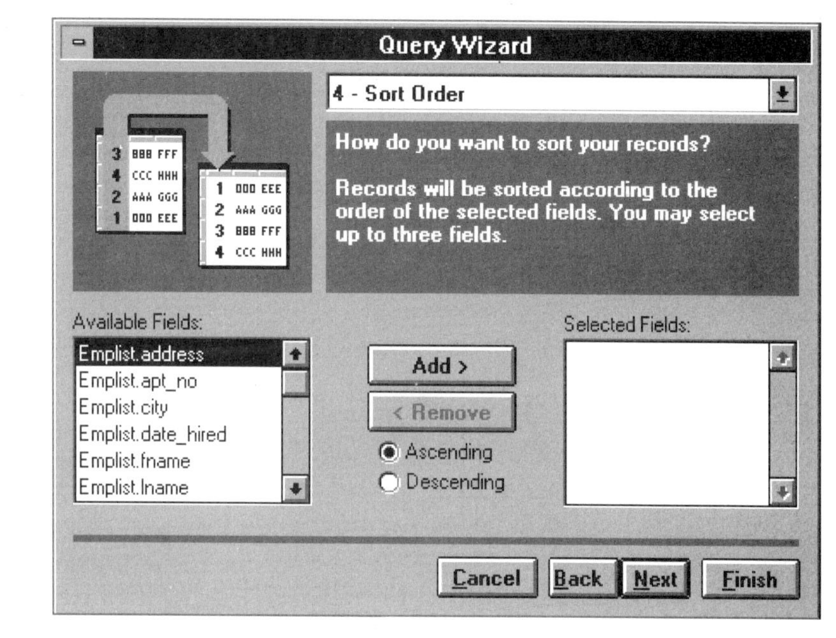

You may base the sort order on as many as three fields. The first field you select is used as the primary basis of the sort order, and the other fields are used as "tie-breakers" when the value in the first field is the same.

To sort alphabetically by name, for example, you must use both the Lname and Fname fields. If you sort only on Lname, then the record for Xavier Smith may come before the record for Aaron Smith; you need to use the Fname as a tie-breaker when Lname is the same in two records.

Likewise, if you wanted to sort names alphabetically by state, you could use the State, Lname, and Fname fields as the basis of the sort. All the records from the same state would be listed together. Within each state, records would be listed by Lname; and if Lname is the same in several records, they would be ordered on the basis of Fname.

To specify sort order, select fields from the Available Fields list, and click the Add button to add them to the Sort Order list; use the Remove button to remove a field from the Sort Order list.

You can select the Ascending or Descending radio button for each of the fields you add, if you are sorting on multiple fields. For example, you can sort records in descending order by ZIP code; and within each ZIP code, you can sort in ascending alphabetical order by last name and first name.

As in other Field Pickers, move buttons appear to the left of items in the Selected Fields list, and you can click and drag these buttons to change the order of fields used as the basis of the sort order.

Filtering the Data

The next dialog box, shown in Figure 4.3, lets you specify criteria that determine which records will be included in the result. Records that do not match the criteria are filtered out of the result. Do not create any filter if you want the query result to include all the records in the table.

If you do want to use a filter, you usually will want to create a simple one that uses just one criterion. For example, you may want to display just the records for people who live in California.

To create a simple filter, use only the top set of controls of this dialog box. Select a field name from the Field drop-down list and an operator from the Operator list. In most cases, you must also enter a value in the Value text box, although some operators do not require a value here.

For example, to isolate the records with addresses in California, you would select **Emplist.state** from the Fields drop-down list, select **equals** from the Operator list, and enter **CA** in the value text box.

Notice that the field begins with the name of the table followed by a dot. For example, the State field of our sample Emplist table has the name **Emplist.state**. This is necessary when you are working with multiple tables, but you can ignore it when working with a single table.

The operators you can select from are Equals, Not Equals, More Than, Less Than, Is Blank, Contains, and In. Most of these operators are followed by a single value, though Is Blank does not use a value, and In is

FIGURE 4.3

Creating a simple expression

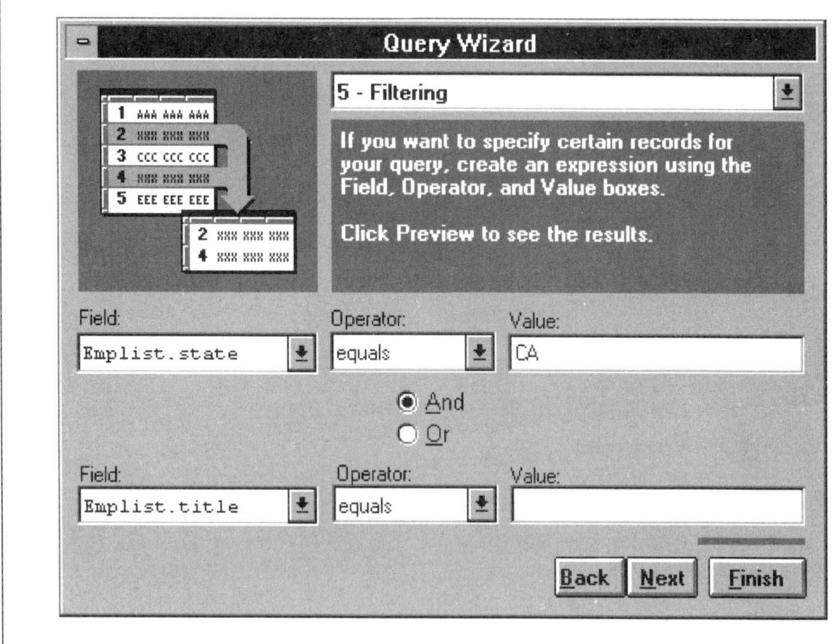

followed by a list of values separated by commas and is true if any of the listed values is in the field. More sophisticated operators are available when you use the Query Designer, and are discussed later in this chapter.

Using Complex Logical Expressions The Wizard also lets you create complex criteria, which are made up of two simple criteria. Just use the lower set of controls to create the second expression, and select the And or the Or radio button to specify whether the two expressions are related using logical AND or logical OR:

- If a complex expression is made up of two simple expressions related by the AND operator, the entire expression is true only if *both* simple expressions are true.
- If a complex expression is made up of two simple expressions related by the OR operator, the entire expression is true if *either* of the simple expressions is true.

We do not always use the words AND and OR as precisely in ordinary speech as we must in specifying query criteria. For example, if we want to see the records from two states, we might say that we want the employees from New York and New Jersey, or we might say that we want the employees from New York or New Jersey. In queries, you must use OR in this case.

Remember that the AND operator excludes records. For example, the expression **State equals CA AND Probation IsTrue** will match fewer records than the expression **State equals CA** alone.

On the other hand, the OR operator includes more records. For example, the expression **State equals CA OR Probation IsTrue** will match more records than the expression **State equals CA** alone.

Previewing the Result of the Expression If you click the Preview button, Visual FoxPro displays a Browse window with the records that match the expression, as shown in Figure 4.4. You can scroll through this window to make sure the expression is finding the records that you actually want.

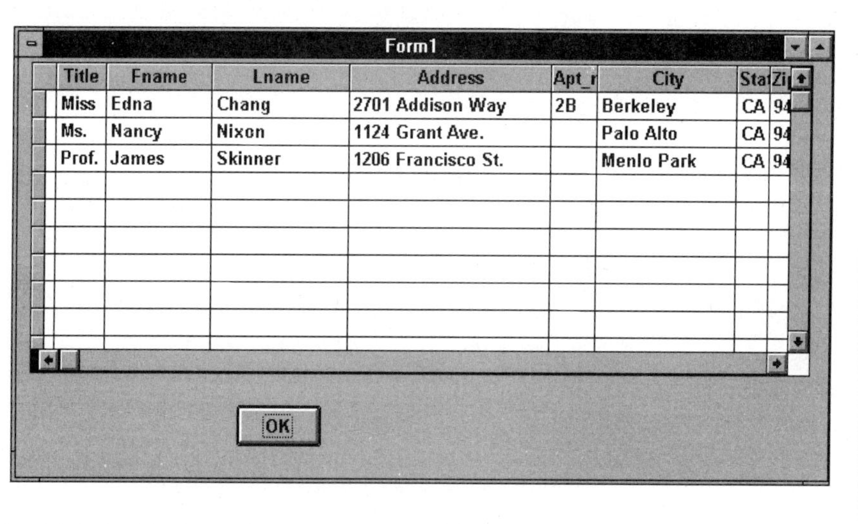

FIGURE 4.4

Previewing the result of a complex query

Saving the Query

The final dialog box, shown in Figure 4.5, gives you three options: save the query and return to the Command window; save the query and run it, displaying its result in a Browse window; or save the query and use the Query Designer to modify it. Like the previous step, it also includes a Preview button.

FIGURE 4.5

The final dialog box of the Query Wizard

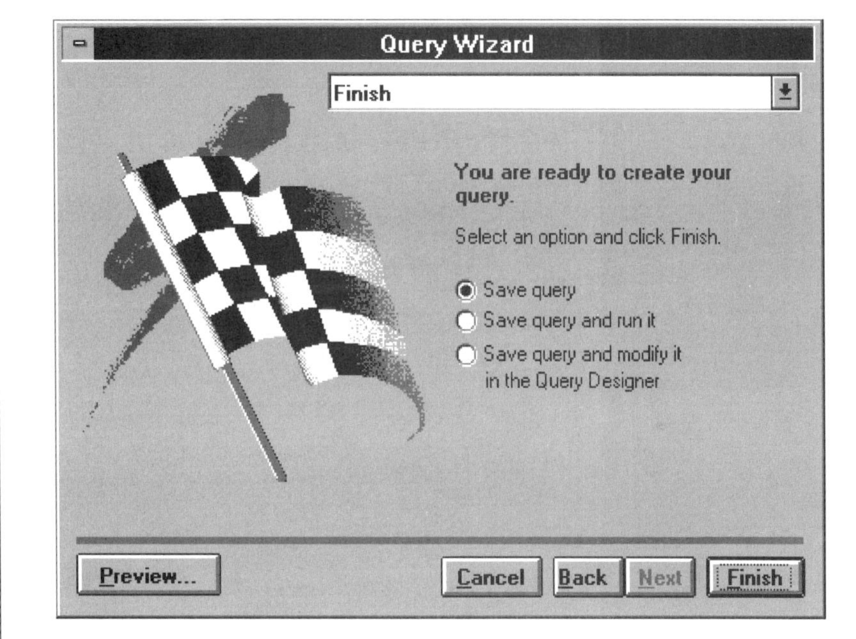

When you click Finish, Visual FoxPro displays the Save As dialog box to let you name the query and specify its directory location. By default, queries have names ending in the extension QPR, which stands for Query Program.

As you will see later in this chapter, queries actually are programs, and you use them by running them as you do other programs.

▸ The Query Designer

You can use the Query Designer at any time to modify a query that you have created earlier. Choose File ➤ Open, and use the Open dialog box to select the query. As you have just seen, you can also proceed directly to the Query Designer from the last dialog box of the Query Wizard to modify the query that you've created there.

The Query Designer is so easy to use, however, that you may prefer to use it to create the query from scratch rather than using the Wizard. Choose File ➤ New or click the New tool, select the Query radio button, and click the New File button.

Adding a Table

When you create a new query in this way, Visual FoxPro displays the Add Table Or View dialog box, shown in Figure 4.6, where you can select a table to base the query on; views are used with FoxPro databases and are covered in Chapter 16. To select a free table, click the Other button to display the Open dialog box and make your selection there.

FIGURE 4.6 ▸

The Add Table or View dialog box

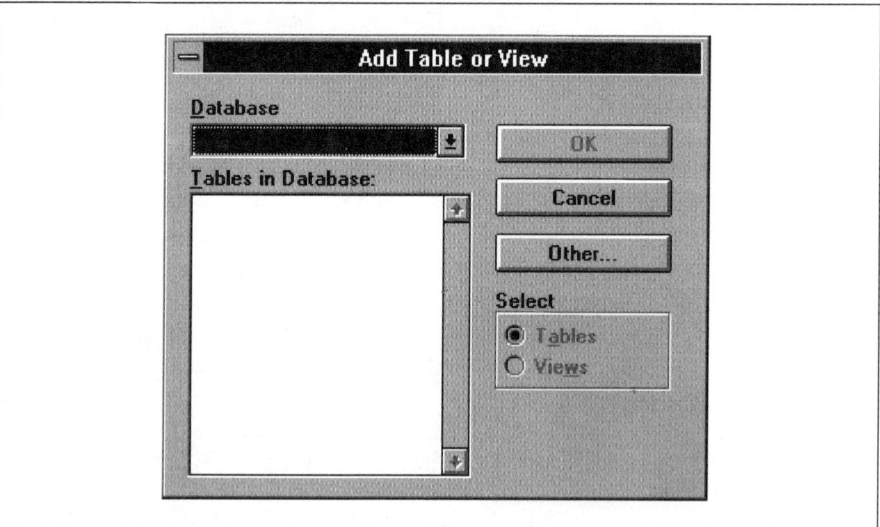

The table that you select is included in the panel at the top of the Query Designer, as shown in Figure 4.7.

FIGURE 4.7

A table is included in the Query Designer

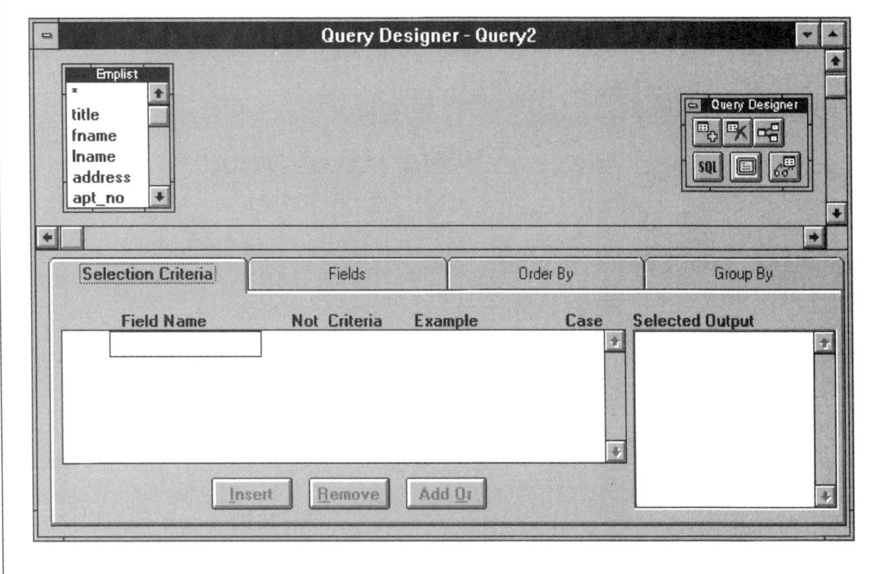

You can also add or remove tables at any time:

- Choose Query ➤ Add table or click the Add Table button on the Query toolbar to display the Add Table Or View dialog box, which you use to select a table.

- Be sure that the table you want to remove is selected in the Query Designer. Its title bar should be highlighted; if it is not, you can simply click it to select it. Then choose Query ➤ Remove Table or click the Remove Table button on the Query toolbar to display the Add Table Or View dialog box, which you use to select a table.

These options are useful when you are working with a relational database, but when you are working with a single table, you should simply add the table when you create the query. Do not include multiple tables in the query unless you understand relational databases, covered in Chapter 12.

Chapter 15 covers advanced features of the Query menu, which are not necessary for the sort of simple queries that you will use as a beginner. For now, you can hide the toolbar by clicking its upper-left corner.

The Query Designer has four panels, which are roughly equivalent to the dialog boxes of the Query Wizard that were covered earlier. Display any panel by selecting its name from the Query menu or simply by clicking its tab.

The Selection Criteria Panel

The Selection Criteria panel, shown in Figure 4.8, works like the Filtering dialog box of the Wizard, with a few minor differences.

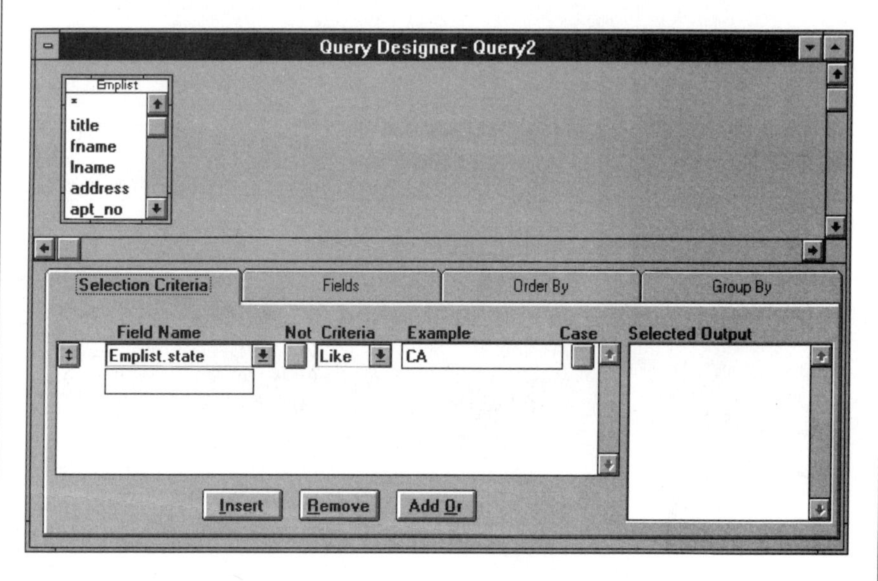

FIGURE 4.8

The Selection Criteria panel of the Query Designer

To enter a simple criterion to determine which records will be matched, use the Field Name drop-down list to choose a field name and the Criteria list to choose an operator; then enter the value you want to match in the Example text box.

For example, to find all the records from California, you would choose **Emplist.state** as the field name and **Like** as the Criteria operator, and enter **CA** in the Example box.

As you can see, the operators used here are a bit different from the operators used in the Wizard. Use the Criteria drop-down list to choose among the following operators:

- **Like:** finds a match if the letters at the beginning of the field match the example. For example, **Emplist.lname Like Smith** will find a match if a record has the name Smithson or the name Smithers, as well as if it has the name Smith.

- **Exactly Like:** finds a match only if the value in the field is identical to the example. Thus, **Emplist.lname Exactly Like Smith** will find a match only if a record has the name Smith, not if it has the name Smithson or Smithers.

- **More Than:** finds a match if the value in the field is greater than the example. May be used with Date, DateTime, and Character fields as well as with numbers. Thus, **Emplist.lname More than O** will find a match if a record has a last name beginning with O or any letter that follows it in the alphabet.

- **Less Than:** finds a match if the value in the field is less than the example. Like More Than, it may be used with Date, DateTime, and Character fields as well as with numbers.

- **Between:** finds a match if you enter two values in the Example column, separated by a comma, and the value in the field is greater than or equal to the first value and less than or equal to the second. For example, **Emplist.date_hired Between 01/01/95, 12/31/95** would find records for all employees hired in 1995.

- **In:** finds a match if the value in the field is the same as any value in the list of values you enter in the Example column (again separated by commas). For example, **Emplist.state In NY, NJ, CT** would find records for all employees from New York, New Jersey, or Connecticut.

Delimiters If you generate a query using the Query Wizard and then modify it using the Query Designer, you will find that the values in the Example columns have delimiters around them that reflect the data type.

FoxPro uses the following delimiters:

- Character values are surrounded by single or double quotation marks or by square brackets; for example, "CA" or 'CA' or [CA].
- Date and Datetime values are surrounded by curly brackets; for example, {09/01/95}.
- Logical values are surrounded by dots; for example, .T.
- Number values do not use delimiters, for example, 25.

You can ignore these delimiters when you are modifying a query generated by the Wizard. In general, you can leave them out when you are creating a query using the Query Designer, but you must include the dot delimiters to query a logical field.

▸▸ NOTE

The only examples you can use to query a logical field are .T. or .F. Of course, these must be used with the Like (or the Exactly Like) operator.

The More Than and Less Than Operators The More Than and Less Than operators may cause a bit of confusion.

In general, they do not find a match if the value is identical: for example, **Emplist.wage More than 6.25** would not include records where the wage was exactly equal to 6.25; if you want to include those records, you should use the criterion **Emplist.wage More than 6.24** instead.

However, if you are working with a character field, a value is "more than" the example if it has any additional characters. Thus, **Emplist.lname More than O** would find a match for any name that begins with O and has other characters following it, but it would not find a match if a record had only the character O in the Lname field.

The Not Check Box You can reverse any criterion by selecting the Not check box. For example, to find records from every state *except* California, use the same query to find records from California described above, but also click the Not box. A check is displayed to show that the box is selected, as illustrated in Figure 4.9.

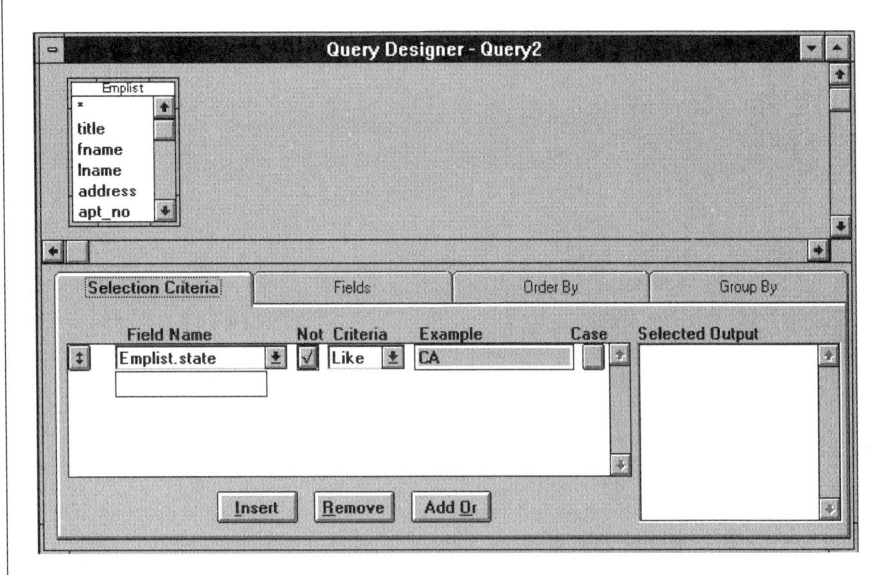

FIGURE 4.9

Using the Not check box

Case-Sensitive Queries By default, queries are case-sensitive. For example **Emplist.lname Like SMITH** will not find records with **Smith** in them. To make a query match regardless of capitalization, select the Case check box. Since each line of the query has this box, you can make some conditions but not others case-sensitive in queries that have multiple conditions.

Queries with Multiple Conditions To create a complex query based on multiple conditions, enter each condition on a separate line.

By default, these conditions will be related using a logical AND, which means there is a match only if all of the conditions are true.

To relate the conditions using a logical OR, so that a match will be found if any condition is true, click the Add Or button. The word OR is added on a separate line, and you can enter an additional condition on a separate line, as shown in Figure 4.10.

FIGURE 4.10

Using a logical OR

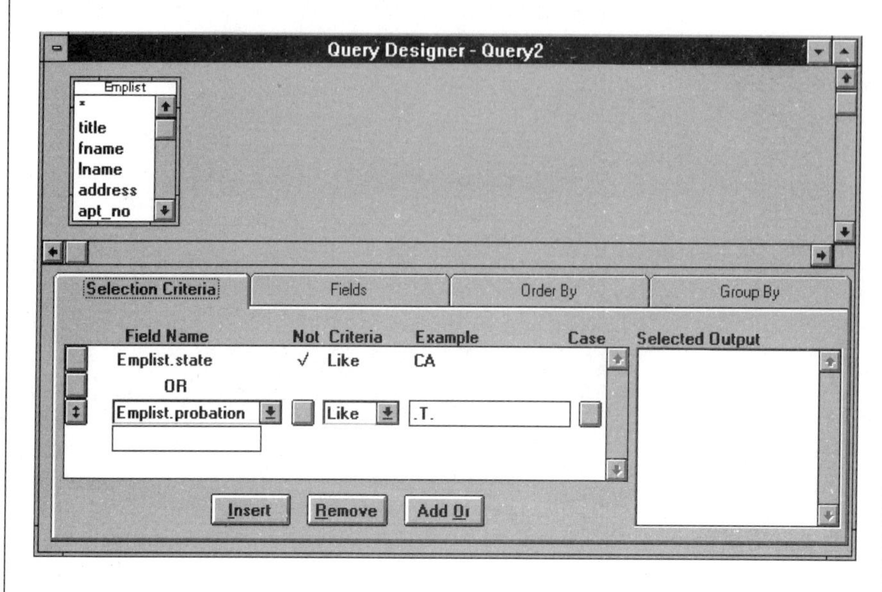

►► **WARNING**

If you mix logical AND with logical OR conditions in the same query, you may get unexpected results unless you understand the *order of precedence* that the query uses to evaluate conditions. Order of precedence is discussed in Chapter 9. For beginners, it is safest to use all ANDs or all ORs in a single query.

When you are working with multiple criteria, you may want to modify the list of criteria in the following ways:

- **Inserting a line:** select a line and click the Insert button to insert a new line above it.
- **Deleting a line:** select a line and click the Remove button to delete it.
- **Changing the order of lines:** click and drag the mover box to the left of any line to change its order.

The Selection Criteria panel also includes a Selected Output list, which includes the fields that you select in the Fields panel and can be used to change their order.

Although the Selection Criteria panel is a bit more complex than the Filtering dialog box of the Query Wizard, the next two panels you will look at are virtually identical to the equivalent dialog boxes of the Wizard.

The Fields Panel

Use the Fields panel, shown in Figure 4.11, to specify which fields will be included in the query's result. Use this panel as you do the Field Picker: Move the fields you want to include from the Available Fields list to the Selected Output list.

FIGURE 4.11 

The Fields panel of the Query Designer

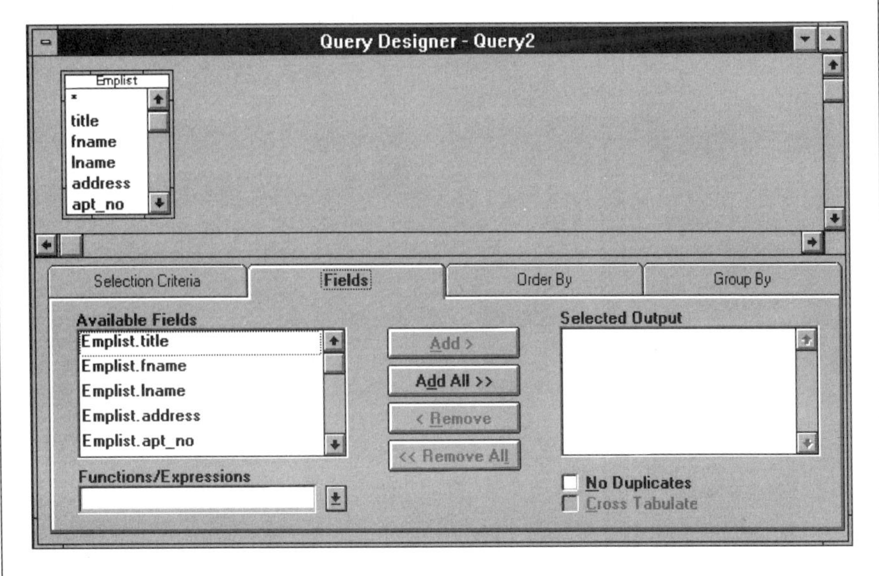

If you are creating a grouped query, you can also include functions or expressions in the result, by selecting them from the Functions/Expression drop-down list and clicking Add. Grouped queries are covered in Chapter 15.

In addition, you can select the No Duplicates check box to remove duplicate records: records must have the same value in every field to be considered duplicate. This option is particularly useful if the query is based on multiple tables, as you can sometimes create many duplicate records when you join two tables.

The Order By Panel

Use the Order By panel, shown in Figure 4.12, to specify the sort order of the result. Add fields to the Ordering Criteria list and use each to sort in Ascending or Descending order, just as you do using the Wizard. The only difference is that you can use an unlimited number of fields as the basis of the sort.

FIGURE 4.12

The Order By panel of the Query Designer

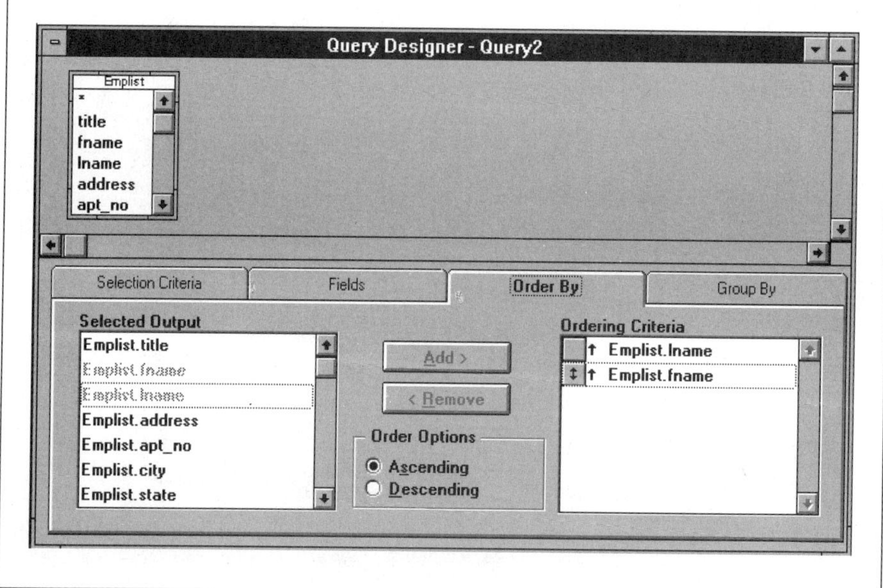

The Group By Panel

The Group By panel is used to create grouped queries. It is covered in Chapter 15.

▸▸ Running the Query

When a query is displayed in the Query Designer, you can run it by choosing Query ➤ Run Query or by clicking the Run button of the main toolbar. As you know, you can open a query to display it in the Designer, and so you can run it in this way at any time.

However, it is generally easier to run a query using the Program menu. A query is actually a program: in fact, it is stored in a file with the extension QPR, which stands for Query Program. When you run a query or other program, Visual FoxPro "pseudo-compiles" it, converting the original programming code to a form that can run more quickly. The pseudo-compiled form of a query is stored in a file with the same name as the query and the extension QPX.

You can run any program by choosing Program ➤ Do to display the Do dialog box, shown in Figure 4.13. Use this like the Open dialog box to select the file, and click Do to run it.

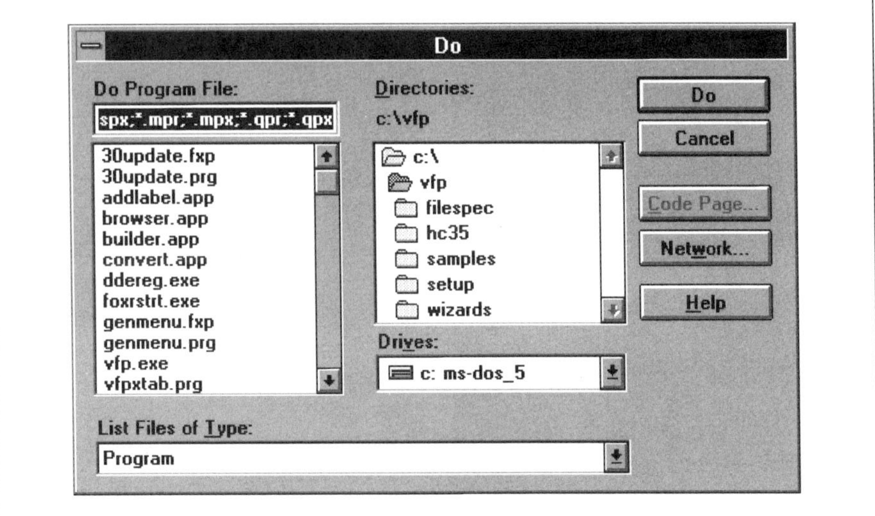

FIGURE 4.13 ▸ *The Do dialog box*

▸▸ Using the Query

When you run a query, its result is displayed in a Browse window, and you can use it just as you do a table, with the exception that a query result is read-only; it is used to view data in the table but not to modify it. You can use the added options of the View menu and the Table menu to work with the result of the query, and you can click and drag to resize or change the order of its columns, as you do with a table. Figure 4.14 shows a query to display all records that are not from California in alphabetical order by name; the window has been maximized and the columns have been resized so you can see the name and state fields.

FIGURE 4.14

The result of a query

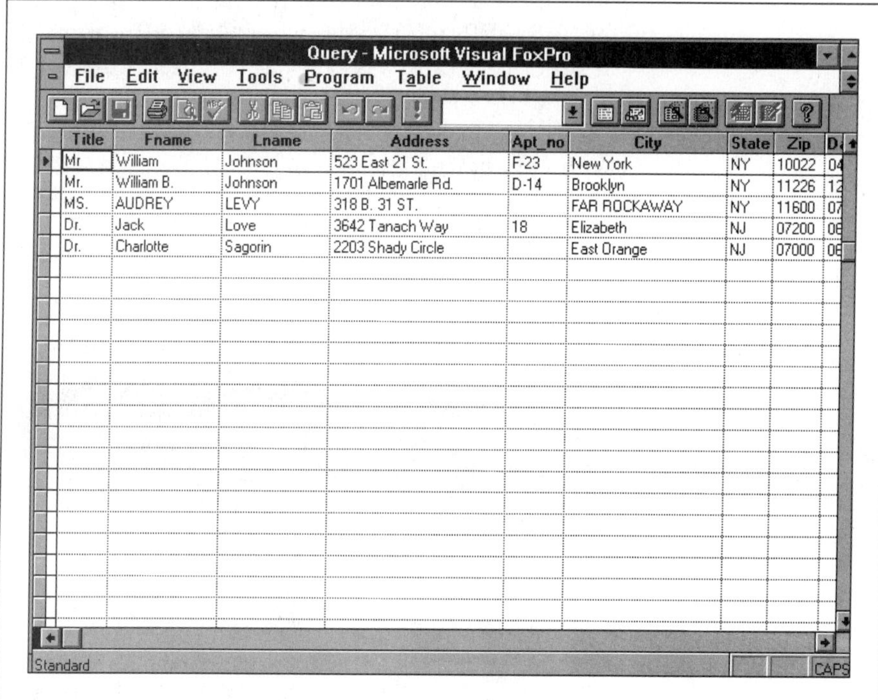

►► **NOTE**

You can also direct the result of the query to a report, labels, a table, and several other file types. It is not generally good practice to save the output of a query in a table, because it is difficult to maintain two copies of the data, and you may use the table even after it is outdated. Chapter 15 looks at redirecting output of a query.

If you close the Browse window, the query itself remains open, and you can browse it again by choosing View ➤ Browse Query.

Because a query remains open in this way, it can sometimes interfere with your opening a table. If you try to open a query's underlying table while the query is still open, Visual FoxPro will display the warning shown in Figure 4.15.

FIGURE 4.15

An open query can prevent you from opening a table.

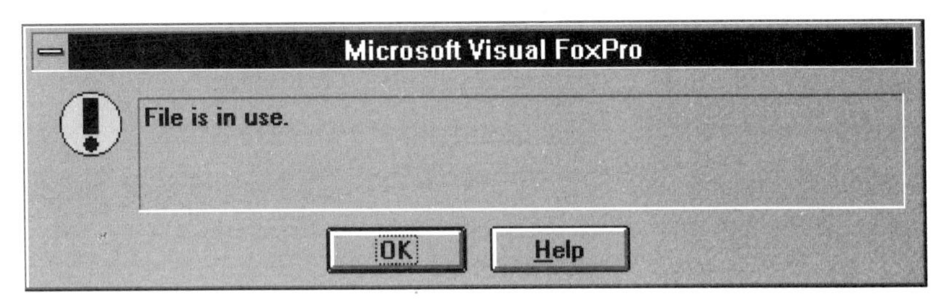

►► **NOTE**

If you have this problem, an easy way to close the query is to enter CLOSE DATABASES in the Command window. After entering this command, you will be able to open the table in the usual way.

If you open the table first, it does not interfere with running the query. So if you want to browse the entire table and the result of a query at the same time, you should browse the table before running the query.

►► Sample Queries

In this section you can try creating a couple of sample queries, to get a feel for the capabilities of the Query Wizard and Query Designer. These exercises again use the Emplist sample database table created in Chapter 2.

► Using the Query Wizard

Probably the most common reason you will use queries as a beginning Visual FoxPro user is to isolate a set of records that meet certain criteria. Try creating a simple query using the Query Wizard to isolate records for all employees in the Emplist table who are from California. Then modify it using the Query Designer to include records for California employees who are also on probation. This is the sort of query that you will use commonly in practice.

You can arrange the records in the result in alphabetical order by name. To do this, you must use both the Lname and the Fname field to determine the sort order, with the Lname field listed first.

1. Choose File ➤ New, select the Query radio button of the New dialog box, and click the Wizard button. When Visual FoxPro displays the Wizard Selection dialog box, select Query Wizard.

2. Visual FoxPro displays Step 1 of the Query Wizard. If the Emplist table was open when you began, it will appear in the Tables list, and its fields will be listed in the Available Fields list. Otherwise, click the … button to the right of the Database/Tables drop-down list and use the Open dialog box to select Emplist.

3. Click the Add All (>>) button to include all the fields from the table in the result of the query. Then click Next. The Wizard skips Steps 2 and 3, the Relationship and Groupings steps, which are available only for relational databases.

4. When Visual FoxPro displays the Step 4—Sort Order window, double-click the Emplist.lname field in the Available Fields list to add it to the Sort Order list. Then double-click the Emplist.fname field to add it under the Lname field, as shown in Figure 4.16. This will sort the records first by last name and then by first name. Click Next.

5. Visual FoxPro now displays Step 5—Filtering to let you enter the criterion for the query. Use only the upper set of controls. Choose Emplist.state from the Fields drop-down list and leave Equals as the operator. In the Value text box, enter **CA**, as shown in Figure 4.17.

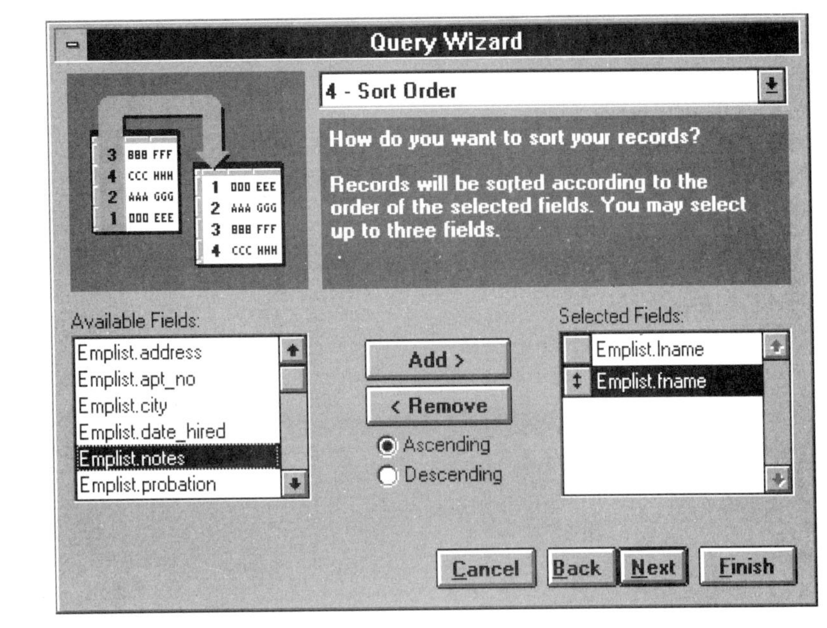

FIGURE 4.16

Specifying the sort order of the records

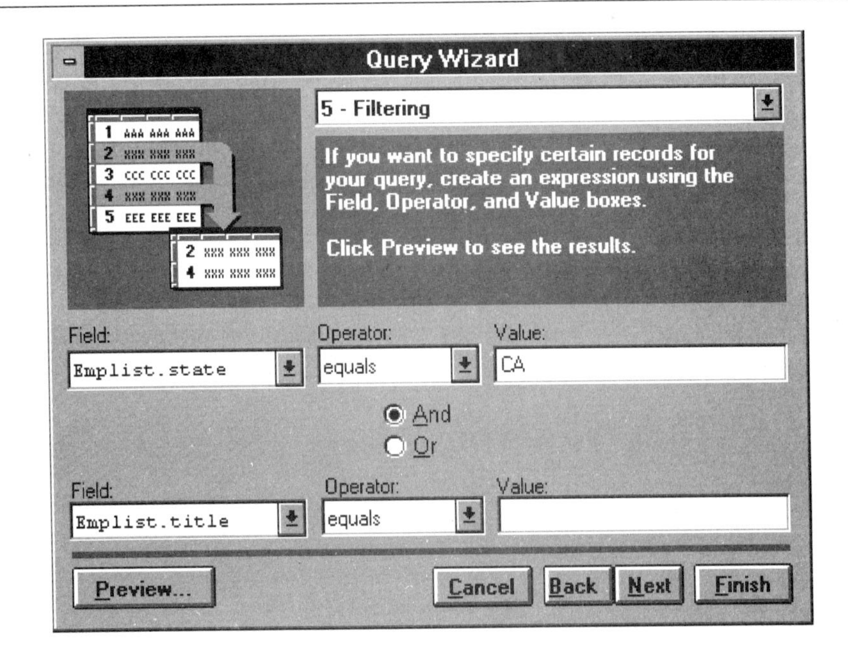

FIGURE 4.17

Specifying which records to include

6. Click Next. In the Final step, select the "Save query and run it" radio button and click Finish to create the Query. When Visual FoxPro displays the Save As dialog box, enter the name **Cal_emps** in the File Name text box, be sure that the LEARN-FOX directory is open, and click Save.

7. Visual FoxPro displays the result of the query. Notice that the names are in alphabetical order, and scroll right to confirm that all the records are from California, as shown in Figure 4.18. Then close the Query window.

FIGURE 4.18

The result of the first sample query

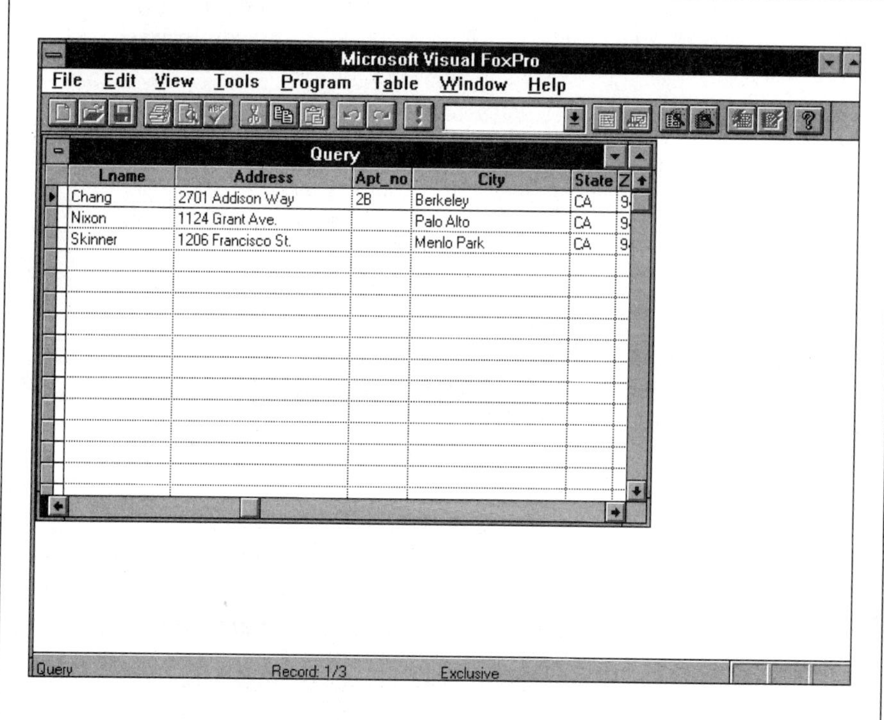

▸ Modifying the Query

Now you can use the Query Designer to modify this query so that it also uses the Probation field as a criterion.

1. To modify the query, choose File ➤ Open and use the Open dialog box to select **cal_emps.qpr**. (You will have to use the List

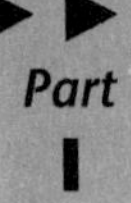

Files Of Type drop-down list and perhaps the directory list to display it.)

2. Visual FoxPro displays the definition of this query in the Query Designer. The Selection Criteria panel is already displayed, but you might want to look at the other panels before using it, to see that they are based on the selections you made using the Wizard. Display the Selection Criteria panel again when you are done.
3. Click the Add Or button to add the Or operator on the second row.
4. On the third row, select Emplist.probation from the Field Name list, leave Like as the criterion, and enter **.T.** in the Example box; be sure to include the dot delimiters.
5. Click the Run button of the main toolbar to display the result. Scroll right to verify that all records are from California and are on probation.
6. Choose File ➤ Save As and save the modified query with the name **cal_prob**. Then close the Query Designer.

▶ Creating a Query Using the Query Designer

Next, try creating a query from scratch using the Query Designer.

The one common use of a query that you have not tried yet is to isolate certain fields of a table. For example, if you are telephoning everyone on your mailing list, you would probably find it easier to work with the result of a query that includes only the first name, last name, and telephone number of each person on the list, rather than working with the entire table. You might also want to list names alphabetically.

In the following exercise, you will create a query to list employees by ZIP code. It will include only the first and last name, Zip, and State fields. It will be sorted on state and ZIP code, so you can see at a glance how employees are distributed geographically; and the sort order will also include Lname, so that employees in the same ZIP code are listed alphabetically:

1. Choose File ➤ New, select the Query radio button of the New dialog box, and click the New File button. When Visual FoxPro displays the Add Table Or View dialog box, click the Other button

and use the Open dialog box to add the Emplist table. Visual Fox-Pro displays the Query Designer.

2. Click the Fields tab to display the Fields panel. As shown in Figure 4.19, double-click the following fields in the Available Fields list to add them to the Selected Fields list: Emplist.state, Emplist.zip, Emplist.lname, and Emplist.fname. Be sure to add the fields in the order shown here: State, Zip, Lname, and then Fname.

FIGURE 4.19

Specifying which fields should be included

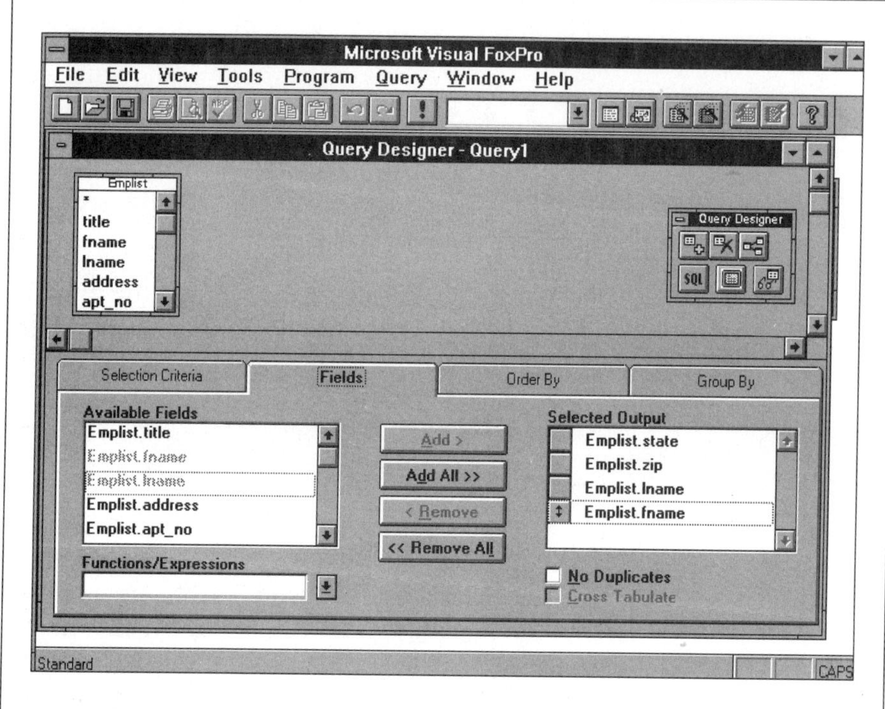

3. Click the Order By tab. Then double-click the State, Zip, Lname and Fname fields in the same order that they are listed in the Selected Output list to add them all to the Ordering Criteria list.

4. Click the Run button of the main toolbar to display the result shown in Figure 4.20. When you are done looking at it, close the Query window. Then close the Query Designer window. Visual FoxPro asks if you want to save the query; choose Yes. In the Save As dialog box, enter the name **St_zip** and press Enter.

FIGURE 4.20

The result of the modified query

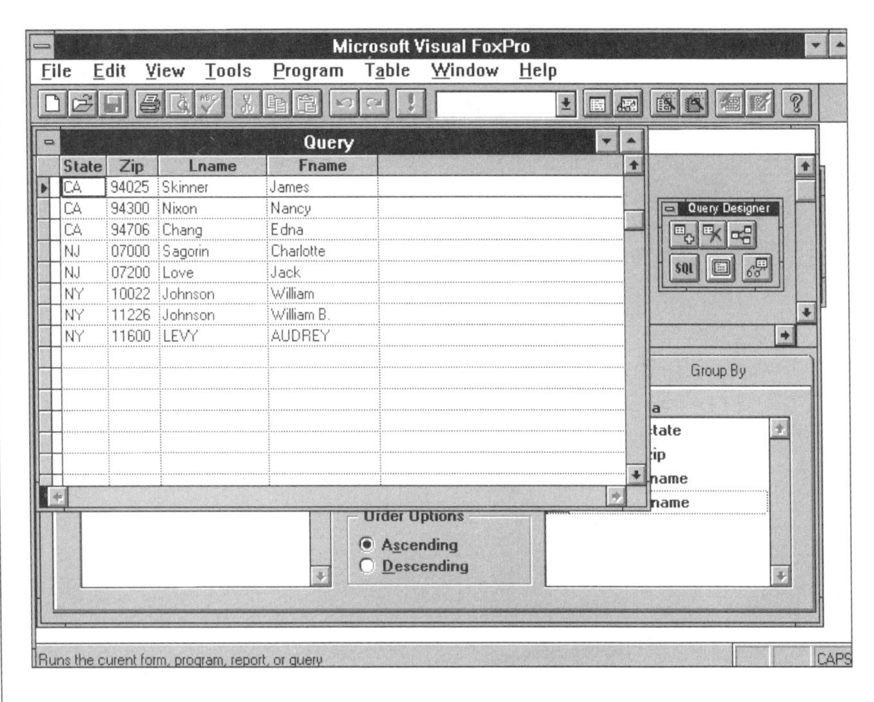

▶▶ To Sum Up

In this chapter, you looked at both the Query Wizard and the Query Designer. You learned to use them to create typical queries of the sort you'll work with often, determining the sort order of the records, the fields, and the records that are included in the result. In the following chapters, you will learn how to use forms to control how your data is displayed on the screen during data entry and to use reports and mailing labels to control how data is printed.

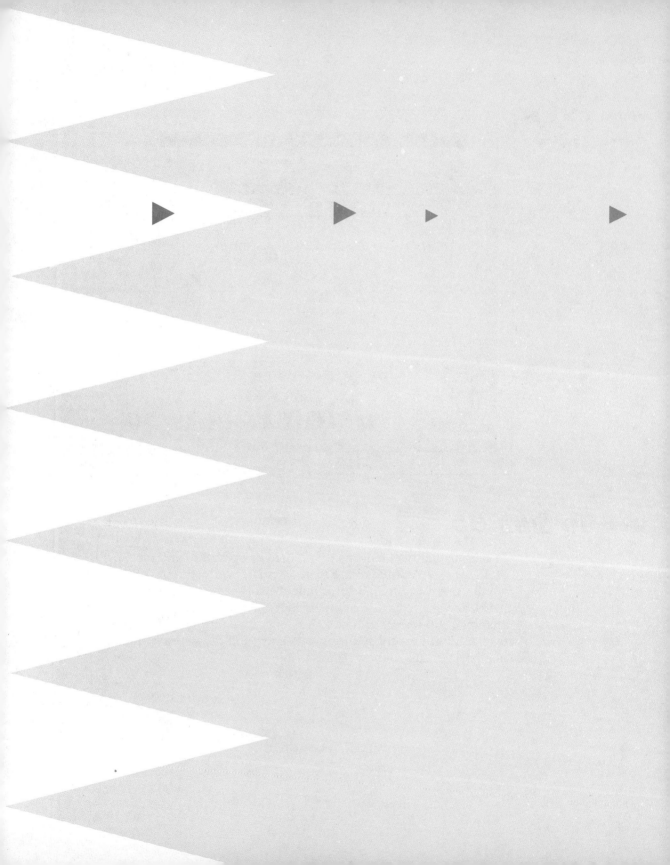

CHAPTER 5

Using Forms to Speed Up Your Work

▸▸ FAST TRACK

▶ ***To create an AutoForm,*** **120**

open the table that it is based on and click the AutoForm button of the toolbar.

▶ ***To create a form using the Wizard,*** **121**

use the first step to choose the fields that will be included. Use the second step to choose the style. Use the third step to choose the sort order. Use the final step to add a title and generate the form.

▶ ***To run a form,*** **125**

choose Program ➤ Do to display the Do dialog box. Choose Form from the Type drop-down list, select the form in the Files list, and click the Do button.

▶ ***To move through the table using a form,*** **126**

click the Top button to display the first record in the table. Click the Prev button to display the record before the current record. Click the Next button to display the record after the current record. Click the End button to display the last record in the table.

▶ ***To locate a record using a form,*** **126**

click the Find button to display the Search Record window.

To add or edit a record using a form, **126**

click the Edit button to edit the current record. Click the Add button to add a new record; Visual FoxPro adds a blank record to the end of the table, and makes it the current record so you can edit it. In either case, Visual FoxPro dims all the other buttons and adds Save and Revert buttons to the form. Thus, you can only add or edit one record at a time using the form, and you must explicitly save or discard the change one record at a time.

To print records using a form, **127**

click the Print button to display a dialog box that lets you print the current record or all records either to the printer or to a Page Preview window.

To close a form, **127**

click the Close button, press Esc or choose File ➤ Close, or choose Close from the form's Control menu.

▶▶ *Fill-in-the-blanks* data entry forms are one of the most useful features of any computerized database management system. Like their paper equivalents, they tell the user (who might be anyone from the company owner to a clerical temp hired just to enter a specific batch of records) exactly what information is needed. Visual FoxPro gives you two simple tools that anyone can use to create such forms: the AutoForm feature and the Form Wizard, both of which you'll learn how to use in this chapter. Both tools can make it easier for you to work with your own applications or to provide an easy-to-use interface for novices who are doing data entry. In addition, you will look briefly at how to customize forms, using the Form Designer, in Chapter 17.

Like a query, a form is a Visual FoxPro program. Its pseudo-compiled version is kept in a file with the extension SCX. When you use Auto-Forms or the Form Wizard, Visual FoxPro generates the appropriate programming code for you and creates the SCX file.

▶▶ AutoForms

To create an AutoForm, you simply open a table and click the Auto-Form button of the main toolbar. Visual FoxPro takes a moment or two to create the form, and then displays a data entry form that includes all the fields in the table.

In general, the form includes the field name and a text box to let you enter data in each field. For logical fields, it includes a check box instead of a text box. The box will be checked if the value is .T. and empty if it is .F.; you can alter its value simply by clicking it, as you do with any check box. For Memo fields, it includes a scrollable text box; if the memo is too large to fit in the box, the scroll bar is activated so you can view it all. The form also includes buttons that make it easy to

perform such basic operations as viewing, editing, and adding data; you'll learn about working with forms a little later in this chapter.

AutoForms are given names made up of the initial letters of the file name, followed by an underscore and a number. For example, if you create an Autoform for the Emplist table, Visual FoxPro gives it the name Emplis_1.SCX. If there is already a form with this name, Visual FoxPro names the new one Emplis_2.SCX, and so on.

▶▶ The Form Wizard

The Form Wizard is very straightforward and easy to use, and it gives you several extra options that are not available in AutoForms. Most people—including developers—find it easiest to create forms by using this Wizard for the basics and customizing the form it generates.

To start the Form Wizard, choose File ➤ New, select the Form radio button, and click the Wizard button, or simply click the Form Wizard button of the main toolbar. You'll see the Wizard Selection dialog box, which lets you choose between the two available types of Form Wizard.

The One-to-Many Form Wizard is used with relational databases and is covered in Chapter 13. When working with single-table databases, you should use only the Form Wizard, as we'll do in this chapter.

▶ Choosing Fields

The first step of the Form Wizard, shown in Figure 5.1, lets you choose which fields are included in the form. It works like the Field Pickers you have used in earlier chapters; use the buttons to move the fields you want to include from the Available Fields list to the Selected Fields list. In deciding which fields to include, or whether to include all of them, consider the form's purpose and who will be using it. The sample form created in this chapter, for example, does not include the Notes field, on the assumption that it might have confidential notes, which you would not want a data-entry person to see.

FIGURE 5.1

Step 1 of the Form Wizard—choosing fields to include in the form

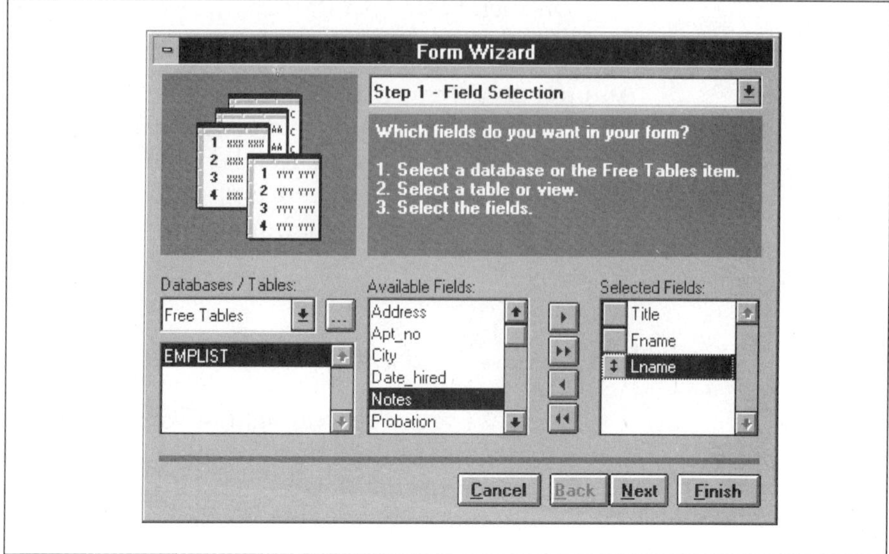

► Choosing a Style

The next step, shown in Figure 5.2, lets you choose the style and button type of the form. These options do not affect the way the form behaves, only its appearance.

FIGURE 5.2

Step 2 of the Form Wizard—specifying a style

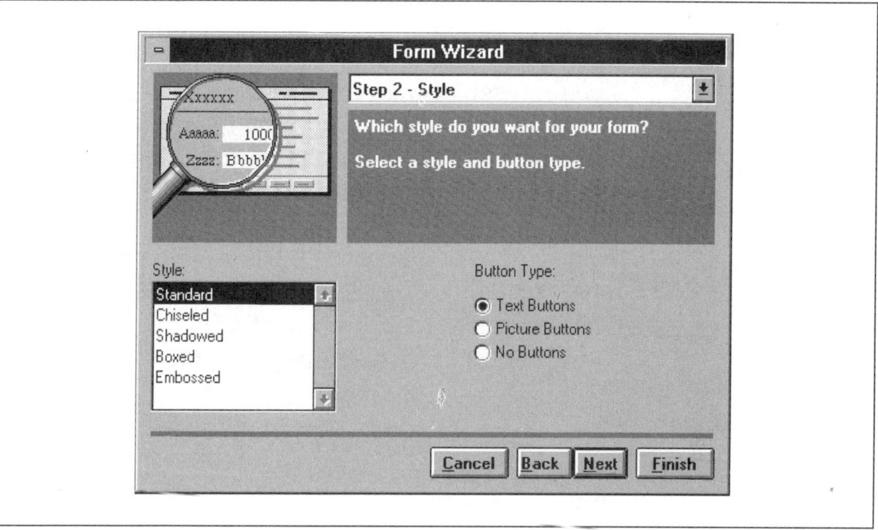

The Style list gives you several options for how fields will be displayed, such as boxed and shadowed, and for the type of button (if any) to use. If you choose the Picture radio button, arrows will be used on the buttons that you use to move among records, rather than words such as Next and Prev. If you choose No Buttons, they will not be included.

In the upper-left corner of the dialog box, you can preview an illustration of each style as you select it.

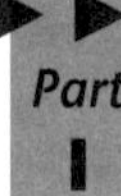

▶ Choosing Sort Order

The next step, shown in Figure 5.3, lets you specify the sort order of the records, and works just like the Sort Order dialog box of the Query Wizard. Use the Add and Remove buttons to move fields from the Available Fields list to the Sort Order of Records list. Use the radio buttons to specify whether each field is sorted in Ascending or Descending order.

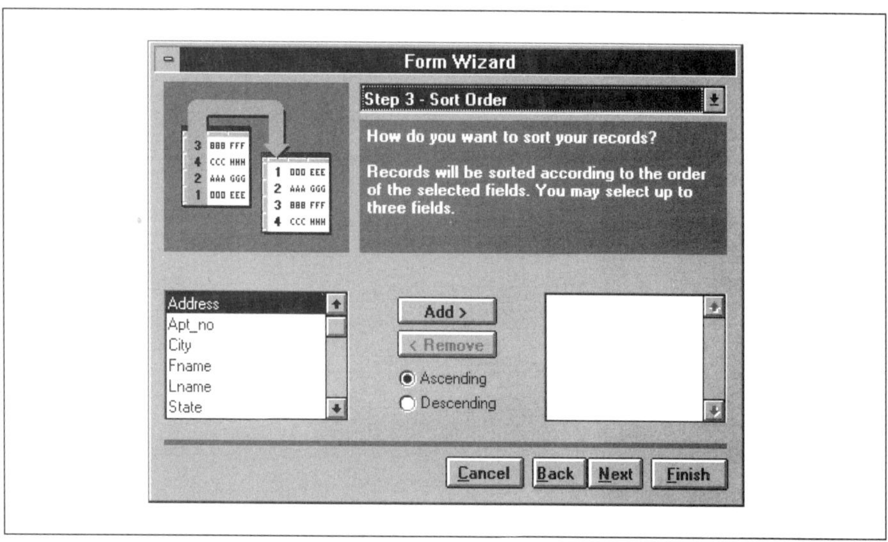

FIGURE 5.3 ▶

Step 3 of the Form Wizard—specifying sort order

Specifying Sort Order can make it easier to find records when you are using the form. For example, it would be easier to look up an employee if the form for the Emplist table were sorted in alphabetical order by name.

▸ Generating the Form

The final step, shown in Figure 5.4, lets you enter a title that will be displayed at the top of the form. The radio buttons give you the option of saving the form, saving it and running it immediately, or displaying it in the Form Designer, so you can customize its design. The Form Designer is primarily intended for application developers; features of it that can be useful to Visual FoxPro users are covered in Chapter 17 of this book.

FIGURE 5.4 ▸

The final step of the Form Wizard

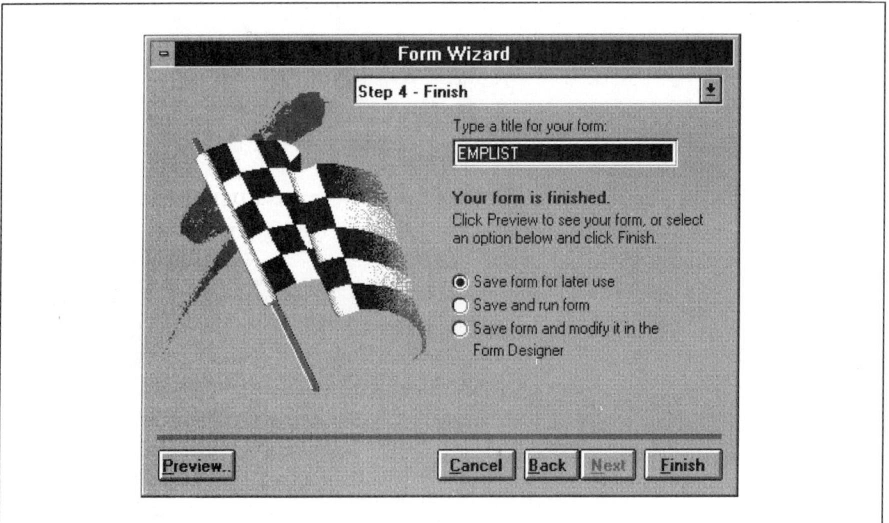

After you click Finish, Visual FoxPro displays the Save As dialog box to let you name the form. As it generates the form program, Visual Fox-Pro displays a dialog box that records its progress.

▸▸ Using Forms

AutoForms and forms created using the Wizard are used in the same ways.

Running a Form

A Visual FoxPro form is a program, like a query, and you run it in the same way. Choose Program ➤ Do and use the Do dialog box to select the form.

NOTE

You'll need to select Form from the List Files Of Type drop-down list in the Do dialog box to display the form programs. Form programs are not displayed if you leave the default Program file type.

Using the Form's Control Panel

AutoForms and forms created using the Wizard have the same set of buttons at the bottom of the form, sometimes called its *control panel*, which make it easy to work with the form. Figure 5.5 shows an ordinary control panel of a form, and Figure 5.6 shows how the control panel looks if you created the form using the Wizard and selected Picture rather than Text as the style of the buttons.

FIGURE 5.5

The control panel with text buttons

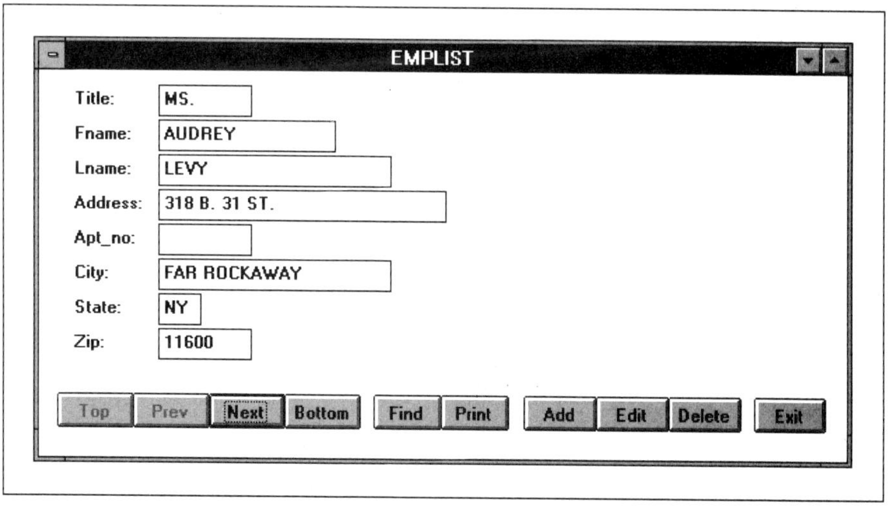

EMPLIST

Title: MS.
Fname: AUDREY
Lname: LEVY
Address: 318 B. 31 ST.
Apt_no:
City: FAR ROCKAWAY
State: NY
Zip: 11600

Top | Prev | Next | Bottom | Find | Print | Add | Edit | Delete | Exit

FIGURE 5.6

The control panel with picture buttons

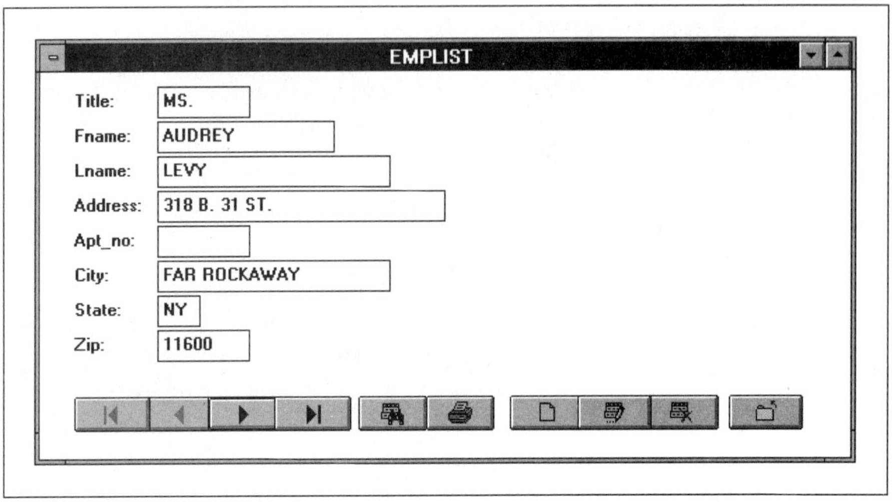

EMPLIST

Title: MS.
Fname: AUDREY
Lname: LEVY
Address: 318 B. 31 ST.
Apt_no:
City: FAR ROCKAWAY
State: NY
Zip: 11600

Moving through the Records

To move through the records:

- Click the Top button to display the first record in the table.
- Click the Prev button to display the record before the current record. If you are already viewing the first record, this button is not available.
- Click the Next button to display the record after the current record. If you are already viewing the last record, this button is not available.
- Click the End button to display the last record in the table.

Locating a Record

You can also move through the table by clicking the Find button to display the Search Record window. Use this like the Find dialog box disussed in Chapter 3.

Adding and Editing Records

To edit the current record, click the Edit button.

To add a new record, click the Add button. Visual FoxPro adds a blank record to the end of the table, and makes it the current record so you can add data to it.

In either case, Visual FoxPro dims all the other buttons and adds Save and Revert buttons to the form.

Thus, you can only add or edit one record at a time using the form, and you must explicitly save or discard the change one record at a time. This makes errors less likely, and it is particularly useful if you are using the form in an application that you are developing for beginners.

Printing Records

Select the Print button to display a dialog box that lets you print the current record or all records either to the printer or to a Page Preview window. (Chapter 6 discusses how to use the Page Preview window.)

Closing the Form

Click the Close button, press Esc or choose File ➤ Close, or choose Close from the form's Control menu to close the form and return to the FoxPro interface (or to an application you've developed that uses this form; see Chapter 24 for information about using forms in applications).

►► Sample Forms

To get accustomed to using forms, first try creating an AutoForm. Then, using the Wizard, you'll create a form that does not display the Notes field and that lists the records in alphabetical order.

1. If necessary, choose File ➤ Open and use the Open dialog box to open the Emplist table. Then click the AutoForm button of the main toolbar to create the AutoForm. When Visual FoxPro displays the form, try using its features, and when you are done, close the Form window.

2. Now, to create a form using the Wizard, choose File ➤ New, select the Form radio button of the New dialog box, and click the Wizard button. Select the Form Wizard in the Wizard Selection dialog box.

3. If the Emplist table is not already displayed in the Field Selection step of the Wizard, click the … button to the right of the Databases/Tables drop-down list and use the Open dialog box to select the table. Then click the button with two right arrows on it to add all the fields to the Selected Fields list. Scroll through the Selected Fields list to display the Notes field and double-click it to remove it from this list.

4. Click Next to go to Step 2. Select Shadowed as the style. Leave Text Buttons selected as the button type.

5. Click Next to display the Sort Order step. Add Lname and Fname to the Selected Fields list.

6. Click Next to display the Finish step. Click the Preview button. After looking at the preview of the form, click Return to Wizard.

7. In the Finish step of the Wizard, enter the title **Employee Data** and select the "Save and run form" radio button; then click Finish. In the Save As dialog box, leave the default name, Emplist.scx, and click Save. After a pause, Visual FoxPro displays the form shown in Figure 5.7.

8. Try using the features of this form, and close the Form window when you are done.

9. Now, use the program menu to display all forms. Choose Program ➤ Do and select Form from the Files of Type drop-down list; and then select Emplist.scx from the File list, using the directory list to select the Learnfox directory if necessary. Close the form when you are done using it.

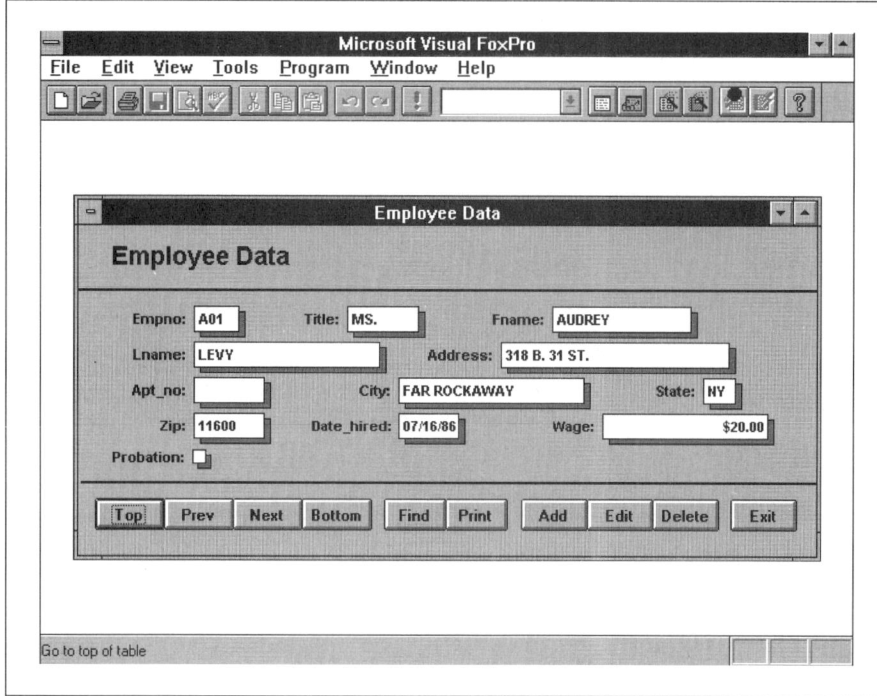

FIGURE 5.7

Using the form

►► To Sum Up

Now, you have learned to work with all the basic features of Visual FoxPro that create screen output. In the next two chapters, you will look at the most important types of printed output—reports, mailing labels, and form letters.

CHAPTER 6

Using the Report Wizards

▸▸ FAST TRACK

▶ ***To preview the report,*** *142*

click the Preview button of the final step of the Wizard. You should always preview a report before clicking the Finish button of this step to generate it.

▶ ***To create a grouped report with totals,*** *145*

Select the Group/Total Report Wizard from the Wizard selection dialog box. Most steps of this Wizard are equivalent to steps in the Report Wizard, but it also has a step that lets you choose the fields that will be used as the basis of the grouping and also specify whether the report includes totals for each group and a final total.

▶ ***To print a report,*** *148*

choose File ➤ Print to display the Print dialog box. Select Report from its Type drop-down list, and use the ... button to the right of its File box to display the Open dialog box, which you can use to select the report to be printed.

▶▶ *Visual FoxPro* offers three main tools for producing reports on your data: AutoReports, the Report Wizards, and the Report Designer. As you might expect after working with similar tools elsewhere in the program, these report tools are designed to meet a range of needs from very simple and very limited to more complex and more versatile. This chapter covers AutoReports, which are adequate when all you need is a columnar listing of data in the fields you've queried, and the Report Wizards, which you can use for many reports that you will have to create in order to manage your own data.

The Report Designer is a powerful tool with many features and is discussed in detail in Chapter 17. However, it is also easy to use and accessible to beginners if they have already used other Windows report writers, and it has many features that you may want to use to enhance reports that the Wizards generate. For example, the Wizards use the fields' names as their labels, and you will often want to edit these names; in a formal report, you want the label "Last Name" rather than "Lname." You may also want to enhance reports by adding extra text or lines or other graphics.

This chapter is designed to give you a quick tour of the basic steps for creating reports in Visual FoxPro, using AutoReports and the Report Wizards. When you want to learn more about producing reports, proceed to the discussion of the Report Designer in Chapter 17 to get a basic idea about how you can customize a report, and do the exercises in that chapter, which customize the reports that you create with the Wizards here in the ways that you will actually need in your own work. (Chapter 17 tells you more about the Report Designer than you'll probably want to learn right away, and there's no need to study all of the features at once.)

If you feel like exploring and you are familiar with report writers from other Windows applications, you can go directly to Chapter 17 after finishing this chapter, and do the exercises in its Report section. You may find it easy to pick up the essential features of the Report Designer simply by doing these exercises.

▶▶ AutoReports

AutoReports are the simplest to create but offer the least flexibility in presenting your data.

Create an AutoReport as you do an AutoForm: Open a table and then click the AutoReport button on the main toolbar.

Like Auto Forms, Auto Reports include all the fields of the table and use the field names as labels.

Reports are given the extension FRX. AutoReports are given names made up of the initial letters of the file name, followed by an underscore and a number; for example, Emplis_1.FRX or Emplis_2.FRX.

▶▶ NOTE

Visual FoxPro can also use reports created by earlier versions of dBASE, which have the extension FRM.

▶▶ Using the Report Wizards

To use the Report Wizards, create a new report as you do other files, by choosing File ➤ New and selecting the Report radio button of the New dialog box. When you click the Wizard button of this dialog box, it displays the dialog box shown in Figure 6.1, which lets you select among the available Report Wizards:

- The Report Wizard creates reports that display data either in columns or one record after another.

FIGURE 6.1

Selecting a Report Wizard

- The Group/Total Report Wizard creates columnar reports, with summary information at the end of the report. It also lets you group the report—for example, to list the employees from each state together—and to include summary information for each group.
- The One-to-Many Report Wizard lets you create reports based on multitable relational databases, and it is covered in Chapter 16.

You can also display this dialog box by clicking the Report Wizard button of the main toolbar.

► Using the Report Wizard

The Report Wizard is the simplest option. It lets you create the two basic types of reports that you need most frequently: reports that list the fields in columns, with one record to each row and field names at the top of each column; and reports that list the records one after another, with field names to the left of each field. In the exercises at the end of this chapter, you'll create sample reports in both the columnar and the row layouts.

Selecting Fields

The first step of the Wizard, shown in Figure 6.2, lets you select the fields to be included in the report. It includes a Field Picker like those in other Wizards.

FIGURE 6.2

Step 1 of the Report Wizard—selecting fields to include

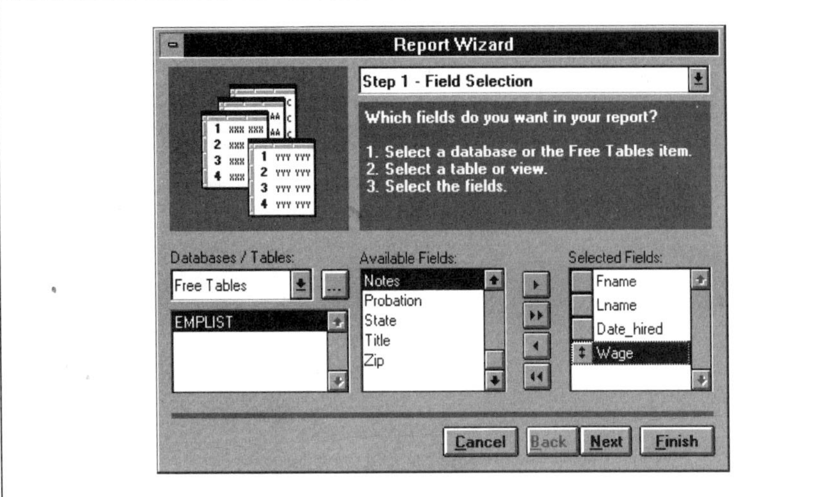

NOTE

You do not choose one of these two types until the third step of the Report Wizard, but you should know which type you plan to use when you select fields to include in the first step. If you are creating a columnar report, you should include few enough fields that the entire report fits on the page. As you will see below, the final step gives you the option of wrapping fields that do not fit in the page width, but this usually does not create an attractive report.

Selecting a Style

The second step, shown in Figure 6.3, lets you select a style for the report: Executive, Ledger, or Presentation, as shown in Figure 6.4. Select each option in turn to see the style illustrated in the upper left of the dialog box. You'll also create an example of each style in the exercises at the end of this chapter.

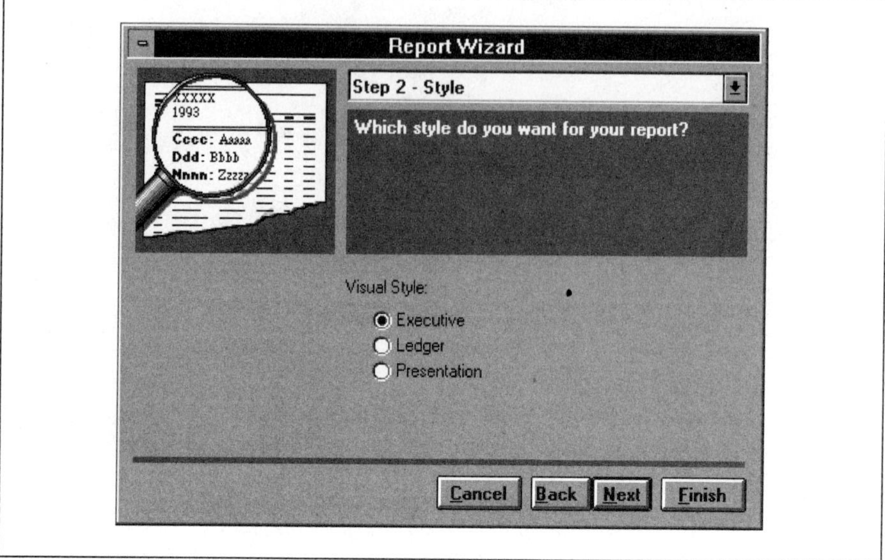

FIGURE 6.3

Step 2 of the Report Wizard—selecting a style

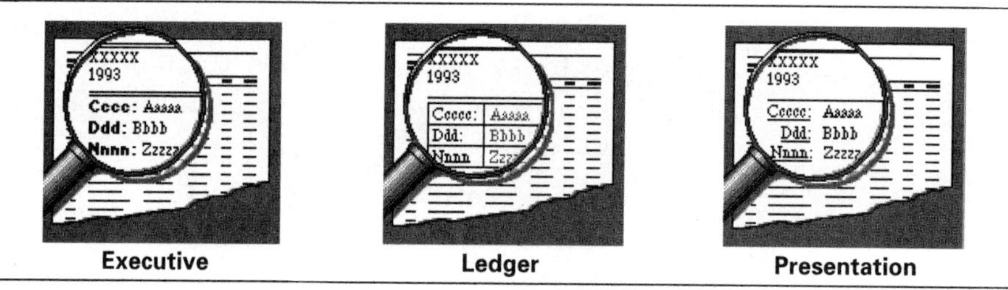

FIGURE 6.4

The Executive, Ledger, and Presentation report styles

Specifying the Layout

The third step, shown in Figure 6.5, lets you specify the report layout. The options that you select are shown in the upper left of the Wizard.

Use the Field Layout radio buttons to specify the basic form of the report:

- **Columns:** Data is arranged in columns, with each record on a row. Field names are above the columns at the top of the page.
- **Rows:** Data is arranged with one field above another and field names to the left of each field.

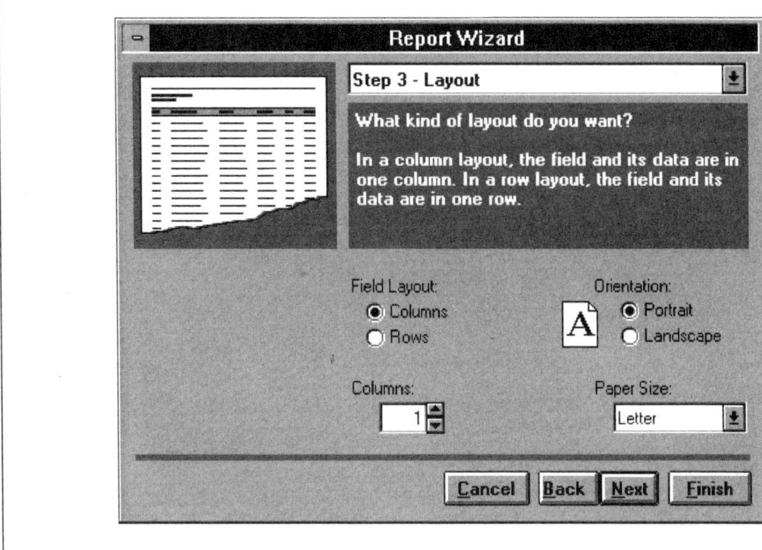

FIGURE 6.5

Step 3 of the Report Wizard—specifying the layout of the fields

Multicolumn Reports You can produce both of these field layouts in either single or multiple columns, by using the Columns spinner control. It's important to realize that the number of columns you specify with this option is independent of your choice of a columnar or row field layout. The entire field layout that you specified is repeated in each column, so if you choose a columnar layout with three fields and select 2 as the number of columns, you'll actually have six columns (two report columns, each comprising three field columns).

If you select Rows as the Field Layout, all the fields are listed one above another in each column. Thus, if you select 2 as the number of Columns and Rows as the Field Layout, the report would have two columns per page and each column would have the fields of the table listed one above another with the name to the left of each field.

If you select Columns as the field layout, all the fields are listed in each report column, with the field name at the top of each field column. You would only do this if the report included a very small number of fields. For example, if you want to print out a telephone list, you could include only fields for first name, last name, and telephone number, and you could select 2 as the number of Columns and Columns as the

Field Layout. Then the report would have two columns per page, and each column of the report would include a columnar listing of names and telephone numbers, as shown in Figure 6.6.

FIGURE 6.6 

Three columns of data within two report columns

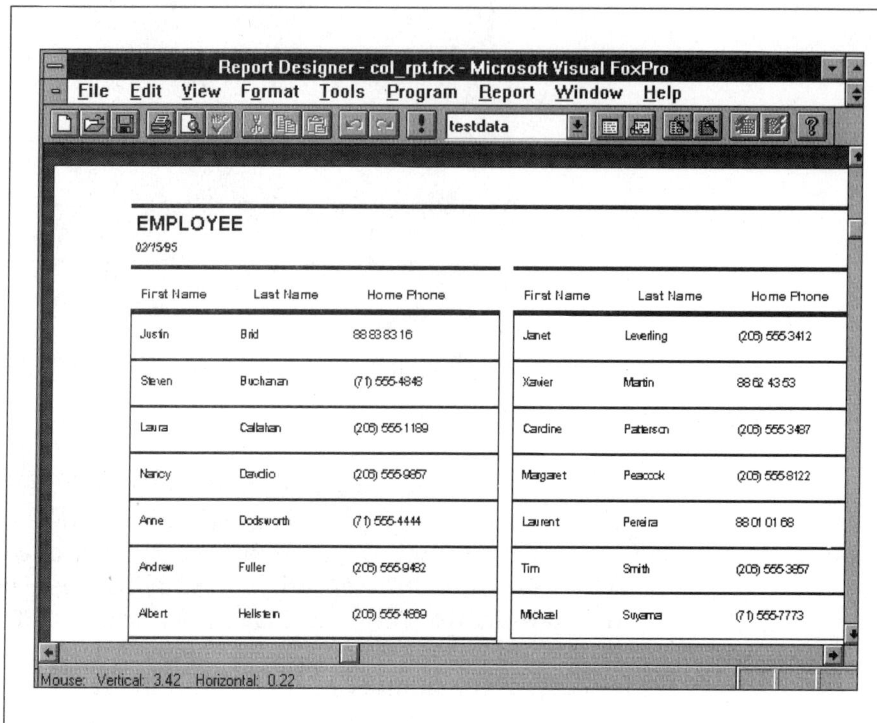

 **TIP**

The combination of Field Layout and number of Columns can be complex, but the illustration in the upper left usually makes it clear. However, this illustration does not take into account the actual size of the field or of the paper you are using, so it cannot tell you if the layout you have chosen actually fits in the page. To see this, use the Preview button of the final step, covered below.

Paper Size and Orientation Use the Orientation radio buttons to select Portrait (the normal text orientation, where the paper is taller than it is wide) or Landscape (where the paper is wider than it is tall). Landscape is particularly useful for columnar reports, to fit more fields across the page.

Use the Paper Size drop-down list to choose among popular paper sizes.

Specifying Sort Order

The fourth step, shown in Figure 6.7, lets you specify the sort order, as you do in other Wizards.

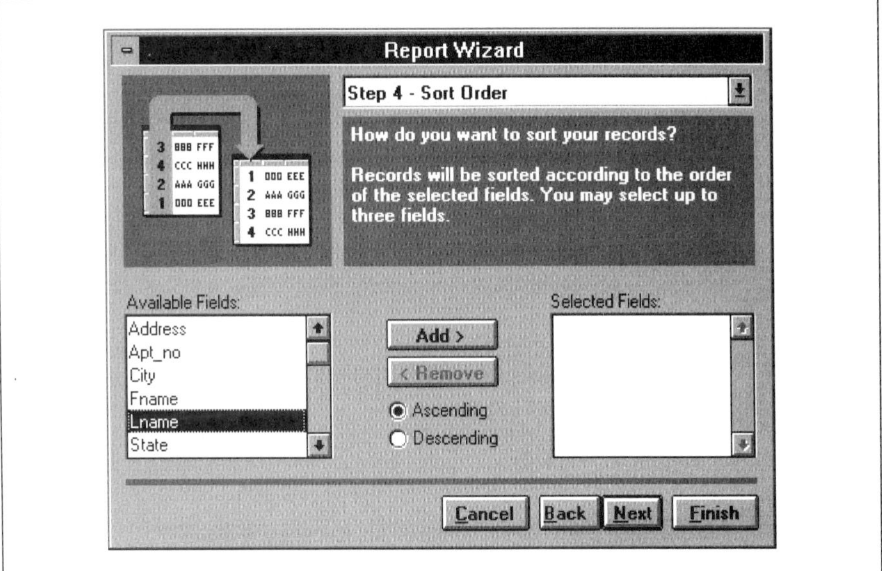

FIGURE 6.7

Step 4 of the Report Wizard—specifying sort order

Generating the Report

The final step, shown in Figure 6.8, lets you enter a title for the report, and specify whether it should be saved for later use or displayed in the Report Designer so that you can customize it, as other Wizards do. It also has a couple of unique features that we'll look at briefly.

FIGURE 6.8

Step 5 of the Report Wizard—generating the report

Wrapping Fields If you use a Column layout, the Wrap Fields check box is selected by default, so that fields that do not fit into the width of the page are wrapped onto following lines. In most cases, however, this feature creates an unattractive and hard-to-read report, as you can see in Figure 6.9.

If you deselect this check box, however, the Wizard simply discards any fields that you included that do not fit the width of the page.

Neither of these alternatives is satisfactory for most reports. You should preview the report to make sure all fields fit before you generate it. If they do not, you will probably want to go back to earlier steps of the Wizard and switch the page orientation to Landscape or remove some fields from the report.

Previewing the Report Click the Preview button of this dialog box to display the report in a Print Preview window, as shown in Figure 6.10. Visual FoxPro takes a moment to generate the report before displaying it and gives it a temporary name that is displayed in the title bar of the Print Preview window.

You can simply click the Preview window with the mouse to display the preview as a whole page, as shown in Figure 6.11. Click it again to display it full size again.

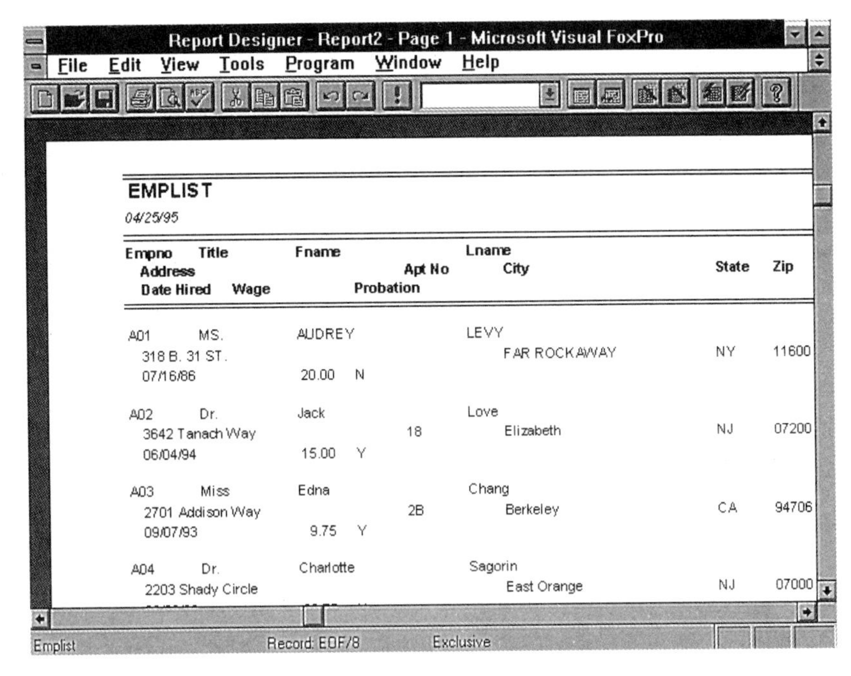

FIGURE 6.9

A report with wrapped fields

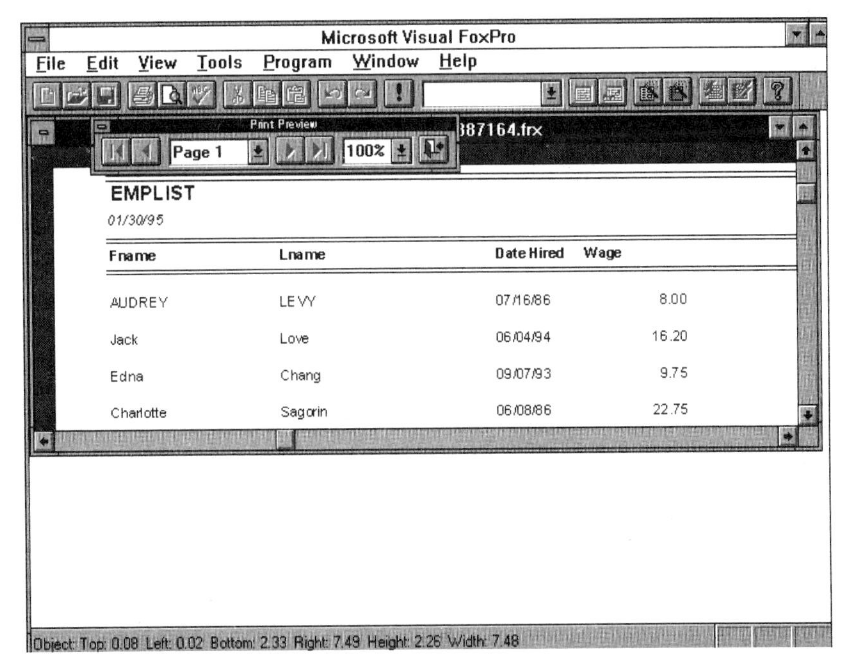

FIGURE 6.10

The Print Preview window

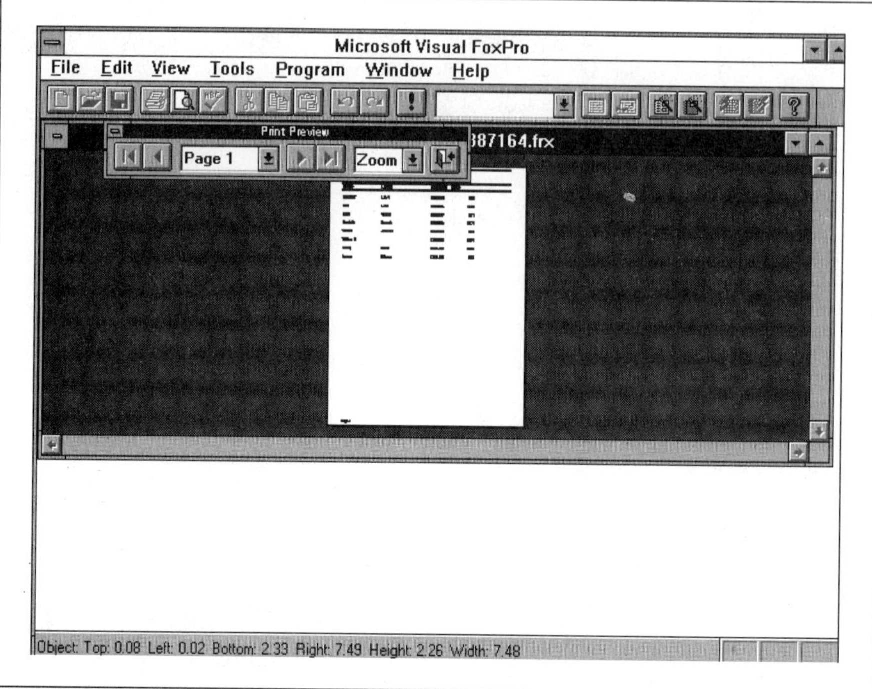

FIGURE 6.11 *Previewing the report as a full page*

Use the Print Preview toolbar to scroll through the report and to view it in other sizes:

- Click the arrow buttons to display the first page, previous page, next page, or final page of the report.
- Use the Page drop-down list to select the page of the report to be displayed.
- Use the Zoom control to display the report in a variety of sizes, from 150% to 10% of its actual size. Select Zoom from this control to display the report so that an entire page can be viewed in the Preview window, regardless of this window's size.
- Click the Close control to close the Preview window and return to the Report Wizard.

NOTE

You should always display a report in the Print Preview window before generating it.

Using the Group/Total Report Wizard

The Group/Total Report Wizard creates a report similar to the Report Wizard's columnar layout, with data listed in columns and the field name at the top of each column. However, it also lets you select up to three fields that will be used to sort and group the data, and it lets you specify summary data to be included for groups. (As with horizontal reports, you may not include more columns than can fit in the width of the page.)

Most of its dialog boxes are also included in the Report Wizard and you can use them as described in the previous section to select fields and sort order, and to preview and create the report.

The Group/Total Report Wizard combines the Style step box of the Report Wizard with some features of its Layout step in the dialog box shown in Figure 6.12. The Layout and Column controls are not needed, since this report always uses column layout and one column. The other controls work as described above.

The new feature of this Wizard is the Groupings step, shown in Figure 6.13, which lets you specify up to three fields used to group the records. For example, you can select State, City, and Zip if you want all the records for the same state to be grouped together, records within the same state to be grouped by city, and records within the same city to be grouped by ZIP code.

NOTE

Records are automatically sorted on the basis of the field they are grouped on. For example, if you are grouping records by state, they are also sorted by state, so that all the records from each state come one after another. The Sort Order step of this Wizard only specifies the order of records *within* each group.

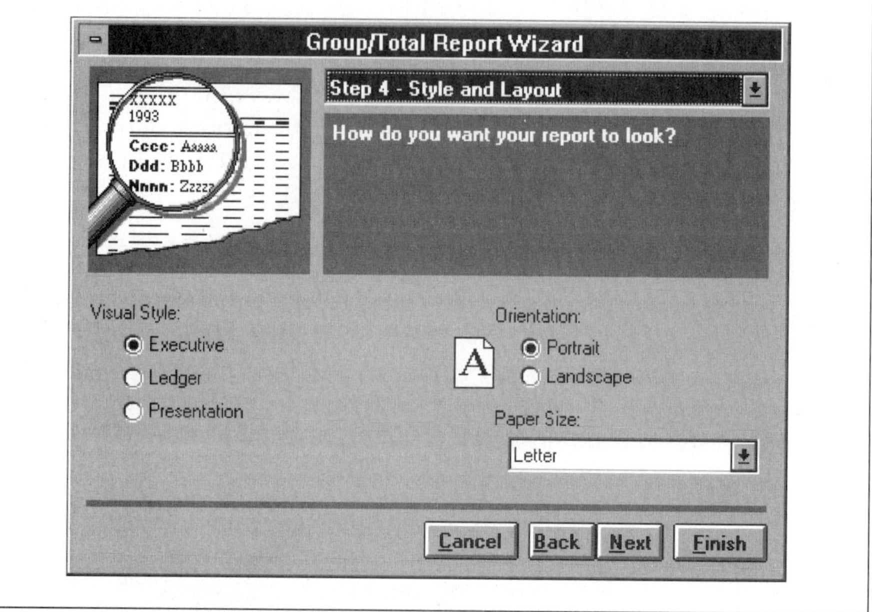

FIGURE 6.12

The Style and Layout step of the Group/Total Report Wizard

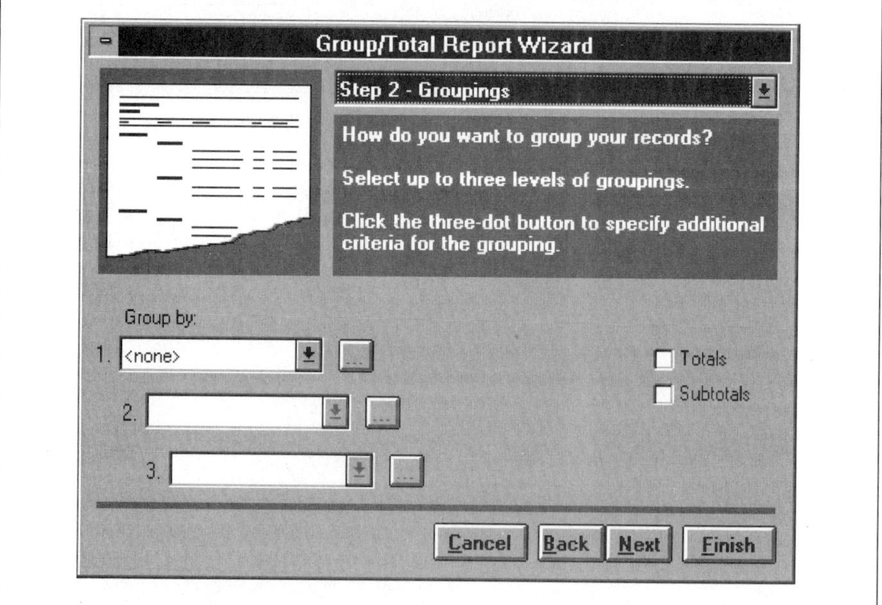

FIGURE 6.13

The Groupings step of the Group/Total Report Wizard

You can click the button to the right of each field that you select to group on to display the Group Modifier dialog box, which gives you more control over the grouping. The options it gives you depend on the data type of the field used for grouping:

- **Character:** If you are grouping on a character field, the Wizard uses the entire field as the basis of the grouping by default. For example, if you group on the city field, it uses the entire name of the city. However, you can use the Group Modifier dialog box shown in Figure 6.14 to group on one or more letters at the beginning of the field name. For example, you might want to group by only the first character of the Lname field, so that all names beginning with the same letter are grouped together.

FIGURE 6.14

The Group Modifier dialog box for character fields

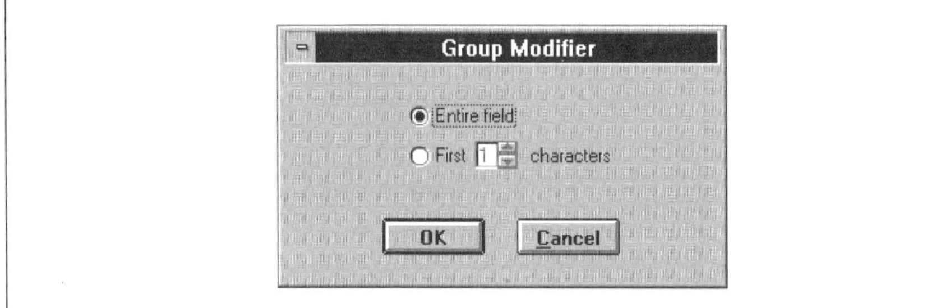

- **Number:** If you are grouping on a number field, Visual FoxPro groups on the exact number by default, but you can use the Group Modifier dialog box shown in Figure 6.15 to group by tens, hundreds, or thousands. For example, to produce a report showing which employees have wages are at the same general level, you could base the grouping on the Wage field and group by 10. Then you would have groups of employees who earn less than $10 per hour, who earn from $10 to $20 per hour, and so on.

FIGURE 6.15

The Group Modifier dialog box for number fields

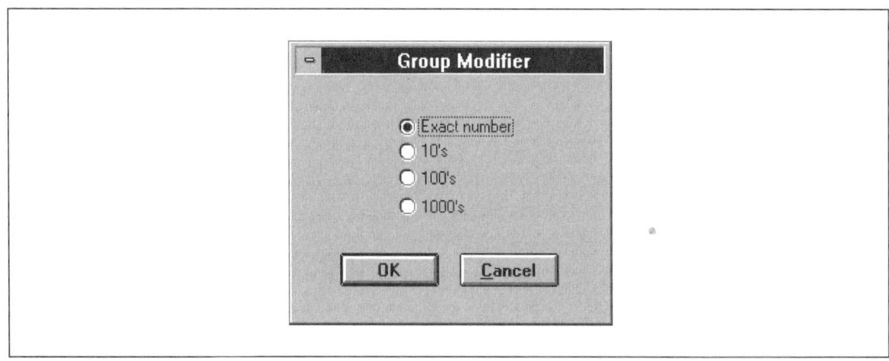

- **Date:** If you are grouping on a date field, Visual FoxPro uses the exact data as the basis of the grouping by default, but you can use the Group Modifier dialog box shown in Figure 6.16 to group on the year, month, or day of the week. For example, if you wanted a report to show which employees were hired each year, you would base the grouping on the Date_hired field and group by year.

FIGURE 6.16

The Group Modifier dialog box for Date fields

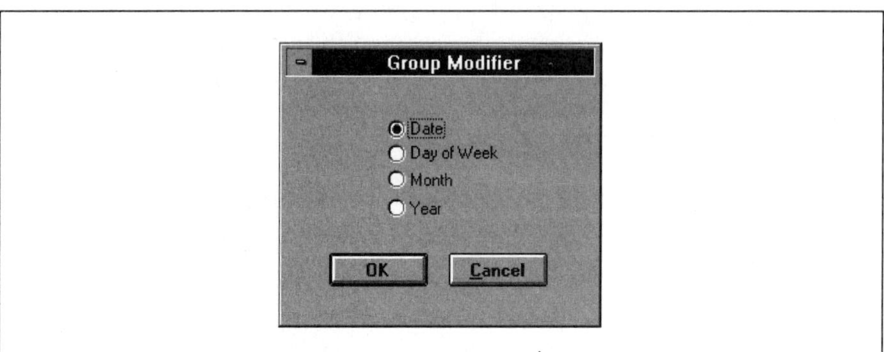

▸▸ Printing Reports

Although it's possible to circulate reports electronically on a network, most reports need to be printed in order to be seen by their intended readers.

▸▸ **NOTE**

Reports are the first type of printed output we are looking at. However, you can also print mailing labels, text files, or the contents of the Command window or Clipboard in the same way.

Choose File ➤ Print or click the Print tool to display the Print dialog box, shown in Figure 6.17. Use the Type drop-down list to select the type of file you are printing—Report in this case. Then click the button to the right of the File text box to display the Print File dialog box, which you use like the Open dialog box to select the file to print.

FIGURE 6.17

The Print dialog box

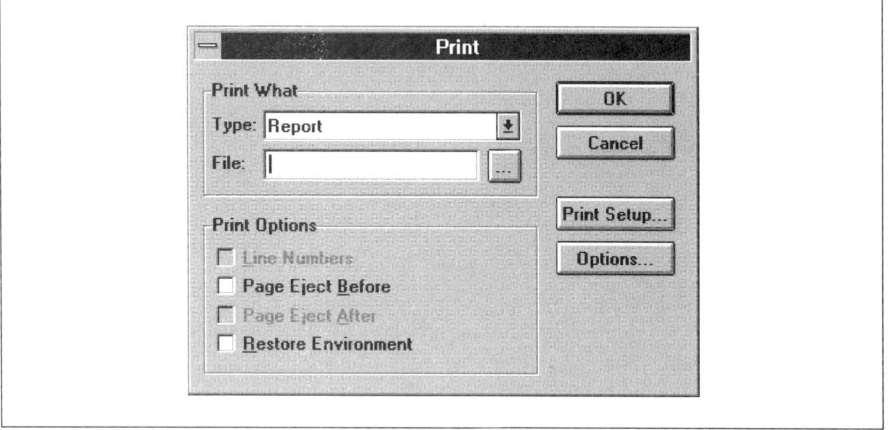

Setting Up the Printer

Click the Print Setup button of the Print dialog box to display the dialog box shown in Figure 6.18.

FIGURE 6.18

The Print Setup dialog box

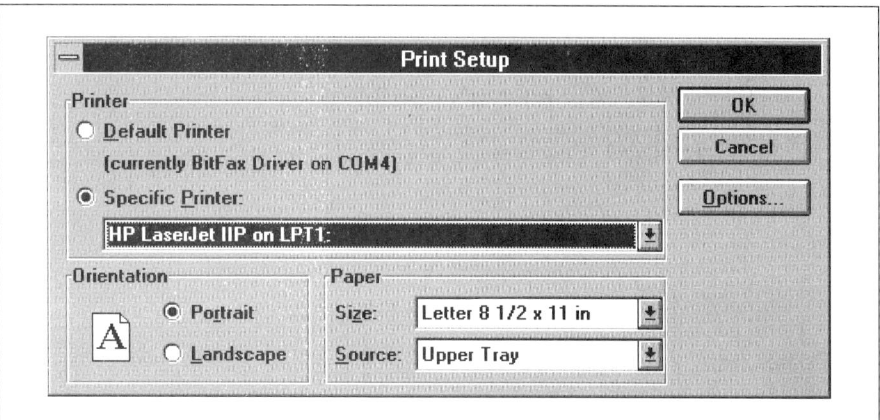

The controls in the Printer area let you choose the device to print to. One radio button lets you select the default printer, which is described under it. The second radio button is connected with a drop-down control that lets you choose among other available printers.

The two radio buttons in the Orientation area let you select either Portrait layout (with the longer dimension vertical) or Landscape (with the longer dimension horizontal).

The drop-down controls in the Paper area let you specify the size of the paper and the source of the paper. (Use the Source control if your printer has several paper trays, if you want to use manual rather than automatic feed, or to choose other paper-feeding options that depend on your printer.)

If you click the Options pushbutton of the Print Setup dialog box, Visual FoxPro displays the Options dialog box; its options depend on your printer. (For example, on some printers, it lets you print graphics with lower resolution, so you can print draft reports more quickly.)

▸ Controlling Which Records Are Included in the Printout

If you click the Options button of the Print dialog box, Visual FoxPro displays the Print Options dialog box, shown in Figure 6.19, which lets you control which records are included in your current printout of the report. For example, you can design a report with general information on all of your employees and then use this dialog box to print that report with only employees from California. Do not confuse this dialog box with the dialog box displayed when you click the Options button of the Print Setup dialog box, which controls options specific to your printer.

To use the Print Options dialog box, you should enter a logical expression in the For or While text box, and so it is covered in Chapter 11, which discusses the use of expressions to filter data.

▸▸ Sample Reports

As exercises, try creating a few sample reports that introduce you to all the major features of the Report Wizards. As the basis of these reports you'll again use the Emplist table, whose structure you defined in Chapter 2 and to which you added data in Chapter 3. If you're feeling ambitious, try proceeding from the final Wizard screen in each exercise

FIGURE 6.19

The Print Options dialog box

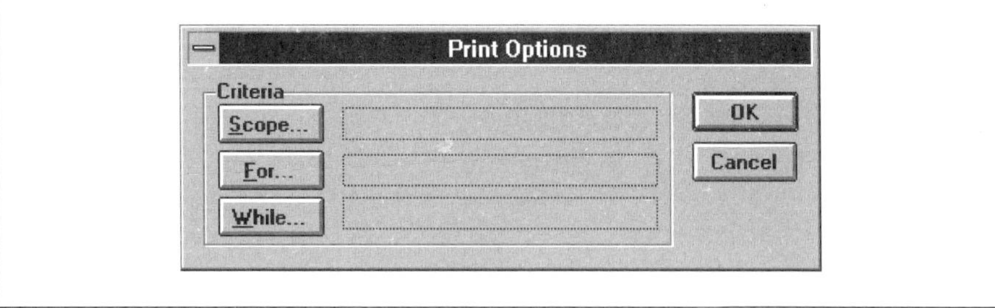

to the Report Designer, where you can explore some of the modifications this tool allows, or proceed to the exercises in Chapter 17 which let you modify these reports.

▶ A Report with Columnar Layout

First, try creating a report that lists a few fields of the table in columnar form, which is often the most useful way of pulling data out of a table. In this exercise, you will create a report listing each employee's name, wage, and date hired, and you will arrange the records in alphabetical order by name.

1. Choose File ➤ New, select the Report radio button of the New dialog box, and click the Wizard button. In the Wizard Selection dialog box, select Report Wizard and click OK.

2. If a table is not already displayed in the first step of the Wizard, click the … button and use the Open dialog box to select the Emplist table. Then double-click the Lname, Fname, Wage, and Date_hired fields to add them to the Selected Fields list, as shown in Figure 6.20. Click Next.

3. Leave Executive selected as the style in Step 2, and click Next to go to Step 3. You can also use the default layout, which has a columnar field layout, a single column to the report, and Portrait orientation. The small number of fields you selected will fit in the paper in this layout.

4. Click Next to display the Sort Order step. Double-click Lname and Fname to add them to the Selected Fields list.

FIGURE 6.20

Selecting fields to include in the sample report

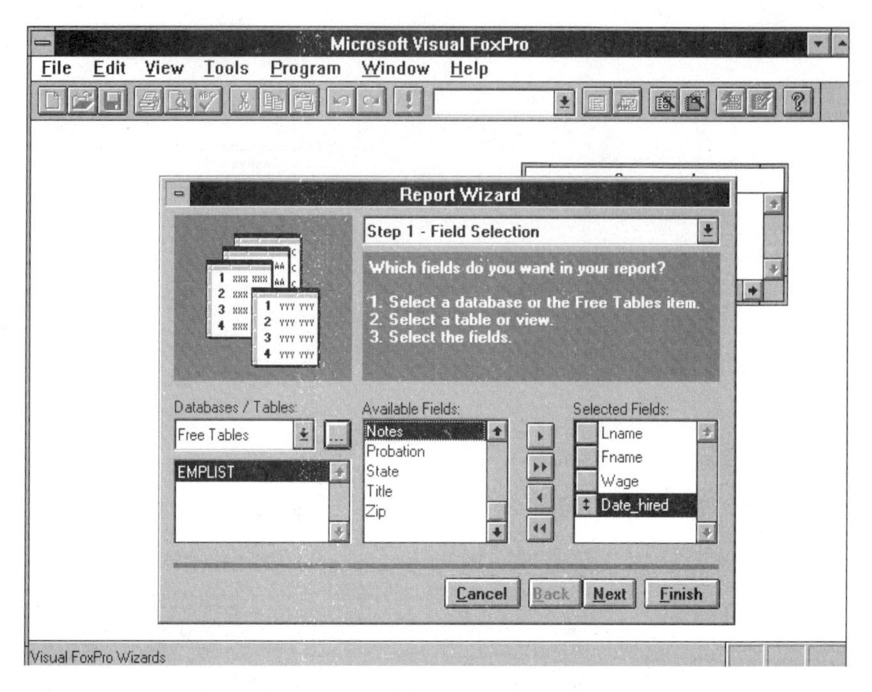

5. Click Next to display the Finish step. As the report title, enter **Employee Wages**. Click the Preview button. After a moment, Visual FoxPro displays the report in a Preview window. Maximize this window to see the report clearly, as shown in Figure 6.21.

6. Close the Preview window to return to the Wizard. Click Finish to create the report. When the Save As dialog box is displayed, enter **empwages** as the report name, and click Save.

7. If you want to print the report, choose File ➤ Print. In the Print dialog box, choose Report from the Type drop-down list. Click the button to the right of the File text box and use the Print File dialog box to select EMPWAGES.FRX. Make sure your printer is turned on and click OK to print the report.

When you previewed this report, you saw that it suppressed repeated values. You have two people with the last name Johnson in the table, and the report includes the first name only for the first, with a blank in the Fname field for the second.

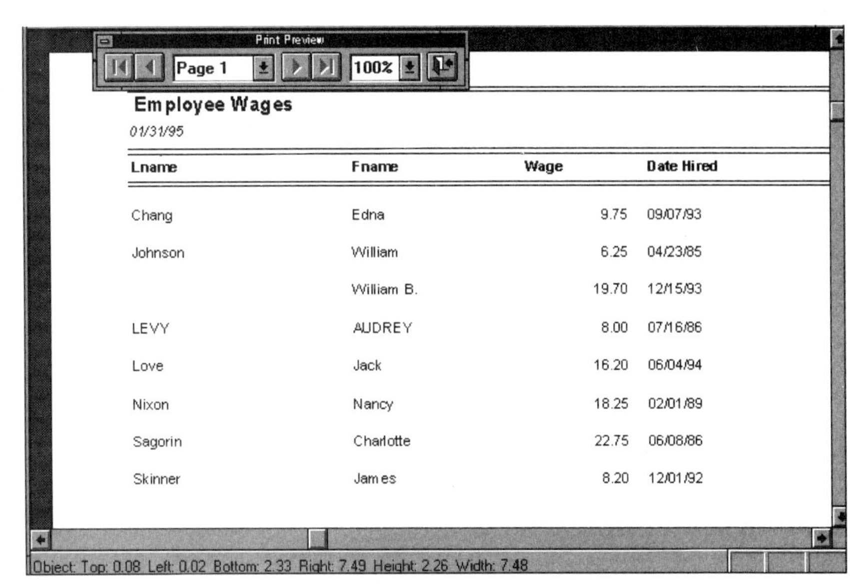

FIGURE 6.21

Previewing the final report

Visual FoxPro's designers made this style the default because it is often useful to suppress repeated values in a columnar report. For example, if you were listing records by state, and you put the state in the first column, the report would list each state name once and leave blank spaces for other records from that state, which makes it very easy to see at a glance which records come from each state.

In this report, however, it would be better to have the name repeated for each record. In Chapter 17, you will see how to include repeated values in the report.

You also saw that the Wizard retains the capitalization in the table, so that one of your records, which was entered in all capital letters, is not properly capitalized. In Chapter 17, you will use the Report Designer to capitalize words properly regardless of how they were entered originally.

A Multicolumn Report with Row Layout

Now, try creating a report that shows all the data on each employee (except the Notes field). Because of the large number of fields included, it would be difficult to fit this report into the width of a page if you used columnar layout. Instead, you will use row layout, but you will use a three-column report to fit the data on fewer pages.

1. Choose File ➤ New. The Report radio button of the New dialog box should already be selected. Click the Wizard button, and double-click Report Wizard in the Wizard Selection dialog box.
2. If necessary, click the … button to the right of the Databases/Tables drop-down list and use the Open dialog box to select the Emplist table. Then click the button with two right arrows on it to add all the fields to the Selected Fields list. Then, scroll through the Selected Fields list to display the Notes field and double-click it to remove it from this list. Finally, click and drag the move boxes in the Selected Fields list so that fields are in the appropriate order, with title, name, and address first.
3. Click Next to go to Step 2 and select Ledger as the style.
4. Click Next to go to Step 3. Select Rows as the Field Layout and 3 as the number of Columns, as shown in Figure 6.22. Notice the illustration of this layout in the upper left of the Wizard.

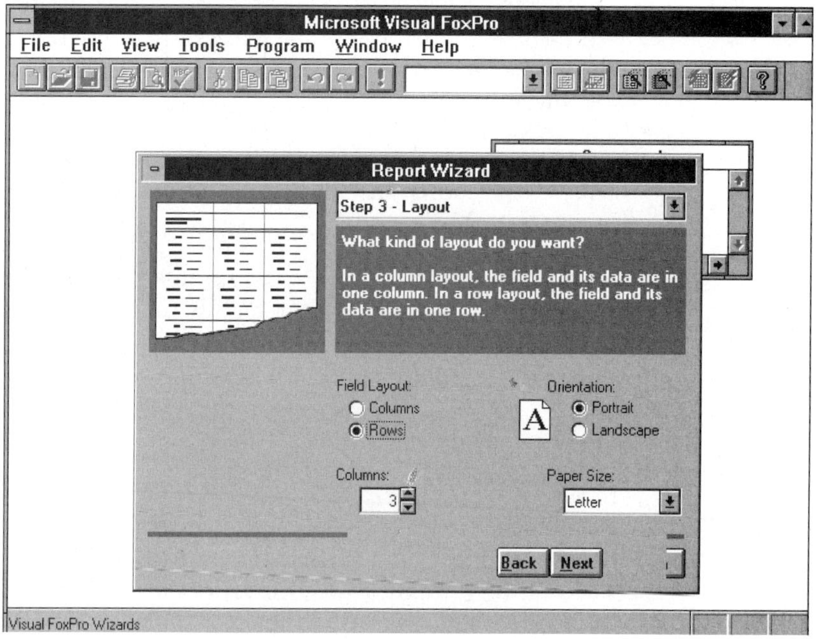

FIGURE 6.22

Laying out the sample multicolumn report

5. Click Next to display the Sort Order step. Add Lname and Fname to the Selected Fields list.

6. Click Next to display the Finish step. As the report title, enter **Employee Report**. Click the Preview button. When Visual FoxPro displays the report Preview window, maximize it. The report is shown in Figure 6.23.

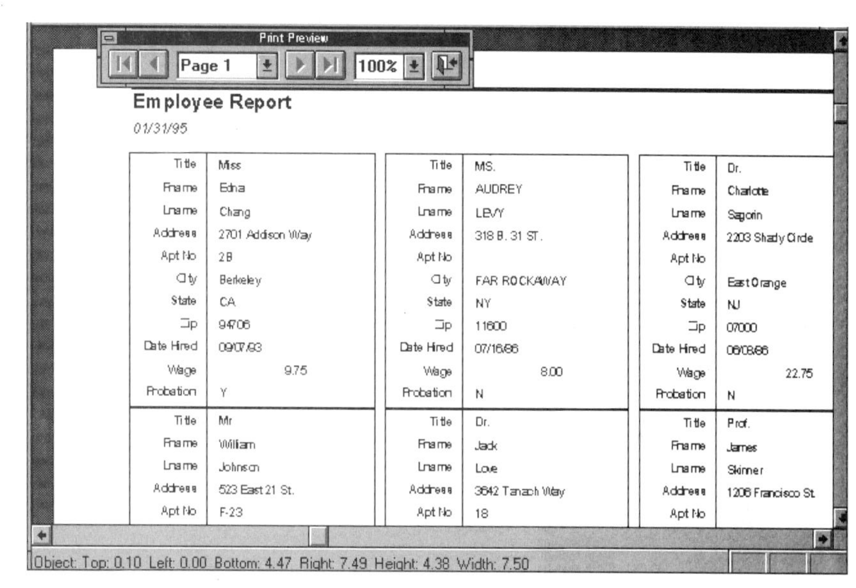

FIGURE 6.23 ▶

Previewing the final report

7. Close the Preview window to return to the Wizard. Click Finish to create the report, and enter **empdata** in the Save As dialog box to name the Report.

Again, if you want to, you can choose File ➤ Print and use the Print dialog box to print the report.

▶ A Grouped Report

Finally, try creating a grouped report with totals. Let's say that you want to compare the average wages of employees in different states. You will include the name, date hired, and wage fields, as you did in the earlier columnar report. You will also group by state and total on wage.

However, because the Group/Total Report Wizard does not include Average as a totaling option you can select, you will sum the values in the Wage field. The sum of hourly wages in a state is a meaningless figure, but you will convert it to an average when you customize the report using the Report Designer in Chapter 17.

1. Click the New button on the main toolbar, make sure the Report radio button of the New dialog box is selected, and click the Wizard button. In the Wizard Selection dialog box, select Group/Total Report Wizard.

2. If a table is not already displayed in the first step of the Wizard, click the ... button to the right of the Databases/Tables drop-down list and use the Open dialog box to select the Emplist table. Double-click the State, Lname, Fname, Date_hired, and Wage fields to add them to the Selected Fields list.

3. Click Next to go to Step 2. Select State as the Group By field, and select both the Totals and Subtotals check boxes, as shown in Figure 6.24.

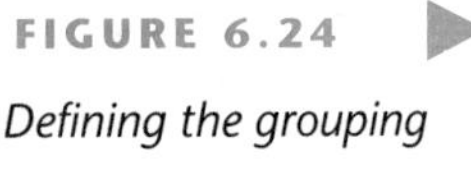

FIGURE 6.24

Defining the grouping

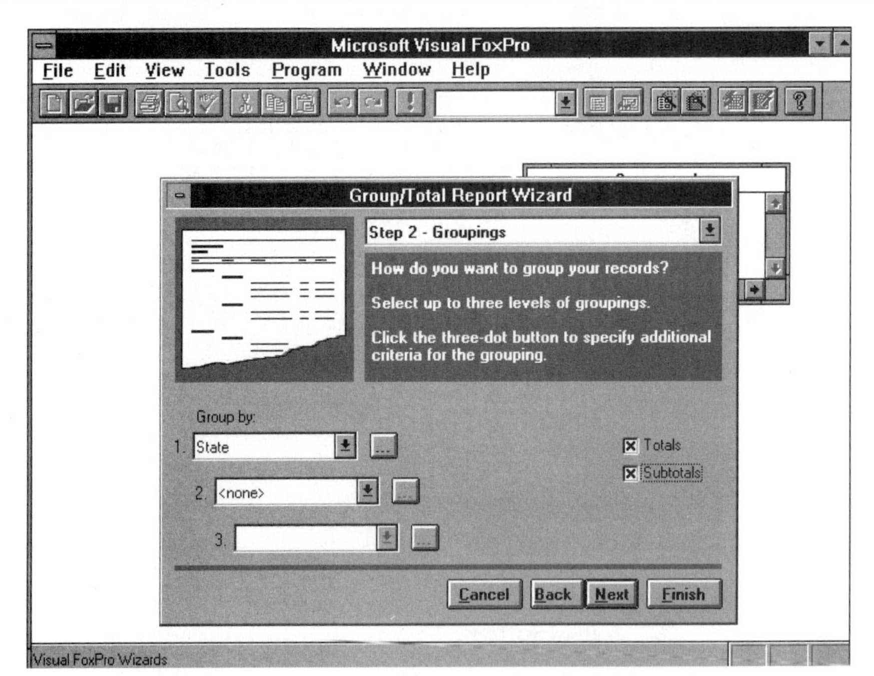

4. Click Next to go to Step 3. Double-click Lname and Fname to alphabetize by name within each state.

5. Click Next to go to Step 4. Select Presentation as the style and keep the default layout.

6. Click Next to display the Finish step. As the report title, enter **Wages by State**. Click the Preview button. After a moment, Visual FoxPro displays the report in a preview window, which you can maximize to see the report.

7. Close the Preview window to return to the Wizard. Click Finish to generate the report. When the Save As dialog box is displayed, enter **st_wages** as the report name, and click Save.

You can see that there are several features of this report that you will want to customize in Chapter 17. Most obviously, totals are meaningless in this context, and you will convert them to averages as well as adding more descriptive captions in the group header and footer.

►► To Sum Up

In this chapter, you learned how to use Wizards to create one form of printed output, reports. You have also seen some of the things that Wizards cannot do, and which features of the reports they generate should be customized using the Report Designer.

The next chapter covers the other form of printed output that most users need to use in managing their own data—mailing labels. It also covers form letters, which are easy to create and which many people find useful.

CHAPTER 7

Working with Mailing Labels and Mail Merge

FAST TRACK

To create mailing labels using the Wizard, **163**

use step 1 to choose the table and the fields that will be included. Use step 2 to choose the label size by selecting the Avery number of the label forms that you use. Use step 3 to lay out the label. Use step 4 to specify sort order. Use the final step to generate the labels.

To lay out the labels, **165**

in the Layout step of the Wizard, double-click field names and click spaces and punctuation marks to add them to the label layout. Click the New Line button at the end of each line.

▶ ***To preview the labels,*** 168

click the Preview button of the final step of the Wizard. You should always preview a label before clicking the Finish button of this step to generate it.

▶ ***To print labels,*** 170

choose File ➤ Print to display the Print dialog box. Here select Labels from the file Type list, and use the … button to display the Open dialog box, which you can use to select the labels to be printed.

In this chapter, to complete your introduction to the basic features of Visual FoxPro, you will look at the two Wizards used for mailings.

The Label Wizard makes it very easy to create mailing labels and other labels; you can also customize these labels in many of the same ways that you customize reports, and so custom labels are covered in Chapter 17.

Visual FoxPro includes another Wizard that is useful in mailings, the Mail Merge Wizard. This tool lets you export data to include in form letters that you create using Microsoft Word or other word processors. Although mail merges are not essential for using Visual FoxPro, they are often handy, and they are certainly easy to use.

Working with Mailing Labels

Create and print labels as you do reports:

- To create a set of labels, choose File ➤ New and use the New dialog box to display the Label Wizard or the Label Designer. The Label Wizard is so much easier to use than the Label Designer that it should always be used to create the labels initially.
- To print labels, choose File ➤ Print to display the Print dialog box. Choose Label from the Type drop-down list; then use the … button to the right of the File text box to display the Open dialog box and use it to select the file you want to print.

Visual FoxPro creates label forms that have the extension LBX. However, it can also work with labels created by earlier Xbase programs, which have the extension LBL.

The Label Wizard

You should always create labels using the Wizard, because of its ease of use. You can modify them using the Label Designer, which is covered in Chapter 17.

Choosing the Table

As in other Wizards, the first step of the Label Wizard lets you choose the table or view to base your labels on, as shown in Figure 7.1. It does not let you choose fields, like the first step of other Wizards, because you will actually lay out fields on a label form in a later step.

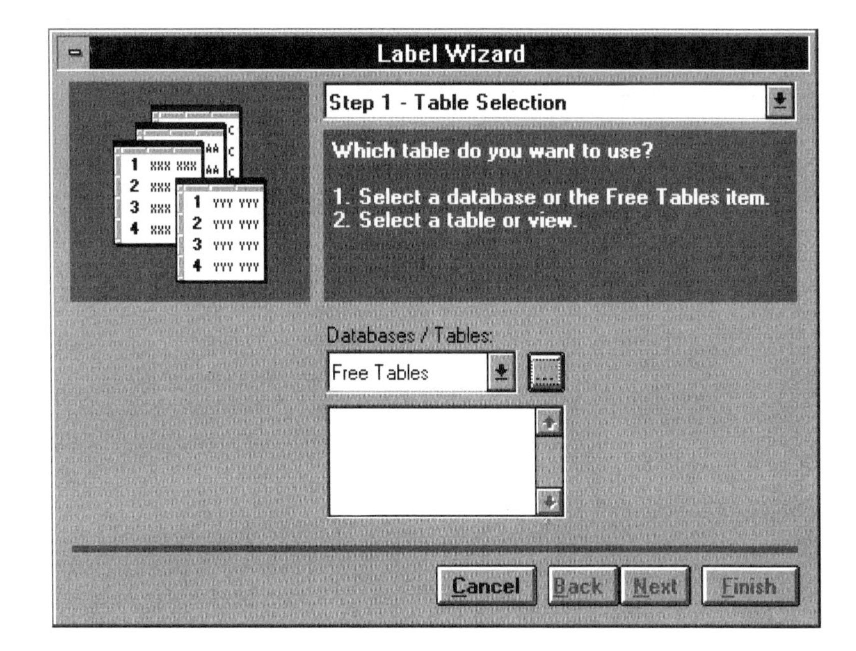

FIGURE 7.1

Step 1 of the Label Wizard—choosing the table

Choosing the Label Size

In the next dialog box of the Label Wizard you select one of the standard label forms by Avery number, as shown in Figure 7.2.

FIGURE 7.2

Step 2 of the Label Wizard—selecting an Avery number

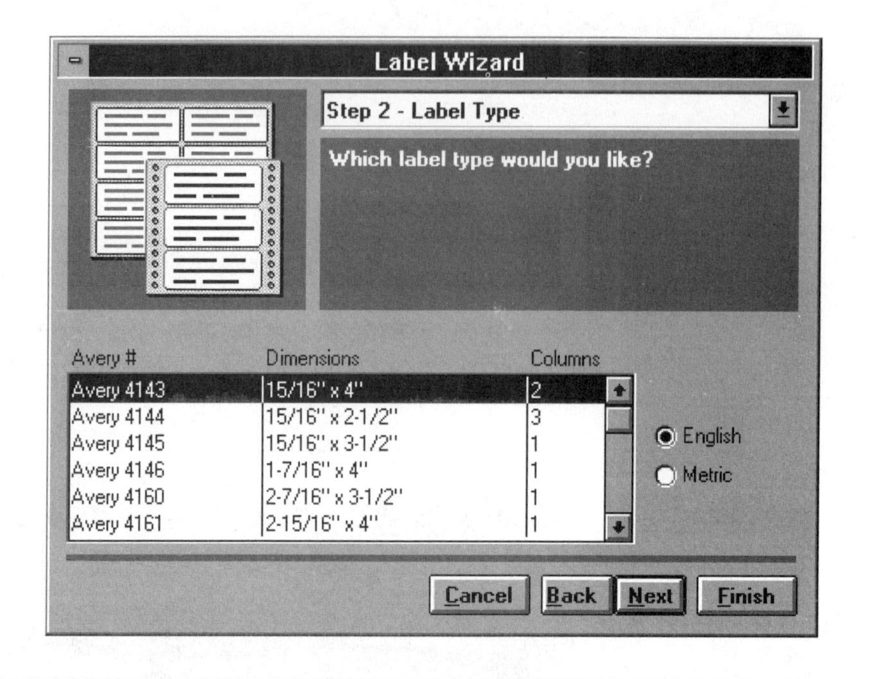

Avery is the most popular brand of label form. Most users will either have Avery label forms or another brand that is compatible in size and layout. Just look on the box of label paper for its Avery number, and select that number in this dialog box.

If your label paper does not have an Avery number, select the option that has the dimensions and number of columns similar to your label paper. If necessary, you can customize the dimensions using the Label Designer when you are done using the Wizard.

►► **NOTE**

Notice that radio buttons let you choose between English (inch) and Metric (millimeter) sizes. The list of Avery labels changes depending on the selection here. Make sure to select the radio button that is appropriate for your label forms.

Laying Out the Label

The next Label Wizard dialog box, shown in Figure 7.3, lets you lay out the label.

FIGURE 7.3

Step 3 of the Label Wizard—laying out a label

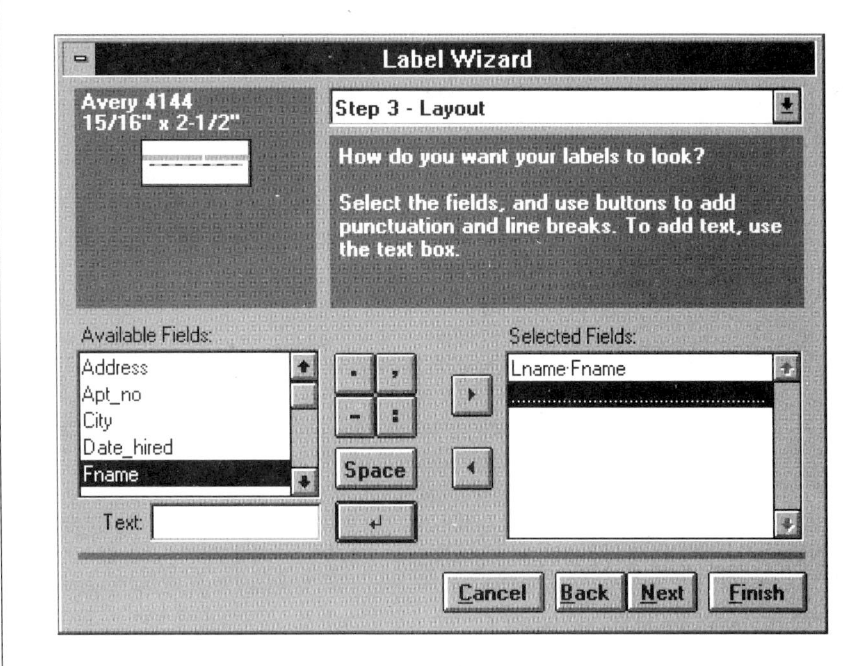

NOTE

While it looks like the Field Picker dialog boxes used in other Wizards, this dialog box works quite differently. Besides choosing the fields to be included, you must also control the layout of the label by placing the fields in the proper location in the Selected Fields box. You can also include text and special characters as well as fields.

Lay out the Selected Fields box as follows:

- Double-click a field name, or select it and click the > button, to add it to the Selected Fields box.
- Click the appropriate buttons to add spaces and special characters, such as period, comma, hyphen, and colon to the Selected Fields list.
- Type text in the Text box and click the > button to add it to the Selected Fields box.
- Click the ↵ button to start a new line in the Selected Fields box.

Remember that you must actually lay out the label in the Selected Fields box. Add spaces between fields, and use the ↵ button to start each new line.

For example, to create a mailing label for a name and address list, you typically would double-click the Fname field, click the Space button, double-click the Lname field, and then click the New Line button to complete the first line of the label before moving on to the address fields. (This is exactly what you'll do in this chapter's exercise.)

In case of error, you can remove objects from the Selected Fields box by selecting them and clicking the < button or by double-clicking them.

The Wizard displays a sample label in the upper-left corner of this dialog box as you lay it out.

Specifying Sort Order

The next dialog box, shown in Figure 7.4, lets you specify sort order. It works like the dialog box used for this purpose in other Wizards. It is common to sort by ZIP code, in order to use bulk rates for large mailings.

Creating the Label Form

The final dialog box, shown in Figure 7.5, includes radio buttons that let you save the label for later use or display it in the Label Designer so you can modify it.

FIGURE 7.4

Step 4 of the Label Wizard—specifying sort order

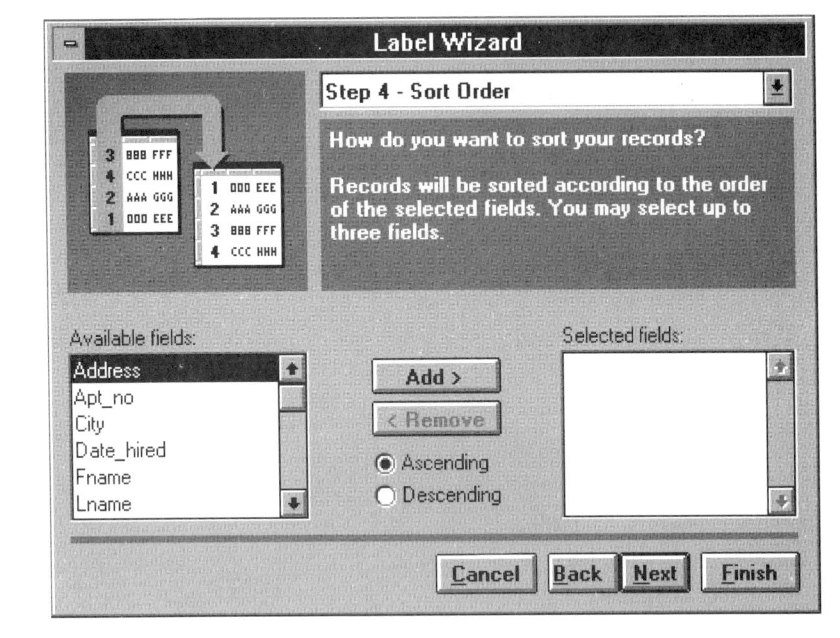

FIGURE 7.5

Step 5 of the Label Wizard—generating the labels

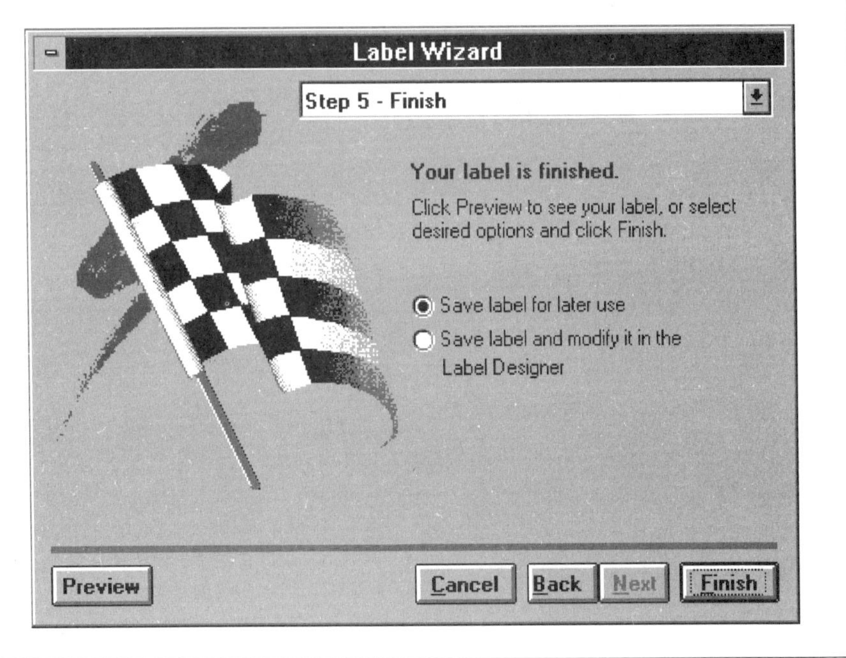

Like the Report Wizards discussed in Chapter 6, the final Label Wizard step also includes a Preview button, which you can use to view the labels in the Page Preview window. You should always preview the labels before clicking the Finish button to generate them.

▶ Sample Labels

Now, try using this Wizard to create a sample set of mailing labels, similar to those you would use in almost any actual application.

1. Choose File ➤ New, select the Label radio button of the New dialog box, and click the Wizard button. If a table is not already displayed in the first step of the Wizard, click the Other button and use the Open dialog box to select the Emplist table.

2. Click Next to display the Label Type step. If you have label forms of your own that you want to try, you can select their Avery number. Otherwise, you can leave the default selection, Avery 4143.

3. Click Next to display the Layout step. Double-click Fname to add it to the Selected Fields list. Click the Space button, and notice that the space is displayed as a small dot in the list. Double-click Lname to finish adding the name, then click ↵ to add a second line to the Selected Fields list.

4. Double-click Address to add it to the second line. Click Space six or seven times. Double-click Apt_no to complete the Address line. Then click ↵ to add a new line to the label.

5. Double-click City. Click the comma (,) button and then click Space. Double-click State, click Space again, and double-click Zip.

6. Click ↵ twice. Then, in the Text box, type **Please open immediately** and click the > button to add it to the label. The final layout is shown in Figure 7.6.

7. Click Next to display the Sort Order step. Double-click Zip to add it to the Selected Fields list.

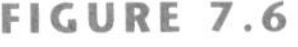

FIGURE 7.6

The label layout

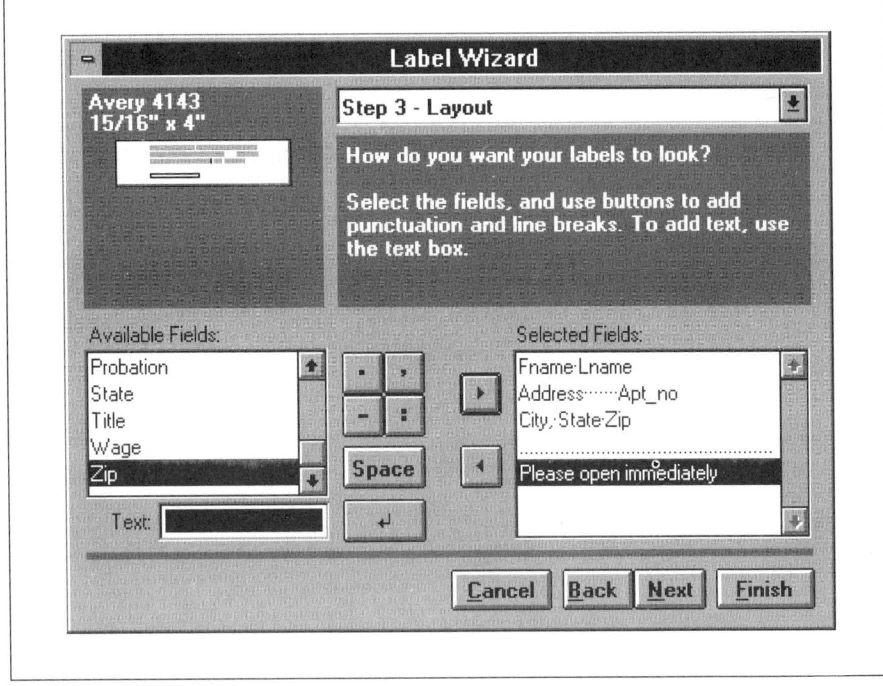

8. Click Next to display the Finish step. Click the Preview button. After a moment, Visual FoxPro displays the labels in a Preview window. Scroll to view them, as shown in Figure 7.7.

FIGURE 7.7

Previewing the labels

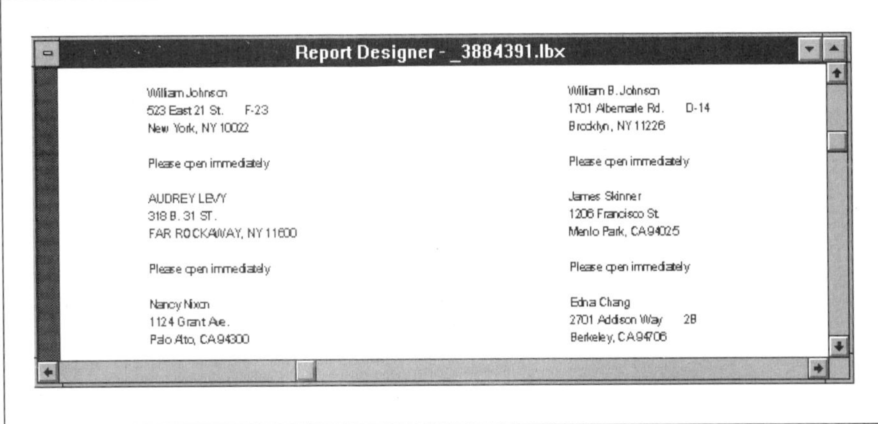

9. Close the Preview window to return to the Wizard. Click Finish to generate the labels. When the Save As dialog box is displayed, enter **standard** as the label name, and click Save.

10. If you want to print the labels, choose File ➤ Print. In the Print dialog box, choose Label from the Type drop-down. Click the ... button to the right of the File text box and use the Print File dialog box to select STANDARD.LBX. Be sure your printer is turned on, and click OK to print.

One defect of these labels is that they do not have the word *Apt* or the symbol # before the apartment number. If you used the Text box to add one of these, it would be displayed for all records, even those that did not have an apartment number. To add this extra text only in records where it's actually needed, you must use one of the FoxPro expressions covered in Chapter 9. You will add this feature to the labels in Chapter 17.

▸▸ Using Mail Merge

Most word processors include a mail merge feature, which lets you create form letters. In general, you type the letter in the usual way, but you include special codes instead of the actual first name, address, and so on. You must also have a list of names and addresses that is kept in a special format in a separate file. When you do the mail merge, the word processor merges the two files and produces a copy of the letter for each name and address in the second file.

The letter or other text that the data is merged into is called the *main document.* The document that holds the names and addresses or other data is called the *data source.*

▸ The Mail Merge Wizard

Mail merges are not actually files in Visual FoxPro, and so you cannot create them by choosing File ➤ New. To use the Mail Merge Wizard, choose Tools ➤ Wizards ➤ Mail Merge.

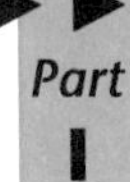

Choosing Fields

The first step of working with the Wizard, shown in Figure 7.8, lets you choose which fields to include in the merge. Use it as you would the Field Pickers of other wizards.

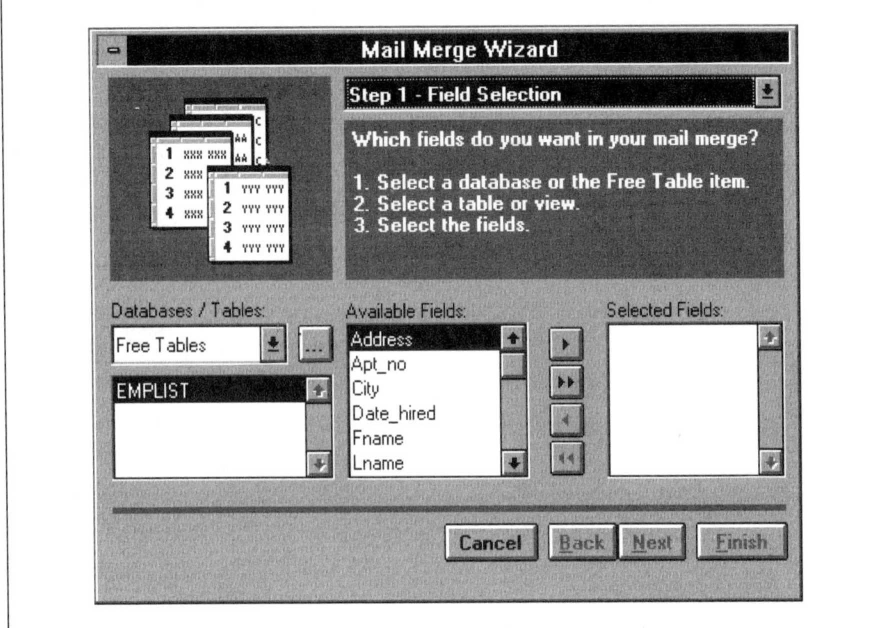

FIGURE 7.8

Step 1 of the Mail Merge Wizard—choosing fields

Choosing a Word Processor

In the second step, the Wizard, shown in Figure 7.9, lets you choose the word processing program you'll use in the merge.

This Wizard creates files that can be used by Word for Windows 6.0 or creates comma-delimited files that can be used for mail merge by other word processors. See the word processor's documentation for details on how to creates mail merge files.

As you will see, the Mail Merge Wizard is particularly powerful if you use it with Word for Windows.

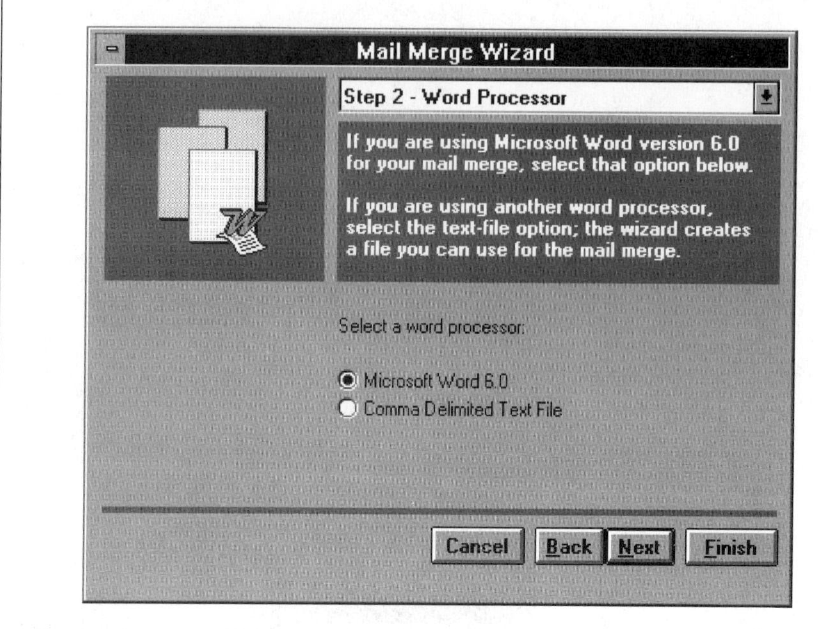

FIGURE 7.9 *Step 2 of the Mail Merge Wizard—choosing a word processor*

If you are using another word processor, the Wizard skips the following steps and goes directly to the final step, which lets you create a file that you can use as the data source of your mail merge.

Choosing a Document

If you are working with Word for Windows, the next step, shown in Figure 7.10, lets you select an existing document or create a new document to merge with the Visual FoxPro data.

If you select the Use Existing Document radio button, you can click the File pushbutton to display the Open dialog box, and use it to select an existing Word document as the main document. Otherwise, the Wizard will create a new Word document, in which you can type the letter.

Choosing a Document Type

If you are working with Word for Windows, the next step, shown in Figure 7.11, lets you choose a document type. In general, it is easier to print labels or envelopes by using the Label Designer than it is by exporting the data to a Word document that is set up to print them.

FIGURE 7.10

Step 3 of the Mail Merge Wizard—specifying a document

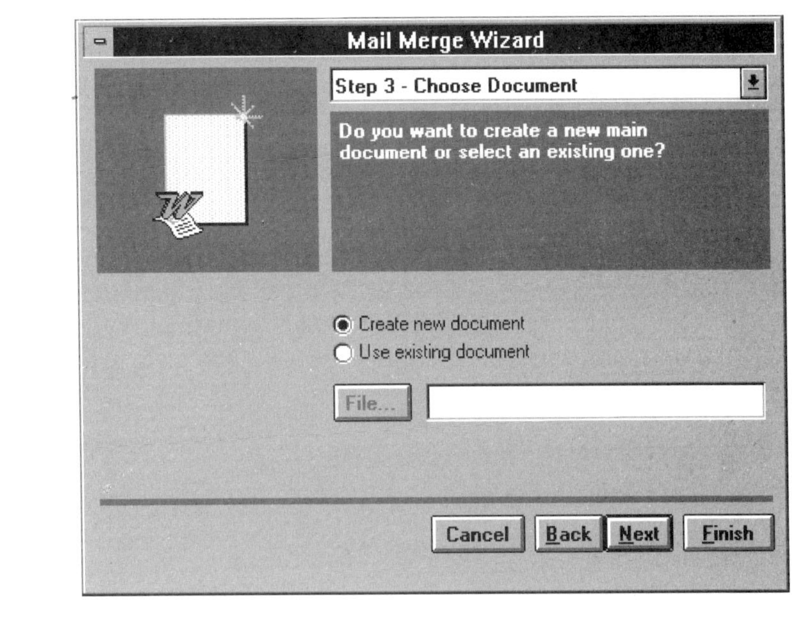

FIGURE 7.11

Step 4 of the Mail Merge Wizard—specifying a document type

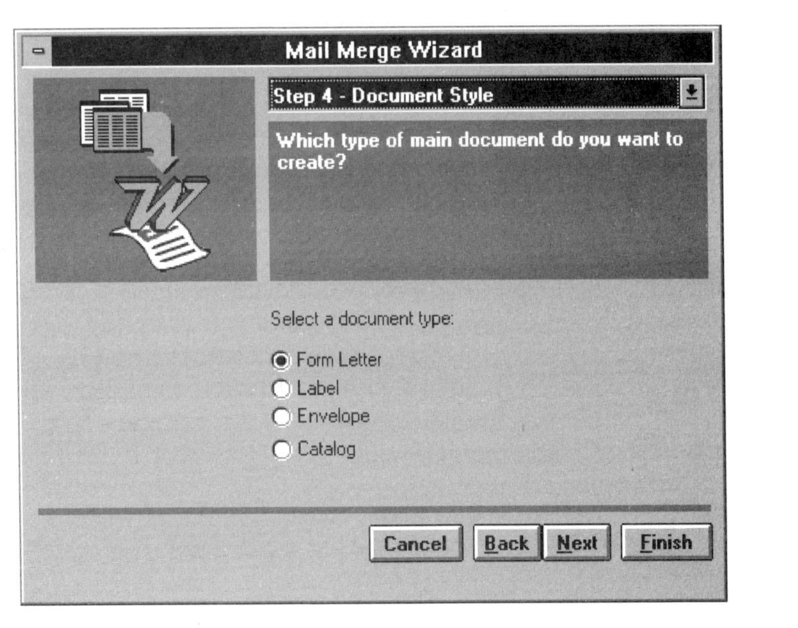

Generating the Merge File

In the final step you simply click the Finish button to generate the file. The Wizard generates a merge file with the data from the Visual FoxPro database you select.

It displays the Save As dialog box to let you name and specify a directory for this data source file.

If you are using Word for Windows, it automatically launches Word in a way that makes it easy for you to do a mail merge. If you are working with another word processor, you must open the program to use this data source in combination with a main document.

► Using the Merge File in Microsoft Word

The Mail Merge Wizard not only starts Word, it also adds a few buttons to Word's interface to make it easy to enter mail merge codes in the document.

Simply type the document as usual, and click the Insert Merge Field button whenever you want to add a code to the document that represents a field in the Visual FoxPro table. Word displays a dialog box that lets you select a field name. It adds a code made up of the field name surrounded by curly brackets, which will be replaced by the contents of the field when you merge the documents.

There is also a list of Word fields in this dialog box, which let you add special codes to perform more sophisticated merges. For example, you can merge data only if some condition is true. For more information, see the Word help system.

Click the Merge to Document button to merge these two documents to form a new Word document, or click the Merge to Printer button to send the merged file directly to the printer, without creating a new Word document to hold it. As a merged document can be very long, if you are working with a large database table, it is generally best to send the merge directly to the printer.

What Next?

Now you have learned all the basic features of Visual FoxPro that you need to manage your data using the easiest methods possible. You can define the structure of a database; add, edit, and view data; use queries to isolate data you want; and create simple forms, reports, and mailing labels. This is all you need to know for many simple database applications.

Now, you can continue your work with Visual FoxPro in several ways.

If you have an application that you can manage with the techniques you have learned so far—such as running a simple mailing list—you might want to get practical experience with that application now, before going any further in this book.

WARNING

Before you decide to "go it alone" using only what you've learned so far, look at the discussion of relational databases in Chapter 12 to see if you might need those techniques to manage your data. The data in many applications must be broken down into multiple tables, and you will create problems for yourself in the long run if you try to manage it in a single table.

How you should go on to use the rest of this book depends on your interests.

Part II covers the use of the Command window, logical expressions, and the Xbase language. If you want to become a power user of Visual FoxPro, you should go on to Part II, because commands and expressions let you use many powerful techniques that you have not yet learned.

Part III covers relational databases. Before you work with any application more complex than a simple mailing list, you should read Chapter 12 to see when you should break up data into multiple tables. The chapters that follow in Part IV cover the different methods of managing relational databases with Visual FoxPro.

Part IV covers Visual FoxPro power tools, such as the Report and Label Designers and the Macro Recorder. Learn these features of Visual FoxPro to customize the reports and labels that you create using the Wizards, which were covered in Part I, and to add more ease and power to your work.

Part V introduces programming and application development. It teaches these topics in a way designed to be useful to people using Visual FoxPro to manage their own data, and also brings you to a point where you are ready to learn to develop professional applications. It is possible to go on to this part after studying Part II.

You can study these parts of the book in whatever order best suits your needs and interests.

Working from the Command Window

PART TWO

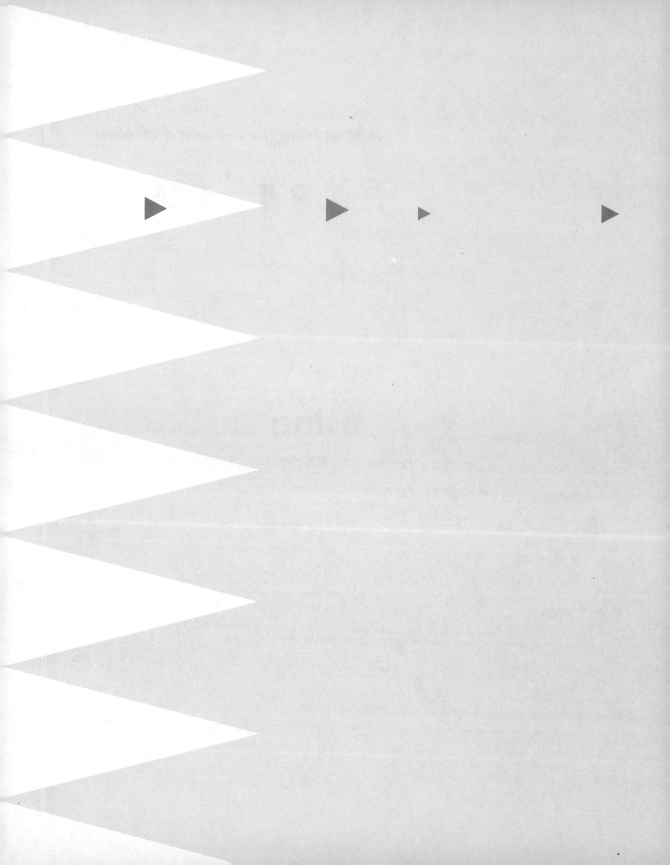

CHAPTER 8

Using FoxPro Commands

▸▸ FAST TRACK

▶ *To create new files from the Command window,* 188

enter **CREATE <file name>** to create a new table. For most other file types, enter a command such as **CREATE QUERY <file name>** to create a new query or **CREATE REPORT <file name>** to create a new report. To create a new text file, enter **MODI FILE <file name>**, and to create a new program file, enter **MODI COMM <file name>**. With these two commands, use a file name that does not already exist; both commands create a new file if there is not already one with the specified name.

▶ *To modify existing files from the Command window,* 189

open a table and enter **MODIFY STRUCTURE** to modify the definition of a table. For most other file types, enter a command such as **MODIFY QUERY <file name>** to modify an existing query or **MODIFY REPORT <file name>** to modify a report. To modify a text file, enter **MODI FILE <file name>**, and to modify a program file, enter **MODI COMM <file name>**; these commands let you modify an existing file if there is one with the name specified.

▶ *To open a table from the Command window,* 192

enter **USE <table name>**.

▶ *To view or edit the data in a table,* 195

first open the table. Enter **BROWSE** to view it in a Browse window in Browse display. Enter **EDIT** or **CHANGE** to view it in Edit display. Enter **APPEND** to view it in a Browse window in Append mode, so that new records will be added continuously at the end of the table.

To move the pointer through a table, 197

enter **GO TOP, GO BOTTOM,** or **GO <record number>** to move the pointer to the first record, the last record, or a record whose number you specify. Enter **SKIP** to move the pointer to the next record. Enter **SKIP <number>** to move the pointer by the specified number of records; for example, enter **SKIP 10** to move to the record ten records after the current record, or enter **SKIP –10** to move to the record ten records earlier.

To mark the current record for deletion or to unmark it, 198

enter **DELETE** or **RECALL**.

To finalize deletions, 199

enter **PACK**.

To view data, 201

enter **DISPLAY** to view the current record or **LIST** to view all records in the table in the main Visual FoxPro window, behind all Visual FoxPro document windows. Use either command with an optional FIELDS clause to view only some fields.

To redirect the output of the DISPLAY or LIST command, 204

add an optional TO PRINT clause to print the current record or all records. Add an optional TO FILE <file name> clause to send the output to a text file.

When you made selections from the menu system in Part I of this book, you saw that Visual FoxPro sometimes generated the equivalent commands in the Command window. These procedural commands were the only way of working with the first versions of dBASE, but there are still reasons to use them in this era of drop-down menus, dialog boxes, and windows.

It is sometimes easier to enter commands than to make selections from the menu system—particularly when you are performing a repetitive task—since you can edit and reenter commands you've already used.

Commands also give you capabilities that are not available using the menu system. For example, you can use many commands with field lists to make them apply to only certain fields of a table, as you will see later in this chapter. You can also use commands with a FOR or WHILE clause followed by a logical expression to make them apply only to certain records, as you will see in Chapter 11. There are also expressions and commands to manipulate data that do not have equivalent menu options. And because many basic commands can be extended by using the same sorts of optional clauses, such as field list, and FOR or WHILE clauses, learning a few features of the Xbase language adds a considerable amount of extra power to your work.

Of course, you must also learn commands if you ever want to do any programming, since a program is, in large part, a list of these commands.

This chapter gets you started with the basic commands used to create files and manipulate data, and it shows you some of the simpler optional clauses that can be added to them.

Although this chapter includes fewer formal exercises than Part I, you should try out each command discussed in this chapter as you're reading about it; that is the only way to be sure you're learning them.

▸▸ Sampling the Command Window

You should begin by trying out a couple of useful commands that will let you sample the Command window. The RUN command lets you run any DOS command in FoxPro's Command window, and SET DEFAULT makes whatever path you specify the current directory.

▸ The RUN Command

If you are familiar with DOS, you may find the Visual FoxPro command RUN very helpful in your work. RUN is a utility that lets you use any DOS command directly from within Visual FoxPro for Windows.

Simply enter the word RUN followed by the DOS command in the Command window.

The result of the DOS command appears in a separate Visual FoxPro Run Command window, which is closed automatically when the command has finished executing.

▸ The SET DEFAULT Command

Another very useful command is SET DEFAULT TO <path>, which makes the path that you specify the current directory, where Visual FoxPro looks for files if you do not specify a directory name.

▸▸ NOTE

Discussions of Visual FoxPro commands often use angle brackets to indicate items that must be filled in with specific information when you run the command. SET DEFAULT TO <path>, for example, indicates that you would enter the words SET DEFAULT TO followed by the actual name of a path, as in the examples below. Do not type the angle brackets themselves or the words in them.

As the path, you can enter any of the following:

- A drive, designated by a letter followed by a colon: for example,

  ```
  SET DEFAULT TO C:
  ```

- The full path name of a directory: for example,

  ```
  SET DEFAULT TO C:\LEARNFOX
  ```

- The path name of a directory without the drive designation, if it is on the current drive. For example, if you are already in some directory on drive C, you can enter

  ```
  SET DEFAULT TO \LEARNFOX
  ```

- The name of a subdirectory of the current directory. For example, if you are already in LEARNFOX and it has a subdirectory named DATA, which has a subdirectory named SAMPLES, you can enter

  ```
  SET DEFAULT TO DATA
  ```

  or

  ```
  SET DEFAULT TO DATA\SAMPLES
  ```

If you are working from the Command window, you can save yourself a considerable amount of typing by using this command rather than typing the full path name of every file you use.

The SET DEFAULT command is equivalent to the Default Directory control of the File Locations panel in the Options dialog box (which you display by choosing Tools ➤ Options), as shown in Figure 8.1. Visual FoxPro has many SET commands, which are equivalent to controls of this dialog box, as discussed in Chapter 19.

▸ Command Window Shortcuts

The following shortcuts will make your work easier:

- **Reusing Commands:** A list of all the commands you have entered or generated by using menus remains available in the Command window throughout your work session. You can use ↑ (or the mouse) to move the cursor to earlier commands, including those that have scrolled beyond the top of the window. Once you

FIGURE 8.1

Options for file locations

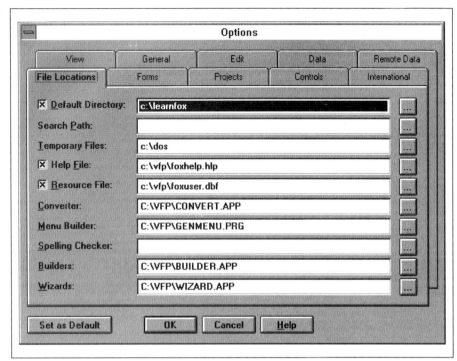

Options

View | General | Edit | Data | Remote Data

File Locations | Forms | Projects | Controls | International

☒ Default Directory:	c:\learnfox
Search Path:	
Temporary Files:	c:\dos
☒ Help File:	c:\vfp\foxhelp.hlp
☒ Resource File:	c:\vfp\foxuser.dbf
Converter:	C:\VFP\CONVERT.APP
Menu Builder:	C:\VFP\GENMENU.PRG
Spelling Checker:	
Builders:	C:\VFP\BUILDER.APP
Wizards:	C:\VFP\WIZARD.APP

Set as Default | OK | Cancel | Help

have found the command you want, just press Enter to reuse it as-is. At that point the command is executed and the cursor returns to the bottom of the list, where a copy of the command is added. If you want to use a variation on the earlier command, you can edit it first, using any of the editing techniques you just learned, and then press Enter to execute it and add it to the list in its revised form.

- **Four-letter abbreviations:** The Xbase language is designed so that you can enter just the first four letters of the keywords of any command. For example, the command MODIFY STRUCTURE is used to display the Table Designer and modify the structure of the open table, but you can simply enter MODI STRU. Of course, this sort of abbreviation applies only to keywords that are part of the language itself, not to names of tables, fields, reports, or to any other names that you create. In the exercises that follow, commands are generally written out in full, to make them easier to understand, but you can save time by using these four-letter abbreviations.

Keep these shortcuts in mind when you do the exercises that follow, and other exercises that use the Command window.

▶ Entering Sample Commands

As your first exercise with the Command window, try using RUN with the DOS command DIR /P to display a directory, pausing when each window is full. Then use SET DEFAULT to change the current directory, and try RUN DIR again to see the difference.

1. You should already have started Visual FoxPro, and the cursor should be in its initial position in the Command window. If it is not, press Esc until you have gotten out of the menu system and returned to the Command window. If for some reason the Command window is no longer on the screen, select Window ➤ Command Window to make it reappear.

2. Type **RUN DIR** and press Enter. Visual FoxPro displays a DOS directory similar to the one illustrated in Figure 8.2. Press a key to continue the listing until the Run window closes.

FIGURE 8.2

Using Visual FoxPro to get a DOS directory

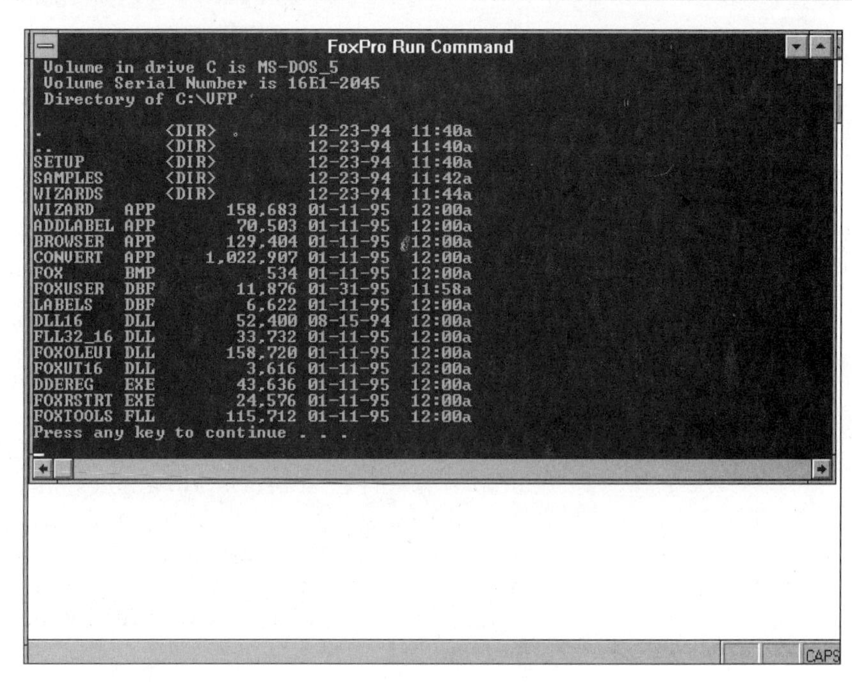

▶▶ **WARNING**

While it runs, Visual FoxPro sometimes creates and uses temporary files whose names are made up of random numbers and letters, with no extension; you may see some of these when you use the RUN DIR command. *Do not delete these files while you are in Visual FoxPro.* Most will be deleted automatically when you quit Visual FoxPro. If any are left, you can delete them in Windows or DOS while Visual FoxPro is not running.

3. Now, try getting a directory of just program files with the extension .EXE. Rather than typing a new command, use conventional Windows editing techniques to edit the first command you entered so that it reads

   ```
   RUN DIR *.EXE /P
   ```

   Then press Enter to display the Run window.

4. Finally, enter **SET DEFAULT TO C:\LEARNFOX** (or specify a different drive or directory name, if that's where you're keeping the sample files of this book). Then press the ↑ key three times and press Enter to use the RUN DIR /P command again. Again, press any key to continue displaying the directory until the Run window closes.

Notice that, when you reuse a command in its original or an edited form, it is added to the end of the list of commands in the Command window.

You can imagine how valuable the ability to edit and reuse commands can be if, for example, you are creating a large number of text files with slightly different names. There are many cases in which it is easier to use and reuse commands than to repeat the same series of menu choices over and over.

▶▶ Working with Files

Now, look at a few basic commands that are used to work with files.

You will see that, in many cases, there are two commands to do the same thing. That is because the Visual FoxPro language is descended from two different languages:

- Xbase: Visual FoxPro includes all the Xbase commands that were available in versions of dBASE through dBASE III+, and most of the additional commands from dBASE IV. These commands are the basis of the Xbase language, originally designed to let users work interactively with their data as well as to let programmers develop applications.
- SQL: Visual FoxPro also includes many commands for manipulating tables from SQL, the Structured Query Language developed to retrieve data on mainframe computers and client-server systems. SQL was originally designed for programmers, but many database management systems now offer an easy-to-use SQL interface; Visual FoxPro's Query Designer generates SQL queries.

Because Xbase was originally designed for users working interactively with their data as well as for programmers, it is generally more useful for working from the Command window. You will see below, for example, that SQL commands for creating and altering tables include features that you would not want to use when you are working interactively with Visual FoxPro. For this reason, this part of the book emphasizes Xbase commands and touches only briefly on SQL commands.

SQL is particularly useful for working with relational databases, and so it is covered in Chapter 15.

▸ Creating A New Table

Rather than choosing File ➤ New and using the New dialog box to create a new table, you can use the command CREATE. If you enter just this command, Visual FoxPro displays the Create dialog box to let you name the table, as it does when you use the menu system, but you can enter:

```
CREATE <file name>
```

to name the table and display the Table Designer in a single step. When you use this command to create a new file, Visual FoxPro automatically adds the extension DBF to the file name you specify.

When you use this command, you must be sure that the table name includes the full path name, or that the path you want to use is already the default directory. If you simply start Visual FoxPro and use a command such as CREATE EMPLIST, FoxPro will store the Emplist table in its home directory, C:\VFP. You must use either a command such as:

```
CREATE C:\LEARNFOX\EMPLIST
```

or a series of commands such as:

```
SET DEFAULT TO C:\LEARNFOX
CREATE EMPLIST
```

to save the file in the directory that you specify.

▶ Modifying the Structure of a Table

As you learned earlier, to change the structure of a table, you must open it and then enter the command MODIFY STRUCTURE to display the Table Designer with the definition of that table.

This command is almost always abbreviated as MODI STRU.

▶▶ WARNING

Remember that, as you learned in Chapter 2, you can lose data by modifying the structure of a table that already contains data.

▶ Creating and Modifying the Structure of a Table Using the Command Window

Visual FoxPro 3.0 also includes commands that let you create and modify the structure of a table without using the Table Designer.

The command to create a table has this basic form:

```
CREATE TABLE <table name>
     (<field name 1> < field type>
                   [<field width> [, <precision>] )
     (<field name 2> . . .)
     . . .
```

and it also includes many other options.

►► NOTE

In this book and other discussions of FoxPro commands, square brackets ([ ]) enclose parts of a command that are optional or required only in certain circumstances. In the CREATE TABLE command, for example, field width and precision need to be defined for some but not all field types. Like the angle brackets used to show placeholders, square brackets must be omitted from your actual commands.

The ALTER TABLE command lets you modify the structure of a table and includes options that let you add a field, alter a field, drop a field, or rename a field.

These are two commands from the Structured Query Language (SQL) that have been added to Visual FoxPro, and are now available in addition to the old Xbase commands CREATE and MODI STRU. Both commands are meant for special uses in programming, however, and when you are working interactively with Visual FoxPro it is much easier to use the Table Designer.

These commands are described in full in Appendix B, in the entries on CREATE TABLE—SQL and ALTER TABLE—SQL.

► Creating and Modifying Other Types of File

Because tables are the basic type of file used with Visual FoxPro, the command CREATE <file name> is used only to display the Table Designer to create a table.

Commands to display the designers used to create other types of files generally require a word representing the file type after the word create. For example:

- **CREATE QUERY <file name>** displays the Query Designer.
- **CREATE REPORT <file name>** displays the Report Designer.

Of course, you can also create any of these by choosing File ➤ New and selecting the appropriate radio button.

Likewise, these files can generally be modified by using MODIFY commands:

- **MODIFY QUERY <file name>** displays the Query Designer.
- **MODIFY REPORT <file name>** displays the Report Designer.

If you use the MODIFY command with the name of a file that does not already exist, Visual FoxPro will create a new file with that name, just as if you had used the CREATE command.

Apart from tables, the exceptions to the usual pattern of commands for creating and modifying files are text files. Both of these have only a MODIFY command, which is used either to create a new file or to alter an existing one:

- **MODIFY COMMAND <file name>** displays an edit window to let you edit a program. If you do not specify an extension, Visual FoxPro assumes PRG. The editor has the preferences that are useful for programming: for example, word wrap is turned off.
- **MODIFY FILE <file name>** displays an edit window to let you edit a text file. If you do not specify an extension, Visual FoxPro assumes TXT. The editor has the preferences that are useful for editing text: for example, word wrap is turned on.

▶▶ TIP

Remember that you can use the four-letter abbreviations for any of these commands. For example, MODI COMM is virtually always used instead of MODIFY COMMAND.

You can avoid confusion if you remember that tables, command files, and text files have commands that are different from other file types. This reflects the historical fact that they were among the first file types available in early versions of Xbase.

►► Working with Data

Once you have opened a table, you can work with its data, either by displaying it in a Browse window or by working directly with the table without displaying it.

► Using the Table in the Background

You can enter the command **USE <table name>** to open a table, rather than choosing File ➤ Open and using the Open dialog box. Remember that you must either use the full path name of the table or have entered the SET DEFAULT command to make the table's directory the default directory before you enter the USE command.

►► **TIP**

The command USE <table name> has the side effect of closing the current table as it opens the one you specify, and it will still close the current file if you don't specify a table to be opened. Thus, the command USE without a table name is often used to close the current table.

When you USE a table, the status bar displays the table's name, the number of records in it, and the number of the current record, but the contents of the table are not displayed. Working from the menu system, you generally must open a Browse window before you can work with the table, but when you work from the Command window, you can work directly with the table in the background. In the rest of this section, you will look a little more deeply at how you USE a table, and at how to do a few things from the Command window that you cannot do with the menu system.

▶▶NOTE

The rest of the exercises in this book use the Emplist table created in Part I. If you began with Part II of this book, go back and do the exercise used to create this table in Chapter 2 and the exercise used to add data to it in Chapter 3.

Commands with Output to the Screen

A handy way of getting information about the file that is currently in use is to enter the command **DISPLAY STRUCTURE** in the Command window (after you have opened the table). This displays the name of the current file and the names, types, and widths of its fields. When the screen is full, Visual FoxPro prompts you to press any key to continue the display. This is one of a number of commands that display information in the Visual FoxPro main window, behind all open document windows, as you can see in Figure 8.3.

FIGURE 8.3 ▶

Displaying the structure of a table

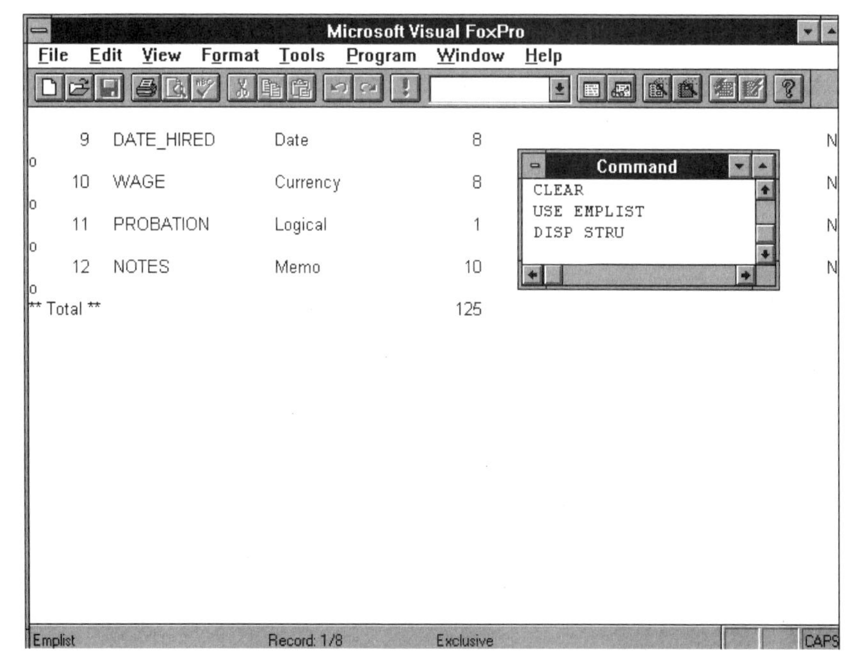

If you use these commands and the screen becomes cluttered, you can enter the command CLEAR to clear all output from the screen.

Try a bit of experimenting to see what is happening in the background:

1. If necessary, enter **CLEAR** to clear the screen. If you have not already done so, choose File ➤ Open and open the file EMPLIST.DBF, and notice that Visual FoxPro generates the USE command in the Command window. If you have changed the default directory, you may find it easier to enter the command USE EMPLIST.
2. Enter **DISP STRU** (short for DISPLAY STRUCTURE) in the Command window. Visual FoxPro displays the structure of the EMPLIST file. Press a key to finish the display.
3. Type **USE** in the Command window to close the current file without opening a new one.
4. To see if the last command worked, type **CLEAR** to clear the screen, and then enter **DISP STRU** again. Since no file is in use, Visual FoxPro displays the Open File dialog box to let you select a table whose structure you want displayed.
5. Rather than selecting a table now, press Esc to close this dialog box. Visual FoxPro displays an error message telling you it cannot execute the DISPLAY STRUCTURE command because no table is in use, as shown in Figure 8.4. This is an example of an alert. Press any key and it disappears.

FIGURE 8.4

A Visual FoxPro alert

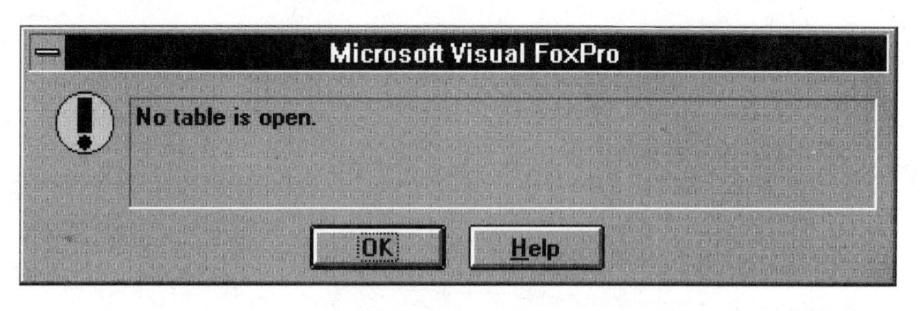

This bit of experimenting should have made you comfortable with the USE command, which is important in combination with many other commands.

▶ Displaying and Editing Data

You learned in Chapter 3 how to browse and edit data using the menu system. Working from the Command window, you can simply USE the table and then:

- Enter **EDIT** (or **CHANGE**) to display the table in Edit display.
- Enter **BROWSE** to display the table in Browse display.
- Enter **APPEND** to display the table in Append mode.

The commands EDIT and CHANGE are exactly equivalent.

TIP

If no table is in use, you can enter the command CHANGE, EDIT, BROWSE, or APPEND in the command window.

It is also possible to add or modify data without using the Browse window. This is useful primarily in programming, to give the programmer complete control over the data and never give the user direct access to the table. However, it is also useful for modifying the contents of multiple records with a single command.

APPEND BLANK and REPLACE

The original method of adding records with Xbase commands requires two steps.

First, enter the command **APPEND BLANK** in the Command window to add a new blank record and make it the current record.

Then use a command such as REPLACE LNAME WITH "SMITH" to enter SMITH in the LNAME field of the current record.

A single REPLACE command can be used to change the values in multiple fields:

```
REPLACE <field name 1> WITH <value 1>,
 <field name 2> WITH <value 2>,
 . . .
```

Because it always works on the current record, you can also use the REPLACE command to modify an existing record.

REPLACE can be very useful if you add an optional Scope clause and a FOR or WHILE clause to change the data in multiple records with a single command. This use of REPLACE is covered in Chapter 11.

Adding a Null Value

There are also times when it is useful to add a *null* value to a field so you can know with certainty whether an entry has been made in that field.

Values that are placed in the fields by default, such as blank spaces in character fields and 0 (zero) in number fields, can also be entered using the keyboard. If you see an entry of 0 in a field recording monthly sales by your employees, for example, you have no way of knowing whether the data-entry person simply has not made an entry in that field yet or whether they entered 0 in that field deliberately because that employee made no sale for the month.

The null value is ASCII character zero, and it cannot possibly be entered using the keyboard; by contrast, a blank space is ASCII character 32, and 0 (zero) is ASCII character 48, and both of these can be entered using the keyboard.

Thus, it is sometimes useful to add .NULL. to a field so you can check later to see whether users have modified that field. For example, you can use a FOR clause (covered in Chapter 11) to isolate the records with the null value in their monthly sales field: these records would include only those who have not had data entered in that field, without including those who actually had sales of 0.

The token representing the null value is made up of the word NULL surrounded by periods. Thus, you can enter this value in a field by using a command such as:

```
REPLACE LNAME WITH .NULL.
```

and you can use this token in the same way in other commands.

Before you can add a null value to a field, you must select the NULL check box for that field in the Table Designer.

The INSERT Command

A more recent addition to the FoxPro language, the INSERT command lets you add a new record and specify the data in it in a single command. It has the general form:

```
INSERT INTO <table name>
     [(<field name 1>, <field name 2> . . .)]
     VALUES (<value 1>, <value 2> . . .)
```

As you can see, the field names are optional. If you leave them out of the command, the values are inserted into the field in their order in the table.

If the table is not already open, it is automatically opened exclusively. INSERT is another SQL command added to Visual FoxPro. Like all other commands discussed here, INSERT has additional options discussed in Appendix B.

▶ Moving the Pointer

If you are working with the table in the background, rather than in a Browse window, you can use commands to control the *pointer* that keeps track of the current record.

You have already seen that, when the table is displayed in a Browse window, the cursor is on the current record. When you are working with commands, it is sometimes useful to move the pointer even when you are not viewing the table. In either case, the status bar displays the word *Record:* followed by the record number of the current record and the total number of records in the table, just to the right of the file name.

Many commands apply to the current record by default. For example, if you enter DELETE in the Command window, the record that the pointer is on is marked for deletion.

It is possible to move the pointer when the Browse window is closed by using the following commands:

- **GO TOP** (or **GOTO TOP**) moves the pointer to the first record.
- **GO BOTTOM** (or **GOTO BOTTOM**) moves the pointer to the last record.
- **GO [RECORD] <number>** (or **GOTO [RECORD] <number>**) moves the pointer to the record with the number indicated. (Again, do not type the square brackets; they simply serve to indicate that the word RECORD is optional.)
- **SKIP <number>** moves the pointer the indicated number of records from the current record. The number can be positive or negative; if the number is omitted, 1 is assumed. Thus, SKIP moves the pointer to the next record and SKIP–1 moves to the previous record.

▸▸ NOTE

In addition to a number, you can use any numerical expression with SKIP or GO RECORD. Expressions are covered in Chapter 9.

These commands are similar (but not identical) to the submenu options displayed when you choose Table ➤ Goto Record, which was discussed in Chapter 3.

▸ Deleting and Recalling Records

As you learned in Chapter 3, Visual FoxPro uses a two-step process of deleting records. Working from the Command window, you first enter DELETE to mark a record for deletion. If a record is already marked for deletion and you decide not to delete it, enter RECALL to unmark it.

PACKing a Table

Enter **PACK** to finalize deletions, so that records marked for deletion can no longer be recalled.

WARNING

Data can be lost if packing is interrupted. Because of this, the Esc key is disabled during packing; pressing Esc will not interrupt the PACK command as it does other commands. Do not turn off the computer while packing is in progress—no matter how long it takes. If you think there is danger of a power failure, back up your table before packing.

You can also use this command with options:

- **PACK MEMO** removes all unused space from the memo file of the table without affecting the records of the DBF file.
- **PACK DBF** removes unused records from the table in the DBF file without affecting the memo file.

NOTE

As you learned in Chapter 3, most Visual FoxPro commands will include records in output regardless of whether they are marked for deletion. You can avoid the problems this causes by PACKing the table before using it with other commands. Chapter 11 discusses other methods of dealing with deleted records.

The ZAP Command

Finally, there is one very dangerous command you should know about: ZAP, which eliminates all records from a file. It is equivalent to deleting all the records of a table and then packing the table, except that it works much more quickly.

After you enter ZAP, your records are gone forever; they cannot be recalled.

This command is useful in programming, where its use can be controlled very precisely. For example, it is common for a programmer to let the user enter records in a temporary file, and then, after the program copies them to the permanent file, it ZAPs the temporary file. In this sort of situation, ZAP makes programs run faster, but it is probably best not to use it from the Command window.

▸▸ WARNING

ZAP is most dangerous in combination with the environment command SET SAFETY OFF. Normally, Visual FoxPro asks if you want to ZAP all your records before it executes this command. However, if you have entered the command SET SAFETY OFF, ZAP will eliminate all your records without giving you any warning. SET commands are covered in Chapter 19.

▸▸ Adding Optional Clauses to Commands

One of the most important benefits of working with the Command window is that for many common commands you can add extra clauses that give you a quick way of performing complex operations. Because the same optional clauses can be used for many different commands, it is very easy to learn and use them.

You will be able to use this sort of optional clause much more powerfully after you have learned about expressions, discussed in Chapter 9. For now, you should look at a few simple optional clauses that can be added to commands, to get the basic idea of this important feature of the Xbase language.

▶ The DISPLAY and LIST Commands

Two commands that are very useful for viewing the data when you are working in the Command window or programming have no equivalent in the menu system:

- **DISPLAY** displays the contents of the current record on the screen, as shown in Figure 8.5.

FIGURE 8.5 ▶

Using DISPLAY

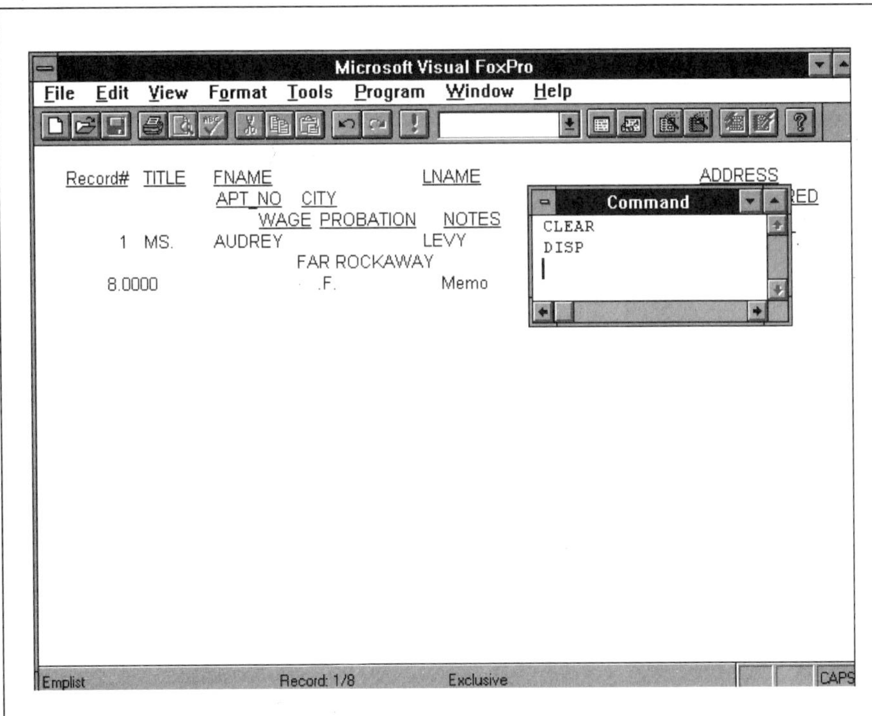

- **LIST** displays the contents of all the records on the screen, as shown in Figure 8.6.

As you can see in the illustrations, both DISPLAY and LIST display records on the screen *behind* Visual FoxPro's windows. If any windows are opened, you might have to hide them to see the records. Both commands display all the field names at the top of the display.

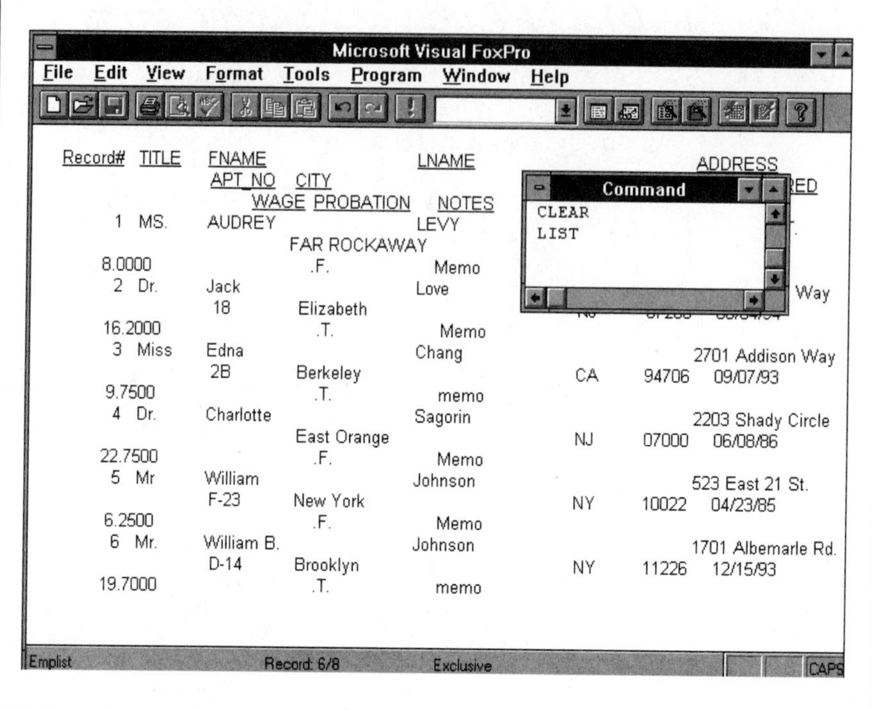

FIGURE 8.6

Using LIST

If all the fields cannot fit across one screen, Visual FoxPro wraps the display to the next line. This makes the output of these commands difficult to read, but you can get a much clearer listing if you add a FIELDS clause.

Adding the FIELDS Clause

You can also use the DISPLAY and LIST commands with the names of the specific fields you want to see. For example, the command

```
LIST FNAME, LNAME, DATE_HIRED
```

would show you only those three fields for all the records in the table, as shown in Figure 8.7. Notice that the field names must be separated by commas. This form of the command lets you choose few enough fields that you can fit them into the width of one screen.

FIGURE 8.7

Using LIST with an optional FIELDS clause

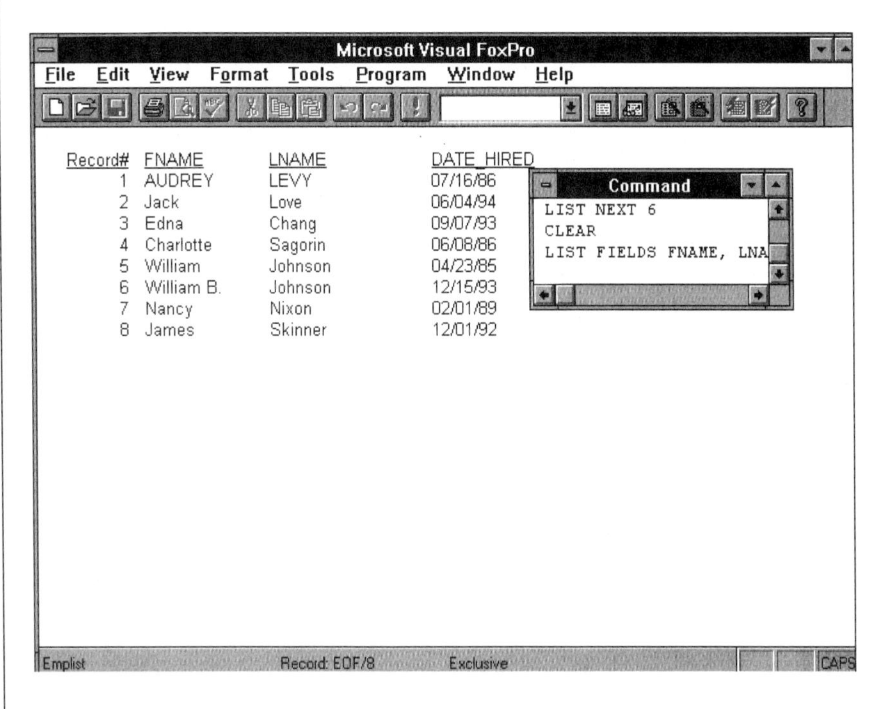

You will see in Chapter 9 that you can use many commands with this sort of field list. In some cases the word FIELDS must also be added before the list of fields. To avoid having to learn which commands require it, it is best to include it whenever it is relevant. Thus, it is easiest to use the command

```
LIST FIELDS FNAME, LNAME, DATE_HIRED
```

here, and this is the form these sorts of commands will take throughout the book.

It is easy to look at individual records in the database by combining GOTO or SKIP commands with the

```
DISPLAY FIELDS <field names>
```

command. Once you get the DISPLAY command right, with the fields you actually want, you can move the pointer to a different record by moving the cursor to the appropriate commands in the Command window and then reusing the DISPLAY command.

Adding the TO PRINT Clause

The limitation of the LIST command is that most tables are too long to fit on a single screen, and the records in the database scroll by on the screen too quickly for you to read them if you use LIST. LIST is genuinely useful, however, if you add TO PRINT at the very end of the command. This sends the listing to the printer as well as to the screen and is usually the easiest way of getting a quick-and-dirty report on the data in your file.

LIST normally displays the record number of each record, but you can make a printed report look better by omitting the record number. Do this by adding OFF after the field list and before the words TO PRINT when entering the LIST command.

For example, if you have a database of names, addresses, and telephone numbers and you want to give someone a printed list of just the names and phone numbers, the easiest way to do it is by entering

```
LIST FIELDS FNAME, LNAME, PHONE OFF TO PRINT
```

(assuming, of course, that these are the field names). This gives you a printed list of all the names and phone numbers in the file, in three columns, with the name of the field at the top of each column. Note that long lists will print continuously, without allowing for page breaks.

►► **TIP**

As a precaution, it is usually best to enter the command without TO PRINT first, to make sure you have the fields you want and that they actually fit into the width of the screen—which is the same as the width of the paper in a standard printer. A long file will take some time to list, but you can press Esc to stop the process. Once you have the fields right, press ↑ to edit the command, and add TO PRINT.

Adding the TO FILE Clause

To improve the appearance of your printout and also make a permanent record of the listing, you can use LIST TO FILE <filename> instead of LIST TO PRINT.

This version of the command creates the same listing in a plain text file (also called an ASCII file). The advantage of this is that you can edit this file with any word processor that reads plain text files. The word processor will automatically handle the page breaks; and if you edit the column headings a bit, add a header or footer for each page, and perhaps change the font, you'll have a very respectable-looking report.

NOTE

Visual FoxPro pads out unused spaces in each field with blank spaces, which are included in the output of the LIST command, so that a given field has the same number of characters in every record, counting the blank spaces. Thus, the fields are lined up in columns only if you use a monospace (also called nonproportional) font, where the same number of characters always take up the same amount of space. To keep the columns lined up properly, you must *not* use a proportional font when you reformat the file where you stored the output of the command, because in proportional fonts different characters take up different amounts of space. This means that the width of each field will depend on which characters it has, and fields with fewer letters will generally take up less space than fields with more letters.

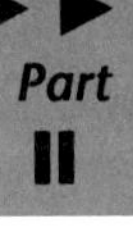

You can use Visual FoxPro's Report Designer, discussed in Chapter 17, to create much more sophisticated reports, but it is often faster to use LIST.

Using LIST

Try this exercise to produce a simple report on employee wages. You should still have the EMPLIST table open.

1. If necessary, enter **CLEAR** to clear the screen. Then enter

   ```
   LIST FIELDS LNAME, FNAME, WAGE OFF
   ```

   The listing is shown in Figure 8.8.

FIGURE 8.8

Using LIST to get a very quick report

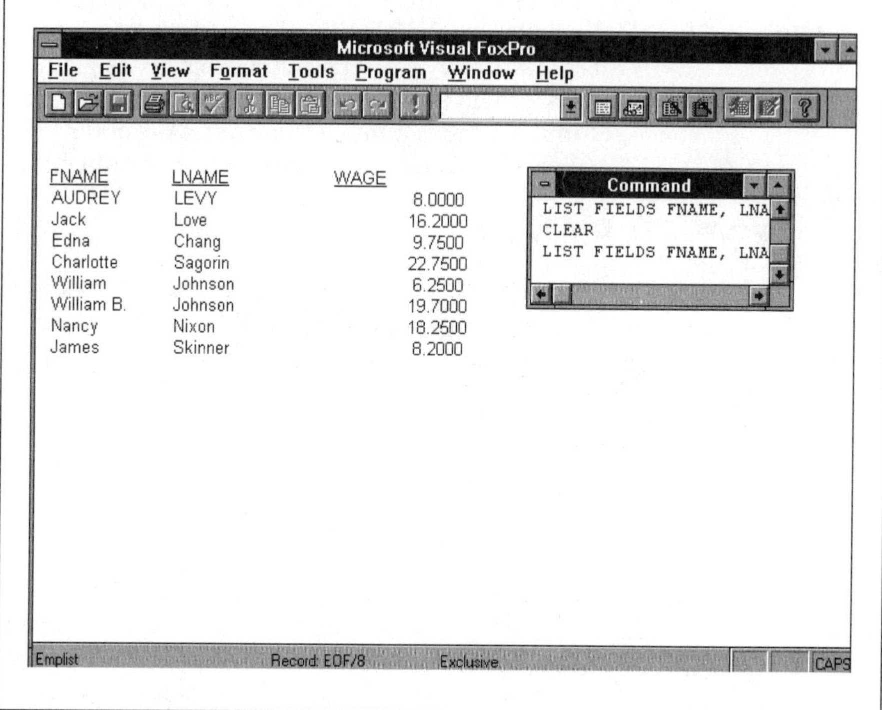

2. If you want to try printing this listing, first make sure your printer is turned on. Then use the conventional editing keys to add **TO PRINT** to the end of this LIST command, and press Enter.

Of course, one of the names is not properly capitalized, and the names are not in alphabetical order. In the chapters that follow, you will learn enough about expressions and indexes to deal with these problems. And in Chapter 11, you will use the LIST command again to produce a more sophisticated report.

► Limiting the Use of the Browse Window

You can also use BROWSE, CHANGE, or EDIT in the Command window with this sort of field list. Specifying fields is particularly useful for fitting all the information you want into the Browse window.

These commands can also be used with options.

The NOEDIT Option

For example, BROWSE, CHANGE, and EDIT can all be used with the NOMENU option to prevent the user from using the menu to change the format of the Browse window. Thus, EDIT NOMENU displays the window in Edit display and lets users edit existing records, but it does not add any options to the View menu that let the user switch to Browse display or change the format of the window in any other way.

BROWSE NOEDIT and the odd command EDIT NOEDIT allow users to add records or mark records for deletion but do not allow them to edit the contents of existing records.

The BROWSE LAST Command

When you select View ➤ Browse, Visual FoxPro generates the command BROWSE LAST. The LAST option of the BROWSE command opens the Browse window with the same display that it had the last time you used it.

This command preserves any changes you made in the Browse window, such as moving or resizing the columns. In addition, if you last used the Browse window in Edit display, BROWSE LAST will open it in Edit display again.

This command can be very useful. For example, if you often telephone people and you change the order of fields in the Browse window so that the telephone number is next to the name, Visual FoxPro will save the setting even after you turn off your computer, and it will display the fields in that order whenever you browse that file using BROWSE LAST.

TIP

To return to the default Browse display, enter the BROWSE command *without* the LAST option in the Command window. You cannot do this using the menu system, which always generates the command BROWSE LAST.

Sampling Browse Options

You may sometimes find it handy to use BROWSE with a fields list, to view only the data you want, and with the NOEDIT option NOEDIT so that you cannot make inadvertent changes in the data. Try using these options:

1. If necessary, open the Emplist table and CLEAR the screen. Then enter

   ```
   BROWSE FIELDS LNAME, FNAME, WAGE NOEDIT
   ```

2. Try editing one of the fields and you will see that it is impossible. Visual FoxPro just beeps and does not change the data. This is because you included NOEDIT in your command.
3. Close the Browse window. Then choose View ➤ Browse Emplist. Notice that Visual FoxPro generates the command BROWSE LAST and that the same options are still being used.
4. Close the Browse window again. Enter **BROWSE** to open the Browse window in its default form.

If you are interested in other options that can be used when you display the Browse window, see BROWSE, EDIT (or CHANGE), and APPEND in Appendix B of this book.

►► Exiting from Visual FoxPro

Finally, to exit from Visual FoxPro, you can use the command QUIT, which is generated in the Command window when you choose File ➤ Exit.

►► To Sum Up

In this chapter, you have begun working with the Command Window interface. You have not only learned the most important menu options and commands that you use for working with tables but you have also learned a key feature of the Visual FoxPro language by seeing how many of these commands can be used with optional clauses. You'll be able to use more types of optional clauses and use them more powerfully after you have learned about Visual FoxPro expressions, which are covered in the next chapter.

CHAPTER 9

Understanding Expressions

FAST TRACK

To display the result of an expression in the main Visual FoxPro window, ***215***

enter **? <expr>.**

To control capitalization, ***222***

use functions such as UPPER(<char exp>) to convert letters to uppercase, LOWER(<char exp>) to convert letters to lowercase, and PROPER(<char exp>) to convert capitalization so that the first letter of each word is uppercase and other letters are lowercase.

To remove unnecessary blank spaces from character data, ***223***

use the functions TRIM(<char exp>) to trim trailing blanks, LTRIM(<char exp>) to trim leading blanks, and ALLTRIM(<char exp>) to trim both trailing and leading blanks.

To convert data types, ***225***

use functions such as VAL(<char exp>) to convert Character data to Numeric data; DTOC(<date exp>) to convert Date data to Character data; DTOS(<date exp> to convert Date data to Character data in ASCII format, yyyymmdd, for use in indexes; CTOD(<char exp>) to convert Character data to Date data; and STR(<number exp>[,<length>][,<decimals>]) to convert Numeric data to Character data.

▶ *To do mathematical calculations,* 230

use the arithmetic operators: + for addition, – for subtraction, * for Multiplication, / for division and either ^ or ** for exponentiation. Use parentheses for grouping.

▶ *To do date calculations,* 232

use the operators + for addition and – for subtraction. In date calculations, numbers represent numbers of days.

▶ *To concatenate text,* 234

use the operators + to combine two character expressions or – to combine two character expressions with all blank spaces moved to the end of the result.

▶ *To create logical expressions,* 237

use the relational operators: = (Equal to), > (Greater than), < (Less than), >= (Greater than or equal to), <= (Less than or equal to), <> or # or != (Not equal to), $ (Contained in: used only for Character data), and == (Identical to: used only for Character data).

▶ *To create complex logical expressions,* 245

combine two logical expressions using the logical operators .AND. (the result is true only if both expressions are true) or .OR. (the result is true if either expression is true). Use .NOT. before a logical expression to reverse its result. Use parentheses for grouping.

An expression is a special sort of calculation used in Visual FoxPro. Expressions not only let you use commands more powerfully to manipulate data. They also let you create more sophisticated indexes and reports, and they add power to almost everything you do in Visual FoxPro, from producing a simple listing of the data in a table to writing advanced programs.

This chapter will give you a thorough background in working with expressions. When you are working with Visual FoxPro in your own applications, you will often create expressions using the Expression Builder dialog box. In most of this chapter, however, you will experiment with expressions by using them directly from the Command window. Not only is it easier to work with sample expressions using the Command window than using the Expression Builder, it also gives you a firmer understanding of expressions, which will make it easy for you to use the Expression Builder in the future.

The ? Command

While you are learning about expressions, you will find it instructive to try them out by using the ? command, which displays an expression in the Visual FoxPro main window, behind all the document windows (like the command LIST, which you used in Chapter 8).

For example, if you enter the command **? "THIS IS A TEST"** in the Command window, the words `THIS IS A TEST` appear in the main Visual FoxPro window, behind the document windows.

The ? command always prints the result of the expression, preceded by a new line. If you use ? without an expression following it, it just prints a new line. This is an easy way to skip a line.

You can also use the command ?? to print an expression without a new line before it.

▶▶ NOTE

Notice that ?, like all other commands, always *evaluates* an expression; that is, it displays the result of the expression. For example, if you enter *? FNAME,* Visual FoxPro prints the contents of the current Fname field, as shown in Figure 9.1. This makes ? very useful for testing complex expressions.

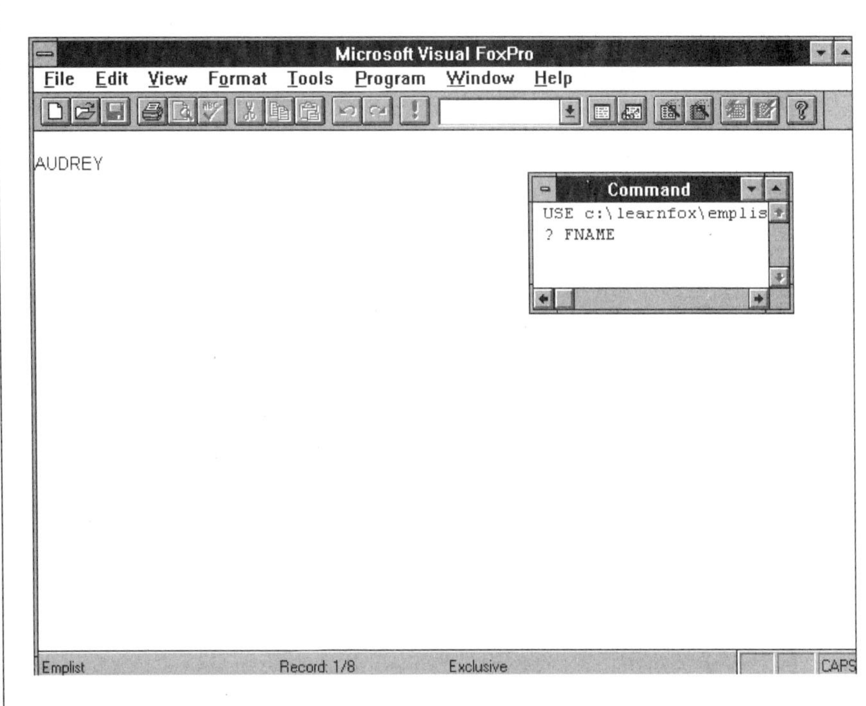

FIGURE 9.1 ▶

Visual FoxPro evaluates expressions used in commands.

▶▶ Components of Expressions

An expression can include several elements:

- Field names
- Variables

- Constants (or literals)
- Functions
- Operators

All of these elements are included in the Expression Builder, shown in Figure 9.2. You can either type them directly in the Expression text box or select them using the Expression Builder controls as follows:

- Use the four drop-down controls at the top of the Expression Builder to select functions and operators of different data types.
- Use the Fields list to select Field names. If you are working with a relational database, you can use the From Table control below this list to select the table whose fields should be displayed here.
- Use the Variables list to select variables.

FIGURE 9.2

The Expression Builder dialog box

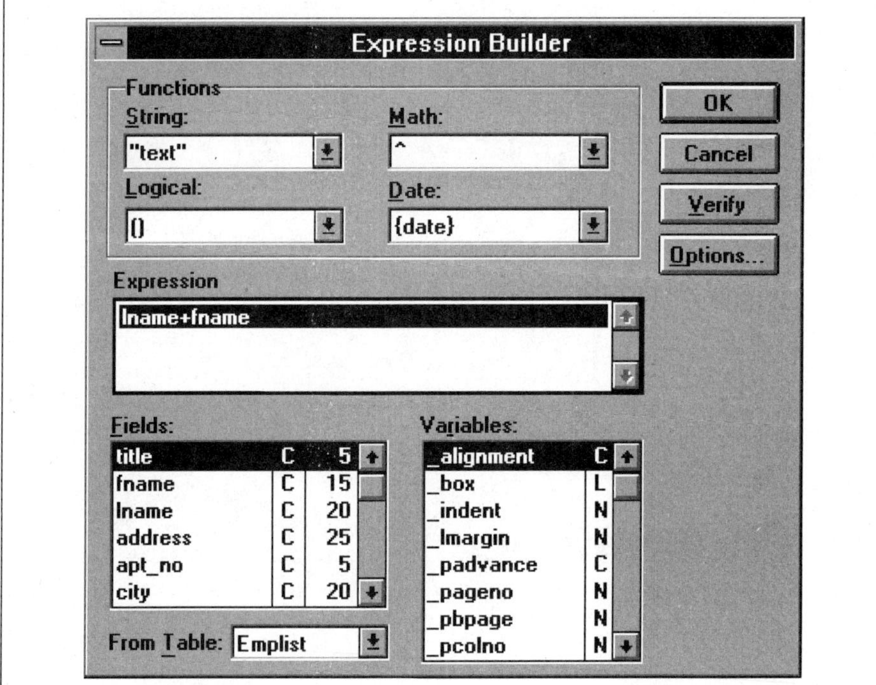

The Expression box shows the expression you've constructed with your selections; you can also type the expression or parts of it directly into this box. You can click the Verify button to check whether the Expression box holds a valid expression—i.e., one that does not contain any errors in syntax. Of course, the fact that an expression is valid does not necessarily mean that it does what you want it to do.

Field Names

Field names, of course, are simply the names of the fields of your database table, such as Fname and Lname. As you can see in the illustration, the names of all the fields in the database you are working with can be selected from the Fields list in the Expression Builder dialog box.

If you are working with a relational database, you can also use the From Table drop-down control to choose which table of the database has its fields displayed in the Fields list. This control is not used when you are working with a simple database that stores data in a single table.

Variables

Visual FoxPro lets you use two types of *variables*:

- System variables are built into Visual FoxPro, always begin with the underscore character, and always have the same meaning. For example, _PAGENO represents the current page of a report, and it can be included in an expression added to the Report Designer. For complete information on system variables, search in the Visual FoxPro Help system for keywords that begin with the underscore character and that do not end with parentheses.
- *Memory variables* are created by the user, are used in more advanced expressions, and are useful primarily in programming. You can learn about them in Chapter 23.

System variables are always included on the scrollable list in the Expression Builder. Memory variables are added to this list after you create them.

▸ Constants

Constants (or *literals*) are letters, numbers, or dates that are used with their literal meaning. For example, if you wanted an expression to actually include the word *Name:* before each person's name, you would use the constant "Name:" as part of that expression. They are called constants because their values are unchanging, unlike the first name and last name, for example, which change for each record.

Constants that are used in expressions must include the following delimiters to indicate their data type:

- **Character constants:** Must be enclosed in double quotation marks, single quotation marks, or square brackets. For example, you could use **"Please"** or **'Please'** or **[Please]** in an expression to make an expression include the actual word *Please*.

▸▸ TIP

If you forget to use delimiters for a character constant, Visual FoxPro will think it is the name of a memory variable or field. If you get a puzzling error message saying that a variable cannot be found, it probably means you mistakenly used a character constant without delimiters.

- **Date and DateTime constants:** Must be enclosed in curly brackets (the { and } characters). If you wanted to create an expression that calculated the number of days to the end of the year, for example, it would include a constant such as **{12/31/95}**.
- **Number constants:** Used without any delimiter. Simply use the number itself.
- **Logical constants:** There are two logical constants, enclosed by dots: .T. represents true, and .F. represents false. However, these are used differently from other constants and are covered in the section on logical expressions later in this chapter.

Constants must be typed directly into the Expression box of the Expression Builder, since the lists of the Expression Builder obviously could not include every constant you might want to use. For example, if you wanted to use the constant 100 in a mathematical calculation, you would have to type **100** as part of the expression.

When you are working with constants, it is important to remember that an entire expression must be of a single data type. Sometimes you must convert literals or fields from the Date or Number data type to the Character data type in order to make them compatible with the rest of the expression. To do this, you must use functions.

▶ The Functions and Operator Drop-Down Controls

The four drop-down lists at the top of the Expression Builder dialog box divide all of Visual FoxPro's functions and operators into four different types, depending on the type of data they work on. The String popup lets you work with character data, the Math popup with numeric data, the Logical popup with logical data, and the Date popup with Date and DateTime data.

Because they are complex, logical expressions are discussed separately later in this chapter.

Figure 9.3 illustrates the string drop-down list. As you can see, there are far too many operators and functions to fit in the display, but you can scroll down to get more.

Notice the word "*text*" at the top of the list. You can select this to add quotation mark delimiters to the Expression text box before entering text in it. Of course, you can also type the quotation marks by hand, while you type the text.

Notice also that some of the functions have commas in their parentheses, showing how many arguments they need. Some have examples in their parentheses, such as *expC*, which shows that a character expression is required.

Functions and operators are the richest and most complex elements of Visual FoxPro expressions, and both are discussed at length below.

FIGURE 9.3

The String drop-down list of the Expression Builder

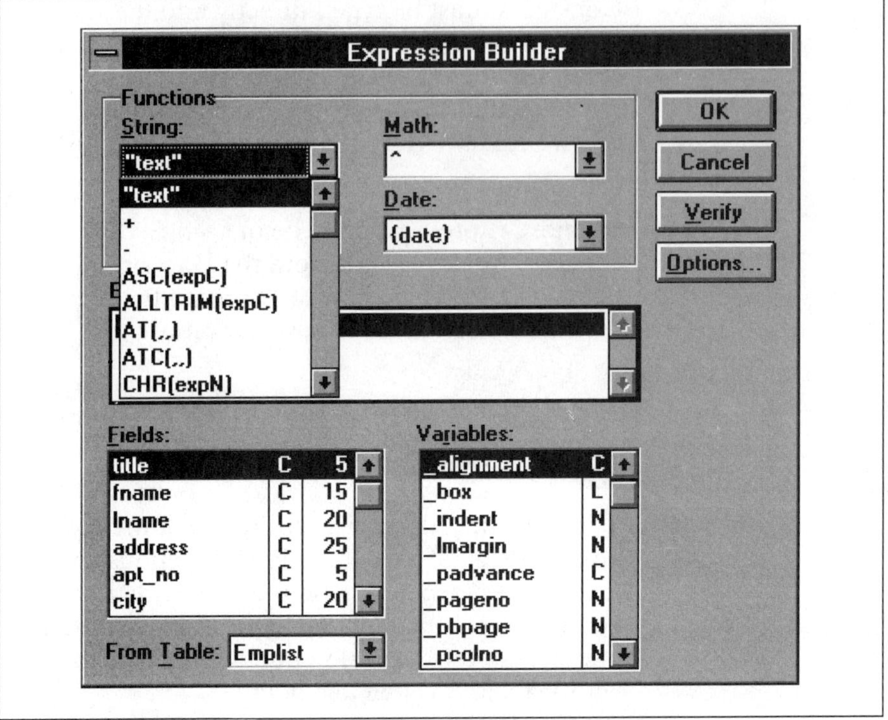

▸▸ **TIP**

For a complete reference guide to the functions you can use with each data type, search for the topic "Commands and Functions by Category" in the Visual FoxPro Help system.

▸ Functions

A *function* returns a value. Usually this means that a function works on a piece of data (known as the function's *argument*) in some way and that the "value" it returns is the data in a new form. The argument appears within the function's parentheses. For example, the function UPPER( ) converts lowercase characters to uppercase, so that UPPER(LNAME) returns the data in the Lname field with all the letters capitalized.

▶▶ **NOTE**

A function does not actually transform or permanently change the data it is working on. It merely lets the expression use the data in this new form.

Some functions return a value that depends on information in your computer system. For example, DATE() returns the current system date. Logical functions, which you will work with at the end of this chapter, return a value of true or false.

Notice that all functions end with parentheses, even functions such as DATE( ) that never use an argument.

Try out the two functions you have learned so far:

1. If necessary, start Visual FoxPro and display the Command window interface.
2. Enter **? UPPER("this is a test")**. Visual FoxPro prints `THIS IS A TEST` on the screen.
3. Enter **? DATE( )**. Visual FoxPro prints the system date, as shown in Figure 9.4.

▶▶ **TIP**

It often makes sense to read the parentheses of a function as if they were the word *"of."* For example, many people find that if they read UPPER(FNAME) as *"the upper of Fname,"* they can more easily keep track of the meanings of the functions.

Visual FoxPro offers a tremendous number of functions, as you will see when you use the scrollable list to choose them. Until you begin programming, though, you can get by with a relatively small number of functions. Some of the most important are listed here.

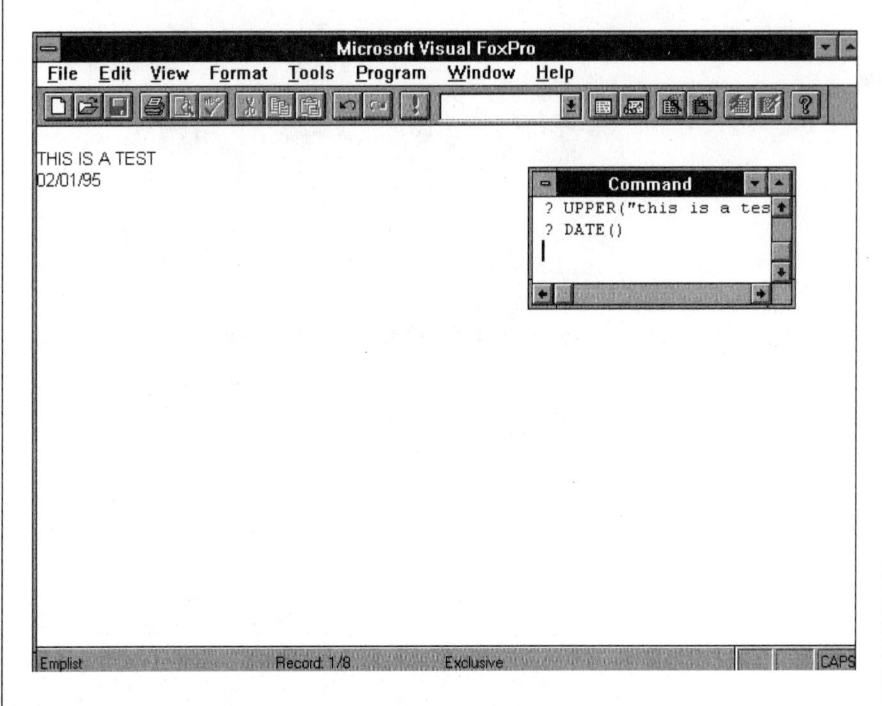

FIGURE 9.4

Using ? to print expressions

Functions to Change Capitalization

You will find the following functions useful for changing the case (capitalization style) of character data. (The abbreviation *char exp* within the arrow brackets stands for *char*acter *exp*ression.)

- **UPPER(<char exp>)** converts letters to uppercase. For example, UPPER(FNAME) returns the contents of the Fname field in all uppercase letters, and UPPER("hEllO") returns the word `HELLO`.
- **LOWER(<char exp>)** converts to lowercase, as you might expect. For example, LOWER(FNAME) returns the contents of the Fname field in all lowercase letters, and LOWER("hEllO") returns `hello`.
- **PROPER(<char exp>)** converts to the capitalization used for a proper name, with the first letter of each word uppercase and the rest lowercase. For example, PROPER(ADDRESS) returns the contents of the Address field with the first letter of each word

capitalized, as you would normally want on mailing labels. PROPER("hEllO") returns `Hello`.

NOTE

These functions act only on letters and do not affect any numbers or special characters that are included in character fields.

Try testing these functions on the fields of your database. Your table should be open. (If it is not, select File ➤ Open to open EMPLIST.DBF.)

1. Enter **?** twice, to skip two lines.
2. Enter **? LOWER(FNAME)** in the Command window. Visual FoxPro prints the Fname field of the current record in all lowercase letters (even though you entered it in all uppercase).
3. Enter **? PROPER(ADDRESS)** in the Command window. Visual FoxPro prints the Address field of the current record with just the first letter of each word capitalized, as shown in Figure 9.5.

Functions for Trimming Blanks

The next group of functions is useful for trimming blanks from character data. This is often necessary because, when you tell it to print the field Lname, for example, Visual FoxPro not only prints the characters that are in the field, it also adds enough blanks at the end to fill the entire width of the field. These are called *trailing blanks.* Likewise, if you convert a numeric field to the character type, Visual FoxPro often adds blanks to the left of the number to pad it out. These are called *leading blanks.* Although there are times when blanks are indispensable (as you will see when you create indexes in Chapter 10), there are also times when you want to get rid of them.

If you want, for example, to produce mailing labels or reports without unnecessary blank spaces in them, you could use these functions:

- **TRIM(<char exp>)** trims trailing blanks.
- **LTRIM(<char exp>)** trims leading blanks.
- **ALLTRIM(<char exp>)** trims both trailing and leading blanks.

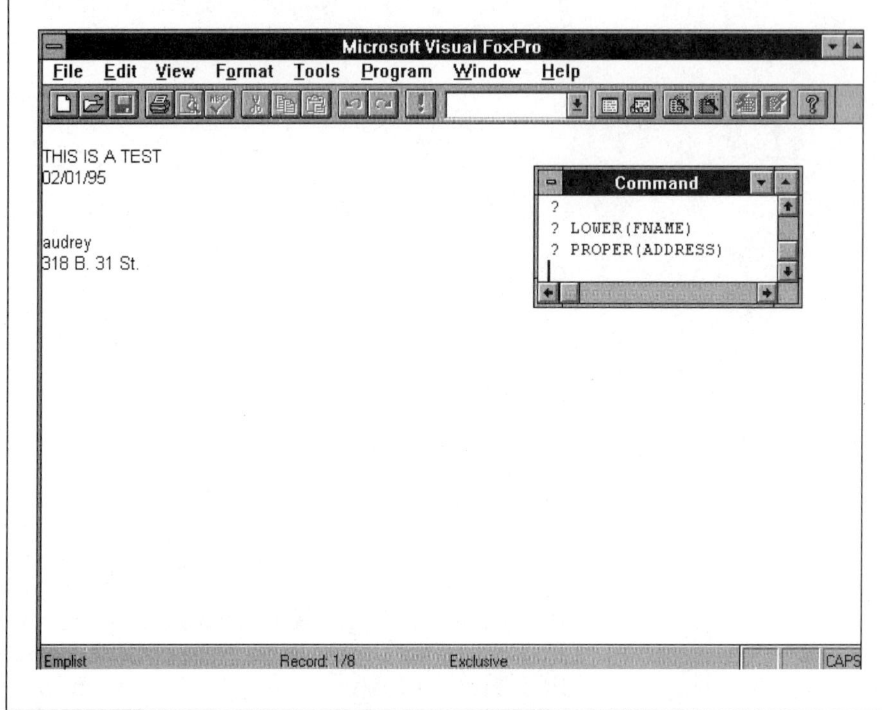

FIGURE 9.5 *Using functions to change the capitalization of character data*

Try these out:

1. Enter **CLEAR** to clear the screen.
2. Enter

   ```
   ? "X" + TRIM("        THIS IS A TEST        ") + "X"
   ```

   Type eight blanks before and after the words THIS IS A TEST. Visual FoxPro will leave the eight blanks between the first X and the words THIS IS A TEST, but there will not be any spaces before the final X.
3. Now enter:

   ```
   ? "X" + LTRIM("        THIS IS A TEST        ") + "X"
   ```

In the second example, there is no space between the initial X and THIS IS A TEST, but there are spaces before the final X, as shown in Figure 9.6.

FIGURE 9.6

Trimming blank spaces

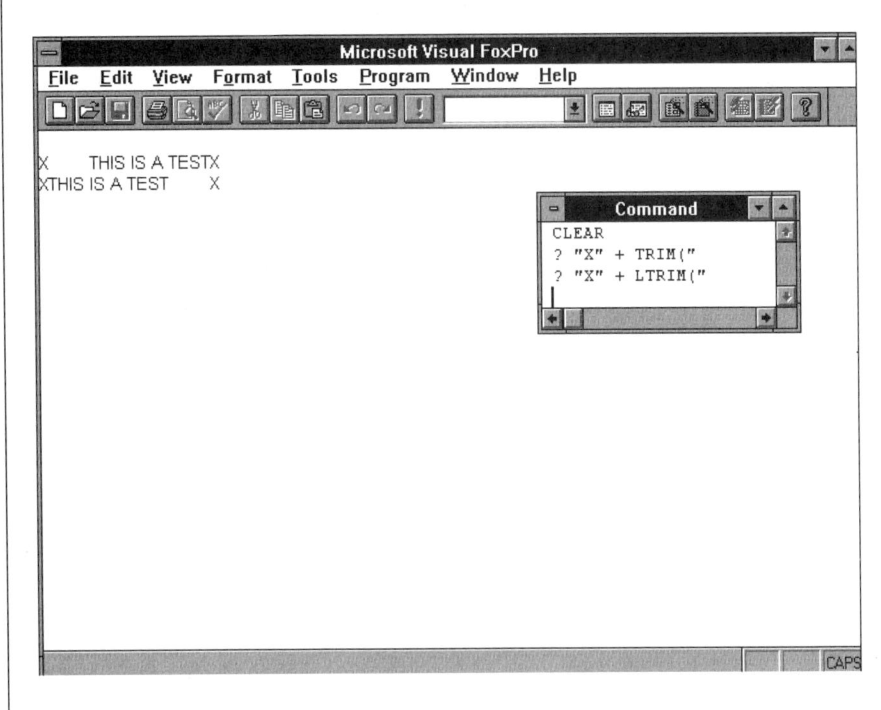

Functions for Converting Data Type

The next group of functions is useful for converting data from one data type to another, which is necessary when you are creating an expression that combines data that is originally of two different types.

- **VAL(<char exp>)** converts character data to numeric data. For example, if you ever wanted, for some strange reason, to perform a calculation using a ZIP code, you could not perform it on Zip directly since that field has been defined as the Character type, but you could perform a calculation on VAL(ZIP).

- **DTOC(<date exp>)** converts date data to character data. For example, DTOC(DATE_HIRED) would return the contents of the Date_hired field as a character string in the same order that dates are normally displayed—in the format mm/dd/yy—although the format can be changed using the View window, as explained in Chapter 8. This function should not be used for indexes, for the reasons explained below.

- **DTOS(<date exp>** converts date data to character data in ASCII format, yyyymmdd, for use in indexes. This function is covered in Chapter 10, which discusses indexes.
- **CTOD(<char exp>)** converts character data to date data. For example CTOD("10/12/90") uses quotation mark delimiters to define 10/12/90 as a literal character string and uses the CTOD() function to convert the string to the Date type. It is identical to {10/12/90}, which uses curly bracket delimiters to define 10/12/90 as being the Date type.

►► NOTE

Older Xbase-compatible programs did not include the curly bracket delimiters for the Date type. The only way to use a date constant was in the form CTOD ("10/12/90"). You will see this form used frequently if you look at older books about dBASE or older programs written in Xbase languages, but now it is rarely used.

- **STR(<number exp>[,<length>][,<decimals>])** converts numeric data to character (sometimes called string) data. Notice the two optional clauses for length and decimals. If these are left out, the default length of the string is 10 spaces and the default number of decimal places is 0. Any extra length is thus padded with leading blanks, and any decimal places are lost.

You will try out a few of these functions in the next section when you use operators to create more complex expressions. For now, try the STR( ) and VAL( ) functions, which are quite commonly used.

1. Enter **CLEAR** to clear the screen.
2. Enter **? WAGE**, and Visual FoxPro prints `8.00`, the contents of the current Wage field (that is, the Wage field for Audrey Levy, the first record entered in the table), indented to allow for the leading blanks in this record.
3. Enter **? STR(WAGE)**, and Visual FoxPro prints `8`, indented nine spaces. This shows the default width for STR( ), with no decimals and ten spaces wide.

4. Enter **? STR(WAGE,5,2)**, and Visual FoxPro prints `8.00`, indented one space. The function returns a value that is five spaces wide (counting the blank tens place and the decimal point as one space each) including the two decimal places, as you can see in Figure 9.7.

FIGURE 9.7

Using STR() to convert a number to characters and VAL() to convert characters to a number

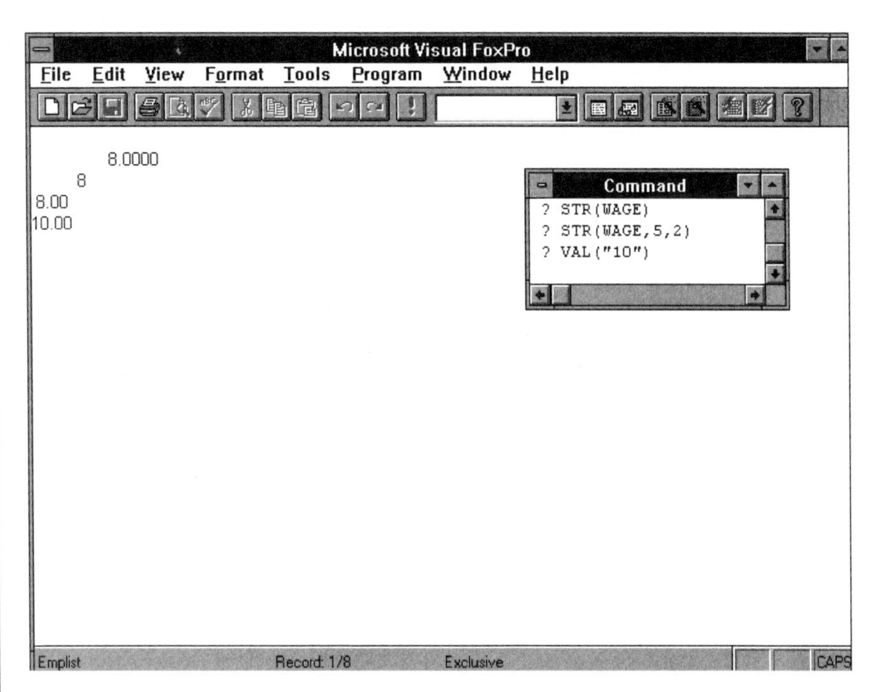

5. Compare the preceding STR( ) examples with VAL( ): Enter **? VAL("10")**, and Visual FoxPro prints `10.00`. By default, it prints two decimal places.

Functions to Work with Dates and Times

Next are a few functions you will want to use on occasion to manipulate dates.

- **DATE( )** returns the current system date (the date in your computer's clock/calendar).

- **DAY( ), MONTH( ),** and **YEAR( )** return the day, month, or year, respectively, of a date in number form. For example, since the date hired for the current record is 04/23/76, MONTH(DATE_HIRED) is `4`.
- **DOW( )** returns the day of the week in number form. For example, since June 14, 1990, is a Thursday, and since Thursday is the fifth day of the week, DOW({06/14/90}) returns `5`.
- **CMONTH( )** and **CDOW( )** return the month or day of the week, respectively, of a date in character form. For example, for the current record, CMONTH(DATE_HIRED) returns `April`.

These date functions can also be used to work with the dates in DateTime expressions. There are similar functions to work with the time portion of a DateTime expression:

- **TIME( )** returns the current system time.
- **HOUR( )** returns the hour from a DateTime expression.
- **MINUTE( )** returns the minute portion of a DateTime expression.
- **SEC( )** returns the seconds portion of a DateTime expression.
- **SECONDS( )** returns the number of seconds between midnight and the current time, as a decimal number with a precision of one one-thousandth of a second. Do not confuse it with SEC().

You have already tried DATE( ). Take a minute now to try out a couple of other date functions:

1. Enter **?** several times to skip lines.
2. Enter **? CDOW({06/06/95})** to get the day of the week for that date. Visual FoxPro prints `Friday`.
3. Enter **? CMONTH(DATE_HIRED)** to print the name of the month when the employee in the current record was hired, as shown in Figure 9.8.

ASCII Conversion Functions

Finally, two other functions you might find instructive, even if they are not necessary, are ASC( ), which returns the ASCII number of any

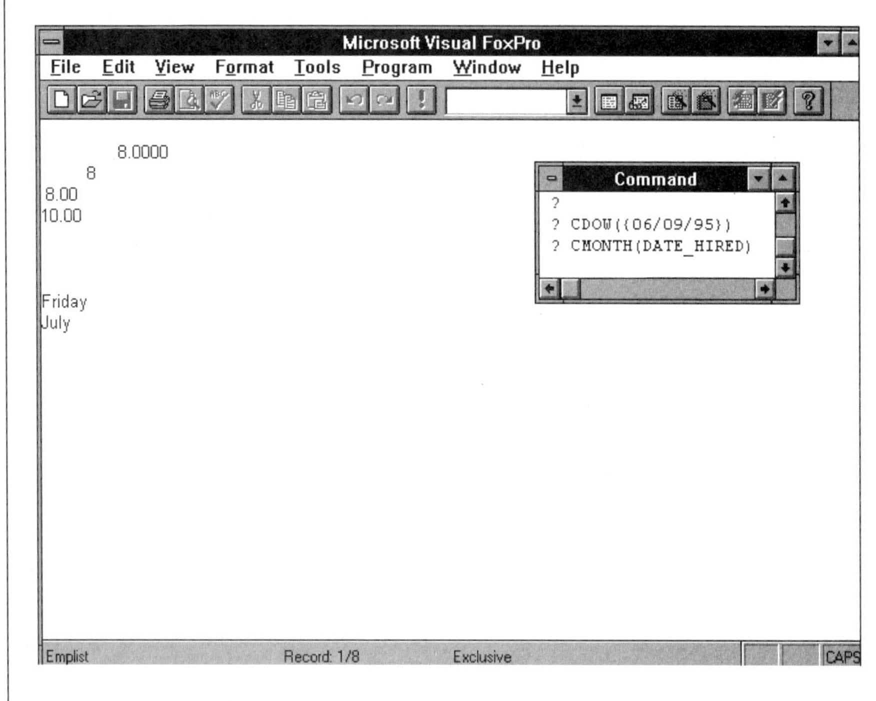

FIGURE 9.8

Using functions to work with dates

character, and the opposite function CHR(), which returns the character for an ASCII number. For example, CHR(65) returns `A`, since the uppercase *A* is ASCII character 65. And ASC("A") returns the number `65`. With these functions and ?, you can use Visual FoxPro as an ASCII chart. For example, ? ASC("z") lets you look up the ASCII number of that character; Visual FoxPro prints `122` in response. These functions are useful in programming. You might also find that experimenting with them now will help you learn the ASCII system.

Nested Functions

You can get more power from the functions described above by using functions within functions. These are sometimes called *nested* functions.

For example, if you use STR( ) to return the number in the Wage field as a character string, it will have leading blanks that you might not want. Since wages are different amounts and some strings may be longer than others, you cannot get rid of all the leading blanks with the

STR( ) function itself. STR(WAGE,5,2), for example, will have a leading blank if the amount is less than ten. You can use LTRIM(STR(WAGE,5,2)) to get rid of these leading blanks.

The double parentheses at the end might seem a bit confusing at first, but if a complex expression confuses you, remember that it is evaluated from the inside out. First look at the innermost function, STR(WAGE,5,2) in this case. Once you understand that this is a number converted into string form, it is easy to see what LTRIM( ) is doing to it.

►► TIP

Within an expression as a whole, the number of left parentheses must be equal to the number of right parentheses. In complex expressions, it is useful to count them to make sure you have not left out anything.

1. Enter **?** several times to skip lines.
2. Enter **? STR(WAGE,10,2)** to see the wage with a number of leading blanks, and then enter **? LTRIM(STR(WAGE,10,2))** to see the same wage without any leading blanks.
3. Enter **? CDOW(DATE( ))**, and Visual FoxPro prints the day of the week that it is today.

► Operators

The word *operators* might sound very technical and forbidding, but even if you have never used a computer before, you are already familiar with some operators, such as + and –, which are used to perform the operations of addition and subtraction in elementary arithmetic. Visual FoxPro includes the usual arithmetic operators and similar operators that are used for strings and dates.

Arithmetic Operators

The *arithmetic operators* are

+	Addition

–	Subtraction
*	Multiplication
/	Division
^ or **	Exponentiation (raising to a power)
( )	Grouping (not a substitute for multiplication)

Most of these signs are probably familiar to you. Like virtually all computer applications and languages, Visual FoxPro uses the asterisk for multiplication, instead of the × sign or the parentheses commonly used in arithmetic or algebra.

Since some computer displays cannot use a superscript to represent an exponent, many programs use the caret: 5^2 indicates that the 2 should be above the line as a superscript, so this stands for 5 squared (5 to the second power). Some programs also use ** (to indicate that exponentiation is a step beyond multiplication). Visual FoxPro lets you use either of these common symbols.

Using Parentheses for Grouping As in algebra, the parentheses are used for grouping, which indicates what is called the *precedence* of operations; that is, the order in which operations are performed. The difference that precedence makes is obvious. For example, (2*3)+5 gives you a different result than 2*(3+5). In the first case, you multiply 2*3 first to get 6 and then add 5, so the final result is 11. In the second case, you add 3+5 first to get 8 and then multiply by 2, so the final result is 16.

NOTE

As you can see, you cannot leave out the multiplication sign in Visual FoxPro as you do in algebra. You cannot use 2(3+5) to indicate that 3+5 is multiplied by 2. The asterisk must always be included to indicate multiplication.

Default Precedence If no parentheses are used, exponentiation takes precedence over multiplication and division, and multiplication and division take precedence over addition and subtraction.

This is the order of precedence you are accustomed to if you studied high school algebra. Think, for example, about the value of the algebraic expression

$$2x^3+4$$

If you're familiar with math, you know not to multiply 2 times x first and then cube the result. Without any thought, you would cube the value of x first, then multiply the result by 2, and then add 4. This is the same order of precedence as in Visual FoxPro: exponentiation, then multiplication or division, and then addition or subtraction.

In general, though, it is a good idea to use parentheses to indicate precedence even if the operations would occur in that order anyway, simply to make the expression easier to read.

For example, (2*WAGE)+4 gives the same result as 2*WAGE+4, but the first expression is easier to understand when you read it. Likewise, because spaces are optional before and after operators, you can use whatever spacing you need to make the expression easy to read: you might find that (2*WAGE)+4 is even easier for you to read at a glance.

Using Visual FoxPro as a Calculator As shown in Figure 9.9, using the arithmetic operators with ? acts as a simple calculator:

1. Enter **CLEAR** to skip a line.
2. Enter **? 2*8**, and Visual FoxPro prints `16`.
3. Enter **? 1/3**, and Visual FoxPro prints `0.33`.

Notice that the Visual FoxPro arithmetic operators print two decimal places by default. You can vary the number of decimal places, however, by using the STR( ) function. For instance, you could use ? STR(1/3,9,8) to print eight decimals.

In addition to the arithmetic operators, Visual FoxPro includes a simple set of date and string operators.

Date Operators

Date operators simply let you add and subtract dates. They are the same as the arithmetic addition and subtraction operators.

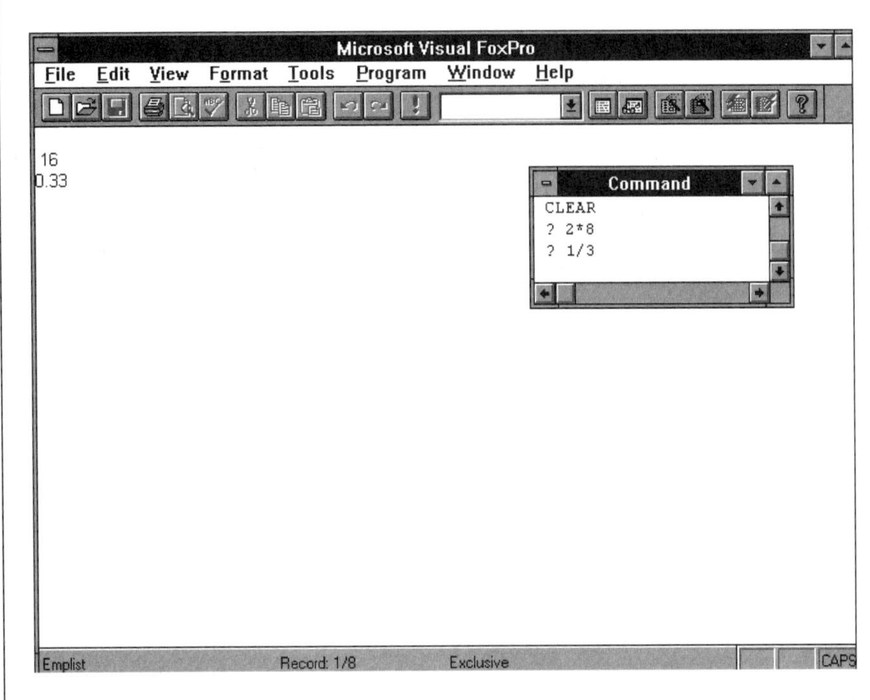

FIGURE 9.9

Using Visual FoxPro expressions as a calculator

Thus, + adds dates. For example, {01/01/96}+90 gives the date that is 90 days into calendar year 1996.

Predictably, – subtracts dates. For example, DATE()–DATE_HIRED gives you the number of days between the current system date and the date hired for the current record; it tells you how long someone has been working for you.

Try these two simple date calculations:

1. Enter **?** several times to skip lines.
2. Enter **? {06/06/96} – {05/06/96}**. Visual FoxPro prints 31, the number of days between the two dates.
3. Enter **? DATE( ) + 7**. Visual FoxPro prints the date a week after the current date.

String Operators

String operators are used to concatenate strings; that is, to put together two strings as one.

- + concatenates strings including blanks.
- – concatenates strings eliminating embedded blanks.

The – to eliminate the blanks is generally used as a shortcut. The expression

```
FNAME-LNAME
```

is similar to

```
TRIM(FNAME)+TRIM(LNAME)
```

There is one difference between the two. TRIM() eliminates the blanks entirely, while the – operator moves the embedded blanks to the end of the string, so the string has the same length as always.

When you work with Visual FoxPro in real applications, you will find it very convenient to use the – operator. This book, though, generally uses the + operator to concatenate strings and uses functions to trim unnecessary blanks. This will help you get accustomed to the trimming functions and give you more insight into what is happening when you concatenate strings.

Printing a Name Notice that the string operators must be fiddled with a bit to print a full name, since a simple – concatenation would not leave a space between the strings; it would give you something like JOHNSMITH. To print a name, you have to include a blank space as a constant. For example,

```
TRIM(FNAME) + " " + TRIM(LNAME)
```

would give you something like JOHN SMITH. The quotation marks may look strange at first, but remember that they are enclosing the blank between them, which is a literal, and that this expression thus concatenates *three* character strings.

Combining Mixed Data Types Even though the different types of operators look the same, you cannot use them to combine characters with dates or numbers. First, you must use functions to convert the data to the same data type. Since forgetting to do this is a very common error, let's make this error on purpose so you can recognize what it looks like.

1. Enter **CLEAR** to clear the screen.

2. Enter

   ```
   ? "Today is " + DATE()
   ```

   Visual FoxPro displays the alert shown in Figure 9.10. Its error message is rather obscure; remember to connect it with this error, which is one of the most common errors you will make when you work with expressions. Press any key to make the alert disappear.

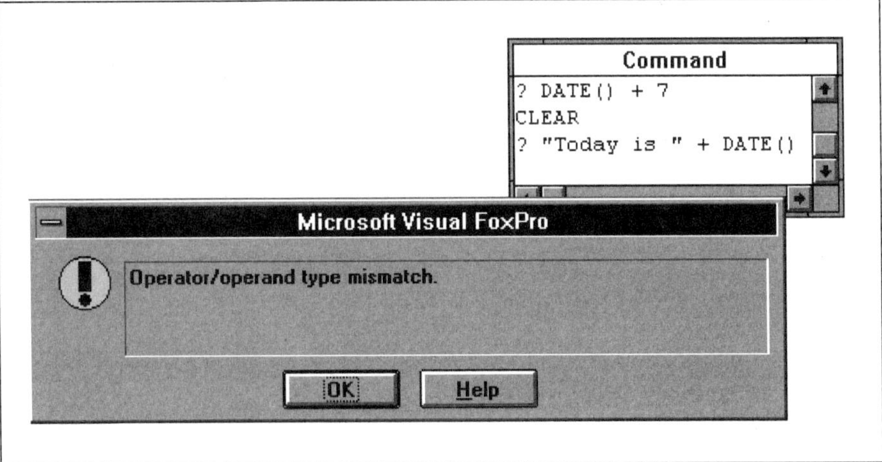

FIGURE 9.10

An alert is displayed if data types are mixed.

What the alert means is that "Today is " is a different data type from DATE( ). Now let's fix the problem.

3. Click OK to remove the alert. Enter

   ```
   ? "Today is " + DTOC(DATE())
   ```

   Visual FoxPro prints a message that includes the current date.

4. Since you are about to start a complex example, enter **CLEAR** to clear the screen. Then enter

   ```
   ? "The hourly wage of " + FNAME + LNAME + " is "
   + WAGE
   ```

Visual FoxPro displays the same alert because WAGE is a different data type from everything preceding it. Press Enter to make the message disappear.

5. Use ↑ to edit the previous command. Enter

```
? "The hourly wage of " + FNAME + LNAME + " is " +
STR(WAGE)
```

Visual FoxPro now prints the expression, but it is filled with unnecessary blanks, and the wage does not have decimals.

6. Edit the command again. Enter

```
? "The hourly wage of " + TRIM(FNAME) + " " +
TRIM(LNAME) + " is " + LTRIM(STR(WAGE,5,2))
```

►► NOTE

Despite the fact that these rather lengthy commands take up more than one line on a printed page, be sure you type them as single commands without pressing Enter until you reach the end of the whole command.

The function TRIM( ) has eliminated the unnecessary blanks, but notice that you had to add a literal blank between FNAME and LNAME so it did not come out AUDREYLEVY. Likewise, remember to include the spaces after *of* and before and after *is*.

7. Edit the command once more to get the capitalization right and to add a dollar sign and a period at the end. Enter

```
? "The hourly wage of " + PROPER(TRIM(FNAME) + " " +
TRIM(LNAME)) + " is $" + LTRIM(STR(WAGE5,2)) + "."
```

The results of this series of commands are shown in Figure 9.11. (The Command window has been moved and resized to show as much of the commands and their results as possible.)

The one other very common error, which you might have made while you were doing this exercise, is using unbalanced parentheses. Fortunately, the alert that tells you about this error is easy to understand.

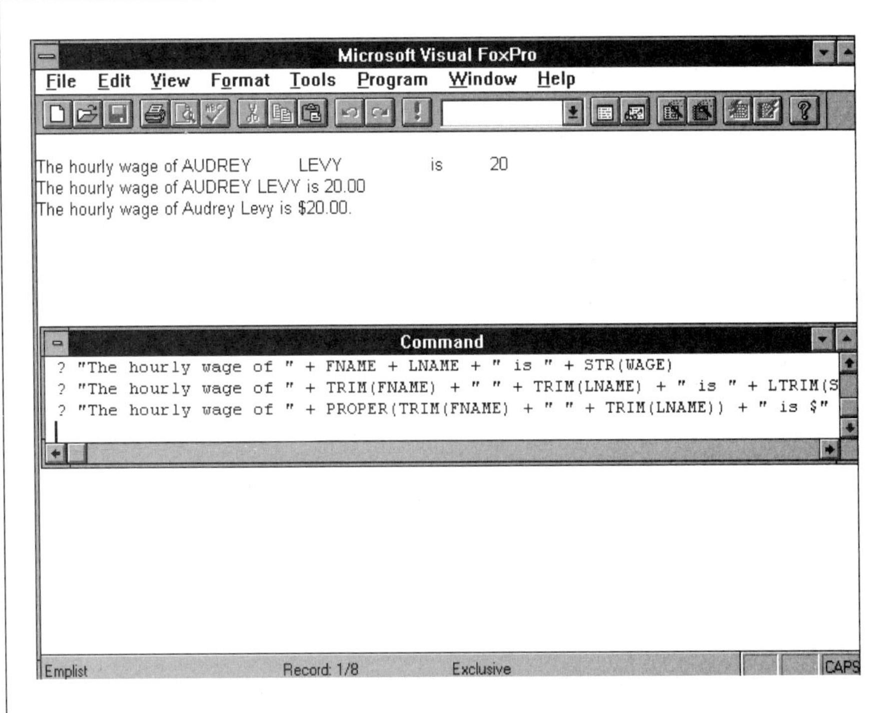

FIGURE 9.11

Getting a string expression right

Working with Logical Expressions

Logical expressions are either true or false.

They are generally used to find an individual record or to isolate records that meet certain criteria. For example, if you wanted to make a query to find the employees who live in California, you would have to use the expression STATE = “CA”.

In Chapter 11, you will examine many different uses of this sort of expression in more detail. For now, just note that it makes Visual FoxPro look at each record to see if the contents of the State field are equal to the letters *CA*. If they are, the expression STATE = “CA” is evaluated as true. If not, the expression is evaluated as false.

TIP

In an actual application, if you think there is any possibility of the state's not being capitalized, you should use the expression UPPER(STATE) = "CA". The examples leave out the UPPER() function to save you the trouble of entering it and because state names are less often miscapitalized than people's names.

► The Result of a Logical Expression

It is important to understand that, when you use a logical expression, Visual FoxPro returns the result True or False. By printing a couple of sample expressions using ?, you can get a firm grasp of how Visual FoxPro evaluates logical expressions:

1. Enter **CLEAR** to clear the screen.
2. Enter **? 1 + 1**. Visual FoxPro prints `2`.
3. Enter **?** to skip another line, and then enter **? 1 + 1 = 2**. Visual FoxPro prints `.T.`, as shown in Figure 9.12.

In the first example, Visual FoxPro evaluates the numeric expression 1 + 1 and comes up with the result 2. The operation it performs to get this result is addition, indicated by the + operator.

In the second example, Visual FoxPro evaluates the logical expression 1 + 1 = 2 and comes up with the result .T., which represents True. The operation it performs to get this result is comparison, indicated by the = operator.

► Logical Functions

Some functions also return .T. or .F. Although they generally are used in programming, logical functions are sometimes handy during ordinary use of Visual FoxPro.

One common example is the function EOF( ), which stands for End-Of-File. As long as the pointer is on one of the records of the file, EOF( ) is false. If you are at the last record, though, and you use the command

FIGURE 9.12

Evaluating a numeric and a logical expression

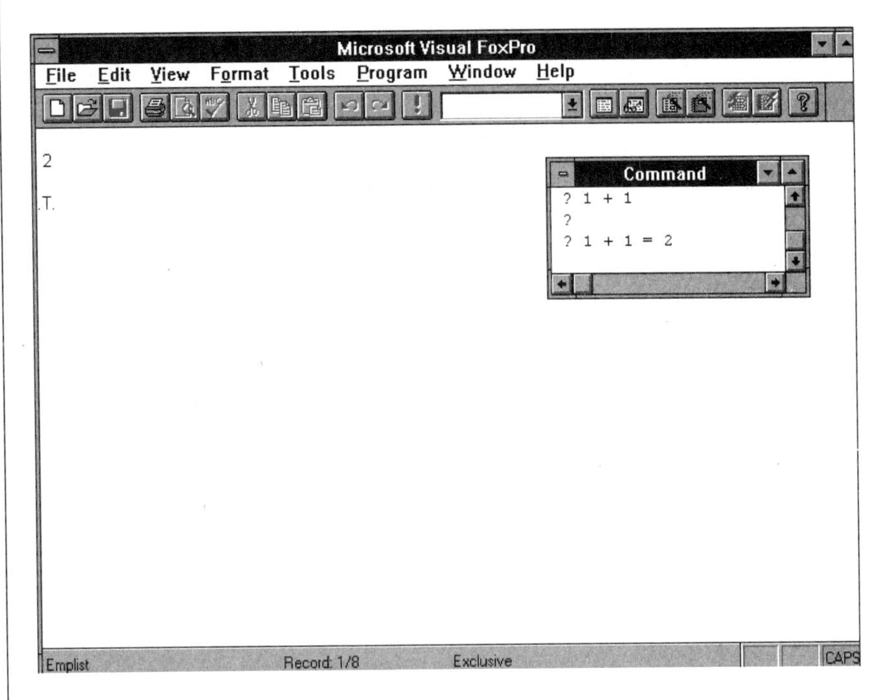

SKIP to move the pointer to the next record, EOF() becomes true, to indicate that you are beyond the point where records exist.

EOF( ) also becomes true if you use commands to locate records and Visual FoxPro does not find what you are looking for. The pointer goes through all of the records looking for the criterion you gave it and passes by the last record without finding it. To indicate this, it makes EOF( ) true. You will use this function in Chapter 25 when you start programming.

Relational Operators

Logical functions and operators are included in the Logical drop-down control of the Expression Builder dialog box, shown in Figure 9.13. Although all the operators on this list are referred to loosely as logical operators, we can think about them more clearly if we divide them into relational and logical operators.

FIGURE 9.13

The Logical drop-down control of the Expression Builder

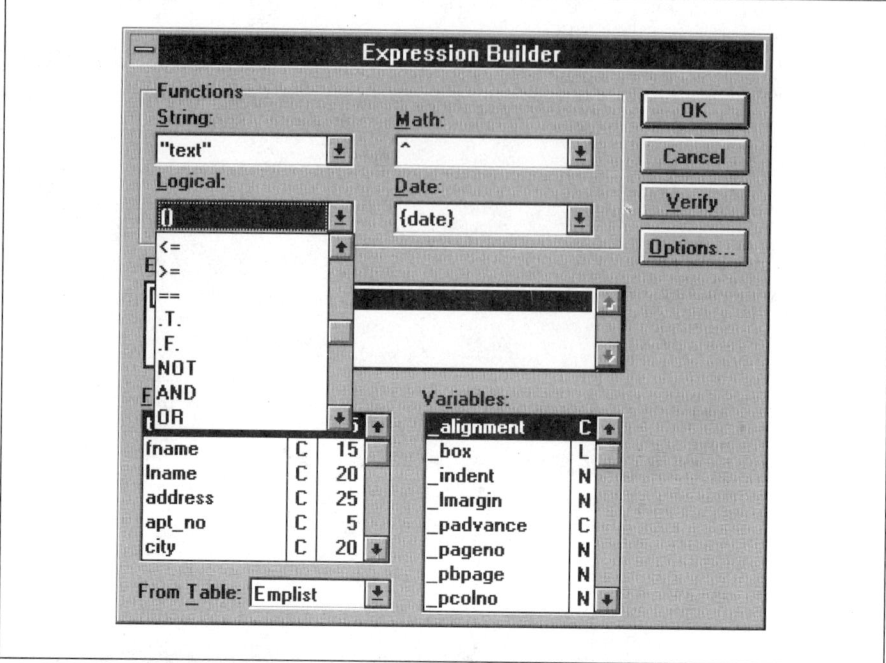

Relational operators are used to make comparisons. You can use them to compare numbers, strings, or dates. The = operator, which you glanced at earlier, is an example.

In combination with commands covered in Chapter 11, you can use expressions such as DATE_HIRED = {10/10/85}, WAGE = 10, or UPPER(LNAME) = "SMITH" to find records in which those fields have those values.

Although you can use relational operators with data of various types, the data being compared must be of the same type.

For example, you could not use UPPER(LNAME) = {10/10/85}. Since there is a character expression to the left of the = and a date expression to the right, Visual FoxPro would display an alert with an error message saying there is a type mismatch, as shown in Figure 9.14.

On the other hand, Visual FoxPro would let you use the expression UPPER(LNAME) = DTOC({10/10/85}) without displaying an error message. Although you obviously will not find someone with this name, the logical expression is valid because it compares two character expressions.

FIGURE 9.14

Alert indicating that there is a data type mismatch

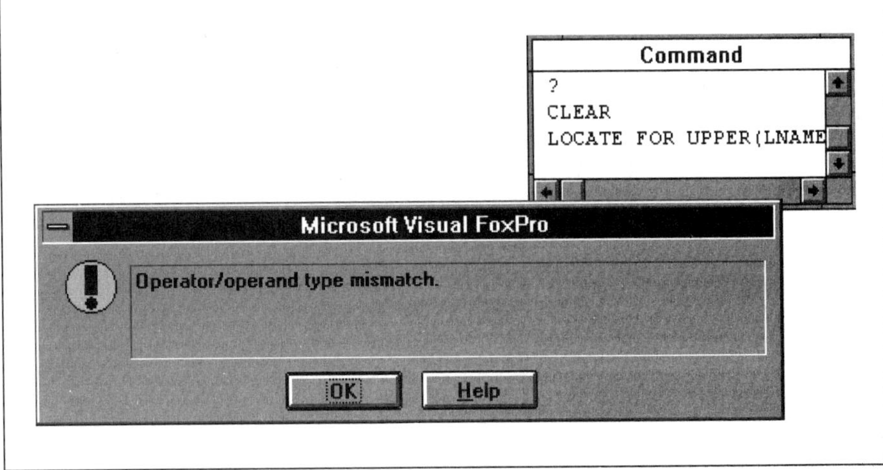

The relational operators are listed in Table 9.1. Most will probably be familiar to you since they are used in mathematics. There are three operators meaning *not equal.* For example, WAGE <> 10, wage # 10, and WAGE! = 10 all mean the same thing: WAGE is not equal to 10. You may use whichever one you find convenient when you are typing from the keyboard. Only one is actually included in the drop-down list.

NOTE

The <> sign, which is commonly used in mathematics, is the only symbol for *Not Equal To* included in the Logical list. The symbol # was common in earlier dBASE-compatible languages, but it is sometimes confusing to beginners, who tend to read an expression like WAGE # 10 as *"wage number 10"* rather than as *"wage not equal to 10."* In Xbase languages, this # sign was meant to represent an equal sign with two vertical lines through it. In addition, ! was added to Visual FoxPro as another way of representing *Not,* which it represents in some computer languages, and it can also be used in combination with = to mean *Not Equal To.*

TABLE 9.1: *Relational Operators*

Operator	Meaning
=	Equal to
>	Greater than
<	Less than
>=	Greater than or equal to
<=	Less than or equal to
<> or # or !=	Not equal to
$	Contained in (used only for character data)
==	Identical to (used only for character data)

Except for $ and ==, you can use all of these operators with character, numeric, or date data. You can use $ and == only for character data.

The $ Operator

The $ symbol is used to search for a substring.

For example, you can use the expression "BROADWAY" $ UPPER(ADDRESS) to find the records of people who live on a street named Broadway. The expression is true if "BROADWAY" is included anywhere in the Address field. You can read this expression as *BROADWAY is contained in upper of ADDRESS.*

This operator applies only to character data; it can be used to search Memo as well as Character fields.

The == Operator

Although the difference may not be obvious, ==, which means *is identical to,* is not the same as =, which means *is equal to.*

For example, if you search for UPPER(LNAME) = "SMITH", Visual FoxPro will find people named SMITHSON and SMITHERS as well as SMITH. This feature of = is generally useful, as you will see. However, when you want only an exact match, you need to use ==.

Since these operators are tricky, you should try them out.

▶▶ NOTE

If you enter the command SET EXACT ON, only strings that are identical will match, even if you use =. To go back to the default method, enter the command SET EXACT OFF. You can also use these commands through the View window, which is discussed in Chapter 22.

1. Enter **CLEAR**. Then enter **? "SMITHSON" = "SMITH"**. Visual FoxPro evaluates the expression as true and prints `.T.`
2. Enter **? "SMITHSON" == "SMITH"**. (You can do this most easily by editing the previous command.) Visual FoxPro evaluates the expression as false and prints `.F.`, as shown in Figure 9.15.

One other point to consider is that in these comparisons, Visual FoxPro uses the second string as the criterion and compares the first string with it. In step 1, for example, it uses "SMITH" as the criterion, and it looks through "SMITHSON" to see that all the letters in "SMITH" are matched. Thus, it would not find that the reverse, "SMITH" = "SMITHSON", is true; when it looks at "SMITH", it would not find that all the letters in "SMITHSON" are matched. Try this out by entering **? "SMITH" = "SMITHSON"**. Visual FoxPro evaluates the expression and prints `.F.`

This example shows why actual queries have the form LNAME = "SMITH" rather than "SMITH" = LNAME. Remember that the Lname field contains SMITH followed by trailing blanks, so only LNAME = "SMITH" is true. Likewise, you can find all the names that begin with the letter *A* by using the criterion UPPER(LNAME) = "A".

▶ Logical Operators

Although the relational operators that were listed in Table 9.1 are loosely referred to as logical operators, this section looks at the logical operators in the stricter sense of the term. These operators, used to create more complex expressions, are shown in Table 9.2.

FIGURE 9.15

Testing the = and == operators

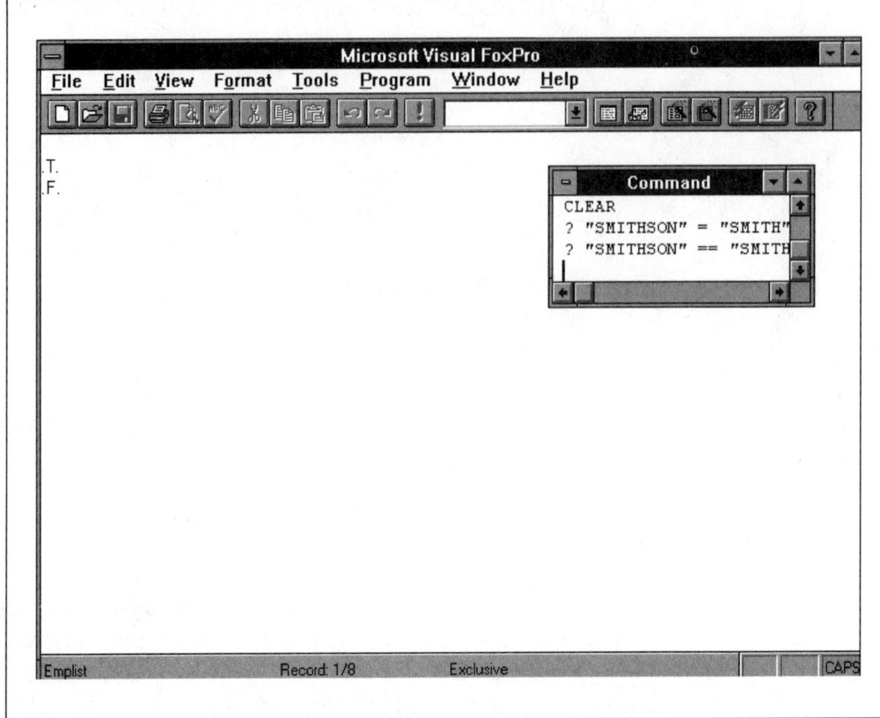

TABLE 9.2: *Logical Operators*

Operator	Meaning
.AND.	Both halves of the expression must be true for the entire expression to be evaluated as true.
.OR.	Either half of the expression must be true for the entire expression to be evaluated as true.
.NOT. or !	The expression that follows must be untrue for the entire expression to be evaluated as true.
( )	Used for grouping.

In earlier Xbase-compatible languages, the AND, OR, and NOT logical operators had to be used with dot delimiters—the period on each side of the word. Visual FoxPro, however, lets you use AND, OR, and NOT with or without delimiters—partly to save you typing but primarily to make the language compatible with SQL (covered in Chapter 15), which was added to version 2 of FoxPro.

This book keeps the dot delimiters since they make it clearer that logical expressions are being used; this is useful when you are learning the language. If you want, you can omit the delimiters to save typing and to become accustomed to both ways of writing logical expressions.

NOTE

This book uses .NOT. for the sake of clarity, but you can use ! instead to save time.

The logical operators are used to build complex expressions. Let's look at a few examples to see how they work.

Using .AND. and .OR.

.AND. and .OR. are both used to build a complex expression out of two or more *logical* expressions. For example, if you wanted to find records of employees who live in California, you would use the expression **STATE = "CA"**. If you wanted to find employees who live in New York, you would use the expression **STATE = "NY"**. And if you wanted to find employees who live in either state, you would combine the two with .OR. to make the complex expression

```
STATE = "CA" .OR. STATE = "NY"
```

As you learned in Chapter 4, the difference between the .AND. and .OR. operators is that .AND. is *ex*clusive (the expression is true only if both halves are true at once, which can exclude a lot of records), and .OR. is *in*clusive (the expression is true if either half is true, so more records are included).

.OR. is thus used for broadening your queries—for example, for finding people from more than one state. .AND. is useful for narrowing your queries by adding more criteria. For example, the expression

```
STATE = "CA" .AND. WAGE < 10
```

would be used to narrow the query so that it finds only some of the employees from California—those with wages less than $10.

Using .NOT.

The use of .NOT. is more obvious. You use it before an expression to reverse the meaning of the expression. For example, **.NOT. STATE = "CA"** could be used to find the records for all the states except California; that is, it would find every record that is left out by the expression **STATE = "CA"**. You simply have to remember to use .NOT. before the entire logical expression it refers to.

▸▸ TIP

If you find these operators confusing, add the words *"it is true that"* when you read the expressions to yourself. Read STATE="CA" .OR. STATE="NY" as *"it is true that the STATE equals CA or it is true that the STATE equals NY,"* and you will not confuse the .AND. with the .OR. operator. Likewise, .NOT. is sometimes clearer if you read it as *"it is not true that."* Thus, it is probably best to read .NOT. STATE="CA" as *"it is not true that the State equals CA."*

Using Parentheses in Complex Expressions

You can combine complex logical expressions with .AND. and .OR. indefinitely, creating more and more complex expressions. When expressions contain more than one of these operators, it is best to group them using parentheses to indicate precedence.

For example, let's say you want to find employees from California and New York who earn less than average wages for the area. We'll assume that the average wage in California is $10 and that the average wage in New York is $11.

To find the records from California, you would use the expression

```
STATE = "CA" .AND. WAGE < 10
```

To find the records from New York, you would use the expression

```
STATE = "NY" .AND. WAGE < 11
```

Thus, to find all the records you want, you would combine these two with .OR. to get

```
(STATE = "CA" .AND. WAGE < 10)
.OR. (STATE = "NY" .AND. WAGE < 11)
```

Order of Precedence

Earlier in this chapter, you saw that if you leave out parentheses, numeric expressions are evaluated in default algebraic order. In fact, all Visual FoxPro expressions are evaluated in the following default order of precedence if you leave out parentheses:

1. Exponentiation
2. Multiplication and division
3. Addition and subtraction
4. Character string concatenation
5. Relational operators
6. .NOT.
7. .AND.
8. .OR.

Some of the reasons for this order of evaluation are obvious. Visual FoxPro has to evaluate numeric expressions before it can compare them. For example, if it is evaluating the expression 1 + 1 = 2, it must use the addition operator + to evaluate 1 + 1 before it can use the relational operator = to see if the entire expression is true.

Likewise, Visual FoxPro must give relational operators precedence over logical operators. For example, if it is evaluating STATE = "CA" .OR. STATE = "NY", it must evaluate STATE = "CA" to see if it is true and must evaluate STATE = "NY" to see if it is true before it can determine if the entire complex expression is true. There is no need to use parentheses to make the order of precedence clearer.

On the other hand, when you get down to the logical operators themselves, things become less obvious. It is possible to leave out the parentheses and rely on the default order of precedence when you are working with expressions that have more than one logical operator. However, doing so creates expressions that are this complex hard to read, which makes errors more likely. Moreover, these errors are often hard to detect since they will only result in your query not finding every record you want and will not produce an error message. For these reasons, it is best always to use parentheses in expressions whenever they may be useful for clarity, even if FoxPro does not need them.

▸ The IIF( ) Function

One function that is invaluable in many situations is IIF(), or "immediate if," which has the form

```
IIF(<log exp.>,<exp1>,<exp2>)
```

This function returns the value of *expression 1* if the logical expression is true or the value of *expression 2* if the expression is false.

Try out this function:

1. Enter **CLEAR** to clear the screen.
2. Enter **LIST FIELDS LNAME, FNAME, IIF(PROBATION, "probation"," ")** to produce the listing shown in Figure 9.16.

Here the IIF function is used to flag employees who are on probation by adding the word "probation" to the right of the name if the Probation field has .T. in it. If the Probation field is .F., it just adds a blank space to the right of the name.

In Chapter 17, you will use this function to add the word *Apt* to mailing labels only if there is a value in the Apt_no field.

FIGURE 9.16

Using the IIF() function

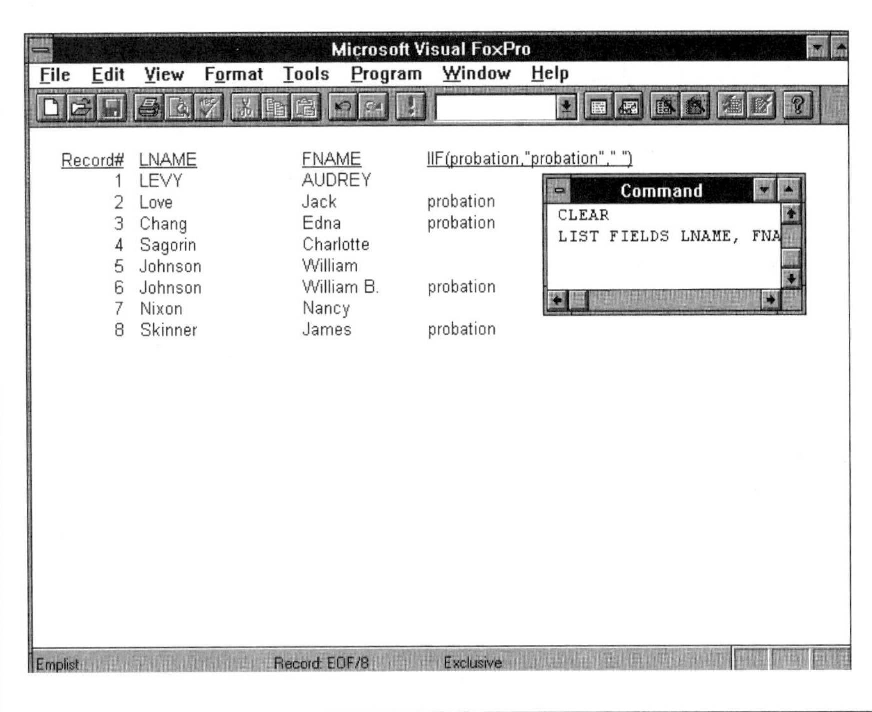

▶▶ To Sum Up

Now you have a thorough understanding of expressions and are ready to apply them. In the next chapter, you will see how to use expressions to create sophisticated indexes, and then, in Chapter 17, you will learn to use expressions to manipulate data in many other ways.

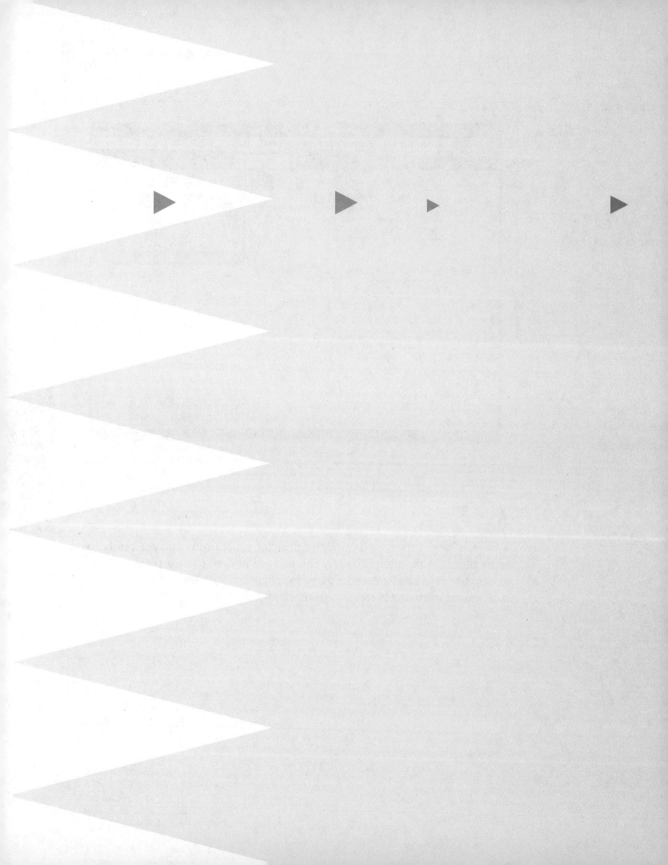

CHAPTER 10

Using Indexes

▶▶ FAST TRACK

▶ ***To create an index tag of the structural compound index file,*** ***258***

display the Table Designer. Enter the tag's name, index type, and the expression that the index is based on.

▶ ***To create an index that does not allow duplicate values to be entered in the field,*** ***260***

select Candidate as the index type.

▶ ***To create an index that displays only one record for each value in the field,*** ***261***

select Unique as the index type.

▶ ***To index on fields of different data types,*** ***262***

index on an expression that uses the functions discussed in Chapter 9 to convert all fields to a single data type. Be sure to use DTOS( ) rather than DTOC( ) to convert Date data to the Character type.

▶ ***To index in mixed ascending and descending order,*** ***263***

index on an expression that subtracts some fields from some large value. For example, to create an index that arranges the records in descending order by wage with people who earn the same wage listed alphabetically, use the expression **STR(1000 - wage) + lname + fname** as the basis of the index.

▶▶ *When* you first created a table in Chapter 2, you saw that the Table Designer includes an Index panel as well as a Table panel. In Part I of this book, you used queries to specify sort order of records. Now that you have learned about expressions, though, you can use *indexes* to determine sort order in much more powerful ways.

▶▶ What Is an Index?

An index of a table is a bit like the index of a book. A book's index lists subjects discussed by the book in alphabetical order and refers you to the pages they are on. Of course, it is much faster to look up something in the index and go directly to the right page than to leaf through the entire book page by page until you find the topic you are interested in.

Similarly, if you are working with a large table, any database program takes a long time to read through the entire file to look up a record. If you had to look up several names in a very long mailing list using FoxPro's Edit ➤ Find As option, for example, there would be annoying delays, because FoxPro would have to read through the entire list to find each name.

If the file were indexed by name, however, the program could find a name very quickly. The index would list just the names in alphabetical order and would contain pointers showing where each name was in the actual table. It is possible to search this sort of ordered list very quickly and retrieve records in large tables without a noticeable delay.

After learning to create indexes and to use them to control the order of records in this chapter, you will learn to do fast indexed searches in Chapter 11.

▶ The Controlling Index

The computer can also use an indexed table in much more powerful ways than a person can use an indexed book. Most important, the computer can list the entire table in the order of any of its indexes. By using the appropriate index, a user can list the records in a table in alphabetical order by name, even though the actual order of the records in the table is different.

Since you can have several different indexes for a single table, you can use the table in more than one order: You can look at the records in alphabetical order to find people's names, and then you can look at the records in ZIP code order to see which people live near each other.

The index that you use at any given time to determine the order in which the records are displayed is called the *controlling index*.

▶ When to Index

Because indexes can speed searches and let you view the records in a different order instantly, beginners are sometimes tempted to index on every field in the table, so that the indexes will be available if they need them.

There is a downside to indexing, however. It takes a bit of extra time to update each index when you are entering or editing data, and a significant amount of time to rebuild each index when you pack the table to remove deleted records permanently. If you have a few indexes, the delay is not noticeable during data entry, but if you have too many indexes, it can begin to slow your data entry and editing significantly.

For this reason, it is best to create indexes only for fields that you have to search through frequently and for fields and expressions that you actually use to order the records.

For example, if you often search for records based on last name and print mailing labels sorted by ZIP code, then you should index on these two fields.

▸ Types of Index Files

Early versions of dBASE and version 1 of FoxPro supported only the *single index file*. Each index was kept in a separate file, with the extension IDX. If you wanted the index to be kept up to date, you had to open each of these index files explicitly whenever you added data to or edited the table.

Opening all these index files not only took extra time, it could also lead to errors—if you forgot to open an index file when you added records to a table, the index would not be updated to include the new records. Later, if you used that index as the controlling index to set the order of the table, these records would disappear.

Version 2 of FoxPro added a second type of index to eliminate this problem. Unlike IDX files, each of which can hold only one index, *compound index* (*CDX*) files can hold multiple indexes in a single file. Each index in a compound index file is called an *index tag*. You can open multiple index tags easily by opening a single file.

Even more important, one compound index file is called the *structural compound index*, and is opened whenever you open the table it applies to. A structural compound index is automatically given the same name as the table, with the extension CDX.

Compound indexes other than the structural compound index are called *independent compound indexes*, and they cannot be given the same name as the table.

For most purposes, it is easiest to use a structural compound index file for all your indexes, so that all the indexes are updated automatically whenever you update the file. You won't have to take the time to open them, and there's no danger of your forgetting to do so.

There are some cases, though, where it makes sense to use an independent compound index file or to use IDX files for your indexes. The one problem with having all of your indexes open at all times is that Visual FoxPro takes some time to update each index when you are entering data. In general, this time is so slight it is not noticeable, but if you have a very large number of indexes open, the time it takes to update them can slow data entry. In addition, Visual FoxPro rebuilds all indexes whenever you pack a table to remove records that are marked for deletion. If you have a very large number of tags in your structural index file, packing could become very slow.

For these reasons, then, if you have a very large number of indexes, it is a good idea to include as tags in the structural compound index file only those indexes you need to keep updated. If you have a group of indexes that you use only once a year to produce reports, keep them in a separate, independent index file. Then you can explicitly use that file and reindex it once a year before producing the reports, without the overhead of maintaining the indexes at all times.

Tags of the structural compound index file are so clearly superior for most purposes that the Index panel of the Table Designer creates them automatically. You must use the Command window to create other types of indexes. This chapter covers indexes created using the Table Designer and touches only briefly on the commands used to create other types of index files.

▶▶ NOTE

As you will see, the View window lets you use indexes from any file type as the controlling index, as long as the index file is open. Remember that if records seem to disappear or appear in incorrect order when you order records on the basis of a certain index, it is probably because the index is not in the structural compound index file, and it has not been updated. See the section "Indexing Commands" later in this chapter for details on how to update it.

▶▶ Creating Indexes

Here you will learn to use the Index panel of the Table Designer to create and modify index tags of the production compound index file. You can also create this type of index file using INDEX ON directly from the Command window, as discussed later in this chapter. As you learned earlier, this file is automatically opened whenever the table is open, so these indexes are always kept up to date.

The Index Panel of the Table Designer

To display the Table Designer using the menu system, open and browse the table and choose View ➤ Table Designer—or simply use the table and enter the command **MODI STRU**. Then click the Index tab to display the panel shown in Figure 10.1.

FIGURE 10.1

The Index panel of the Table Designer

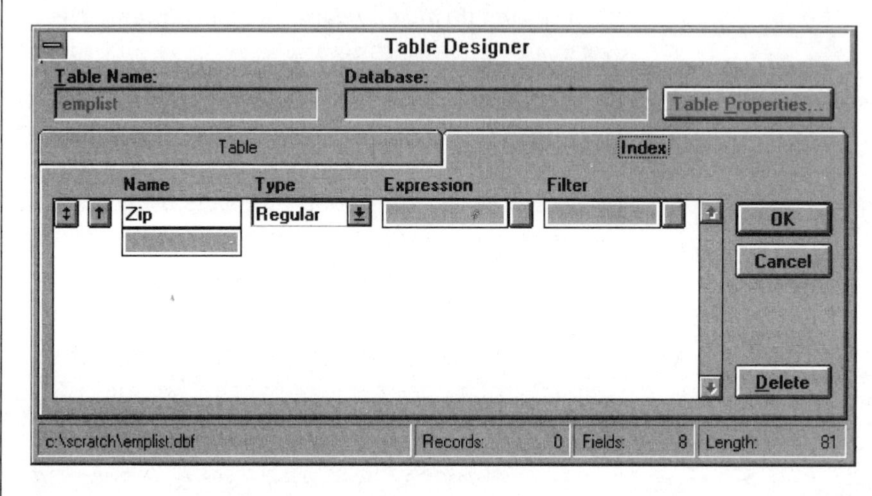

To create a new index tag, enter a name for the tag in the Name column. The name should describe the index, and if the index is based on a single field, it is generally easiest to give it a name that is the same as the field name. In the illustration, the name Zip has been entered, as the name of a tag based on ZIP code.

When you enter a name, controls are displayed in the other columns, and you can use them to define the index.

Ascending and Descending Order

Indexes can arrange the records in either ascending or descending order.

If you index in ascending order on a date field, the record with the earliest date comes first. On a numeric field, the smallest number comes first. On a character field, *A* comes before *Z*.

Descending indexes arrange the records in just the opposite order. This is particularly useful for date fields, where you often want the most recent date to come first.

Ascending order is the default, but you can simply click the button to the left of the Name text box to toggle between ascending and descending order. The button will display either:

- an upward pointing angle, representing ascending order.
- a downward pointing arrow, representing descending order.

NOTE

The button to the far left, with a double-headed arrow on it, is a mover button, like that in the Fields panel, which you can click and drag upward or downward to change the order in which indexes are listed. This change affects only the order of display in this list, not the sorting order.

The order you choose here applies to the entire index expression. You can create an index that is based on some fields in ascending order and others in descending order by using more complex expressions, as discussed later in this chapter.

NOTE

If your index is based on a character field, in either ascending or descending order, by default FoxPro arranges the records based on the ASCII value of their characters rather than arranging them alphabetically. The main difference between the two is that in ASCII order, all the capital letters come before all the lowercase letters. Thus, if records are capitalized incorrectly, they may not be in proper alphabetical order. For example, ABRAHAM would come before Aaron, because the capital B comes before the small a in ASCII order. To be sure of having proper alphabetical order, you must use the Options dialog box or the SET COLLATE command to change collation order, as you will learn later in this chapter.

Index Types

Use the Type drop-down control, shown in Figure 10.2, to select among the three types of indexes that are available for free tables:

FIGURE 10.2

Selecting an index type

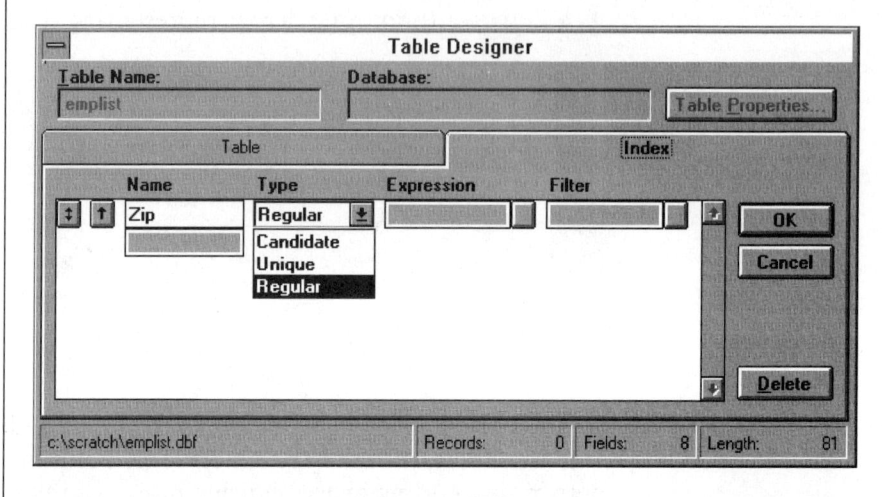

Candidate As you will see in Chapter 16, when a table is part of a FoxPro database, you can create a Primary Key index, meant to be used in a relational database. For reasons that will be clear when you learn a bit of database theory in Chapter 12, a primary key index must have a unique value in each record.

If the table is not part of a FoxPro database, you can create a Candidate index, which can be converted to a Primary Key index if the table is added to a database. (That is, the index is a "candidate" for conversion, even after data has been entered into it.) Like a Primary Key, a Candidate index does not let you enter duplicate values in the field it is based on.

For example, if you create either a Primary or a Candidate index based on an Employee Number field, you will not be able to enter the same employee number in two records.

Both Candidate and Primary Key indexes become important when you are working with relational databases, covered in Part III of this book.

Unique A Unique index displays only the first record in which the expression used as the basis of the index has any value.

For example, if you create a Unique index based on the State field, when you use the table with this index as the controlling index, only one record from each state will be displayed.

Do not confuse the Unique index with the Candidate index. A Candidate index based on the State field, for example, would only let you enter one record in the table from each state, regardless of whether it is used as the controlling index. Thus, you would never want to use State as a Candidate index. A Unique index based on the State field would let you enter as many records as you want from each state; but when you use the table with this index as the controlling index, only one record from each state is displayed. You might want to use this index to list only one record from each state, so you could see at a glance in which states the people in the table lived.

Unique indexes are useful for special purposes, such as listing all the states that your employees live in.

Regular A Regular index does not control what values can be entered or which values are displayed. It simply lets you control the order in which the records are displayed.

This is the type of index you will use most frequently.

Index Expression

You can use the Expression text box to enter the expression that the index is built on, or click the button to its right to display the Expression Builder, which you can use to create the expression. For most indexes, you just need to enter a very simple expression in this text box. In this section you'll see examples both of simple indexes and of more complex expressions that are commonly used for indexes.

An Index Based on a Single Field To create an index based on a single field, simply enter the name of that field in the Expression text box.

For example, if ZIP codes are stored in the Zip field of your table, and you want to create an index to arrange the records in ZIP code order, enter **Zip** as the expression.

An Index Based on Multiple Fields There are times when you must base an index on more than one field. The most common example is an index to order records alphabetically by name. If your index is based on the Lname field alone, then Zazu Smith may come before Aaron Smith when you use it as the controlling index. The index would only order records by last name, and if two people had the same last name, it would leave the records in whatever order they were originally in.

To create most multiple-field indexes that you will actually need in practice, you simply enter an expression made up of the field names with the + sign between them in the Expression text box. For example, to create an index for the sample table based on employee names, enter this expression:

```
LNAME + FNAME
```

It is easier to enter this in the Expression text box than to use the Expression Builder.

Indexing on Mixed Data Types One common reason for using a more complex expression as the basis of an index is to index on mixed data types.

In Chapter 9, you learned that you can only use the + operator to combine fields of the same data type. If fields are of different data types, you must use functions to convert them to the same data type before combining them. Generally, it is easiest to convert them all to the Character data type.

For indexing, always use the function DTOS( ), which converts date data to character data in ASCII format, yyyymmdd.

By way of comparison, note that DTOC( ) would ordinarily return character strings such as 12/31/95 and 01/31/96. Character strings are compared from left to right, so the second of these would come before the first in index order if you used DTOC( ) as part of the index expression. Because 0 comes before 1, Visual FoxPro would never get to comparing the years.

On the other hand, DTOS( ) would return the character strings 19951231 and 19960131, so the first of these would come first: when the dates are in yyyymmdd format, sorting the character strings always puts them in order by date.

Thus, to create an index that lists records by date hired and that lists people who were hired the same date alphabetically, you would use the expression:

```
DTOS(DATE_HIRED) + LNAME + FNAME
```

DTOC( ) is used in most other cases, but not for indexing.

▶▶ **NOTE**

You can use the date field by itself as the basis of a simple index. You must use DTOS() to convert the date to character data only if you are creating a more complex index that combines a date with character data.

See Chapter 9 for more information on functions for converting data type.

Indexing in Mixed Ascending/Descending Order As you know, the button to the left of each index tag in the Table Designer lets you arrange records in either ascending or descending order, based on the entire index expression. But the Table Designer does not give you an obvious way to create an index that has some elements in ascending and some in descending order.

For example, you might want to list employees by wage in descending order, with the highest wage first, but list employees who earn the same wage alphabetically in ascending order. You can do this by combining expressions that index in ascending order with expressions that trick Visual FoxPro into indexing selected fields in descending order.

To reverse the order, simply subtract the value in a date or number field from some large date or number. For example, if you want to list your employees from those with the highest wage to those with the lowest wage, you can enter **1000 – WAGE** as part of the index expression. Of course, the higher the WAGE, the smaller the value of 1000 – WAGE.

To create an index that arranges the records in descending order by wage with people who earn the same wage listed alphabetically, then, you can use the following expression as the basis of this index:

```
STR(1000 - wage) + lname + fname
```

using STR() to convert the numeric expression to character type so it can be combined with the date.

If you wanted to, you could do the same thing with a date field. An index based on the expression {12/31/99} – DATE_HIRED would list the most recently hired employees first. The later the date hired is, the smaller the time between it and the end of the century. To list employees hired on the same date alphabetically, use the expression

```
STR({12/31/99} - DATE_HIRED) + LNAME + FNAME
```

Of course, these indexes would not be needed in a file as small as your sample table, where there are not many people with the same wage or the same date hired, but they could be very useful in larger tables.

Filter

You can create a filtered index that includes only records that match certain criteria. For example, you can create an index that displays only the records of employees from New York state when it's used as the controlling index.

To do this, you must enter a logical expression in the Filter text box of the Table Designer's Index panel, or click the button to its right and use the Expression Builder to create this expression.

This feature of indexes is covered in Chapter 11, which discusses the use of expressions to filter data.

► Collating Sequence

As mentioned earlier, when you create an index of any type that is based on character fields, by default, the index organizes records in ASCII rather than alphabetical order. ASCII order can conflict with alphabetical order in two ways:

- In ASCII order, all uppercase letters come before all lowercase letters. Thus, ASCII order may not be the same as alphabetical order if your data is capitalized inconsistently. For example, the name **SMITH** will come before the name **Sanders** in ASCII order, because the uppercase M comes before the lowercase A.
- In ASCII order, all letters with accent marks come after all letters without accent marks. Thus, foreign words that include accented letters will not be in proper alphabetical order.

If you are working only with English-language data and you capitalize all your data properly, ASCII order will usually be the same as alphabetical order, though there may be problems if your table has unusually capitalized names, such as DeLeon or LaForce. You can avoid these problems by changing collation order from the default ASCII order to the *General* collation order, which alphabetizes correctly in English and most European languages.

▶▶ **NOTE**

You must change collating sequence *before* creating the index. This option determines the collating sequence that any future index will be based on. Changing collation order does not affect indexes created earlier.

To change collating sequence, choose Tools ➤ Options to display the Options dialog box, click the Data tab, and select General from the Collating Sequence drop-down list, shown in Figure 10.3.

FIGURE 10.3 ▶

Using the Collating Sequence drop-down list

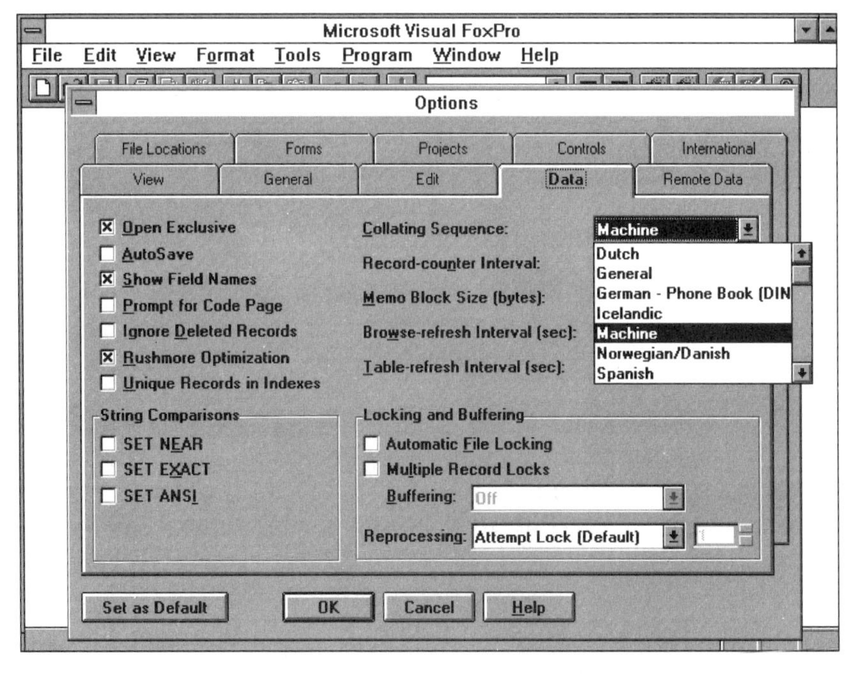

TIP

After you make this selection, General will be the collating order until you exit from Visual FoxPro. Click the Set as Default button of the Options dialog box after selecting General to make it (and any other options you chose in this dialog box) the default setting whenever you use Visual FoxPro in the future.

By default, Machine is selected in this drop-down list, and indexes are sorted in ASCII order. As you can see, it also has options to alphabetize properly in Dutch, Icelandic, Norwegian/Danish, classical Spanish, and other languages. However, the General option will create indexes in proper alphabetical order in English, French, German, modern Spanish, Portuguese, and most other western European languages.

Rather than using this dialog box, you can enter the command **SET COLLATE TO "GENERAL"** in the Command window. To return to the default ASCII collation order, enter the command **SET COLLATE TO "MACHINE"**. The SET COLLATE TO command also has options to create indexes for the other languages included in the Collating Sequence list. The Options dialog box and other SET commands are covered in detail in Chapter 19.

▸ Modifying or Deleting a Tag

You modify an index tag in the same way as you create one. Display the Index panel of the Table Designer and change the definition of the tag.

To delete a tag, select it in the Index panel of the Table Designer and click the Delete button, or enter the command:

```
DELETE TAG <tag name> [OF <CDX file name>]
```

The optional clause [OF <CDX file name] must be used only if identical tag names exist in a number of compound index files. For virtually all index tags, you would simply enter a command such as **DELETE TAG names** (assuming you've named the tag *names*).

▸▸ Indexes Created by the Wizards

When you make a selection in the Sort Order step of the Form, Report, or Label Wizard, it creates an index tag for the table it is based on to display the table's records in that order. The Wizard names this tag in one of two ways:

- If the index is based on a single field, the tag has the same name as the field.
- If the index is based on multiple fields, the tag has a name such as WIZARD_1 or WIZARD_2.

These tags are part of the table's structural compound index file, to make sure they are always updated, so they are displayed in the Index panel of the Table Designer. For example, Figure 10.4 shows the index tags created in the exercises in Part I of this book.

FIGURE 10.4 ▸

Index tags created by the Wizards

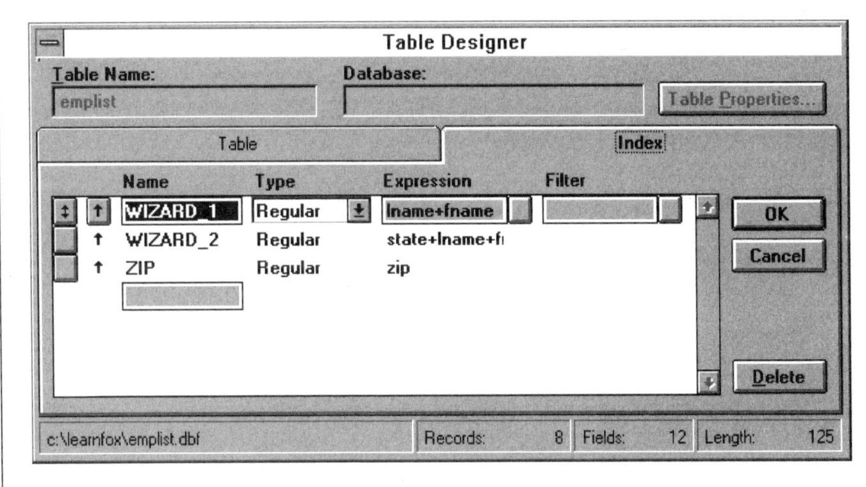

When you created mailing labels, you sorted them in ZIP code order, and the Label Wizard created the index ZIP. When you created a report, you sorted them in alphabetical order by name, and the Report Wizard created the index WIZARD_1 based on Lname+Fname. Finally, when you created a grouped report, you based the grouping on the state and sorted within each state by name; the Group/Total Report Wizard created the index WIZARD_2, based on State+Lname+Fname, since the records have to be sorted primarily by grouping, with the name used as a tie-breaker within each group.

These tags are automatically used by the reports and labels that the Wizard generated, but you can also use them yourself to set index order, in the same way that you use other indexes.

►► **WARNING**

You should not change the name or expression of any index created by a Wizard, or the Wizard will not run properly.

►► Setting Index Order

You can make an index the controlling index that determines the order in which the records are displayed, either by using the View window or by using indexing commands.

► Using the View Window to Set Index Order

To change the order in which the records are displayed, open the table and either choose Window ➤ View or click the View Window tool to display the View window, shown in Figure 10.5.

If you're working with a free table it should be selected in the Aliases list. However, if you are working with a relational database and you have multiple tables open, you may have to select it from this list. If multiple tables are open, each is opened in a different *work area*, as you will learn in Chapter 14.

With the table selected, click the Properties button to display the Work Area Properties dialog box. Use its Index Order drop-down list, shown in Figure 10.6, to select the index.

FIGURE 10.5

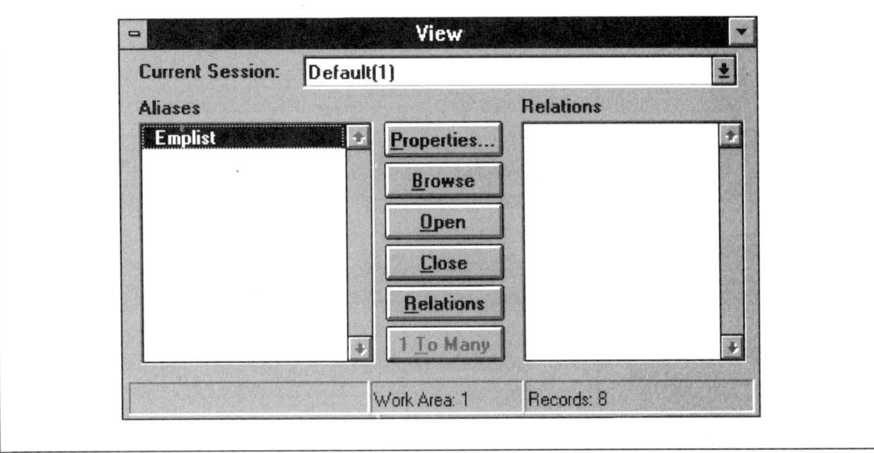

The View window

FIGURE 10.6

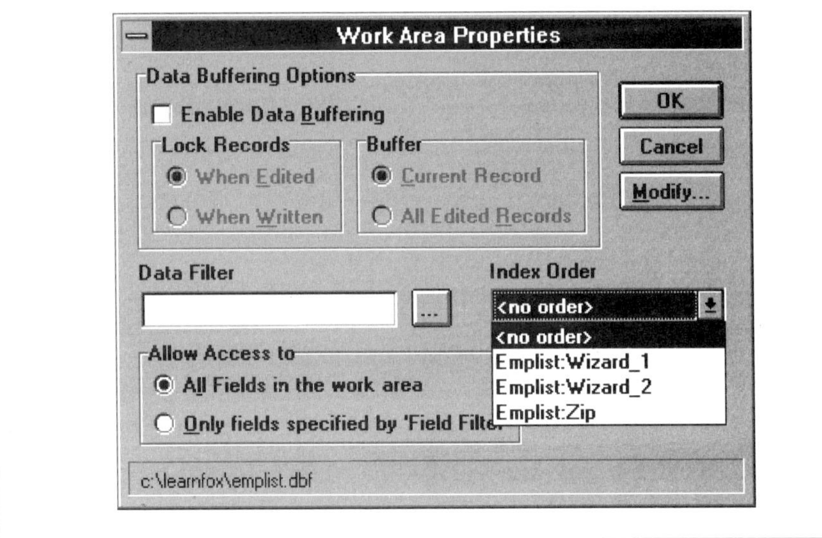

The Work Area Properties dialog box

This list includes all indexes for the table. If the index is part of a compound index file, you'll see the name of the index file, followed by a colon, followed by the name of the index tag. Because the structural compound index file has the same name as the table, tags in it are listed with names such as **Emplist:Zip**.

The index you select will be used as the controlling index until you do any of the following:

- select some other index as the controlling index
- select <no order> from this list, to display the records in the order in which they were originally entered (called their *natural order*), without any controlling index
- close the table or exit from Visual FoxPro

► Using the Command Window to Set Index Order

Specifying the controlling index is another case where it is often easiest to work from the Command window.

To open a table with a tag as controlling index, simply enter the command:

```
USE <table name> ORDER TAG <tag name> [OF <CDX file
name>]
```

As when you delete a tag, you need to include the optional clause **[OF <CDX file name>]** only if identical tag names exist in a number of compound index files. For virtually all index tags, you would simply use a command such as **USE emplist ORDER TAG names**.

To make a tag the controlling index after a table is open, use the command:

```
SET ORDER TO [TAG] <tag name>
```

Again, you can add the optional clause **[OF <CDX file name>]** if identical tag names exist in a number of compound index files. For virtually all index tags, you would simply use a command such as **SET ORDER TO names**.

To return to natural order, enter **SET ORDER TO** without any tag name.

Commands for using single-index files are similar and are discussed in the following section, "Indexing Commands."

►► Indexing Commands

This section includes a brief summary of indexing commands, including commands for single-file indexes as well as for tags of compound index files. This is only meant as a summary, and you can get complete information on these commands from Appendix B.

► Creating Indexes

The basic command for creating indexes is:

```
INDEX ON <expr> TO <idx file name> ¦ TAG <tag name>
[OF <cdx file>] [COMPACT] [ADDITIVE]
```

(This entire command must be entered on one line in the Command window.)

Before you can use this command, the table must be open. The command creates different types of index files as follows:

- If the expression is followed by TO <idx file name>, Visual FoxPro creates an IDX file with the name that is specified. If it is followed by TAG <tag name>, Visual FoxPro creates a tag of the structural CDX index file with the name that is specified.
- If the TAG clause is followed by the optional clause OF <cdx file>, Visual FoxPro will add the tag to the CDX file whose name is specified if that file already exists, or create this CDX file to hold the tag if it does not already exist. If this optional clause is left out, Visual FoxPro uses the structural CDX file to hold the tag. Of course, its name does not have to be specified since it is the same as the name of the table.

The optional keyword COMPACT creates the index in compact format. FoxPro 2.0 added a major improvement in indexing: *compact indexes,* which take up much less disk space than the IDX indexes used by version 1. These smaller indexes not only save you disk space, they also improve performance because Visual FoxPro spends less time reading the index from disk. For the sake of compatibility, IDX index files can still be created in the older format as well as in the new compact format. The compact format is preferable, and this optional clause should always be used to create new single-index files. CDX files all

use compact format, and so this option is not needed with the tag of the CDX file, which is automatically compact.

The optional keyword ADDITIVE creates a new index file or tag without closing indexes that are already open. If you create an index without this option, all index files that are open except the structural compound index are automatically closed. Thus, they are not updated if the table is changed. When you use the dialog box, Visual FoxPro generates the ADDITIVE option so that other index files remain open and updatable.

In addition, this command can have the optional keyword ASCENDING or DESCENDING to specify the sorting order for the index. You can leave this off if you want the index to be sorted in ascending order, since ascending is the default order.

The command can also have an optional FOR <expr> clause and the optional UNIQUE keyword. These do the same thing as the Index Filter pushbutton and the Unique option of the Type drop-down list.

► Setting Index Order

You have already looked at the commands for using an index tag as the controlling index:

- To open a table with a tag as controlling index, enter the command

  ```
  USE <table name> ORDER TAG <tag name> [OF <CDX file name>]
  ```

- To make a tag the controlling index after a table is open, use this command:

  ```
  SET ORDER TO [TAG] <tag name> [OF <CDX file name>]
  ```

In both cases, [OF <CDX file name>] is necessary only if tags in different files have the same name.

There are similar commands for working with single-index files:

- To open indexes when you open a table, enter the command

  ```
  USE <table name> INDEX <index file list>
  ```

  All of the index files in the list will be opened and updated, and the first file in the list will be used as the controlling index, setting the order of records.

- To make an index file the controlling index after a table is open, use this command:

```
SET ORDER TO <idx file name>
```

▶ Reindexing

If records seem to disappear when you use, as a table's controlling index, an IDX file or a tag of an index file that is not the structural compound index file, that index was probably not opened during data entry, and so changes made in the table were not reflected in the index.

To update the index, open the table and the index file and enter the command:

```
REINDEX
```

or display the table in a Browse window, and choose Table ➤ Rebuild Indexes. Either of these methods rebuilds all open indexes, which can take a considerable amount of time.

▶▶ Sample Index Tags

Now you create a sample index and then use it and some of the indexes created by the Wizards to control the order of the records in our sample Emplist table. Even though it duplicates the order created by one of the Wizards, you will find it convenient to create an index to alphabetize by name and to call it **Names**, so it is easy to use in the future.

1. If necessary, open the Emplist table.
2. Choose Tools ➤ Options. Click the Data tab of the Options dialog box. Select General from the Collating Sequence drop-down control, and select OK.
3. Enter **MODI STRU** to display the Table Designer. Click the Index tab. In the Name column for the next tag, enter **NAMES**. Leave Regular as the Type.
4. Click the button in the Expression column to display the Expression Builder. Double-click **lname** in the Fields list. Select **+** from

the String drop-down list. Double-click **fname** in the Fields list to generate the expression shown in Figure 10.7. Select OK to return to the Table Designer, with the new index defined, as shown in Figure 10.8. Click OK to close the Table Designer, and click Yes to make the changes permanent.

FIGURE 10.7 ►

Creating the index expression

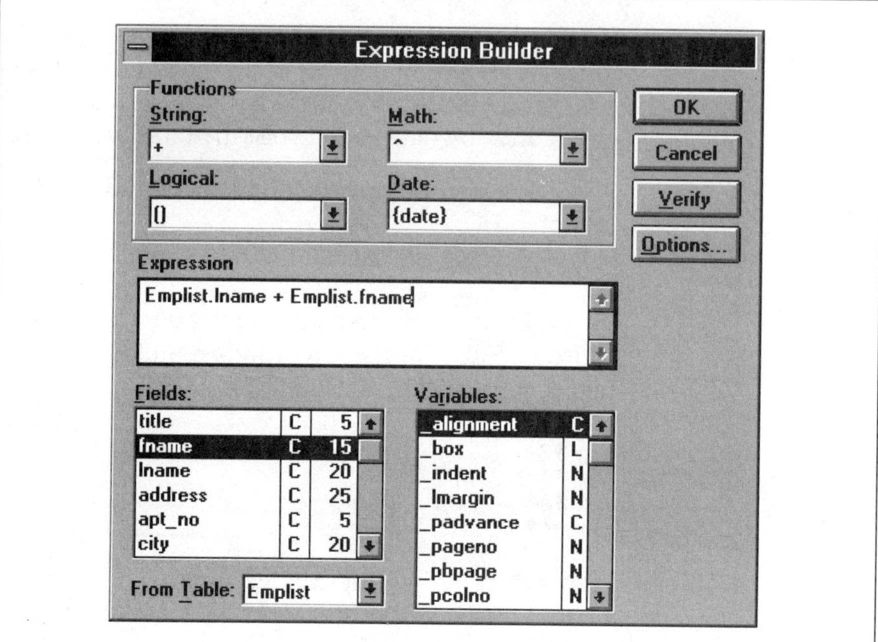

FIGURE 10.8 ►

The new index

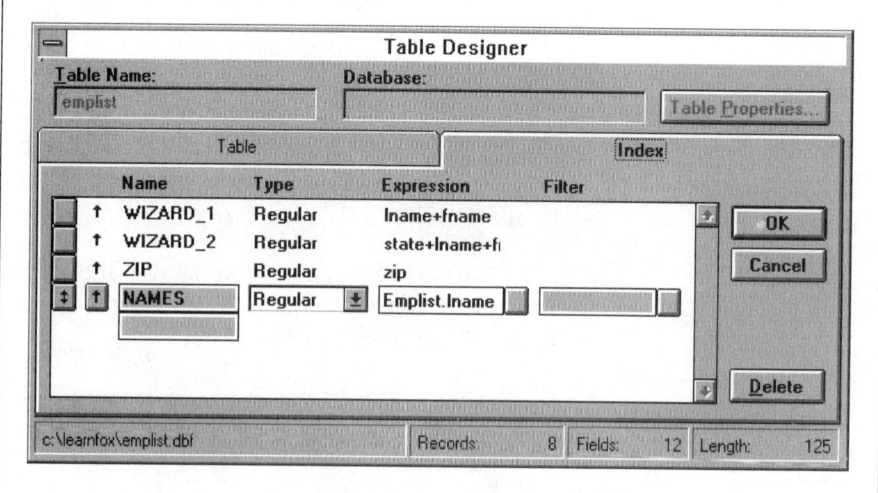

5. Now, to use the indexes, click the View Window button of the main toolbar. Click the Properties button of the View window. Choose Emplist:Zip from the Index Order list of the Work Area Properties dialog box, as shown in Figure 10.9. Select OK to return to the View window and then close the View window.

FIGURE 10.9

Setting index order

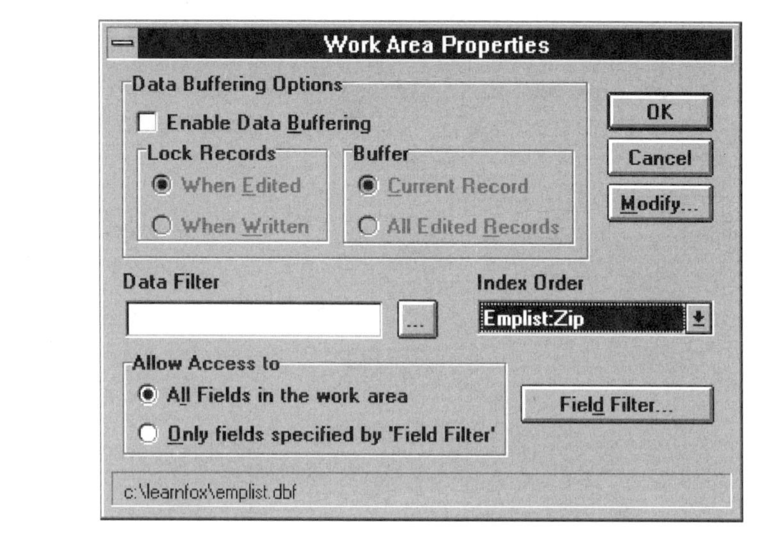

6. Choose View ➤ Browse Emplist. Scroll all the way through the Browse window, so you can see that the records are in ZIP code order.

7. Click the Command window to bring it forward. Enter **SET ORDER TO NAMES**. Click the Browse window to bring it forward: when you do this, Visual FoxPro rewrites the Browse window, and you can see that it is now in alphabetical order by name.

8. Again, click the Command window to bring it forward. Enter **SET ORDER TO**. Click the Browse window to bring it forward; you'll see that the records are now in the order in which they were entered.

▸▸ To Sum Up

Now that you have learned about expressions in Chapter 9 and about indexes in this chapter, you are well on your way to using the FoxPro language to control how your data is displayed. In the next chapter, you will learn how to filter data, to control which records and which fields of a table are displayed. At that point you will understand enough of the language to have complete control over how your data is displayed, and you will be able to display or print out data in just the way you want it by using three or four commands.

CHAPTER 11

Filtering Data

FAST TRACK

To specify which records a command applies to, on the basis of record order, 283

add an optional scope clause to a command. ALL makes the command apply to all records. NEXT <number> makes it apply to the specified number of records, beginning with the record the pointer is on; for example, NEXT 1 makes the command apply to only the current record.

To specify which records a command applies to, on the basis of record content, 289

add an optional FOR <logical expression> or WHILE <logical expression> clause to a command, to make the command apply only to the records for which the logical expression is true.

To prepare to use a WHILE clause, 290

use the table in index order so that all the records for which the WHILE clause is true are together. Move the pointer to the first record where the WHILE clause is true. Then use the command with the WHILE clause.

To speed up a command that includes a FOR clause, 292

in the FOR clause, use an *optimizable expression*—a logical expression based on an indexed field.

To do an unindexed search for a single record, 294

enter the command **LOCATE FOR <logical expression>**.

To do an indexed search for a single record, 296

use the index that the search is based on as the controlling index, and then enter the command **SEEK <expr>**.

To limit which fields are included in the output of a command, 307

add an optional FIELDS clause to the command.

To limit which records are included in the output of a series of commands, 311

enter a logical expression in the Data Filter text box of the Table Properties dialog box or enter the command **SET FILTER TO <logical expression>**. Only records for which the logical expression is true will be used by all following commands.

To limit which fields are included in the output of a series of commands, 312

click the Field Filter button of the Table Properties dialog box and use the Field Picker to select the fields, or enter the command **SET FIELDS TO <field list>**. Only fields that are specified will be used by all following commands.

It is often useful to work with only specific fields and records of your table. For example, you might want to list names and phone numbers of people from a certain state. In Chapter 4, you learned to use queries to isolate fields and records in this way. In this chapter, you will learn more powerful ways to build this sort of filter into FoxPro commands.

This chapter focuses on four optional clauses that you can add to many commands to specify which data in the table those commands apply to.

- The **scope** clause specifies that the command applies only to certain records, based on their location in the table. For example, a command may apply to only the current record or to all the records in the table.
- The **FIELDS** clause specifies that the command applies only to certain fields in the table.
- The **FOR** and **WHILE** clauses specify that the command applies only to records that meet some criterion that you specify by using a logical expression. For example, the command may apply only to records from the state of California. The difference between these two clauses is that you must explicitly use an index and move the pointer to the appropriate location before using a WHILE clause.

In addition to these clauses that you add to individual commands, Visual FoxPro gives you similar methods of restricting the data that all future commands apply to.

The SET FIELDS command lets you use the table as you normally would but includes only the fields that you specify. It is equivalent to adding a FIELDS clause to each subsequent command.

The SET FILTER command lets you use the entire table, just as you normally would, but filters out the records that do not meet the logical criterion that you specify. It is equivalent to adding a FOR clause to each subsequent command.

You can use the View window to specify a filter or fields that all future commands apply to, which is equivalent to using the SET FILTER and SET FIELDS commands.

Because they can be used with many commands, these options add a great deal of power to your work.

►► The Scope Clause

First, you should look at the scope clause, both because it is simple and because it often must be used in combination with FOR and WHILE clauses, as you will see in later sections.

The *scope* of a command merely refers to the number of records that Visual FoxPro searches in the course of performing a command. Many commands can be used with scope clauses.

Descriptions of these commands in Appendix B include the word [*scope*] to indicate where a scope clause goes, with the square brackets indicating that it is optional. The word *scope*, though, is not actually used in the clause. Instead, scope clauses may consist of any of the following words:

- **ALL:** The command acts on all of the records of the table (unless some other clause, such as a FOR or a WHILE clause, restricts it).
- **NEXT <number>:** The command acts on the number of records specified, counting the *current* record (where the pointer is) as the NEXT 1.
- **RECORD <number>:** The command acts on the record whose number is specified. This option is not often useful, as you do not usually know the numbers of particular records in your table.

▶▶ NOTE

Record numbers always refer to the order in which the records appear in the actual table, not to the order in which they seem to appear because an index is being used. Record 1 is the first record you entered in the table, not the first record in alphabetical order or any other index order.

- **REST:** The command acts on the records beginning with the current record and continuing until the last record in the file.

▶ The Default Scope

Commands used to manipulate data have a default scope—the scope that is usually most convenient to use them with. For example, DELETE has a default scope of NEXT 1, since you usually want to delete just the current record. If you use DELETE without specifying a scope, it just deletes the record where the pointer is. But you can also use commands such as DELETE ALL or DELETE NEXT 10 to override the default scope.

In Chapter 8, you learned two commands that both let you view data, the main difference being that one—DISPLAY—lets you view one record and the other—LIST—lets you view the entire table. Now you can see that the main difference between these commands is their default scope. DISPLAY ALL is virtually identical to LIST, and LIST NEXT 1 is virtually identical to DISPLAY (although there are a couple of other, very minor, differences apart from their scope).

▶▶ TIP

One minor difference between the two is that DISPLAY ALL displays records one screen at a time, pausing and asking you to press any key to see the next screen. This difference makes DISPLAY ALL the easiest way of scrolling through data to view it on the screen if you are working from the Command window. LIST is best if you are adding an optional TO PRINT clause.

▶ Using a Scope Clause

The options Table ➤ Delete Records and Table ➤ Recall Records display dialog boxes that include Scope, For, and While pushbuttons, as shown in Figures 11.1 and 11.2. These menu options are equivalent to the commands DELETE and RECALL, discussed in Chapter 8.

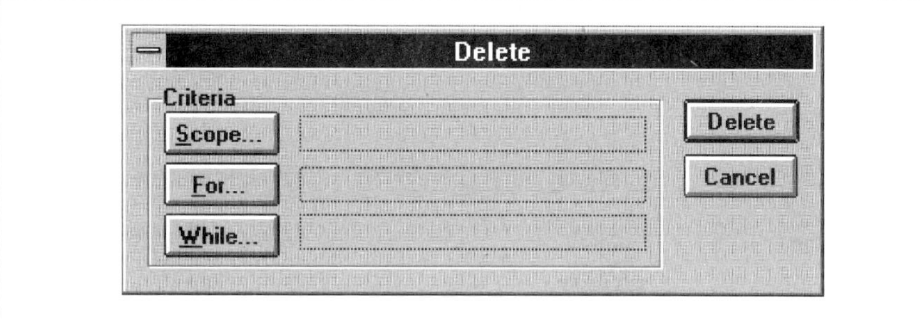

FIGURE 11.1
The Delete dialog box

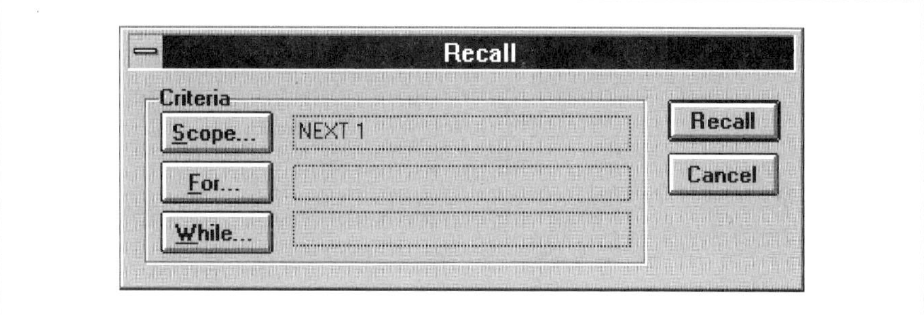

FIGURE 11.2
The Recall dialog box

Selecting the default Delete or Recall pushbutton from these dialog boxes simply marks or unmarks the current record for deletion, just as selecting Table ➤ Toggle Deletion Mark does. The Scope, For, and While check boxes let you mark more than one record at a time.

As an example of how to use the Scope options, try deleting all of your records. Don't worry—remember that this command just *marks* records for deletion, and you can use Recall with a Scope check box to get them all back.

1. If necessary, choose File ➤ Open and use the Open dialog box to open the Emplist table. Then choose View ➤ Browse to display it in a Browse window.

2. Choose Table ➤ Delete Records. When the Delete dialog box appears, select the Scope pushbutton. When the Scope dialog box appears, select the All radio button. Then select OK to return to the Delete dialog box, and select the Delete pushbutton. Notice that the command DELETE ALL has been generated in the Command window, and that darkened rectangles appear to the left of all the records to indicate that they are marked for deletion, as shown in Figure 11.3.

FIGURE 11.3

Using the DELETE ALL command

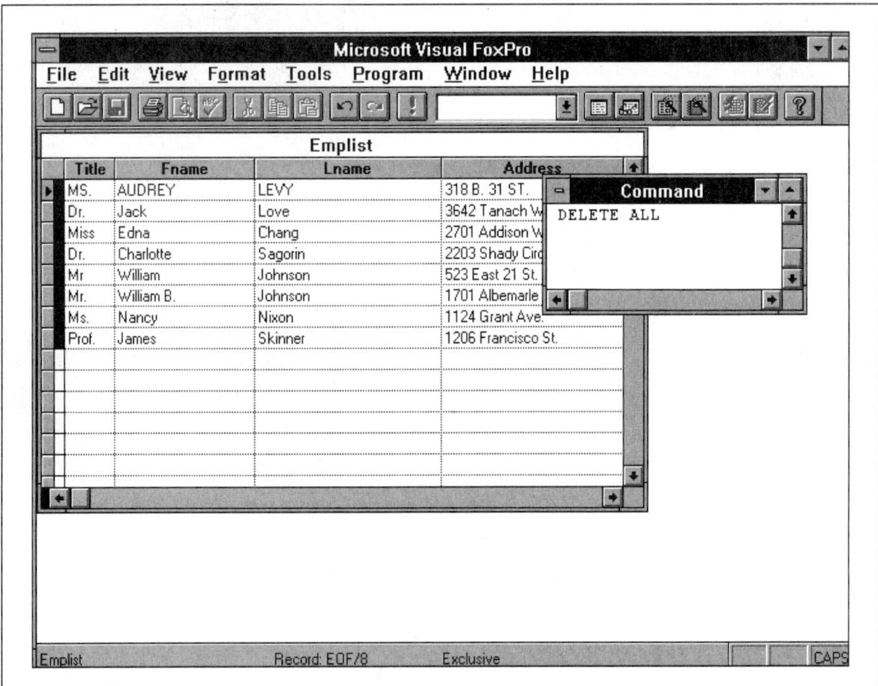

3. Enter **RECALL ALL** in the Command window. The darkened rectangles at the left edge of the Browse window disappear to indicate that the records are no longer marked for deletion. Close the Browse window.

When you first used the Scope check box with either Delete or Recall, the Next radio button was chosen and the default scope 1 was written to its right. Because this is the default scope of the command, just the current record is deleted or recalled if you do not use the Scope check box.

If you experiment a bit more with these menu options, you will see that, with their default scope, they generate the commands

```
DELETE NEXT 1
```

and

```
RECALL NEXT 1
```

However, the NEXT 1 at the end of each of these commands is not necessary. As it often does, Visual FoxPro generates commands with more detail than you actually need. You do not need to specify the default scope for a command if you are working from the Command window. Thus, to mark or unmark the current record from the Command window, simply enter DELETE or RECALL.

▸▸ Using Logical Expressions to Find Records

Now that you have looked at the scope clause, you can look at commands that let you use logical expressions to isolate records that meet some criteria. For example, you might want to add a logical expression to a command to find the record of a person with a certain name or to find all the records with addresses in the state of California. Notice that you want two different types of results from these two examples; for the first you want one record and for the second a whole list of records.

There are two basic uses of logical expressions to find records in Visual FoxPro:

- You can find a single record that meets the criterion. Then, if you want, you can repeat the search to see if there is a second record that meets the criterion. This method is useful for tasks such as looking up someone by name, and repeating the query is useful if you get someone else with the same name the first time you try. Perform this type of search by using the LOCATE or SEEK command.
- You can find all the records that meet the criterion by combining logical expressions with commands that work with the entire table. For example, you can use logical expressions with the LIST command so that records that meet the criterion are included in

the listing. The logical expression can be part of either a FOR or a WHILE clause that is added to the command.

As you can see, there are two commands to let you do either of these things. That is because, in both cases, you have the option of using or not using an index explicitly.

Though this chapter focuses on the FOR and WHILE clause, which are used to work with multiple records, we will also look at LOCATE and SEEK, both because they use indexes in the same ways and because (as you will see) you must use a LOCATE or SEEK command before you can use a WHILE clause.

▸ To Index or Not to Index?

One basic choice you must make before using logical expressions to isolate records is whether to use an index.

There are many cases in which using an index is essential. For example, if you are looking up employees by name in a large table, the delays would be intolerable if you did not use an index and the program had to read through every record in sequence to find each name you wanted.

There are also cases in which an index is not useful. If all of your employees lived in two states, for example, it would be foolish to use an index to search for state names. The program would have to read through about half the file just to read all the records with the state you wanted, and so using an index would not save much time. In this case, maintaining an index is more trouble than it is worth.

Likewise, there is no need to use an index to produce a report if you plan to go do something else while the report is being printed. If a report is printed overnight, for example, time is not a concern, and there is no reason to go to the trouble of maintaining an index.

Implicit versus Explicit Use of an Index

In version 1 of FoxPro, as in other dBASE-compatible programs, you had to use the index explicitly in order to do an indexed search. As you will see, this is a tedious process.

One of the most impressive innovations in versions 2 and later of FoxPro is *Rushmore* technology, which automatically makes use of existing indexes to optimize queries, and which is blindingly fast—up to a thousand times faster than other dBASE-compatible programs. Rushmore substitutes for older forms of indexed query, and it is so much easier to use that it makes them virtually obsolete.

You will learn more about Rushmore later in this chapter, but first you should compare the two older types of queries, for several reasons:

- The older type of indexed query is still included in Visual FoxPro dialog boxes, and so you must learn about it to fully understand the Visual FoxPro interface.
- It also is invariably used in older programs because it was so much faster than an unindexed query, and so you need to learn about it if you ever want to maintain existing programs.
- Finally, although they are rare, there are some occasions in which you can invent ways to do explicitly indexed queries even though Rushmore will not kick in automatically.

FOR and WHILE Clauses

As you know, you can add either a FOR or a WHILE clause to a command to restrict it using a logical expression. The difference between the two is in how indexes are used:

- **FOR clauses:** If you precede the logical expression with the word FOR, you do not need to use the index explicitly. If there is no index to optimize the search, Visual FoxPro does an *unindexed* search. It reads through the entire table in sequence, starting with the first record, to find records in which that expression is true. If there is an index that can be used to optimize the search, Rushmore technology automatically uses it.
- **WHILE clauses:** If you precede the logical expression with the word WHILE, Visual FoxPro assumes you are doing an *indexed* search. You should use this sort of clause to search the field that is currently being used as the basis of the controlling index (or a field that the table is sorted on). Visual FoxPro assumes that the

pointer is already on the first record you want and that all of the records you want follow immediately after that record. It is called a WHILE clause because the search continues only while the criterion remains true.

If you are working in the Command window, there are many different commands you could use with, for example, the clauses FOR STATE = "CA" or WHILE STATE = "CA" in order to build a query into the command. For example, you could use LIST with either of these clauses if you want a listing of only records from California.

Likewise, if you are working from the menu system, you will find that a couple of dialog boxes have For and While buttons, and thus generate commands that include FOR and WHILE clauses. The Delete and Recall dialog boxes, which you looked at earlier, are examples of this.

Preparing to Use WHILE

Using a FOR clause with a command is very simple. You just add the FOR clause to the command; if FoxPro reads through the entire table in sequence to find matching records, there is no opportunity for problems to arise—except for the big problem of the extra time it adds.

Using a WHILE clause is a bit more difficult. You will find it easier to understand by looking at an example.

Let's say you have a very large table and you want to use just the records of the employees whose names begin with the letters *L* through *O*. You could do this by using a command that includes the clause WHILE UPPER(LNAME) >= "L" .AND. UPPER(LNAME) <= "O".

Before you can use this command, though, you must be using the EMPLIST table with the NAMES index active as the controlling index so the names are listed in alphabetical order. Then you must put the pointer on the first record that begins with *L*. Only then can you use a command containing this WHILE clause.

When you use a WHILE clause, Visual FoxPro begins by looking at the current record (where the pointer is) to see if it meets the criterion. If it does, then Visual FoxPro looks at the next record and sees if it meets the criterion. It continues to look at records in this manner until it finds a record that does not meet the criterion (or until it reaches the end of the file), at which point it stops the search.

Think about the pitfalls this process involves; they sometimes come up, and it will be helpful if you can recognize the disease when you see the symptom:

- If you used a WHILE clause on a file that was not indexed, it would not find all the records that matched. They would be scattered through the file, and Visual FoxPro would certainly find a record that did not match before it found every record that did match.
- If you used a WHILE clause without moving the pointer to the first record that matched, it would look at the current record, and if it didn't meet the criterion, it would stop searching without having found *any* records.
- If you had an indexed file and the pointer was on a record that matched but was not the *first* record that matched, the query would find only the records that came *after* that location of the pointer, not those that came before.

None of these problems can occur when you use a FOR clause.

Rushmore Technology

Although WHILE clauses require extra work and can create extra problems, it used to be common to use them because the extra speed you gained by doing an indexed search made all the trouble worthwhile. If you were working with even a moderately large table, commands with FOR clauses would seem to take forever.

The Rushmore optimization technology added in version 2 of Visual FoxPro changes this entirely. If an index exists that can be used to speed the search, Rushmore automatically uses it when you use a FOR clause. You do not have to do the extra work that a WHILE clause requires.

If you want to do fast searches based on the contents of a certain field, it is easiest to create an index tag based on that field as part of the structural compound index file. As you know, Visual FoxPro will automatically maintain the index for you when you modify the table. And whenever you do a query based on this field, Visual FoxPro will automatically use Rushmore technology to optimize the search.

Optimizable Expressions For Rushmore to work, there must be a *basic optimizable expression* as either part or all of the expression the query is based on.

A basic optimizable expression takes one of these two forms:

```
<index expression> <relational operator> <constant>
```

or

```
<constant> <relational operator> <index expression>
```

For example, if you have a NAMES index tag based on the expression UPPER(LNAME + FNAME), either UPPER(LNAME + FNAME) = "SMITH" or "SMITH" = UPPER(LNAME + FNAME) is a basic optimizable expression.

Notice, though, that the index expression must exactly match the expression on which the index is based; if your table has an UPPER-(LNAME + FNAME) index, it does not make UPPER(LNAME) = "SMITH" an optimizable expression. You have to do the extra work of typing FOR UPPER(LNAME + FNAME) = "SMITH" to save all the preparation you would have to do before using the clause WHILE UPPER(LNAME) = "SMITH".

The relational operators for basic optimizable expressions are

=, <, >, <=, >=, <>, #, !=

Basic optimizable expressions cannot include $ or ==.

If only part of the query expression is optimizable, Rushmore optimizes the query to the extent possible. For example, suppose you have an index tag based on Date_hired but none based on State. If you used a command with the clause FOR DATE_HIRED > {01/01/90} .AND. STATE = "CA", Visual FoxPro could only partially optimize the search.

Disabling Rushmore There are rare occasions when you should disable Rushmore: If a command with an optimizable FOR clause modifies the index key the FOR clause is based on, the group of records Rushmore selects becomes outdated as the command is executed, so you could get an inaccurate result using Rushmore. You can disable

Rushmore by adding the clause NOOPTIMIZE at the end of a command that can use it or by entering the command SET OPTIMIZE OFF, which disables it until you enter SET OPTIMIZE ON.

You can also use the Rushmore Optimization check box of the Data panel of the Options dialog box, shown in Figure 11.4, to disable and enable Rushmore. Selecting and deselecting this checkbox is equivalent to entering SET OPTIMIZE ON and OFF. To use this checkbox, choose Tools ➤ Data to display the Options dialog box and then click its Data tab.

FIGURE 11.4

The Data panel of the Options dialog box

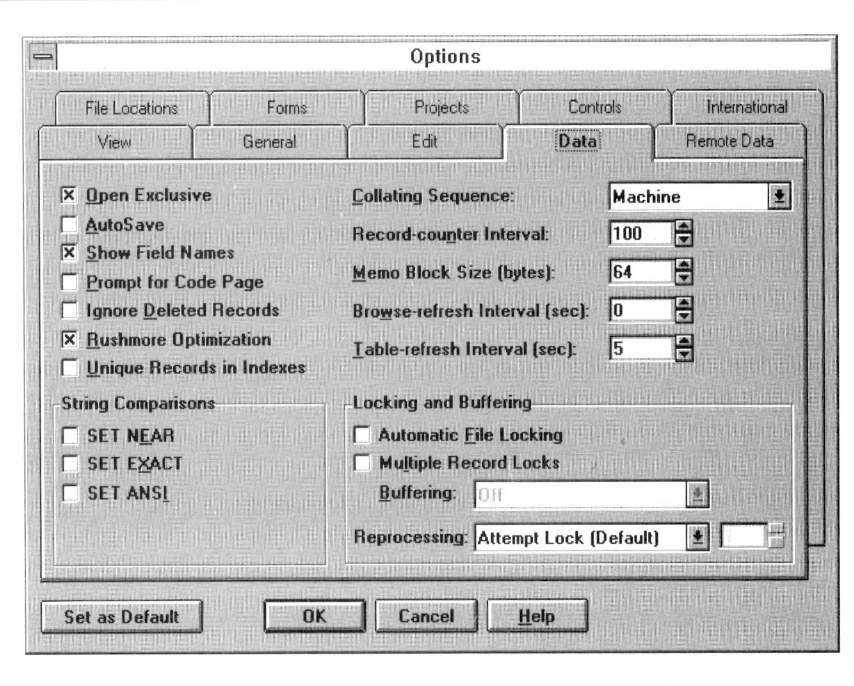

NOTE

Rushmore is automatically disabled if a WHILE clause is included in a command, even if the command also contains a FOR clause that could use Rushmore.

The circumstances where Rushmore could be used but is not, however, are very rare. A FOR clause optimized by Rushmore can be used in virtually every case in which a WHILE clause was used in the past. If the index exists that lets you use the WHILE clause, you can almost always use a FOR clause with an optimizable expression instead—although you might have to use a slightly different expression, as you saw in the examples using the NAMES index.

One of the most important exceptions involves sorted tables, which can use WHILE clauses even though there is no index that can be used to optimize a FOR search.

► Finding a Single Record

Now that you have looked at the issues involved in using indexes, you can learn to use the commands to do a search for a single record. One of these commands explicitly uses an index and the other does not.

An Unindexed Search for a Single Record

The most common way of querying for a single record is to use the command LOCATE FOR <logical expr>.

For example, to find the record for somebody named Johnson, you would enter the command LOCATE FOR UPPER(LNAME) = "JOHNSON". It is useful to include the UPPER( ) function, to find the name regardless of how it is capitalized in the table.

If there is no index based on UPPER(LNAME), the LOCATE FOR command begins with the first record in the table and reads through it sequentially until it finds a match, regardless of where the pointer is when you begin. If it does not find any record that matches, Visual FoxPro displays the message `End of Locate Scope`.

In addition, the pointer will be set at the end-of-file position, so the function EOF( ) is true, and Visual FoxPro also sets the function FOUND( ) to false. It is useful to test the values of these functions in programming.

The CONTINUE Command If LOCATE FOR finds a matching record but you also want to see the next record that meets the criterion, enter the command CONTINUE.

Sampling the Locate Command Try these two commands, which are used frequently in the everyday work of looking up records:

1. Select File ➤ Open. When the Open dialog box appears, select EMPLIST.DBF. In order to see the pointer being moved by the commands, open the Browse window by selecting Table ➤ Browse.

2. Click the Command Window tool to bring the Command window forward. In the Command window, enter **GO TOP** to be sure that you are starting the search at the beginning of the table. Then enter **LOCATE FOR UPPER(LNAME) = "JOHNSON"**. Click the Browse window to rewrite it, and you can see that the pointer moves to the first record with the last name of Johnson, as shown in Figure 11.5.

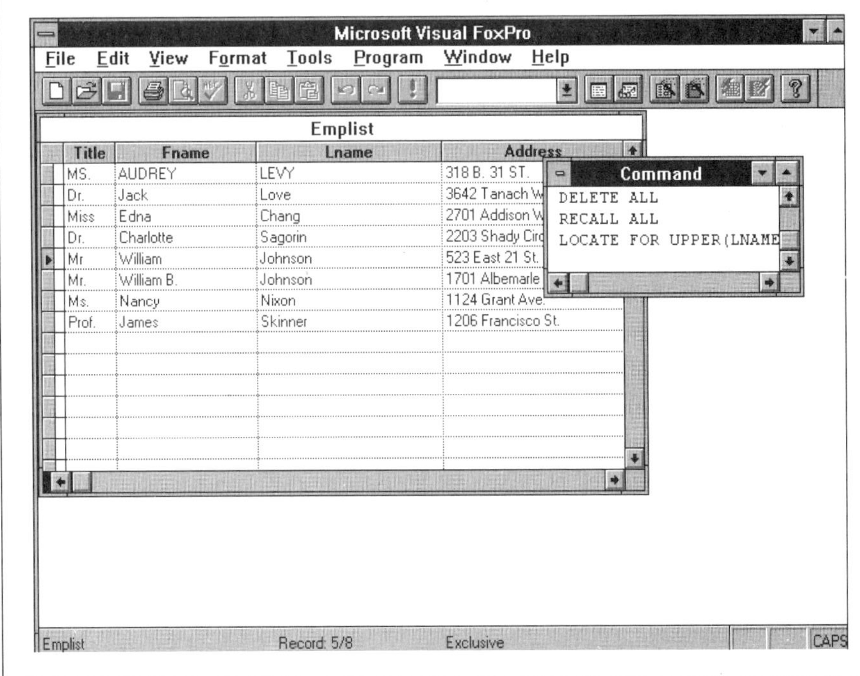

FIGURE 11.5

Using LOCATE to find a record

3. Click the Command window to bring it forward, as shown in the illustration. Enter **CONTINUE**. Click the Browse window. The pointer moves to the next record with the last name of Johnson.

If you had wanted to be more explicit, you could have entered the full form of the command:

```
LOCATE ALL FOR UPPER(lname) = "JOHNSON"
```

The word ALL is the scope of the command, but it does not have to be included because it is the default scope.

Of course, this exercise in using LOCATE and CONTINUE does not seem very useful when you are working with a file this small, where you can see the two Johnsons as soon as you open the Browse window. These commands are essential, however, when you are working with a larger file that has people named Johnson scattered all through it. CONTINUE lets you jump through the file to all the matching records.

►► TIP

You can also use LOCATE and CONTINUE, without opening the Browse window, to move the pointer without the data being visible to the user. This is often essential in programming, when you want the user to be able to search for a given record to view or edit it but don't want to give the user access to the actual table.

Indexed Searches for a Single Record

SEEK is a shortcut method for finding the first record in an indexed table that matches the criterion. It is generally used before you use a command with a WHILE clause based on the same criterion.

Before you use SEEK, the table must be indexed on the field your query is based on, and that index must be active as the controlling index. Since this must be an indexed search, Visual FoxPro can always find the first matching record very quickly, even in a very large table. Because it uses the index to find the record, SEEK searches the entire table; that is, it does not just begin where the pointer is.

If SEEK does not find a match, the pointer is put at the end of the file, EOF( ) becomes true, and FOUND( ) becomes false.

TIP

Normally, the pointer moves to the end of a file if the search is unsuccessful. But if you use the command SET NEAR ON before using SEEK, the pointer is placed at the record that comes nearest to matching; then you can browse nearby records. This is very useful if, for example, you misspelled a name. SET commands are covered in Chapter 19.

Since SEEK works only on the indexed field, it lets you enter the criterion in an easy way. Rather than entering the entire logical expression, as you do in the command:

```
LOCATE FOR LNAME = "Johnson"
```

you use the Names index as the controlling index and simply enter:

```
SEEK "Johnson"
```

Visual FoxPro assumes that you want to find the value "Johnson" in the field or fields currently used as the controlling index.

Remember that there is a match as long as the beginning of the string you are searching matches, so this criterion will be true as long as the last name is Johnson, even though the index is based on both last and first name.

Try this command:

1. Enter **SET ORDER TO NAMES** to make it the controlling index. Click the Browse window to confirm that records are listed alphabetically by name.
2. Enter **SEEK "Love"** in the Command window. Click the Browse window to rewrite it. Visual FoxPro has moved the pointer to the proper record, as shown in Figure 11.6.

After you have done a SEEK in this way, the index is still open as the controlling index, and the pointer is on the first record with the value you want. As you will see in the following section, this leaves you ready to use a command with a WHILE clause.

FIGURE 11.6

Using SEEK

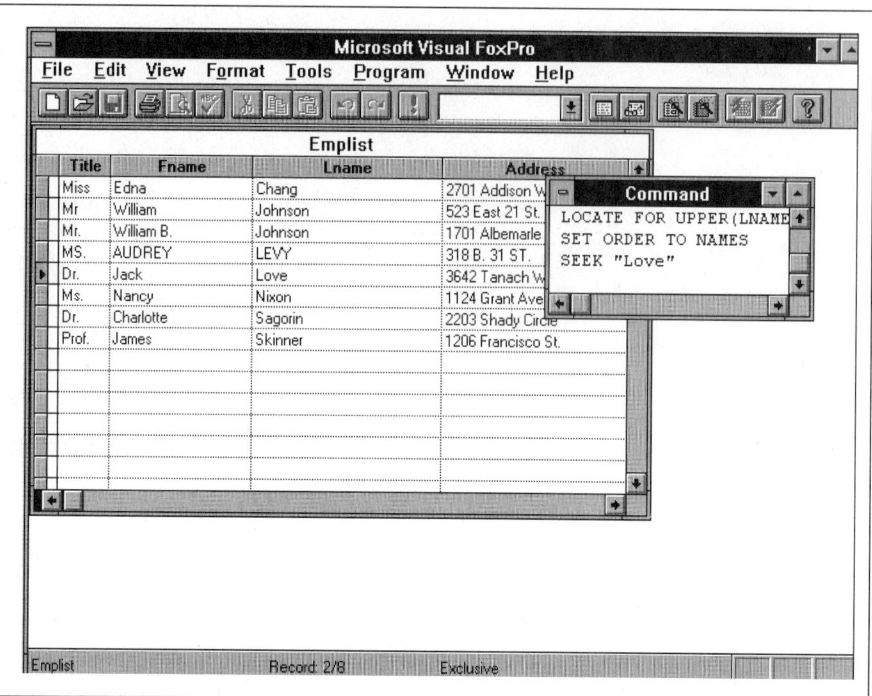

►► NOTE

There is no need to use a command like CONTINUE with SEEK. If you want to find the next single record that meets the criterion after you have used a SEEK, all you need to do is look at the next record in the Browse window! Since this is a search on the key field of the index, the next record that matches the criterion (if there is one) is simply the next record in the file.

► Isolating Multiple Records

When you want to work with all the records in a table that match some criterion, many database management programs require you to create a query as a new object, separate from the table.

One of the advantages of using the Visual FoxPro Command Window interface is that, instead of going through this unwieldy process, you can add a FOR or a WHILE clause to many commands and, in essence, build the query into the command.

Using a FOR Clause to Find Multiple Records

As you know, no preparation is needed before using a FOR clause; just add **FOR <logical exp>** to the command.

As an exercise, you can use the menu option that lets you add a FOR clause: Choose Table ➤ Delete Records, click the For button, and use a For clause to mark all the records from California for deletion.

This exercise emphasizes one extra point: that the FOR clause filters the ordinary output of the command. Because the default scope of DELETE is NEXT 1, it ordinarily applies only to the current record. Thus, if you just add the FOR clause, Visual FoxPro will only look at the current record to see whether the For condition applies.

To make the command apply to all the records, you must use the ALL scope as well as the FOR clause.

Try it both ways so you can see clearly that, in this case, you must use a scope clause with the FOR clause.

1. If necessary, choose File ➤ Open and use the Open dialog box to open the Emplist table. Then choose View ➤ Browse to display it in a Browse window. To see the result more clearly, scroll right through the Browse window until you can see the State field, and then click and drag the heading of the State column left to make it the first column.

2. Choose Table ➤ Delete Records to display the Delete dialog box. Click the For pushbutton to display the Expression Builder. In the Expression box, enter **STATE = "CA"** (or use the Fields list to select State, the Logical control to select =, and the String control to select "Text", which places the delimiters in which you type the letters **CA**).

3. Click OK to return to the Delete dialog box, with this condition entered in its For text box, as shown in Figure 11.7. However, this

dialog box still uses the default scope of NEXT 1. Click Delete to run the command; and notice that no records are marked for deletion, because Visual FoxPro checked only the current record to see if it matched the For condition.

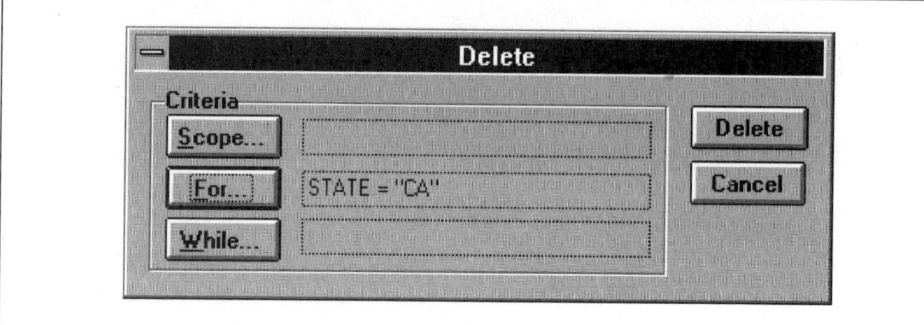

FIGURE 11.7

Entering the For Condition

4. Choose Table ➤ Delete Records to display the Delete dialog box again. Click the For button and use the Expression Builder to enter the Condition **STATE = "CA"**, as you did in step 2. After returning to the Delete dialog box, click the Scope button. Select the All radio button in the Scope dialog box, and click OK to return to the Delete dialog box.

5. The Delete dialog box now has both the For condition and the Scope you want, as shown in Figure 11.8. Click the Delete button, and all the records in the table from California have black boxes to their left to indicate that they are marked for deletion. Click the Command window to see the command that was generated, as shown in Figure 11.9.

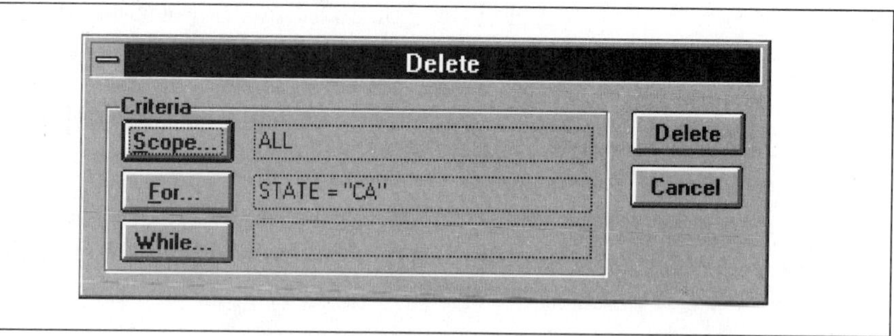

FIGURE 11.8

Entering both the For condition and the scope

FIGURE 11.9

All records from California are marked for deletion.

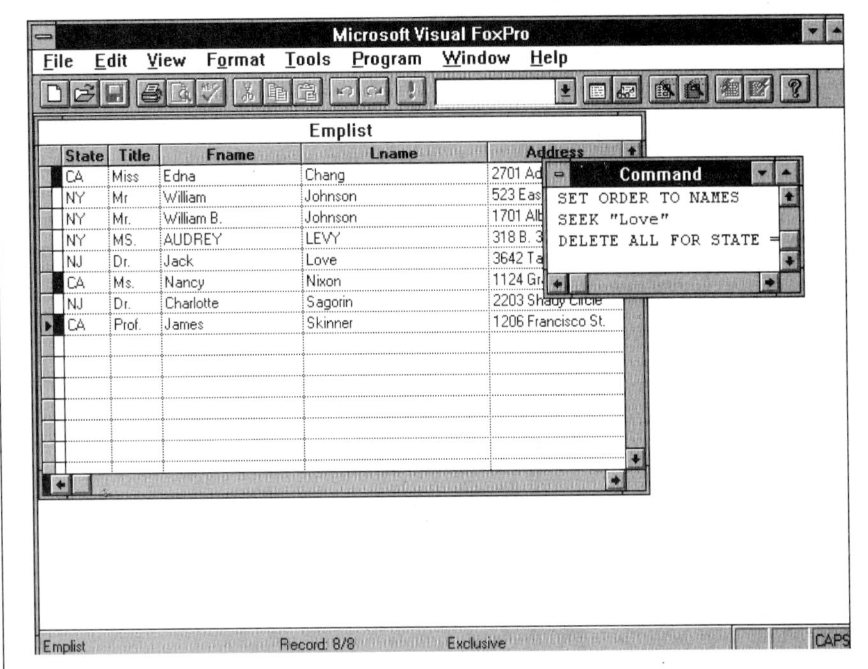

6. Now, to undo the damage you just did, enter the command **RECALL ALL**.

In later sections of this chapter, you will look at some uses of the FOR clause from the command line—for example, added to a LIST command.

Using a WHILE Clause

To use a WHILE clause to filter records, you must perform the preliminaries first: Use the file with an index and place the pointer on the first matching field.

Even though this table is not indexed on the State field, you can use a WHILE clause to delete all the records from California if you remember that California residents have ZIP codes beginning with a 9. You will use the ZIP index created in Chapter 10 and use the criterion Zip = "9" to mark all the California records for deletion. Notice how convenient it is that Zip is a character field and matches the criterion even if there are other characters after the 9. After making the ZIP index tag the controlling index, you can use the command SEEK "9" to find the first record from California. Then you can use the clause WHILE STATE = "CA" to find all of the records from California.

1. The Emplist table should still be open and displayed in a Browse window. If it is not, open and browse it.

2. To use the proper index, enter **SET ORDER TO ZIP**. Click the Browse window, and notice that records are now in ZIP code order.

3. Click the Command window to bring it forward. Enter the command **SEEK "9"**. (Remember to include the quotation marks, because Zip is a character field.) Click the Browse window, and notice that the pointer has moved to the first California record, as shown in Figure 11.10.

FIGURE 11.10

Moving the pointer to prepare to use WHILE

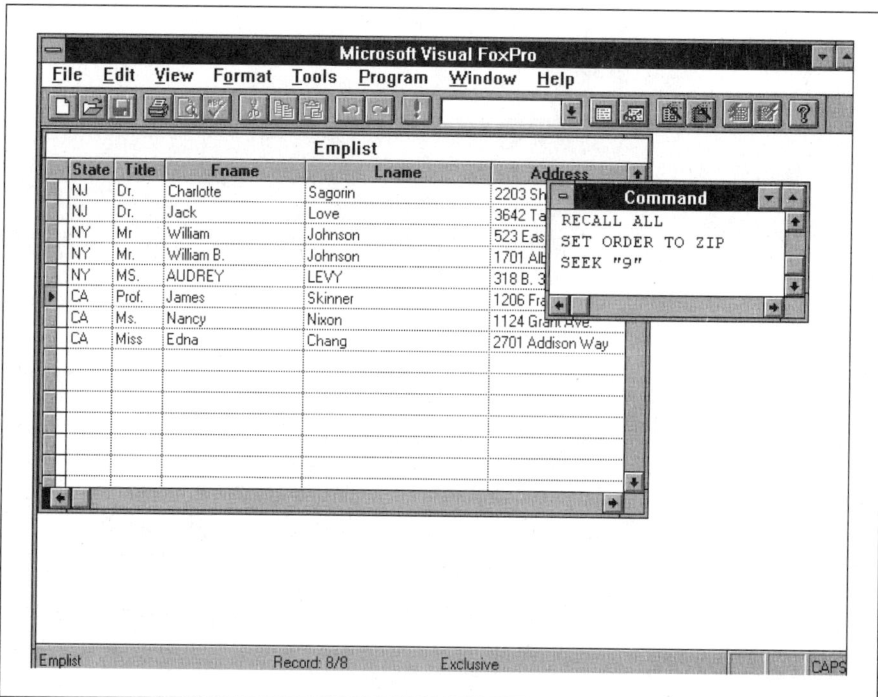

4. Now, enter the command **DELETE ALL WHILE STATE = "CA"**. All the records from California are marked for deletion, as shown in Figure 11.11.

FIGURE 11.11

Using the WHILE clause

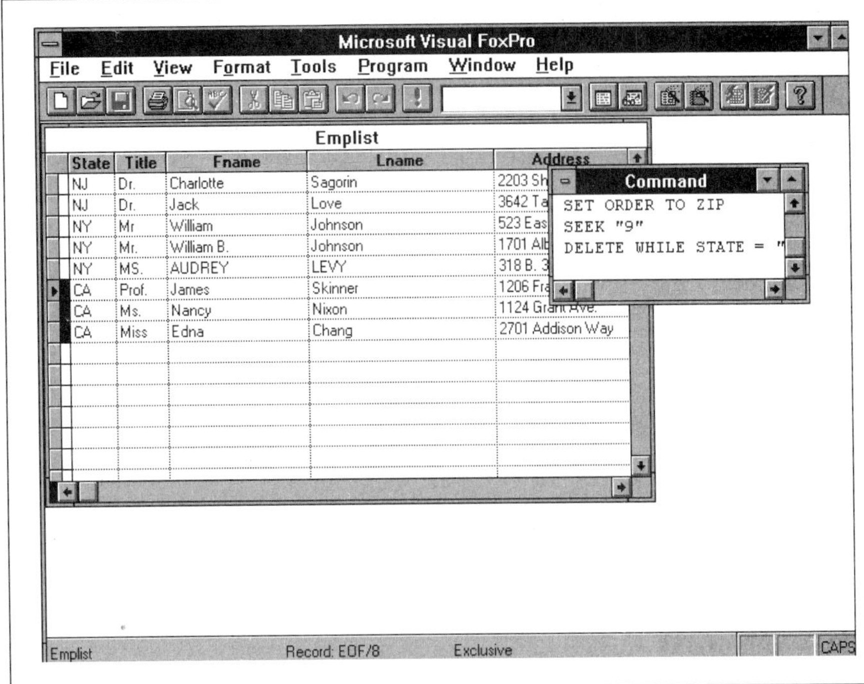

5. Again, to undo the damage, enter the command **RECALL ALL**. All the records are unmarked.

This exercise used an unusual method of moving the pointer to the first California record before using the WHILE clause. The purpose was simply to show that while the records must be in proper order before you use the WHILE clause, they do not necessarily have to be ordered using an index that is based on the field used in the logical expression of the WHILE clause.

Of course, you could have used the Table ➤ Delete Records and Table ➤ Recall Records instead of the DELETE and RECALL commands, but you have become comfortable enough with these commands to see that, once you have learned them, it is easier to enter commands than to work from the menu system.

Logical Expressions for Other Data Types

It is very simple to search fields of most data types, using the equal, greater-than, and less-than operators with both of these data types. The

= operator is used most commonly when you are searching Character fields, and the >, <, >=, and <= operators are most common when you are searching Numeric fields.

However, you must use different techniques to search Memo and Logical fields.

Memo Fields You can use the "included-in" operator, $, for Character fields, but it is most commonly used to find a substring in a memo.

In the next exercise, for example, you will look for employees who are connected with the Christmas fund-raising drive. The only trick to this query is figuring out all the different ways you might have entered the data in the Memo field. You need to search for both XMAS and CHRISTMAS in both uppercase and lowercase. Even then, you should read each memo individually since one says that the employee *cannot* help with the fund-raising.

Logical Fields When you are basing a query on a logical field, you do not need to use a logical expression. You may recall that logical expressions are evaluated as true or false. The content of a logical *field,* however, is already one of these values (.T. or .F.). Thus, to find all the people in the EMPLIST table who are on probation, you can use a query with FOR followed by the logical field Probation. Visual FoxPro will evaluate this logical field just as it would evaluate any logical expression: as true or false. Likewise, you could use the criterion FOR .NOT. PROBATION to find the records of employees who have .F. in the field.

Using BROWSE FOR To try out logical expressions for these data types, the following exercise uses the BROWSE command with a FOR clause.

1. The Emplist table should already be open. Enter:

   ```
   BROWSE FOR "XMAS" $ UPPER(NOTES) .OR. "CHRISTMAS" $
   UPPER(NOTES)
   ```

   Of course, you should enter this command on a single line.

2. In the resulting Browse window, double-click each record's Notes field to see that all match the criterion of the query, as shown (for example) in Figure 11.12. When you are done, close the Browse window.

FIGURE 11.12

Using a FOR clause with a Memo field

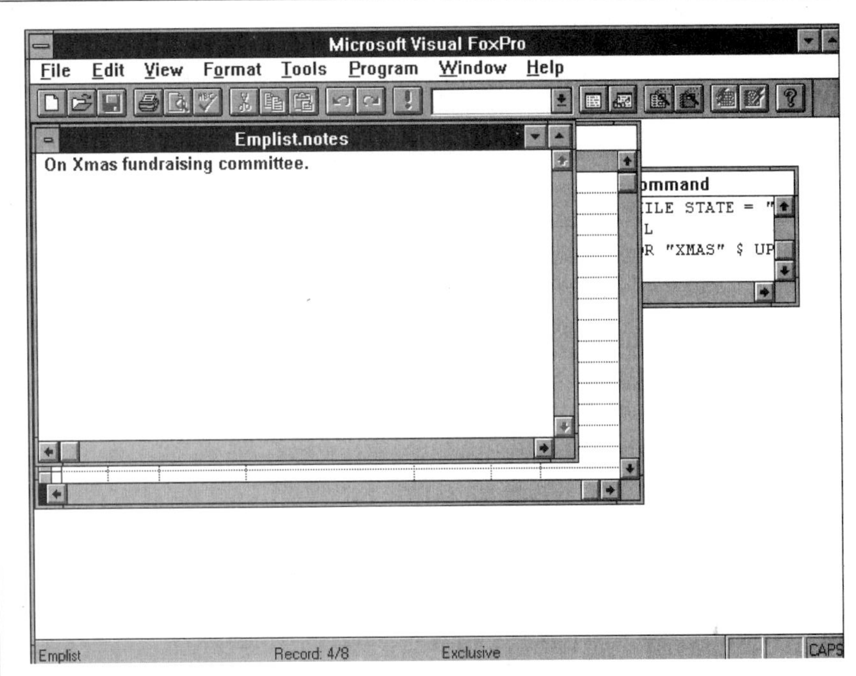

Now, try a query for the logical field. Remember that, if you simply use the field name PROBATION, Visual FoxPro evaluates it as .T. or .F., just as it would evaluate a comparison as .T. or .F.

1. Enter **BROWSE FOR PROBATION**.
2. Scroll to see the Probation field and confirm that all of them are .T., as shown in Figure 11.13. Close the Browse window.

   When you were looking at the Memo fields, you might have noticed that *fund raising* was spelled in three ways: fund raising, fund-raising, and FUNDRAISING. This gives you an idea of what you are up against when you are searching Memo fields.

FIGURE 11.13

Using a FOR Clause with a Logical field

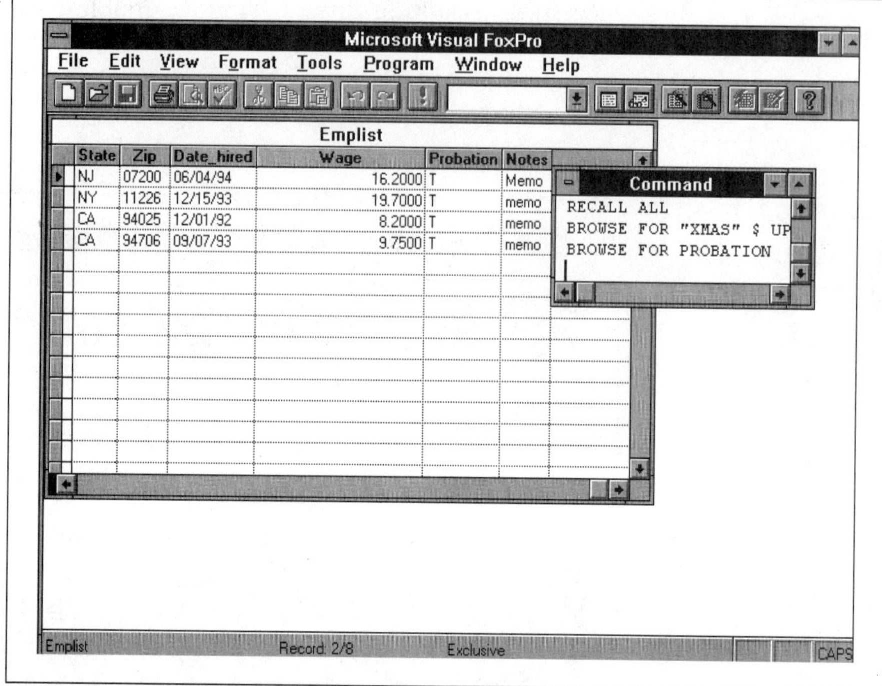

Combining FOR and WHILE Clauses

It is possible to use a command with both a FOR and a WHILE clause, just as it is possible to use a command with a FOR and a scope clause.

LOCATE FOR may also be used with an optional WHILE clause.

If you use both a FOR and a WHILE clause, the WHILE clause takes precedence. The command carries out the search for the FOR condition only as long as the WHILE condition remains true. This is the same thing that happens when you use both a FOR and a scope clause; the command carries out the search for the FOR condition only within the specified scope.

For example, if you have used the ZIP index as the controlling index of the table and have placed the pointer on the first record from California, you can use the command LOCATE FOR UPPER(LNAME) = "JOHNSON" WHILE STATE = "CA" to search for the name Johnson only in the records from California.

▶▶ NOTE

Although it is possible to use both a FOR and a WHILE clause in a command in this way, it can be confusing and should generally be avoided. It is never absolutely necessary, as it is necessary to combine a FOR and scope clause to override the default scope of some commands.

▶▶ The FIELDS Clause

So far, you have looked at how to use scope, FOR, and WHILE clauses to specify which *records* of the table are included in the output of commands. You can also restrict which *fields* are included in the output of commands by adding a FIELDS clause.

For most commands, a FIELDS clause usually contains either the word FIELDS followed by a list of fields or it simply contains the list of fields. In either case, commas must be included to separate each of the fields or expressions in the list.

Typically, after opening the Emplist table, you could use a command such as

```
LIST FIELDS fname, lname
```

or simply use the command

```
LIST fname, lname
```

to get a listing of only the names of your employees.

However, some commands require the word FIELDS. For example, if you enter **BROWSE FIELDS fname, lname**, Visual FoxPro will display a Browse window with only these two columns, but if you enter **BROWSE fname, lname**, it will display an error message saying there is an unrecognized phrase in the command.

▶▶ TIP

To avoid confusion, it is easiest always to use the word FIELDS if you are working from the Command window.

▸ Using Expressions in FIELDS Clauses

You can use a FIELDS clause with expressions as well as with field names.

With a BROWSE command, you must create a calculated field as part of the field list. For example, if you had a monthly salary field named MON_SAL, you could include the yearly salary in a Browse window by using a command such as

```
BROWSE FIELDS fname, lname, year_sal = mon_sal*12
```

By including **year_sal = mon_sal*12** in the field list, you create a calculated field named year_sal and define its value as mon_sal * 12. This sort of calculated field is read-only.

With a LIST command, you can simply use expressions as part of the FIELD list. For example, to improve the appearance of the result, you can use the PROPER() function with all the fields you are using in a LIST command, to capitalize the listing properly. Likewise, in a later exercise, you will use PROPER(TRIM(FNAME) + " " + LNAME) to improve both capitalization and spacing of a LIST command.

▸▸ Using Data and Field Filters

You have learned the basic techniques for finding either one record or all the records that match a criterion:

- To search for a single record without explicitly using an index, use LOCATE and CONTINUE.
- To search for a single record that explicitly uses the index, use SEEK.
- To search for all matching records without explicitly using the index, use a FOR clause.
- To search for all matching records explicitly using the index, use a WHILE clause.

These techniques are the workhorses you will constantly use when you are working with Visual FoxPro commands.

However, there will also be times when you want to perform a long series of commands, all of which apply only to records that meet some criterion and all of which apply only to certain fields. It would be unwieldy to add FOR and FIELDS clauses separately to each of these commands.

For this reason, Visual FoxPro also gives you the option of setting a data filter and of setting a field filter. You can do both of these either by using the Work Area Properties dialog box or by using a SET command. After you have done this, the records and fields that you do not want to use are filtered out indefinitely, until you remove the filter.

Using the Work Area Properties Dialog Box

You can set a data filter or field filter by displaying the View window. Make sure the table you want to filter is selected in the Aliases list. If you are working with a single table, it will always be selected, but you may have to click the table in the list to select it if you are working with a relational database with multiple tables. (Chapter 14 covers the use of the View window to manage relational databases.)

Click the Properties button of the View window to display Work Area Properties dialog box, shown in Figure 11.14. As you can see in the illustration, this dialog box includes a Data Filter and a Field Filter control.

Creating a Data Filter

To create a data filter, enter a logical expression in the Data Filter text box or click the button to its right to display the Expression Builder, which you can use to generate the expression. After you select OK, the filter will continue to be active until you display this dialog box again and delete the filter.

Creating a Field Filter

You can also use the View window in much the same way to set a field filter. Click its Properties button to display the Work Area Properties dialog box, and then click the Field Filter button to display the Field Picker shown in Figure 11.15. Use the Field Picker in the usual way to specify the fields list.

FIGURE 11.14

The Work Area Properties dialog box

FIGURE 11.15

The Field Picker for field filtering

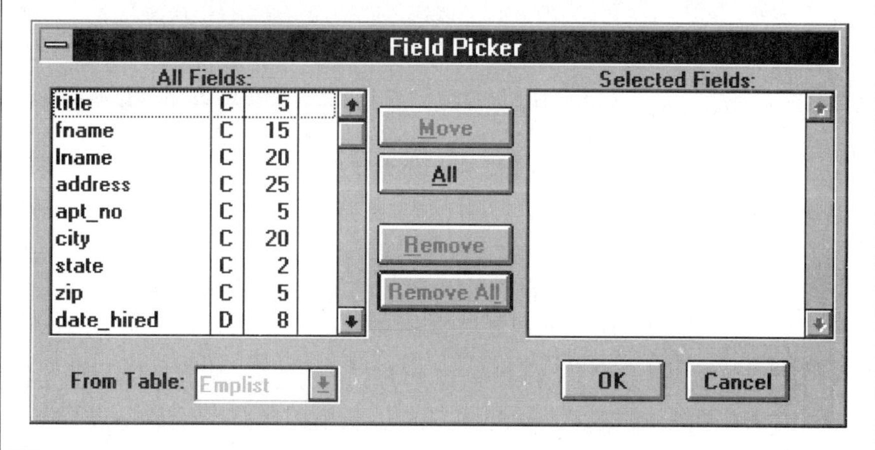

The difference between a data and a field filter is that a data filter remains in force until you remove it permanently. When you use a field filter, however, the radio buttons in the Allow Access To area of the Work Area Properties dialog box let you temporarily disable it and use all the fields, and then enable it again to reuse the field filter.

Once you've created a field filter, you can use these two radio buttons at any time to use all the fields again or just to use the fields specified by the filter.

NOTE

When you first create a field filter, you must select the Only Fields Specified By Field Filter radio button to enable the filter. If you just use the Field Picker to create the filter, it will not have any effect.

Using the Command Window

You can also create data and field filters from the Command window.

The SET FILTER Command

To create a data filter, enter

```
SET FILTER TO <logical exp>
```

You can remove the filter by entering the command SET FILTER TO without any logical expression included; you might want to read this as *set filter to nothing.*

TIP

In some cases, filters are useful for simplifying commands. Even if you want to use the criterion only once, it is sometimes easier to understand what you are doing if you use a filter to set up the criterion, then use the command, and then remove the filter. This is part-icularly true if the command has many other clauses besides the FOR clause. When you have multiple criteria that would have to be combined, creating a complex and difficult-to-understand logical expression, it may also be easier to use a filter for one criterion and a FOR clause for the other.

The SET FIELDS Command

The basic command to create a field filter is **SET FIELDS TO <field list>**. The field list is made up of field names separated by commas.

The SET FIELDS TO command can also be used in combination with the commands SET FIELDS OFF, which temporarily turns off the field setting and uses all the fields again, and SET FIELDS ON, which turns on the fields setting again. These commands are equivalent to the radio buttons in the Allow Access To area of the Work Area Properties dialog box.

▸▸ **NOTE**

In other Xbase languages and in earlier versions of FoxPro you had to use the command SET FIELDS ON to activate the setting after using the command SET FIELDS TO <field list> to specify the fields that were included. In Visual FoxPro 3.0, you can just use the command SET FIELDS TO <field list> both to specify the field list and to activate the setting; then you can use SET FIELDS OFF and SET FIELDS ON later to temporarily deactivate and activate the setting. This change can lead to confusion at first if you are accustomed to earlier versions of FoxPro or if you are working with older programs.

Use the command

```
SET FIELDS TO ALL
```

to undo the **SET FIELDS TO <field list>** and make all of the fields in the current table active permanently.

Using Calculated Fields in Filters You can also include calculated fields in a SET FILTER command's field list, as you do in the Field list used with a single command, by using the statement:

<calculated field name> = <expression>

instead of one of the field names. This statement names the field and assigns it a value.

NOTE

Many SET commands are deactivated by using them without any argument following TO. For example, you learned earlier that you can enter SET FILTER TO without any expression following it to deactivate a SET FILTER TO <expression> command and use all the records again. The SET FIELDS command does not work in this way. If you enter SET FIELDS TO without any argument, Visual FoxPro does not include any fields in the commands that follow. You must use SET FIELDS TO ALL to include all fields.

For example, if you had a monthly salary field named MON_SAL, you could include the yearly salary in the fields list by using this command:

```
SET FIELDS TO fname, lname, year_sal = mon_sal*12
```

In all later commands, you would refer to this field by the name year_sal.

Using Field Skeletons If you have a large number of fields in a table, you might find it convenient to use a *field skeleton* to refer to a number of them.

A field skeleton is made up of one or more literal characters plus the two wildcard characters:

- ? refers to a single character
- * refers to any number of characters

They are used in the clause ALL LIKE <skeleton> ¦ EXCEPT <skeleton>. Thus, you could use the command

```
SET FIELDS TO ALL LIKE ?NAME
```

to include only the FNAME and LNAME fields of your table. And you could use the command:

```
SET FIELDS TO ALL EXCEPT ?NAME, A*
```

to include all fields but to leave out the FNAME and LNAME fields and all fields whose names begin with the letter A.

▸▸ Applications of Filters

Now you have a thorough background on the use of filters and have looked at some of the ways that they can be applied in practice. This section covers some other practical applications of filters that are often useful.

▸ Filtered Reports and Labels

You can use a FOR, WHILE, or scope clause to restrict the records that are included when you print a report or mailing labels, either using the menu system or the Command window.

After you choose File ➤ Print to display the Print dialog box, select Label or Report from the Type drop-down list, display the file name in the File text box, and click the Options button to display the Print Options dialog box, shown in Figure 11.16.

FIGURE 11.16

The Print Options dialog box

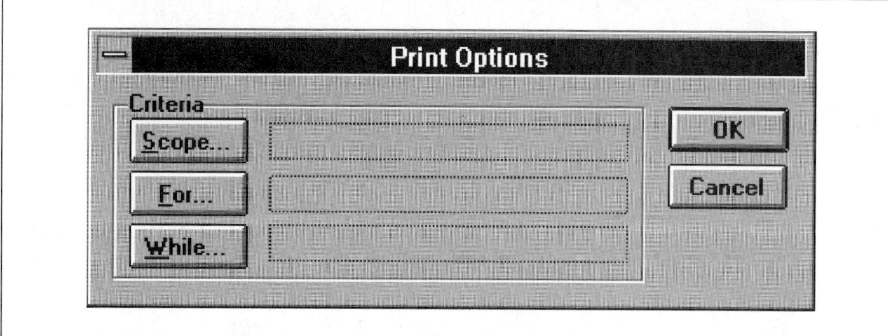

You can click the Scope button to display the Scope dialog box, shown in Figure 11.17, and use it to specify a scope for the command, though this is not often useful for printing reports. You can click the For or While button to display the Expression Builder, and use it to enter a logical expression to restrict the records included in the report. It is often useful to add a For clause to a report; for example, you can produce the reports you designed in Chapter 6 so that they only include employees from California—or, using a more complex expression, so they only include employees from California who are on probation.

FIGURE 11.17

The Scope dialog box

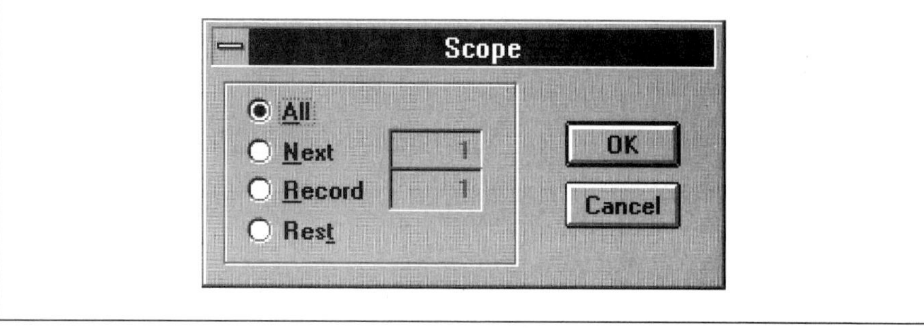

Working from the Command window, you can add a FOR, WHILE, or scope clause to the command used to print reports. Again, it is usually best to add a FOR clause, so the command has the form:

```
REPORT FORM <file name> [TO PRINT] [FOR <log exp>]
```

If the optional TO PRINT clause is left out, the report is simply displayed on the screen.

WARNING

If you have created a data filter for a table using the View Window or the SET FILTER command, it will also apply to reports based on that table. If you want to print the report as you designed it, with all the records in the table, remove the filter before printing it.

Try using the Command window to print the Empdata report that you created in Chapter 6, to see the opportunities and pitfalls that are involved:

1. Enter **REPORT FORM \learnfox\empdata**. The report is displayed with all records included.
2. Enter **CLEAR** and then edit the earlier command to read **REPORT FORM \learnfox\empdata FOR state = "CA"** and press Enter. The report is displayed with only records from California, as shown in Figure 11.18. (Only one column is displayed, because in this small sample table there are so few records from California.)

FIGURE 11.18

Using a filtered report

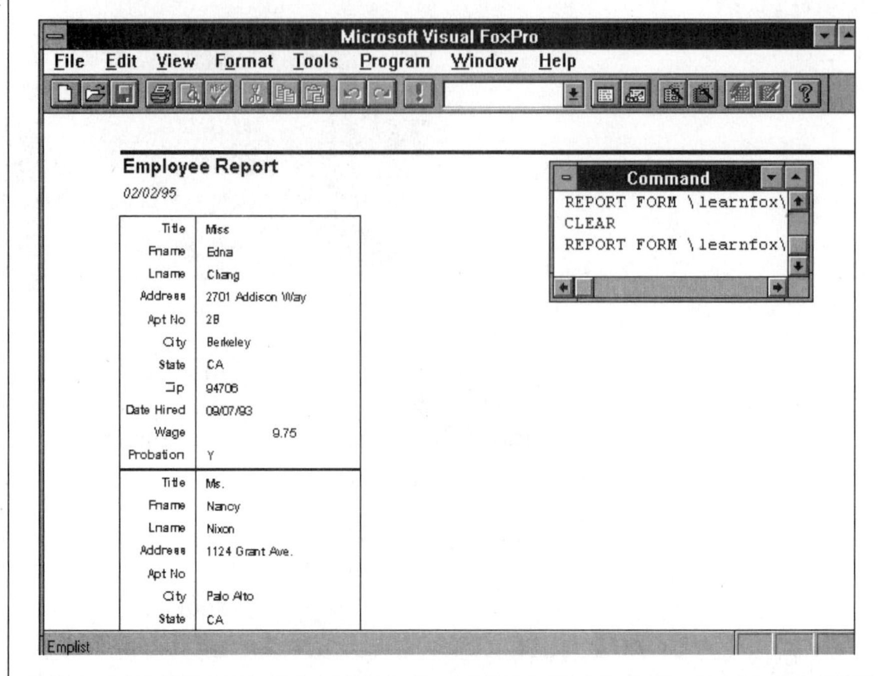

3. Enter **CLEAR**. Then enter **SET FILTER TO state = "CA"**. Now, imagine that you have done other work since setting the filter and you print the report in the ordinary way. Reuse your original report command, **REPORT FORM \learnfox\empdata**. This time, only records from California are included.

4. Enter **CLEAR**. Enter **SET FILTER TO** to remove the filter. Now you can produce the full report by reusing the command **REPORT FORM \learnfox\empdata**.

▸ Manipulating Data Using the REPLACE Command

One of the most time-saving uses of FOR, WHILE, and scope clauses is to manipulate data using the REPLACE command, since it lets you change the data in a large number of records with a single command.

Chapter 8 introduced the basic form of this command:

```
REPLACE <field name 1> WITH <value 1>
   [, <field name 2> WITH <value 2> ...]
```

which simply places the specified values in the specified field or fields of the current record. Of course, it is easier simply to type the values in the table than it is to use this version of the command, but you can use the REPLACE command much more powerfully now that you know about expressions and about the optional clauses you can use with REPLACE.

You can see now that the default scope of this command is NEXT 1. It is very useful when it is used with the scope of ALL; it lets you change or fill in the value in the field (or fields) that you specify in every record in the database.

For example, say that you have already entered thousands of records in your table, and then you modify its structure to add a new logical field to determine whether you should continue mailing to each person. The field is named MAILTO, and it should initially be true for every record, until you have a reason to stop mailing to that person.

After adding the field, instead of using the keyboard to type **T** in each record, you can use the command

```
REPLACE ALL mailto WITH .T.
```

to enter data in thousands of records effortlessly.

NOTE

Notice that you must use delimiters around the value used in the REPLACE command, because it is an expression, even though you do not use delimiters when you enter the value directly in the table. Here, you use the dot delimiters for a logical value. Likewise, you would include the quotation marks for a character field in a command such as REPLACE ALL state WITH "CA", even though you do not have to use quotation marks when you type the value into a character field.

The REPLACE command can also be used with a FOR or WHILE clause, to specify which records should be changed.

For example, if you decide to stop doing mailings to everyone in your list from California, you can follow the previous command with the command:

```
REPLACE ALL mailto WITH .F. FOR state = "CA"
```

Finally, because the value you replace the field with is an expression, you can use a calculation as the value—even a calculation based on the field itself. For example, if you wanted to give all your employees a 10 percent raise, you could use the command:

```
REPLACE ALL wage WITH wage * 1.1
```

which would replace the value in the wage field of every record with a value that is 10 percent greater than its current value (1.1 times its current value).

To give a raise only to certain employees, you could use a command such as:

```
REPLACE ALL wage WITH wage * 1.1 FOR state = "CA"
```

►► **WARNING**

It is sometimes impossible to undo the changes that this command makes. For example, if you have already entered .T. and .F. in the Mailto field of many records, there is no way of recovering the original values in the fields after you use the command REPLACE ALL mailto WITH .T. You should be sure that you fully understand the change you want to make before using this command. If you have any doubts, back up the table before using a REPLACE command.

► Building a FOR Clause in an Index

You saw in Chapter 10 that the Index panel of the Table Designer dialog box contains a Filter text box with a button to its right that you can use to display the Expression Builder. You can use this control to add a FOR clause to the INDEX command, to create indexes that include only the records that meet a certain logical criterion.

For example, you can create an index that includes only records of employees who live in California. Whenever you update the table with that index active, records will be used in future commands only if they are from California. Anytime you want to query for records in California, all you have to do is use the table with this index as its controlling index, and records not from California will be ignored.

You can do the same from the Command window by using the INDEX command with a FOR clause, as follows:

```
INDEX ON <expr> TAG <tag name> FOR <log expr>
```

The INDEX command can only have a FOR clause—not a WHILE or a scope clause.

Dealing with Deleted Records

In Chapter 3, you learned that records that are marked for deletion are included in reports, mailing labels, and other output unless you PACK the table to remove these records permanently.

Visual FoxPro also includes records that are marked for deletion in the output of commands if you filter data, and this can sometimes create problems. For example, if you use a FOR clause to find the records of certain people you want to telephone, Visual FoxPro will include records you have marked for deletion, and you might end up telephoning people you thought you had scratched off your list.

You now know enough to be able to handle these problems in several ways.

The most obvious technique is to choose Table ➤ Remove Deleted Records or use the PACK command before you use any command where deleted records might cause a problem. This method does not take any thought, but it can waste time if you are working with a large table. If you delete records frequently and use these commands frequently, you might have to pack your table dozens of times, which means significant delays.

A more efficient way to handle the problem is to use the SET DELETED command. You can access this command through the menu system by choosing Tools ➤ Options to display the Options dialog box and clicking its Data tab to display the panel shown in Figure 11.19; then select the Ignore Deleted Records check box. You can also use this command through the Command window. If you enter SET DELETED ON, commands that select records will not include any records that are marked for deletion. If you enter SET DELETED OFF, the commands will again include records marked for deletion.

FIGURE 11.19

The Data panel of the Options dialog box

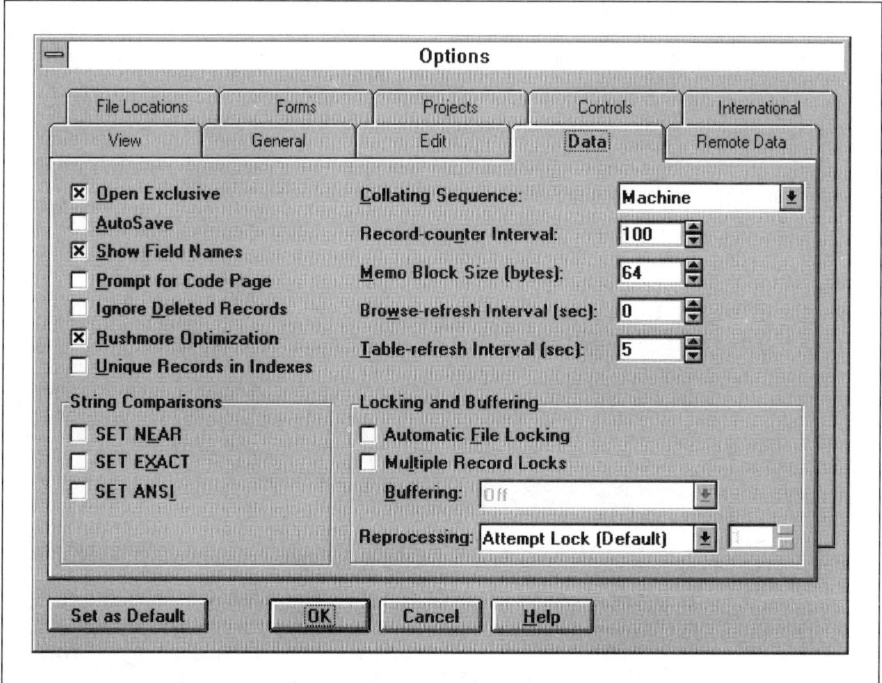

►► **TIP**

Many people find the SET DELETED command confusing since SET DELETED ON is the command that turns *OFF* the deleted records. It is easy to remember if you realize what it means: Set on the feature that eliminates deleted records.

You can also deal with the problem of deleted records by using the function DELETED( ) in combination with a command. If a record is marked for deletion, DELETED( ) returns .T.; if it is not, DELETED( ) returns .F. Thus, by adding .AND. .NOT. DELETED( ) to a logical expression, you can create a query that leaves out records marked for deletion. For example, you can use the command

```
BROWSE FOR STATE = "CA" .AND. .NOT. DELETED()
```

to display a Browse window with only California records, but to make sure that it omits any records in the table that are marked for deletion.

You can access DELETED( ) through the Logical control of the Expression Builder, and so you can also generate this function if you are working with the menu system.

Finally, you can create an index that ignores deleted records by using .NOT. DELETED as the index's FOR clause. It is generally not worthwhile to create an index solely for this purpose, but if you are creating an index with a FOR clause for some other reason, you might want to add AND .NOT. DELETED( ) to the logical expression that you are using in the FOR clause.

As you can see, there are many ways of accomplishing the same task when you are using Visual FoxPro. The Xbase language grew gradually, with more commands and functions to let you do things more conveniently. There is no need to learn all of the commands and functions; many of them just do the same things in different ways that different users prefer. Just be aware of them and learn the ones that let you do what you want in a way that is easiest for you.

The Easiest Possible Report: LIST with Options

You have finally learned enough that you can begin to do things the easy way.

In Chapter 8, you used the command LIST to create the simplest possible report—easier than anything you can do with the menu. You can also use LIST in combination with a FOR clause and a field list to create rather precise custom reports without using the Report Designer. Of course, the appearance of the report will not be as attractive as if you had used the Designer, but LIST is the easiest way to get a quick printout of your data for your own use—for example, if you simply want to print out names and phone numbers of people who live in California so you can telephone them today.

Try listing names and wages for employees from California:

1. Enter

   ```
   USE \LEARNFOX\EMPLIST ORDER NAMES.
   ```

2. Enter

   ```
   LIST FIELDS LNAME, FNAME, WAGE, FOR STATE = "CA" OFF
   ```

►► **NOTE**

Remember that OFF used with the LIST command simply makes the command leave out the record numbers, which you do not want in an alphabetical listing. OFF can be used immediately after LIST, but it often comes at the end of a LIST command—only TO PRINT and TO FILE must come after it—so, to avoid confusion, you must remember that it has nothing to do with the preceding clauses.

3. To make the listing look nicer, you can combine the first and last names so that the listing has a single name column. Enter

   ```
   LIST FIELDS PROPER(TRIM(FNAME)+" "+(LNAME)), WAGE,
   FOR STATE = "CA" OFF
   ```

If the listing on the screen, shown in Figure 11.20, looks good to you, you can add TO PRINT at the very end of the command to get a quick printout of the data you need, or add TO FILE <file name> to save the listing in a text file.

If you want a report that includes page breaks, page headers and footers, and the like, you can add TO FILE <file name> after OFF to save the output of the report in a plain ASCII text file. Most word processors can import text files, and they can add any formatting you want to the data. You can change the headings above the columns and even use a variety of fonts for them.

FIGURE 11.20

Using LIST with options to create a report

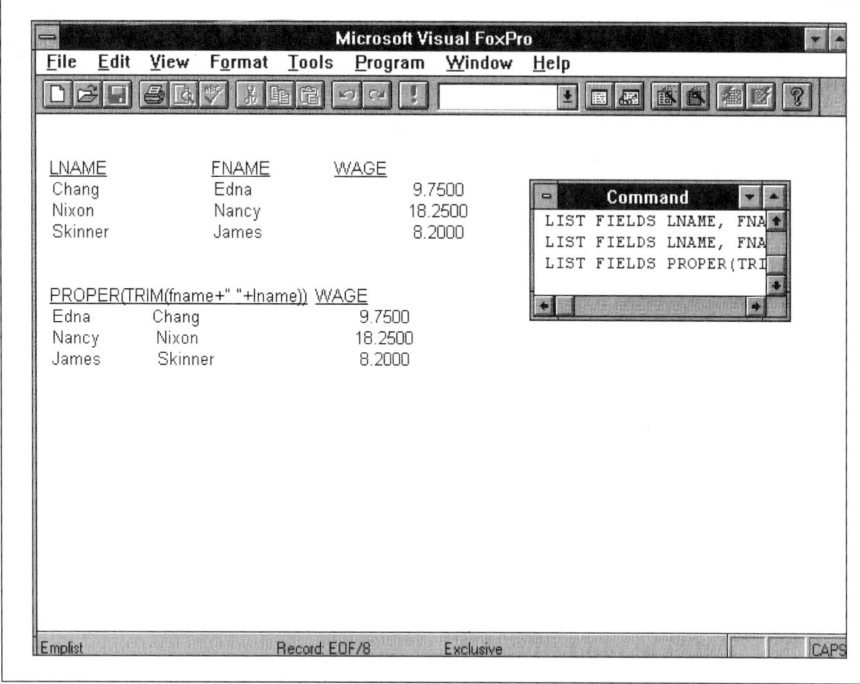

WARNING

Do not use proportional fonts for the data of a text file generated by Visual FoxPro. Remember that Visual FoxPro pads the space between columns by using the blank character. Proportional fonts use less space for blanks than for other characters, so they will not align the columns properly. Of course, you can use proportional fonts to add a report title.

Homemade Queries

Likewise, rather than going through the steps of the Query Wizard or the panels of the Query Designer to specify the fields and records that you want to display and the order in which you want to list them, you can simply enter a series of commands such as:

```
USE C:\LEARNFOX\EMPLIST ORDER NAMES
SET FILTER TO STATE = "CA"
SET FIELDS TO LNAME, FNAME
```

After you use these three commands, all commands that follow will use the Lname and Fname fields of the EMPLIST table in alphabetical order—just as if you had created a query that uses these features of the table. Since these commands give you direct access to the table, you can update your data after using them.

Once you are accustomed to using the Command window, you'll find that it is easier to type these three lines than it is to click your way through a long series of menu selections and dialog boxes to create a query that displays the same data.

►► To Sum Up

You can see now how worthwhile it is to know about Visual FoxPro commands and about the different types of expressions and clauses that can be used with many of them. Although they have taken you a bit of time to learn, the extra power they give you will more than repay you for the trouble. As you have just seen, a one-line command can produce an entire report for you; three lines of commands can take the place of three dialog boxes of a Wizard, and can do a better job than the Wizard does.

Now you have learned the basic features of the Xbase language that you need to manipulate your own data. If you find the language interesting, you may want to skip directly to Part V of this book, beginning with Chapter 23, which covers features of the language used in programming. Or you may want to continue with Part III, which covers relational databases, and Part IV, which covers Visual FoxPro utilities, before going on to programming.

Working with Relational Databases

PART THREE

CHAPTER 12

Understanding Relational Databases

FAST TRACK

▶▶ So far, you have worked only with single-table databases, which are sufficient for some simple business applications. In this chapter, you will learn how to determine when to use multitable or *relational* databases and how to break down data into multiple tables. After learning a bit of simple database theory in this chapter, you will be able to go on to the other chapters in Part III, which teach you how to work with relational databases using Visual FoxPro:

- Chapter 13 shows you how to use the Query Wizard as the simplest way to use relational databases.
- Chapter 14 shows you how to use the View window to open multiple tables and relate them. You can easily save and restore the settings in the View Window.
- Chapter 15 shows you how to use the Query Designer, which generates SQL commands. You looked at the Query Designer in Chapter 4, but there you only used it to work with one table. Now, you will use it with multiple tables and look at the programming code that it generates to relate the tables and manipulate their data.
- Chapter 16 shows how to use Visual FoxPro databases to create persistent relationships between tables, the most powerful way of working with multitable databases in Visual FoxPro, but also the trickiest.

It is possible to manage your data using just the Query Wizard: if you want to do things the easy way, you can just read Chapter 13 after finishing this chapter. The other three chapters let you add power to your work.

In any case, though, you should begin by reading this chapter to learn why relational databases are needed and why data is broken up into multiple tables—issues that are important regardless of the database management system you use.

Even if you have no immediate need to use them in your work, you should know when relational databases are used. While a single-table database may be all you need now, you will probably need a relational database for some application that you want to work with in the future. You will be much better off if you recognize immediately that the application demands a multitable database, rather than trying to squeeze it into a single table and creating endless difficulties for yourself.

►► Why Relational Databases Are Used

When businesses first began to computerize, they discovered an unexpected benefit of abandoning their paper files: they could avoid unnecessary repetition of data.

When records were kept on paper, different departments of large businesses kept records that repeated the same data. For example, the Payroll department might keep records on a form that included each employee's name, address, and wages. The Benefits department might keep records on a form with each employee's name, address, and eligibility for benefits. The Human Resources Development department might keep records on a form with each employee's name, address, and training. In a large business with many departments, basic information such as the name, address, and social security number of each employee might be repeated dozens of times.

This repetition required extra data entry: the names and addresses had to be entered a dozen times, and if an employee moved, a dozen different forms had to be updated. Inevitably, there were also anomalies in the data, as some forms were updated incorrectly.

Computer scientists developed a number of methods of avoiding this repetition, and the relational database eventually emerged as the method of choice.

Before you can set up a relational database, you must *normalize* the data—break it down in a way that minimizes repetition. In the example above, you obviously would want to keep the employee's name, address, and other basic data in one table, like your Emplist table, the records of wages in a second table, which you might call the Wages table, the records of eligibility for benefits in a third table, the records of courses taken in a fourth table, and so on.

You relate these tables by using some common *key field*, such as Employee number. FoxPro can use the key field to join the tables. For example, by seeing which records have the same Employee number, it can find the name and address in the Emplist table that applies to each record in the Wages table.

Databases organized in this way are called *relational* because the key field links or relates the tables. Next we'll look at the different types of relationship that can exist between tables.

▸▸ Data Normalization

Data normalization involves breaking down complex data into several tables. More advanced books include detailed discussions of the theory of database normalization. What you actually need to know in practice, though, is generally just a matter of common sense.

You simply need to remember that your goal is to eliminate unnecessary repetition of data. You can do this by looking for two different types of relationship between fields that can create unnecessary repetition if the data is kept in a single table: the *many-to-one* relationship and the *many-to-many* relationship. Both of these are discussed in detail below.

▸ The Many-to-One Relationship

Later in this chapter, you'll modify our sample Emplist database to keep a record of how many hours the employees worked each week. As you will see, this is an example of a many-to-one relationship—there are many weekly wage entries for each one employee.

Your first impulse, before you think about it, might be simply to add extra fields to the Employee table to hold the number of hours worked and the date that the week ends. If you just added these extra fields to the same table, though, you would have to repeat the entire record each week. Figure 12.1 shows a simplified version of what the table would look like if you set it up in this way.

FIGURE 12.1

Incorrect database design

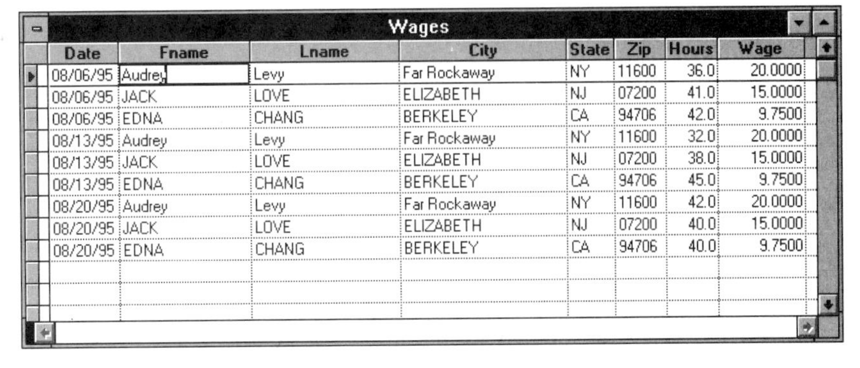

Wages

Date	Fname	Lname	City	State	Zip	Hours	Wage
08/06/95	Audrey	Levy	Far Rockaway	NY	11600	36.0	20.0000
08/06/95	JACK	LOVE	ELIZABETH	NJ	07200	41.0	15.0000
08/06/95	EDNA	CHANG	BERKELEY	CA	94706	42.0	9.7500
08/13/95	Audrey	Levy	Far Rockaway	NY	11600	32.0	20.0000
08/13/95	JACK	LOVE	ELIZABETH	NJ	07200	38.0	15.0000
08/13/95	EDNA	CHANG	BERKELEY	CA	94706	45.0	9.7500
08/20/95	Audrey	Levy	Far Rockaway	NY	11600	42.0	20.0000
08/20/95	JACK	LOVE	ELIZABETH	NJ	07200	40.0	15.0000
08/20/95	EDNA	CHANG	BERKELEY	CA	94706	40.0	9.7500

You can see that you would need nine records to record three weeks of work-hours for just three of your employees, and that most of the data, such as the name and address, is repeated in several records. You can imagine how much unnecessary data there would be in this table if you had to record years and years of weekly work-hours for all of your employees: apart from the disk space needed to store the repeated data, think of the extra time needed to enter it.

On second thought, you might want to add 52 additional fields to each record, one for each week's work hours. This would also create problems, though. The table would be so large that it would become unwieldy to work with. If new employees were hired, they would have blank spaces in all of the earlier weeks. And, of course, after the 52 weeks ended, you would have to add another 52 fields to the table for the next year's worth of work hours.

The reason these problems arise is that there are many weeks of work-hours to record for each employee. This is what is called a many-to-one relationship.

The way to break down the data is to separate the one from the many—that is, separate the data that you need to record only once, such as the employee's name and the address, from the data that changes and needs to be recorded each week, such as the hours worked and the date that the week ends. Place the data in two separate tables.

The Key Field

In order to break the data down into two tables, you must have a way of relating the records in one table to the records in another, so you know which work hours go with which employee. The two tables are related by using what is called a *key field*, which is shared by both tables.

The simplified example in Figure 12.2 shows how the key field is used. Here, the same data that was recorded in Figure 12.1 is broken down into two tables, which are related by using Empno (short for Employee Number) as a key field. To see how many hours a given employee worked each week, you have to look on the Emplist table first to find her employee number. Then you have to look at the Wages table to see how many hours the employee with that number worked each week. Of course, the computer can relate the two tables to each other in this way almost instantly.

FIGURE 12.2

Correct database design

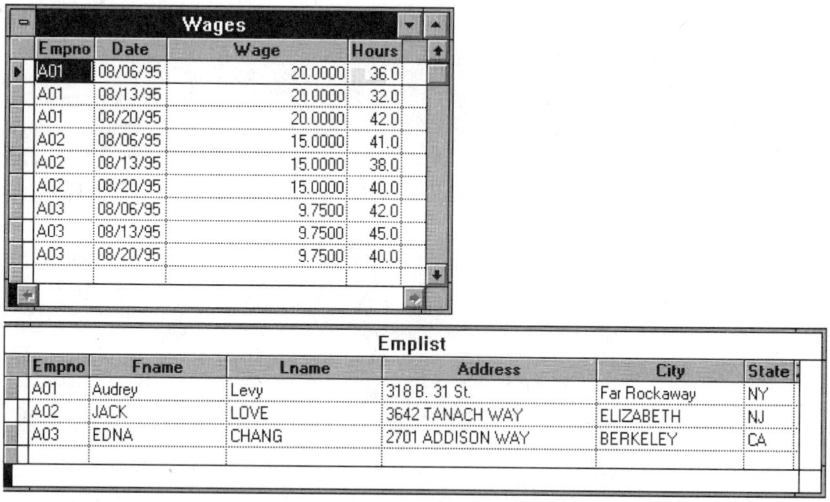

Wages

Empno	Date	Wage	Hours
A01	08/06/95	20.0000	36.0
A01	08/13/95	20.0000	32.0
A01	08/20/95	20.0000	42.0
A02	08/06/95	15.0000	41.0
A02	08/13/95	15.0000	38.0
A02	08/20/95	15.0000	40.0
A03	08/06/95	9.7500	42.0
A03	08/13/95	9.7500	45.0
A03	08/20/95	9.7500	40.0

Emplist

Empno	Fname	Lname	Address	City	State
A01	Audrey	Levy	318 B. 31 St.	Far Rockaway	NY
A02	JACK	LOVE	3642 TANACH WAY	ELIZABETH	NJ
A03	EDNA	CHANG	2701 ADDISON WAY	BERKELEY	CA

The key field must be handled differently in the "one" table, where it is a *primary key*, and in the "many" table, where it is a *foreign key*.

The Primary Key A primary key, such as the Empno field in the Emplist table, must be unique. It cannot be duplicated in more than one record in this table. If two employees had the same employee number, for example, there would be no way of knowing which one of them corresponded to a wage record with that employee number.

The primary key field must also be unchanging. If you ever change its value in a record on the "one" side of the relation, you will have no way of relating the records on the "many" side to it.

WARNING

If you change the value of a primary key field in the "one" table that has already been used in related records in the "many" table, you will cause massive loss of data. For example, if you change an Empno in the Emplist table of the sample application, you would no longer know which employee is referred to by all the records with that Empno in the Wages table. Those records would become virtually useless. Though you can take precautions to avoid changing or deleting primary key fields, you should always keep a backup of the data in the "one" table of a many-to-one relationship, since accidental data loss can occur because of system failure.

You should use some arbitrary value, such as an employee number, in a primary key field, and you should never use a meaningful value, such as the person's name. Why not? Because a meaningful value might be duplicated, and it might change. For example, two people may have the same name; furthermore, people sometimes change their names.

NOTE

Although it is meaningful, the social security number is acceptable as a primary key field since it is arbitrarily assigned to be unique and unchanging for each person.

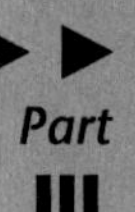

The Foreign Key If you think about how the key field is used to relate data in a many-to-one relationship, you will see that it does not have the same requirements in the "many" table as it does in the "one" table, where it is the primary key.

The primary key cannot be repeated in more than one record of the "one" table. For example, two employees cannot have the same employee number in the Emplist table.

However, this key can be repeated in the "many" table, and it usually is. Obviously, you can use the Wages table to record the hours of many weeks of work for each employee, and all of these records must have the same employee number.

The prime requirement for values of the key field that you enter in the "many" table is that they must already exist in the "one" table. For example, you should not enter the hours for an employee in the Wages table unless that employee is already listed in the Emplist table: if you enter an Empno in the Wages table and there is no record with that Empno in the Emplist table, you will not know whom to pay the wages.

A record in the "many" table with a key that does not exist in the "one" table is called an *orphan record.*

Because a key field such as the employee number in the Wages table is a primary key from another table, it is called a *foreign key*.

The Benefits of Relational Databases

The amount of space and data entry that you save is not obvious when you look at Figures 12.1 and 12.2, because only a few weeks are recorded. You can begin to appreciate the use of multitable databases if you imagine several years worth of employee records. Placing the database in one table, as in Figure 12.1, would mean repeating each employee's name and address (and any other data that you have) hundreds of times. Breaking the database down into two tables would mean that you only need to repeat the Employee Number, not the entire name and address. Over the course of a few years, you will save yourself the trouble of entering a tremendous amount of repetitious data.

Of course, you save even more trouble if there are several one-to-many relationships to keep track of, as there often are in an actual business. You have to keep track not just of the number of hours that each employee works but also of other data, such as the benefits they have used and the training courses they have taken. As Chapter 1 of this book pointed out, an employee's moving could cause you a major chore, if you had to change the employee's address in a dozen different files (as businesses had to do when records were kept on paper). On computer, though, you just have to change the address in the Employee file; all the other files have the Employee number, which relates them to the Employee file and lets them use the address that is there.

It is hard to believe that anyone would set up a database like the table illustrated in Figure 12.1, where the repetition is so obvious. But there are less obvious cases where the same principle applies, and (as database consultants sometimes see) people do make this error if they are not deliberately looking for the one-to-many relationship between data.

For example, you might see a database to do mailings and solicit contributions that is made up of a single table with fields for the name and address of each person on the mailing list and fields for the date and amount of the contribution. When the user does the first mailing using this list, it is not obvious how much trouble this database design will cause. You can imagine, though, that when somebody gives a second contribution, the data-entry person would be puzzled for a moment and then would probably decide to create an entire new record for that person. Then, when the mailing labels were generated again, there would be two mailing labels for that person. After a few mailings, the program would have so much repetition that it would be unworkable.

To avoid this sort of problem, you have to look in advance for possible one-to-many relationships and break down the data to avoid repetition.

Common Sense

Finally, when you are designing a relational database, you should always use common sense to decide how far to go in normalizing your data. There are times when it is easier to maintain some repetitive data than it is to break down the database into more tables and have a more complex application to work with.

An obvious example is city, state, and ZIP code information. If you wanted to remove as much repetition from your data as possible, you would keep only the ZIP code in the table that holds the name and address, and you would have a separate table with ZIP codes, cities and states. Then, if two people had the same ZIP code, you would not have to enter the city and state of that ZIP code twice. You could simply type in the ZIP code, and the city and state would be entered automatically, if it had been entered in a previous record.

If you had a very large database, with many people from each ZIP code, it might be worthwhile to normalize it in this way. In most applications, however, where you have only a few ZIP codes with multiple people living in them, the time and disk space you would save by keeping the city and state in a separate table are not worth the extra effort of creating an extra table and an extra relationship.

It is very common to keep the city and state in the same table with the rest of the name and address. This sort of practice is often preferable, even though the data is not perfectly normalized.

▸ The Many-to-Many Relationship

Most of the relational databases that you actually need to create will involve the one-to-many relationship. If you run a membership organization, for example, each member may pay many years' dues. If you run a consulting business, each client may hire you for many jobs. If you want to record your purchases of supplies, each supplier may make many sales.

In all of these cases, you have many transactions with each person you deal with. You will want to break down your database into one table to hold some sort of identification number (member number, client number, or something similar) and the name and address of each person you deal with, and a second table to hold the identification number, and the date and amount of each transaction.

You should be aware, though, that there are also many databases that involve many-to-many relationships. A typical example is the enrollment of students in classes. Each student can take many classes, and each class can have many students enrolled.

Normalizing the Data

A database with a many-to-many relationship is not hard to work with in practice. The first step is to break it down into two different one-to-many relationships.

In the case of students and classes, for example, you would create a database like the simplified one shown in Figure 12.3, where there is one table with data about the students, one table with data about the classes, and one table of enrollments, which links the other two.

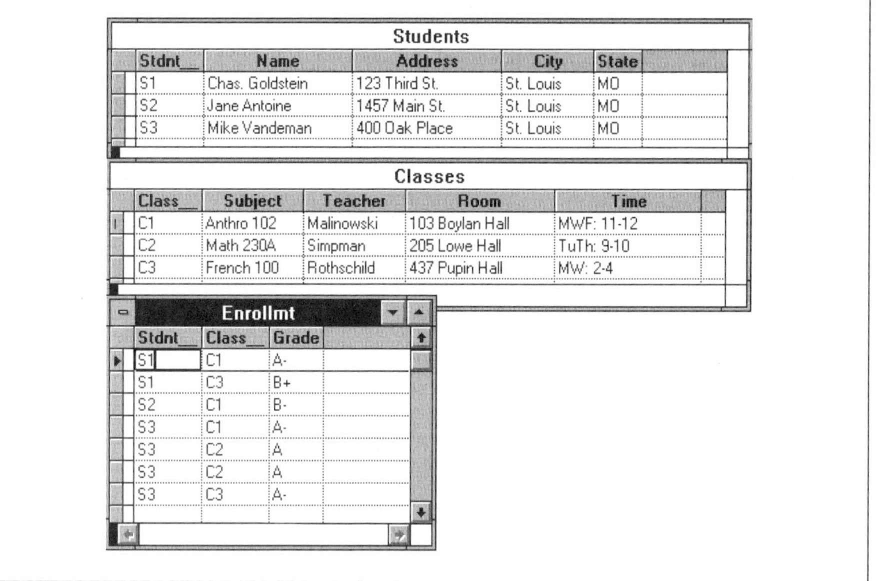

Students

Stdnt_	Name	Address	City	State
S1	Chas. Goldstein	123 Third St.	St. Louis	MO
S2	Jane Antoine	1457 Main St.	St. Louis	MO
S3	Mike Vandeman	400 Oak Place	St. Louis	MO

Classes

Class_	Subject	Teacher	Room	Time
C1	Anthro 102	Malinowski	103 Boylan Hall	MWF: 11-12
C2	Math 230A	Simpman	205 Lowe Hall	TuTh: 9-10
C3	French 100	Rothschild	437 Pupin Hall	MW: 2-4

Enrollmt

Stdnt_	Class_	Grade
S1	C1	A-
S1	C3	B+
S2	C1	B-
S3	C1	A-
S3	C2	A
S3	C2	A
S3	C3	A-

FIGURE 12.3

A database with a many-to-many relationship

You can see in this figure that students are in a one-to-many relationship with enrollments: each student can be enrolled in many classes. Likewise, classes are in a one-to-many relationship with enrollments: each class can enroll many students. The many-to-many relationship between students and classes is contained in these two one-to-many relationships.

In Figure 12.3, you can find all the classes that any student is enrolled in. For example, to find Chas. Goldstein's classes, you first look on the Student table to find that he is student S1. Then you can see on the Enrollmt table that he is enrolled in classes C1 and C3. Finally, looking at the Classes table, you can see that the two classes he is enrolled in are Anthropology 102 and French 100, and you can also see who their instructors are, where they meet, and so on.

Likewise, you can see all the students who are enrolled in any class. French 100, for example, is Class C3, as you can see from the Classes table. Looking in the Enrollmt table, you can see that students S1 and S3 are enrolled in it. And you can look at the Student table to find the names and addresses of these two students.

At a minimum, this sort of "linking" table must have two fields: the primary key fields of the two tables it is linking. The Enrollmt table must

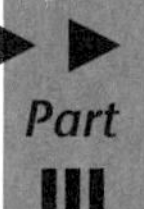

have Stdnt_ and Class_ to link the tables of Students and Classes. In many cases, it also has other fields. The Enrollmt table has one for the Grade, for example, since there is one grade for each student enrolled in each class.

Since you must break it down into two separate one-to-many relationships, managing a database with a many-to-many relationship does not require any skills beyond those you need to manage many-to-one relationships. It is just a more complex variation on the same theme.

This book deals only with multitable databases that have one-to-many relationships. After you have had some practical experience working with these, though, you should not have any trouble applying the same techniques to databases with many-to-many relationships.

It is important that you know in advance when to use each of these two relationship types, in order to avoid confusion in case you ever do run across a database with a many-to-many relationship.

When to Use a Many-to-Many Database

A seemingly minor difference in company policy could change the database from many-to-one to many-to-many.

If your company assigns one salesperson to each of its customers, for example, then you have a typical many-to-one relationship. Each salesperson deals with many customers, but each customer deals with just one salesperson. There should be a separate database for each salesperson: one table would have the customer number and the customer names, addresses and so on, and a second table would have the customer number and the dates and amount of each sale.

On the other hand, if your company lets any of its salespeople deal with any of its customers, then you are working with a many-to-many relationship. Each salesperson deals with many customers and each customer deals with many salespeople.

Because there is a many-to-many relationship, you would have to break up this database into three tables. As shown in Figure 12.4, there would be one to hold the salespeople's social security numbers, names, addresses, and all the other data that you just need to keep once for each salesperson. A second table holds the customer numbers, names, addresses, the contact person, and other data that you need just once for each customer. Finally, one table would record sales: each record contains just the social security number of the salesperson, the Customer number of the customer, the amount of the sale, and the date of the sale. (Notice, incidentally, that this database uses the social security number instead of an employee number, as many real applications do.)

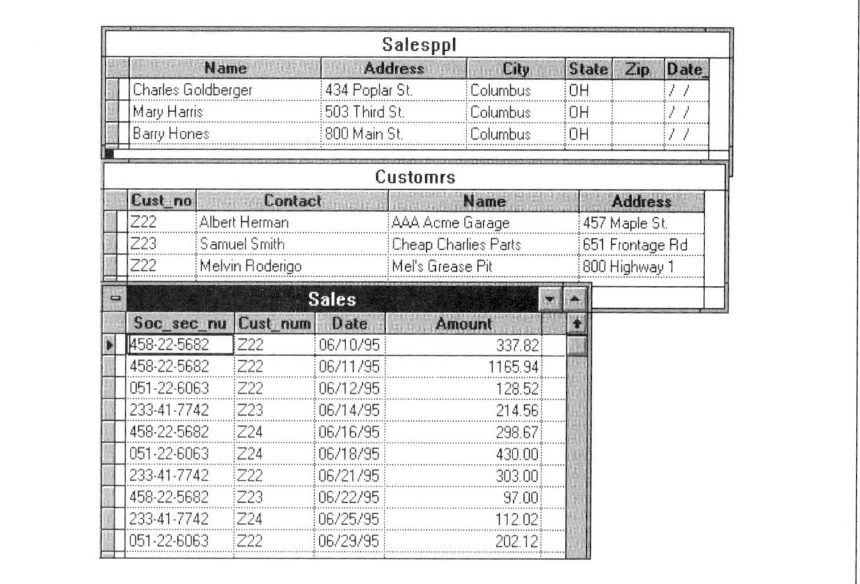

Salesppl

Name	Address	City	State	Zip	Date_
Charles Goldberger	434 Poplar St.	Columbus	OH		/ /
Mary Harris	503 Third St.	Columbus	OH		/ /
Barry Hones	800 Main St.	Columbus	OH		/ /

Customrs

Cust_no	Contact	Name	Address
Z22	Albert Herman	AAA Acme Garage	457 Maple St.
Z23	Samuel Smith	Cheap Charlies Parts	651 Frontage Rd
Z22	Melvin Roderigo	Mel's Grease Pit	800 Highway 1

Sales

Soc_sec_nu	Cust_num	Date	Amount
458-22-5682	Z22	06/10/95	337.82
458-22-5682	Z22	06/11/95	1165.94
051-22-6063	Z22	06/12/95	128.52
233-41-7742	Z23	06/14/95	214.56
458-22-5682	Z24	06/16/95	298.67
051-22-6063	Z24	06/18/95	430.00
233-41-7742	Z22	06/21/95	303.00
458-22-5682	Z23	06/22/95	97.00
233-41-7742	Z24	06/25/95	112.02
051-22-6063	Z22	06/29/95	202.12

FIGURE 12.4

A change in policy requires a many-to-many relationship.

How to Use a Many-to-Many Database

In using this database, you would probably want to look at the two one-to-many relationships separately. For example, you might want one report to calculate the commissions that you owe; you would need the name and address of each salesperson plus the date and amounts of that person's sales for the month. To generate this report, you would only need to use the Salesppl table and the Sales table, and you would list many sales for each employee.

Looking at Figure 12.4, you can begin to appreciate the work that you save by computerizing. It would be impossible to break down the data in this way and to keep track of so complex a database without the help of a computer. Imagine trying to track down all of Mary Harris' sales by looking through a long Sales file for every occurrence of her social security number. If you were still keeping records on paper, you would

have to duplicate the entry of some data. You might have to enter each sale once in the file of the salesperson who made the sale, so that you could produce a report to determine the employee's commission. Then you might want to enter the same sale in the file of the customer who made the purchase, so that you could produce a report to track the trends of your sales to each of your customers.

On computer, though, it is easy to produce a report on your employee's sales from a multitable database such as this. You would simply fill out a report form to generate a report from the Salesppl and the Sales tables, as you will learn to do in this section.

Many-to-many relationships sound complicated when you describe them, but they are clearer when you are actually working with concrete cases that you know about—with your own salespeople and customers, for example. It is best not to add this extra complication when you are first learning to use multitable databases. But once you have experience working with multitable databases based on one-to-many relationships, you should not have much trouble applying the same skills to many-to-many relationships.

▸▸ Other Types of Relationships

A few other relationship types are possible in addition to the two fundamental types that you have looked at, many-to-one and many-to-many relationships. These should be easy to understand based on the principles that you have already learned.

▸ One-to-One Relationships

Visual FoxPro and other database management systems all let you create *one-to-one relationships*.

For example, you could conceivably keep employee names and addresses in one table and use a second table to hold the date each person was hired, a memo on that person, and other data that is in a one-to-one relationship with name and address. You would have to add an employee number to both files and relate them to see the name of the person a particular date or memo applied to.

This is not something you should normally do. When there is a one-to-one relationship among fields, it is usually best to keep all the data in one table. If you want to view only some of the fields—only the name and address, for example—you can create a query or use a SET FIELDS command to display them. This is usually much easier than keeping the data in several tables and relating them.

There are cases, though, in which you might want to create a one-to-one relation between two files that you had not anticipated using together, assuming they have some field, such as social security number, that you can use as the key. For example, if you have a list of prospective customers that includes social security numbers but not telephone numbers, and another larger list (such as a mailing list of a very large company) that includes social security and telephone numbers, you could join the two to produce a result with all the records in the first list and matching telephone numbers from the second list. In cases like this, one-to-one relationships can be very useful to merge data that you get from different sources.

One-to-Many Relationships

One-to-many relationships are identical to many-to-one relationships in terms of the data they handle and how the data is normalized. For example, you could take the two sample tables we are working with, enter the same data in them, and then relate them in either a many-to-one or a one-to-many relationship.

The only difference is your choice of which table to use as the *parent table* and which one to use as the *child table.* (The parent is the table on which the relationship is based, and the child is where we look up records that are related to each record in the parent table.)

It is normally best to use a many-to-one relationship—that is, to make the "many" table the parent. For example, it is simplest to use the Wages table as the parent table and the Emplist table as the child table, because you can find one and only one record in the Emplist table that is related to each record in the Wages table. Thus, you can join the two tables in a table like the one shown in Figure 12.5, where each record has data in each field. It is usually easiest to work with this sort of joined table.

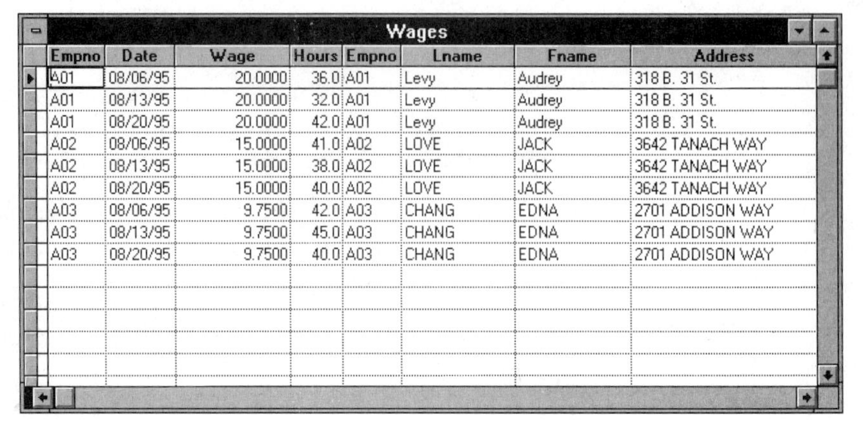

Wages

Empno	Date	Wage	Hours	Empno	Lname	Fname	Address
A01	08/06/95	20.0000	36.0	A01	Levy	Audrey	318 B. 31 St.
A01	08/13/95	20.0000	32.0	A01	Levy	Audrey	318 B. 31 St.
A01	08/20/95	20.0000	42.0	A01	Levy	Audrey	318 B. 31 St.
A02	08/06/95	15.0000	41.0	A02	LOVE	JACK	3642 TANACH WAY
A02	08/13/95	15.0000	38.0	A02	LOVE	JACK	3642 TANACH WAY
A02	08/20/95	15.0000	40.0	A02	LOVE	JACK	3642 TANACH WAY
A03	08/06/95	9.7500	42.0	A03	CHANG	EDNA	2701 ADDISON WAY
A03	08/13/95	9.7500	45.0	A03	CHANG	EDNA	2701 ADDISON WAY
A03	08/20/95	9.7500	40.0	A03	CHANG	EDNA	2701 ADDISON WAY

FIGURE 12.5

A many-to-one relationship

On the other hand, if you used the same data in a one-to-many relationship, you would use the Emplist table as the parent table and Wages as the child table. You could have any number of records in the child table for each record in the parent table, from zero up to a very large number. If you joined the two tables, you would get a result like the one in Figure 12.6.

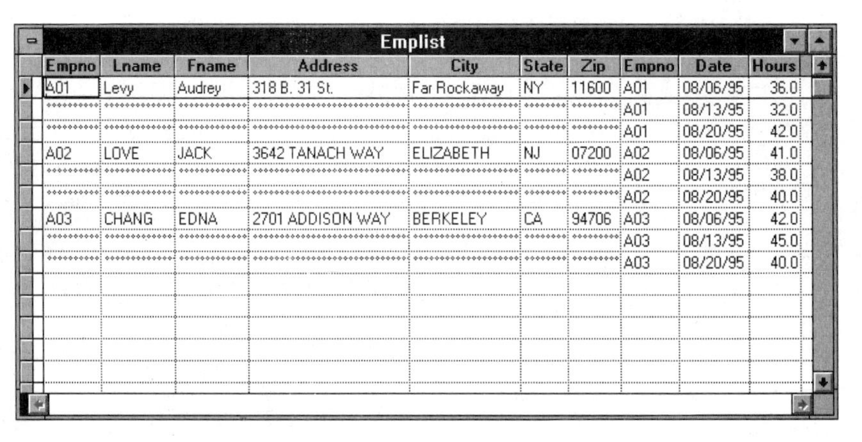

Emplist

Empno	Lname	Fname	Address	City	State	Zip	Empno	Date	Hours
A01	Levy	Audrey	318 B. 31 St.	Far Rockaway	NY	11600	A01	08/06/95	36.0
							A01	08/13/95	32.0
							A01	08/20/95	42.0
A02	LOVE	JACK	3642 TANACH WAY	ELIZABETH	NJ	07200	A02	08/06/95	41.0
							A02	08/13/95	38.0
							A02	08/20/95	40.0
A03	CHANG	EDNA	2701 ADDISON WAY	BERKELEY	CA	94706	A03	08/06/95	42.0
							A03	08/13/95	45.0
							A03	08/20/95	40.0

FIGURE 12.6

A one-to-many relationship

The one-to-many relationship is not as easy to use as the many-to-one relationship for most purposes, but there are times when it is better.

For example, if you wanted to produce a report on wages with the name and address of the employee at the top of each page and all of the wage records for that employee listed below, it would be easiest to use a one-to-many relationship.

More Complex Data

There are also many cases in business applications where data is more complex than any of the relationships you have looked at so far. However, you can always analyze these cases by looking for many-to-one and many-to-many relationships, and ultimately breaking them up into a large number of many-to-one relationships.

Invoices for sales of products are a typical example. There can be many invoices for each customer but only one customer for each invoice. This is a typical many-to-one relationship. You need a Customer table to hold basic data on each customer and an invoice number. You also need an Invoice table that includes the customer number, the invoice number, the date, and other data on each sale.

There can also be many products sold on each invoice, and many invoices for each product. This is a typical many-to-many relationship, which can be broken down into two many-to-one relationships. To link the Invoice table and a Products table, which has the product number, name, description, price, and other data on each product, you need an Invoice Line table. This would include the invoice number, the product number, the quantity purchased of that product, and perhaps other data that applies to the line, such as a specially negotiated discount for this sale.

To produce an invoice you would create a report, based on the Invoice Line table, that includes only those records in this table that have the invoice number you specify.

To produce the heading of the report, you would find the record in the Invoice table that has this Invoice number. The date from this record would go at the top of the report. You also use the Customer number from this record of the Invoice table to look up the record with this number in the Customer table, which gives you the Customer name and address to place at the top of the report. The date from the Invoice table also goes at the top of the report.

Listed below this heading, in the detail band of the report, are all the products purchased. To find these, use a query to isolate all the records with this invoice number in the Invoice Line table. Use the product number in each of these records to look up the name, description, and price of each product in the Products table, and include these fields on each invoice line. In addition, include the quantity purchased (and discount, if any) from the Invoice Line table on each line, and add an expression that multiplies quantity by price (applying any discount that may be in effect) to get total price for that line.

Finally, in the summary band of the report, include an expression that sums the total prices calculated for all the lines of the report to calculate the total bill for the entire invoice. The summary band can also add tax and shipping.

Though this invoice sounds complicated, it is not difficult to work with once you relate all the tables properly. You must relate the Invoice table with the Customer table using the customer number (Custno) field as a key, relate the Invoice table with the Invoice Line table using the Invoice number as the key, and relate the Invoice Line table with the Products table using the Product number as the key. All of these are many-to-one relationships.

▸▸ Preparing the Sample Application

In the following chapters, you will learn several ways of relating tables. In all of them, you will use the same sample application, which lets you record wages of the employees whom you have already entered in the Emplist table. In this section, you will create the tables used in this sample application, so you can use them in exercises in the chapters that follow.

▸ Analyzing the Problem

As you learned earlier in this chapter, recording the employees' wages involves a many-to-one relationship, because each employee can earn many weeks of wages. Thus, in addition to the Emplist table that you have been working with so far, you must create a Wages table.

As with other many-to-one relationships, there may be any number of records for each employee in the Wages table, including zero records for a new employee who has not yet been paid. There must be one and only one record for each employee in the Emplist table.

The Wages Table

As you saw in the examples earlier in this chapter, the Wages table includes an employee number field (Empno), which is a foreign key used to relate it to the Emplist table. It also includes fields to hold the Date of the week whose wages are stored in the record, the number of Hours worked that week, and the hourly Wage. There is no need to record the total earned, as it can be calculated by multiplying hours worked and the hourly wage.

Why do we have to include a field for the hourly wage in this table, rather than keeping the employee's wage in the Emplist table? This is necessary for most businesses because the hourly wage can change.

Some businesses may be set up in a way that only requires the hourly wage to be stored in the Emplist table. If you gave employees raises only at the end of the year, for example, and if you archived old records in both tables at the end of each year and kept a separate Wages table for each year, you could keep the hourly wages only in the Emplist table. If you wanted to look up how much an employee earned in a certain week several years ago, you could do so by using the archived database for that year.

In each of these archived databases, there would be a one-to-one relationship between employees and hourly wages. Each employee could earn only one hourly wage for the year. Thus, you could store the amount of the hourly wage in the Emplist table.

If you keep the same database over many years and give employees raises at different times of the year, however, the employee is in a one-to-many relationship with the hourly wage. Each employee can earn many different hourly wages over the years.

The hourly wage for each week must be kept in a separate table from Emplist. If it were in the Emplist table, and you changed it when the employee got a raise, you would no longer be able to calculate how much that employee earned during past pay periods.

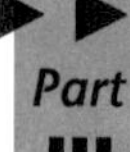

Notice that the hourly wage is also in a one-to-many relationship with the weekly wage, because each worker earns the same hourly wage for many weeks, and so the same figures for hourly wages will be repeated in record after record of the Wages table. It would be possible to eliminate this repetition by keeping the hourly wage in a separate table and relating it to the Wages table, but this is one of those cases where common sense must take precedence over the rules of database normalization. The extra complexity involved, and the extra work of entering another primary and foreign key field to create an additional relationship, would obviously outweigh the effort saved by not entering the hourly wage for each week.

Thus, the hourly wage for each week should be kept in the Wages table, in addition to the date, the hours worked, and the employee number.

The Emplist Table

A Current Wage field should also be kept in the Emplist table. When an employee's wage is raised, there is no logical place to record the raise in the Wages table. The raise must be recorded in the Emplist table.

When each week's wages are entered, the Current Wage value from the Emplist table is entered into the (hourly) Wage field of the Wages table.

The Emplist table must also have an Empno field added to hold the employee number, which is used as a primary key.

These are the only changes needed in the Emplist table.

Using an Index to Create a Primary Key

Visual FoxPro includes two index types that can be used for the primary key field. These can be selected from the Index panel of the Table Designer, as shown in Figure 12.7.

- **Primary:** This type is added to the list only when the table is part of a FoxPro database. (As discussed in Chapter 16, the term *database* in Visual FoxPro 3.0 refers to a particular file type in addition to its more general meaning.) Visual FoxPro does not allow repetition of values in this field, so it may be used as a primary key. It can also be used to create persistent relationships with other tables in the database.

FIGURE 12.7

Types of indexes

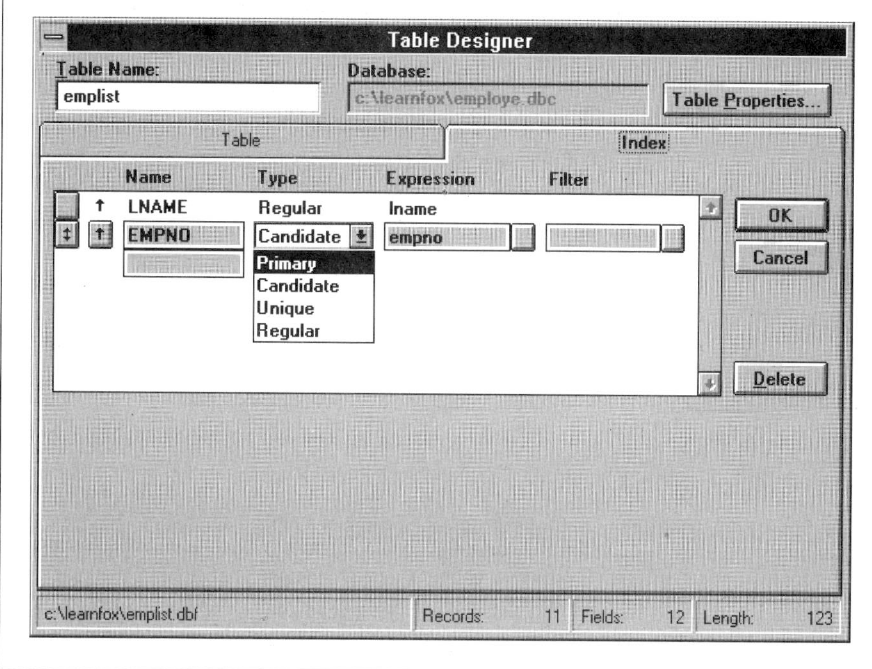

- **Candidate:** This type is available whether or not the table is part of a database. Visual FoxPro does not allow repetition of values in the field, so it can later be converted to the primary key index if the table is added to a database.

The illustration shows the Table Designer as it is displayed when you are modifying the structure of a table that you have added to a Visual FoxPro database. You'll learn about other features of this form of the Table Designer in Chapter 16.

When you use a Visual FoxPro database in that chapter, you will create a primary index for the Employee Number field. For now, you can create a Candidate index for the Employee Number, which also prevents you from entering repetitive data in this primary key field.

Creating and Modifying the Tables

Before relating the two tables, you must create a Wages table with the employee number, date, and wage, and you must add an employee

number field to the Emplist table, which already has the basic data on employees.

Creating a Wages Table

First, create and enter data in the Wages table as follows:

1. Choose File ➤ New, select the Table radio button, and click the New File button. When Visual FoxPro displays the Create dialog box to let you name the table, enter the name **WAGES**.

2. Visual FoxPro displays the Table Designer. Create a database with the fields shown in Figure 12.8. Then select OK.

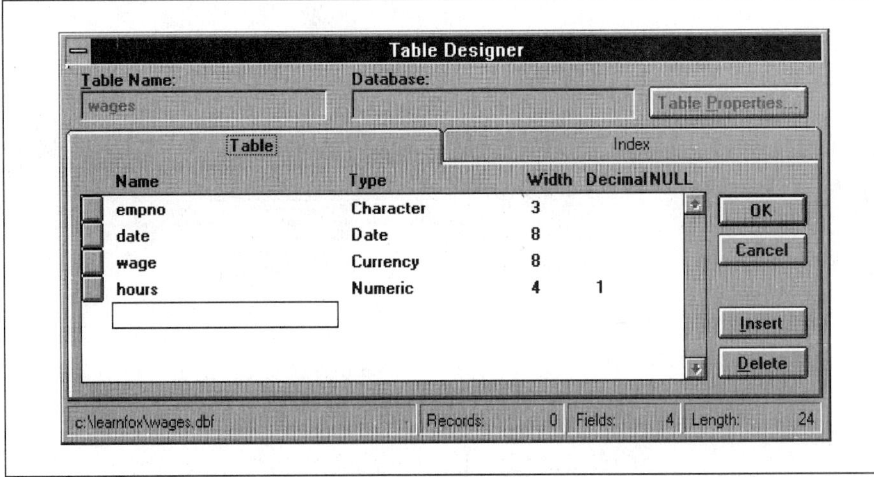

FIGURE 12.8 ▸

Structure of the Wages table

3. Visual FoxPro asks if you want to input data records now. Select Yes. When the Wages window appears, enter the following sample records, whose use will become clear to you in a moment:

Empno:	A01
Date:	08/06/95
Wage:	20.00
Hours:	36.0

Empno:	A01
Date:	08/13/95
Wage:	20.00
Hours:	32.0

Empno:	A01
Date:	08/20/95
Wage:	20.00
Hours:	42.0

Empno:	A02
Date:	08/06/95
Wage:	15.00
Hours:	41.0

Empno:	A02
Date:	08/13/95
Wage:	15.00
Hours:	38.0

Empno:	A02
Date:	08/20/95
Wage:	15.00
Hours:	40.0

That's three weeks of wages for two employees, as shown in Figure 12.9. Close the Wages window.

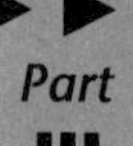

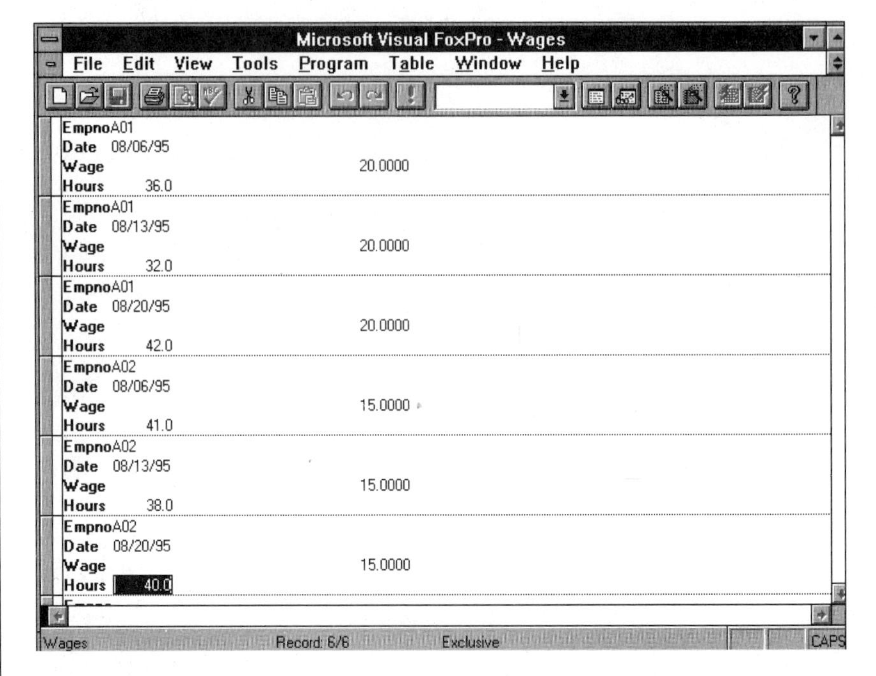

FIGURE 12.9

Data entered in the Wages table

Modifying the Emplist Table

Now, modify the structure of the Emplist table to add fields for employee number and wages, as follows.

1. First, open the Emplist table. Choose File ➤ Open. In the Open dialog box, select Tables from the List Files of Type drop-down list and if necessary open the LEARNFOX folder. Then double-click Emplist in the file list.

2. Enter **MODI STRU** in the Command window to display the Table Designer. Then move the highlight to the Fname field and select Insert to add a new field. Change the name of the field that is added from NewField to **empno**, keep its type as Character, and change its width from 10 to 3.

3. Next, scroll down and click the Probation field. Then click the Insert button to add a new field above it. Change its name from NewField to **Wage** and select Currency as its Type, as shown in

Figure 12.10. Click OK to close the Table Designer, and click Yes to make the structure changes permanent.

FIGURE 12.10

Modifying the structure of the Emplist table

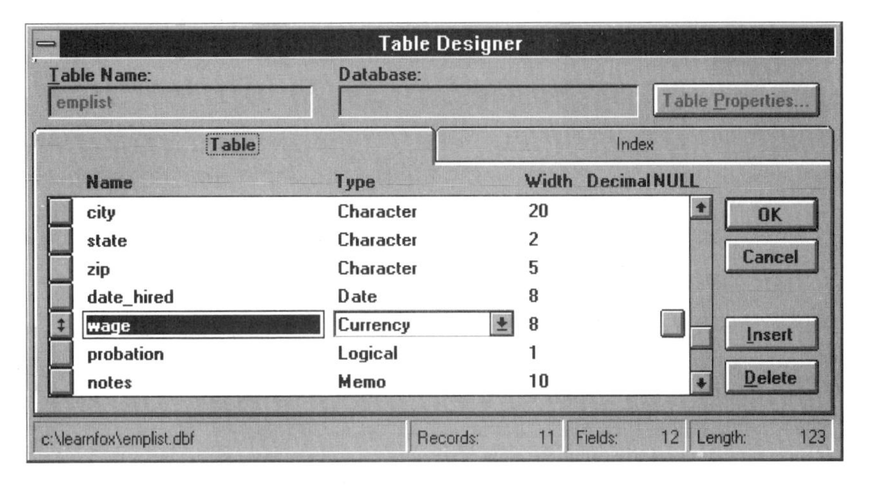

Now, you need to add employee numbers and wage amounts to the Emplist table. Since this is the file on the "one" end of the one-to-many relation, the employee numbers must be unique.

1. Enter **BROWSE** to display it in a Browse window.
2. Add the numbers from A01 to A11, as employee numbers, as shown in Figure 12.11, and also add the wages shown in this figure. In the figure, the Wage field has been placed next to the Empno field, so both are visible, but you do not have to move the fields when you enter data. When you are done, close the Browse window, saving the changes.
3. Finally, to create an index on the primary key field, enter **MODI STRU**. Click the Index panel of the Table Designer. As the name of the new index, enter **EMPNO**. As the type, select Candidate. As the Expression, enter **empno**. Click OK to close the Table Designer and click Yes to make the changes permanent.

Now you have the sample tables that you need for the exercises on relational databases.

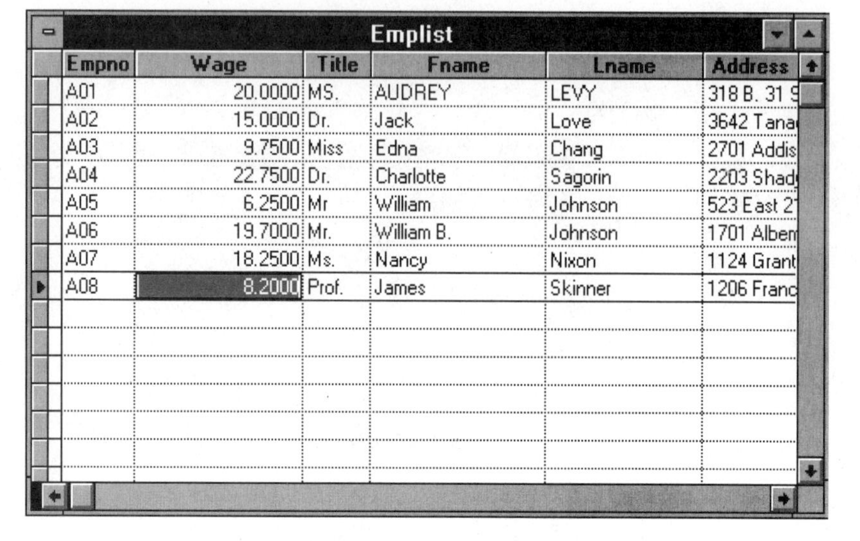

Emplist

Empno	Wage	Title	Fname	Lname	Address
A01	20.0000	MS.	AUDREY	LEVY	318 B. 31 S
A02	15.0000	Dr.	Jack	Love	3642 Tana
A03	9.7500	Miss	Edna	Chang	2701 Addis
A04	22.7500	Dr.	Charlotte	Sagorin	2203 Shad
A05	6.2500	Mr	William	Johnson	523 East 2
A06	19.7000	Mr.	William B.	Johnson	1701 Alber
A07	18.2500	Ms.	Nancy	Nixon	1124 Grant
A08	8.2000	Prof.	James	Skinner	1206 Franc

FIGURE 12.11

Entering new data in the Emplist table

▸▸ To Sum Up

In this chapter, you learned enough about database theory to understand when relational databases must be used and to use commonsense methods to normalize data so it can be stored in multiple tables.

You also created the tables for a sample application, which you will use in the next four chapters to explore the different ways that Visual FoxPro lets you work with relational databases, beginning with the simplest and proceeding to the most sophisticated.

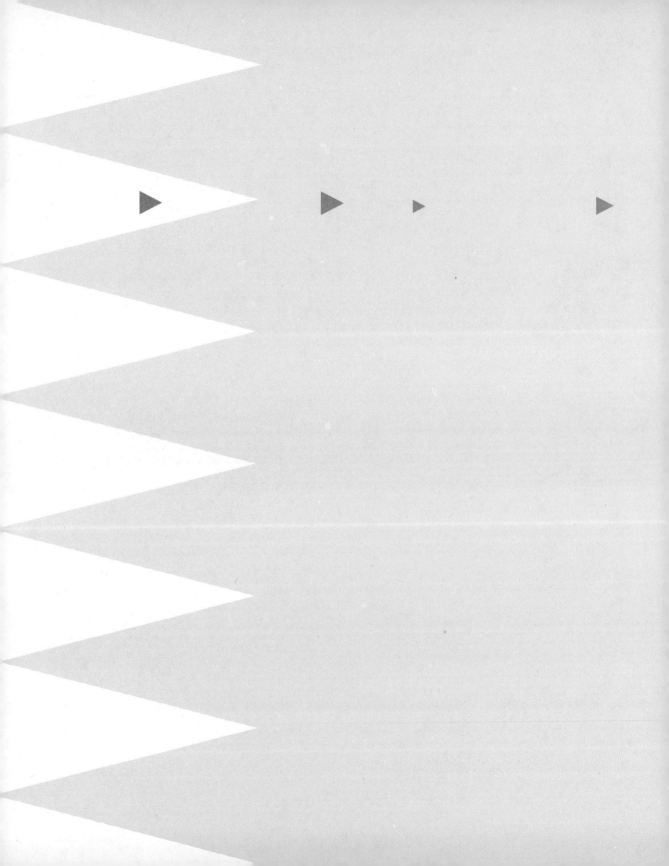

CHAPTER 13

Relational Wizardry

▸▸ FAST TRACK

▶ ***To use the One-to-Many Form Wizard,*** ***361***

use the first step to choose the fields from the "one" table, which is the Main table of the form. Use the second step to choose the fields from the "many" table, which is the related table of the form. Use the third step to specify the relationship between the two tables. The result is a form that has the selected fields from one record of the "one" table in its top half, and the selected fields from all the related records of the "many" table listed in its bottom half.

▶ ***To use the Query Wizard with a relational database,*** ***366***

add and select fields from multiple tables in step 1 of the Query Wizard. When you do this, you can access Step 2 of the Wizard, which lets you define the relationships among tables. Use the drop-down controls to select the fields in two tables that the relationship is based on, and click the Add button to add them to the list below.

▶ ***To use the One-to-Many Report Wizard,*** 370

as with the One-to-Many Form Wizard, use the first step to choose the fields from the "one" table, use the Wizard's second step to choose the fields from the "many" table, and use the third step to specify the relationship between the two tables. In addition, specify style and layout as you do with the ordinary Report Wizard. The result is a report that has the selected fields from the "one" table listed one above another, with the name to the left of each, with the selected fields from all related records of the "many" table listed in columnar layout below each record of the "one" table.

▶ ***To create many-to-one reports,*** 373

create a query based on a many-to-one relationship. Display it in the Query Designer. Choose Query ➤ Query Destination and send the result of the query to a report.

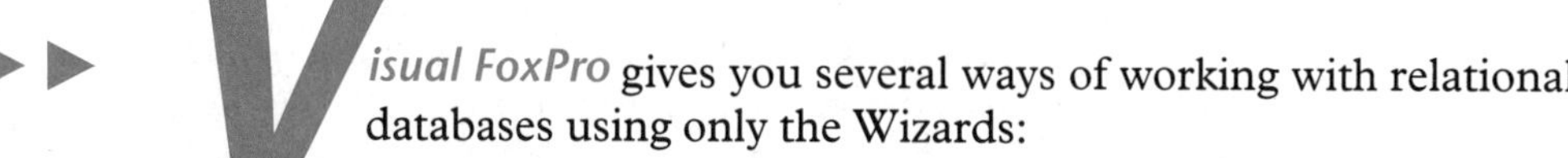

Visual FoxPro gives you several ways of working with relational databases using only the Wizards:

- **The Form Wizard:** You can use this tool to join the tables in a one-to-many relationship, producing a form that has a record from the "one" table with all matching records from the "many" table below it. For example, you can have the name and address from the Emplist table in the top half of the form, and all the wage records for that employee listed in the bottom half.
- **The Query Wizard:** You can use this tool to join the tables in a many-to-one relationship, so that the result has fields from the "one" table matched with each record from the "many" table. For example, you can display all records from the Wages table and have the name and address from the Emplist table added to each record.
- **The Report Wizard:** You can use this tool to join the tables in a one-to-many relationship, producing a report that lists each record from the "one" table with all the records from the "many" table below it—for example, the names and addresses from the Emplist table, with all the records from the Wages table below each.

These Wizards alone are enough to let you manage a simple relational database, such as the sample database you have created to record data on employee wages.

▸▸ Entering and Viewing Data Using the Form Wizard

The One-to-Many Form Wizard displays fields from a record in the "one" table in its top half, and corresponding records from the "many" table in its bottom half. For example, it might display an employee's name and address in its top half and all the wage records for that employee in its bottom half.

Because this form is laid out as a typical one-to-many database, as described in Chapter 12, all records in the "one" table are displayed. This table is called the *main table* of the form, and the "many" table is called the *related table*.

The buttons on the form that is generated, which let you add or edit data, apply to either the main table or the related table—whichever the cursor is in at the time you click the button. Thus, if you use this form to enter data in the "many" table, you can be sure the data is valid; you would only enter a new record in the "many" table if you can use the form to display a corresponding record in the one table.

▸ Using the Wizard

The One-to-Many Form Wizard is similar to the Form Wizard that was covered in Chapter 5. The differences should be easy to understand in light of the discussion of database theory in Chapter 12.

Choosing Fields from the Main Table

Step 1, shown in Figure 13.1, lets you choose fields from the main table. Use it in the same way you've selected fields in other Visual FoxPro dialog boxes. Select the table from the list or use the ... button to the right of the control and use the Open dialog box to select it. Then use the Field Picker to select which fields to include.

Remember that the main table must be the table on the "one" side of the one-to-many relationship—the Emplist table in our example. One record from this table will be displayed in the top half of the form.

FIGURE 13.1

Step 1 of the One-to-Many Form Wizard—choosing fields from the main table

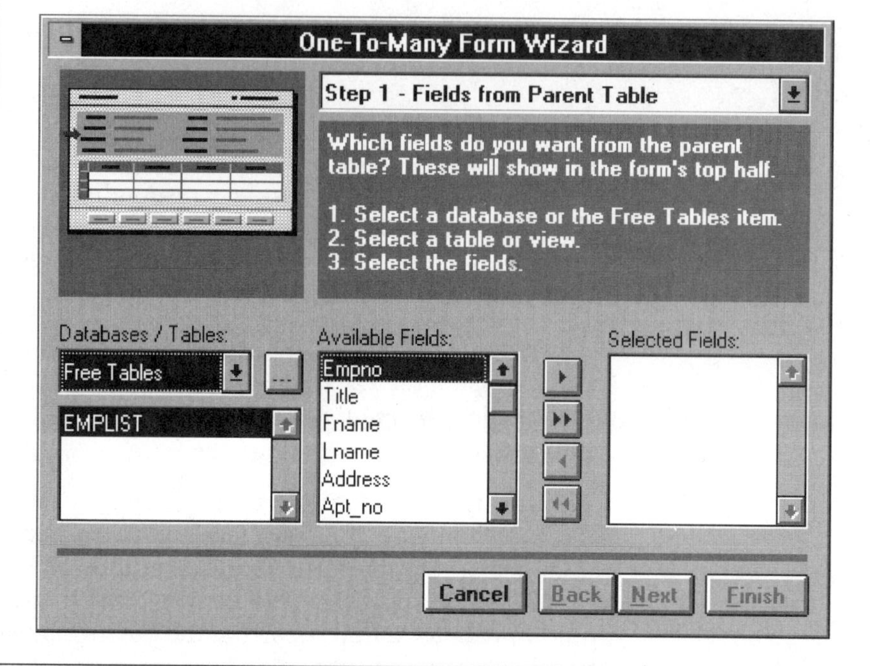

Choosing Fields from the Related Table

Step 2, shown in Figure 13.2, lets you choose fields from the related table. Use it in same way that you use Step 1, but choose the table that is on the "many" side of the one-to-many relationship—the Wages table in our example. All of the records from this table that correspond to the record in the top half will be displayed in the bottom half of the form.

Specifying the Relationship

Use Step 3, shown in Figure 13.3, to specify the relationship. Simply use the drop-down controls to select the key fields from the two tables.

Remaining Steps

The remaining steps are the same as those of the Form Wizard, covered in Chapter 5.

Step 4 lets you choose a Style, such as Standard, Chiseled, or Shadowed, and to choose either Text buttons, Picture buttons, or no buttons.

FIGURE 13.2

Step 2 of the One-to-Many Form Wizard —choosing fields from the related table

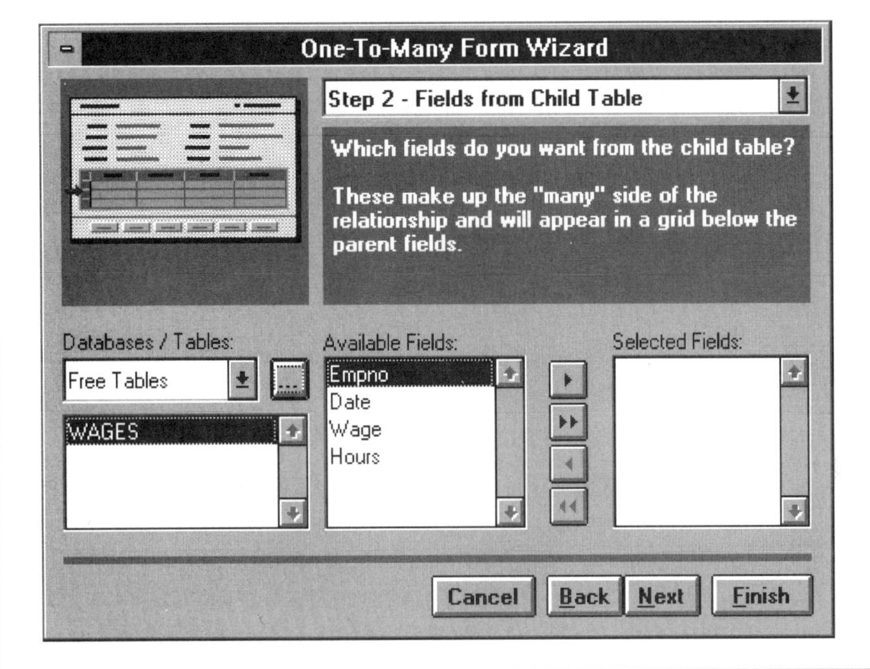

Step 5 lets you specify sort order. Only fields from the main table are available.

The final step lets you enter the title and generate the form.

Creating a Sample Form

Try creating a form for your sample applications:

NOTE

Chapter 12 included exercises where you modified the Emplist table, created a new Wages table, and entered some sample data in them. If you have not yet done so, do the exercises in the section "Creating and Modifying the Tables" at the end of that chapter, before you go on with the exercises in this chapter.

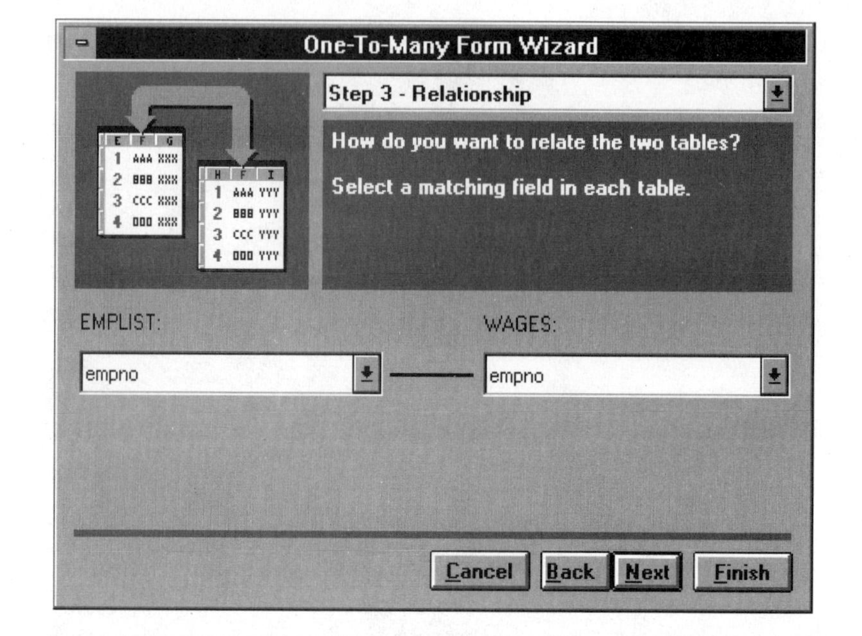

FIGURE 13.3

Step 3 of the One-to-Many Form Wizard —specifying the relationship

1. Choose File ➤ New, select the Form radio button, and click the Wizards button. In the Select Wizards dialog box, select One-to-Many Form Wizard.

2. In Step 1 of the Wizard, click the … button to the right of the Database/Tables control and use the Open dialog box to choose Emplist as the main table. Double-click Empno, Fname, Lname, and Wage to add them to the Selected Fields list. Click Next.

3. In Step 2, click the … button to the right of the Database/Tables control and choose Wages as the related table. Double-click Empno, Date, Hours, and Wage to add them to the Selected Fields list in that order. Click Next.

4. In Step 3 the Wizard suggests that the Empno field from both tables be used as the basis of the relationship. Keep this relationship. In Step 4 keep the default style, and go to Step 5 to specify the sort order.

5. Double-click Lname and Fname to use them as the basis of the sort order. Click Next to go to the final step.

6. As the title of the form, enter **Wage Data**. Select the Save And Run Form radio button, and click Finish. In the Save As dialog box, enter **Wagedata** as the form's name, and click Save.

7. After a moment, Visual FoxPro generates the form shown in Figure 13.4. Try using it to view the sample data and enter new data. Most important, try adding a new record to the "many" table by placing the cursor in that table and clicking the Add button. Close the form when you are done.

FIGURE 13.4

The form for wage data entry

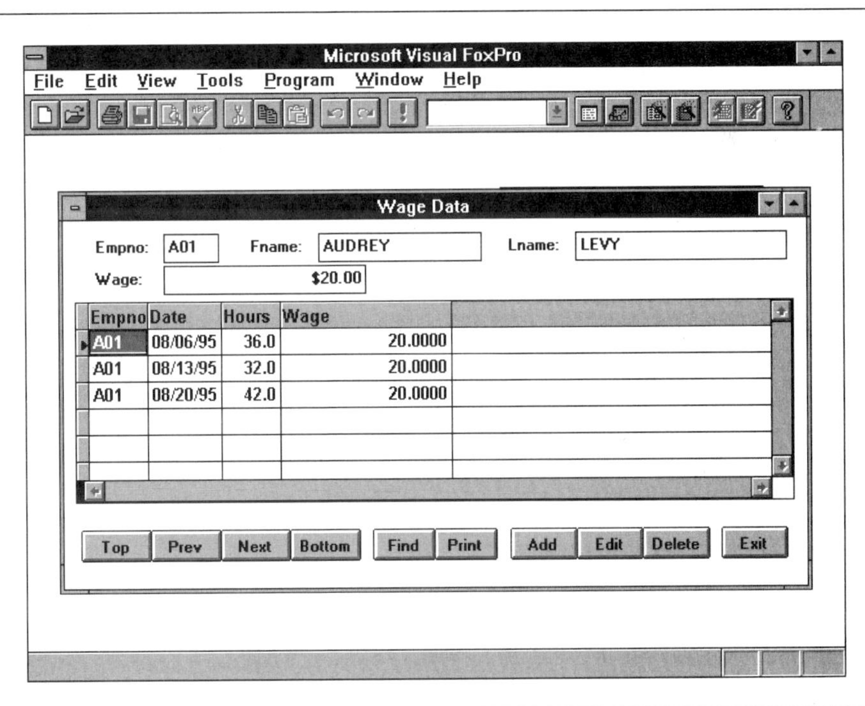

You can see that, with the addition of this form, you can guarantee that data you enter in both the "one" and the "many" table is valid, in keeping with the rules you learned in Chapter 12:

- **The "one" table:** For data to be valid, each record must have a unique entry in the Primary Key field. By using this field as the basis of a Candidate index, you guarantee that its data is valid, regardless of how you enter it.

- **The "many" table:** For data to be valid, each record must have a value in its key field that corresponds to a value already entered in the key field of the "one" table. You can be sure that its data is valid by using the one-to-many form for all data entry in the many table.

▸▸ **WARNING**

There is danger to the integrity of your data if you edit the key field in a record of the "one" table that already has corresponding data in the "many" table. For example, if you change the value of Empno A01 in the Employee table, and there are already entries with Empno A01 in the Wages table, you will no longer know which employee these wage records apply to. To avoid this problem, it is best never to edit the value in the key field of the "one" table. If you must do so, edit it using the one-to-many form, so you can be sure that there are no corresponding records in the "many" table.

▸▸ Using the Query Wizard to Work with Relational Databases

It is very easy to use the Query Wizard to display the data in a relational database.

You use it to create a many-to-one relationship. Each line in the query result contains data from a record in the "many" table and matching details from the "one" table. For example, a query of your sample application would contain a record with the data from each record in the Wages table, with details from the Emplist table, such as name and address, added to each.

▸ Relating the Tables

In general, you use the Query Wizard with relational databases in the same way that you learned to use it with single tables in Chapter 4.

However, in the first step, you add two or more tables to the Table list and select the fields from both that you want to include in the query's result.

When you include multiple tables in a query, you can access Step 2 of the Query Wizard, shown in Figure 13.5, which you use to relate them. Use the drop-down controls to choose the fields that are the basis of the relationship, and click the Add button to add them to the list below.

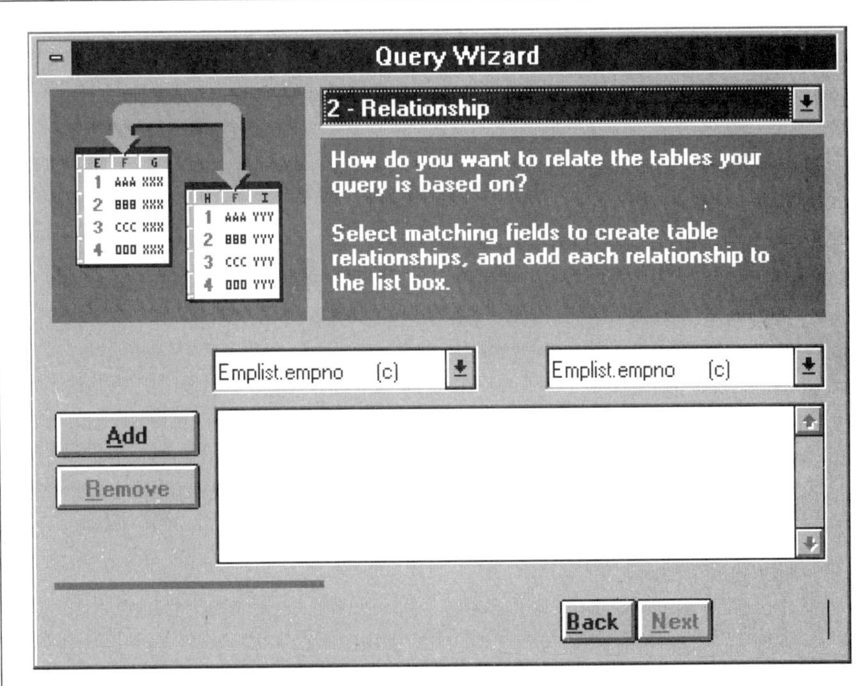

FIGURE 13.5

Specifying a relationship

You can also specify multiple relationships using this Wizard. In the example of a many-to-many database discussed in Chapter 12, there was one table for Students, one for Classes, and one for Enrollments. To work with this database using the Wizard, you would specify the relationships both between the Students and Enrollments tables and between the Classes and Enrollments tables, adding both relationships to the list below. You can include fields from all these tables in the result.

Once you have related tables and specified which fields to create, you use the Query Wizard just as you would if you were working with a single table.

▶ Creating a Sample Relational Query

Now, try using the Query Wizard to create a query that displays the weekly wages of your employees.

1. Choose File ➤ New, select the Query radio button, and click the Wizards button. When Visual FoxPro displays the Wizard Selection dialog box, click the Query Wizard button.

2. In the first step of the Wizard, click the button to the right of the Database/Tables control and use the Open dialog box to add the Emplist table to the list; then click this button again and add the Wages table to the list.

3. Click the Emplist table to display its fields, and double-click the Emplist.fname and Emplist.lname fields to add them to the Selected Fields list. Then click the Wages table, and double-click the Wages.date, Wages.wage, and Wages.hours fields to add them to the Selected Fields list, as shown in Figure 13.6. Then click Next.

4. Visual FoxPro displays the next dialog box of the Wizard, which lets you specify how the tables are related. It suggests the Emplist.empno and Wages.empno fields as the common key, because they have the same name in both tables. Click the Add button, to display the relationship, as shown in Figure 13.7. Then click Next.

5. At this point in an actual query, you might want to use the Sort Order or Filtering step to sort or filter the data. In this exercise, you can just click the Finish button to go to the final step, and click the Preview button to view the result of the query, as shown in Figure 13.8.

6. Click OK to close the Preview window. In the final dialog box, click Finish. Visual FoxPro displays the Save As dialog box; enter the name **Wage_emp** and click Save.

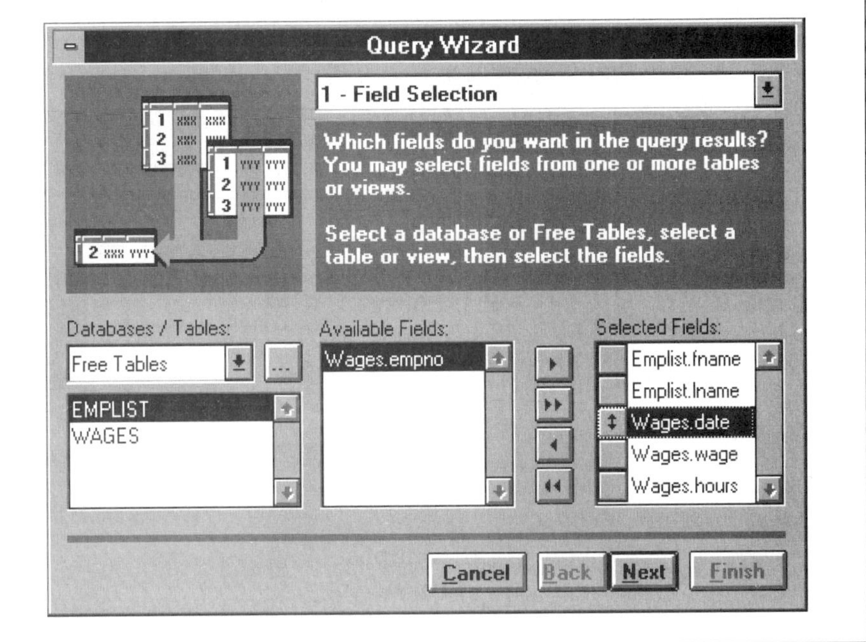

FIGURE 13.6

Including fields from multiple tables in the query

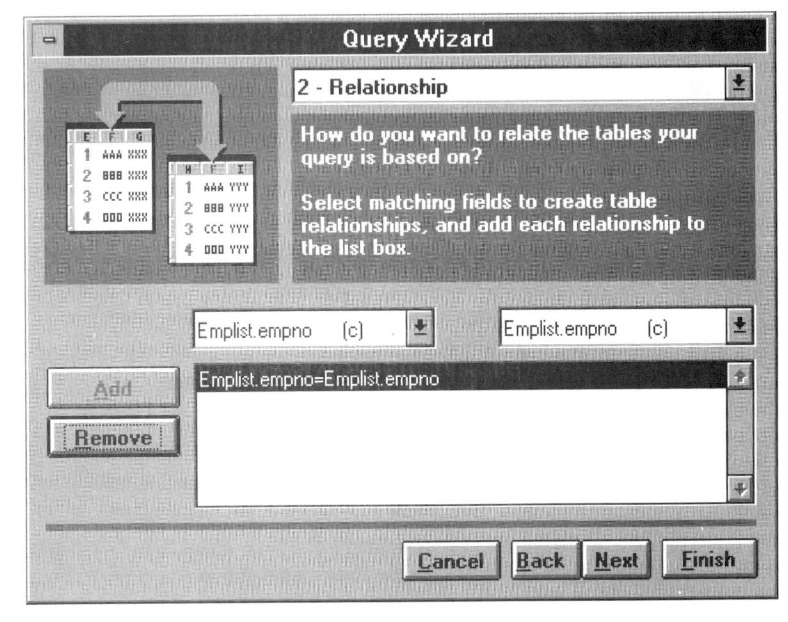

FIGURE 13.7

Defining the relationship

FIGURE 13.8

The result of the query

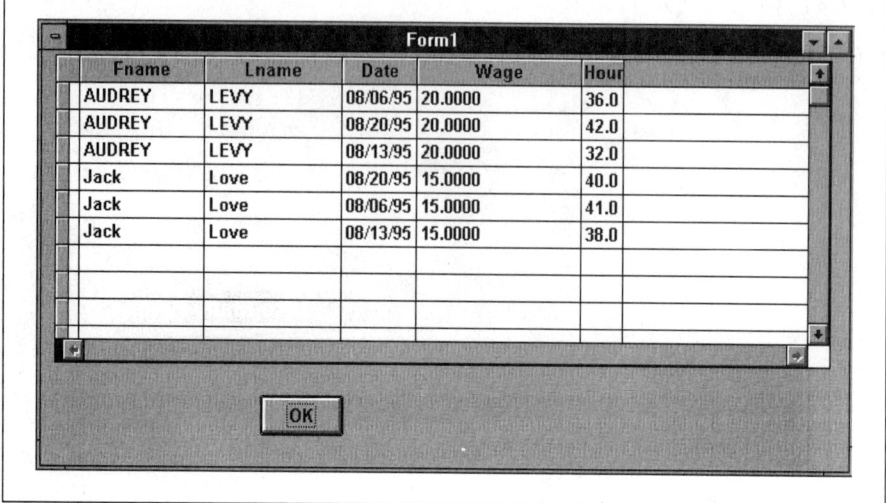

Fname	Lname	Date	Wage	Hour
AUDREY	LEVY	08/06/95	20.0000	36.0
AUDREY	LEVY	08/20/95	20.0000	42.0
AUDREY	LEVY	08/13/95	20.0000	32.0
Jack	Love	08/20/95	15.0000	40.0
Jack	Love	08/06/95	15.0000	41.0
Jack	Love	08/13/95	15.0000	38.0

As you can see, the name of each employee is filled in to the left of that employee's wage data. Because you entered three weeks of wages in the Wages table, each Employee's name and other data is displayed three times, though you only had to enter it once in the Employee table. You can see how much data entry time a relational database would save if you were recording the wages of dozens of employees for a year.

▸▸ **NOTE**

Notice also that the result of a query includes a record only if there is a record with that Empno in both of the tables. Records in the Emplist table that do not have matching Wage records are left out of the result.

▸▸ *Using the One-to-Many Report Wizard*

The One-to-Many Report Wizard is very similar to the One-to-Many Form Wizard. Its first three steps are used in the same way, to select fields from the main table and the related table and to specify the relationship, and its Sort Order step is also similar to that of the Form Wizard. However, its Style step, shown in Figure 13.9, is similar to the Layout step of the Report Wizard, which was covered in Chapter 6. Its Finish step also includes a Preview button and wrap-around check box, like the Finish step of the Report Wizard.

FIGURE 13.9

The Layout step

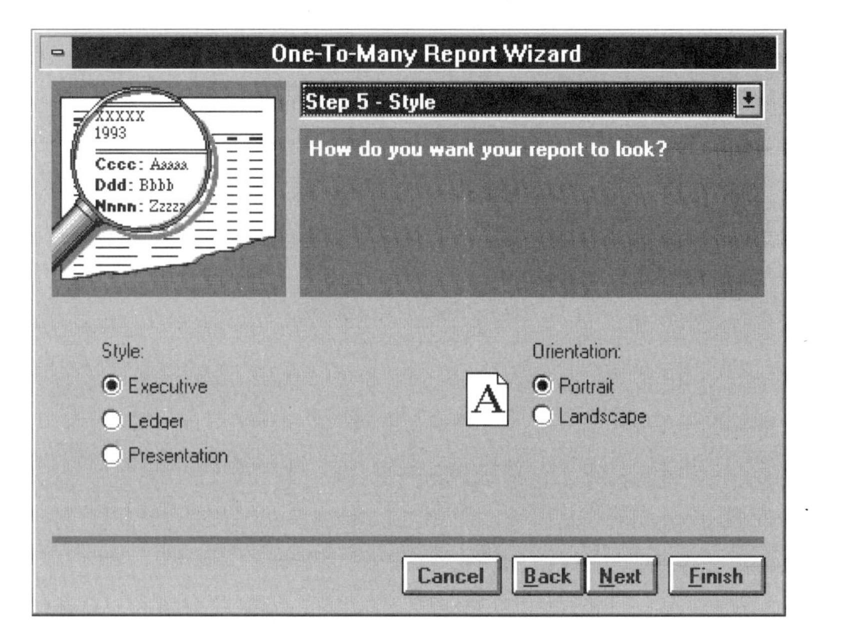

The report that is generated includes the fields from the "one" table that you included listed above one another, with the name of each to its left. Under the fields for each record are the values from all the corresponding records of the "many" table, listed in columnar form, with the field name at the top of each column.

Because the fields from the "one" table are listed one above another, you only have to worry about data wrapping if there are a large number of fields in the "many" table. This is not a problem in your sample database.

▸ Creating a Sample Report

Because the One-to-Many Report Wizard is so similar to other Wizards that you have already learned about, you should have no trouble creating a sample report:

1. Choose File ➤ New, select the Report radio button, and click the Wizards button. In the Wizard Selection dialog box, select One-to-Many Report Wizard.
2. In Step 1 of the Wizard, click the … button to the right of the Database/Tables control and use the Open dialog box to choose Emplist as the main table. Double-click Fname and Lname to add them to the Selected Fields list, as shown in Figure 13.10. Click Next.

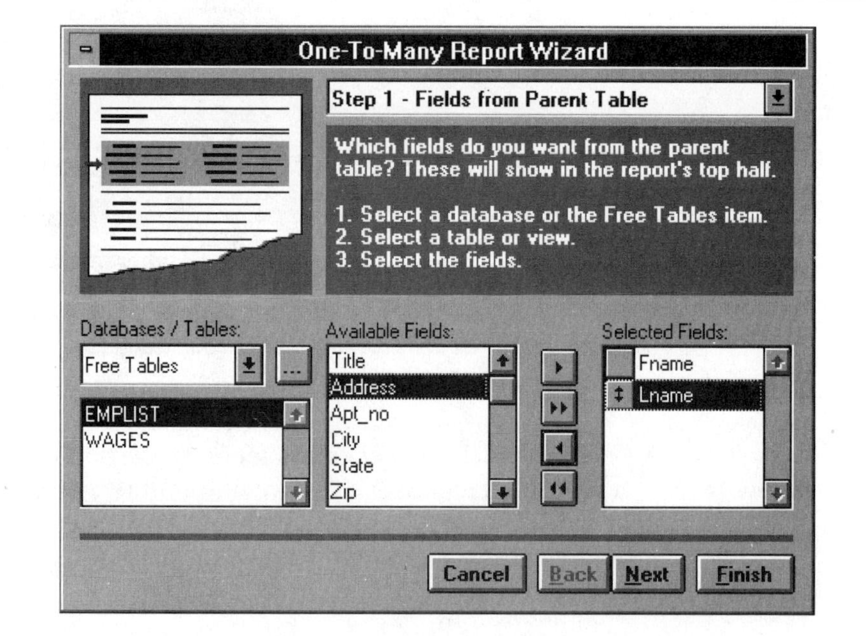

FIGURE 13.10 ▸ *Adding fields from the parent table*

3. In Step 2, click the … button to the right of the Database/Tables control and choose Wages as the Related table. Double-click Emp-no, Date, Hours, and Wage to add them to the Selected Fields list, as shown in Figure 13.11. Click Next.

FIGURE 13.11

Adding fields from the child table

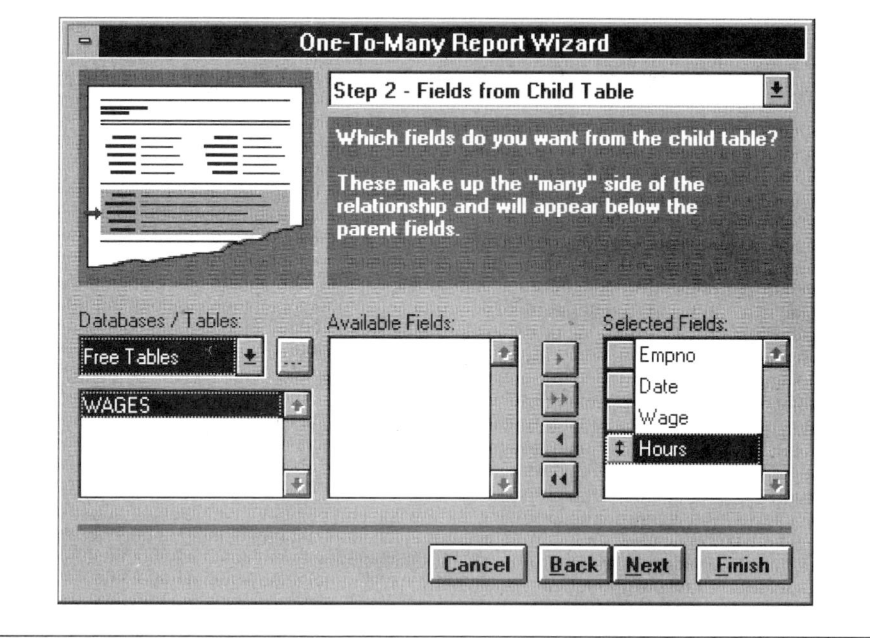

4. Keep the suggested relationship in Step 3. In Step 4, double-click Lname and Fname to use them as the basis of the sort order. Click Next to go onto Step 5, where you should keep the suggested style and layout. Click Next.

5. In the final step, enter **Wages By Employee** as the title of the report. Click the Preview button to view the sample report, as shown in Figure 13.12. (You may want to close the Print Preview toolbar, as in the illustration, to see more of the report.) Close the Preview window and click Finish to generate the report. Use the Save As dialog box to name it **Empwages**.

If you want, you can also choose File ➤ Print and print this report in the usual way.

▶ Many-to-One Reports

You might also want to create many-to-one reports on a relational database. For example, you might want a columnar report, where each row

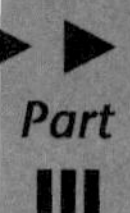

FIGURE 13.12

Previewing the sample Wages by Employee report

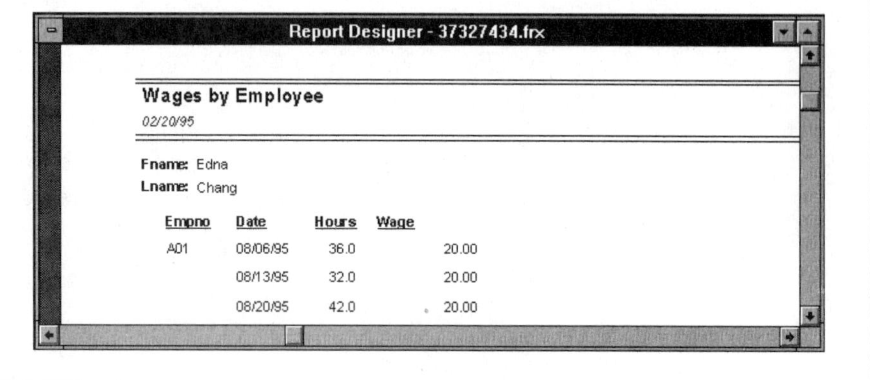

includes a record from the wage field plus the name of an employee who earned that wage, like the query that you created earlier in this chapter.

You cannot do this solely with the Wizards. However, if you create the query to relate the two tables, as you did above, and then display it in the Query Designer, you can then choose Query ➤ Query Destination to redirect the result of the query. Visual FoxPro displays the Query Destination dialog box, and you can click its Report button to direct the result of the query to a report, and then click its Wizard button to use the Report Wizard to design that report.

The Query Destination dialog box is covered in Chapter 15, which discusses how to use the Query Designer to work with relational databases.

►► To Sum Up

In this chapter, you learned to work with relational databases in the easiest way possible, using only the Wizards. You learned how to guarantee the integrity of your data by using the form created with the One-to-Many Form Wizard for data entry in the "many" table, how to view data using the Query Wizard, and how to design printed output using the One-to-Many Report Wizard.

The basic database theory that you learned in Chapter 12 and the skills you learned in this chapter are enough to let you manage simple relational databases, such as your sample application. Now you can go on to use relational databases in your own work, or you can continue with Chapters 14, 15, and 16, which teach you to manage relational databases in more sophisticated and powerful ways.

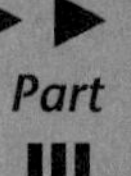

CHAPTER 14

Using the View Window

▸▸ FAST TRACK

To create a view, **382**

while using the View window, choose File ➤ Save and use the Save As dialog box to name the View file, or enter **CREATE VIEW <file name>**. View files have the extension VUE.

To open a view, **382**

choose File ➤ Open and open it as you do other files, or use the command **SET VIEW TO <file name>**.

To open multiple tables simultaneously, **383**

use the Open button of the View window, and each table will automatically be opened in a new work area. From the Command window, enter a command such as **SELECT B** to work in an unused work area before entering the command **USE <table name>** to open the table.

To refer to fields in the tables of a relational database, **384**

simply use the field name to refer to fields of the table in the current work area, as you always have. For tables open in other work areas, use the table name followed by the dot or arrow operator followed by the field name.

▶ ***To create a many-to-one relationship,*** ***387***

open the necessary tables in different work areas. Use the "one" table with an index based on its Primary Key field as its controlling index, and select the work area of the many table. Then click the Relations button and use the Expression Builder to specify the field in the "many" table that is related to the controlling index of the "one" table, or enter the command **SET RELATION TO <field name> INTO <"one" table name>**.

▶ ***To use fields from multiple tables in a single command,*** ***390***

use the command with an optional FIELDS clause, whose field list refers to fields in multiple tables.

▶ ***To use fields from multiple tables in a series of commands,*** ***394***

use the Properties dialog box to create a Field Filter that includes fields from both tables, or use the command **SET FIELDS TO** with a field list that refers to fields in multiple tables. In either case, enter the command **SET FIELDS GLOBAL** to make the commands that follow use fields from all tables.

▶ ***To create a one-to-many relationship,*** ***399***

use the View window to set up the relationship as you would for a many-to-one relationship, and then click its 1 To Many button.

In this chapter, you will look at how to work with relational databases using the View window. You should read Chapter 12, which covers basic database theory, before reading this chapter. Here, you will learn how to use the View window to create a sample relational database, but first you must understand why relational databases are used and how their data is normalized (broken down into multiple tables)—the basic concepts of relational database theory that were covered in the earlier chapter.

The View Window: An Overview

Using the Command Window interface, you can choose Window ➤ View or click the View Window tool at any time to display the View window, shown in Figure 14.1. This window lets you set up a special view of your data. You can open multiple tables and define relationships among them.

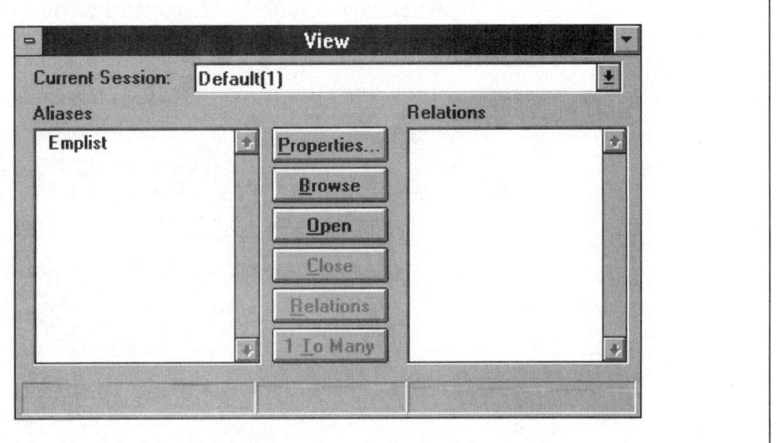

FIGURE 14.1

The View window

In addition, as you can see in the illustration, the View window includes a Properties button that lets you use the Work Area Properties dialog box, shown in Figure 14.2, for each of the tables you open. You learned in Chapter 10 of this book to use the Work Area Properties dialog box to work with indexes, and in Chapter 11 to use this dialog box to set a filter that determines which records the user can access (in the same way that a FOR clause does) or to set fields so that the user can access only certain fields in the table.

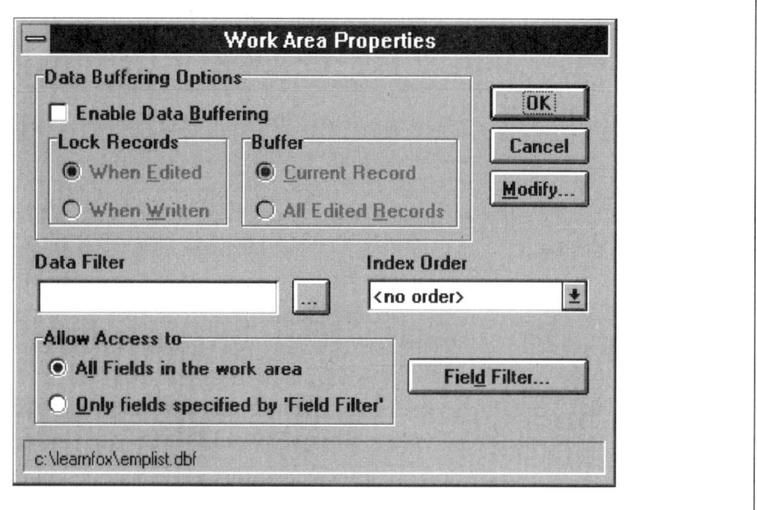

FIGURE 14.2 *The Work Area Properties dialog box*

NOTE

You should not confuse the View window with the View Designer, which is covered in Chapter 16. As you learned in Chapter 8, Visual FoxPro uses commands from both the Xbase and the SQL languages; the View window generates Xbase commands, and the View Designer generates SQL commands. Views created using the View Designer are called SQL views, to distinguish them from the views covered in this chapter.

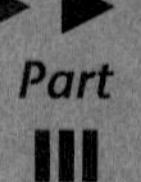

▶ Saving and Opening Views

After setting up a view, you can also save this view in a file and use it whenever you want. Views are kept in files with the extension VUE.

To save a new view, simply choose File ➤ Save when you are working in the View window. Visual FoxPro displays the Save As dialog box to let you name it. After you have named it, you can simply choose File ➤ Save to save any changes you make in it.

▶▶ **NOTE**

You *cannot* create a VUE file by choosing File ➤ Open and selecting the View radio button of the New dialog box. Doing this opens the View Designer, covered in Chapter 16, which you use to create a SQL view. The only way to create a VUE file is by opening the View window and then saving the view you create.

To open a view that you created and saved previously, simply choose File ➤ Open to display the Open dialog box. Then select View from the List Files of Type drop-down list to display VUE files, and open the view as you do any other file. Visual FoxPro will display the View window and will use all the tables, relationships, and other settings in all of its panels.

▶ Commands to Work with Views

You can also work with views by entering the following commands in the Command window:

- **CREATE VIEW <file name>** saves the current environment in a VUE file.
- **SET VIEW TO <file name>** restores a view previously saved in a VUE file.
- **SET VIEW ON** opens the View window.
- **SET VIEW OFF** closes the View window.

When you use the menu system to save or restore a view, Visual FoxPro generates the appropriate command.

►► Setting Up a Relational Database

To relate two tables using Visual FoxPro, you open them both at once. In other parts of Visual FoxPro that you've worked with in this book, you have always found that the current table is automatically closed when you open a new file, but the View window lets you open multiple tables in different work areas.

► Using Work Areas

As you can see in Figure 14.3, you can open multiple tables in the View window's Alias list. Each of these is opened in a numbered work area. In the past, you were only able to open one table at a time—when you opened a table, the table that was open previously was closed automatically. Work areas are simply a device to let you open several tables simultaneously. If you select a different work area before opening a table, it does not close the table that was open previously.

FIGURE 14.3

The View window's work areas

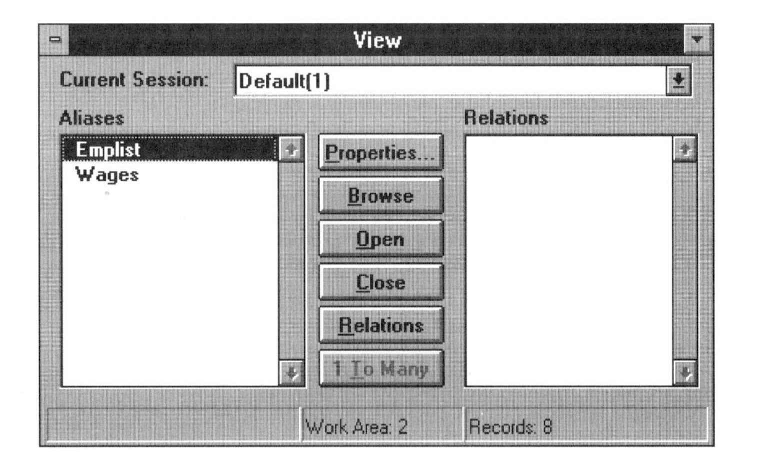

In earlier versions of FoxPro, there were 10 work areas, each designated using a letter from A to J or a number from 1 to 10. In Visual FoxPro 3, the list includes 145 work areas designated by numbers. You can still refer to the first 10 by the letters A to J, but you must refer to the rest using numbers.

The current work area is selected (highlighted) in the list. You will see in a moment how you can move among work areas and open a different table in each of them.

Using Data in the Current Work Area

You can always use data from the table in the current work area in all the same ways you have used tables in the past. For example, you can refer to its fields simply by using the field names, as usual.

Using Data in Other Work Areas

No matter which work area you are in, though, you can use the fields of any table that is open in any work area by referring to it in the following ways, all of which use either the arrow operator or the dot operator, which are described in a moment:

- The appropriate number (from 1 to 255), followed by the dot operator or the arrow operator and the field name.
- The appropriate letter (from A to J), followed by the dot operator or the arrow operator and the field name.
- The file name (or alias), followed by the dot operator or the arrow operator and the field name.

▸▸ **NOTE**

Programmers sometimes open tables with an alias to make it easier to follow the code. You can do this by using the command USE <tablename> ALIAS <alias name>, after which you can refer to the table by its alias rather than its name. If you are not programming, you will almost always use the table name rather than an alias in the third of these methods.

All of these methods use either of the two following operators:

- The dot operator is simply a period. Using the dot operator, for example, you could refer to a field as Emplist.fname.
- The arrow operator is made up of two characters, a hyphen followed by a greater-than sign. Using the arrow operator, you could refer to the same field as Emplist->fname.

Only the arrow operator was used in early Xbase languages. The dot operator was added in Visual FoxPro for compatibility with SQL, and it is now the more common of the two, since it saves typing.

Using Work Areas in the View Window

To select a work area in the View window, simply click it.

If you double-click a work area with a table open in it, Visual FoxPro selects the work area and also displays that table in the Browse window.

If you double-click a work area with no file open, Visual FoxPro displays the Open dialog box to let you use a table in that work area.

Using the keyboard, you can move the highlight among the work areas using ↑ and ↓ or the other cursor keys. Pressing Enter is equivalent to double-clicking the current work area.

Commands to Select a Work Area

You can also move among work areas by using the command SELECT followed by any of methods of referring to the work area.

For example, if you have the EMPLIST file open in Work Area 1, you can select that work area by entering any of the following:

```
SELECT A
SELECT 1
SELECT EMPLIST
```

Once you have selected the work area, you can use the table it contains in the same way you have always used tables.

▶▶ **NOTE**

Notice that the dot or arrow operator is not used to move among work areas; it is used only to refer to fields that are not in the current work area.

Commands to Close Tables

Close tables in the same ways you have learned in the past.

To close a single table, select its work area and enter the command USE without any file name following it.

To close all open tables, enter one of the following commands:

- **CLOSE TABLES** closes all tables in all work areas and selects Work Area 1.
- **CLOSE ALL** closes all tables in all work areas, selects Work Area 1, and also closes certain windows, such as the Form Designer, Label Designer, Query Designer, and Report Designer.

▶▶ **NOTE**

Leaving tables open can cause unexpected results later on. Remember that closing the View window does not close the tables you have opened in its work areas. Be sure to close all tables explicitly when you are done working with a view.

▶ Setting Relations

If you wanted, you could open different tables in different work areas to make it easy to look at different lists when you are working on several at the same time. You could then move back and forth among the work areas and use the table in each one without having to open it every time. You could still use the dot or arrow operator to access a table in another work area, even though it is unrelated to the table in the current work area. You would get the data from the record where you left the pointer the last time you were working on that table.

You get the most power from the multiple work areas, however, when you use the View window to set a relationship between two tables so the pointer in one moves automatically whenever you move the pointer in the other.

How SET RELATION Works

You must use a many-to-one relationship when you set a relation in the View window. You open both files, make the work area of the "many" file the current work area, and then set the relation into the "one" file.

You will find it easier to understand how to set a relation if you consider the nature of the one-to-many relationship of your data.

The Emplist table contains one record for each employee, and the Wages table can contain many records for each employee.

While you are working with a view based on a many-to-one relationship, when you scroll through the records in the Wages file, you can find corresponding data for the Emplist file; as you look at each week's wages, for example, you can also look at the name of the person who has that employee number.

▶▶ NOTE

The SET RELATION command actually lets you relate files by record number as well as by key field, but this feature is not really useful. To create a genuine relational database, you must set the relation into an indexed key field.

Thus, there are two requirements for setting a many-to-one relationship:

- You must be in a work area of the table that is on the "many" side of the many-to-one relation when you set the relation and when you use the relational database.
- The file on the "one" side of the many-to-one relation must be indexed on the key field (in this case, on the employee number field). Visual FoxPro uses this index to look up the name of the person with the same employee number as the current record in the WAGE file.

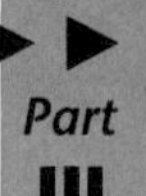

You'll see exactly how to do this when you do the exercise in the next section, "Relating the Tables."

Before you do this exercise, you must create a Wages table and modify the structure of the Emplist table by adding Employee numbers to it. If you have not already done so, go back to the exercises in the section "Creating and Modifying the Tables" at the end of Chapter 12. You must do these exercises before you can do any of exercises in this chapter.

Relating the Tables

Now, try using the View window to open both tables simultaneously and relate them.

1. Enter **CLOSE ALL** to close any open tables or queries. Choose Window ➤ View or click the View Window tool to display the View window. Click the Open button and use the Open dialog box to open the Wages table.

2. Next, click the Open button and open the Emplist table. Click the Emplist table to select it, and click the Properties button to display the Properties dialog box. Use its Index Order drop-down list to select the Emplist:Empno index, making it the controlling index. Select OK to return to the View window.

Now you are ready to set the relation. Remember that you must be in the work area of the table on the "many" side of the relation and set the relation into the table on the "one" side of the relation. This is because Visual FoxPro needs to look into the EMPLIST file to find one record that matches each record in the WAGES file.

1. Click Wages in the Work Areas list to generate the command SELECT 1. Then click the Relations button. Notice that WAGES, the name of the current table, appears in the panel on the right with a line leading to the space under it. This space is the location for the file you'll set the relation into.

2. Click EMPLIST to select it as the table the relation is set into. The Expression Builder appears, to let you choose the expression in WAGES that corresponds to the indexed expression in EMPLIST. Notice that you can use any expression from the table on the "many" side of the relation but that you must relate it to the

expression used as the controlling index in the file on the "one" side of the relation. Visual FoxPro should suggest empno as the expression; if it does not, double-click **EMPNO** in the fields list to add it to the SET RELATION text box. Select OK to return to the View window. Now that the relation is set, EMPLIST appears under WAGES, with the line leading into it, as in Figure 14.4.

The command

```
SET RELATION TO empno INTO emplist ADDITIVE
```

is generated. The ADDITIVE clause means that, if other relations were set earlier, this relation does not replace them but is set in addition to them. This clause is important when you are using complex data that requires multiple relations among tables.

FIGURE 14.4

Relation of WAGES set into EMPLIST, shown in the View window

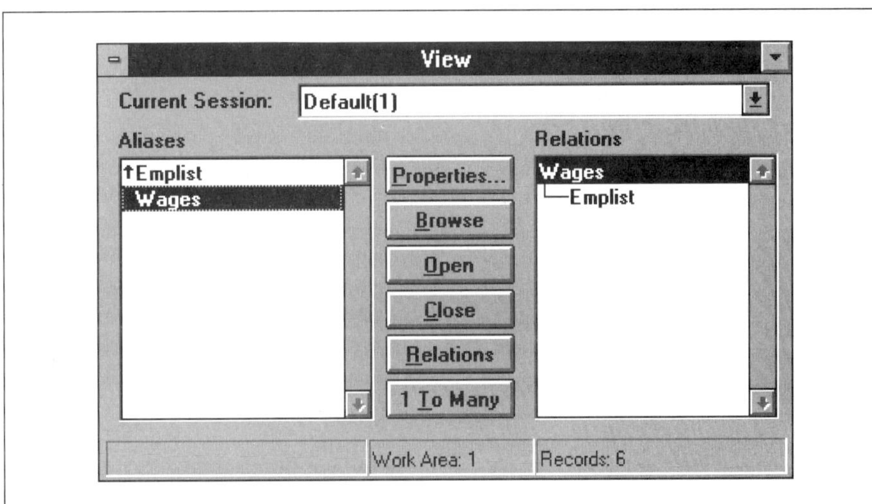

▶▶ Using a Relational Database

Now that you have set the relation, you can begin to make use of this relational database. First, you will create a Browse window of the sort you could use for entering and viewing data. Then you will use a command with a Fields check box to include fields from both files.

► Browsing Related Tables

As you will remember, you can use many Visual FoxPro commands with field lists. When you are using a view with related tables, you can use these commands with a list that includes fields from both tables. You just need to use the dot or arrow operator to refer to fields in the file that is not in the current work area. As you learned in the last section, you should always arrange to have the file for the "many" side of the relation in the current work area, so that Visual FoxPro can automatically move the pointer in the file the relation is set into, finding the one record there that corresponds to the record in the current file.

One particularly worthwhile command to use with relational databases is BROWSE FIELDS <field list>, since the Browse window you set up is saved and reused automatically each time you choose View ➤ Browse <table name>, generating the command BROWSE LAST. If you use BROWSE FIELDS <field list> once to create the Browse window, the Browse window will be displayed in the same way whenever you choose View ➤ Browse, as long as the View window is unchanged.

As an exercise, try creating a Browse window that includes the Empno, Fname, Lname, and Wage fields of the EMPLIST file, all the fields of the WAGES file, and a field based on an expression that calculates total wages by multiplying hourly wage times hours worked, to see how easy this makes data entry. Having the Empno fields from both files will let you see clearly that the fields added to the Browse window from the EMPLIST file correspond to the current record in the WAGES file. It will also show you an important pitfall to avoid when you are working with relational databases.

►► **WARNING**

As you learned earlier, the key field from the file on the "one" side of any one-to-many relation must be protected from being changed accidentally; otherwise, it can cause irrecoverable loss of data. The Empno field from the EMPLIST file is included in the Browse window in this exercise only for instructional purposes. You can use the Browse command to specify that fields are read only to avoid this danger. For more information, see Appendix B.

1. Make sure the work area of the WAGES file is still the current work area.

2. In the Command window, enter

```
BROWSE FIELDS EMPNO, DATE, WAGE, HOURS, TOT_PAID =
WAGE * HOURS, EMPLIST.EMPNO, EMPLIST.LNAME, EMP-
LIST.FNAME, EMPLIST.WAGE
```

all on one line to get the Browse window you see in Figure 14.5. (In the illustration, some fields are narrowed and the window is expanded, so you can see them all.) Notice that each record you entered in the WAGES file has the corresponding employee number, last name, and first name from the EMPLIST file added to it.

FIGURE 14.5

Browsing fields from two related tables

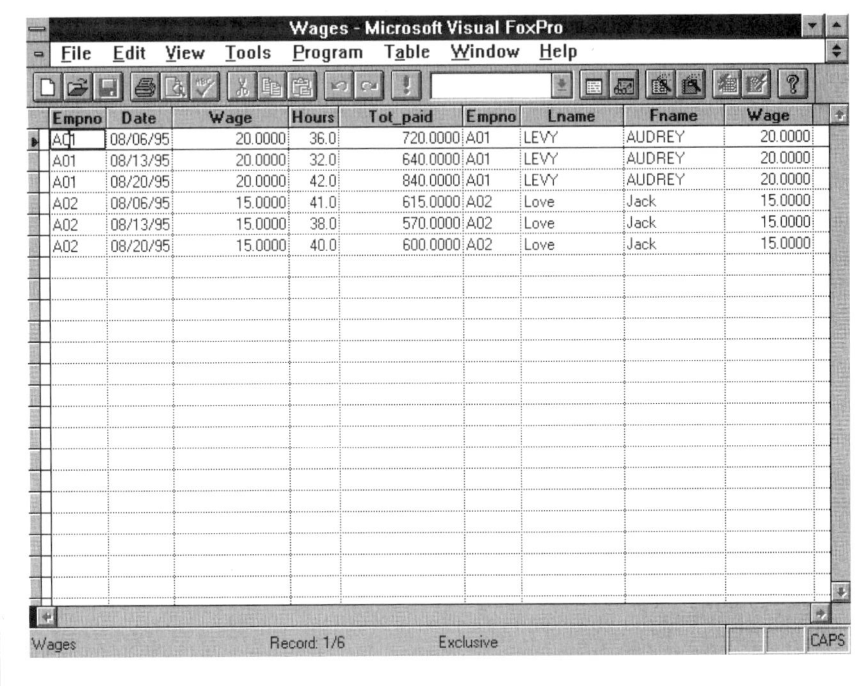

3. Add a new record: choose Table ➤ Append New Record. In the first Empno field (which you may remember is the Empno of the HOURS file), type **A03**. The corresponding EMPLIST fields

Empno, Lname, Fname, and Wage, are instantly filled in, as shown in Figure 14.6. To finish filling in the record, type **08/06/95** as the Date, **9.75** as the Wage (which is the same value as the Wage in the Emplist table) and **42** as Hours.

4. For comparison, see what happens if there is no corresponding record in the EMPLIST. Choose Table ➤ Append New Record. Type **A23** in the Empno field. The fact that no corresponding Empno, Lname, Fname, and Wage appear lets you know you have made an error in data entry. You have begun to enter wages for a worker who does not exist in your list of employees. Correct the error by editing A23 so it is A03 instead. When you move the cursor to the Date field, the Empno and name appear. As the date, enter **08/13/95**, as the Wage, **9.75**, and as Hours, enter **45**.

5. Now, imagine that you make a very dangerous error. If it is not already there, move the cursor to the next field in the same record—the Empno field that comes from the EMPLIST file. Change this number from A03 to A23.

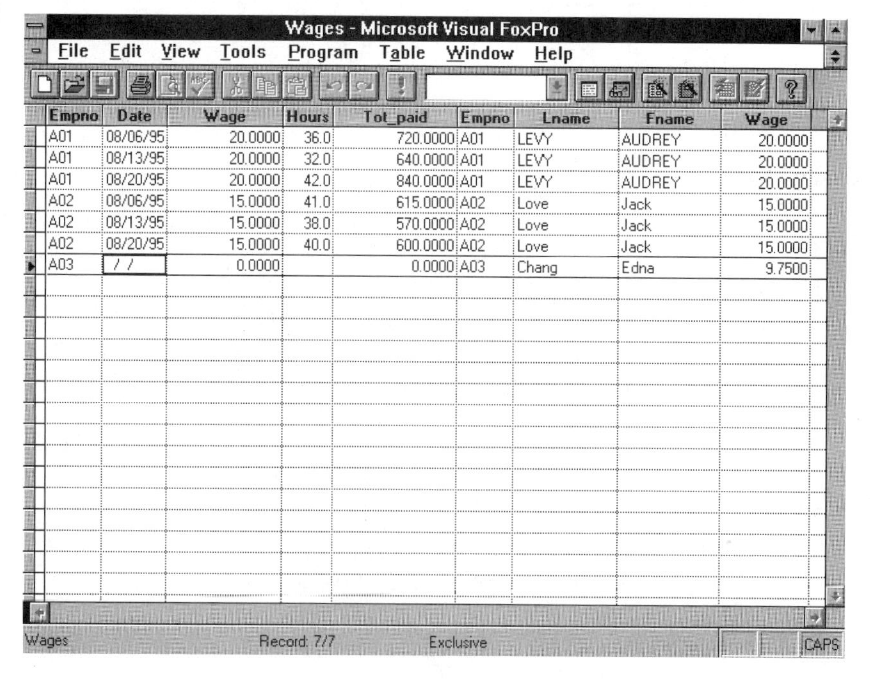

FIGURE 14.6

Fields that correspond to the Empno you enter are automatically filled in.

There is no second Empno and no name for the last record as shown in Figure 14.7.

You have just edited the EMPLIST file by mistake, so it no longer has a record there with the Empno of A03. Fields disappeared because there is no longer a record in the EMPLIST file that corresponds to these records in the HOURS file. In a real application, this could involve a disastrous loss of data.

1. To fix this mistake, click the View Window tool or choose Window ➤ View. In the View window, double-click Emplist to generate the command SELECT B and open a Browse window. In the new Browse window, you can see that Edna Chang now has an Empno of A23.

FIGURE 14.7

The data vanishes.

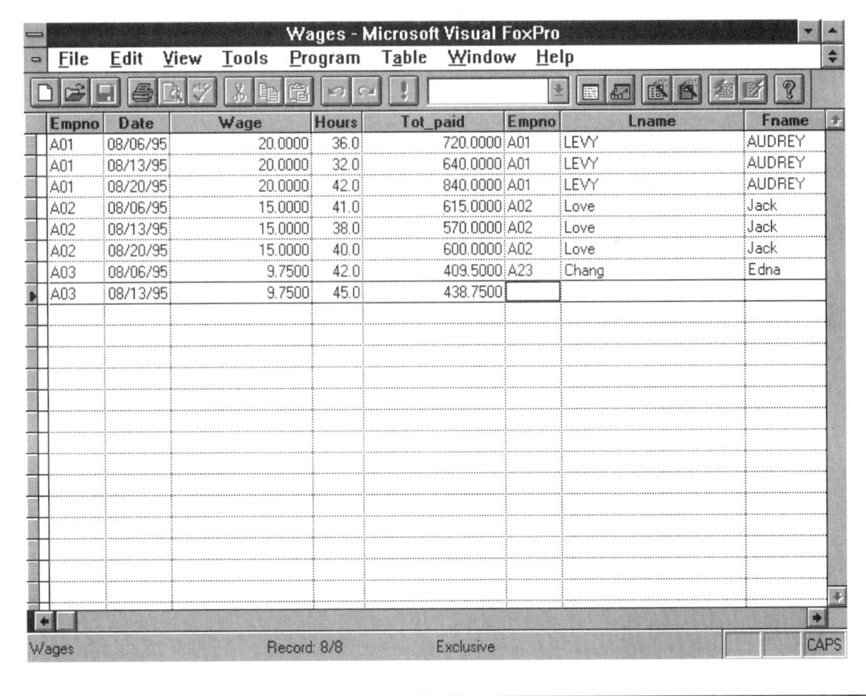

Empno	Date	Wage	Hours	Tot_paid	Empno	Lname	Fname
A01	08/06/95	20.0000	36.0	720.0000	A01	LEVY	AUDREY
A01	08/13/95	20.0000	32.0	640.0000	A01	LEVY	AUDREY
A01	08/20/95	20.0000	42.0	840.0000	A01	LEVY	AUDREY
A02	08/06/95	15.0000	41.0	615.0000	A02	Love	Jack
A02	08/13/95	15.0000	38.0	570.0000	A02	Love	Jack
A02	08/20/95	15.0000	40.0	600.0000	A02	Love	Jack
A03	08/06/95	9.7500	42.0	409.5000	A23	Chang	Edna
A03	08/13/95	9.7500	45.0	438.7500			

2. With luck, you remember that this number should be A03. Edit the file so Edna Chang again has number A03 and close this Emplist Browse window, saving the change. Now, click the Wages

Browse window to bring it forward again. The Empno, Lname, and Fname reappear in the records where they were missing.

To avoid this potentially disastrous error, you should not include the key field of the "one" table in this sort of Browse window. If you do include it, make it read-only by including **:R** after its name in the field list, as follows:

1. Close all Browse windows.
2. Enter the command

   ```
   BROWSE FIELDS EMPNO, DATE, WAGE, HOURS, TOT_PAID =
   WAGE * HOURS, EMPLIST.EMPNO:R, EMPLIST.LNAME, EM-
   PLIST.FNAME, EMPLIST.WAGE
   ```

3. Try to edit the Empno field, and you will see that you cannot.

▸ Using the SET FIELDS Command

Rather than using a Fields list as part of each command, as you just did with the BROWSE command, it is much easier to use the Set Fields pushbutton of the Setup window to specify a list of fields that is always included when the view is used.

You learned in Chapter 11 that you use two commands to set fields:

- To specify the fields, use the command SET FIELDS TO <field list>.
- Use the commands SET FIELDS ON and SET FIELDS OFF, which determine whether Visual FoxPro makes use of the field list you specified.

When you are working with a relational database, you use two additional commands, which work a bit like SET FIELDS ON ¦ OFF:

- **SET FIELDS GLOBAL** makes Visual FoxPro use fields from all related tables that are in the field list.
- **SET FIELDS LOCAL** makes Visual FoxPro use only fields from the current table that are in the field list.

▶▶ NOTE

For compatibility with earlier versions of FoxPro, LOCAL is the default. To use a field list with a relational database, you must use the command SET FIELDS GLOBAL in addition to SET FIELDS TO <field list>.

Once you have created a field list, you have completed setting up the relational database in the View window. In the following exercise, you will use all the fields from both tables, but you may want to use only certain fields in some actual applications. Choose whichever fields it is easiest to work with by default.

1. If necessary, close all open Browse windows, and choose Window ➤ View or click the View Window tool to open the View window.
2. Click the Properties button in the View window to display the Work Area Properties dialog box, and then click the Field Filter button of this dialog box to display the Field Picker.
3. Click the All button of the Field Picker to add all the fields of the Wage table to the Selected Fields list. Then select Emplist in the From Table drop-down list, and click the All button to add all its fields to the Selected Fields list, as shown in Figure 14.8. Click OK to return to the Setup dialog box and OK to return to the View window.
4. Click Wages to make it the current table. To make it easier to see your work, close the View window: remember that its settings remain in force regardless of whether it is displayed. In the Command window, enter **CLEAR** to clear the screen if necessary. Enter **LIST**. Visual FoxPro lists only fields from the Wages table, as shown in Figure 14.9.
5. Enter SET FIELDS GLOBAL. Then enter LIST again. Visual FoxPro lists the fields from both tables, as shown in Figure 14.10.

```
CREATE VIEW c:\learnfox\wageentr.vue
```

Now, you will not have to do the work of opening and relating tables when you use this database.

FIGURE 14.8

Specifying the fields to include

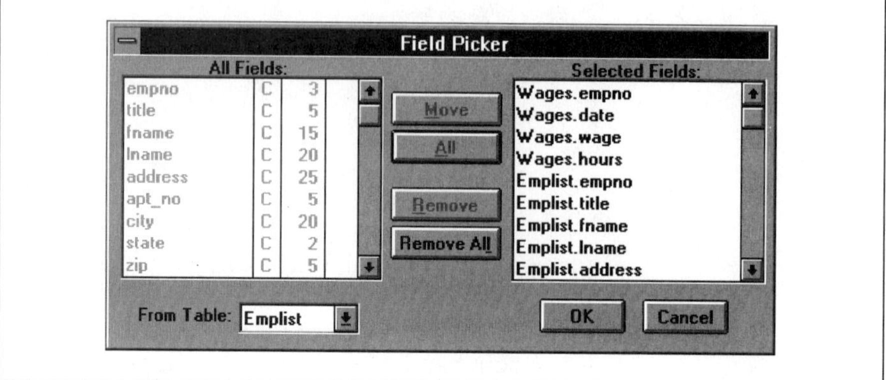

FIGURE 14.9

By default, Visual Fox-Pro uses only fields from the current table.

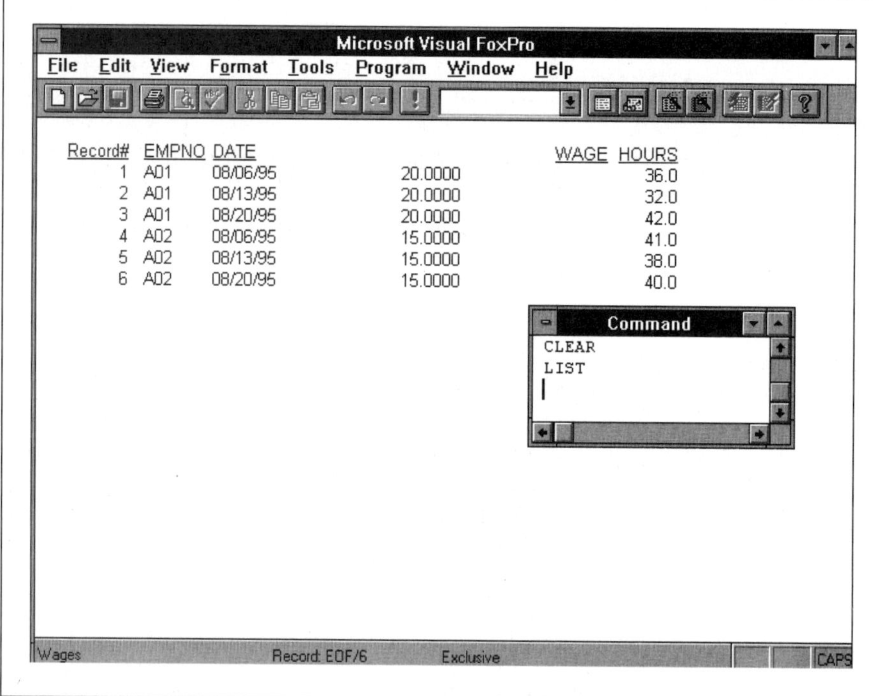

FIGURE 14.10

After SET FIELDS GLOBAL, Visual FoxPro uses fields from all tables.

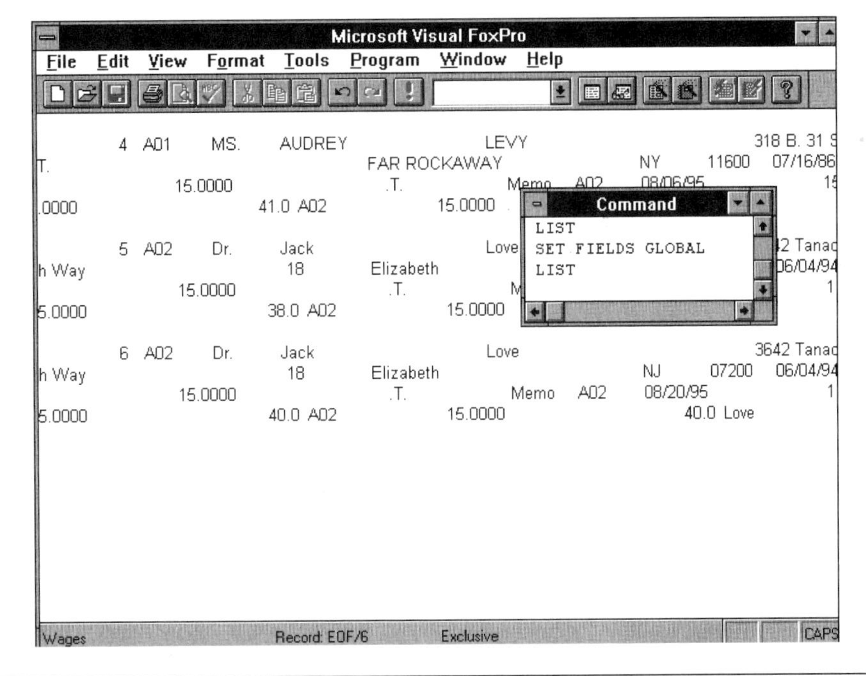

NOTE

FoxPro does not currently save the GLOBAL setting when you save the view. You must enter the command SET FIELDS GLOBAL whenever you use the view, in order to use the fields from all tables in the view.

Saving the View

Now that you have related the tables and selected the fields you want to use, you should save this view. Then you can close it and reuse it as an exercise.

1. To save the view, choose Window ➤ View or click the View Window tool to open the View window again. Then choose File ➤ Save As; Visual FoxPro displays the Save As dialog box. Type the name **WAGEENTR**, make sure the directory is still C:\LEARNFOX\, and select Save.

2. Enter CLOSE ALL. All tables are closed, as you can see by looking at the Aliases list of the View window.

3. Choose File ➤ Open. In the Open dialog box, select View from the List Files of Type drop-down list, and (if necessary) select C:\LEARNFOX\ as the directory. Select WAGEENTR.VUE from the scrollable list and select the Open pushbutton. Note that Visual FoxPro generates the command SET VIEW TO c:\learnfox\wageentr.vue.

4. Now, choose View ➤ Browse to generate the command BROWSE LAST. The Browse window you set up to display fields from the two files reappears. This is still the last configuration of the Browse window that you used. Close the Browse window.

You can see that it is as easy to open a view—with up to 145 files and the relations among them—as it is to open a single table. You can imagine how convenient this is if you have to switch among 10 different views of your data in the course of the day or if you are writing a program that constantly switches from one view to another.

▶ Some Words of Warning

The most important thing you should have learned from these exercises is how much damage you can do by modifying the indexed key field of the database the relation is set into. If you do this by mistake, you could end up with a list of wages and employee numbers without having any way of finding out which employee has a given employee number. Or you could end up with lists of customer numbers, sale dates, and amounts of money owed to you without having any way of finding out the names, addresses, or phone numbers of the customers you have to bill.

Never include a key field of this sort in the Browse window in the way you did in the exercise. That example was meant to teach you graphically about a danger you need to avoid. If you do need to include this sort of key field, you can make it a read-only Browse field. Do not even include this sort of key field in the Browse window you use to update the file itself; instead, use a Browse window with all the *other* fields. This way, you can change the name and address but you cannot change the employee number or customer number even by mistake. Moreover, do not delete records in this file unless you are archiving all of your old data at a new cycle of data entry. If you do delete a record in this file, you will not be able to use the corresponding records in the related file. Finally, always keep your data backed up, in case the mistake does occur despite your precautions.

In fact, because of this danger, the best way to use a relational database is by writing a program that adds the key field automatically and never lets the user change it. It is better yet if the user never even sees it.

▶▶ Setting One-to-Many Relations

The View window lets you set one-to-many relations as well as the many-to-one relations you have already learned about. Setting a one-to-many relation is easy.

First, you must set a relation just as you did earlier, using the View window or the SET RELATION command, with the file on the "one" side of the relation as the parent (controlling) file. Whenever you are in the work area of a file that is a parent file, the 1 To Many pushbutton of the View window is activated, and you can select it to use the Establish 1-To-Many Relationship dialog box, shown in Figure 14.11.

FIGURE 14.11 ▶

The Establish 1-To-Many Relationship dialog box

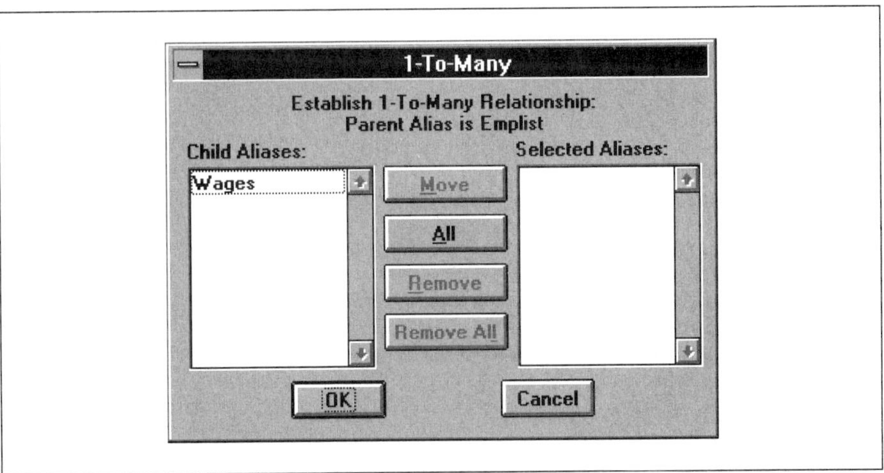

As you can see, the name of the parent file—the file whose work area was selected when you called up this dialog box—is listed at the top of the dialog box. All of its child files are listed in the Child Aliases box, and you can move any of them to the list of Selected Aliases in order to specify that they are part of a one-to-many relation.

► A Sample One-to-Many Relationship

As an example of a one-to-many relation, try creating a view with the EMPLIST file as the parent file and the WAGES file as the child file, since there can be many entries in the WAGES file for each employee in EMPLIST:

1. Open the View window to see the result of the commands that you enter. Then click the Command window to bring it forward. If you have not already done so, enter **CLOSE ALL** to close the previous view.

2. Now, enter **USE EMPLIST**. Enter **SELECT B** and **USE WAGES**. The WAGES file must be indexed to set a relation into it, so enter **INDEX ON EMPNO TAG EMPNO**. Now, to set the relation, enter **SELECT EMPLIST** and then **SET RELATION TO EMPNO INTO WAGES**.

3. Now, click the View window to bring it forward. To see what you have done, choose Window ➤ View. Click the 1-To-Many pushbutton to use the Establish 1-To-Many Relationship dialog box, and select the All pushbutton to move the name of the WAGES file to the list of selected aliases. Then select the OK pushbutton. This generates the command SET SKIP TO, which is covered later in this chapter, and the line between Emplist and Wages is altered to show that it is a one-to-many relationship, as shown in Figure 14.12.

4. That is all it takes to establish a one-to-many relation. Save this view in case you want to use it again: Choose File ➤ Save As, enter the name **EMPWAGES**, and select Save. Then close the View window to return to the Command window.

► The Browse Window for a One-to-Many Relationship

Now, you will use the BROWSE FIELDS command as an exercise in using this relational database. Remember that EMPLIST is the file in the

FIGURE 14.12

A one-to-many relationship in the View window

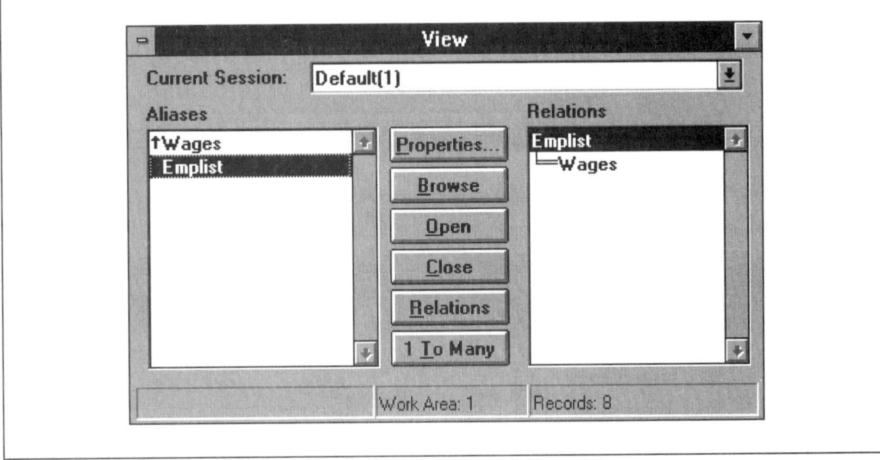

current work area, so you can refer to its fields by name. To refer to the fields in the WAGES file, though, you must use the arrow or dot operator.

1. In the Command window, enter **BROWSE FIELDS LNAME, FNAME, WAGES.DATE, WAGES.HOURS, WAGES.WAGE**, to display the Browse window shown in Figure 14.13.
2. When you are done, close the Browse window and enter **CLOSE ALL to close the view. Remember that, since you saved it, you can open this view again at any time.**

You can see in the illustration that when you browse tables in a one-to-many relationship, fields from the parent file appear only once. If there are multiple records in the child file, the blank spaces under the fields of the parent file are filled in or shaded.

The SET SKIP Command

Notice that when you created a one-to-many relationship, the command SET SKIP TO WAGES was generated in the Command window.

The command SET SKIP TO <list of table aliases> specifies that the parent file in the current work area is in a one-to-many relation with all of the tables whose aliases (or names) are listed. The file names in the list must be separated by commas if there is more than one, and all

FIGURE 14.13

Browsing fields of a one-to-many relation

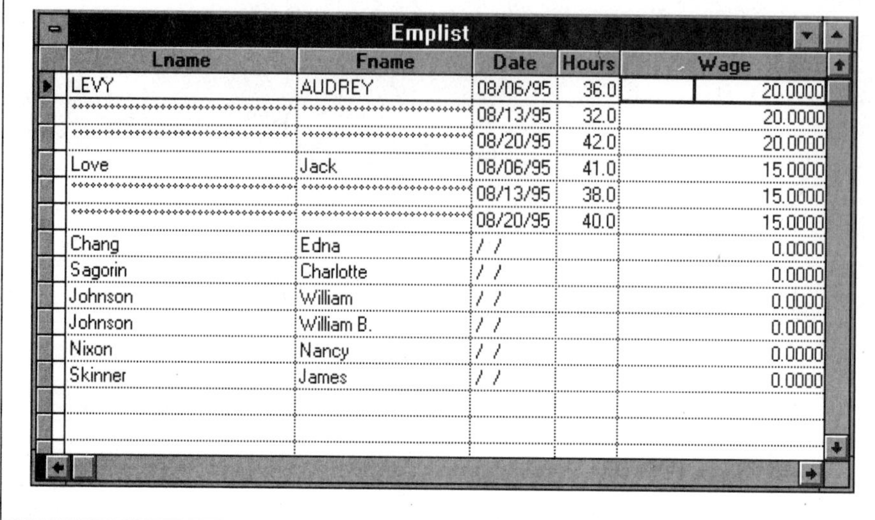

must already have been made child files of the file in the current work area. For more information about SET SKIP TO, see Appendix B.

▸▸ To Sum Up

In this chapter, you looked at how to use the View window to set up a relational database and to save the settings in the View window in a VUE file, so they are in effect again whenever you open that VUE file.

In the next chapter, you will look at another method of working with relational databases in Visual FoxPro, the View Designer, and at the SQL programming code it generates.

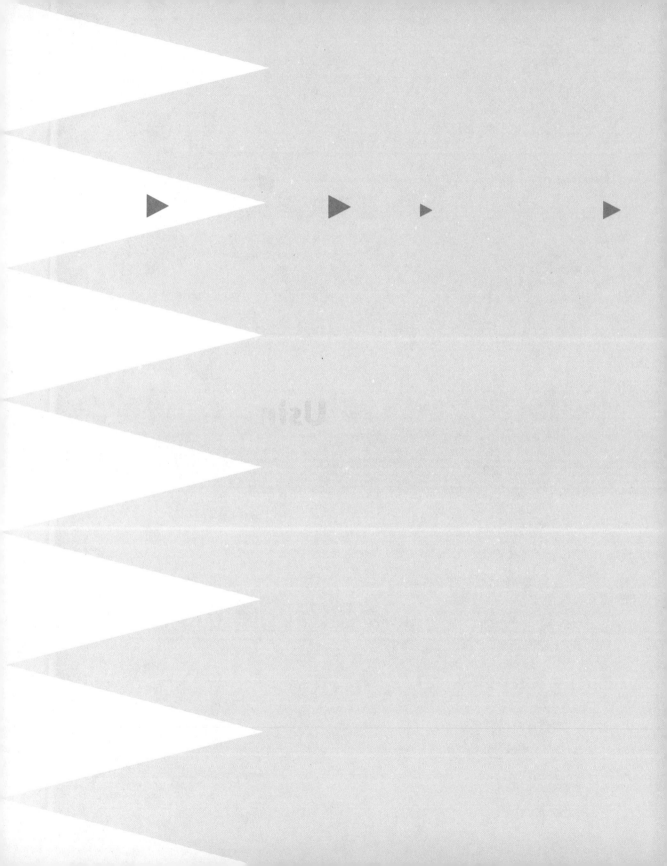

CHAPTER 15

Using Queries and SQL

▸▸ FAST TRACK

▶ ***To add multiple tables to the Query Designer,*** **410**

click the Add Table button or choose Query ➤ Table. Click the Other button of the Add Table or View dialog box to add a table that is not part of a FoxPro database.

▶ ***To join two tables,*** **412**

use the Join Condition dialog box, which is displayed automatically if you add a table to a query that already has tables included in it. Use the dialog box controls to select the common key fields of the two tables, and the operator used to compare them. If you are joining two tables in a relational database that has been set up properly, you should always be able to use the Like operator.

▶ ***To remove a join,*** **414**

click the line that represents the join in the Query Designer to select it, and then choose Query ➤ Remove Join Condition or simply press Del.

▶ ***To add a new join among tables that have already been added to the query,*** **415**

either click the Add Join tool of the Query toolbar to display the Join Condition dialog box and use it to specify the join condition, or use the Selection Criteria panel to specify the Join condition, or click and drag from the field in one table that the join is based on to the related field in the other table.

To change a join condition that you specified earlier, **415**

either double-click the line that represents the join to display the Join Condition dialog box and change its specifications, or use the Selection Criteria panel to modify the join condition.

To create a grouped query, **418**

use the Functions/Expressions control of the Fields panel to choose a summary function (such as the SUM( ) or AVG( ) functions) and the field it applies to; then click Add to add it to the selected output. Use the Group By panel to choose the field or fields that the grouping is based on. The result will have one record for each group, which includes the summary for that group.

To view the SQL code that the query generates, **426**

click the SQL Window button of the query designer toolbar, choose Query ➤ View SQL, or choose View SQL from the Query Designer shortcut menu to open the SQL Window that contains this code.

To run a query, **427**

if you are still using the Query Designer, click the Run button of the main toolbar, choose Query ➤ Run Query, or choose Run Query from the Query Designer shortcut menu. If you have closed the Query Designer, choose Program ➤ Do and use the Do dialog box to select the query program.

Early versions of the Xbase language supported only the procedural commands for using relational databases that were described in Chapter 14; you had to use a series of steps to open and relate the tables explicitly before you could extract the data that you needed from them. Beginning with version 2.0, the FoxPro language has incorporated features of SQL, the Structured Query Language. SQL is the industry standard for working with relational databases in mainframe environments, and it is now also being added to more powerful microcomputer database management systems.

SQL lets you query relational databases with a single command, without doing all the preliminary housekeeping work of setting a relation. Several SQL commands are now a part of the FoxPro language and can be used like any other command in Visual FoxPro.

You can also use the Query Designer to relate and query multiple tables. Visual FoxPro generates a SQL SELECT command based on the selections you make there; you can copy and paste this command and use it elsewhere.

You have already looked briefly at the Query Designer in Chapter 4, where it was used with a single table; this chapter will cover it in more detail, emphasizing how it is used with relational databases, and will also discuss the SQL code that it generates.

The Disadvantages of SQL Queries

Because they use only a single line of code, SQL SELECT commands run more quickly than the series of procedural commands covered in Chapter 14, and so they are preferred by developers who are interested in optimizing the performance of their programs. However, there are two major disadvantages of using the queries to join tables.

Queries versus Views

First, the result of a query is read-only. You can look at the result in a Browse window, but you cannot update its data.

As you will see in the next chapter, though, you can overcome this problem by using the View Designer to create a SQL view that is part of a database, rather than using the Query Designer to create a SQL query.

Because they can only be used when you are working with Visual FoxPro database files, SQL views are covered in the next chapter. However, the View Designer works like the Query Designer, and you will be able to use what you learn in this chapter when you work with SQL views.

Including Only Records That Appear in Both Tables

A problem with both SQL queries and SQL views that is harder to get around, however, is that the result includes only records that are found in both of the original tables.

In the previous chapter, you saw that you could use the View window to create a query that includes all the records in the "many" tables and matching records in the "one" table, or all the records in the "one" table and matching records in the "many" table. You cannot do either of these using the Query Designer.

There are times when it is useful to include all the records in the "one" table—for example, if you have a database recording the sales of a number of salespeople, and you want a report on all the salespeople, including those who have not made any sales.

In addition, if there is any danger of data entry error, it is best to include all the records in the "many" table, even if there is no equivalent in the "one" table. This should not make any difference in the result; if data was entered correctly, as you know, there should be a record in the "one" table for each record in the "many" table. However, if there was a data-entry error and an orphan record was entered in the "many" table, it is best to display it when you use the relational database, so you can see (for example) that there is a record of hours worked without a name and address of an employee who worked them. Once you see this error, you can try to correct it.

SQL queries will not display orphan records. If one exists, you may go for months without seeing the error and trying to find out who the orphan record applies to. If it is a record of the number of hours that someone worked for you, the employee is likely to complain. But if it is a record of the number of hours that you worked for a client, you may never bill that client!

Thus, when you use SQL queries to relate tables, you should be especially careful that there are no orphan records in the "many" table. SQL queries and SQL views are best used by developers, who can use programming techniques to control data entry.

▸▸ The Query Designer

As you learned in Chapter 4, you create a query using Query Designer in the same way you create other Visual FoxPro files, by choosing File ➤ New or clicking the New tool, selecting the Query radio button, and selecting either the New File or the Wizard button, or by entering the command CREATE QUERY <query name> in the Command window.

You can also modify queries in the usual way, by choosing File ➤ Open or clicking the Open tool and selecting the query in the Open dialog box or by entering MODIFY QUERY <query name> in the command window.

Queries are stored in files with the extension QPR, and Visual FoxPro assumes this extension if you do not include one in a command.

When you create or modify a query, Visual FoxPro displays the Query Designer, shown in Figure 15.1. In Chapter 4, you learned to use this window with a single table; Visual FoxPro either includes the currently open table in it or, if no table is open when you create it, displays the Open dialog box so you can open one. In this chapter, you will learn to use Query Designer with multiple tables, as shown in the illustration.

▸ Working with Multiple Tables

You can add additional tables to the Query Designer by any of these methods:

- Choose Query ➤ Add Table.

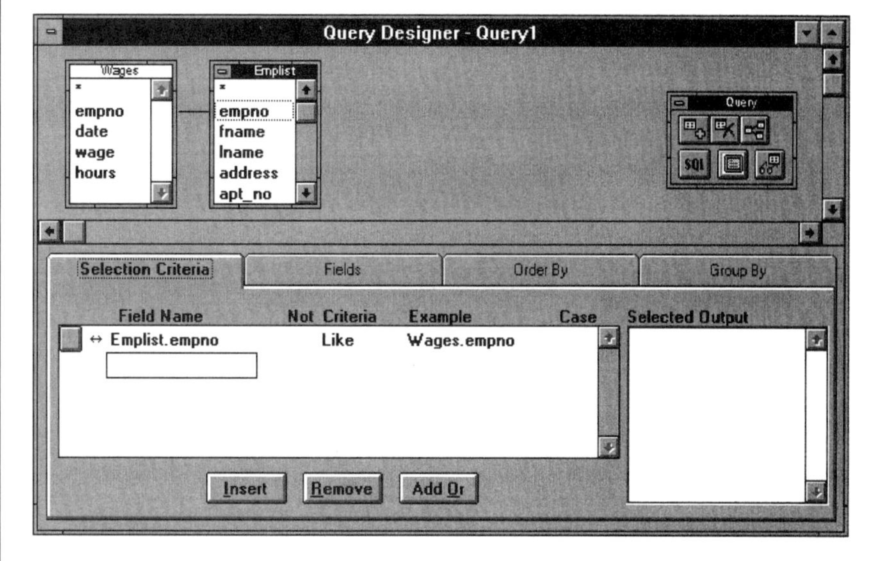

FIGURE 15.1

The Query Designer window

- Right-click the Query Designer and choosing Add Table from its shortcut menu.

- Click the Add table button of the Query toolbar.

In any case, FoxPro displays the Open dialog box, which you use in the usual way to select the table to be added.

Removing Tables

Likewise, to remove a table, you first select it by clicking it to highlight its title bar. Then do any of the following:

- Choose Query ➤ Remove Table.
- Right-click the Query Designer and choose Remove Table from its shortcut menu.

- Click the Remove Table button of the Query toolbar.

Moving Tables

You can move any table in this panel simply by clicking and dragging its title bar, if doing so makes the query easier to work with.

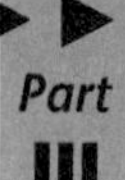

Specifying a Join Condition

If there is already a table in the Query Designer and you add another, Visual FoxPro displays the Join Condition dialog box, shown in Figure 15.2, which you must use to specify the way in which the new table is related to another table in the Query.

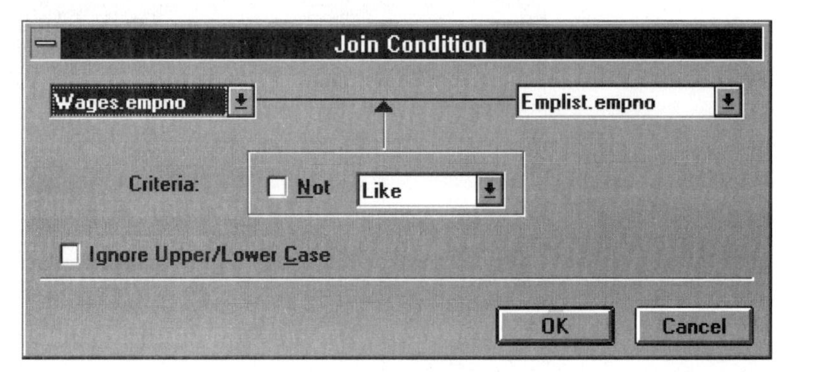

FIGURE 15.2

The Join Condition dialog box

This dialog box includes three drop-down list boxes:

- Use the list on the left to select a field from the table already included in the Query.
- Use the list on the right to select a field from the table you just added.
- Use the center list to select the relation between the fields: LIKE, EXACTLY LIKE, MORE THAN, or LESS THAN. These comparison options were covered in Chapter 4 and are equivalent to FoxPro operators that you learned in Chapter 11, as shown in Table 15.1. You can also use the Not check box to invert any of these relations, and the Ignore Upper/Lower Case check box to make them find a match regardless of case.

As Table 15.1 shows, LIKE is similar to the = operator, which finds a match between two strings if the second has all the characters in the first. EXACTLY LIKE is similar to the == operator, which finds a match only if the second string has all the characters in the first and no other characters. For example, LIKE would find a match if SMITH were in one field and SMITHSON were in the other, but EXACTLY LIKE would not.

TABLE 15.1: *SQL Comparisons and Equivalent Operators*

Comparison	Operator
Like	=
Not like	<>, #, !=
Exactly like	==
Greater than	>
Greater than or equal to	>=
Less than	<
Less than or equal to	<=

Use LIKE to Join Tables in a Relational Database When you specify the join condition, Visual FoxPro displays default values in the list boxes that are usually the values you need, including the LIKE operator.

You should always set up relational databases so that you can use LIKE in the center control, without using the Not or the Ignore Upper/Lower Case check boxes. As you learned in Chapter 12, you should use the same value in the key fields of the two tables you are relating.

For example, using our sample database, you would want the records in the two tables to be joined whenever EMPNO in the EMPLIST file is LIKE EMPNO in the WAGES file.

If the primary and the foreign keys have been entered correctly in the two tables, LIKE should join the tables properly.

Avoid the Other Operators EXACTLY LIKE, MORE THAN, LESS THAN, and the Not or Ignore Case check boxes may be used when you need to join tables that were not set up to function as a relational database, in order to merge data from tables that you get from a variety of sources. In addition, they are commonly used in queries that are meant to filter data, as you saw in Chapter 4. You should not need

them when you are joining files of a relational database on the basis of a common key field.

►► **WARNING**

Note that when you join tables, using some of these criteria can produce a result with a very large number of records. For example, if you have 100 employees and 50 weeks of wage records for each, joining them using LIKE will produce a result with 5000 records—the 5000 records in the Wages table, each joined with data from one record in the Emplist table. If you check the Not check box, however, each of the 5000 wage records will be joined with the 99 employee records that do not have the same number, instead of with the single employee record that has the same number, which will give you a result with almost half a million records. In this case, the information in the records is useless; but even if you have joined tables to produce useful information, you usually do not want to deal with half million records of it. When you do a join using criteria other than LIKE or EXACTLY LIKE, you should estimate how many records will result: if the result is too large, use filter conditions to isolate only those records you want.

Working with the Join

After you specify the join condition, the new table is added to the top of the Query Designer, and the fields of the two tables that are the basis of the join condition are connected by a line. As you can see in Figure 15.3, the join condition is also automatically entered in the Selection Criteria panel.

Removing the Join To remove the join, first click the connecting line to select it; once selected, it will become thicker and darker, as shown in Figure 15.3. Then choose Query ➤ Remove Join Condition or simply press the Del key.

FIGURE 15.3

The join is selected.

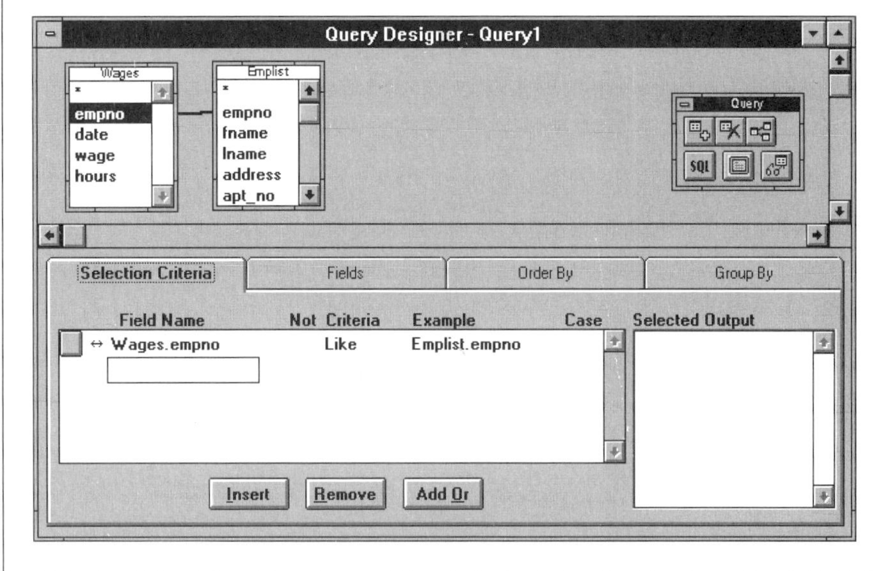

Adding a New Join You can create a new join among tables that have already been added to the query, in several ways.

- Click the Add Join tool of the Query toolbar to display the Join Condition dialog box, and use it to specify the join condition.
- Use the Selection Criteria panel to specify the join condition, as described below.
- Click and drag from the field in one of the join's tables to the related field in the other table. Visual FoxPro adds a line representing the join between the two fields, without displaying the Join Condition dialog box. You can display this dialog box as described below, in the section on the Selection Criteria panel.

Modifying the Join Condition To change a join condition that you specified earlier, double-click the line that represents the join to display the Join Condition dialog box again. Change the specifications in the same way that you originally entered them.

Alternatively, you can use the Selection Criteria panel to edit the join condition, as described below.

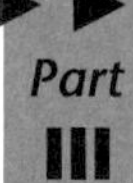

The Selection Criteria Panel

All the join conditions you create in this way are listed in the Selection Criteria panel that is initially displayed on the bottom half of the Query Designer.

Because your sample database includes only two tables, you need to use only one join condition. If you were working with more complex data, broken up into a larger number of tables, you would have to use multiple join conditions.

You can create or modify a join condition by using the drop-down lists and the Not check box to change the fields and criteria in this panel, as you learned to do in Chapter 4.

You can also use this panel to specify selection criteria that filter the result of the query, as you learned to do in Chapter 4. For example, in addition to the join condition, you can add a selection criterion to display only records from California.

After you run a query, a list of the fields you selected as output is also included in this panel.

The Fields Panel

To specify which fields are included in the result of the query, click the Fields tab or choose Query ➤ Output Fields to display the Fields panel of the Query Designer, shown in Figure 15.4. Use the Field Picker in the usual way to select the fields you want to include.

Fields are output in the order in which they listed in the Selected Output list. You can change their order by clicking and dragging the boxes to the left of the fields in this list upward or downward.

Select the No Duplicates check box if you want records with duplicate data to be excluded from the result. The Cross Tabulate check box is used to create crosstabs, which are covered in Chapter 18.

If you are creating a grouped query, you can also use the Functions/Expressions control of this panel to create a calculated field for each group. Use this drop-down list to select one of the following summary functions:

- **COUNT( ):** The number of records that have values entered in the field.

FIGURE 15.4

The Fields panel of the Query Designer

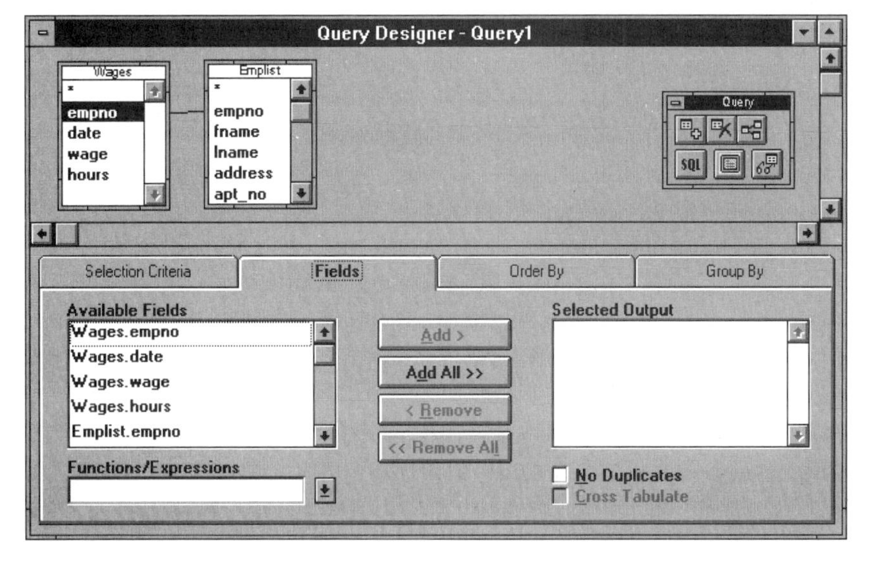

- **SUM( ):** The sum of all the values entered in the field.
- **AVG( ):** The average of all the values entered in the field.
- **MIN( ):** The smallest value entered in the field.
- **MAX( ):** The largest value entered in the field.
- **COUNT(DISTINCT):** The number of records that have different values entered in the field.
- **SUM(DISTINCT):** The sum of all different values entered in the field.

Each of these options also lets you select the field that the calculation will be applied to, which is used in the same way as the submenu of a menu. After making the selection, click the Add button to add it to the Selected Output list.

This calculation will be applied to each group you specify in the Group By panel. For example, if you select Average as the function and Wage from its sub-menu in this panel, and you select State as the field to group on in the Group By panel, the result will include the average wage for each state.

Grouped queries are discussed at greater length below in the section on the Group By panel, and there is also an exercise using a grouped query.

The Order By Panel

You can specify the order in which records should be listed as a result of the query by clicking the Order By tab or choose Query ➤ Order By to display the Order By panel, shown in Figure 15.5. The Selected Output list includes all the fields you included in the result in the Fields panel. Add one or more of these to the Ordering Criteria list to use it as the basis of the sort. Use the radio buttons to specify whether each field is sorted in ascending or descending order.

FIGURE 15.5

The Order By panel of the Query Designer

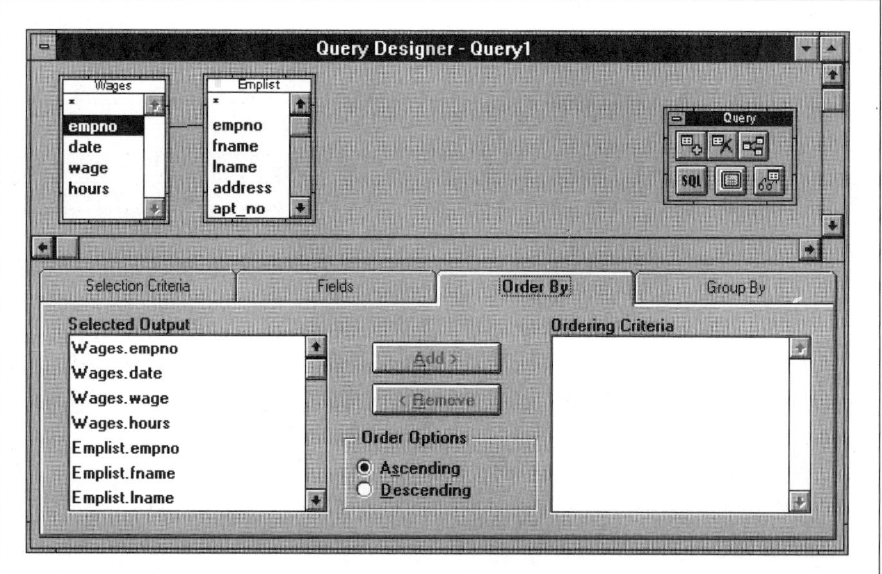

The Group By Panel

To group records, click the Group By tab or choose Query ➤ Group By to display the Group By panel, shown in Figure 15.6. Add the fields on which you want the grouping to be based to the Group By Fields list.

Groupings are useful for queries that include calculations. You indicate the calculation by using the Functions/Expressions drop-down list of

FIGURE 15.6

The Group By panel of the Query Designer

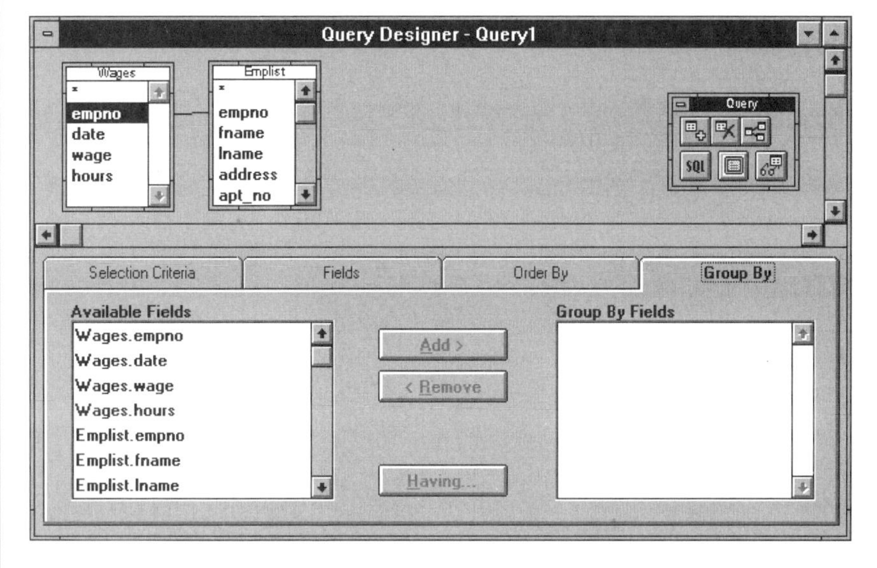

the Fields Panel. The result of the query includes one record for each group, and it includes this calculated value for the group in each record.

For example, if you group by state, the result of the query will include one record for each state. You could also use the Functions/Expressions list to select the Average function, and select Wage as the field to average. Include this field in the output, and the result will include a value that is the average wage for that state.

If you add fields to group on, the Having button is enabled. Click it to display the Having dialog box, shown in Figure 15.7, which lets you specify a filter condition to limit the records included in the grouping. As you can see, the filters are the same as the ones included in the Selection Criteria panel and used to filter records, but here they filter which records are included in the calculation of the grouping. For example, if you were finding the average wage by state, you could also use the filter condition Emplist.date_hired More Than {01/01/95}, so that the result would give you the average wages for recently hired employees from each state.

FIGURE 15.7

The Having dialog box

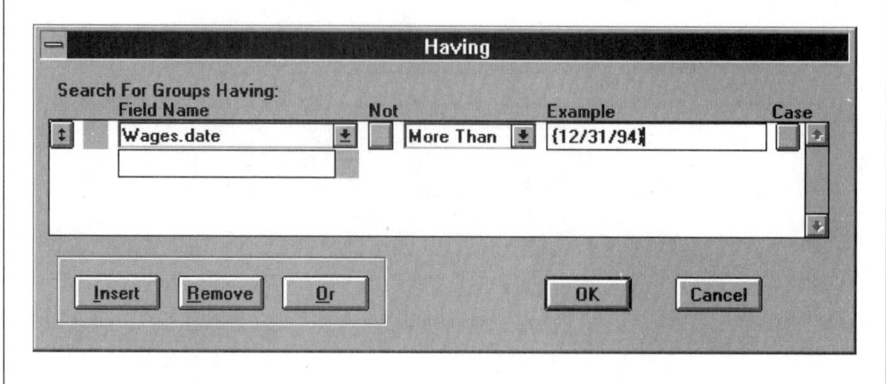

▸▸ **NOTE**

If you select fields to include in the result that have different values in different records within the grouping, the result will simply include the value from the first record in each group, which will probably be meaningless or misleading. For example, if you are finding the average wages for employees in each state, and you include the Fname and Lname field, the result will simply include the name of the first employee in each state, creating the impression that you have calculated the average wage for only that employee. It is up to you to include only meaningful fields in the result—such as the State and the Average Wage in the example.

Groupings are particularly useful when you are working with relational databases, because you can do a calculation on records in the "many" table that is grouped so you have a result for each record in the "one" table. In your sample application, for instance, there are many Wage records for each employee, and you can create a query that is grouped on Empno to find the total hours worked for each employee, as you will do in the exercise below. Any field from the "one" table can be meaningfully included in the result: in the example, you would probably want to include the name of each employee.

Directing Output

To specify where the result of the query will appear, click the Query Destination tool of the Query toolbar or choose Query ➤ Query Destination to display the Query Destination dialog box, shown in Figure 15.8.

FIGURE 15.8

The Query Destination dialog box

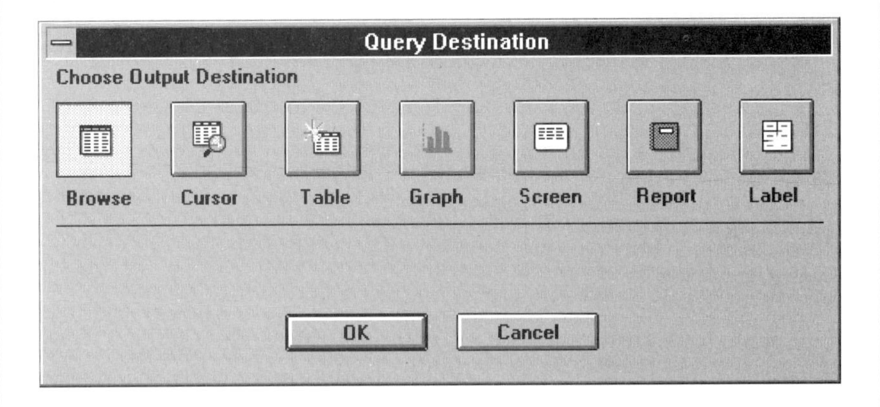

There are seven options, and this dialog box changes for some of them to let you enter the additional information that they need.

Browse

If you click the Browse button, the result is displayed temporarily in a Browse window. This is the default that you have been working with so far.

Cursor

If you click the Cursor button, the result is sent to a cursor. As you learned in Chapter 4, a cursor is like a table except that it exists only temporarily. As long as it remains open, you can use this cursor in the same ways as any table—for example, you can use the usual commands to browse it or list its records—but once you close it, it is discarded.

When you select this button, a Cursor Name text box is added to the Query Destination dialog box, as shown in Figure 15.9. Name the cursor and use its name in commands as you would a table name.

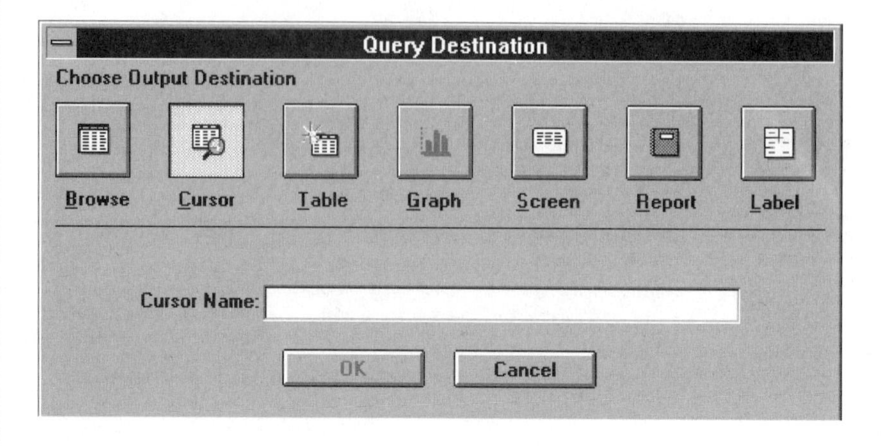

FIGURE 15.9

Sending the result to a cursor

Table

If you select the Table button, the Query Destination dialog box is displayed as shown in Figure 15.10. Enter a table name in the text box (the name of the Query is suggested) or click the button to its right and use the Open dialog box to specify the name and location of the query.

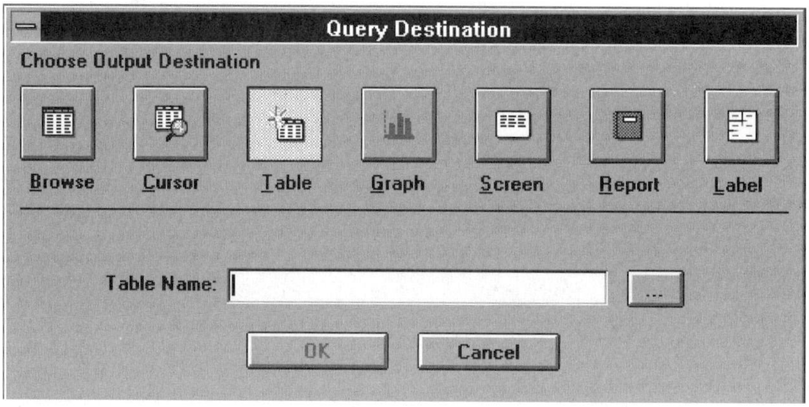

FIGURE 15.10

Sending the result to a table

WARNING

If you select an existing table as the destination of the query, its existing contents will be overwritten without warning when you run the query.

Though beginners are tempted to send the result of a query to a table, keeping two tables that hold the same data can lead to errors. For example, at a later time, you may edit a record in the table that holds the query result by mistake, instead of editing it in the main table, or you might use the table that holds the result of the query without realizing that the data in the main table has been changed since you created it.

For your own use, it is generally better to keep the result in a cursor rather than a table, and to run the query to create the cursor again every time you need it.

It is useful to store the result in a table if you want to give the data to someone else.

Graph

If you select the Graph button, the result is displayed in a graph created using Microsoft Graph, a mini-application that is bundled with Visual FoxPro.

Screen

If you select the Screen button, the output is displayed in the main Visual FoxPro window, like the output of a LIST command. The Query Destination dialog box is displayed as shown in Figure 15.11.

As you learned in Chapter 8, when you use commands that send output to the screen in this way, you can add an optional TO PRINT or TO FILE <file name> clause, to send the output to a printer or to a text file at the same time. The options in the Secondary Output area of this dialog box let you do the same things.

The check boxes in the Options area of the dialog box let you specify whether the result includes field names as the heading of each column and whether the result is displayed one screen at a time (like a DISPLAY command) or continuously (like a LIST command).

FIGURE 15.11

Sending the result to the screen

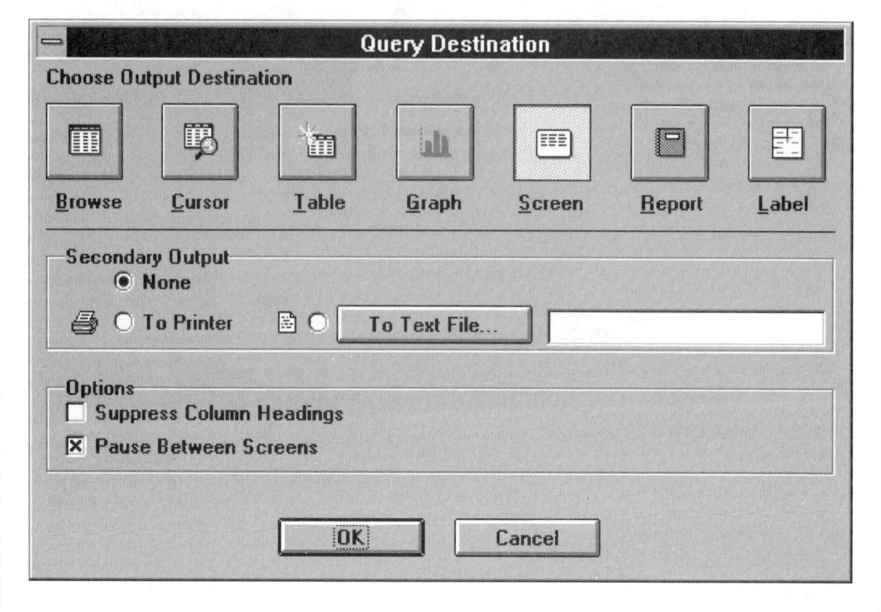

Report

If you click the Report button, the result is displayed in a new or existing report form. The Query Destination dialog box is displayed as shown in Figure 15.12.

To specify which report is used, you may:

- Click the Open Report button and use the Open dialog box to select an existing report.
- Enter the name of an existing report in the text box to the right of this button.
- Click the Wizard button to the right of the text box and use the Wizard to create the report.

The check boxes immediately below control the report's output options. Select Page Preview to display it in a Preview window rather than printing. Select Console On to display it on the screen while it is being printed. Select Eject Page Before Report to make the printer eject a

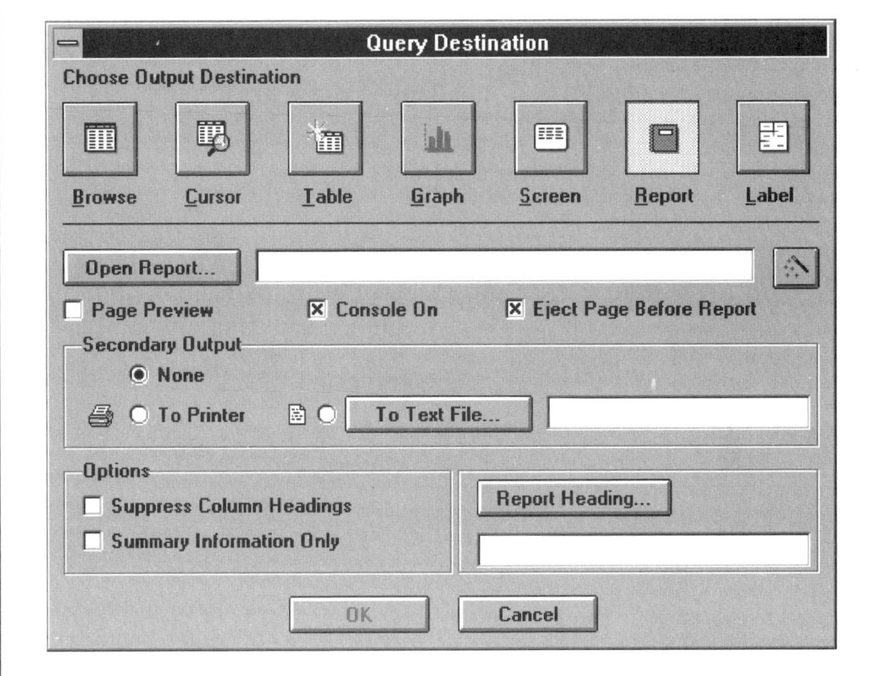

FIGURE 15.12

Sending the result to a report

page before it begins printing; you can deselect this check box if there is not a partially completed page in the printer.

The Secondary Output area works as it does if you select the Screen button, as described above.

The check boxes in the Options column let you suppress the use of the field name as a heading or produce a report with summary information only. The Report Heading button displays the Expression Builder, which you can use to create a heading; or simply enter the heading in the text box under it.

Label

If you click the Label button, the result is sent to an existing label form. The Query Destination dialog box is displayed as shown in Figure 15.13. Click the Open Report button and use the Open dialog box to select an existing report, or enter the name of an existing report in the text box to the right of this button.

FIGURE 15.13

Sending the result to labels

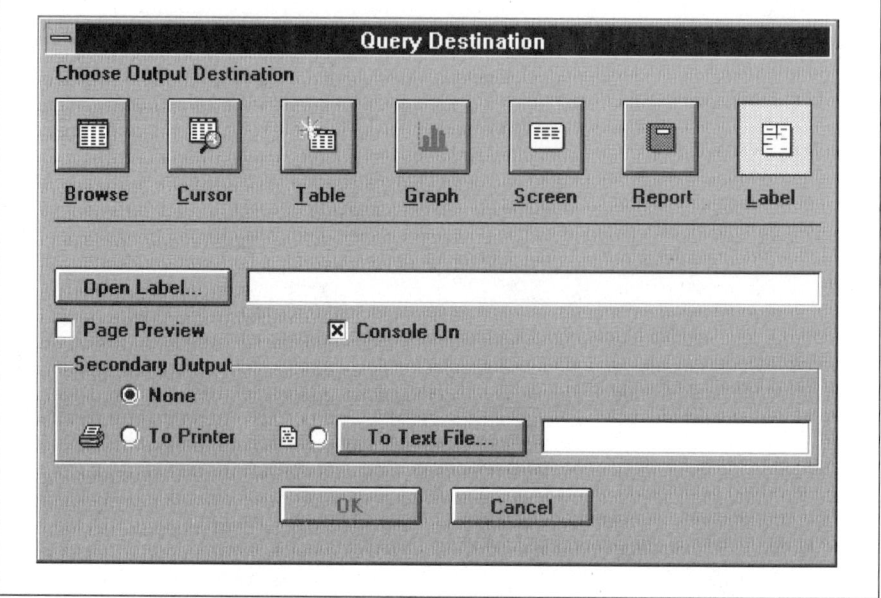

Select the Page Preview check box to display the labels in a Preview window rather than printing them. Select Console On to display it on the screen while it is being printed.

The Secondary Output area works as it does if you select the Screen button, as described above.

▸ Viewing SQL Code

You can click the SQL Window button of the Query Designer toolbar, choose Query ➤ View SQL, or choose View SQL from the Query Designer shortcut menu to open the SQL window, which contains the code generated by the selections you made in the Query Designer, shown in Figure 15.14. These options are all toggles; if the SQL window is already open, they hide it.

The SQL language is discussed later in this chapter.

FIGURE 15.14

The SQL window

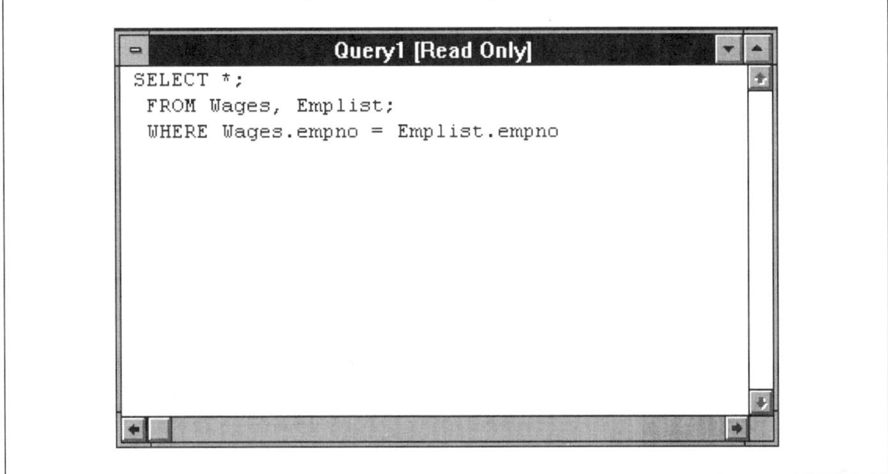
Query1 [Read Only]
SELECT *;
FROM Wages, Emplist;
WHERE Wages.empno = Emplist.empno

Maximizing the Table View

Click the Maximize Table View button of the Query toolbar to make the top pane, which displays the tables, fill the entire Query Designer window. This is only necessary if you are looking at a complex database with so many tables that you cannot see them all when this pane is its ordinary size.

Running the Query

After you have selected all the options you want, it's time to run the query. Either click the Run button of the main toolbar, choose Query ➤ Run Query, or choose Run Query from the Query Designer shortcut menu to run the query and send its output to the destination you specified—or to a Browse window, if you did not specify a destination.

Sample Queries

Now, you should solidify what you have learned by trying a few sample queries that relate tables. Before you can do these exercises, you must

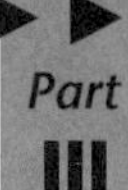

have done the exercises in the section "Creating and Modifying the Tables" at the end of Chapter 12, to create a Wages table and add employee numbers to the Emplist table. If you have not yet done so, go back and do those exercises before continuing here.

▶ Relating Tables

As an exercise in using the Query Designer window, you will set up the same many-to-one relation between the Wages table and the Emplist table that you created using the View window in Chapter 14, and then you will browse fields of this relational database, as you did earlier using the BROWSE FIELDS command.

1. Choose File ➤ New. Select the Query radio button, and click the New File button to use the Query Designer. Visual FoxPro displays the Open dialog box so you can select a table. Select WAGES.DBF and click OK.

2. Now, click the Add Table button of the Query toolbar. Select EMPLIST.DBF in the Open dialog box, and click OK. Visual FoxPro displays the Join Condition dialog box. By default, Wages.empno should be displayed on the left, Like should be selected as the condition, and Emplist.empno should appear to the right, as shown in Figure 15.15. If these items are not there by default, use the drop-down lists to select them. Click OK to return to the Query Designer. Notice that the criterion you just created is displayed in the Selection Criteria list, and that the two tables are connected with a line to indicate the join, as shown in Figure 15.16.

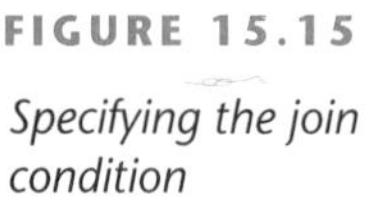

FIGURE 15.15 ▶

Specifying the join condition

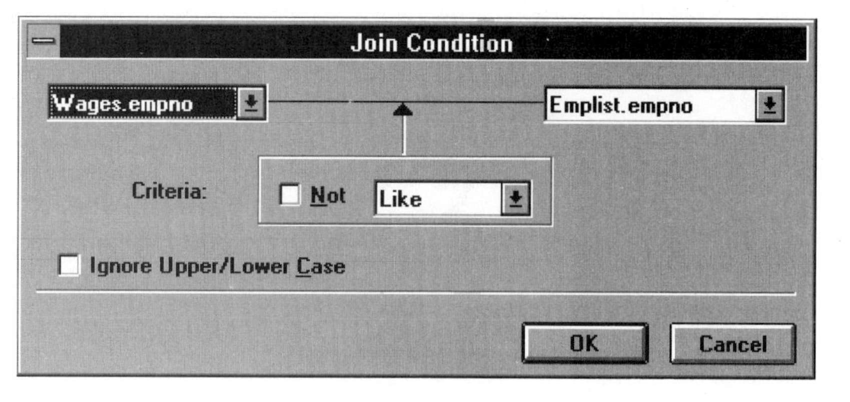

FIGURE 15.16

The join is displayed in the Query Designer.

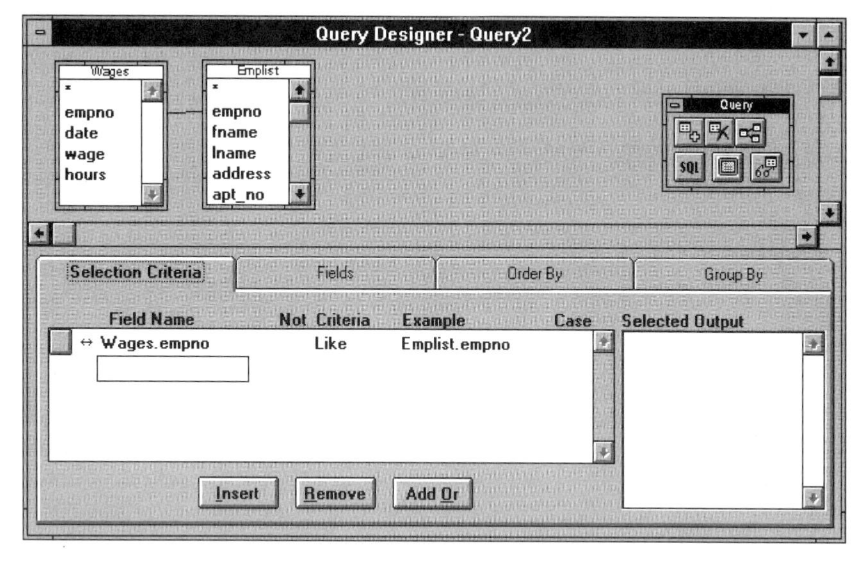

3. Click the Fields tab. Use the Field Picker to move Emplist.lname, Emplist.fname, Wages.date, Wages.wage, and Wages.hours to the Selected Output list.

4. Click the Order By tab. Double-click Emplist.lname and Emplist.fname to move them to the Ordering Criteria list. Then select OK.

5. Choose File ➤ Save. As the query name, enter Wage_emp and click Save. Click the Run button. Visual FoxPro displays the result of the query in a Browse window (the default destination), as shown in Figure 15.17. (Columns are narrowed slightly in the illustration, so they all are visible.)

6. Now, to see that the result of the query is kept in a cursor, press Esc to close the Browse window. Press Esc again to close the Query Designer. Enter **LIST** in the Command window. Visual FoxPro lists the result of the query, as shown in Figure 15.18.

7. You can continue to use this query result with any commands that you would use with an open table, including commands with optional clauses. For example, enter **CLEAR** and then enter **LIST FOR LNAME = "L"**. Visual FoxPro lists the records in the result whose last name begins with L, as shown in Figure 15.19.

FIGURE 15.17

The result of the Wage_emp query

Query

Lname	Fname	Date	Wage	Hours
CHANG	EDNA	08/06/95	9.7500	42.0
CHANG	EDNA	08/13/95	9.7500	45.0
LOVE	JACK	08/20/95	15.0000	40.0
LOVE	JACK	08/06/95	15.0000	41.0
LOVE	JACK	08/13/95	15.0000	38.0
Levy	Audrey	08/06/95	20.0000	36.0
Levy	Audrey	08/13/95	20.0000	32.0
Levy	Audrey	08/20/95	20.0000	42.0

FIGURE 15.18

The result of the Wage-emp query can still be used.

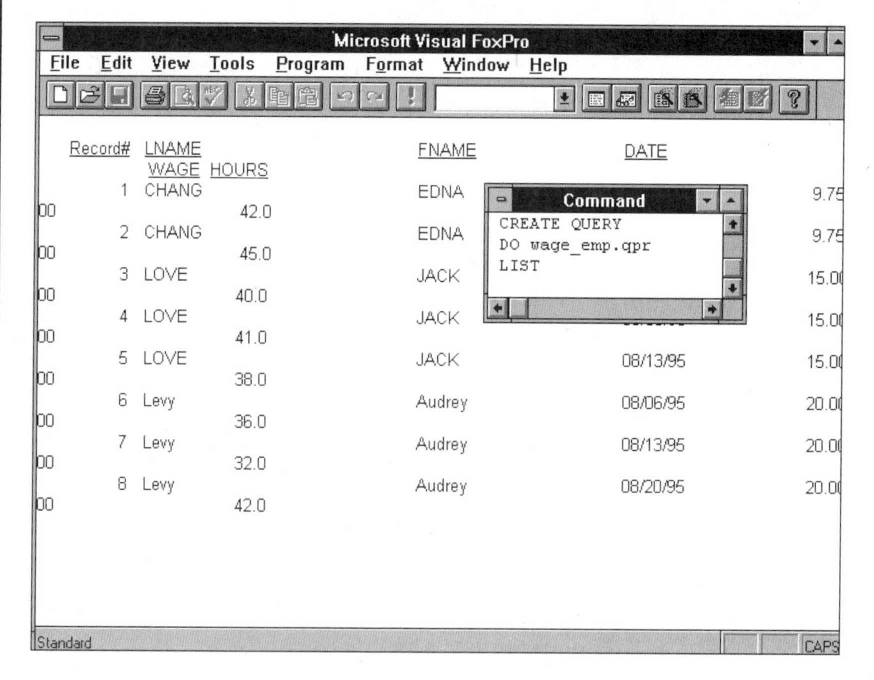

FIGURE 15.19

Using the query result with a filter

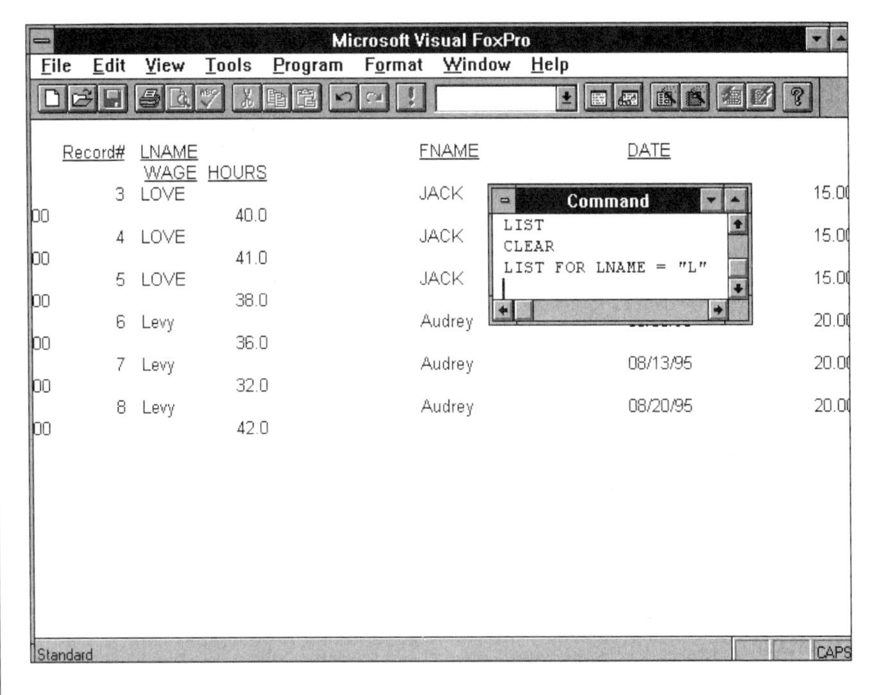

8. Now, enter **USE**. Then enter **LIST**. Because the cursor is no longer open, Visual FoxPro displays an Open dialog box so you can open a table. Press Esc, and press any key to remove the Alert.

You see that you not only use a cursor just as you use a table, you also close it just as you do a table. Once the cursor is closed, it is gone forever, but you can generate a new one simply by running the query again.

One-to-Many and Many-to-One Queries

Now, if you want, you can do the following exercise to verify that with SQL queries there is no difference in the result of queries based on many-to-one and one-to-many relationships. This exercise creates the same query as the one above, except that it begins by using the Emplist table and relates the Wages table to it. Despite the switch from a many-to-one to a one-to-many relationship, there is no difference in the result.

1. Choose File ➤ New. Select the Query radio button and click the New File button. When Visual FoxPro displays the Open dialog box, select EMPLIST.DBF and click OK.

2. Click the Add Table button of the Query toolbar. Select WAGES.DBF in the Open dialog box, and click OK. Visual FoxPro displays the Join Condition dialog box, with Emplist.empno displayed in the list box to the left, Like selected as the condition, and Wages.empno selected in the list box to the right. Click OK to return to the Query Designer, with the join you defined displayed in it, as shown in Figure 15.20.

FIGURE 15.20

The selection criterion

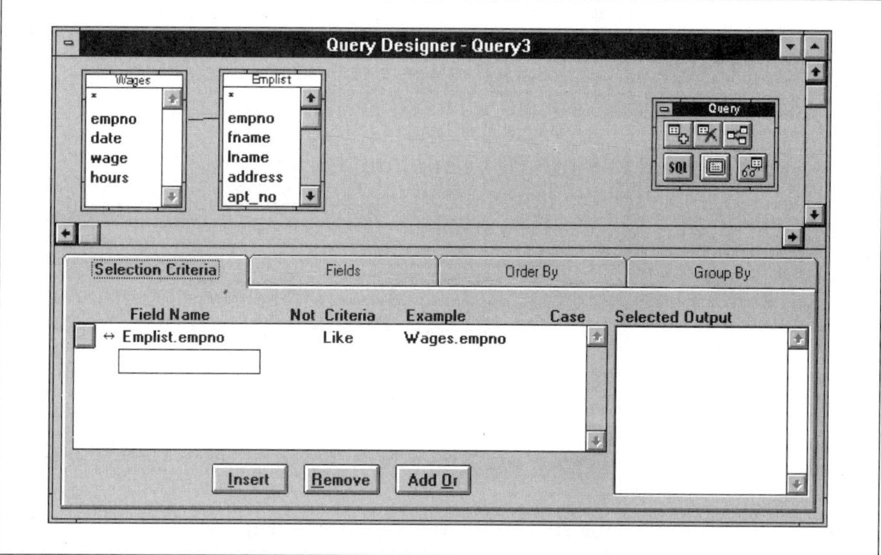

3. Now, repeat steps 3 and 4 from the previous exercise to specify the fields to be included and their sort order. Then click the Run button. Visual FoxPro displays the result shown in Figure 15.21, exactly the same as the result of the previous exercise. Close the Browse window and close the Query Designer without saving this query.

FIGURE 15.21

The result of the modified query

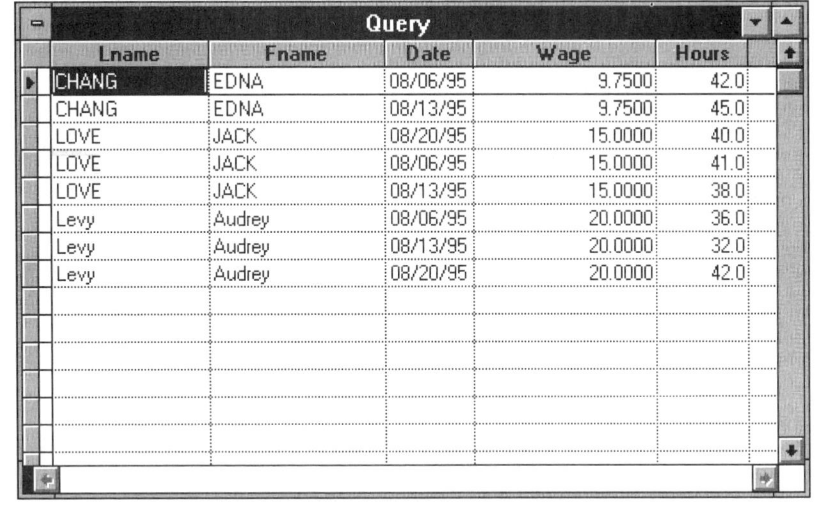

Query

Lname	Fname	Date	Wage	Hours
CHANG	EDNA	08/06/95	9.7500	42.0
CHANG	EDNA	08/13/95	9.7500	45.0
LOVE	JACK	08/20/95	15.0000	40.0
LOVE	JACK	08/06/95	15.0000	41.0
LOVE	JACK	08/13/95	15.0000	38.0
Levy	Audrey	08/06/95	20.0000	36.0
Levy	Audrey	08/13/95	20.0000	32.0
Levy	Audrey	08/20/95	20.0000	42.0

▶ Filtered Joins

When you are using the Query Designer with a relational database, you can use additional selection criteria to filter the result, just as you learned to do in Chapter 4. Try a couple of examples: first, create a query that displays the wages and names of all employees who are not from New York state, and then create one that displays the wages and names of all employees from New York or New Jersey.

1. Choose File ➤ Open, and use the Open dialog box to open the Wage_emp query that you created a moment ago. When Visual FoxPro displays the Query Designer, choose File ➤ Save As. In the Save As dialog box, enter **N_nywage** as the new document name, and click Save to return to the Query Designer.

2. In the second line of the Selection Criteria list, click the Field Name box and use the drop-down list to select Emplist.state. Click the Not box to its right to select it. In the Example box, enter "**NY**". Choose File ➤ Save to save the change.

3. The query is shown in Figure 15.22. Click the Run button to display the result in a Browse window, as shown in Figure 15.23. As expected, the result uses the same join as the earlier example, but

now it only includes records with NY in the State field. Press Esc to close the Browse window.

FIGURE 15.22

A query with a join and filter

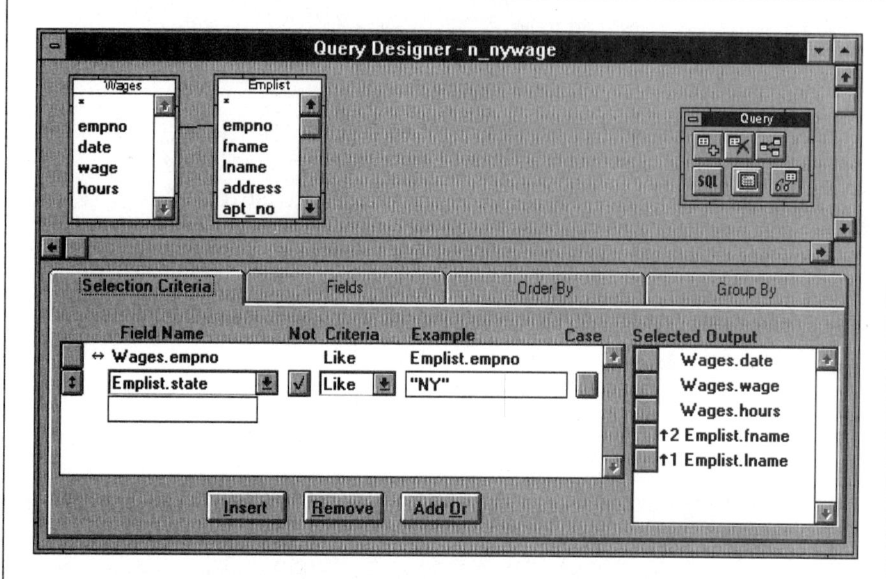

FIGURE 15.23

The result of the Nynjwage query

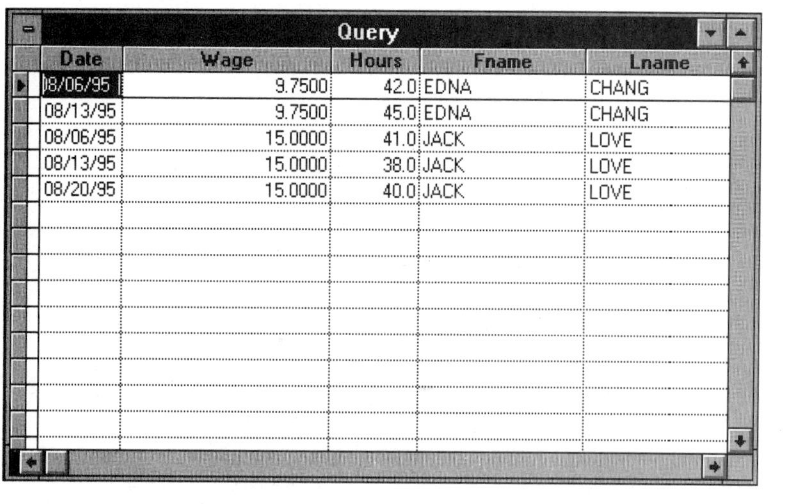

Query

Date	Wage	Hours	Fname	Lname
08/06/95	9.7500	42.0	EDNA	CHANG
08/13/95	9.7500	45.0	EDNA	CHANG
08/06/95	15.0000	41.0	JACK	LOVE
08/13/95	15.0000	38.0	JACK	LOVE
08/20/95	15.0000	40.0	JACK	LOVE

4. Now, rename the query and change it again. Choose File ➤ Save As. In the Save As dialog box, enter **Nynjwage** as the new name, and click Save.

5. In the Query Designer window, click the Not box of the criterion you just entered to deselect it, so it now includes states with the value NY in them.

6. Click the Add Or button to add a line with OR in it. Then, in the fourth line of the Selection Criteria list, click the Field Name box and use the drop-down list to select Emplist.state, and enter "**NJ**" in the Example box. Choose File ➤ Save to save the changes.

7. The query is shown in Figure 15.24. Click the Run button to display the result, as shown in Figure 15.25. Press Esc to close the Browse window.

FIGURE 15.24

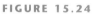

A query with a join and a complex filter

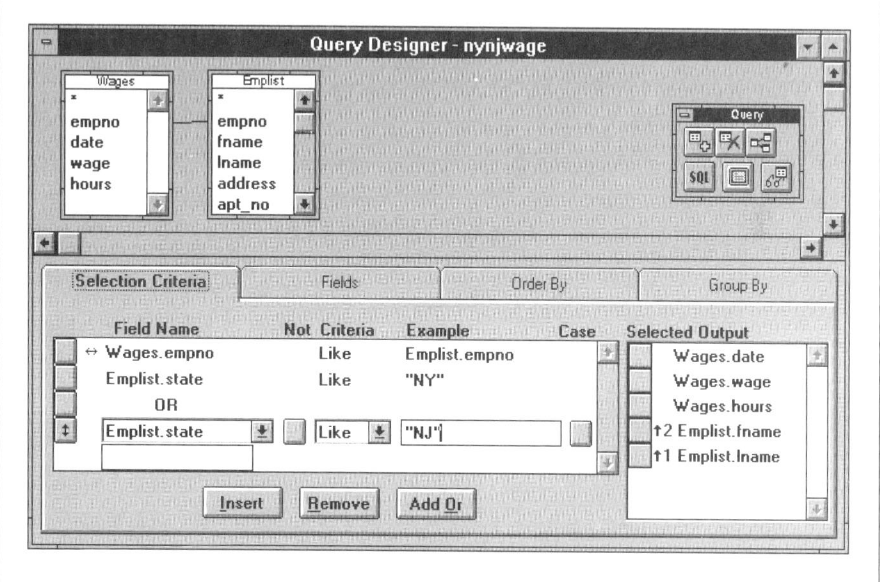

As you can see, it is no more difficult to use a query to isolate records of a relational database than it is to isolate records of a single table. Simply enter one line of the selection criteria panel to relate the tables. Then enter additional lines in the usual way to specify which records are included.

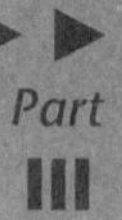

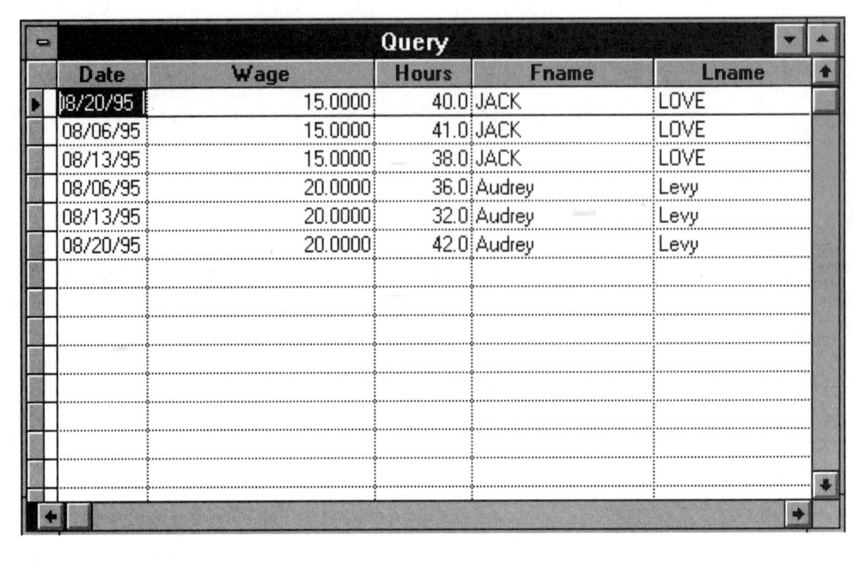

Query

Date	Wage	Hours	Fname	Lname
08/20/95	15.0000	40.0	JACK	LOVE
08/06/95	15.0000	41.0	JACK	LOVE
08/13/95	15.0000	38.0	JACK	LOVE
08/06/95	20.0000	36.0	Audrey	Levy
08/13/95	20.0000	32.0	Audrey	Levy
08/20/95	20.0000	42.0	Audrey	Levy

FIGURE 15.25 ▸ *The result of the Nynjwage query*

▸ A Grouped Query

As mentioned earlier, grouped queries are particularly useful with relational databases, in order to perform calculations on data in the "many" table with a result for each record in the "one" table. Try creating a grouped query to find the total hours worked by each employee:

1. Choose File ➤ New, make sure the Query radio button is selected, and click New File. In the Add Table Or View dialog box, click the Other button and select the Wages table. Select OK to proceed to the Query Designer.

2. Click the Add Table button. Click the Other button of the Add Table Or View dialog box, and select the Emplist table. Click OK. The Join Condition dialog box suggests joining the tables by using the Empno field of both and the Like criterion; click OK to accept this suggestion.

3. Display the Group By panel of the Query Designer and double-click Wages.empno to add it to the Group By Fields list.

4. Display the Fields Panel. Double-click Emplist.empno, Emplist.fname, and Emplist.lname to add them to the Selected Output list. From the Functions/Expressions control select Sum, and select Wages.hours from the submenu. Click the Add button to add it to the Selected Output list, as shown in Figure 15.26.

FIGURE 15.26

Specifying the fields included in the grouped query

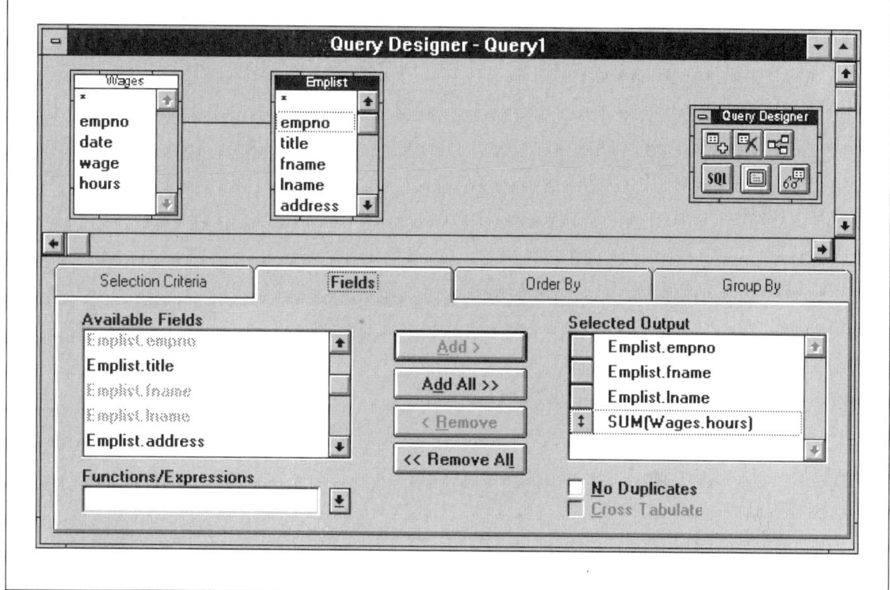

5. Choose File ➤ Save. As the Query name, enter tot_wage, and click the Save button. Then click the Run button to display the result. After you have looked at it, close the Browse window and Query Designer.

As you can see, the result has only two records, because you have only entered Wage records for two employees. Each record has the employee number, name, and total hours worked by that employee.

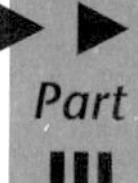

▶▶ The SQL SELECT Command

Although the SQL SELECT Command has many options its basic features are easy to understand.

If you open the Wage_emp query that you created earlier and then click the SQL button of the Query toolbar, Visual FoxPro will display the code shown in Figure 15.27.

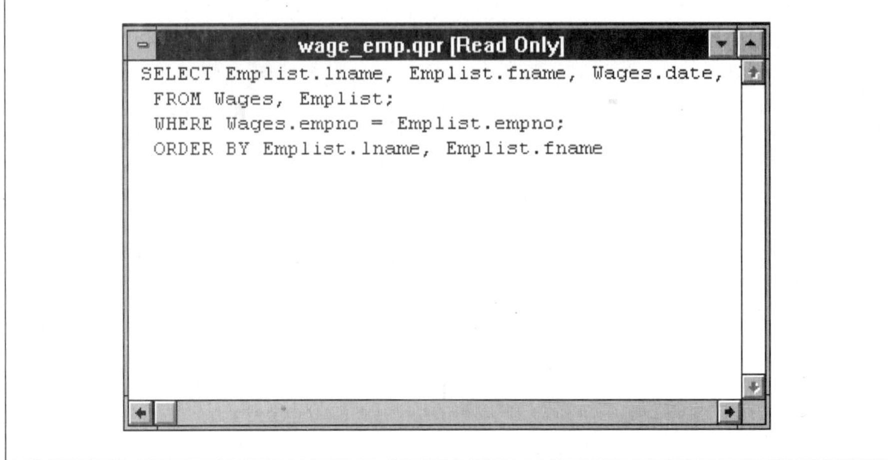

wage_emp.qpr [Read Only]
SELECT Emplist.lname, Emplist.fname, Wages.date,
FROM Wages, Emplist;
WHERE Wages.empno = Emplist.empno;
ORDER BY Emplist.lname, Emplist.fname

FIGURE 15.27 ►

The SQL SELECT command that was generated by the Wage_emp query

As you can see, the command includes three clauses:

- **SELECT <field list>** specifies the fields to be included in the result. Field names all include the table name, followed by a dot, followed by the field name, and they are separated by commas.
- **FROM <table list>** specifies the tables used by the query. Table names are separated by commas.
- **WHERE <logical expression>** specifies the join condition used to relate the tables. As you will see in a moment, this clause can also include logical expressions used to filter the data.

Although this command is listed on several lines to make it easier to read, it is actually just a single command. The semicolon at the end of each line indicates that the following line is a continuation of the same command.

TIP

Though this is a read-only file, you can use the usual editing methods to copy the code out of this window and paste it into the Command window or into a program. If you paste it into the Command window, you must delete the line breaks and the semicolons so it is all on one line.

Likewise, if you open the Nynjwage query and then click the SQL button, Visual FoxPro will display the code shown in Figure 15.28. You can see that this has the same clauses as the previous command, but that the WHERE clause has multiple conditions. Notice that the OR condition is in parentheses, and that all the conditions between the word AND and the end of the command are nested in parentheses, so that everything that follows is in a logical AND relationship with the initial WHERE condition that relates the two tables.

▶ Other Features of the SELECT Command

The SELECT command has many options. Its complete syntax is:

```
SELECT [ALL ¦ DISTINCT] [<alias1>] <select item>
     [,[<alias>,] <select item>...]
     FROM <table> [<alias2>][,<table> [alias3>]...]
     [[INTO <destination>] ¦ [TO FILE <filename>
          [AD   DITIVE] ¦ TO PRINTER]]
     [NOCONSOLE]
     [PLAIN]
     [NOWAIT]
     [WHERE <join condition>
          [AND <join condition>...]
          [AND ¦ OR <filter condition>
          [AND ¦ OR <filter condition>...]]]
     [GROUP BY <group column> [,<group column>...]]
     [HAVING <filter condition>]
     [UNION [ALL] <SELECT command>]
     [ORDER BY <order item> [ASC ¦ DESC]
          [,<order item> [ASC ¦ DESC]...]]
```

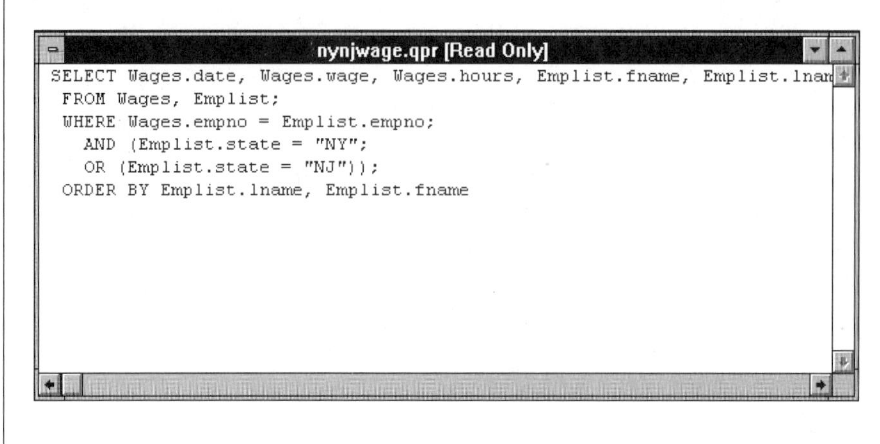

nynjwage.qpr [Read Only]
SELECT Wages.date, Wages.wage, Wages.hours, Emplist.fname, Emplist.lnam
FROM Wages, Emplist;
WHERE Wages.empno = Emplist.empno;
AND (Emplist.state = "NY";
OR (Emplist.state = "NJ"));
ORDER BY Emplist.lname, Emplist.fname

FIGURE 15.28

The SQL SELECT command that was generated by the Nynjwage query

You can see that some of these options are equivalent to features of the Query Designer that you already understand. For example, the ORDER BY clause is equivalent to the Order By panel of the Query Designer, and the GROUP BY option is equivalent to the Group By panel.

All of the options of this command are described in Appendix B. Here, you should look at a couple of particularly useful ones.

The Destination of the Query

The INTO or TO clause determines where the results of the query go:

- **INTO CURSOR <cursor name>:** Stores the results in a temporary table.
- **INTO DBF <filename>** or **INTO TABLE <filename>:** Stores the results in a permanent table.
- **INTO ARRAY <array name>:** Stores the results in an array of memory variables (arrays are a programming feature not covered in this book).
- **TO FILE <file name> [ADDITIVE]:** Stores the results in the file that is named. If the file does not exist, Visual FoxPro creates it. If it does exist, the command overwrites it, unless you use the

optional keyword ADDITIVE, which appends the results to the data already in the file.

- **TO PRINTER:** Prints the results.
- **TO SCREEN:** Displays the results on the screen, like the output of a LIST command.

If no destination option is used, as in the generated commands you looked at above, the results are displayed in a Browse window without being stored in a named cursor. As you have seen, though, they are kept in an unnamed cursor that can be used like any other cursor.

Including Expressions in the Result

Instead of field names, you can use expressions in the list of items that follows the word SELECT.

For example, if you wanted all of the results to be capitalized properly, you could copy the SQL command into a program or into the Command window, as described above, and then edit the list to read **Proper(Emplist.lname)** instead of **Emplist.lname**, and so on.

Likewise, you could add an expression to calculate total wage in the same way.

Excluding Duplicate Values

There are two options that can be used within the SELECT clause, between the word SELECT and the list of fields or other select items.

- **ALL** includes all the records in the result.
- **DISTINCT** eliminates duplicate records, and is equivalent to selecting the No Duplicates check box of the Fields panel of the Query Designer.

ALL is the default option and is used if neither option is specified.

Including All Records from the Many Table

As you have seen, you cannot use the Query Designer to include all the records in the "many" table of a many-to-one relationship, even those that do not have a matching record in the "one" table.

If data was entered properly, this should not make a difference. There should not be any records in the "many" table without an equivalent in the "one" table. However, it is a good idea to display all records from the "many" table to catch data-entry errors; if a record is entered in the "many" table that does not have an equivalent in the "one" table, you are better off seeing it in the result of a query, so you can correct the error, rather than having it hidden and never learning that the error exists.

You can simulate a query that includes all records of a table in a result by using the UNION clause of the SELECT command. In this clause the keyword UNION is followed by a second SELECT command, whose result is united with the result of the first SELECT command. When you use a UNION clause:

- Both SELECT commands must have the same number of Select items listed after them, and the corresponding items in the list must have the same data type and width.
- You can include an ORDER BY clause only in the final SELECT, and this order applies to the entire result.

The Wage_emp query that you created earlier had the following code:

```
SELECT Emplist.lname, Emplist.fname, Wages.date,
        Wages.hours, Wages.wage ;
     FROM Wages, Emplist ;
     WHERE Wages.empno = Emplist.empno
```

To include all records from the "many" file (Wage), you can modify the query as follows:

```
SELECT Emplist.lname, Emplist.fname, Wages.date,
        Wages.hours, Wages.wage ;
     FROM Wages, Emplist ;
     WHERE Wages.empno = Emplist.empno
UNION ;
SELECT SPACE(20), SPACE(15), Wages.date,
        Wages.hours, Wages.wage ;
     FROM Wages ;
     WHERE Wages.empno NOT IN
     (SELECT Emplist.empno FROM Emplist)
```

The UNION clause says that you should include two fields of blank spaces and the data from the Wage file for every record in the Wages table whose Empno is not in the Employee table.

NOTE

The example uses the SPACE( ) function to return a number of blank spaces that is the same as the width of the Emplist.lname and Emplist.fname fields, though you could also simply use character strings made up of these spaces surrounded by quotation marks. The SPACE( ) function is used only to save the trouble of counting individual blank spaces as you type.

Other SQL Commands

Visual FoxPro includes the following SQL commands in addition to SELECT:

- **INSERT:** lets you add records to a table.
- **CREATE TABLE:** lets you create a table using a command rather than using the Table Designer.
- **CREATE CURSOR:** lets you create a cursor, a temporary table like the one you can create using a query.

All of these commands are covered more detail in Appendix B.

To Sum Up

In the previous chapter and this chapter, you looked at views and relational queries, the only two ways to relate tables that were available in earlier versions of Visual FoxPro. In the next chapter, you'll look at databases, a new and very powerful feature of Visual FoxPro 3.0 that lets you create permanent relationships between tables.

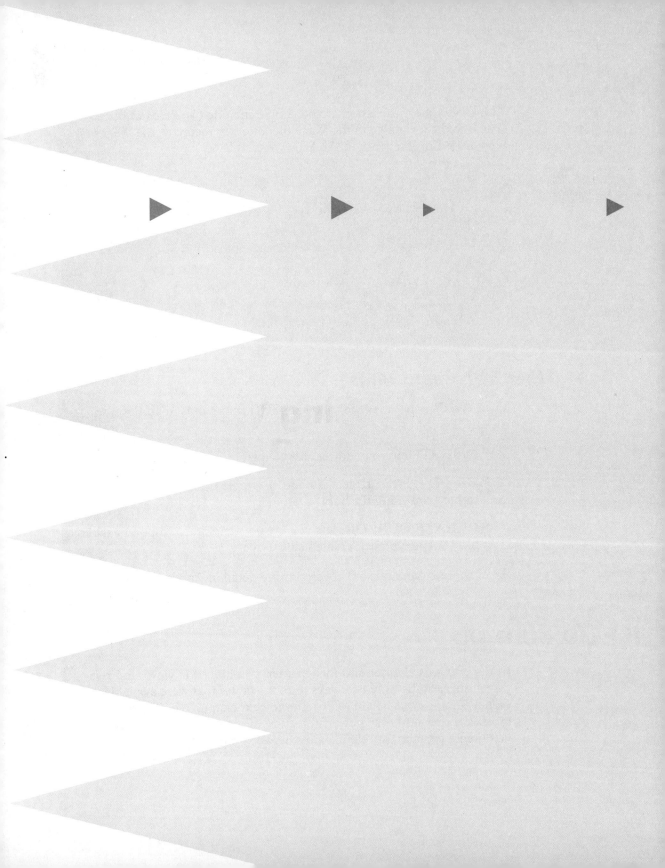

CHAPTER 16

Using Visual FoxPro Databases

▸▸ FAST TRACK

choose File ➤ Open and open it as you do any other file. All open databases are included in the Database drop-down control on the toolbar, and you can make any one the current database by selecting it from this list.

click the Add Table button or choose Database ➤ Add Table to add an existing Free table to the database. Click the New Table button or choose Database ➤ New Table to create a new table that is part of a database.

click the New Local View or New Remote View button, or choose Database ➤ New Local View or Database ➤ New Remote View. Use the View Designer to define the view in the same way that you use the Query Designer, and also to specify update options.

make sure the "one" table of a one-to-many relationship has a Primary Key index, and that the "many" table has an index that can be used as a Foreign key. In the Database Designer, click and drag from the Primary Key index in the "one" table to the index being used as the Foreign Key in the "many" table. Visual FoxPro displays the Edit Relationship dialog box, which should have the proper field names displayed in the drop-down lists and should say that the Relationship Type is One To Many. You can select a different index, if necessary.

To delete a database, **462**

use the command DELETE DATABASE <file name> [DELETE TABLES]. If you use the DELETE TABLES option, all the tables in the database are also deleted permanently from the disk. If you do not use this option, the tables become free tables. Views in the database are automatically deleted permanently when you delete a database.

To free tables if you have accidentally deleted the database in some other way, **462**

enter the command **FREE TABLE <table name>**.

To validate data entered in a table that is part of a database, **464**

use the Field Properties area of the Table Designer. In the Validation Rule text box, enter a logical expression which must be true for Visual FoxPro to allow data entry. In the Validation Text text box, enter an expression which Visual FoxPro displays as an error message if the user tries to enter data that violates the validation rule.

To create a default value for a field that is part of a database, **465**

enter an expression in the Default Value text box of the Field Properties area of the Table Designer. This value is automatically displayed in the field when a new record is appended, and you can edit it.

▶▶ **T**he word *database* has a special meaning beginning with Visual FoxPro 3.0. In addition to the common meaning, a collection of tables used to store data for a single application, the word "database" was often used in early versions of FoxPro to refer simply to a table. In fact, the extension DBF, which is used for tables, stands for *d*ata*b*ase *f*ile. Beginning with Visual FoxPro 3.0, however, the term *database* refers to a special file, with the extension DBC, which you can use to organize multiple tables and views and to create persistent relationships among them. In other words, Visual FoxPro's "database" file type is a tool for managing relational databases. This chapter discusses how to use this powerful new feature, and then uses it to organize our sample relational database.

▶▶ When to Use a Database

The database feature has several important advantages over other methods of working with relationally organized data in Visual FoxPro:

- Databases allow you to create persistent relationships among tables and to display all of these relationships schematically. This makes them particularly valuable if you have very complex data broken up into multiple tables, as in Figure 16.1, which shows the schema of the sample database distributed with Visual FoxPro. Clearly, if you have this many tables, it is difficult to keep the relationships among all of them in mind, each time you use the View window or Query Designer to relate the tables for a different purpose. It is much easier to create a single schema with all the relationships among the tables, like the one in the illustration, and to have the relationships displayed automatically whenever you create a view.

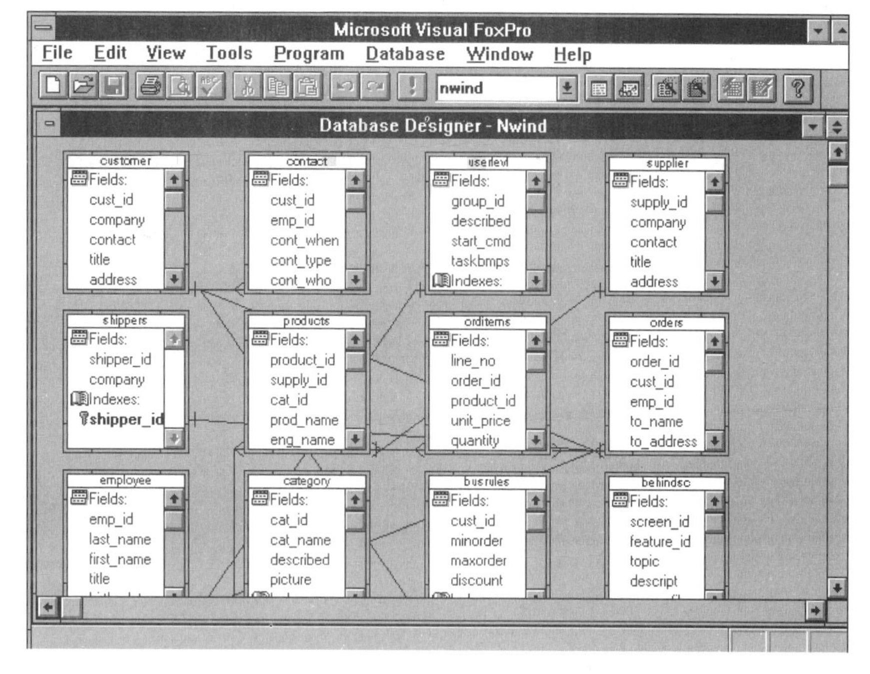

FIGURE 16.1

A sample database schema

- Databases let you create updatable SQL views, which work like the SQL queries discussed in Chapter 15 but are not read-only. This is useful for developers, who want to use SQL to optimize performance, and also for users who prefer using SQL views to work with their data, rather than using the View window. You can also use these views as the basis of queries, reports, and other files, just as you do tables.
- When a table is part of a database, *data dictionary* features are added to the Table Designer so that you can create long names, validity checks, and default values for fields.

However, Visual FoxPro databases have the disadvantages of being complex and a bit unwieldy to use.

Because databases are an advanced feature of Visual FoxPro, you cannot use Wizards to create and modify them, and this makes them a bit more difficult to work with than other Visual FoxPro files.

Databases are a bit unwieldy because you cannot use a table that is part of a database without using the database first. All Visual FoxPro tables are either *free tables* or are included in a database. Up to this point, you have only worked with free tables. If you choose File ➤ Open and try to open a table that is part of a database, though, Visual FoxPro will display the error message shown in Figure 16.2.

FIGURE 16.2

You must open the database before opening a table in it.

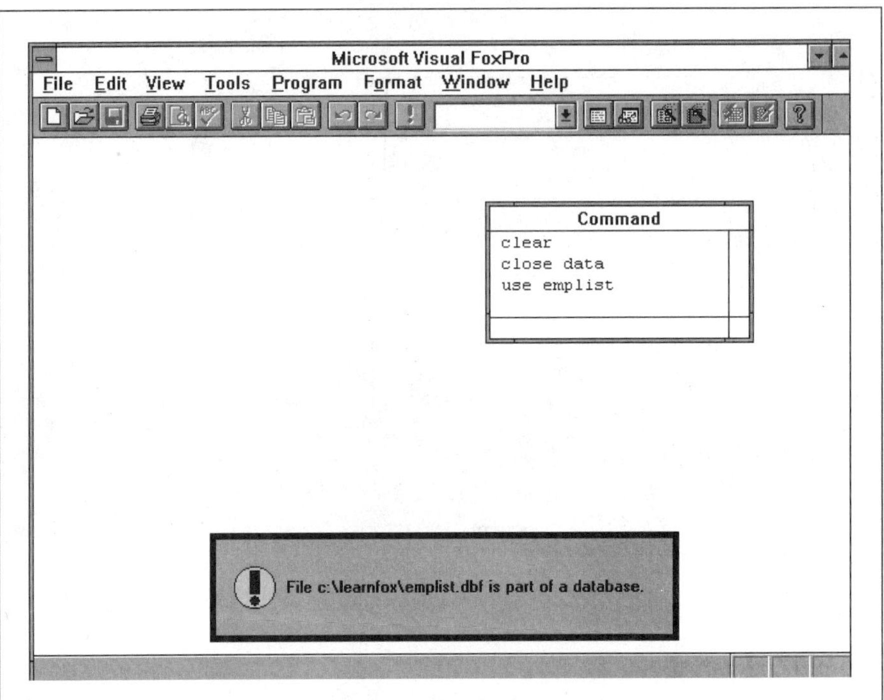

►► **TIP**

From the Command window, you can use a table belonging to a database that is not open by using the database name and table name, separated by the ! delimiter, to refer to the table. For example, if the Emplist table is part of the Employee database, entering the command USE EMPLOYEE!EMPLIST lets you open the table without opening the database.

Given these advantages and disadvantages, it makes sense to use a Visual FoxPro database to manage a complex application, made up of many tables. It is the easiest way to create and keep track of a large number of relationships.

Just as obviously, it does not make sense to use the database feature if your data is stored in a single table. You get no benefit from the extra work of creating and opening the database.

Whether to use Visual FoxPro databases to manage a simple relational database is a matter of preference. After you've used a database to manage your sample data in this chapter, you'll know whether you prefer it to using the View window or Query Designer.

▶▶ Setting Up a Database

Create a Visual FoxPro database as you do other files: choose File ➤ New or click the New button to display the New dialog box, select the Database radio button, and click the New File button. Visual FoxPro displays the Create dialog box to let you name the new database.

▶▶ TIP

As with other objects, you can create and name the database in a single step from the Command window. Enter the command CREATE DATABASE <file name>.

▶ Opening and Closing Databases

When you first create a database, it becomes the current database, and its name is displayed in the toolbar's list box. For example, the database name Nwind appears in the toolbar you saw in Figure 16.1.

You can open existing databases as you do other files, by choosing File ➤ Open or clicking the Open button and using the Open dialog box, or by entering the command **OPEN DATABASE <file name>**.

Opening Multiple Databases

You can open multiple databases simultaneously. The names of all open databases are added to the Database drop-down list in the Visual FoxPro toolbar, as shown in Figure 16.3, and you can select any one to make it current. You can also enter the command **SET DATABASE TO <database name>** to make any open database current.

FIGURE 16.3

The Database drop-down list

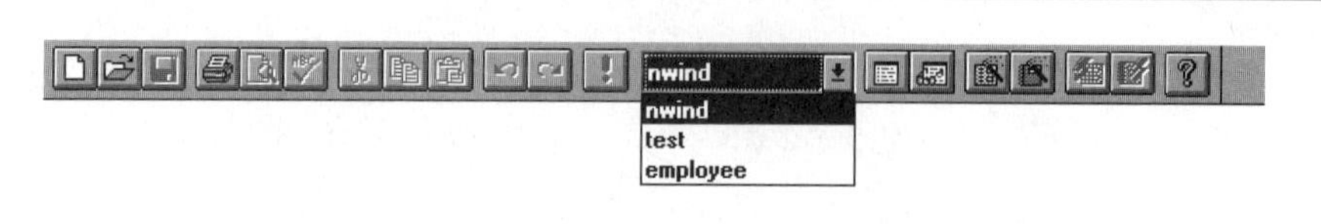

Closing Databases

To close all open databases, use the following commands:

- **CLOSE DATABASES** closes all databases and all tables and selects Work Area 1.
- **CLOSE ALL** closes all databases and all tables and selects Work Area 1; it also closes certain windows, such as the Form Designer, Label Designer, Query Designer, and Report Designer.

▸ The Database Designer

You can work with the tables of the current database just as you have always worked with tables. For example, you can USE them and BROWSE them. However, you can also work with them more powerfully if you use the Database Designer. Immediately after you have created a database, Visual FoxPro displays the Database Designer with no tables in it, as shown in Figure 16.4.

To perform routine work with the tables in the database, you can use the Database menu, the Database toolbar, or the database's shortcut menu.

FIGURE 16.4

The Database Designer for a new database

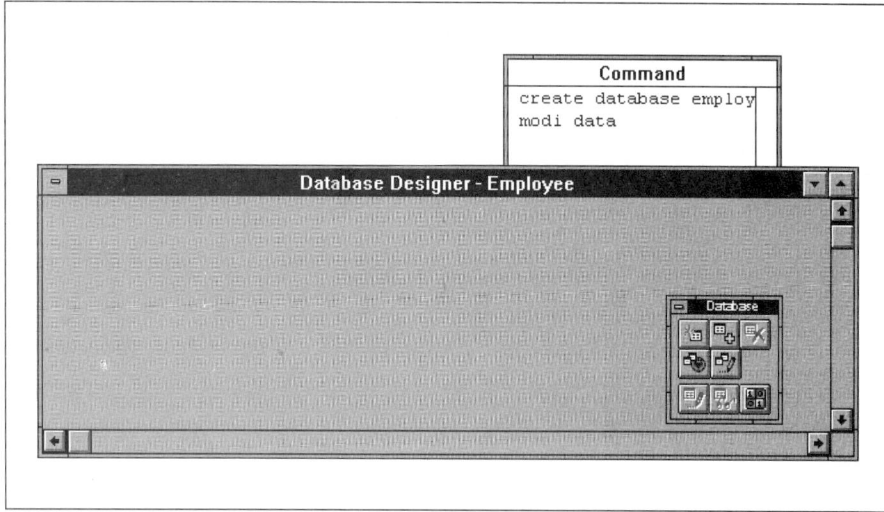

Creating a New Table

To create a new table, you can do any of the following:

- Choose Database ➤ New Table.
- Right-click the database and choose New Table from the shortcut menu.

- Click the New Table tool of the Database toolbar.
- Choose File ➤ New, click the New tool of the main toolbar, or use the CREATE command to create the table, just as you always have. If a database is open, this new table will be included in it, even if the Database Designer is not displayed.

In any case, Visual FoxPro displays the Create dialog box to let you name the table (unless you named it in the Command window), and then displays the Table Designer in an expanded form that lets you use Visual FoxPro's data dictionary features, which will be discussed later in this chapter.

Adding a Table

To add an existing table to the database, do any of the following:

- Choose Database ➤ Add Table.
- Click the Add Table button of the Database toolbar.
- Right-click the database and choose Add Table from its shortcut menu.

Visual FoxPro displays the Open dialog box to let you select an existing table.

You can also enter the command **ADD TABLE <table name>** to add a table to the currently open database, even if the Database Designer is not displayed. If you do not include the table name (or if you include a ? instead of the table name), Visual FoxPro displays the Open dialog box to let you select the table to add.

You can only add free tables to a database. You cannot add a table that is already part of another database. You must remove it from one database—for example, by using the command REMOVE TABLE, which is discussed below—before you can add it to another database.

Creating a View

To create a SQL view that is part of the database, do any of the following:

- Choose Database ➤ New Remote View or Database ➤ New Local View.
- Right-click the database and choose New Remote View or New Local View from the shortcut menu.

- Click the New Remote View or New Local View tool of the Database toolbar.
- Choose File ➤ New, click the New tool of the main toolbar, select the View radio button of the New dialog box, and create the view as you do other objects.
- Enter the command **CREATE SQL VIEW <file name> [REMOTE]**. Using this command without the REMOTE option creates a local view. This command also has options that let you

create connections to remote data sources and use a SQL SELECT statement to define the view from the command line; these options are covered in Appendix B. However, it is generally easier to omit them and use the Select Connection or Datasource dialog box to create connections and the View Designer to define the view. If a database is open, this new view will be included in it, even if the Database Designer is not displayed.

NOTE

Do not confuse the command CREATE SQL VIEW <file name> with the command CREATE VIEW <file name>, which creates a VUE view file, of the sort covered in Chapter 14, from the current environment.

If you are creating a remote view, Visual FoxPro displays the Connections dialog box, which lets you specify the data source or create a connection to a server.

If you are creating either a local or a remote view, Visual FoxPro displays the View Designer, which is similar to the Query Designer described in Chapter 15. The special features of SQL views are discussed later in this chapter.

You cannot add an existing view to the database, as you can a table, because a SQL view must be created as part of a database. There are free tables to add, but there are no free views.

Working with Tables and Views

A table or view is displayed in the Database Designer as a list of fields, with the table or view name in its title bar. Tables also include a list of indexes following the field list.

You can manipulate tables and views as you do other objects in Windows applications:

- To move a table or view, click and drag its title bar.
- To resize a table or view, click and drag its left or right side to make it narrower or wider, its top or bottom to make it taller or shorter, or one of its corners to change both dimensions at once.

As in other Windows applications, the pointer is displayed as a two-headed arrow, indicating the directions you can click and drag, when it is in position to resize the object.

You can also right-click the Database Designer and choose Collapse All from its shortcut menu to display only the title bars of all the tables and views, as shown in Figure 16.5; choose Expand All from the shortcut menu to restore them to their previous size. Of course, this feature is most useful in a very complex database.

FIGURE 16.5

Collapsing tables and views

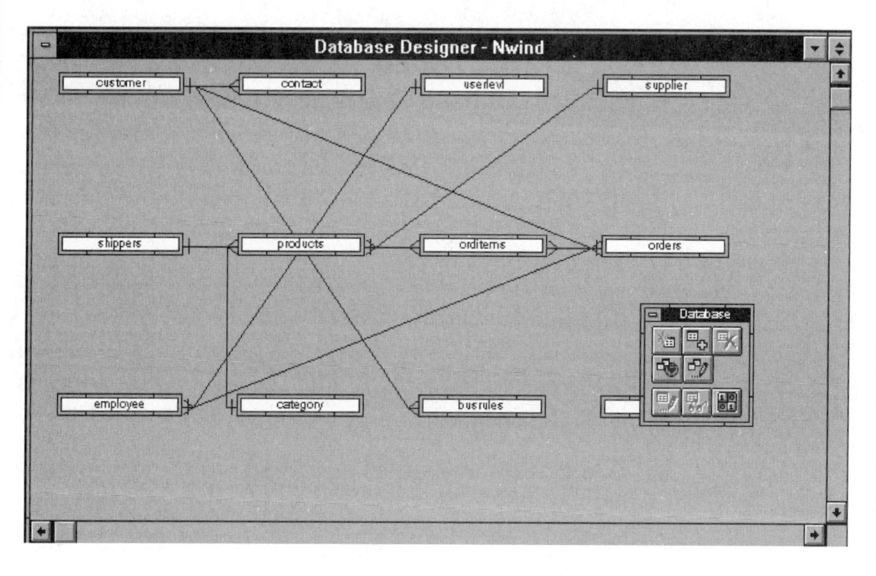

Browsing and Modifying Tables and Views You can use the Database menu or toolbar to browse or modify tables and views. First, click a table or view in the Database Designer to highlight it and then:

- Choose Database ➤ Browse or click the Browse Table tool of the Database toolbar to display the data of the table or view in a Browse window, or simply double-click the table or view in the Database Designer to display it in a Browse window. If you do any of these, a Table menu is added to the menu bar, which you can use to work with the data in the Browse window in all the ways that you have already learned to do, regardless of whether you are browsing a table or a view.

- Choose Database ➤ Modify or click the Modify Table tool of the Database toolbar to modify the table or view. If a table is selected, Visual FoxPro displays the Table Designer, and if a view is selected, Visual FoxPro displays the View Designer to let you change its specifications.

You can also right-click the table or view to display its shortcut menu, shown in Figure 16.6, and then use the menu to browse or modify the file.

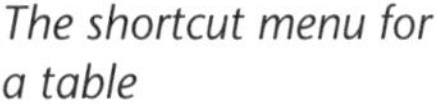

FIGURE 16.6

The shortcut menu for a table

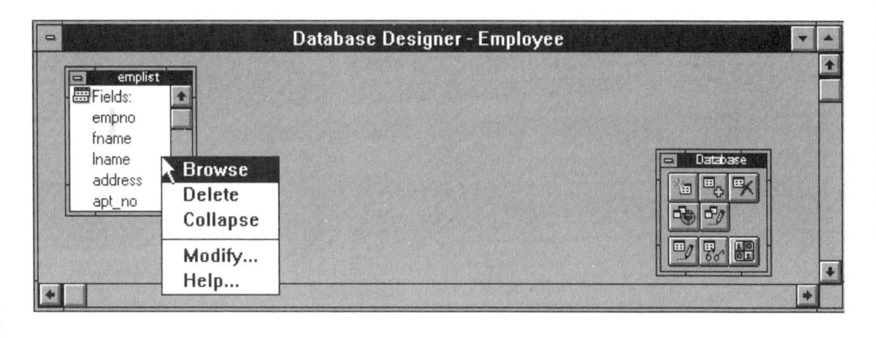

Of course, you can also browse or modify tables in the other ways you learned earlier, in Chapters 2, 3, and 8: for example, USE the table and then enter BROWSE or MODI STRU.

NOTE

After adding a table to a database, you can modify it to display the Table Designer with the data dictionary features (discussed later in this chapter) that were not available when you created it as a free table.

Removing or Deleting a Table Select a table and choose Database ➤ Remove or click the Remove Table button of the Database toolbar to display the dialog box shown in Figure 16.7, which gives you the option of either removing a table from the database or deleting it from the disk.

FIGURE 16.7

Removing or deleting a table

▸▸ **NOTE**

If you remove a table from a database, it becomes a free table, and you can work with it without first opening the database.

You can also use the command REMOVE TABLE <table name> [DELETE] to remove or delete a table. If you omit the optional DELETE, the table is removed from the database and becomes a free table.

Deleting a View Select a view and choose Database ➤ Remove or click the Remove Table button of the Database toolbar to delete it from the disk. Alternatively, use the command DELETE VIEW <view name>.

Since a view must be part of a database, you cannot remove it from the database without deleting it permanently.

Other Methods of Working with Tables Once you have opened a database, you can also work with its tables in any of the other ways that you have already used.

For example, if you click the Browse button of the database toolbar to browse a table, you also open the table, just as if you had entered a USE command; its name and others appear in the status bar, and it remains open until you close it. You can manipulate it using all of the Visual FoxPro commands that you ordinarily use to work with data.

Likewise, as long as a database is open, whether or not the Database Designer is displayed, you can work with its tables using all the methods and commands you have already learned.

▶ Creating a Persistent Relationship

One of the most important benefits of databases is the ability to create persistent relationships among tables. When you use the View Designer to create views of the data, these relationships are automatically included: you do not have to define them for each view.

To create a persistent one-to-many relationship between two tables, first you must create the necessary indexes. In a one-to-many relationship, the "one" table must have a primary key index, and the "many" table must have an index that can be used as a foreign key, holding the same values as the primary key in the "one" table.

In the Database Designer window, table lists include both the tables' fields and their indexes. To create a one-to-many relationship, click and drag from the Primary Key index in the "one" file to the index being used as the Foreign Key in the "many" table. Visual FoxPro displays the Edit Relationship dialog box, shown in Figure 16.8. This should have the proper field names displayed in the list boxes and should say that the Relationship Type is One To Many. You can use the drop-down lists to select a different index, if necessary.

FIGURE 16.8

The Edit Relationship dialog box

If you drag from the index in the "many" file to the primary index of the "one" file, instead of clicking and dragging in the opposite direction, Visual FoxPro will create a one-to-one relationship. You cannot use the Edit Relationship dialog box to change this; you must begin again and re-create the relationship.

After you have created a one-to-many relationship, the indexes it is based on are connected, as shown in Figure 16.9. Notice that the line divides into three branches on the "many" side of the relationship.

FIGURE 16.9

The line between indexes represents the relationship.

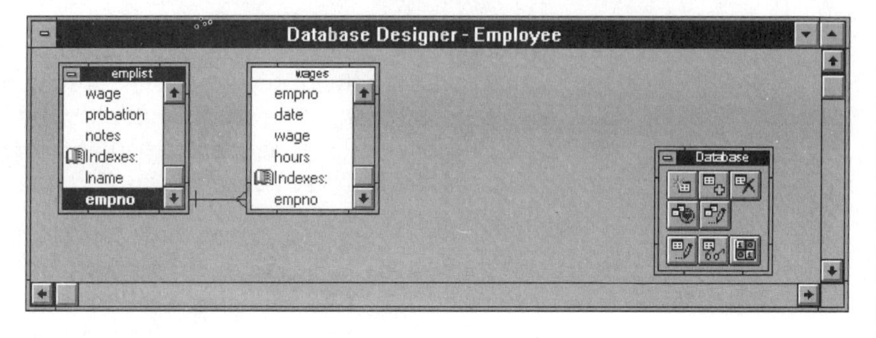

Editing a Relationship

After you have created a relationship, you can select it by clicking the line that represents it: the line becomes thicker to indicate that it is selected. Then you can choose Database ➤ Edit Relationship to display the Edit Relationship dialog box again and use the drop-down lists to change the indexes on which the relationship is based.

Alternatively, you can right-click the relationship to display its shortcut menu, shown in Figure 16.10, and choose Edit Relationship from it.

FIGURE 16.10

The shortcut menu for a relationship

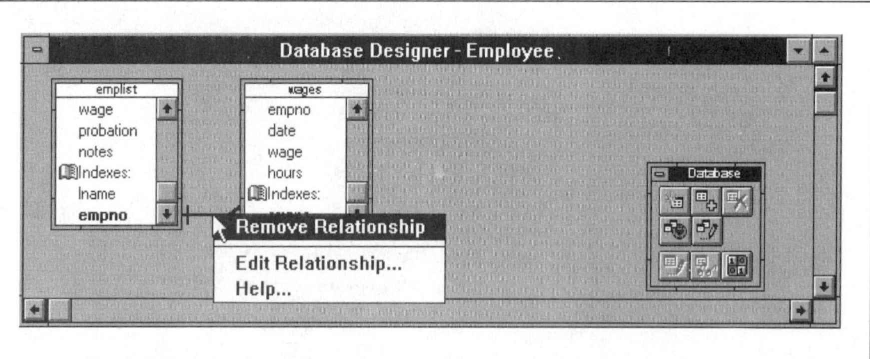

Removing a Relationship

To remove a relationship, right-click the line that represents it and choose Remove Relationship from its shortcut menu, or simply select the line and press Del.

Creating a Relationship Using SQL Statements

You can also create persistent relationships by writing SQL statements. Because this method is generally more difficult than the Database Designer technique that you just learned, we won't discuss it in detail here. Briefly, the steps are these:

1. If it does not already exist, create the appropriate primary key in the "one" table by using the PRIMARY KEY clause of the ALTER TABLE or CREATE TABLE command.
2. Then use the FOREIGN KEY … REFERENCES clause of the ALTER TABLE or CREATE TABLE command to create a foreign key in the "many" table and to indicate the "one" table that it is related to.

For more information, see ALTER TABLE or CREATE TABLE in Appendix B.

▶ Packing a Database

As you will see in a moment, a database is actually stored in a table, like an ordinary DBF table, which lists the tables and views in the database.

When you remove a table or view from a database, the record for that table or view is marked for deletion, but is not removed entirely from the table used to store the database.

To remove the records marked for deletion permanently, choose Database ➤ Cleanup Database, or enter the command **PACK DATABASE**.

Before you can pack a database, the following conditions must be met:

- It must be the current database.
- It must be opened exclusively.
- None of its tables or views may be open.

You do not need to worry about packing a database unless you have removed a large number of tables and views from it.

► Deleting a Database

You might want to delete a database when you are done working with it and have archived the data. As a beginner, you might also try working with a database in an application, and then decide that it is easier to manage your data using free tables.

To delete a database, use the command **DELETE DATABASE <file name> [DELETE TABLES]**.

If you use the DELETE TABLES option, all the tables in the database are also deleted permanently from the disk. If you do not use this option, the tables become free tables.

Views in the database are automatically deleted permanently when you delete a database.

► Freeing a Table

When you add a table to a database, Visual FoxPro creates a reference to the database in the table's DBF file, which prevents anyone from using the table unless the database is also in use.

If you use the DELETE DATABASE command to delete a database, Visual FoxPro removes these references from the tables that were in the database, and so they can be used as free tables. Likewise, when you remove a table from a database, Visual FoxPro removes this reference from it to make it a free table.

If you mistakenly delete the DBC file in some other way (for example, if you use Windows to delete it), these references will remain in its tables, and you will not be able to use them as free tables.

However, you can remove the database reference from a table, and thus use it as a free table, by using the command **FREE TABLE <table name>**. You can only use this command if no database is open.

Inside the Database

Although you don't need to understand all the details of how Visual FoxPro handles databases internally, it may be useful for you to see that a database is stored in an ordinary Visual FoxPro table.

For example, later in this chapter, you will create a database including the sample Emplist and Wages tables, and you will name it Employee. You could view the table in which this database is stored with these commands:

```
CLOSE ALL
USE \LEARNFOX\EMPLOYEE.DBC
BROWSE
```

Visual FoxPro will display the contents of the EMPLIST.DBC table in a Browse window, as shown in Figure 16.11. This lists all files used by the database, and the fields in all its tables and views. Notice that the database itself is object 1; the Emplist table is object 5 and has object 1 (the database) as its parent object, and its fields are objects 6 through 19 and have object 5 (the Emplist table) as their parent.

FIGURE 16.11

Browsing the table used to store the database

Employee

Objectid	Parentid	Objecttype	Objectname
1	1	Database	Database
2	1	Database	TransactionLog
3	1	Database	StoredProceduresSource
4	1	Database	StoredProceduresObject
5	1	Table	emplist
6	5	Field	empno
7	5	Field	fname
8	5	Field	lname
9	5	Field	address
10	5	Field	apt_no
11	5	Field	city
12	5	Field	state
13	5	Field	zip
14	5	Field	date_hired

►► **WARNING**

Do not edit the data in this Browse window unless you understand fully how databases are stored in tables.

You can also display this information on the screen or send it to a printer or a file by entering the command DISPLAY DATABASE or LIST DATABASE, or you can display just the names of the tables in the current database by entering the command DISPLAY TABLES or LIST TABLES. For more details on these commands and their options, see Appendix B.

►► The Table Designer

As you learned earlier, when you create a new table or modify an existing table that is part of a Visual FoxPro database, Visual FoxPro lets you use an enhanced version of the Table Designer.

► Using the Table Panel

The Table panel of the Table designer includes *data dictionary* features, which let you establish properties of fields that apply whenever you use them. If you are developing a complex application, it is obviously easier to define these properties once, when you are defining the structure of the table, than it would be to set them up each time a user enters data.

The Field Properties Area

As you can see in Figure 16.12, the Table Designer for tables that are part of a database has a Field Properties area, which is not available in the Table Designer when you're working with free tables (as discussed in Chapter 2). You can enter expressions in the four text boxes in the left half of this area, or click the button to the right of each to display the Expression Builder and use it to generate expressions, to define the following properties:

- **Validation Rule:** Enter a logical expression that must be true before Visual FoxPro will allow data entry. For example, if you pay your employees a wage of between $5 and $60 per hour, you can

FIGURE 16.12

The Table Designer for database tables

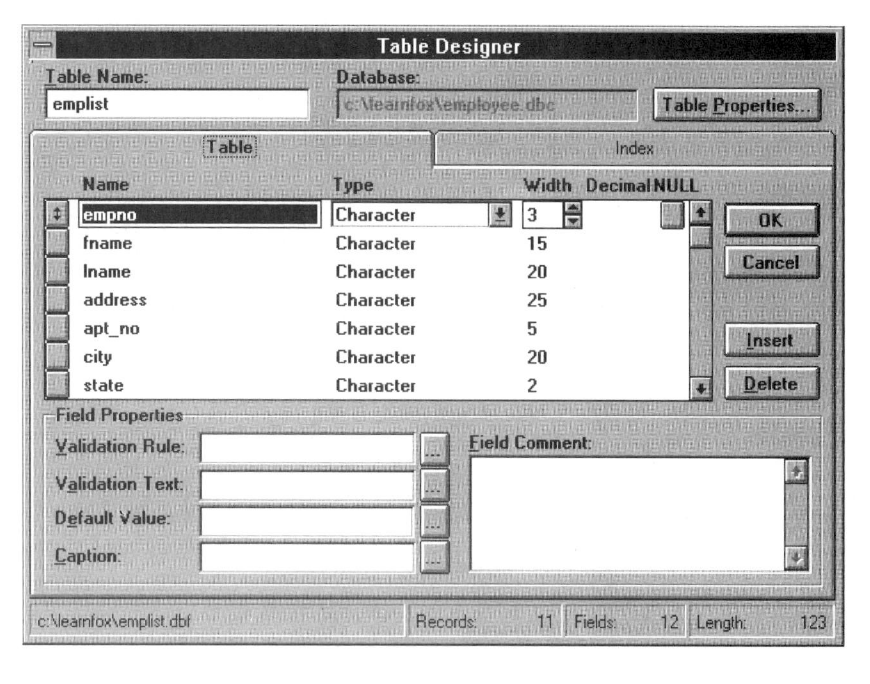

use the expression **>=5 .AND. <= 60** as a validation rule for the Wage field.

- **Validation Text:** Enter an expression for Visual FoxPro to display as an error message if the user tries to enter data that violates the validation rule. For example, as validation text to accompany the rule mentioned above, you could use "**The Hourly Wage must be between $5 and $60.**" Usually, the expression used as validation text is simply a character string, like this one, but there are also times when you might want to use a more complex expression that includes values of fields, the current date, or the like. For example, if the entry in a date field had to be at least earlier than the date it was entered, you could use the expression **<DATE( )** as its validation rule, and the expression "**The entry must be before** " **+ DTOC(DATE( ))** as its validation text.

- **Default Value:** Enter an expression to be used as the default value of the field; it will be automatically displayed in the field when a new record is appended. This value can be edited, like any

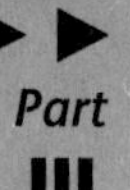

other. Remember that when you are entering data and press Tab to move from one field to another, the current value in the field is highlighted, so anything you type overwrites it. This means it's as easy to edit a default value as it is to enter data in a blank field. For this reason, it saves time to enter a default value even if you need that value in fewer than half of your records. For example, if one-third of the people in your list live in California, you can still save a bit of data entry time by using "**CA**" as the default value in the State field.

- **Caption:** Enter an expression that will be used as the caption of the field in forms by default, instead of the field name.

In addition, you can use the Field Comment text box to enter notes on the field for your own use. These comments do not affect the performance of the program.

The properties of each field are displayed in this area when that field is highlighted in the fields list.

Long Field and Table Names

The Table Designer also lets you enter names of up to 128 characters for the fields and the table itself. Simply type these names in the Table Name text box, in the upper-left corner of the Table Designer, and in the Name column for the field.

► Table Properties

If the table is part of a database, the Table Designer also includes a Table Properties button in its upper-right corner, which you can click to display the Table Properties dialog box, shown in Figure 16.13.

Record-Level Validation Rules

Use the Validation Rule and Validation Text boxes of this dialog box to create record-level validation rules. These are rules that cannot be defined at the field level, because they apply to more than one field in the record.

FIGURE 16.13

The Table Properties dialog box

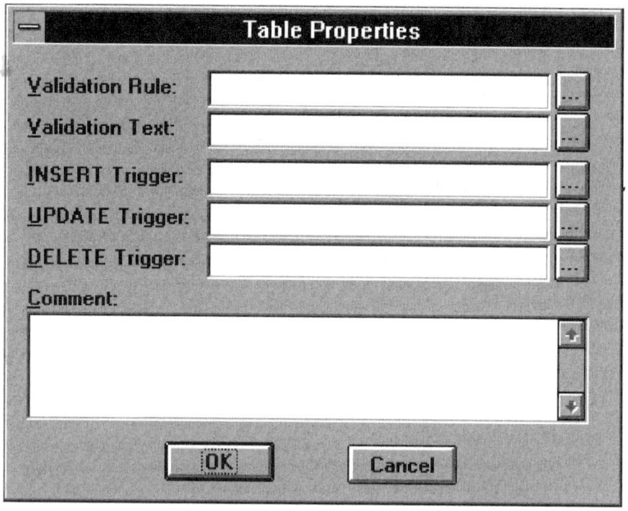

For example, if you had fields for DATE_HIRED and BIRTH_DATE, you could check that employees are over 18 years old by using this validation rule:

```
(DATE_HIRED - BIRTH_DATE) / 365 >= 18.
```

Enter an expression in the Validation Text box for FoxPro to display when the validation rule evaluates as false.

Triggers

The other three text boxes of this dialog box are used to create *triggers*.

A trigger is a logical expression that Visual FoxPro evaluates when someone deletes, inserts, or modifies a record. If the expression evaluates as false, Visual FoxPro does not allow the change.

Triggers are used primarily in programming. For more information, see the CREATE TRIGGER command in Appendix B.

▶ Using the Index Panel

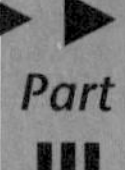

Finally, if the table is part of a Visual FoxPro database, the Type drop-down list of the Index panel of the Table Designer includes the option Primary, as shown in Figure 16.14, which lets you create a primary index.

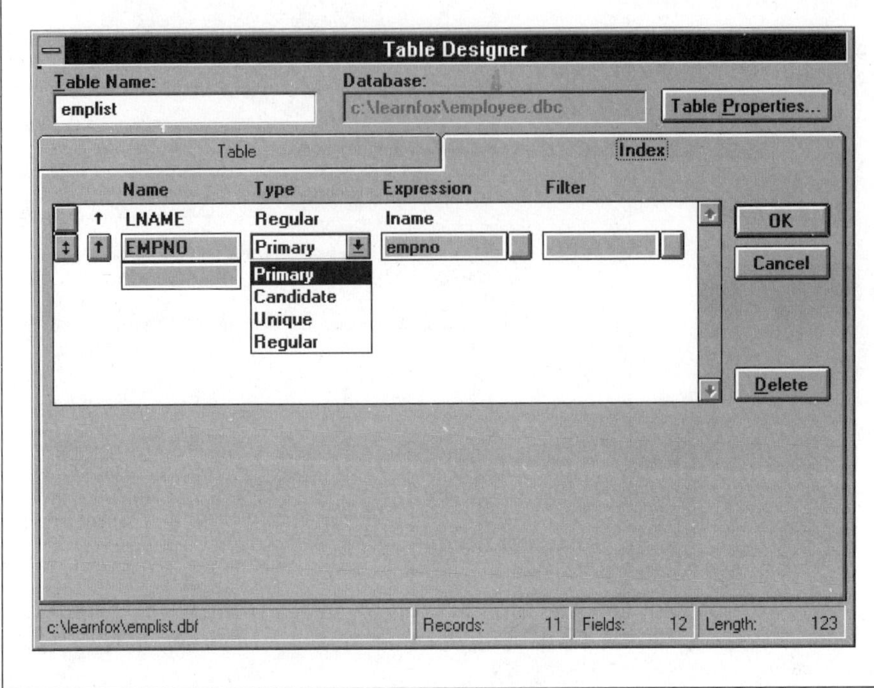

FIGURE 16.14 Creating a primary index

Like a candidate index, a primary index does not allow duplicate values to be entered in the field. It can also be used to create persistent relationships among tables, as described above, in the section "Creating a Persistent Relationship."

▸▸ The View Designer

The View Designer works just like the Query Designer, covered in Chapters 4 and 15, except that:

- SQL views are updatable, unlike queries, which are read-only. When you change the data in a SQL view, Visual FoxPro updates the data in the tables it is based on.
- SQL views can only be saved as part of a database, unlike queries, which are saved in independent QPR files. Though you can create

a view without having a database open (by using File ➤ New or the CREATE VIEW command), you cannot save it.

- SQL views can include tables stored on remote servers, without downloading their data to your own computer. Changes you make on your computer are sent back to the server. You have seen that remote tables can be added to a Visual FoxPro database; these tables can also be used in views of the database.

The main difference between the View Designer and the Query Designer is the View Designer's Update Criteria panel, which lets you control how data in remote tables is updated, in order to avoid conflicts with other users on the network.

▶▶ NOTE

If you are working solely with local tables, you do not have to use the Update Criteria panel. Simply design SQL views as you do queries.

▶ Saving and Naming Views

To save a view while you are working with the View Designer, choose File ➤ Save.

The first time you save the view, Visual FoxPro displays the Save dialog box, shown in Figure 16.15. Visual FoxPro also displays this dialog box to let you rename a view, if you choose File ➤ Save As while you are working with the View Designer.

FIGURE 16.15 ▶

The Save dialog box for views

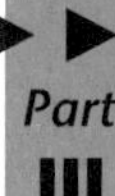

Because a SQL view can only be saved as part of a database, this dialog box does not include controls that let you choose the directory and drive of the file; and the length of the file name also is not limited by the usual naming conventions. Simply enter a name of up to 128 characters.

You can also choose File ➤ Save As when you are working with the View Designer and use this dialog box to save the view under a different name.

▸ Using the Update Criteria Panel

If you are working on a network and your view includes remote tables, you can use the Update Criteria panel of the View Designer, shown in Figure 16.16, to specify how source tables should be updated, in order to avoid conflicts with other users.

FIGURE 16.16 ▸

The Update Criteria panel

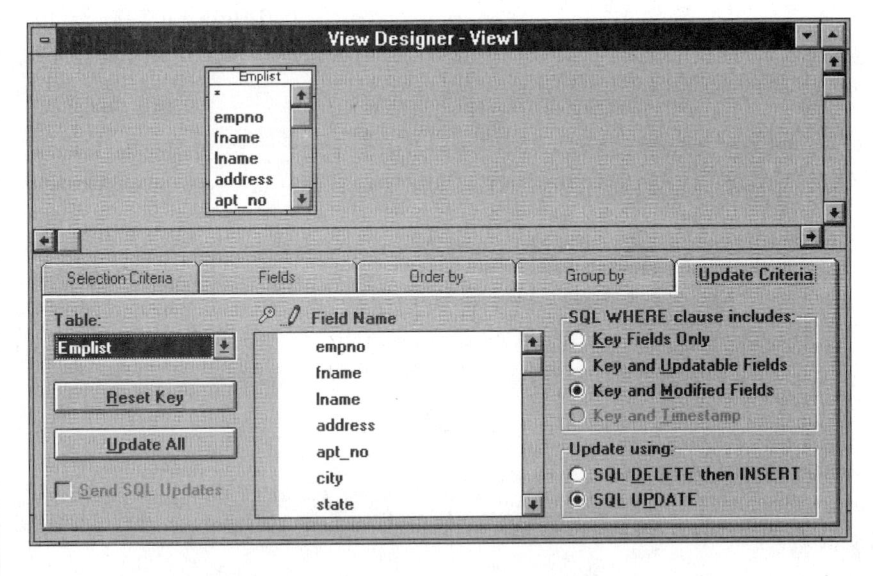

If a view contains only local tables stored on your own computer, you do not need to use this panel.

Making a Remote Table Updatable

In order to have any changes you make in a view sent to the remote table, you must select the Send SQL Updates check box. Because a table can be updated only if it has a key field, this button is not enabled unless there is a key field specified in the Field Names list, as described below.

Making Fields of a Remote Table Updatable

In addition to making the table updatable, you must use the Fields list to specify that its fields are updatable. By default, all tables in the view are included in this list. You can use the Table drop-down list to include only fields from specific tables.

Specifying Key Fields A table must have a key field for any of its fields to be updatable.

When you first display the Update Criteria panel, key fields have a check in the Key column to the left of the Field Name list.

You can change this default and specify whether any field is a key field by clicking the key column to its left. The first time you click the column, a check box will be displayed for that field. Click this box to add or remove the check that makes it a key field.

To eliminate any changes you made and restore the default key fields, click the Reset Key button.

Specifying Updatable Fields Once a table has a key field, you can make any of its fields updatable by clicking the Pencil column to its left. The first time you click this column, a check box is displayed: click the box to add a check mark and make the field updatable. If there is already a check in the box, clicking it will remove the check and make the field read-only again.

Click the Update All button to add checks in the Pencil column of all fields that can be updated, making them all updatable. If a table does not have a key field, this button will not make its fields updatable.

Preventing Conflict with Other Updates Data can be lost when multiple users are working on a single table, if two users update the same record at the same time.

For example, let's say that one user changes the address in a record, and a second user is changing the spelling of the first name in that record at the same time. The first user saves the record with the new address. Then, a moment later, the second user saves the record that has the new first name but that still has the old address, which overwrites the new address that the first user entered.

To avoid this problem, Visual FoxPro checks the record in the remote data source before saving it, to see if any other changes have been made in it since it was retrieved into the view.

The SQL Where area of the Update Criteria panel determines how Visual FoxPro checks the record in the data source, and has the following options:

- **Key Fields Only:** Updates the record if there has been no change in the key field.
- **Key And Updatable Fields:** Updates the record only if there has been no change in the key field or in any of the updatable fields of the view.
- **Key And Modified Fields:** Updates the record only if there has been no change in the key field or in any of the fields that have been modified in the view.
- **Key And Timestamp:** Updates the record only if there has been no change in the key field and if the timestamp on the remote record has not changed.

Key And Modified Fields is the default option. It is generally preferable to Key And Updatable Fields, because it is faster to look for changes only in fields that have actually been modified in the view than in all updatable fields that can possibly be modified.

▸▸ **WARNING**

The Key Fields Only option should only be used in special circumstances. It can result in data loss, as described at the beginning of this section.

Controlling the Update Method The two radio buttons in the Update Using area let you control the update method on the remote server. You can use the SQL DELETE command to remove the original of the record that has been changed from the remote table, and then the SQL INSERT command to add the altered record to the remote table. Or you can use the SQL UPDATE command, assuming that it is supported by the remote server, to modify the data in the remote table.

▶▶ Creating a Sample Database

Now, try creating a Visual FoxPro database, adding your sample tables to it, and taking advantage of some of its special features.

1. Choose File ➤ New. When Visual FoxPro displays the New dialog box, select the Database radio button and then click the New File button. In the Create dialog box, enter **employee** as the database name, make sure that **learnfox** is the current directory, and click the Create button.

2. Visual FoxPro creates the database and makes it the current database, with its name displayed in the database list box on the toolbar. In the Command window, enter **MODIFY DATABASE** (or **MODI DATA**) to open the Database Designer window.

3. Click the Add Table button of the Database toolbar, use the Open dialog box to select emplist.dbf as the table to add to the database, and click OK.

4. Click the Add Table button again, and use the Open dialog box to select Wages.dbf as the table to add to the database. Both tables are contained in the Database Designer, as shown in Figure 16.17.

5. Now, click the Emplist table to select it—its title bar must be highlighted—and then click the Modify Table button of the Database toolbar. When Visual FoxPro displays the Table Designer, click the Index tab to display the Index panel, and use the Type drop-down list to convert the Empno index to a primary index, as shown in Figure 16.18. Then click OK, and click Yes to make the structural changes permanent. The Wages table should already be indexed on the Empno field.

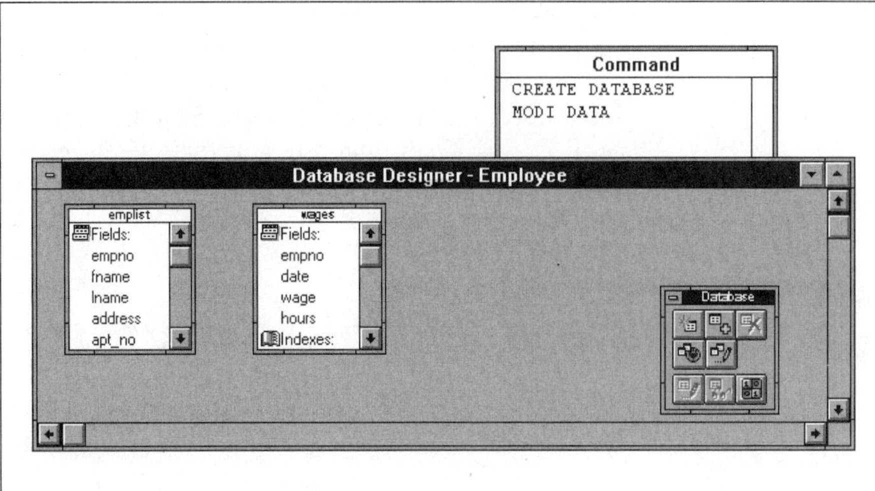

FIGURE 16.17 *The tables have been added to the Database Designer.*

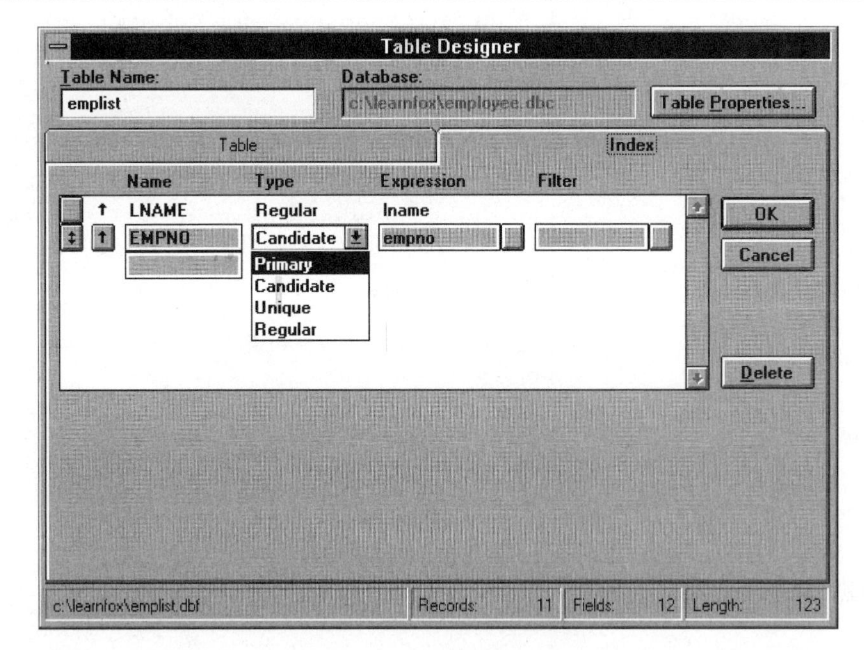

FIGURE 16.18 *Creating the primary index*

6. Now, scroll down through the Emplist table, and also through the Wages table if necessary, so you can view the Empno indexes of both: the Empno index of the Emplist table should have a key to

its left, to indicate that it is a primary index. Click the Empno index of the Emplist table, hold down the mouse button, and drag to the Empno index of the Wages table. When you release the mouse button, Visual FoxPro displays the Edit Relationship dialog box, shown in Figure 16.19. If you clicked and dragged accurately, Empno should be displayed in both list boxes as the index to use as the basis of the relationship; if it is not, use the drop-down list to select it. Select OK. The relationship is displayed in the Database Designer, as shown in Figure 16.20.

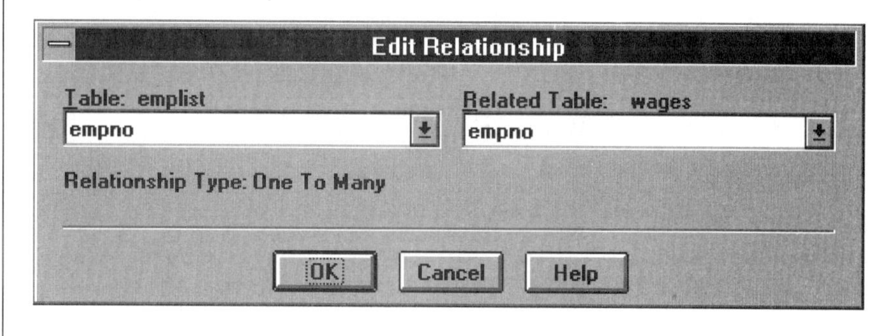

FIGURE 16.19

Creating the relationship

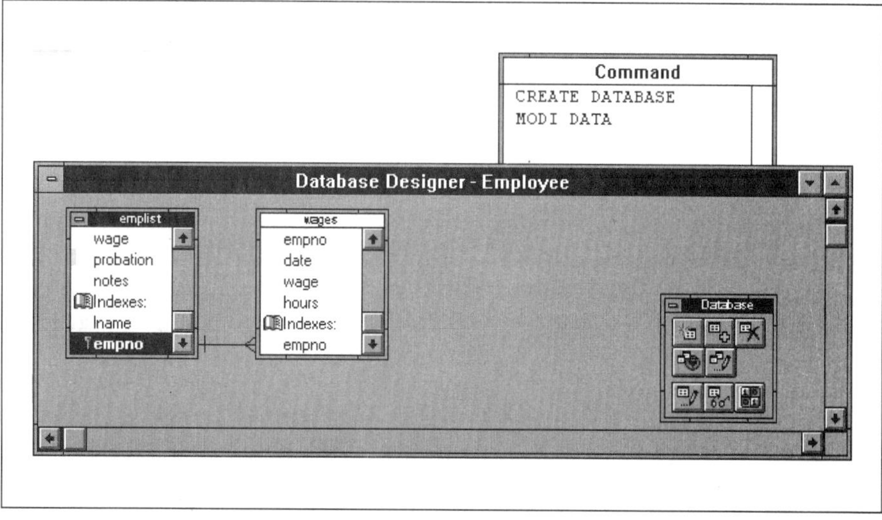

FIGURE 16.20

The Database Designer displays the relationship.

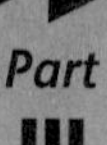

7. Now, click the New Local View button of the Database Designer. When Visual FoxPro displays the Add Table or View dialog box, select Emplist as the table to include.

8. Click the Add Table button of the View toolbar. In the Add Table or View dialog box, select Wages as the table to add, and click OK. The Wages table is added, with its relationship to the Emplist table already established, as shown in Figure 16.21.

FIGURE 16.21

The tables are related automatically.

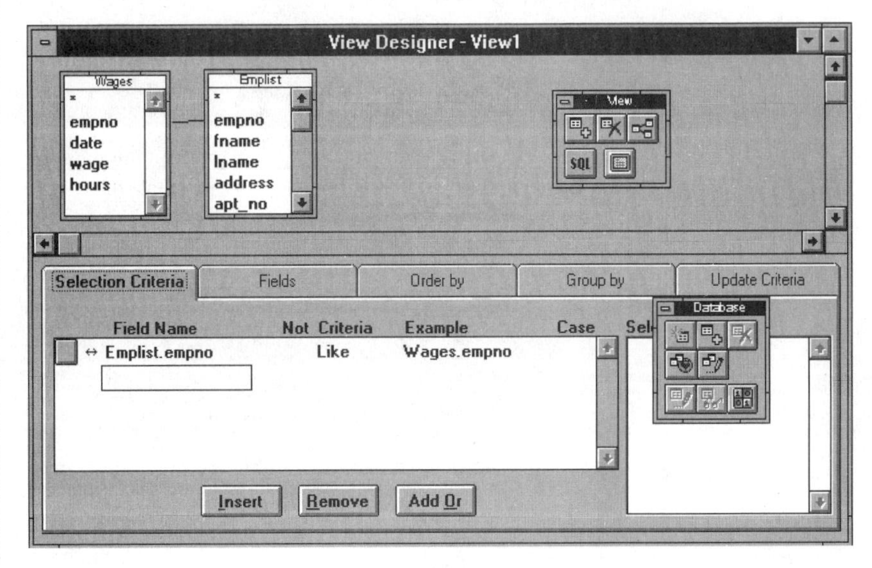

9. Now, try creating a general-purpose view that includes all the fields in both tables. Click the Fields tab, and then click the Add All button of the Fields panel to include all fields in the output. Choose File ➤ Save. In the Save dialog box, enter the view name **General View: all fields from both tables**, and click OK. The view is added to the Database Designer.

10. Click the View Designer to bring it forward, and then choose Close from its Control menu to close it.

11. Double-click the field list for the new view to browse it, and scroll through the Browse window to verify that it includes all the fields.

You can try editing some fields to verify that they are updatable, but be sure not to edit key fields.

▶▶ TIP

You can use this general-purpose view as a basis of other views. Remember that when you create a new view, Visual FoxPro lets you select either a table or a view to include in the View Designer. If you begin by including this view, you can add filters or remove fields from the output, without going through the extra step of adding a second table each time you create a new view.

▶▶ To Sum Up

In this chapter, you have looked at Visual FoxPro databases, the most sophisticated method the program offers for handling relational data. Now that you have looked at all the methods that Visual FoxPro has for handling relational databases, you can go on to Part IV of this book, which covers Visual FoxPro utilities.

PART FOUR

CHAPTER 17

Customizing Reports, Labels, and Forms

FAST TRACK

To add controls to a report, 491

click the appropriate tool of the Report Controls toolbar and click and drag to place the control on the report. If you add a field expression or picture control, Visual Fox-Pro displays a dialog box to let you define it.

To select controls, 493

click a single control to select it. Hold down the Shift key while you click multiple controls to select them all. Click and drag around a group of controls to select them all.

To move a control, 493

click and drag it.

To delete a control, 493

select it and press Del.

To define a text control, 495

use the control's dialog box, which is displayed when you place it; you can also double-click the control to display its dialog box at any time. Enter a field name or expression in the Expression text box, or click the button to its right to use the Expression Builder to generate the expression. Click the Format button to display the Format dialog box, which you can use to specify how the field's content is displayed.

In Chapter 5 you learned how to use the Form Wizard, in Chapter 6 you learned how to use the Report Wizards, and in Chapter 7 you learned how to use the Label Wizard. In your work with Visual FoxPro, you will probably want to customize the reports generated using the Wizards, and you may want to customize forms and labels. For example, you might want to add extra text or pictures to many reports for distribution; you will at least want to edit the field names that the Wizard uses as the labels for data and replace them with more descriptive names.

This chapter covers both the Report Designer and the Label Designer thoroughly. It includes exercises where you use these Designers to customize the reports and labels created in earlier chapters using the Wizards; these exercises demonstrate the techniques that you need most frequently in your practical work.

NOTE

Because the Report Designer has more features than most users need to learn about, this chapter is designed to be used more as a reference than as a tutorial. If you've worked with other Windows report-writing software, you may want to start with the exercises at the end of the chapter (in the section "Customizing Sample Reports") and then go back to earlier sections to study the features that you need to learn more about. You may find that you can pick up the essential features of the Report Designer just by doing these exercises.

The Form Designer has many features in common with the Report and Label Designers, but it also has many advanced features that only developers should use. This chapter will cover some of the basic features of the Form Designer that you might want to use to modify forms you have created using the Form Wizard. For example, it is easy to rearrange the fields of the form or to add text or pictures to it.

▶▶ Using the Report Designer

To customize a report you've created using the Wizard, choose File ➤ Open and use the Open dialog box to select the report. Visual FoxPro displays it in the Report Designer, and you can modify it.

You can also use the Report Designer to create a report from scratch, by choosing File ➤ New to display the New dialog box, selecting the Report radio button and clicking its New File tool. In general, however, it is easier to use the Wizard for the basics—at least for choosing which fields to place in the report—and then to customize the report it generates.

Choose File ➤ Save at any time to save changes you made to the report. (If you are creating a report from scratch and it has not been named, Visual FoxPro displays the Save As dialog box to let you name it the first time that you save it.) To rename the report at any time, select File ➤ Save As to use the Save As dialog box. When you save a report, Visual FoxPro adds the extension FRX to the name you give the report.

▶▶ TIP

It is a good idea to save changes periodically when you are working on a complex report, so you do not lose your work in case of a power failure or some other accident.

To close the Report Designer and save changes, you can simply press Ctrl+W. To discard changes, select File ➤ Close, select Control ➤ Close, or press Esc. Visual FoxPro then gives you the option of saving or discarding changes.

▸▸ **NOTE**

dBASE, FoxBASE, and other earlier dBASE-compatible programs saved report forms with the extension FRM. If you are running older applications on Visual FoxPro, it will be able to use these FRM reports without any trouble and will include them in the list of report forms for you to choose from. The only possible confusion arises when you are working from the Command window, where you can enter the report's name without the extension. If there are two reports with the same name, Visual FoxPro will use the one with the FRX extension and ignore the one with the FRM extension.

▸ An Overview of the Report Designer

The Report Designer is shown in Figure 17.1. As you can see, a Report menu is added to the menu bar when you are using this window so you can add a title or summary to the report, group its data, and create a Quick Report; additional options are also added to the View menu so you can display the report in Design or Preview mode, display the data environment, and display the toolbar. You can also access many of these options by right-clicking the report to display its shortcut menu.

In addition to the extra menu options, Visual FoxPro lets you use the three floating toolbars shown in the illustration to work with reports.

- Use the Report Controls toolbar to add expressions, text, graphics, or pictures to the report. All of these are called either *controls* or *objects.*
- Use the Layout toolbar to align, resize, or place controls within the report.
- Use the Color Palette to specify the color of controls.

If these toolbars are not displayed when you first open the Report Designer, you can display them by choosing View ➤ Report Controls Toolbar, View ➤ Layout Toolbar, and View ➤ Color Palette Toolbar.

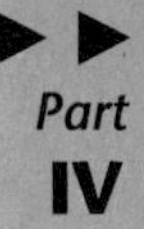

FIGURE 17.1

The Report Designer

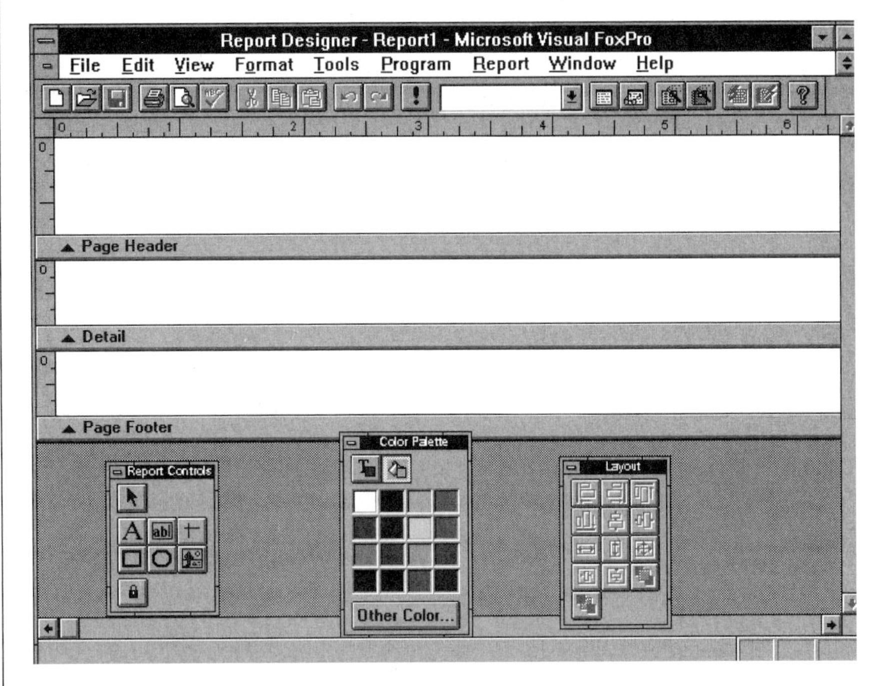

Notice also that the report is divided into bands, labeled Page Header, Detail, and Page Footer. As you will see, you can add additional bands to hold a report title or summary and to group data. The band to which you add controls determines how they are displayed in the final report; for example, controls added to the Page Header band are displayed as a header at the top of each page when you print the report.

The Report Bands

As you have seen, the Report Designer window is divided into bands. Reports always include a page header, detail, and page footer band.

The header and footer, of course, appear at the top or bottom of each page. If you have created a report without a header or footer, this band will be empty.

The detail band contains examples of the data you want included in the report. You enter the data in the detail band just once, but the final, printed report repeats it for each record that is included.

The report may also include the following bands (if it does not, you can use the Report menu to add them):

- **Title:** The report title appears only once, at the beginning of the report, unlike the header, which is repeated at the top of each page.
- **Summary:** The report summary appears at the end of the report, unlike the footer, which is repeated at the bottom of each page. It is common for the summary to include some calculation—for example, the total number of workers and the total payroll.
- **Groupings with headers and footers:** Groupings let you divide your data. For example, you can group all the employees from each state.

You add these bands using the Report menu, which is described in detail later in this chapter.

You can change the size of a band simply by clicking and dragging its border (which has its name on it) up or down.

Report Band Dialog Boxes

You can also double-click a band's border to display its dialog box. Figure 17.2 illustrates the detail band's dialog box, and others are similar. Type a number in the Height text box or use the spinner to its right to specify the band's height, and use the radio buttons to specify whether it is in inches or centimeters.

By default, the Constant Band Height check box in the detail band's dialog box is not selected, so that the detail band expands to accommodate all the data in it. Select this check box to keep the band a constant height. (Of course, this means you need to make it large enough to fit all fields, leaving a gap below smaller fields.)

You can click the buttons to the right of the Run Expression controls to display the Expression Builder, where you enter an expression that Visual FoxPro will run whenever the user tabs into or out of this band. This is an advanced feature meant for developers.

Page Preview

While you are working with a report, you will find it convenient to display it in a Page Preview window occasionally (by choosing View ➤

FIGURE 17.2

The Detail band's dialog box

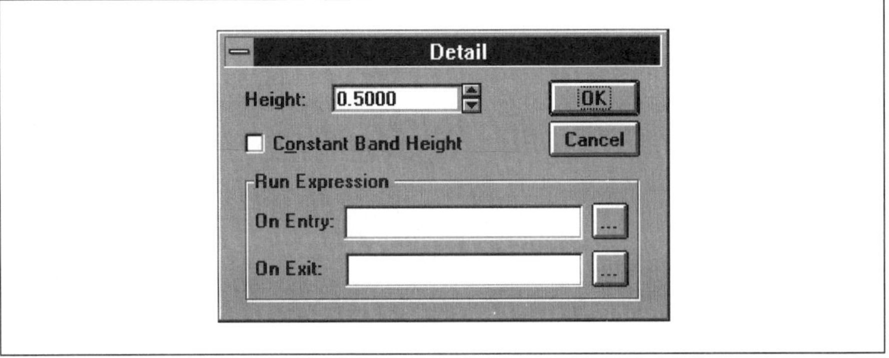

Preview), so you can see exactly what the printed report will look like. It is sometimes difficult to imagine the report's eventual appearance by looking at the banded layout.

Choose View ➤ Design to return to the Report Designer.

The Data Environment

In a moment, you will learn how to add fields and other controls to a report. Before you add fields, however, their table must be part of the report's *data environment.*

In early versions of the Xbase language, the data environment of a report was not saved, and so you had to open the report's underlying table explicitly (with a USE command) before you could use the report form to produce the report. Saving the data environment with the report lets you produce the report with a single command.

NOTE

If you are working with a report that you generated using a Wizard, the tables that it is based on are already included in its data environment.

You can control the data environment by choosing View ➤ Data Environment to display the Data Environment window, shown in Figure 17.3. As you can see, this window includes field lists for the tables that are used as the basis of the report. If you are working with a relational database, as discussed in Part III of this book, it will include field lists for multiple tables and show their relationships.

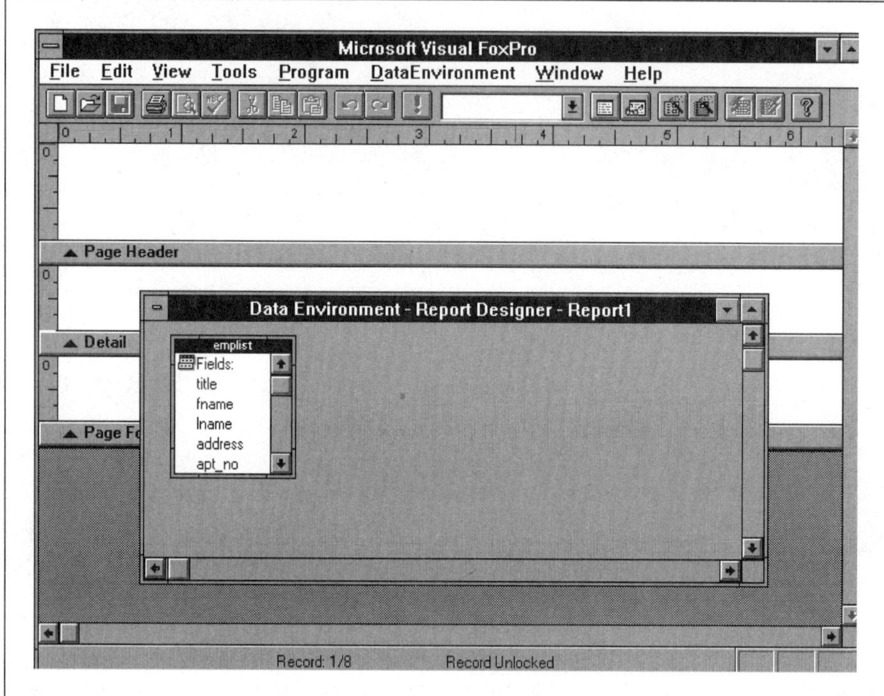

FIGURE 17.3 *The Data Environment window*

When this window is displayed, a DataEnvironment menu is added to the main menu bar, so you can add or remove tables:

- Choose DataEnvironment ➤ Add to add a table or view to the data environment. Visual FoxPro displays the Add Table or View dialog box. If you are working with Visual FoxPro databases, you can choose a database name from the Database drop-down to control which tables are displayed; Visual FoxPro databases are used for relational databases and are discussed in Chapter 16. You can also click the Other button to display the Open dialog box and use it to select the table to add; use this option if you are not working with a relational database.

- Click a table in the Data Environment window to select it and choose DataEnvironment ➤ Remove to remove it from the data environment. You should not do this without a good reason. If you remove a table whose fields are used in the report, Visual FoxPro will make you select the table explicitly before printing the report.
- Click a table in the Data Environment window to select it and choose DataEnvironment ➤ Browse to display the data in that table in a Browse window. If you are working with a report based on a complex relational database with many tables, this option can sometimes be a convenient way of reminding yourself what is in each table.

If you are working with Visual FoxPro databases, covered in Chapter 16, you can use the Add Table Or View dialog box to add views as well as tables.

▶▶ Working with Controls

Any report bands can include text, fields or field expressions, lines, rectangles, rounded rectangles and pictures. All of these controls are treated as objects, which you can select and then modify, move, or delete in the ways described below.

▶ Adding Controls

The Report Controls toolbar, shown in Figure 17.4, is used to add controls as follows:

- **Pointer:** Click the Pointer tool to return the pointer to its usual form after using some other tool. This tool is sometimes called the selection tool because when the pointer is in this form, you can select any control by clicking it.

- **Label** (or **Text**) **tool:** Click the Label tool to add text. The pointer becomes an insertion bar, and you can click any location in the Report window to place a cursor there. Then just type your text.

- **Expression tool:** Click the Expression tool to add a field or an expression. Then click any location in the report to display the

Report Expression dialog box, discussed later in this chapter. When you use this dialog box, the field or expression is placed in the location where you clicked.

- **Line tool:** Click the Line tool to add lines. The cursor becomes a cross made of a vertical and a horizontal line. Move the cross to one end of the line you want to draw, click and drag to draw the line, and release the mouse button when you reach the other end of the line. Lines must be horizontal or vertical (not diagonal).

- **Rectangle tool:** Click the Rectangle tool to add rectangles. The cursor becomes a cross made of a vertical and a horizontal line. Move it to one corner of the rectangle you want to draw, click and drag to draw the rectangle, and release the mouse button when you reach the other corner of the rectangle.

- **Rounded Rectangle tool:** Click the Rounded Rectangle tool to add rectangles with rounded corners. Click and drag to draw as you do when you are adding rectangles.

- **Picture tool:** Click the Picture tool to add pictures. The pointer becomes a cross made of a vertical and a horizontal line. Click and drag to draw a rectangle that will be used as the picture frame, just as you do when you are using the rectangle tool. When you release the mouse button, Visual FoxPro displays the Report Picture dialog box, used to specify the file or field that contains the picture or OLE object. OLE objects are covered in Chapter 22.

- **Button Lock Tool:** By default, when you click any of the tools described above, it lets you place only one control. If you click the Button Lock tool, however, the next tool that you click will remain selected indefinitely, making it a bit easier to place the same type of control several times. Any tool you select will work this way until you deselect the Button Lock tool by clicking it again or by clicking the Pointer tool.

As you move the pointer within the Report Designer window, a line is displayed on the rulers at the top and left of this window. This shows you exactly where you are placing these controls.

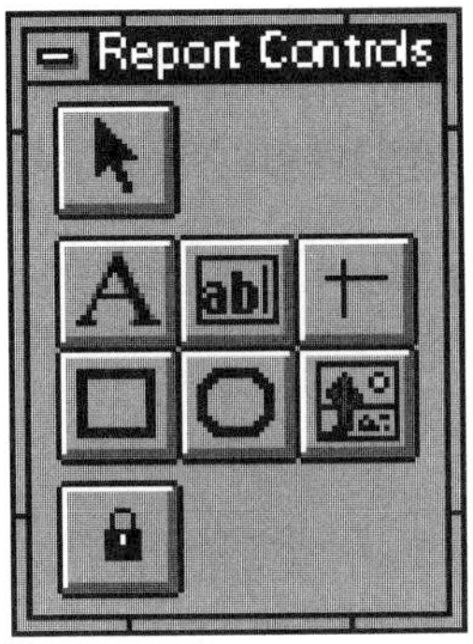

FIGURE 17.4

Report Controls tools

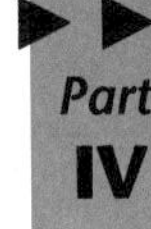

Manipulating Controls

First you will look at the basic ways to select and manipulate a single control. Then you will look at more advanced techniques, such as selecting multiple controls and displaying the dialog box used to specify a control's properties. You may want to create a sample report, add a few controls, and try out these manipulations, checking the Page Preview window to see their effect in the report you are designing.

Selecting a Control

To select a control in the Layout window using the mouse, put the pointer on it and click. To select more than one control at once, hold down Shift as you are clicking on the controls. Handles (small rectangles) appear at the ends, edges, or corners of a control to indicate that it is selected.

Moving a Control

To move a control, click and drag it. Release the mouse button when the control is located where you want it.

Deleting a Control

Pressing Del or Backspace deletes a control that is selected.

Resizing a Control

To resize a control, select it and then click and drag one of its handles. For example, you can drag the handle at the top or bottom of a rectangle to make it taller or shorter, drag the handle on either side of a rectangle to make it wider or narrower, or drag the handle in any corner to make larger or smaller in both dimensions. You can even use this method to resize fields or expressions that you added to the report.

► Selecting Multiple Controls

To select multiple controls, simply hold down the Shift key as you select a new control; controls that were selected previously will not be deselected.

You can also select multiple controls by creating what is called a *selection marquee.* Using a mouse, begin with the pointer outside the controls you want to select; then, hold down the mouse button and drag to create a box (the marquee) around the controls. Select the controls within the marquee by releasing the mouse button.

► Copying and Pasting Controls

You can use the Edit menu in the ordinary way to cut or copy and paste controls. After selecting the control or controls, just select Edit ➤ Cut or Edit ➤ Copy. Then you can move the cursor and select Edit ➤ Paste to paste whatever was cut or copied to the new location.

Sometimes it is easiest to do this by opening multiple report windows. For example, imagine that you need to create a report with features similar to some that you have already laid out on an earlier report. After selecting File ➤ New to create the new report form, select File ➤ Open and open the report from which you want to borrow features. Select the controls you need, and select Edit ➤ Copy. Then close that report window and paste the controls in the proper location in the new report.

► Control Dialog Boxes

Every report control has a dialog box associated with it that you can use to specify its properties. You can display a control's dialog box by double-clicking it or by right-clicking it and choosing Properties from its shortcut menu. You must use a dialog box when you add a field or picture control; both are covered below. Other report controls have simple dialog boxes.

Text Control Properties

The dialog box for a text control is shown in Figure 17.5.

FIGURE 17.5

The dialog box for a text control

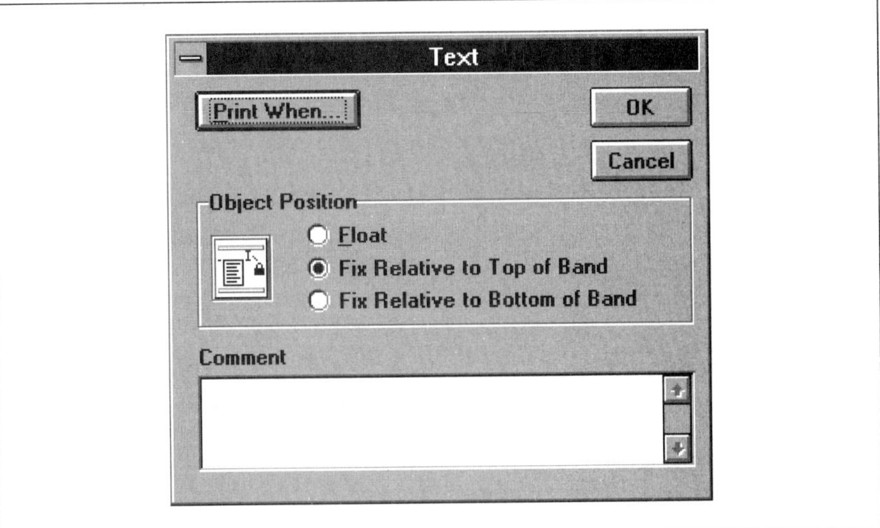

TIP

Notice that you cannot change a text control's font using this dialog box. To change font, select the text control and select Format ➤ Font to display the Font dialog box.

Positioning the Text Control if the Band Expands Use the radio buttons in the Object Position box to specify where the control will be located if the band must expand to accommodate some other control (for example, to accommodate the text in a memo field) when it is printed.

By default, the text control remains the same distance from the top edge of the band if it stretches, but you can select Bottom to keep it a fixed distance from the bottom of the band.

Adding a Comment Use the Comment text box to enter information about the control (or to edit information you entered earlier); this information is not displayed in the report and is purely for your own use. It might be a description of the control or any other text you want to enter as a reminder for yourself or a message to other people working on the report.

Specifying When the Control Prints If you select the Print When pushbutton in the Text dialog box, Visual FoxPro displays the Print When dialog box, shown in Figure 17.6.

FIGURE 17.6

The Print When dialog box

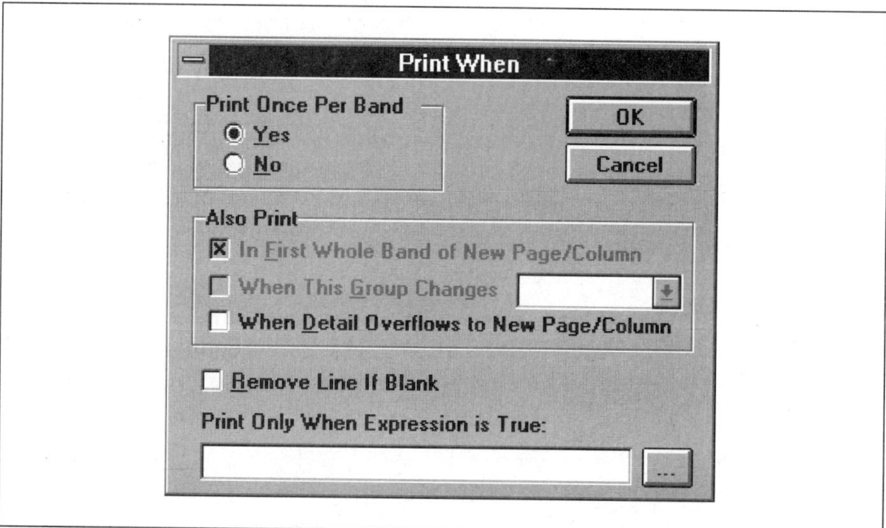

The radio buttons in the Print Once Per Band box let you specify whether or not the control should be printed repeatedly if the band is stretched.

The check boxes in the Also Print box let you print the text control when the group changes or when the detail is on a new page or column. (Grouping data is covered later in this chapter.)

Enter an expression in the Print Only When Expression Is True text box or click the button to its right to display the Expression Builder. You can enter a logical expression to have the text control printed only if it is true. For example, if you are working on a membership table, you can print *Overdue* to the left of members' names only if their dues are not paid.

Selecting the Remove Line If Blank check box deletes the line if nothing is printed in it, so that lines are not skipped. This is useful in combination with the Print Only When Expression Is True check box.

Rectangle or Line Control Properties

The dialog box for a rectangle or line control is shown in Figure 17.7. It has the same options as a text control, but it also has a Stretch Downward area with three radio buttons:

- **No Stretch:** the line or rectangle remains the same size, regardless of whether the band or any object in it stretches.
- **Stretch Relative To Tallest Object in Group:** The line or rectangle stretches so it remains larger than the tallest object in the group. This is useful if the rectangle is drawn around a group of controls, and it must expand to hold the largest of them.
- **Stretch Relative to Height of Band:** The line or rectangle expands whenever the band expands to accommodate any control. This is useful if you draw rectangles around a number of controls in the band, and you want them all to stretch whenever the band stretches, so that the boxes remain the same size, even if some controls become larger and others do not.

Rounded Rectangle Control Properties

The dialog box for a Rounded Rectangle control is shown in Figure 17.8. It has the same options as a rectangle control, but it also includes five picture buttons with Style options that specify the rounding of the rectangles corners, from the least rounded on the left to the most rounded on the right. The second from the left is the default option.

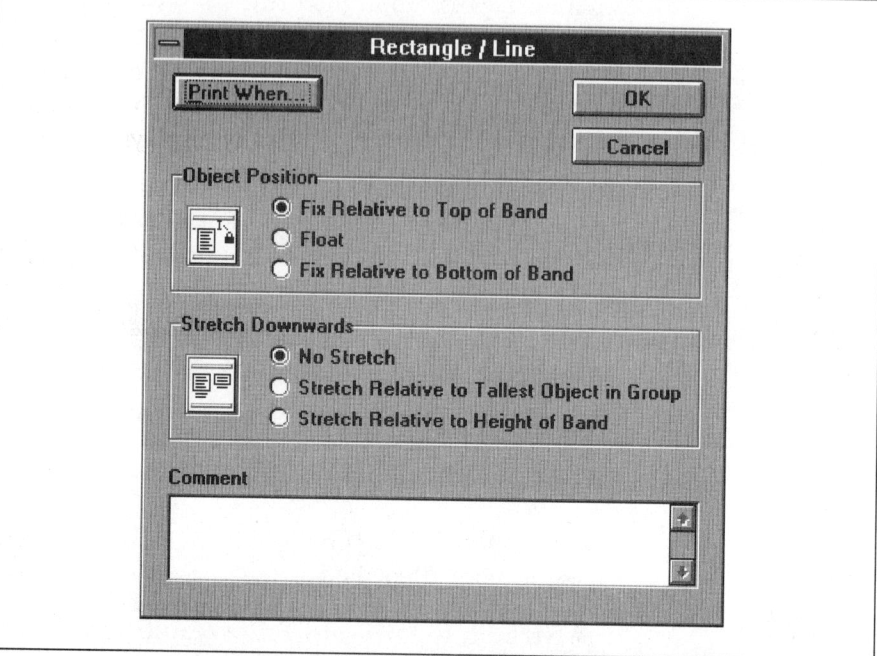

FIGURE 17.7

The dialog box for a rectangle or line control

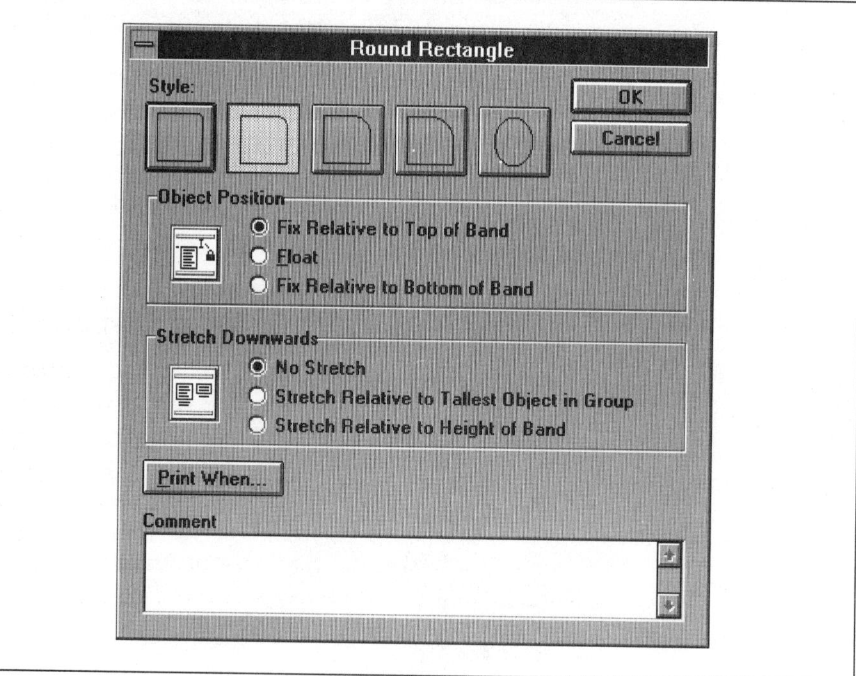

FIGURE 17.8

The dialog box for a rounded rectangle control

▶ Using Fields and Expressions in Reports

You can display the dialog box of a field control at any time, just as you do with other controls. In addition, when you first place a field in a report, Visual FoxPro automatically displays the Report Expression dialog box, which is shown in Figure 17.9.

FIGURE 17.9

The Report Expression dialog box

Report Expression

Expression: [...] OK

Format: [...] Cancel

Calculations... Print When...

Object Position

Float

Fix Relative to Top of Band

Fix Relative to Bottom of Band

Stretch with overflow

Comment

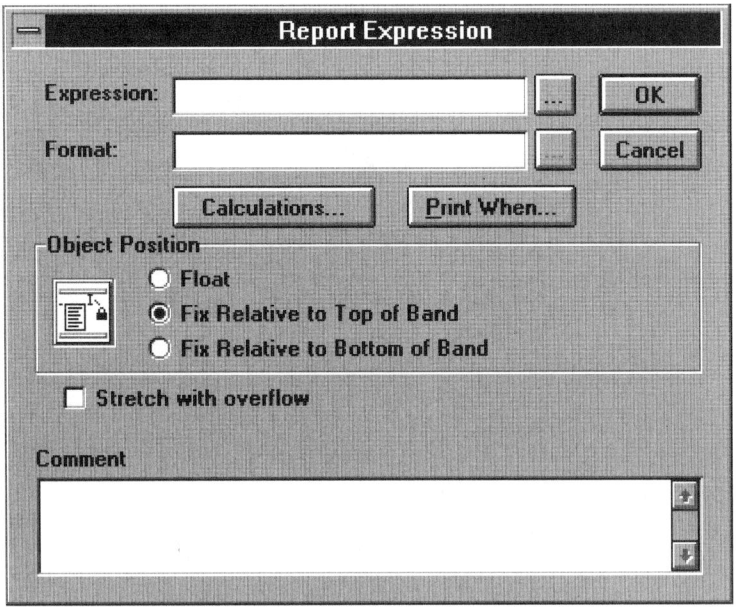

Notice that you do not change a field control's font by using this dialog box. To change the font, select the field control and select Format ➤ Font to display the Font dialog box.

When you are adding a new field or expression to the report, you must type the field name or expression in the Expression text box or click the ... button to call up the Expression Builder and generate the expression. The Expression Builder is discussed in Chapter 9.

This dialog box also includes important options that let you specify the format of fields or expressions and create calculated fields.

Formatting Fields

The Format pushbutton of the Report Expression dialog box calls up the Format dialog box shown in Figure 17.10, which lets you format the field you are placing in a variety of ways. As you can see from the illustration, this dialog box includes three radio buttons to indicate the data type of the field that is being formatted—Character, Numeric, or Date. The Editing Options check boxes change according to the data type of the field being formatted. The options for all the data types are summarized in Table 17.1.

FIGURE 17.10

The Format dialog box

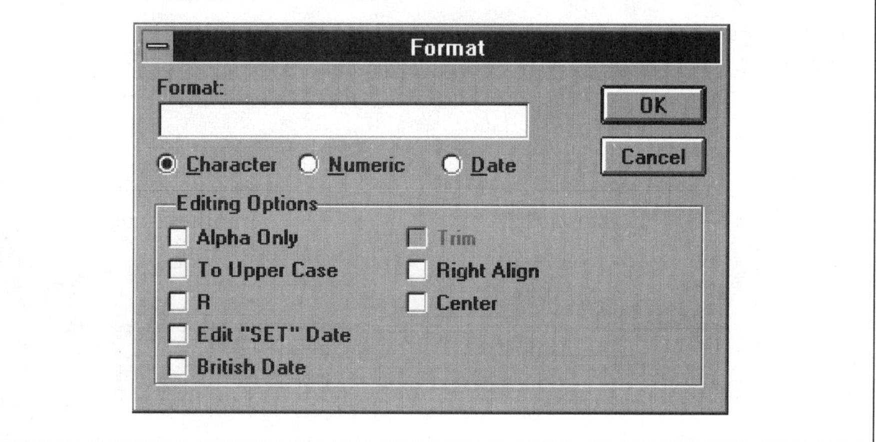

TABLE 17.1: *Editing Option Check Boxes Available for Formatting Data*

Radio Button Selected	Check Boxes Available	Effect
Character	Alpha Only	Allows only letters.
	To Upper Case	Capitalizes letters.
	R	Nonformatting characters are not stored, although they are displayed.
	Edit "SET" Date	Displays the date using whatever format is determined by the current SET DATE command (an environment command covered in Chapter 8).

TABLE 17.1: *Editing Option Check Boxes Available for Formatting Data (continued)*

Radio Button Selected	Check Boxes Available	Effect
	British Date	Displays the date in the European format, dd/mm/yy.
	Trim	Trims both leading and trailing blanks.
	Right Align	Right-justifies data.
	Center	Centers data.
Numeric	Left Justify	Left-justifies data.
	Blank If Zero	Prints nothing if the expression's value.
	(Negative)	Prints negative numbers in parentheses, as they usually are in accounting.
	Edit "SET" Date	Displays the date using whatever format is determined by the current SET DATE command.
	British Date	Displays the date in the European format.
	CR If Positive	CR (which stands for Credit) appears after all positive numbers.
	DB If Negative	DB (for Debit) appears after all negative numbers.
	Leading Zero	Pads the length of the field with leading zeros.
	Currency	Displays the expression in currency format.
	Scientific	Displays the expression in scientific (exponential) format.
Date	Edit "SET" Date	Displays the date using whatever format is determined by the current SET DATE command.
	British Date	Displays the date in the European format.

In addition to the options that are available through check boxes, you can enter templates in the Format text box at the upper left of the dialog box to format an expression on a character-by-character basis. A *template* is a series of symbols that control the format of the entry. The special formatting characters are summarized in Table 17.2. Any character that's not one of these special characters can also be used in a template as a literal, which means the character itself will appear in the formatted expression. For example, you can format social security numbers using the template 999-99-9999. In this case, the 9s are symbols that let the user enter only numbers, and the hyphens are literals.

TABLE 17.2: *Special Characters for Format Templates*

Character	Effect
A	Displays only letters.
L	Displays only logical data.
N	Displays only letters or numbers.
X	Displays any character.
Y	Displays logical data.
9	Displays only numbers when used with character data, or displays numbers and signs when used with numeric data.
#	Displays numbers, blanks, and signs.
$	Displays a dollar sign in a fixed location before a numeric value (if the value includes leading blanks, there will be a space between the dollar sign and the number).
$$	Displays a floating dollar sign before a numeric value (if the value includes leading blanks, the dollar sign will move right so there is no space between it and the number).
*	Uses asterisks to fill the leading blanks of a numeric value (this is often used on printed checks).
.	Shows the location of a decimal point.
,	Adds commas to separate values to the left of the decimal point.

Creating Calculated Fields

Clicking the Calculations button of the Report Expression dialog box calls up the Subtotal or Calculate Field dialog box shown in Figure 17.11, which lets you create calculated fields that summarize the values in a number of records. As you can see, this dialog box contains eight radio buttons that let you select the calculation to be performed on the field:

- **Nothing:** No calculation is performed.
- **Count:** Counts the number of fields.
- **Sum:** Totals all the values of the field.
- **Average:** Finds the average value in the field.
- **Lowest:** Finds the lowest value in the field.
- **Highest:** Finds the highest value in the field.
- **Std Deviation and Variance:** Performs these statistical calculations.

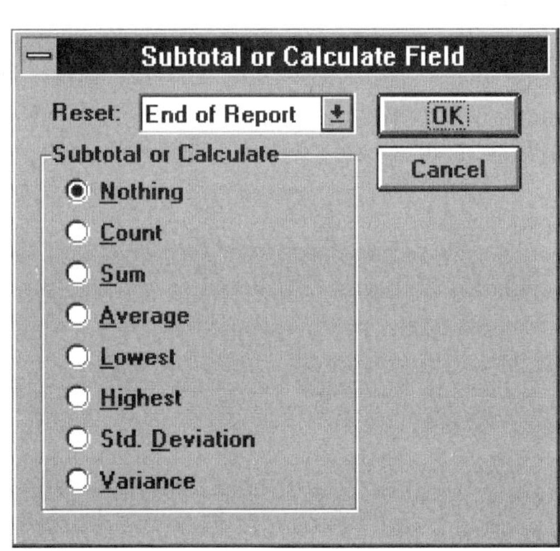

FIGURE 17.11

The Subtotal or Calculate Field dialog box

For example, if you had WAGE as the field expression in the Report Expression dialog box and you checked the Calculate check box and then selected the Average radio button in the Calculate dialog box, you would create a calculated field that finds the average wage.

▸▸ NOTE

The default calculation in the Calculate dialog box is Nothing. Thus, if you do not select the Calculate check box and use this dialog box, no calculation is performed.

The Calculate dialog box includes a Reset drop-down list, which determines when the calculation will be done. In Group Bands, the calculation is done for each group by default. For other bands, the default is End of Report, which does the calculation only once, at the end. You can select End of Column or End of Page from the drop-down list to calculate the data for each page or each column. For example, select End of Page if you want to put a total in the page footer. If you have grouped data, you can also select the name of any of your groups from the list and perform the calculation for each group. The calculated field would be placed in the group header or footer. In any of these cases, you must place the field in the appropriate place—for example, in the report summary or the page footer band—and select the calculation you want.

Other Features of the Report Expression Dialog Box

The other features of the Report Expression dialog box are similar to the features of the dialog boxes for other report controls, which were covered earlier in this chapter in the section "Text Control Properties." However, there are a few significant differences we need to look at.

Printing or Hiding Repeated Values The Print When button displays the Print When dialog box, which is similar to the one for text control properties (discussed earlier), except that instead of the Print Once Per Band box it has a Print Repeated Values box.

If you select the No radio button in the Print Repeated Values area of this dialog box, and the value of the field is the same for more than one record, then only the first occurrence of the value is printed.

For example, if you have a report that is indexed by state, you might want to put the State field at the far left of the report and select this option so that each state's name appears only once.

Stretching the Control In addition to using the options in the Object Position box to specify whether the field remains a constant distance from the top or bottom of the band, as you do with other controls, you can use the Stretch With Overflow check box to specify whether to keep the field a constant height or let it stretch to accommodate extra text.

Selecting this text box lets the control expand to let the data wrap to the next line for the records where its contents do not fit on a single line. This is particularly useful for Memo fields. Of course, you need to anticipate the effect this will have on other controls in the band.

Using Expressions This section has focused on adding fields, but you should remember that a field is a type of expression, and more complex expressions also are often useful in reports. Some are covered in the section "Some Useful Expressions in Reports and Labels" later in this chapter.

Using Pictures and Other OLE Objects in Reports

To add a picture to a report, click the Picture tool and then click and drag in the layout window to draw a frame for the picture. When you release the mouse button after drawing the frame, Visual FoxPro displays the Report Picture dialog box shown in Figure 17.12. You can also display this dialog box by double-clicking an existing picture, as you do with other controls.

There are two fundamentally different types of pictures that you might want to add to a report:

- A picture from a file remains the same throughout the report, and is normally added in the Report Title, Report Summary, Page Header, or Page Footer band. For example, you might want to add a company logo to the report title or to the header of each page.

FIGURE 17.12

The Report Picture dialog box

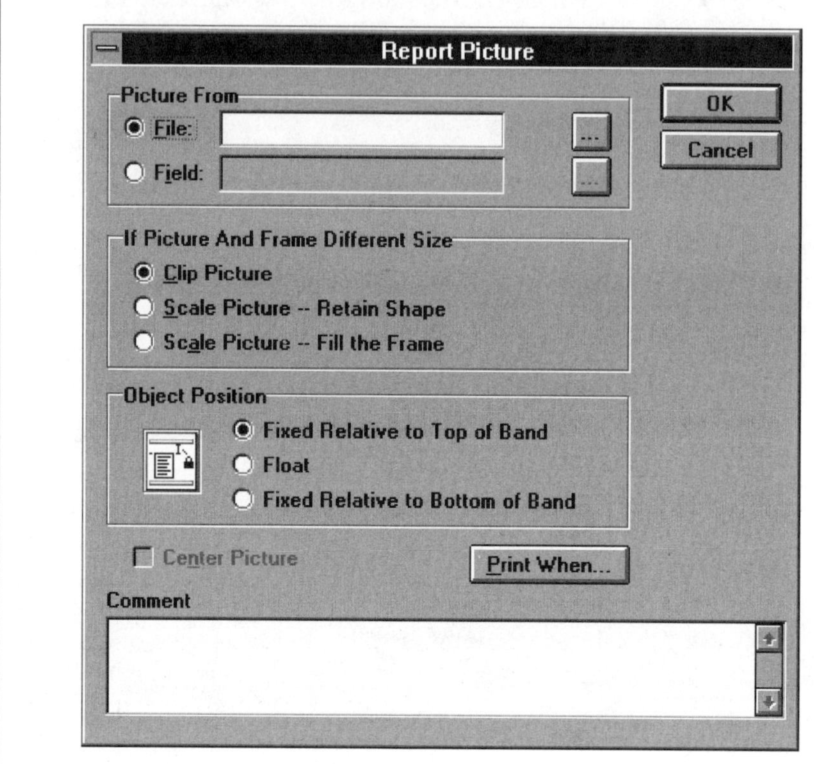

- A picture in a General field is different for each record of the report, and is normally added in the Detail band (or, particularly if you are working with a relational database, in the Group Header or Group Footer band). For example, if you have a General field with a picture of each of your employees, you could add it in the detail band to include a picture next to each employee's name and address.

As you can see from the figure, the radio buttons at the top of the Report Picture dialog box let you choose which of these to add.

Adding a Picture from a File

Pictures from a file that will be added to reports must be in bitmap format, which has a BMP or DMP extension, or in Windows Icon format, which has an ICO extension.

TIP

The Paintbrush utility, which is included with Windows, creates pictures with the BMP format, and is the easiest and most accessible way of creating pictures to include in reports.

If you select the File radio button, enter the name of one of these file types in the text box to its right, or select the pushbutton to its far right to display the Open dialog box.

Use this like any Open dialog box to select the picture file. The only difference is that you can click the Preview button to display the picture in the Picture area of the Open dialog box.

Adding a Picture from a Field

If you select the Field radio button, you can enter the name a General field that contains bitmap graphics or select the Field pushbutton to display the Choose Field/Variable dialog box and use it to select the desired field or a variable of the General data type.

Formatting Pictures

Other features of the Report Picture dialog box let you control the display of pictures from either a file or a field.

The If Picture And Frame Different Size area lets you specify what will be done if the picture does not fit precisely in the frame. If the picture is larger than the frame, the radio buttons give you these options:

- **Clip Picture:** The picture retains its original dimensions. The upper-left corner of the picture is aligned at the upper-left corner of the frame. Any portions of the picture's lower or right edge that do not fit in the frame are not displayed.
- **Shrink Picture—Retain Shape:** The picture is resized so that all of it can be displayed, and it fills as much of the frame as possible without its shape being changed.

- **Shrink Picture—Fill the Frame:** The picture is resized so all of it can be displayed filling the entire frame. If the picture is not the same shape as the frame, it is stretched horizontally or vertically.

On the other hand, if the picture is smaller than the frame, it will be displayed in the frame's upper-left corner by default; however, if you select the Center Picture check box, it will be centered within the frame instead.

In addition to these features, the Report Picture dialog box has Object Position options, a Print When check box, and a Comment text box, all of which work as they do in the dialog boxes for other report controls, covered earlier in this chapter, in the section on Text Control Properties.

▸ Formatting Controls

You can format most controls on the report by using the Format menu or the Layout toolbar. You can also determine their color by using the Color Palette toolbar.

The Format Menu

The Format menu contains many options that are only enabled when you've selected one or more controls. Many of its features are also included on the Layout toolbar. It includes the following options:

- **Align:** Displays a submenu that lets you specify how the selected controls should be aligned. For example, you can align their top edges, bottom edges, left edges, or right edges. The options on this submenu are also available in the Layout toolbar, covered in the next section.
- **Size:** Displays a submenu that lets you give the selected controls a uniform size. Select the To Tallest or To Shortest option to make them all the same height as the tallest or shortest one, or select To Widest or To Narrowest to make them all the same width as the widest or narrowest control. Alternatively, select To Grid to size them all so they fit within an imaginary grid. The options on the Size submenu are also available in the Layout toolbar, covered in the next section.

- **Horizontal Spacing** and **Vertical Spacing:** Both display a submenu that lets you control the spacing of the selected objects. You can select Make Equal to equalize the horizontal or vertical spacing between all the objects, or select Increase or Decrease to increase or decrease the spacing uniformly.
- **Bring to Front:** Brings the control(s) to the front so they cover other controls. This option is also available in the Layout toolbar, covered in the next section.
- **Send to Back:** Sends the control(s) to the back so they are covered by other controls. This option is also available in the Layout toolbar, covered in the next section.
- **Group:** Groups the selected controls so they can all be manipulated (for example, cut or moved) as if they were a single control.
- **Ungroup:** Separates grouped controls so they must be manipulated individually once again.
- **Snap to Grid:** This option, which is selected by default, automatically aligns the upper-left edge of controls to an imaginary grid of lines, so they are lined up more accurately.
- **Set Grid Scale:** Displays the Ruler/Grid dialog box, shown in Figure 17.13, which lets you control the fineness of the grid to which controls are automatically aligned if Snap to Grid is on.

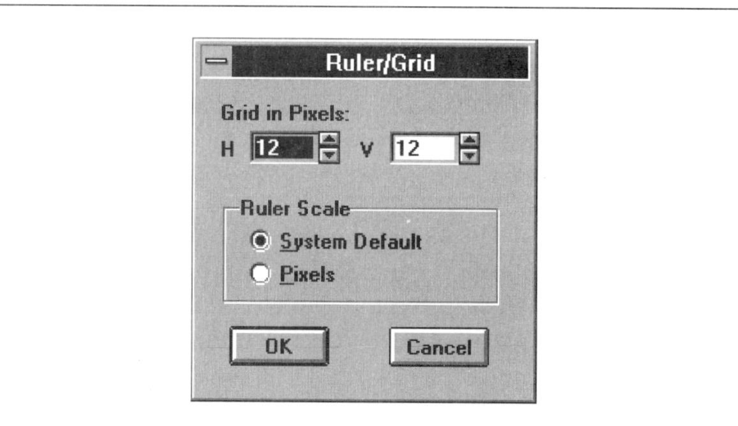

FIGURE 17.13

The Ruler/Grid dialog box

- **Font:** Displays the Font dialog box, shown in Figure 17.14, to let you determine the font of the selected control(s). (This option is enabled only for text and field controls.)

FIGURE 17.14

The Font dialog box

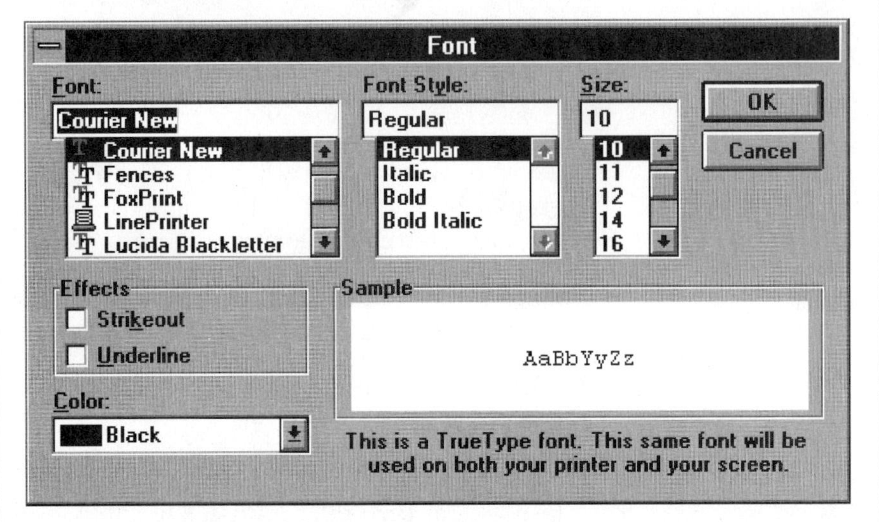

- **Text Alignment:** Displays a submenu that lets you select the justification and spacing of text. You can left-justify, center, or right-justify, and you can single-space, 1½-space, or double-space. (This option is enabled only for text and field controls.)

- **Fill:** Displays a submenu of fill patterns, shown in Figure 17.15, that you can select to fill rectangles or rounded rectangles.

- **Pen:** Displays a submenu, shown in Figure 17.16, that lets you select the type of line that will be used for a line, rectangle, or rounded rectangle. The default Hairline draws a thin line; the point sizes draw progressively thicker lines. You also have the option of lines made of dots, of dashes, or of combinations of dots and dashes. The None option, which eliminates the border, is useful if the control is filled with a pattern.

- **Mode:** Displays a submenu with two choices, to let you determine whether controls located behind the selected control(s) will be visible. Opaque (the default) hides such controls and Transparent shows them.

FIGURE 17.15

Fill patterns for rectangles and rounded rectangles

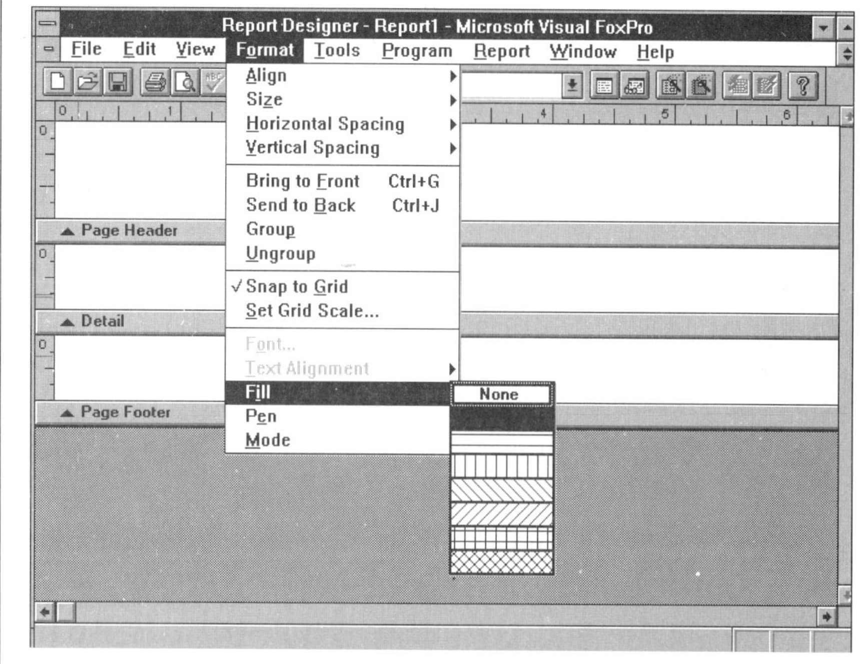

FIGURE 17.16

The Pen submenu

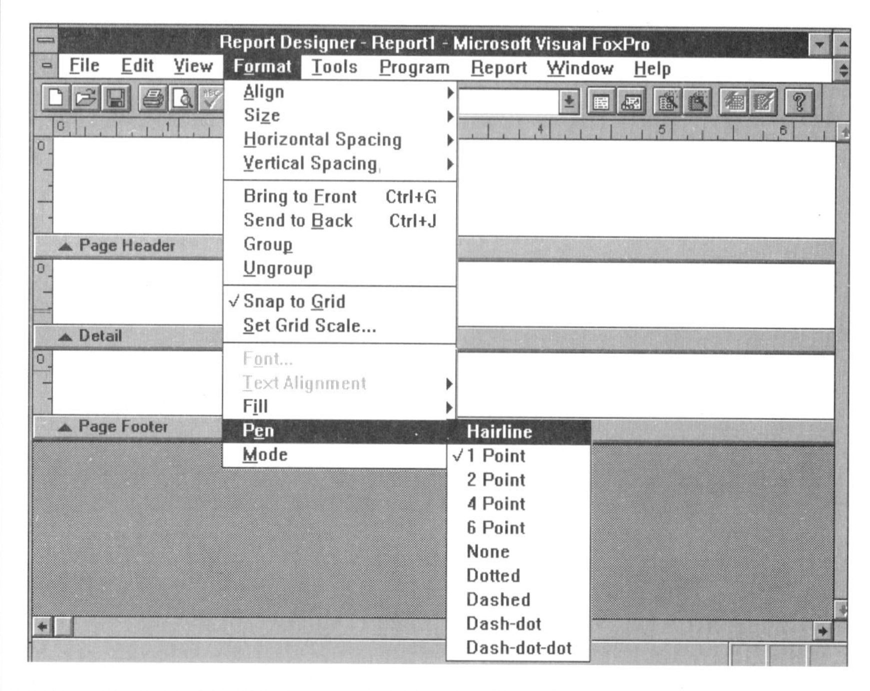

The Layout Toolbar

The Layout toolbar, shown in Figure 17.17, gives you an easier way to use some of the options of the Format menu. It includes the following buttons:

- **Align Left Sides:** Arranges the selected controls so that their left edges are lined up.

- **Align Right Sides:** Arranges the selected controls so that their right edges are lined up.

- **Align Top Edges:** Arranges the selected controls so that their top edges are lined up.

- **Align Bottom Edges:** Arranges the selected controls so that their bottom edges are lined up.

- **Align Vertical Centers:** Arranges the selected controls so that they are centered one above another.

- **Align Horizontal Centers:** Arranges the selected controls so they are centered one next to another.

- **Same Width:** Resizes the selected controls so they are all the same width

- **Same Height:** Resizes the selected controls so that they are all the same height.

- **Same Size:** Resizes the selected controls so that they are all the same height and width

- **Center Horizontally:** Centers the selected control(s) horizontally, so that they are equally close to the left and right edges of the report.

- **Center Vertically:** Centers the selected control(s) vertically, so that they are equally close to the top and bottom edges of the band.

- **Bring to Front:** Brings the selected control(s) to the front so that they cover other controls.

- **Send to Back:** Sends the selected control(s) to the back so that they are covered by other controls.

FIGURE 17.17

The Layout Toolbar

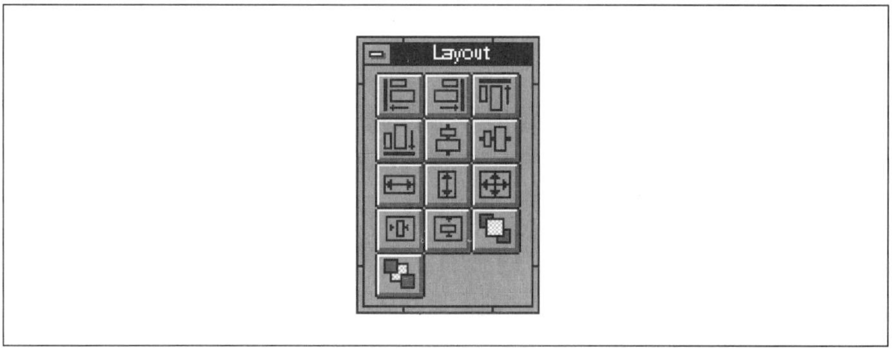

The Color Palette

Use the Color Palette, shown in Figure 17.18, to change the colors of objects.

FIGURE 17.18

The Color Palette

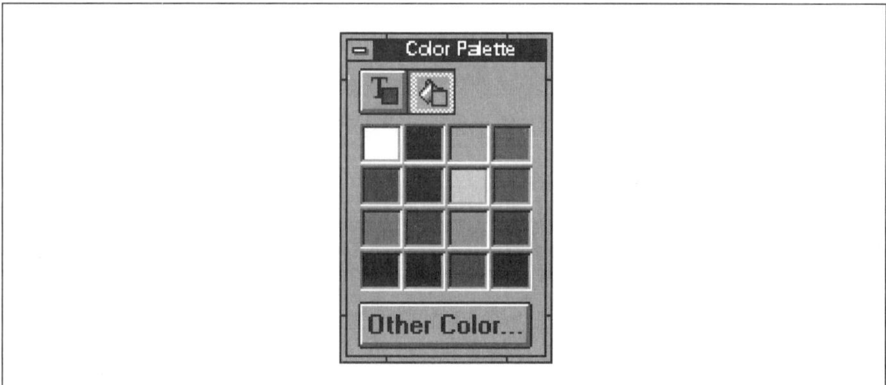

Select the Foreground Color button to make your selection apply to the foreground color of the object; for example, to the letters of text controls.

Select the Background Color button to make your selection apply to the background color of the object; for example, to the box behind the letters of text controls.

After you select one of these buttons, it appears to be "pressed." Then you can click any of the color buttons to apply that color to the foreground or background of all selected controls.

Click either the Foreground or the Background Color button again to deselect it.

►► The Report Menu

The Report menu, added to the main menu bar when you display the Report Designer, includes several features that are invaluable for laying out a report.

► Adding a Title or Summary

Choosing Report ➤ Title/Summary displays the Title/Summary dialog box shown in Figure 17.19, which lets you add a title or summary band to the report.

FIGURE 17.19 ►

The Title/Summary dialog box

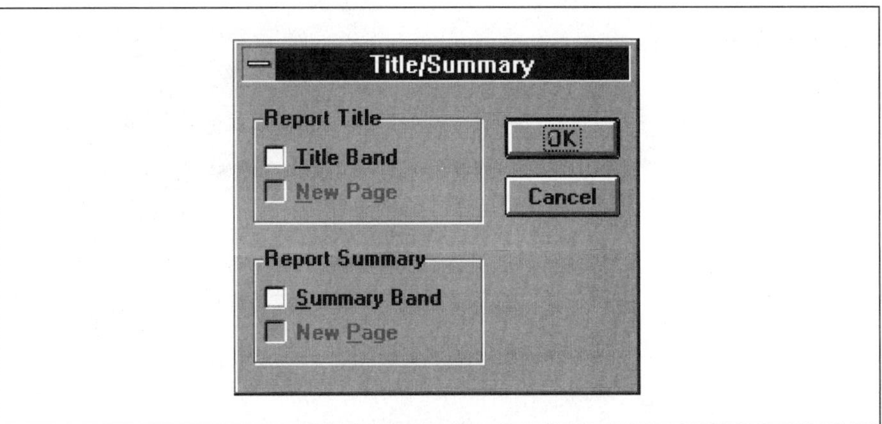

As you can see in the illustration, there are two check boxes under both Report Title and Report Summary. Checking the first adds a title band or summary band to the Report Designer. You can work in these bands the same way you work in other bands. Once you add one of these bands, the New Page check box under it is enabled: checking it makes Visual FoxPro print out the report title or summary on a separate page.

You might want to use the title band not just for a one- or two-line title but for an abstract of the report. This is one case in which you would want it to appear on a separate page.

Of course, the title actually appears below the header of the first page, even though the title *band* is above the page header band. Similarly, Summary actually appears above the footer of the last page, even though its band is below the page footer band.

Creating Grouped Reports

Selecting Report ➤ Data Grouping lets you group data. A grouped report might, for example, print the data for each state separately, and it could include a header and footer for each state. Often the group footer includes a calculated field that summarizes the data in the group.

When you add a grouping, new bands appear in the Layout Report window to hold the group header and footer. You can work with these bands in the same ways you work with any other bands.

Selecting Data Grouping calls up the Data Grouping dialog box, shown in Figure 17.20. As you can see, this dialog box lets you add, change, or delete a grouping. The scrollable list represents groups that have already been added; you can select a group from the list to change or delete. This list can include up to 20 levels of groupings. For example, you can group by state, by city within each state, and so on. In the illustration, records have been grouped by state; within each state, they are grouped by city; and within each city, they are grouped by ZIP code. Notice how these groupings are added to the report, visible behind the dialog box in the illustration. You resize them and add controls to them in the usual ways.

A new, blank line is always included at the end of the Group Expression list to let you add a grouping. You can type the expression you want the group to be based on in the text box in this list, or select the pushbutton to its right to call up the Expression Builder to create the expression. Usually the grouping expression is something simple—a field name such as STATE. You might also want to use a simple expression such as UPPER(STATE), if there is a chance that the state names are not all capitalized.

FIGURE 17.20

The Data Grouping dialog box

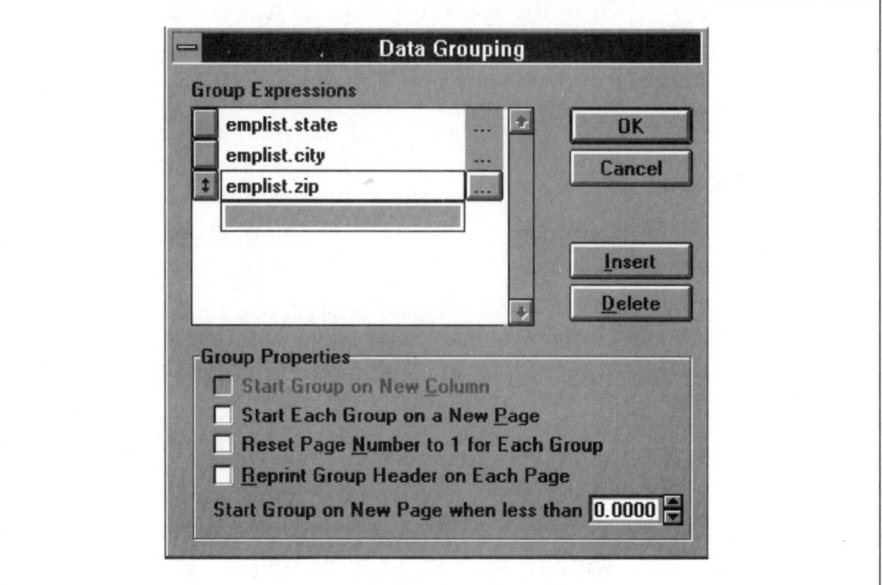

Click and drag the move buttons to the left of the items in this list to change the order of the grouping, and use the Insert and Delete buttons to insert or remove groupings, as you do in the Table Designer.

Remember that groupings that are lower on this list are incorporated within higher groupings. Thus, if you want to group records by state and within each state by ZIP code, STATE must be the first Group Expression and ZIP the second.

Group Properties

Select any item in the Group Expressions list of the Data Grouping dialog box, and use the controls below to specify the properties of that group. You can use the following options:

- **Start Group on New Column:** Makes each group start on a new column (available only on multicolumn reports).
- **Start Each Group on a New Page:** Makes each new group start on a new page.

- **Reset Page Number to 1 for Each Group:** Makes each group start on a new page and resets the page number so that the numbering for each group begins with page 1.
- **Reprint Group Header on Each Page:** If the group occupies more than one page, the group header is printed at the top of each page when this check box is selected.

The Importance of Indexing

There is one important precaution to take if you use data groupings: You must index your data properly to make sure the data is grouped correctly. If you group on State without indexing, for example, Visual FoxPro prints a new group footer and header each time it comes to a record in which the state is not the same as it was in the previous record. The options on the menu system just make the report print the previous group's footer and the new group's header whenever there is a change in the data in the expression you are grouping on.

NOTE

It is also possible to sort your data in the appropriate order, but this is a much clumsier method than indexing.

For example, what if you want to group by state but also want the names of the employees within each state to be alphabetized? You have to index on UPPER(STATE+LNAME+FNAME) or some equivalent expression. The index itself must put the records in the right order for the grouping.

If you generate a report using the Grouped Report Wizard, it automatically creates the indcx you need, as you saw in Chapter 10.

Adding Variables

Selecting Report ➤ Variables lets you add memory variables to the report form. This is a sophisticated report feature that is used primarily in programming. Memory variables are discussed in Chapter 23. If you add a memory variable to a form, its content changes depending on the value you give the memory variable, so you can change this feature of the report by giving the memory variable a different value, without redesigning the report.

▶ Using a Default Font

Choose Report ➤ Default Font to display the Font dialog box, which you can use in the usual way to select a font, a font style, and a font size. This font will be used as the default for all controls that include text, such as field and text controls.

▶ Restricting Network Access

Choose Report ➤ Private Data Session to prevent other users on a network from accessing the table while you are working on the report design.

▶ Creating a Quick Report

Choosing Report ➤ Quick Report calls up the Quick Report dialog box, shown in Figure 17.21. While it is not as effective as the Report Wizard, you can use this dialog box to place field data in the report automatically so you do not have to place each field expression individually.

The two Field Layout picture buttons let you choose whether you want the fields arranged in column layout, with the fields placed in the detail band one next to another, from left to right; or in row layout, with the fields placed in the detail band one above another, from top to bottom. (If you use form layout, the detail band will automatically stretch to hold all the fields.)

This dialog box also contains four check boxes:

- **Titles:** Determines whether the field name will be placed above each field (column layout) or to the left of each field (form layout).
- **Fields:** Displays a Field Picker dialog box to let you choose which fields are initially displayed in the quick report.
- **Add Table to Data Environment:** Includes the table in the Data Environment of the report.
- **Add Alias:** Inserts an alias in the names of all fields used as labels in the report.

FIGURE 17.21

Quick Report dialog box

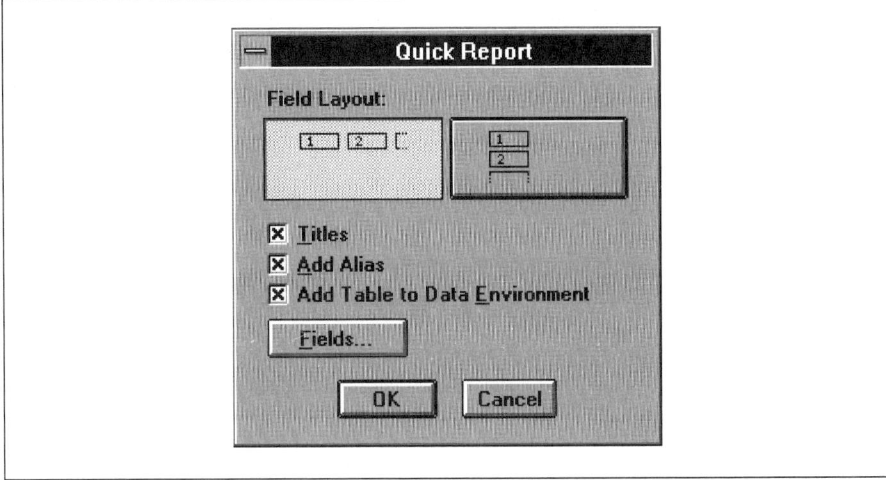

The initial quick report includes fields but not more complex field expressions.

Running the Report

Choose Report ➤ Run Report to display the Print dialog box, which you can use in the usual way to print the report.

Page Setup and Multicolumn Reports

When you are using the Report Designer, you can choose File ➤ Page Setup to display the Page Setup dialog box, shown in Figure 17.22. This dialog box lets you control several features of the page layout; the most important is the number of columns on the page.

Creating Multicolumn Reports

In the Columns area, use the Number control to create multicolumn reports. If you select 2 or higher, you can also use the controls below it to specify the width and spacing of the column.

FIGURE 17.22

The Page Setup dialog box

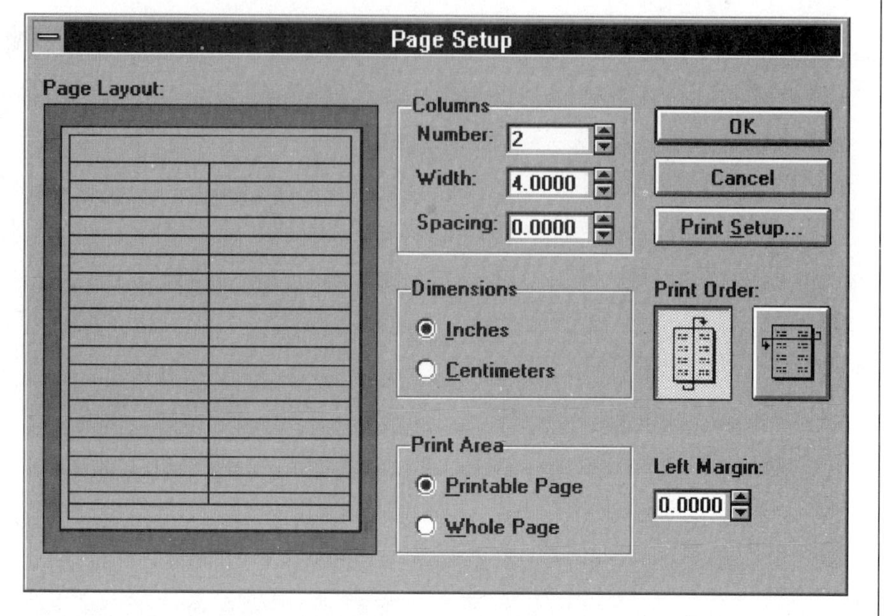

When you create a multicolumn report in this way, the Report Designer displays a detail band that is only wide enough for one column of the report, as shown in Figure 17.23. The layout you design here will be repeated in each column of the report.

With multiple columns the Report Designer also adds a Column Header and Column Footer band, which you can use in the same way as page header and page footer bands. The header or footer is the same width as the column and is repeated for each column.

When you are working with a multicolumn report, you can also use the Print Order buttons of the Page Setup dialog box to specify whether the records should be printed down the columns or across the rows. For example, if the records are in alphabetical order by name, you can select the button on the left to have the names listed alphabetically down the first column, to continue at the top of the second column, and so on. You can select the button to the right to list the names alphabetically across the top row, to continue at the left of the second row, and so on.

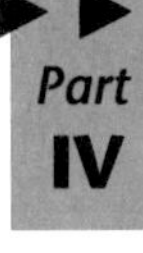

FIGURE 17.23

Designing a multicolumn report

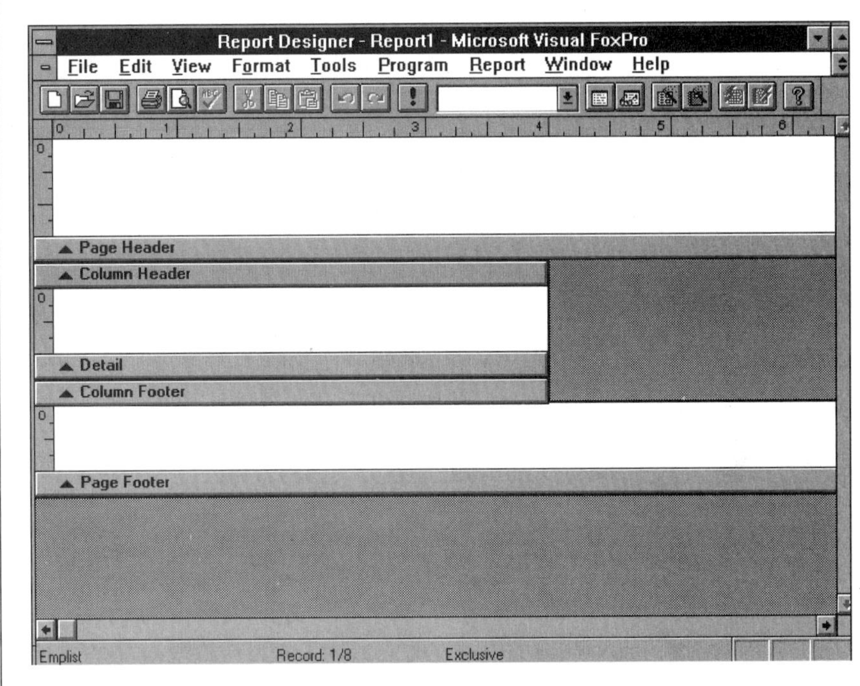

Setting Margins

You can also use the Print Area and left Margin controls of this dialog box to specify whether the design is printed on the entire page or on the printable page and whether it is printed with a margin.

Most printers cannot print on the entire page; typically, they can only print up to a quarter inch away from each edge of the page. If you select Printable Page, the Report Designer lets you lay out controls only on an area as large as your printer can print, so that a control at the right edge of the report design (for example) will be printed as far right as your printer can go. If you select Whole Page, on the other hand, placing a control at the right edge of the report design would mean that it should be printed at the right edge of the paper, though that is probably impossible for your printer; you would have to design your report so no controls are closer to the edge of the page than your printer can handle. Needless to say, it is usually much easier to select Printable Page, so that the Report Designer handles this detail for you.

You ordinarily want to print a report with a left margin such as 1 inch or 1¼ inch, larger than the nonprintable area on the left edge of the report. If you use the margin spinner to specify a margin, a control on the left edge of the report layout will be placed at the margin. Again, this is generally easier than placing the controls in the report in locations that allow for the left margin.

►► Using the Label Designer

The Label Designer is virtually identical to the Report Designer, except that it is used to work on labels. Label files have the extension LBX.

There are two ways of using the Label Designer. As discussed in Chapter 7, the easiest way is to create the labels using the Label Wizard and then use the Designer to customize the design. To use this method, choose the "Save label and modify it in the Label Designer" option in the final step of the Label Wizard.

Though it is more difficult, you can also create labels from scratch. To do this, choose File ➤ New, select the Label radio button, and click the New File button. Visual FoxPro displays the New Label dialog box, shown in Figure 17.24. Use this dialog box to select an Avery Number, as you did in the first step of the Label Wizard.

FIGURE 17.24 ►

The New Label dialog box

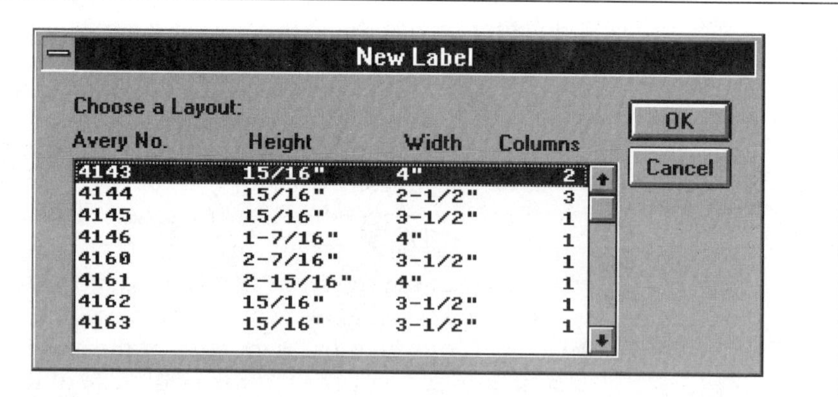

Avery No.	Height	Width	Columns
4143	15/16"	4"	2
4144	15/16"	2-1/2"	3
4145	15/16"	3-1/2"	1
4146	1-7/16"	4"	1
4160	2-7/16"	3-1/2"	1
4161	2-15/16"	4"	1
4162	15/16"	3-1/2"	1
4163	15/16"	3-1/2"	1

When you click OK, Visual FoxPro displays the Label Designer, shown in Figure 17.25.

FIGURE 17.25

The Label Designer

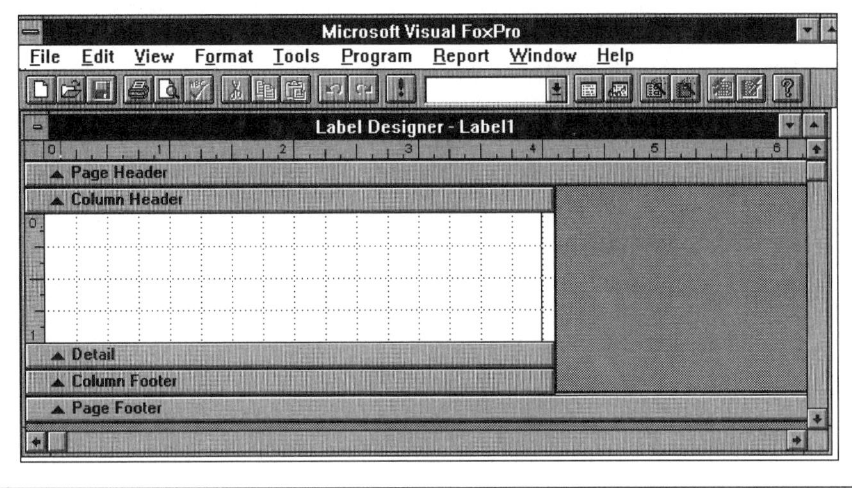

As you can see, the Label Designer is the same as the Report Designer. It is simply used to create a multicolumn report with the number of columns and the size of the detail band adjusted to produce labels that fit the Avery form you selected. The header bands are present, because they are always included in the Report Designer, but they are reduced to zero size, since these labels do not have headers.

You can adjust the size of the detail band, use the tools to add additional fields, graphics, or pictures to the label, and work with the label in any other way that you work with reports.

WARNING

You should remember, though, that it is not appropriate to use some features of the Report Designer when you are working on labels. For example, data groupings or headers and footers are obviously inappropriate. Yet they are included on the Report menu for the Label Designer, because it is identical to the menu for the Report Designer.

In addition, you generally cannot add fields to labels in the same way that you do to reports. The Wizard generates the expressions needed to display the fields without unnecessary spacing. For example, Figure 17.26 shows the labels you generated using the Wizard in Chapter 7, and you can see that they use expressions that include the ALLTRIM( ) function to remove unnecessary blank spaces, as you learned to do in Chapter 9.

FIGURE 17.26

The Label Wizard uses expressions to trim blank spaces.

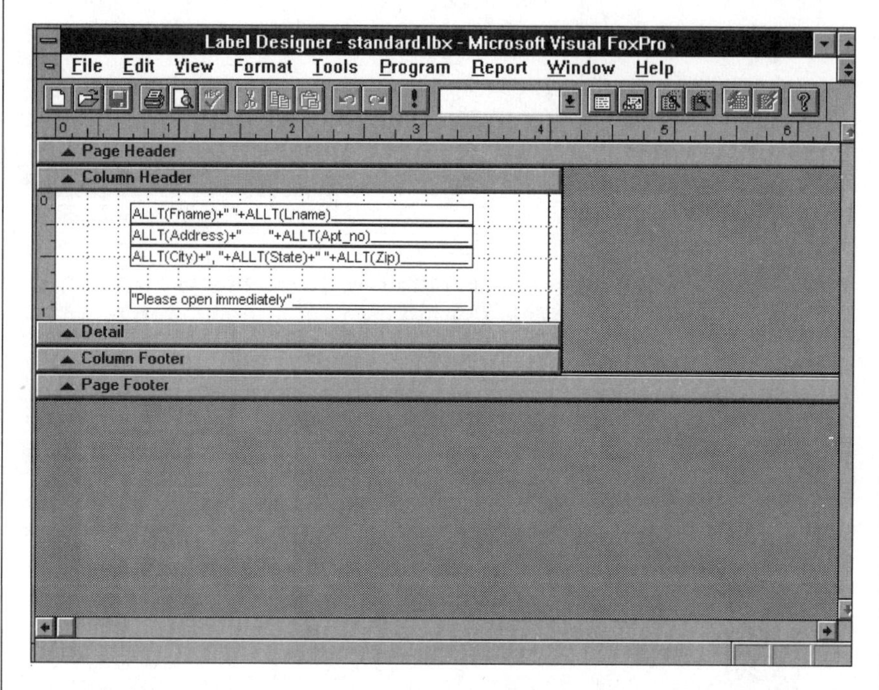

Because it is so much easier than entering expressions by hand, it is generally best to lay out labels using the Wizard. Then, you can use the Label Designer to easily add pictures, graphics, or other enhancements to the label. Either use the final dialog box of the Wizard to display your label in the Label Designer, or select File ➤ Open at any later time and use the Open dialog box to display it in the Label Designer and customize it.

Some Useful Expressions in Reports and Labels

As you are designing reports and mailing labels, you will find many cases where expressions, rather than simple field names, are useful. Here are a few examples of how you can use expressions in reports and labels, but you should always be on the lookout for others as you work with the Report and Label Designers.

Correcting Capitalization

If there are any inconsistencies in the way that your data is capitalized, you should use the PROPER( ) or UPPER( ) function to correct capitalization. This is not as important on mailing labels, which are used individually, but it is essential in reports, where records are listed one after another.

Including a Page Number

One system variable is very useful in reports. You can include a page number in an expression by selecting _PAGENO from the list of memory variables in the Expression Builder. This variable is included automatically when you create a report using a Wizard, but there may be times when you need to add it by hand.

Trimming Blank Spaces

As you have seen, if you design labels from scratch using the Label Designer, you should not simply place the fields on the label. Because some fields have contents that are different lengths, there will be gaps between the first and last name and between the city and state. Instead, you should use expressions such as:

```
TRIM(FNAME) + " " + LNAME
```

to display the name. The TRIM( ) function removes all trailing blanks from the first name. You must explicitly include a blank space between two quotation marks in the expression to add a space between the first and last name. The LNAME field does not require the TRIM( ) function, because nothing follows it.

Likewise, to display the city, state, and ZIP, use an expression such as:

```
TRIM(CITY) + " " + STATE + " " + ZIP
```

Here, you do not need to TRIM( ) the state name, because all state names are the same length and do not include trailing blanks. You do have to include blank spaces between the fields.

▸ The Immediate If

One complex function that is often useful in both reports and labels is IIF( ), the immediate-if function, which takes the form:

```
IIF(<log exp>,<exp1>,<exp2>)
```

and returns the value of the first expression if the logical expression is true or the value of the second expression if the logical expression is false.

In our sample application, you are producing mailing labels for a table that has a separate field for apartment number. People who do not live in apartments have nothing entered in this field.

On labels that have apartment numbers, you want the address, followed by the word **Apt.**, followed by the apartment number. On labels that do not have apartment numbers, though, you do not want the word **Apt.** included. To get this result, you can enter an expression such as:

```
TRIM(ADDRESS) + " " + IIF(APTNO = " ", " ", "Apt. ")
+ APTNO
```

This expression prints the contents of the address field with trailing blanks trimmed for every record. Then it prints a blank space. Finally, it uses IIF( ) to print **Apt.** followed by a space only when it is appropriate.

The logical expression in this function, **APTNO =** " ", is true if the APTNO field has no entry in it. In this case, IIF() returns the second expression, which is simply a blank space. On the other hand, if there is an entry in the APTNO field, this logical expression is false, and so IIF( ) returns the word **Apt.**

Finally, the expression includes the contents of the APTNO field for all records, but if there is no entry in the field, this just adds a few extra blank spaces at the end of the line.

In one of the exercises below, you will add this expression to customize the labels you created using the Wizard.

IIF( ) can also be used to add a special message on some mailing labels. For example, you might want to add an extra line on the labels sent to magazine subscribers whose subscriptions have expired, by adding a line to it with an expression such as:

```
IIF(EXP_DATE < DATE(), "Your last issue unless you
renew", " ")
```

assuming that the field EXP_DATE holds the expiration date. If the expiration date is "less than" the current date—that is, if it has already occurred—the label includes a line with this warning. Otherwise, this line just includes a blank space.

IIF( ) is also useful in reports. For example, if you are phoning members of an organization to request donations, you might produce a columnar report that includes all fields for the name, phone number, and last donation of all the people who have given donations in past, plus a column with an expression such as:

```
IIF(LAST_DONAT > 100, "MAJOR DONOR", " ")
```

So the words MAJOR DONOR are displayed next to the names and phone numbers of people who have given more than 100 dollars, to let the phone solicitors know that they are big donors.

Commands to Produce Reports and Labels

If you are working from the Command window, you design and produce reports and labels using similar commands.

To work with reports, use the commands:

- **CREATE REPORT <file name>** to display the Report Designer to create a new report.

- **MODIFY REPORT <file name>** to display the Report Designer to modify an existing report.
- **REPORT FORM <file name> [TO PRINT]** to produce a report that has already been designed. If you do not include the optional TO PRINT clause, the report is just displayed in the main Visual FoxPro window, behind all document windows. This report can also include an optional scope, FOR, and WHILE clause, and other optional clauses that are covered in detail in Appendix B.

To work with labels, use identical commands with the word LABEL instead of REPORT. For example, to print labels that you have already designed, enter **LABEL FORM <file name> TO PRINT**.

▸▸ Customizing Sample Reports and Labels

Now that you have looked at the Report Designer and Label Designer, you should use them to customize the sample reports and labels that you created in Chapters 6 and 7.

These exercises will let you use the features of the Report and Label Designers that are most useful in practical work. You can also try on your own to customize these reports in other ways.

▸ Customizing the Employee Report

First, try customizing the employee report that you created in Chapter 6 and saved with the file name Empdata.

This is a general report showing most of the data on each employee, and it requires only the customization that you will find is needed in most reports. You will change field names that are used as labels where it is necessary, and you will use the PROPER( ) function to capitalize data correctly.

Remember that this is a three-column report. When you display it in the Report Designer, you will view only one report column; that is, only one example of the layout of the data. To see how this data is repeated on the page, choose File ➤ Page Setup to display the report's

Page Setup dialog box, shown in Figure 17.27, and consult the preview in the Page Layout illustration.

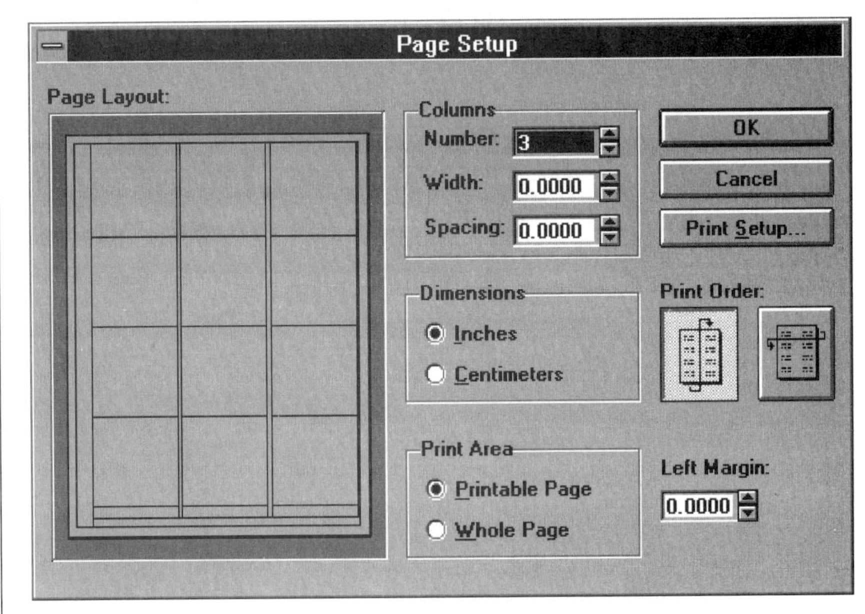

FIGURE 17.27

The Page Setup dialog box for the Empdata report

1. Choose File ➤ Open and use the Open dialog box to display the Empdata report in the Report Designer. If necessary, maximize the Report Designer, so you have more space to work in. Close the Layout and Color Palette toolbars if they are displayed, because you won't need them.

2. Now, edit the labels for the Fname and Lname fields. Click the Label tool of the Report Controls toolbar. Click the word **Fname** to place the insertion bar in it, and edit it so it reads **First name**. Likewise, click the Label tool, click **Lname** and edit it to read **Last name**. Click the Pointer tool to return the pointer to its usual form.

3. Now, double-click the Field control that represents the title field, to display its dialog box. Its expression is **TITLE**. Edit it to read **PROPER(TITLE)**, as shown in Figure 17.28.

FIGURE 17.28

Correcting capitalization

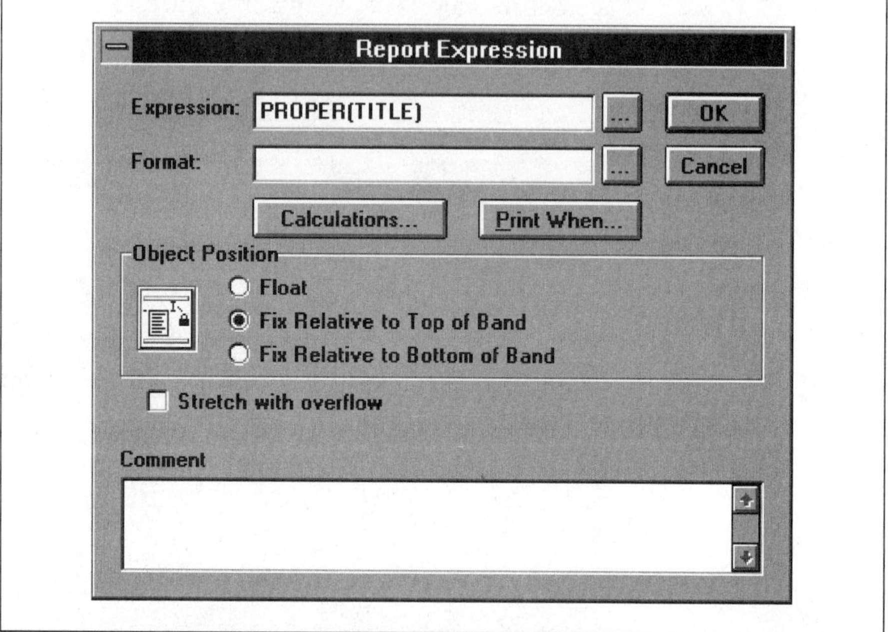

4. Do the same for the Fname, Lname, Address, and City fields. Double-click each one to display its dialog box, and add PROPER( ) to the expression, so they are capitalized correctly.
5. The final report design is shown in Figure 17.29. Choose File ➤ Save to save these changes. Then choose View ➤ Preview to display the output of the report in a Print Preview window. When you are done looking at it, close the Preview window and the Report Designer.

When you display the report in the Preview window, notice the changes you have made. You have improved the field labels and capitalization of the report generated by the Wizard in a way that will be useful in most reports you actually work with.

▸ Customizing the Wage Report

Now, you should customize the Wage report that you created in Chapter 6. There, you saw that this report suppressed repeated values. You have two people with the last name Johnson in the table, and the report

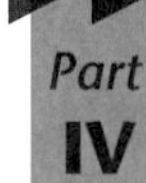

FIGURE 17.29

The final design of the Emp data report

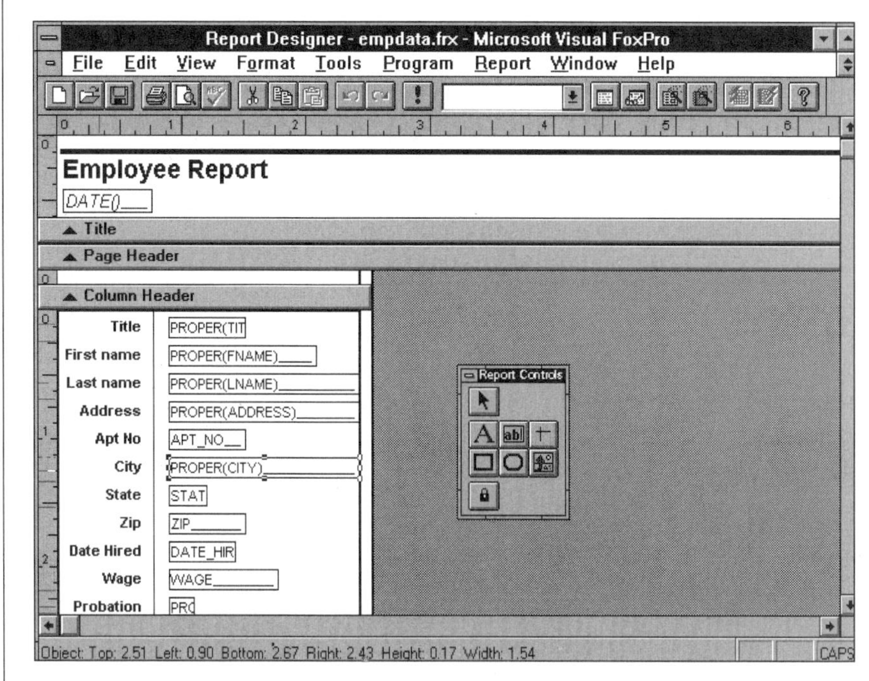

includes this last name only for the first, with a blank in the Lname field for the second.

It is often useful to suppress repeated values in a columnar report. If you were listing records by state and put the state in the first column, for example, the report would list each state's name once and leave blank spaces in the state column for the rest of the records from that state, making it very easy to see which records come from each state. In the Wage report, however, you do not want the name suppressed if two people happen to have the same last name. You should customize this report by changing the Print Repeated Values property.

Like the Employee report generated by the Wizard, this report also retains the capitalization in the table, and uses field names as labels; and you should also customize these features just as you did in the previous section.

When you display this report, notice that the field names that are used as labels are in the Page Header band, and the fields themselves are in the detail band. Thus, field names are displayed at the top of each page, and the values in the field are listed in the body of the page.

1. Choose File ➤ Open and use the Open dialog box to display the Empwages report in the Report Designer. If necessary, maximize the Report Designer. The Layout and Color Palette toolbars should be hidden, and the Report Controls toolbar should be displayed.

2. Edit the labels for the Lname and Fname fields, as you did in the previous exercise. Click the Label tool, click **Lname** and **Fname** to place the insertion bar in them, and edit them to read **Last name** and **First name**. When you click the Pointer tool to return the pointer to its usual form, these labels will be properly aligned over the fields.

3. Likewise, as you did in the previous exercise, double-click the Field control that represents the Lname to display its dialog box, and edit the expression so it is **PROPER(LNAME)**. Then click the Print When button, and select the Yes radio button in the Print Repeated Values area of the Print When dialog box, as shown in Figure 17.30. Close the Print When and Report Expression dialog boxes.

FIGURE 17.30

Printing repeated values

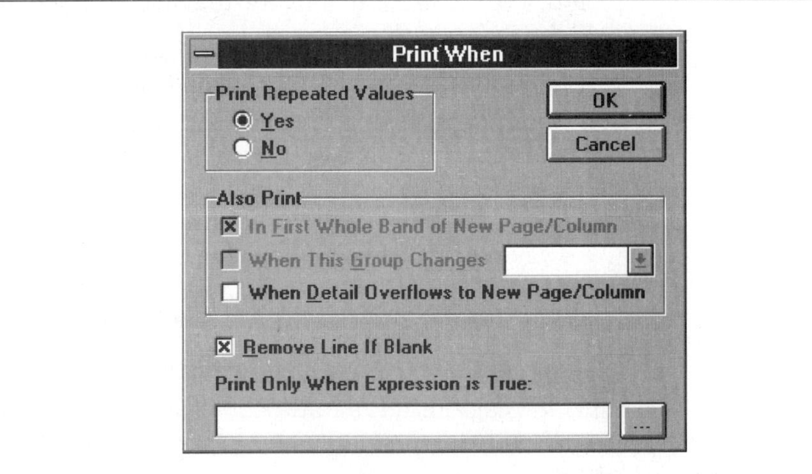

4. Change the properties of the Fname field in the same ways that you did the Lname field.

5. The final report design is shown in Figure 17.31. Choose File ➤ Save to save these changes. Then choose View ➤ Preview to display the output of the report in a Print Preview window, as shown in Figure 17.32. When you are done looking at it, close the Preview window and the Report Designer.

FIGURE 17.31

The final design of the Employee Wages report

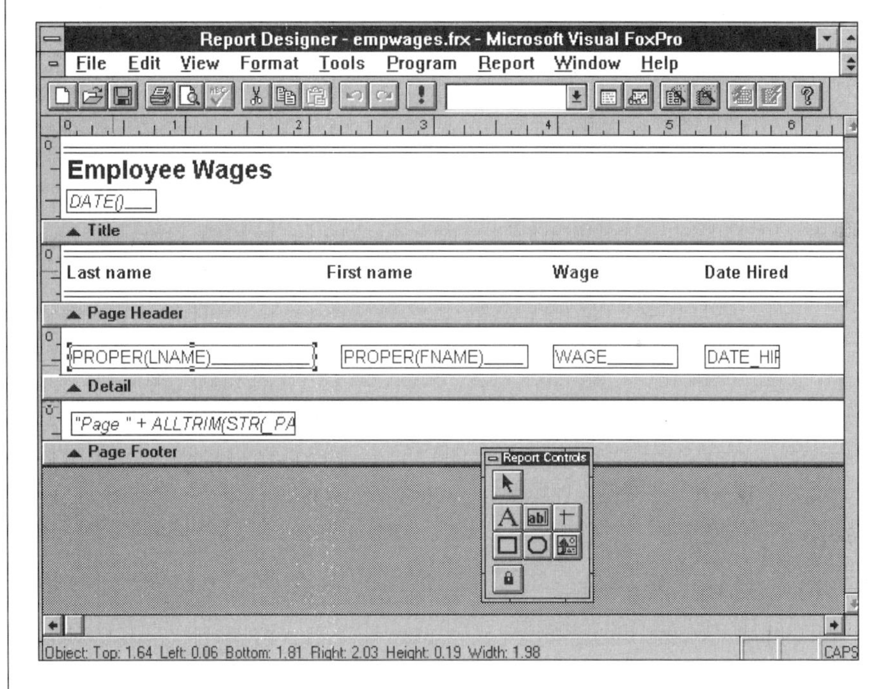

In an actual report, you would probably also want to change the Print Repeated Values property of other fields in the report. Even if there were no problem with repeated values initially, there might be when you printed the report at a later time, after adding more data. Remember, the default for this property is to *suppress* repeated values, and often you'll want to display them.

▶ Customizing the Wages by State Report

Finally, you should customize the grouped report that you created in Chapter 6, which lists employees, their date hired, and their wages by

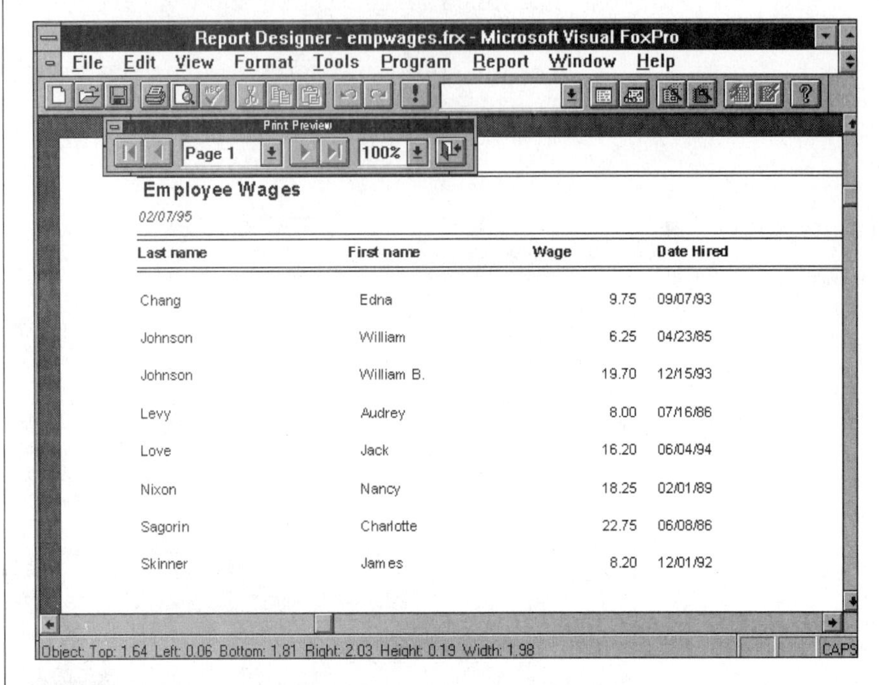

FIGURE 17.32 *Previewing the Employee Wages report*

state. As you remember, you wanted to include the average wage for each state in the group footer, but instead, you had to total the figures in the wage column, because the Wizard did not include an Average option.

In this exercise, you will change the group footer to include an average and add text to describe it. You should also customize the report to correct capitalization and field labels, as you did for the reports in the previous exercises, but this exercise will not repeat the step-by-step instructions for doing these things.

In step 3 of this exercise, be sure you double-click the Wage field in the Group Footer: STATE band, not in the Detail band.

1. Choose File ➤ Open and use the Open dialog box to display the St_wages report in the Report Designer. If necessary, maximize the Report Designer.

2. As you did in the previous two exercises, edit the labels for the Lname and Fname fields, change the expressions of these fields

by adding the PROPER( ) function to capitalize them correctly, and use the Print When dialog box for each so that repeated values are not suppressed.

3. In the Group Footer band, double-click the Wage field to display its Report Expression dialog box. Click its Calculations button to display the Subtotal or Calculate Field dialog box, and select its Average radio button, as shown in Figure 17.33. Close these dialog boxes when you are done with them.

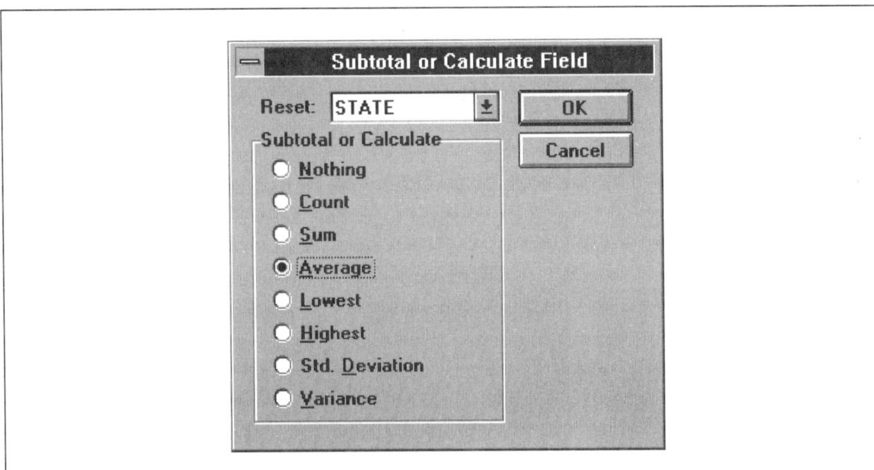

FIGURE 17.33

Changing the Group Total to a Group Average

4. Now, double-click the Expression at the left of the Group Footer band, which says **Subtotal for**, to display its dialog box. Edit the expression so it reads **[Average wage for employees from]+ ALLT(STATE) +[:]**, as shown in Figure 17.34. (This expression uses the square bracket as the text delimiter, like the expression generated by the Wizard, but you can use the quotation mark delimiters instead if you prefer them.) After returning to the Report Designer, resize the text control so it is large enough to display all this text.

5. You must change the report summary band in the same way that you did the group footer band. Double-click its Wage field, and change it from a total to an average, in the same way you did in step 3. Likewise, double-click the text that says **Grand total** to

FIGURE 17.34

Changing the text in the Group Footer

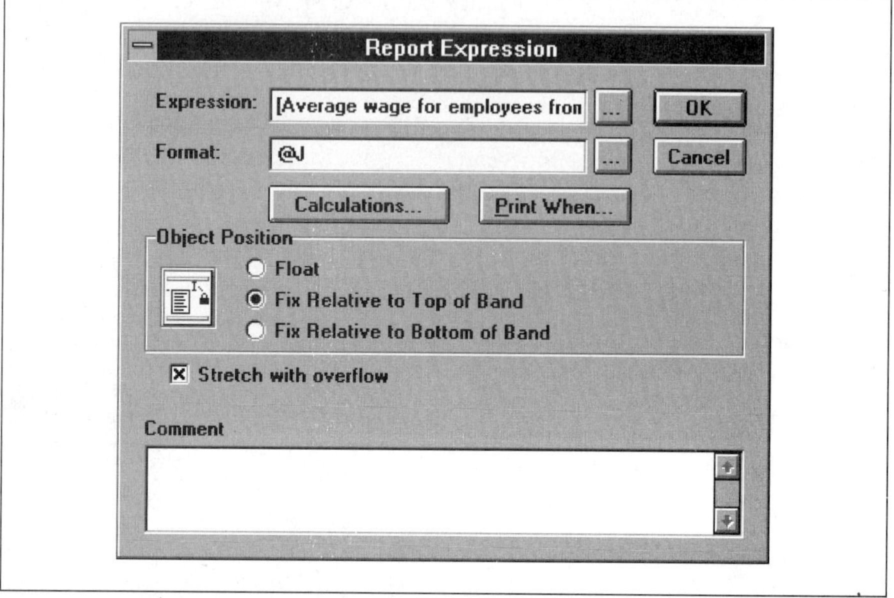

display its dialog box, and edit its expression to read **[Average wage for all employees:]**. Resize the text control so it is large enough to display all this text.

6. The final report design is shown in Figure 17.35. Choose File ➤ Save to save the changes. Then choose View ➤ Preview to display the output of the report in a Print Preview window. When you are done looking at it, close the Preview window and the Report Designer.

▸ Customizing Mailing Labels

If you want, you can customize labels by using the PROPER( ) function, so that names and addresses are all capitalized in the same way. This is not always necessary for labels, as it is for reports, however; because the public sees only one label at a time, inconsistent capitalization is not obvious.

As an exercise in using expressions in labels, you should customize the labels you created in Chapter 7 by adding the IIF( ) function, so **Apt.** is included before the Apartment number, only for records that actually have an apartment number. As you learned earlier in this chapter, in

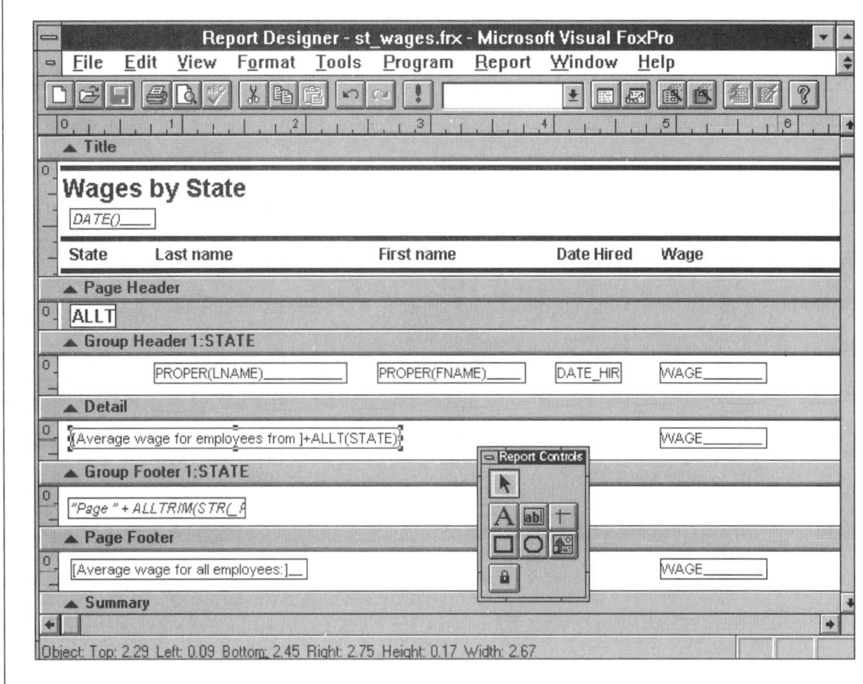

FIGURE 17.35

The final design of the Wages by State Report

the section on "Some Useful Expressions in Reports and Labels," you can do this by using the following expression:

```
TRIM(ADDRESS) + " " + IIF(APTNO = " ", " ", "Apt. ")
+ APTNO
```

Though TRIM( ) is all that is necessary to get rid of trailing blanks, the Wizard generates expressions using the ALLTRIM( ) function. It is easier to edit the expression if you use ALLTRIM( ) instead of TRIM( ) in the exercise.

Choose File ➤ Open and use the Open dialog box to display the Standard labels in the Label Designer.

Now, double-click the expression on the label's second line, which includes the Address and Apt_no fields, to display its Report Expression dialog box, and edit the expression to read **ALLT(address) + " " + IIF(APTNO = " ", " ", "Apt. ") + ALLT(aptno)**. Click OK.

3. The final label design is shown in Figure 17.36. Save the changes, and choose View ➤ Preview to display the labels in a Print Preview window. When you are done looking at it, close the Preview window and the Label Designer.

FIGURE 17.36 ►

The final design of the labels

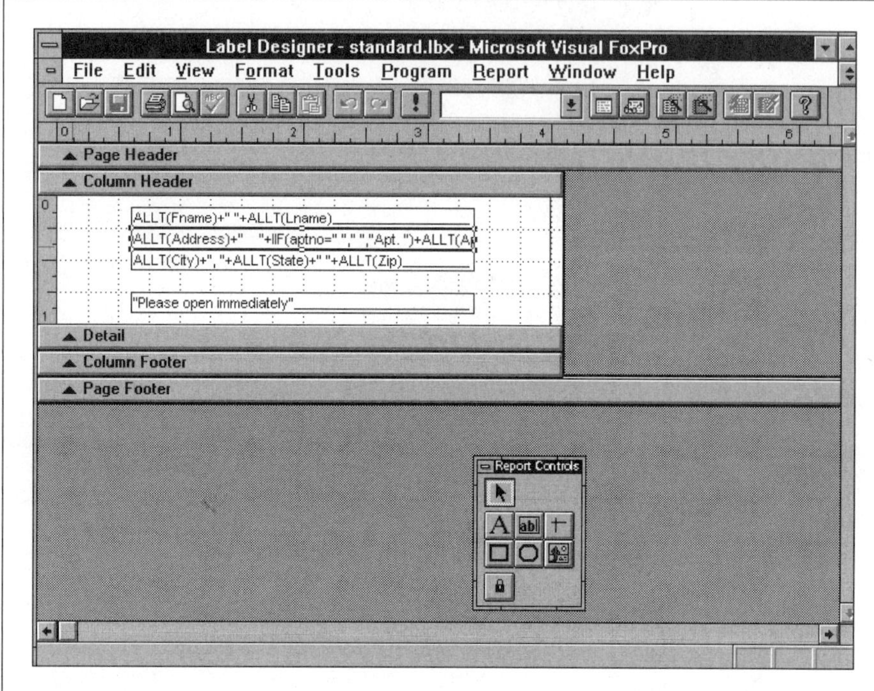

As you can see, the labels are printed with the word **Apt** included in the address only if there is an apartment number. You will find this expression useful in many mailing labels that you work with, and you may find other expressions using IIF( ) useful in reports as well.

►► Using the Form Designer

You can modify a form you created using the Form Wizard as you do other files: enter the command **MODIFY FORM <file name>** or choose File ➤ Open and open the form to display it in the Form Designer, shown in Figure 17.37.

FIGURE 17.37

The Form Designer

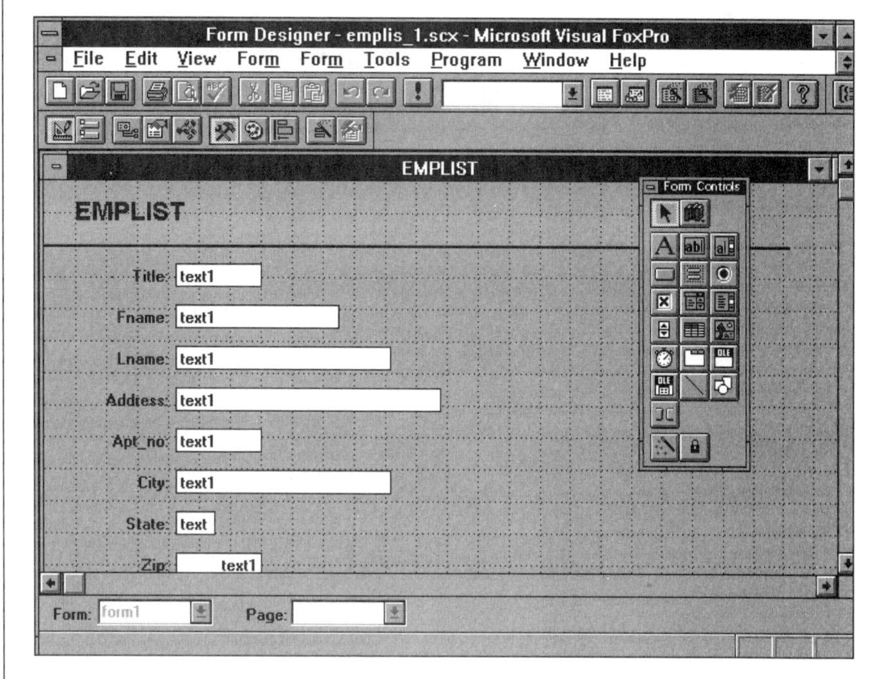

The Form Designer is one of the more advanced and more complex features of Visual FoxPro. For example, it lets you write code to create entirely new properties of controls, as well as change existing properties, such as size and color. This section, however, will show you some of the simple ways of working with forms that ordinary users might find useful to modify forms generated by the Form Wizard.

Manipulating Controls

You can select and manipulate controls in the Form Designer as you do in the Report Designer.

Click a control to select it. Hold down the Shift key while you click to select multiple controls. Click and drag around a group of controls to select them all.

Once controls are selected, you can click and drag their handles to resize them, or press Del or Backspace to delete them.

▸▸ **NOTE**

You can also click and drag the edges of the form itself to resize it.

You can also simply click and drag a control to move it.

When you are working with the Form Designer, you can use the Layout toolbar to align controls and use the Color Palette toolbar to change their colors just as you do when you are working with reports.

These simple techniques are often useful for modifying forms generated by the Form Designer. For example, it is often useful to move the controls on the form so that they take up less space; this lets you reduce the size of the form as a whole, making it easier to work with.

▸ Changing Tab Order

If you move controls in a way that changes their order in the form, then you also should change their tab order, so that the cursor still moves from the top to the bottom and from left to right when the user presses the Tab key.

For example, if you drag the fields on your sample form so that Lname is above Fname, the cursor will still move to Fname first, unless you change tab order, and this will confuse the user.

To specify a new tab order, choose View ➤ Tab Order or click the Tab Order tool. Visual FoxPro displays a box to the left of each control. Hold down the Shift key and click the boxes in the order that you want the user to tab through the controls. As you click them, Visual FoxPro fills these boxes in with numbers that represent the tab order, as shown in Figure 17.38. When you are done, click Reorder to make this the new tab order, or click Cancel to retain the original tab order.

▸ Working with the Properties of Objects

One major difference between the Form Designer and the Report and Label Designers is that the form, as do all the objects, has a Properties window attached to it in the form. This window describes all of the

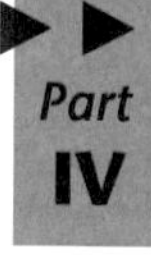

FIGURE 17.38

Specifying tab order

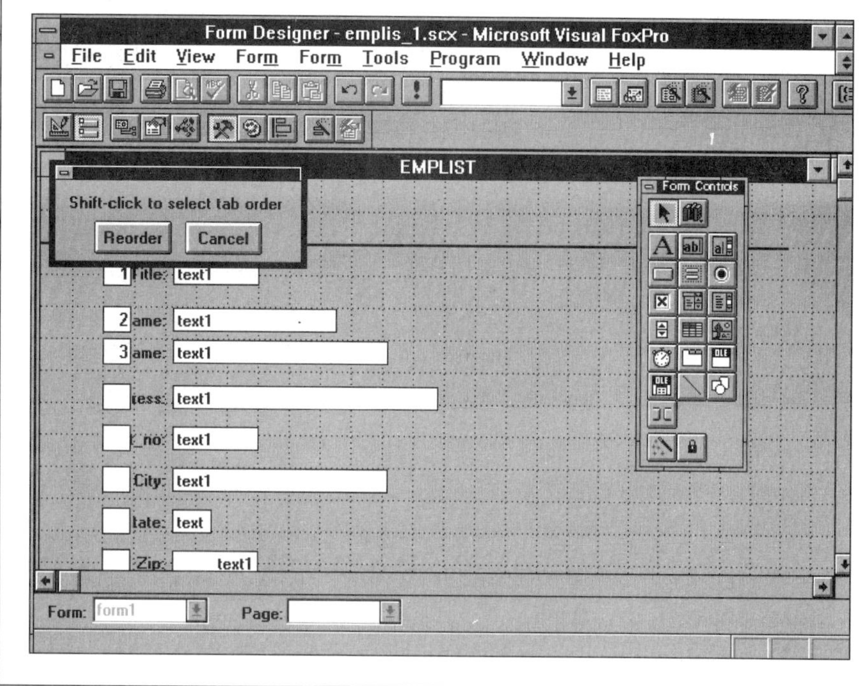

properties of the form or object, including its color, its size, the text if it is a label, and the field or expression it is attached to if it is a text box.

To display the Properties window, do any of the following:

- Choose View ➤ Properties Window to display the properties of the currently selected object.
- Right-click the form or a control and choose Properties from its shortcut menu to display its properties.

Once the Properties window is open, it displays the properties of the form as a whole or of any object in the form that you select.

Using the Properties Window

The Properties window is shown in Figure 17.39.

You can use the Object drop-down to select the form or any object on it, in order to display its properties and to select it in the Form Designer.

FIGURE 17.39

The Properties window

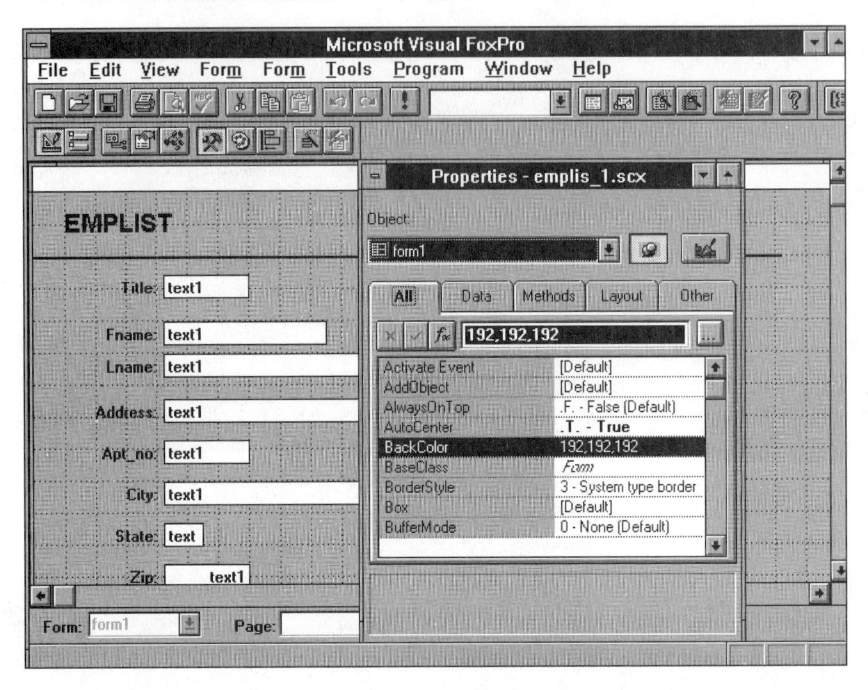

Use the tabs to display the panels where the properties are listed. The All tab displays all of the properties of the object. To make it easier to find properties, the other tabs display just some of the properties listed in the All tab, as follows:

- **Data:** The Data tab displays properties that specify how the object works with the data it holds. The most important of these is the ControlSource property of a text field or of another control that is used to enter data (such as a drop-down list or a check box).
- **Methods:** The Methods tab displays properties that specify how the object reacts to different events, such as a mouse click. Attaching methods to objects is essential to object-oriented programming.
- **Layout:** The Layout tab displays properties that specify how the object looks, such as its color and size. One very important property listed in this tab is the Caption, which specifies the text held in a text control (or on other controls that include text, such as command buttons).

- **Other:** The Other tab displays miscellaneous properties of the object, including its name. Many of these properties specify the class it is a member of; classes are an advanced feature of object-oriented programming.

A help line is displayed at the bottom of the Properties window, describing the use of the property that is highlighted. You can select various properties and look at this help line to get an idea of all the properties available for each type of object.

You must use the Properties window when you add a new label or new field to the form.

Adding or Editing a Label

You may want to modify a form generated by the Wizard by adding new text to it, or by editing existing text, such as the form title or the label of a field.

You cannot add or edit a label in a form as you do in a report or in labels. Instead, you must change the Caption property of the label.

To add new text to a form:

1. Click the Label tool of the Form Control toolbar.
2. Click and drag on the form to place the text. Visual FoxPro gives it a default caption, such as Label3, and this is displayed in the new label that is placed in the Form.
3. Display the Properties window and display the Caption Property for the new control, which you can find in its Layout tab. As you can see in Figure 17.40, when you select this property, the caption is also displayed in a text box above the Property list.
4. Use the usual Windows editing techniques to edit the text in this label box. Click the check tool to its left to keep the changes, or click the X tool to its left to discard the changes.
5. If necessary, click the FontName or FontSize properties to display a drop-down control above the property list that lets you select among available fonts and sizes. To specify other features of the typeface, select the FontBold, FontItalic, FontOutline, Font-Shadow, or other stylistic features from the Property list, and use

FIGURE 17.40

Editing a caption

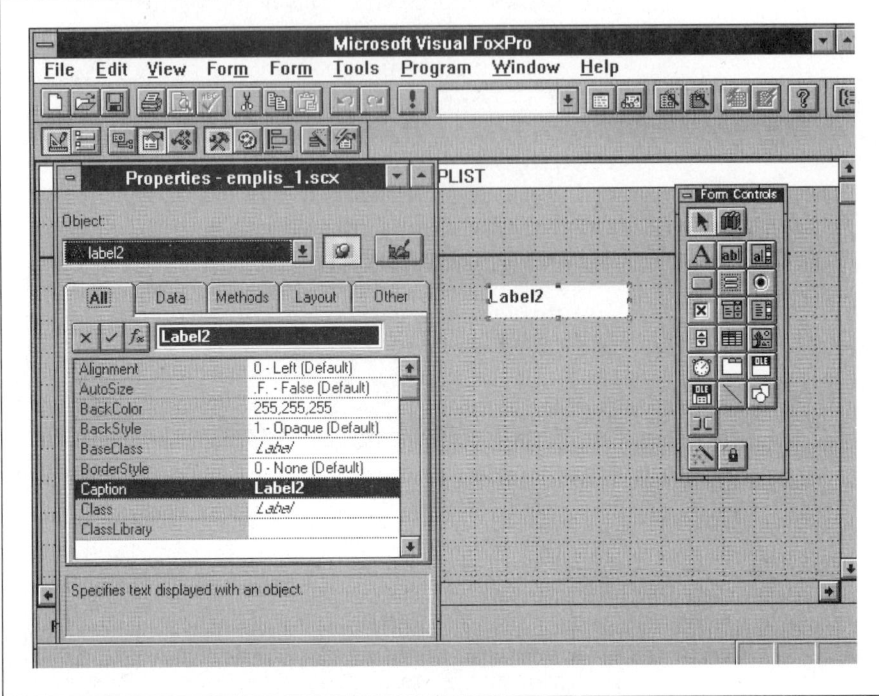

the drop-down above the Property list to select .T.—True to use that feature, or .F.—False to remove it.

Edit an existing label in the same way. Display its properties. Then edit the Caption property to change the text in the label, and use the FontName, FontSize, and other properties as necessary to change its typeface.

This method should be useful to edit field names generated by the Wizard—for example, to edit Fname so that it reads First Name.

Adding a Field to a Form

The way you add a field is a bit like the way you add a label.

First, you must make sure that the table is in the form's data environment. You can control the Data Environment just as you do with reports, but choosing View ➤ Data Environment to display the Data Environment window and choosing DataEnvironment ➤ Add to add a table to it. However, if you are modifying a form created by the Wizard, it should already have the data environment you need.

To add the field:

1. Click the Text Box tool of the Form Control toolbar.
2. Click and drag on the form to place the text box. Visual FoxPro displays it with a default name, such as Text3.
3. Display the Properties window and display the ControlSource property for the new control, which you can find in its Data tab. By default, there is not any field used as the ControlSource; however, when you select this property, you can use a drop-down control above the Property list to select any field in the form's data environment, as shown in Figure 17.41. The data in the field you select will be displayed in the text box.

FIGURE 17.41

Selecting a control source

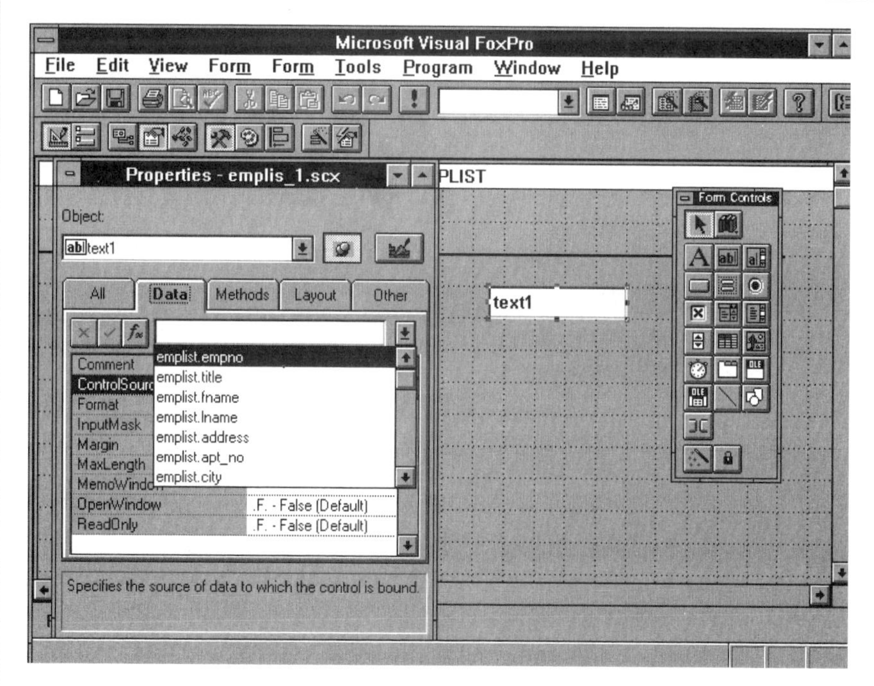

You can also control the typeface of the field by using the same properties used to control the typeface of a label, as described in the previous section.

In addition to placing a text box to display the contents of the field itself, you will probably also want to place a label with the name of the field or some description of it, using the methods described in the previous section. A text box does not have a Caption property that you can use to add a label to it.

Adding a Check Box to a Form

Other controls used for data entry are placed in much the same way as fields. Some, such as list boxes or drop-down controls, are a bit more complex, because you must specify the items that the user can choose from to enter data in the field. A check box is one of the simplest, and you can use it to represent a field of the logical data type as follows:

1. Click the Checkbox tool of the Form Control toolbar.
2. Click and drag on the Form to place the check box. Visual FoxPro displays it with a default label, such as Check1.
3. Display the Properties window and display the ControlSource property for the new control, which you can find on its Data tab. Use the drop-down control above the Property list to select a logical field in the Form's data environment. The box will be checked if the field is true or empty if it is false.
4. Select the Caption property in the Layout tab, and edit the caption to say something meaningful (such as **Probation** if this checkbox represents the probation field of your Emplist table). If necessary, change its typeface as you do for labels.

You can use the same method to edit the caption of check boxes that the Wizard places to represent logical fields.

Adding OLE Objects to a Form

There are two types of OLE objects you can add to a form:

- **OLE Bound Control:** Displays the OLE objects stored in a General field. This is called a *bound control*, because its contents changes as you move through the record of the table; the content depends on (or is "bound to") the record that is being displayed.

- **OLE Container Control:** Displays an OLE object that remains the same regardless of which record is displayed. You might want to use this, for example, to display a company logo at the top of the form.

Add a bound control to a form as you do other fields:

1. Click the OLE Bound Control tool of the Form Control toolbar.
2. Click and drag on the form to place the box that will hold the OLE control.
3. Display the Properties window and display the ControlSource property for the new control. Select the ControlSource property, and use the drop-down control above the Property list to select a General field in the form's data environment.

You add an unbound control to a form in much the same way that you add one to a report:

1. Click the OLE Container tool of the Form Control toolbar.
2. Click and drag on the form to place the box that will hold the OLE control.
3. Visual FoxPro displays the Insert Object dialog box, which you can use in the ways described in Chapter 22 to create a new OLE object or to add an OLE object that already exists in a file.

►► To Sum Up

In this chapter, you looked in detail at how to use the Report Designer and the Label Designer, and you looked at some of the most important features of the Form Designer, which are of practical use to Visual FoxPro users who want to modify forms generated by the Form Wizard. Now that you have looked at these three major Visual FoxPro tools, which have some features in common, you will go on in the next chapter to look at cross-tabs and graphs.

CHAPTER

18

Working with Cross-Tabs and Graphs

▸▸ FAST TRACK

▶ ***To create a cross-tab using the Wizard,*** ***553***

use the first step to select at least three fields—one for the row labels, one for the column labels, and one that holds numeric data to be totaled in the data cells. In the second step, click and drag these field names to the row, column, and data boxes. Use the third step to indicate what sort of total, if any, should be included for each row.

▶ ***To create a cross-tab using the Query Designer,*** ***556***

use the Fields panel to select the fields to be used as the row and column labels, and use the Function/Expression control to select the summary expression that will be included in the data cells. Then select the Cross Tabulate check box. The fields you chose as the row and column labels will automatically be used in the Order By panel as the basis for sorting and in the Group By panel as the basis for grouping. The settings in these panels will be dimmed, since they all must work together to create the cross-tab. You can still enter selection criteria to determine which records are included in the cross-tab.

▶▶ *Cross-tabs* and graphs are two very different methods of summarizing large amounts of data in a way that is easy to understand at a glance. In Visual FoxPro, both are specialized types of queries, which you can create using either Wizards or special features of the Query Designer. It is often most convenient to create one by using the Cross Tab Wizard or the Graph Wizard and then use the Query Designer to modify it—for example, by adding selection criteria that restrict which records are being used.

Both cross-tabs and graphs are most useful when you are analyzing large amounts of repetitive data, of the sort that should be stored in a relational database, and so the examples in this chapter use data from the sample relational database that is distributed with Visual FoxPro. Part III of this book covered relational databases; if you have not yet read those chapters, you may not understand all the details of these exercises. However, you can still go through their steps: You should have no trouble understanding the sample cross-tabs and graphs themselves.

▶▶ *What Is a Cross-Tab?*

A cross-tab, or cross-tabulation, is a very powerful way of summarizing data in rows and columns. If you had a database that recorded the sales made by different salespeople to customers in different states, for example, you might want to create a cross-tab showing the total sales by each salesperson in each state. The cross-tabulation could have a salesperson's name at the left of each row, and a state's name at the top of each column, and each cell of the cross-tab could show the total sales made by that salesperson in that state.

Or, instead of calculating the sum, you could use this cross-tab to calculate the average sale for each salesperson in each state, the total number of sales by each salesperson in each state, or the maximum or minimum sale by each salesperson in each state.

This is a much more powerful way of looking at data than ordinary queries, because you can look either across the rows to see each salesperson's sales, or down the columns to see the sales in each state, while ordinary summary queries just let you view one of these. Thus, a cross-tab is grouped in two ways, while ordinary queries can be sorted and grouped in only one way. In the example, data is grouped both by salesperson and by state, but in an ordinary query, it could only be grouped by one or the other.

This cross-tab could also include a Total column with the total sales by each salesperson. Note that cross-tabs can only total rows. If you wanted to show total sales for each state, you would have to create a separate cross-tab with the state name at the left of each column and the salesperson's name at the top of each row.

Cross-tabs are a powerful tool, and Visual FoxPro makes them easy to create and use.

▶▶ Creating Cross-Tabs

You can create a cross-tab using either the Cross-Tab Wizard, which is one of the Query Wizards, or the Query Designer.

The Wizard is easier to use, but its disadvantage is that it lets you display only sums in the cross-tab cells. Once you understand how to work with cross-tabs in the Query Designer, however, you can easily get around this limitation by using it to modify cross-tabs generated by the Wizard.

▶ The Cross-Tab Wizard

Choose File ➤ New, select the Query radio button, and click the Wizard button. When Visual FoxPro displays the Wizard Selection dialog box, select Cross-Tab Wizard.

Selecting Fields

The first step, shown in Figure 18.1, lets you select fields and works like the Field Pickers of other Wizards.

FIGURE 18.1

Step 1 of the Cross-Tab Wizard—selecting fields

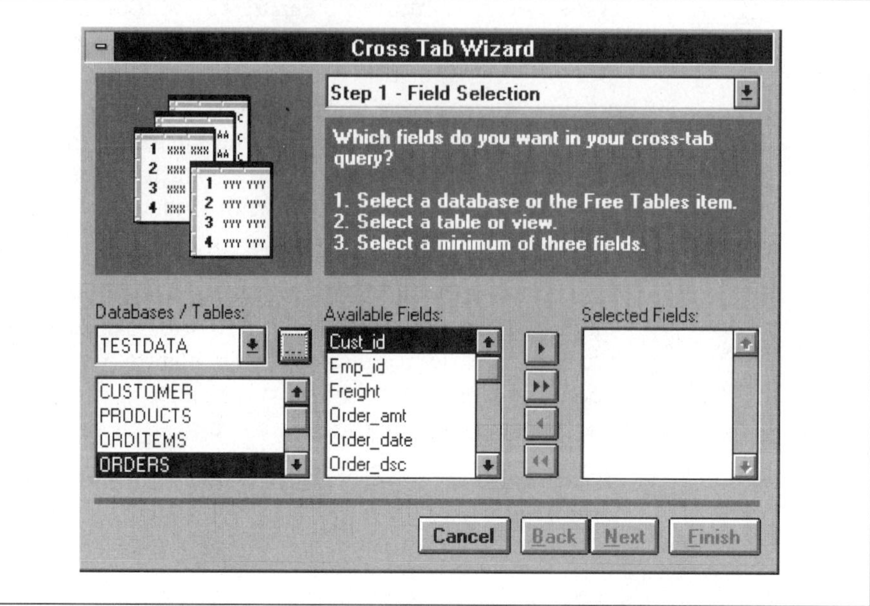

You must choose at least three fields: one for the column headings, one for the row headings, and one that is used as the basis of the calculations in the cells. For example, if you wanted to calculate total sales by each salesperson in each state, you would select the state name, to be used as the row heading, the salesperson name, to be used as the column heading, and the sales amount field, to be used as the basis of the calculation in the cell.

Laying Out the Cross-Tab

The second step, shown in Figure 18.2, lets you lay out the cross-tab by clicking and dragging fields. If you want to total on a category, you must place it in the rows.

Selecting Totals

The third step, shown in Figure 18.3, lets you specify what sort of total should be included for each row. The radio buttons let you select the sum of the data in each row, the number of cells containing data in each row, or the percentage of the table total in each row.

FIGURE 18.2

Step 2 of the Cross-Tab Wizard—laying out the cross-tab

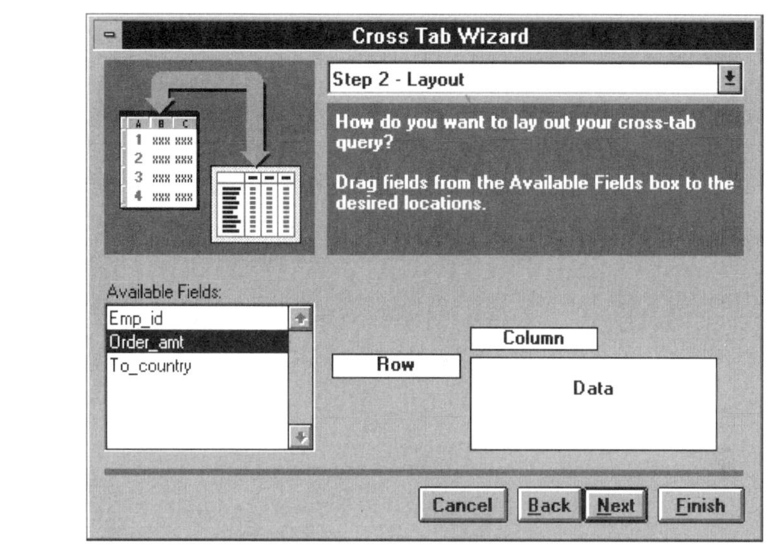

FIGURE 18.3

Step 3 of the Cross-Tab Wizard—totaling data for each row

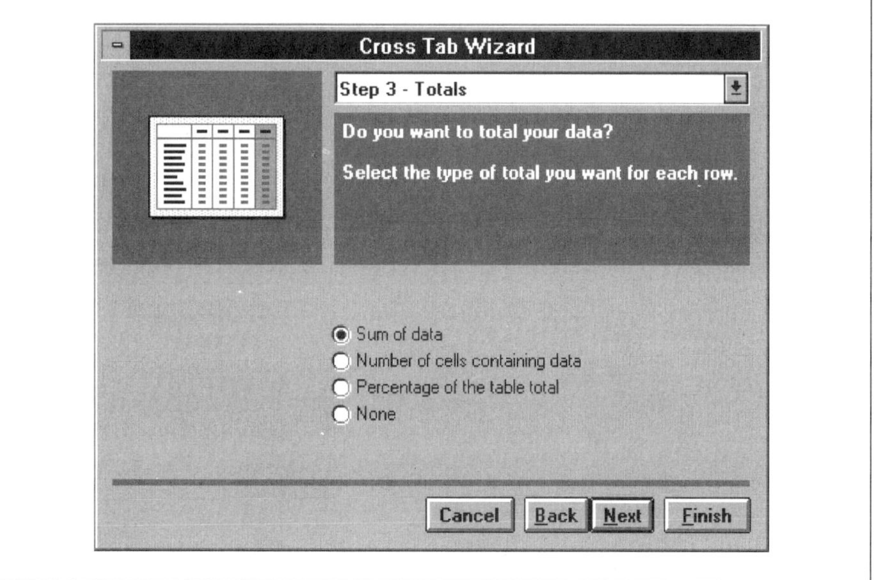

These totals are useful in some but not all cases. For example, if you were cross tabulating the sales made by each sales person in each state, you might want a total column that lists the sum of the sales by each salesperson, or you might want a total column that lists the percentage of total sales in each state. However, you probably would not want a total column if the cross-tab included average sales in each state.

Creating the Query

The fourth step, shown in Figure 18.4, lets you create the query, and is similar to the Finish step of other Wizards. Use the radio buttons to save the query for later use, to save and run the query, or to save the query and modify it in the Query Designer.

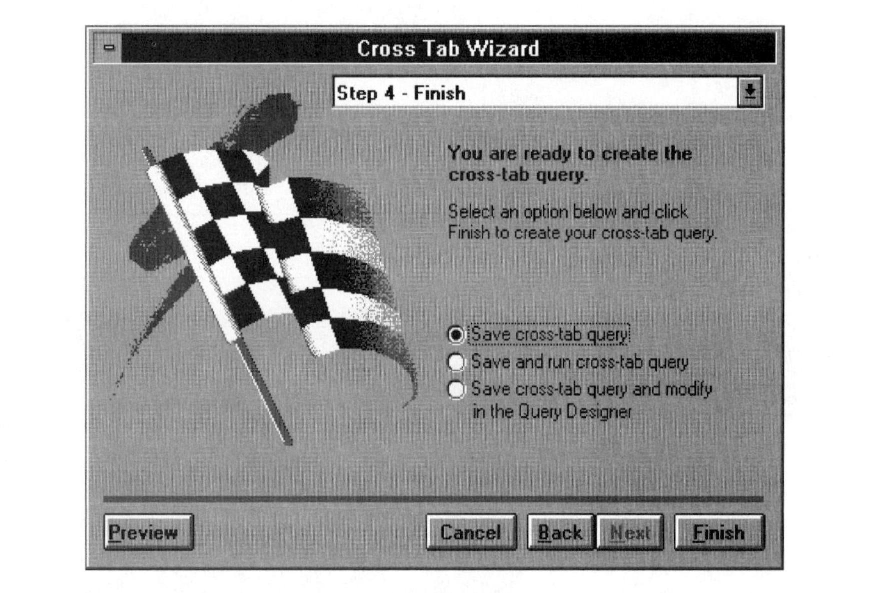

FIGURE 18.4 ▸ *The Finish step of the Cross-Tab Wizard*

Click the Preview button to view the result of the query in a preview window. As with other query types, it is always best to preview a cross-tab before creating it, so you can go back and modify earlier steps of the Wizard if the result is not what you planned.

▸ Creating a Cross-Tab Using the Query Designer

Now that you have seen how to create a cross-tab using the Wizard, it should be easy to understand how you create one using the Query Designer.

The key to creating the cross-tab is the Fields panel. Here, in the Selected Output list, you add the fields that are to be used as the basis of the rows and columns. You also add to this list an expression that will be used as the summary calculations in the cells of the cross-tab.

Once you have added the fields and expression that make it possible to create a cross-tab, the Cross Tabulate check box is enabled.

If you check this box to create a cross-tab query, the fields are dimmed, as shown in Figure 18.5. Settings that are necessary to this cross-tab query are automatically entered in the Order By and Group By panels, and are also dimmed.

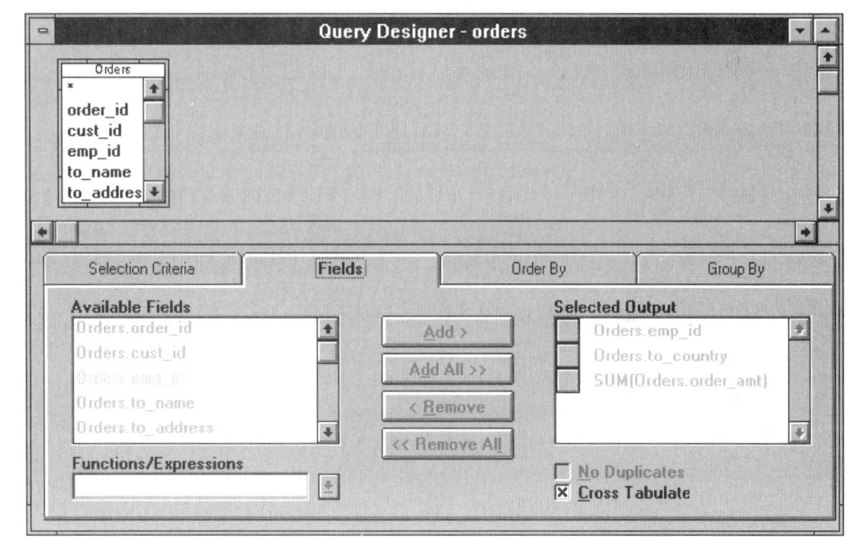

FIGURE 18.5

The Fields panel for a cross-tab query

The Order By panel, shown in Figure 18.6, automatically sorts on the fields that are the basis of both the rows and columns. Unlike other queries, Cross-Tabs have two different sort orders; both the row headings and the column headings are sorted.

Likewise, the Group By panel, shown in Figure 18.7, groups on both these fields. In an ordinary grouped query, the result has a single row for each value in the Group By field. In a cross-tab, there is one row for each value in one of the Group By fields, and one column for each value in the other.

FIGURE 18.6

The Order By panel for a cross-tab query

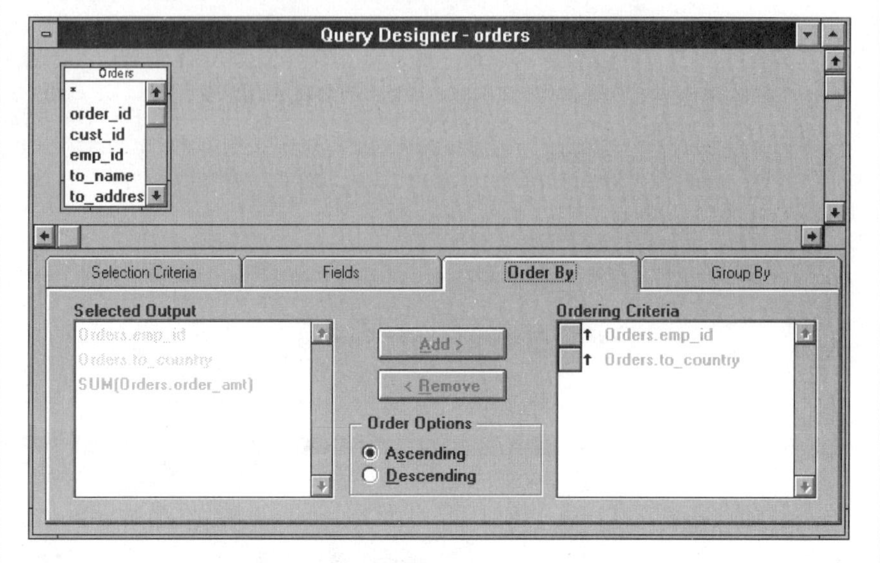

FIGURE 18.7

The Group By panel for a cross-tab query

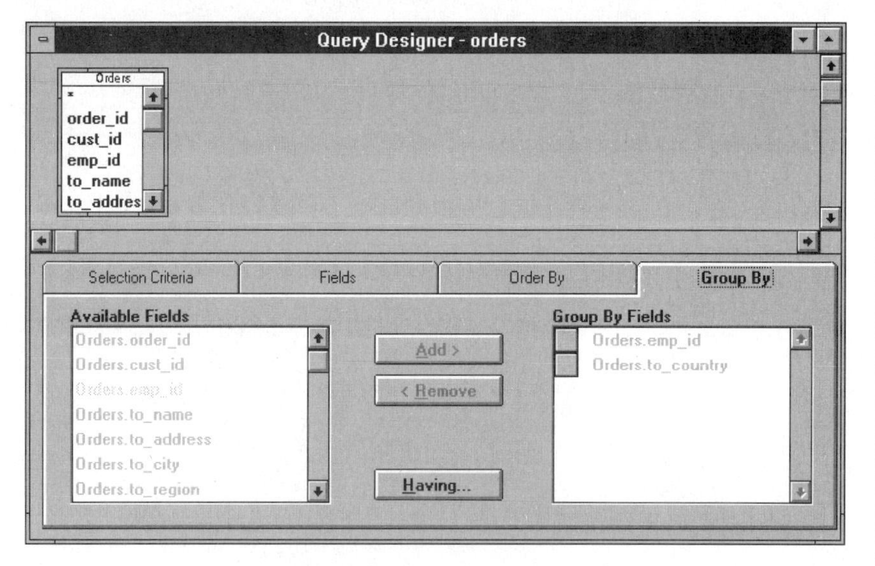

When you select the Cross-Tabulate check box in the Fields panel, the settings in the Order By and Group By panel are entered automatically, and the settings in all three panels are dimmed, because all these panels must work together to create the cross-tab.

You can still use the Selection Criteria panel as you do in an ordinary query to create a filter that specifies which records of the table are included in the cross-tab.

As always, click the Run button or choose Query ➤ Run Query to view the result of the query.

►► Modifying a Cross-Tab Using the Query Designer

If you create a cross-tab using the Wizard and modify it using the Query Designer, the fields and summary function that you specified using the Wizard are entered in the Fields panel, and the equivalent settings are entered in the Order By and Group By panel, as they would be if you had created the Query using the Query Designer, as described above.

The Cross Tabulate check box is selected, and so the features of these three panels are dimmed.

It is easy to use the Selection Criteria panel to modify a cross-tab generated by the Wizard. As you learned above, this panel is still accessible when the Cross Tabulate check box is selected, and you can use it to create a filter that determines which records the cross-tab includes, just as you would with an ordinary query.

To make any other modifications in a cross-tab generated by the Wizard, you must deselect the Cross Tabulate check box, to make all of the query's controls accessible again. After you make your changes, select the Cross Tabulate check box again.

Most of the selections you can modify in these panels change the nature of the cross-tab so completely that it is easier to start from scratch using the Wizard than to modify a feature in the Query Designer. There is one feature that you can usefully modify in this way, however. The Wizard automatically displays the sum of the data in the cells of the cross-tab it generates. You cannot use it to display an average or other summary function.

You can change this summary function easily using the Query Designer. After generating a cross-tab in the Wizard and displaying it in the Query Designer:

1. Deselect the Cross Tabulate check box to make all of its settings accessible.
2. Remove the SUM(<field name>) function from the Selected Output list of the Fields panel, by double-clicking it or by selecting it and clicking Remove.
3. Use the Functions/Expressions drop-down control to create a new summary function, using a function such as AVG(), MIN(), MAX(), or COUNT() instead of SUM(). Click Add to add this function to the Selected Output list.
4. Select the Cross Tabulate check box. The settings are dimmed again.

This change is a simple substitution of some other summary function for the SUM() function, and so it cannot create any problems but can add significantly to the power of the queries that you generate using the Wizard.

▸▸ A Sample Cross-Tab

The following exercise uses sample data distributed with Visual FoxPro, in the database named Testdata.dbc, which is in the directory \VFP\SAMPLES\DATA. You will create a sample cross-tab that uses only the Orders table of this database. Create it using the Wizard to display the total orders sold by each employee in each country, and then modify it using the Query Designer to display the largest order sold by each employee in each country.

1. Choose File ➤ New. In the New dialog box, select the Query radio button and click the Wizard button. In the Wizard Selection dialog box, be sure that Cross-Tab Wizard is selected and click OK.
2. In the first step of the Wizard, click the … button to display the Open dialog box. Select Table/DBF from the List Files of Type

drop-down control. Use the Directories list to open the directory \vfp\samples\data. Select the database named Orders.dbf, and click OK.

3. Visual FoxPro returns to the Wizard, with all the tables of this database listed, and the Orders table selected. Double-click the fields Emp_id, Order_net, and To_country in the Available Fields list to move them to the Selected Fields list. Click Next.

4. In the Layout step, drag Emp_id to the Row box, To_country to the Column box, and Order_net to the Data box, as shown in Figure 18.8. Click Next.

5. In the Totals step, select the None radio button, and click Next. In the Finish step, select the "Save and run cross-tab query" radio button, and then click Finish. In the Save dialog box, keep the default query name, use the Directories list to select your \Learnfox directory, and click Save. When Visual FoxPro displays the result, maximize the Query window, as shown in Figure 18.9. After you have looked at the result, close the window.

You can see that the result displays the total sales by each employee in each country. Now, try using the Query Designer to change the query so that it displays the largest sale by each employee in each region.

1. Choose File ➤ Open and open the Orders query that you just created. If necessary, click the upper-left corner of the Query toolbar to hide it, since you will not need it in this exercise.

2. Click the Fields tab of the Query Designer. Deselect the Cross Tabulate check box. Double-click SUM(Orders.order_net) to remove it from the Selected Output list. In the Function/Expressions drop-down list, choose MAX() and choose Orders.order_net from the submenu. Then click Add to add it to the Selected Output list, as shown in Figure 18.10.

3. Select the Cross Tabulate check box, and you'll see that all the fields displayed in the panel are dimmed again. Click the Run button, and maximize the result, as shown in Figure 18.11. Close the Query window. Then close the Query Designer and select Yes to save the changes.

FIGURE 18.8

Laying out the cross-tab

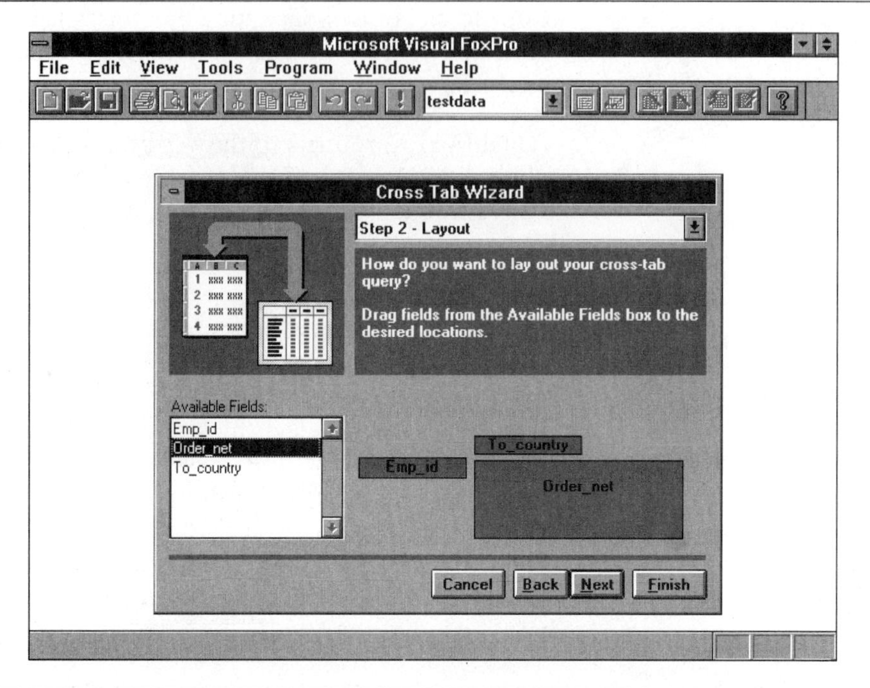

FIGURE 18.9

The result of the cross-tab query

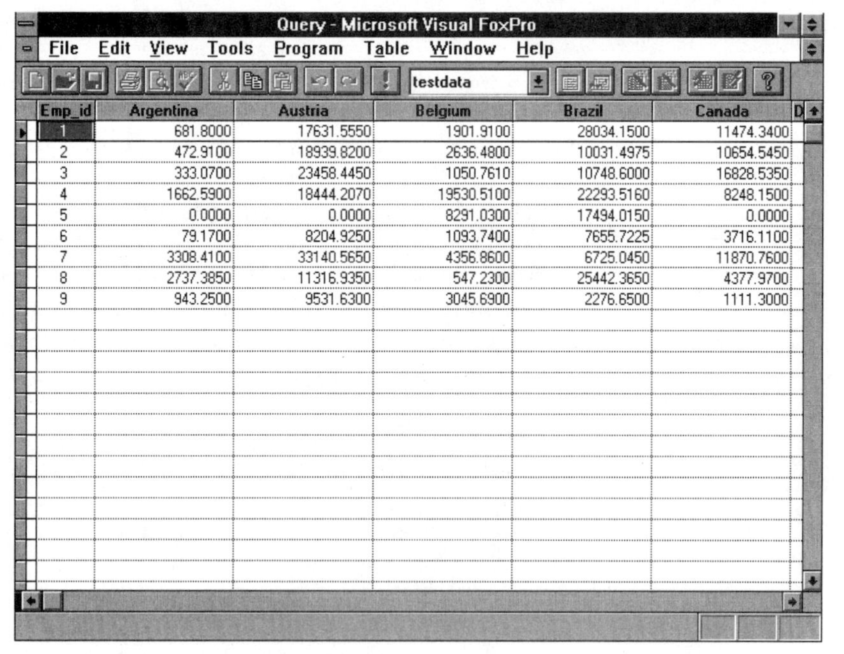

Emp_id	Argentina	Austria	Belgium	Brazil	Canada
1	681.8000	17631.5550	1901.9100	28034.1500	11474.3400
2	472.9100	18939.8200	2636.4800	10031.4975	10654.5450
3	333.0700	23458.4450	1050.7610	10748.6000	16828.5350
4	1662.5900	18444.2070	19530.5100	22293.5160	8248.1500
5	0.0000	0.0000	8291.0300	17494.0150	0.0000
6	79.1700	8204.9250	1093.7400	7655.7225	3716.1100
7	3308.4100	33140.5650	4356.8600	6725.0450	11870.7600
8	2737.3850	11316.9350	547.2300	25442.3650	4377.9700
9	943.2500	9531.6300	3045.6900	2276.6500	1111.3000

FIGURE 18.10

Changing the Summary function

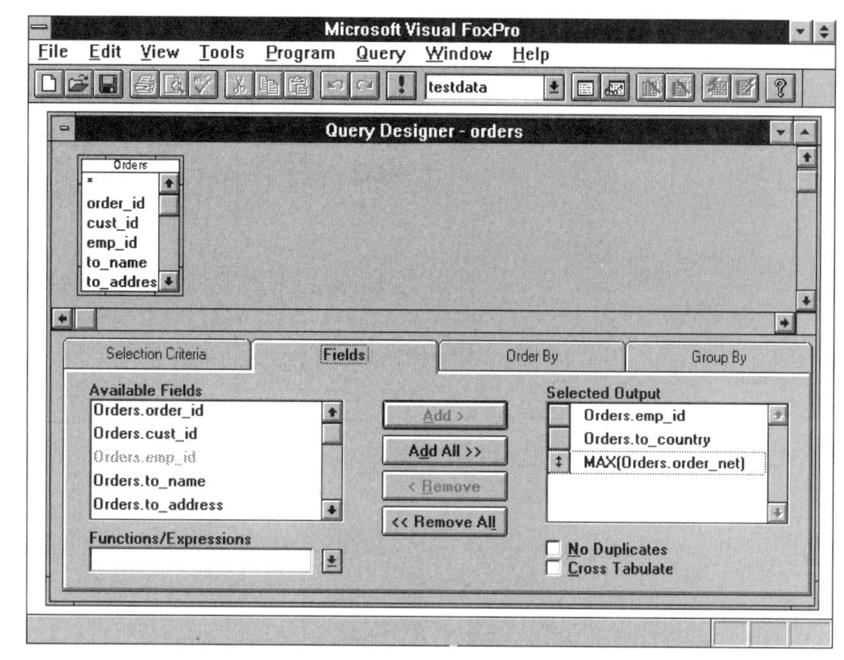

FIGURE 18.11

The Result of the New Query

Orders_a - Microsoft Visual FoxPro

File Edit View Tools Program Table Window Help

Emp_id	Argentina	Austria	Belgium	Brazil	Canada
1	681.8000	6637.5800	798.1300	14422.3700	4272.5300
2	472.9100	5766.7800	1579.2200	2015.1700	4054.2400
3	333.0700	8551.0550	725.3100	1751.9600	3049.9300
4	657.9700	5675.1800	3408.3000	3669.3600	2314.8700
5	0.0000	0.0000	4547.2000	11943.8600	0.0000
6	79.1700	2431.4500	1093.7400	2807.9150	1249.1300
7	1831.5000	10028.0700	3648.9600	1995.4100	10714.4900
8	2215.8600	4685.2200	547.2300	13015.3700	1944.6100
9	929.6500	6829.2600	1662.2400	1268.0700	1111.3000

The most important changes that you will have to make to cross-tabs using the Query Designer are either to change the summary function, as you just did, or to add selection criteria, as you learned to do in Chapter 15. Use the Selection Criteria panel just as you do for ordinary queries, to restrict the records that the cross-tab includes. For example, add the criterion **Probation like .T.** to the cross-tab you just created to get the same cross-tabulation for only those employees who are on probation.

You can create any cross-tab you need by using the method of this exercise: first, create the cross-tab using the Wizard, and then modify it if necessary using the Query Designer.

▸▸ Creating Graphs

Graphs offer the most purely visual way of presenting numeric data. A pie chart, for example, can show at a glance what percentage of the total each component of a budget represents; or a line graph can track the sales of a product over time.

You can create a graph either by using the Graph Wizard, which is one of the Query Wizards, or by using the Query Designer and using the Query Destination dialog box to send the result to a graph.

Most graph types let you display either a single data series or multiple series. For example, if you were graphing sales of a single product during a single period in different regions of the country, you would be working with a single data series. If you were graphing the sales of two or three different products in each region of the country, you would be working with multiple data series. In this case, you would probably want to use a bar graph with two or three bars for each region, each representing the sales of a different product. It is also common to produce line graphs with several lines, each representing a data series.

▸ The Graph Wizard

Choose File ➤ New, select the Query radio button, and click the Wizard button. When Visual FoxPro displays the Wizard Selection dialog box, select Graph Wizard.

Selecting Fields

The first step, shown in Figure 18.12, lets you select fields and works like the Field Pickers of other Wizards.

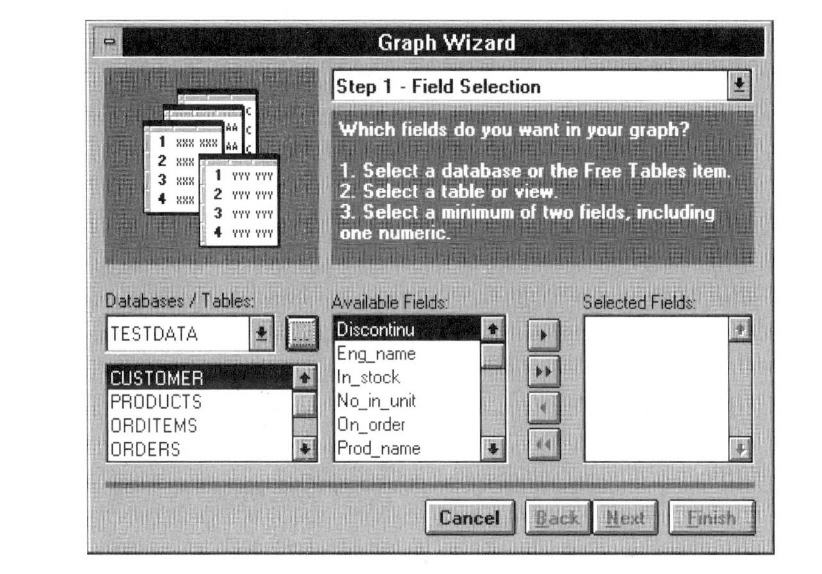

FIGURE 18.12

Step 1 of the Graph Wizard—selecting fields

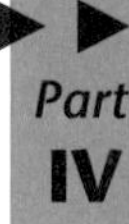

You must select at least two fields—one numeric field that holds the quantity you are graphing, and one field that is displayed as the graph's labels. For example, if you wanted a graph of your employees' wages, you would choose Wage as the field holding the values to be graphed and Empno as the field holding the labels.

Select more than one numeric field to create graphs with multiple data series.

Laying Out the Graph

The second step, shown in Figure 18.13, lets you lay out the graph, by clicking and dragging fields.

The fields you selected in step 1 are included in the Available Fields list. Click the field you want to use as the basis of the labels and drag it to the Axis box. Click one or more numeric fields whose values you want to graph and drag them to the Data Series list.

FIGURE 18.13

Step 2 of the Graph Wizard—laying out the graph

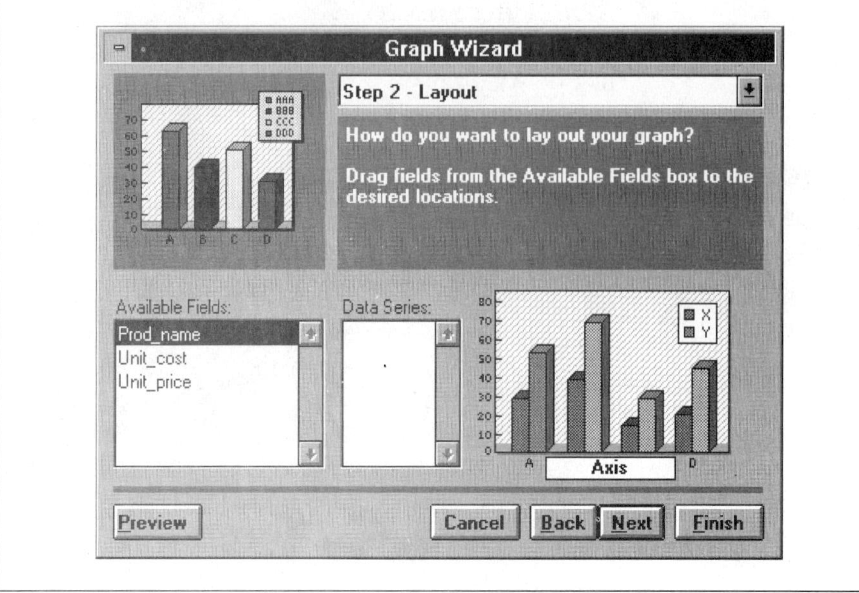

Selecting a Graph Style

The third step, shown in Figure 18.14, lets you specify a graph style. The illustrations on the buttons make it clear what the options are.

Although the illustrations on most of these buttons show multiple data series, virtually all of them can be used with either single or multiple data series. A pie graph can be used with only one data series, and a high-low graph must be used with two data series.

Creating the Graph

The fourth step, shown in Figure 18.15, lets you create the graph and is a bit different from the finish step of other Wizards.

The radio buttons give you two choices:

- Save the graph to a table: If you select this radio button, the Wizard generates the graph when you click Finish, after prompting you to enter the name of a table to save its specifications in.
- Save and create a query with the graph: If you select this radio button, the Wizard generates a query with the specifications of the

FIGURE 18.14

Step 3 of the Graph Wizard—selecting a Graph Style

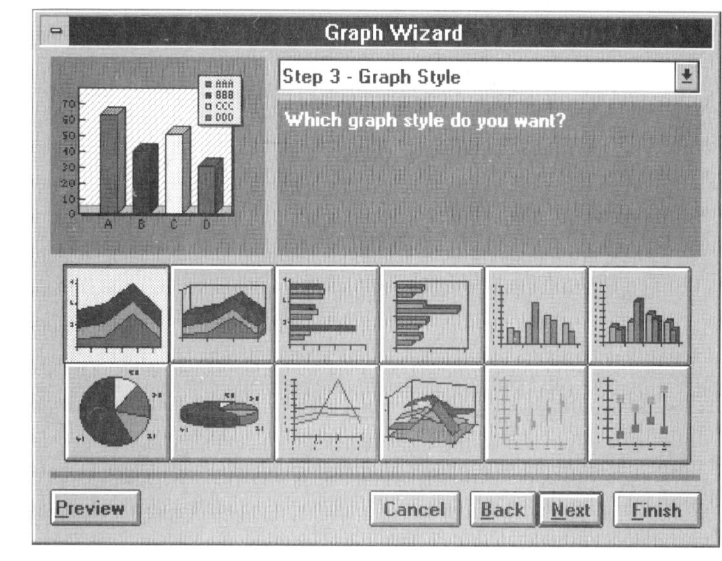

FIGURE 18.15

The Final step of the Graph Wizard

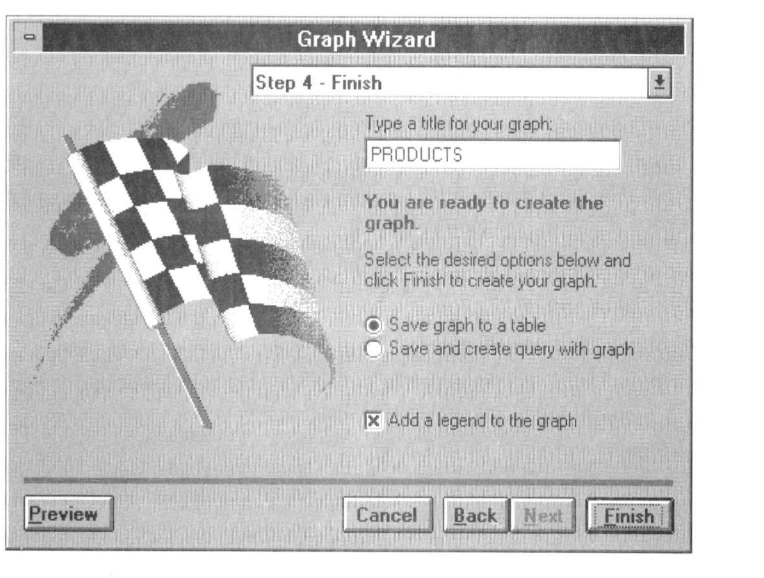

graph when you click Finish, and it displays the Query Designer to let you modify the query. You must run the query to display the actual graph.

In addition, the check box lets you choose whether to include a legend for the graph.

Enter a title for the graph as you do in the Finish step for other types of files. As in other Wizards, click the Preview button to view the graph in a preview window.

► Creating or Modifying a Graph Using the Query Designer

The simplest method of creating a graph using the Query Designer is very similar to creating the query using the Wizard:

1. Use the Fields Panel of the Query Designer to select the fields included in the graph. As you learned earlier, you must select one field to use as the graph's labels and one or more numeric fields to use as the data series.
2. Choose Query ➤ Query Destination and click the Graph button of the Query Destination dialog box, which was covered in Chapter 15.

When you run the query, Visual FoxPro displays Step 2 of the Query Wizard, the layout step described above, with the fields you selected included in its fields list. Click and drag these fields to the Data Series list and the Axis label box, just as you do when creating a graph using the Wizard.

After you have used this step to lay out the graph, you can access Step 3 of the Wizard to select the Graph Style. When you display the Finish step, only the "Save graph to a table" radio button is selected and cannot be changed; when you click Finish, the Graph is generated and displayed.

The important advantages of using the Query Designer to create a graph are:

- You can use the Selection Criteria panel of the Query Designer to create a graph that includes only the records of the table that you specify. Simply enter selection criteria as you do for any query, as covered in Chapters 4 and 15.

- You can use the Functions/Expressions drop-down of the Fields panel in combination with the Group By panel to include a calculation as one of the values that is graphed—for example, to include the maximum or average value in some field. Create a grouped query as you learned to in Chapter 15.

These are the same advantages that you have if you use the Query Designer rather than the Wizard to create a Cross-Tab, as you learned earlier in this chapter.

You can also gain these advantages if you use the Query Designer to modify a graph that you created using the Wizard. Select the "Save and create a query with the graph" radio button in the Finish step of the Wizard. When you click Finish, the Fields panel of the Query Designer is displayed, with the fields you selected in the Wizard already included in its Selected Output list, and you can modify it by adding selection criteria or calculations.

NOTE

Graphs generated using Visual FoxPro are OLE objects. The graph is created by Microsoft Graph, a mini-application that is bundled with a number of Microsoft products, and displayed as an OLE object in Visual FoxPro. You can activate the source application by double-clicking the graph, as you can with other OLE objects. You can then use Microsoft Graph to alter the design of the graph—for example, by moving or editing labels.

Creating a Sample Graph

The sample graph you create in this exercise will use data from the Testdata database, the same sample database distributed with Visual FoxPro that was used in the previous exercise. You will use the Products table of this database, and create a bar graph with two data series, which lets you compare the unit cost and the unit price of the products you sell.

1. Choose File ➤ New. In the New dialog box, select the Query radio button and click the Wizard button. In the Wizard Selection dialog box, select Graph Wizard and click OK.

2. In the first step of the Wizard, click the … button to display the Open dialog box. Select Database from the List Files of Type drop-down, open the directory \vfp\samples\data, select the database Testdata.dbc, and click OK to return to the Wizard.

3. Select the Products table. In the Available Fields list, double-click the Prod_name, Unit_cost, and Unit_price fields to add them to the Selected Fields list. Click Next.

4. In the Layout step, drag Unit_cost and Unit_price to the Data Series list, and drag Prog_name to the Axis box, as shown in Figure 18.16. Click Next.

FIGURE 18.16

Laying out the graph

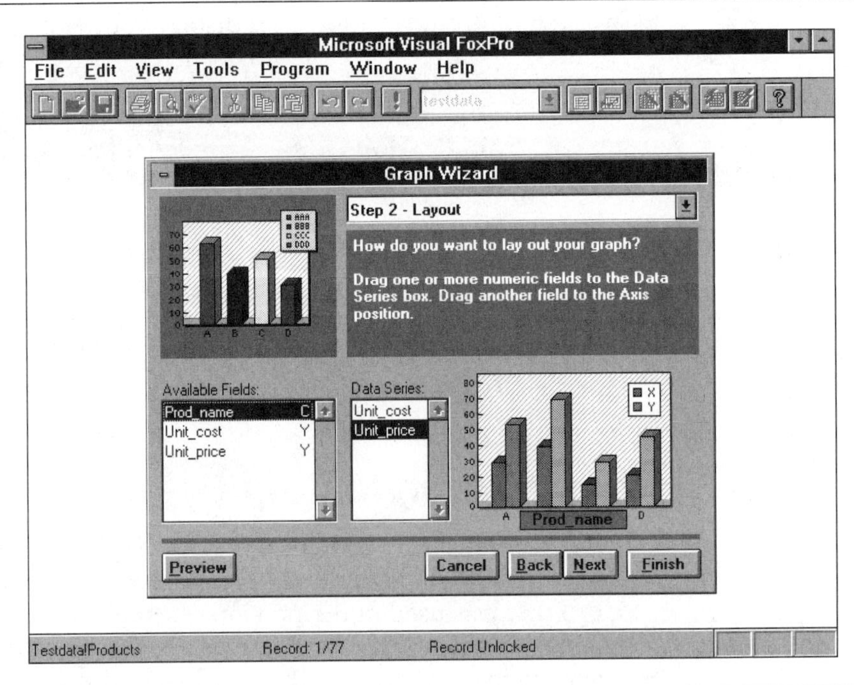

5. In the Graph Style step, select the three-dimensional vertical bar graph (the button on the far right of the upper row) and click Next. In the Finish dialog box, type the title **Cost and Price of Products**. Click the "Save and create query with graph" radio button, and click Finish. Leave the default name in the Save dialog box, but select \learnfox as the directory, and click Save. After a few moments, Visual FoxPro displays the graph. Close the graph window when you are done.

If you want to try using Microsoft Graph, double-click the graph window and experiment with this mini-appplication by using it to modify this graph.

►► To Sum Up

In this chapter and the previous one you've learned how to use the Visual FoxPro tools that let you display your data more effectively: reports, labels, forms, cross-tabs, and graphs. The next four chapters cover tools that let you customize Visual FoxPro to make it easier to work with.

CHAPTER 19

Customizing the Working Environment

▸▸ FAST TRACK

- ***To customize the Visual FoxPro environment using the menu system,*** ***576***

  choose Tools ➤ Options to display the Options dialog box, and select settings in its panels; click the Set As Default button to make all selected options the default used whenever you start Visual FoxPro.

- ***To delete or overwrite files without a warning,*** ***581***

  deselect the Confirm File Replacement check box of the General panel, or use the equivalent command, SET SAFETY OFF. This feature can be useful in programming, but to avoid accidental data loss you should never SET SAFETY OFF when you are using the Visual FoxPro interface to work directly on your own data.

- ***To hide records that are marked for deletion,*** ***584***

  select the Ignore Deleted Records check box in the Data panel or enter the command SET DELETED ON.

- ***To place the pointer on the nearest matching record if there is no exact match when you use the FIND or SEEK command,*** ***586***

  select the SET NEAR check box from the Data panel or enter **SET NEAR ON**.

- ***To create indexes in alphabetical order,*** ***587***

  choose General from the Collating Sequence drop-down list of the Data panel, or enter the command SET COLLATE TO GENERAL. Indexes will use proper alphabetical order in English, French, German, modern Spanish, Portuguese, and other western European languages.

▶ ***To choose the default drive and directory that will be used for all file input and output,*** *589*

use the Default Directory control of the File Locations panel. Select the check box and then click the ... button to display the Select Directory dialog box, and use the drop-down list to select a drive and directory, as you do in the Open dialog box. This control is equivalent to the command SET DEFAULT TO <letter of drive>:<directory path>.

▶ ***To specify the way currency and other numbers are displayed,*** *597*

use the Currency and Numbers area of the International panel. Use the Currency Format control to choose whether the currency symbol (such as the $ symbol) goes before or after the amount of currency. Enter any character in the Currency Symbol text box to have it replace the default $ sign. Enter any character in the 1000 Separator text box to have it replace the comma that is used by default to separate thousands, millions, and so on. Enter any character in the Decimal Separator text box to have it replace the period that is used as a decimal point by default. Use the Decimal Digits text box or spinner control to specify the number of digits displayed to the right of the decimal point.

Visual FoxPro lets you customize your working environment by using the Options dialog box. This dialog box is similar to those of other Microsoft applications, though many of its individual options apply specifically to Visual FoxPro. Many of these options are equivalent to SET commands of the Visual FoxPro language, which let you control the working environment.

Using the Options Dialog Box

Choose Tools ➤ Options to display the Options dialog box, shown in Figure 19.1.

Click any of the tabs of this dialog box to display a panel with options in that category. When you click a tab, its panel is brought forward, and the other tabs appear to be above and behind it.

NOTE

All of the selections you make in the Options dialog box remain in effect until you exit from Visual FoxPro. You can also click the Set as Default button to make all of your selections the default settings that will be used automatically whenever you start Visual FoxPro.

You can get complete information on any option in this dialog box by displaying the option's panel and clicking Help. This chapter will discuss options that are important to the average user and will give you a brief overview of all the panels, so you have a general idea of all the options that are available.

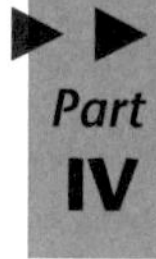

FIGURE 19.1

The Options dialog box

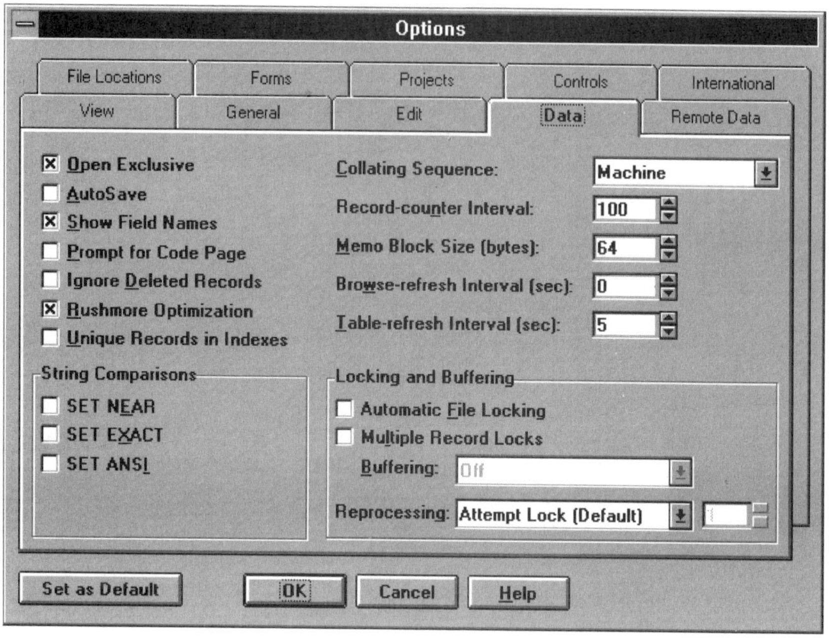

This section also discusses the most important and interesting SET commands that are equivalent to some of these options. You can get complete information on SET commands by searching in the Visual FoxPro Help system for the word SET, or you can get more information on the most interesting and important commands by looking under SET in Appendix B.

▸▸ The View Panel

The View panel, shown in Figure 19.2, controls which features of the desktop are displayed.

▸ The Status Bar

Use the Status Bar check box to display or hide the status bar. This is equivalent to the command SET STATUS BAR ON ¦ OFF.

FIGURE 19.2

The View panel

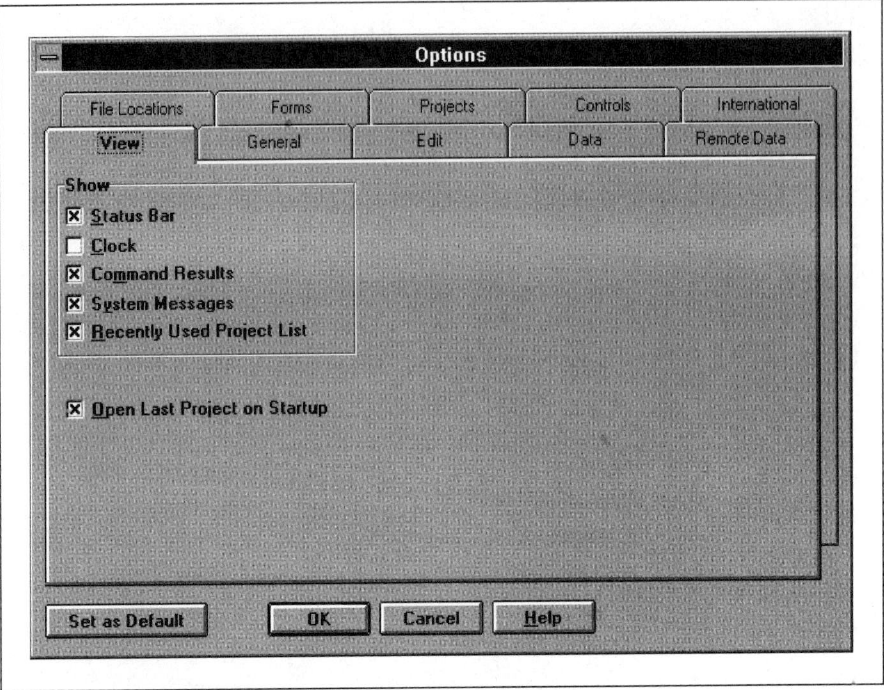

▸▸ NOTE

Visual FoxPro for Windows also supports the command SET STATUS ON ¦ OFF, which displays and hides a character-based status bar like the one used in FoxPro for DOS, rather than the usual Windows status bar. If Visual FoxPro displays this character-based status bar, you entered SET STATUS ON by mistake. To correct the error, just enter SET STATUS BAR ON to display the Windows status bar and automatically remove the "DOS" status bar.

▸ The Clock

The Clock check box lets you use and adjust the system clock. When the check box is checked, the system time is displayed on the screen. The command equivalent is SET CLOCK ON ¦ OFF. By default, the clock is displayed in the upper-right corner of the Visual FoxPro main window.

You can also display the clock at the far right of the status bar by using the command SET CLOCK STATUS.

You can also control where on the screen the time is to be displayed by using the command

```
SET CLOCK TO <row, col>
```

Use a number (or numeric expression) to represent the row and column where the clock should be located.

Command Results

Use the Command Results check box to determine whether certain commands display information about their status, and how frequently this information is displayed.

This option is selected by default, so that Visual FoxPro displays messages telling you (for example) how many records have been indexed when you use the INDEX command, and it displays the value of a memory variable when you use a command to assign a value to it.

This check box is equivalent to the command SET TALK ON or OFF.

You can also control the interval at which this information is displayed by using the command SET ODOMETER TO <number>.

System Messages

The System Messages check box determines whether certain system messages are displayed and is equivalent to the command SET NOTIFY ON ¦ OFF.

Projects

The View panel also includes two check boxes that control whether recently used projects are added to the File menu, and whether the last project used is opened when you start Visual FoxPro. Projects are a feature of Visual FoxPro used primarily by developers to organize files and compile them into applications, and they are covered in Chapter 25.

►► The General Panel

The General panel, shown in Figure 19.3, controls miscellaneous settings.

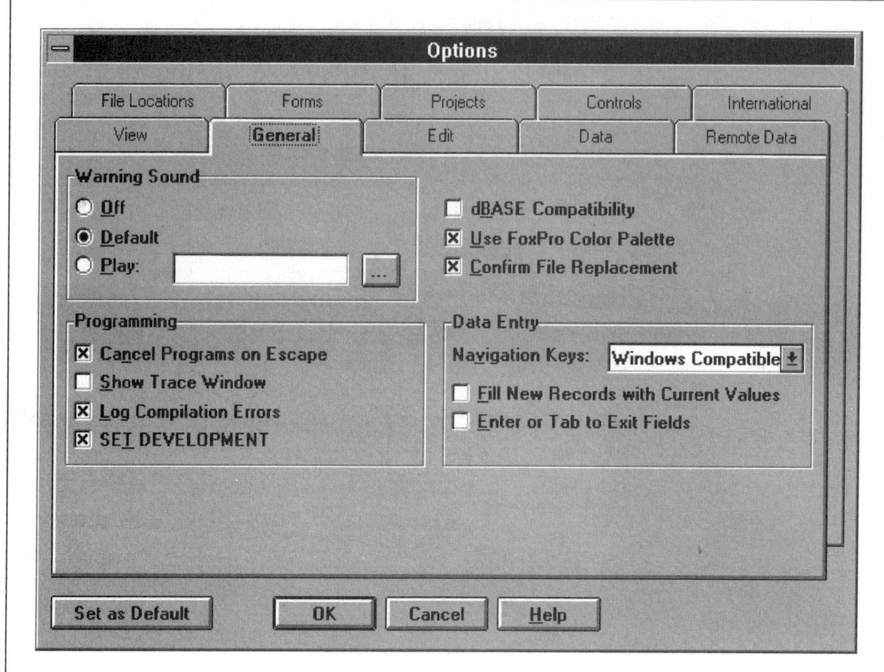

FIGURE 19.3

The General panel

► Warning Sound

The Warning Sound area controls whether Visual FoxPro beeps when you have filled a field with data, moving the cursor to the next field automatically. Select the Off radio button to stop it from beeping, or select the Play radio button and then click the … button to select a WAV file to be used instead of the default beep.

Use the command SET BELL ON or OFF to enable or disable the warning beep. To control how the warning beep sounds, use the command SET BELL TO <frequency, duration>, with a frequency from 19 to 10000 to change its pitch and a duration from 1 to 19 to determine how long it lasts.

WARNING

This setting is useful mainly in programming. You may be tempted to SET BELL OFF when you are entering data in Visual FoxPro tables, because the beep can be annoying; but you will find that if you do, the data you are entering in one field sometimes runs into the next field without your realizing it. SET BELL OFF is useful in programs where you have built in some other way of controlling this problem.

dBASE Compatibility

The dBASE compatibility check box can be used to make Visual FoxPro more compatible with dBASE IV programs that use certain commands. For more information, search the Visual FoxPro Help system for the equivalent command: SET COMPATIBLE DB4.

Confirm File Replacement

If you deselect the Confirm File Replacement check box or use the equivalent command, SET SAFETY OFF, Visual FoxPro will delete or overwrite files without asking you for confirmation.

WARNING

Setting Safety off can be useful in programming. For example, a program might copy data from a temporary data-entry table to a permanent table; since the data is saved automatically, it is reasonable to delete all records from the temporary file without confirmation from the user; in fact, having to confirm the deletion would only confuse the user. However, you should never SET SAFETY OFF when you are using the Visual FoxPro interface to work directly on your own data, to avoid accidental data loss.

▶ Data Entry

The Navigation Keys drop-down list in the Data Entry area lets you use either Windows-compatible keystrokes or the keystrokes used by default in FoxPro for DOS. For example, with Windows-compatible keystrokes, you can press Enter to select the default button (usually the OK button) of a dialog box; but using DOS-compatible keystrokes, you must press Ctrl-Enter to select the default button. If you use other Windows applications, it is best to use Windows-style keystrokes in Visual FoxPro.

If you select the Fill New Records with Current Values check box, Visual FoxPro adds the values in the current record to new records you append to the table. This can save time if you are entering repetitive data.

▶ Programming

By default, you can interrupt program execution by pressing Esc. If you deselect the Escape check box of the Programming area, or use the command SET ESCAPE OFF, the user can no longer interrupt a program in this way. This feature is useful if you have set up a program for a user and do not want the user to be able to interrupt it and return to the Visual FoxPro interface simply by pressing the Esc key. However, you should not use it until the program is thoroughly debugged, so you can interrupt it during development.

Other check boxes in this area control more advanced programming utilities.

▶▶ The Edit Panel

The Edit panel, shown in Figure 19.4, controls options used to edit text files, program files, and memo fields. It includes the following options:

- **Drag-and-Drop Text Editing:** Determines whether drag-and-drop editing is enabled.
- **Word Wrap:** Determines whether the word-wrap feature is enabled. Word wrap is on by default for text files and memo fields but is off by default for program files.

FIGURE 19.4

The Edit panel

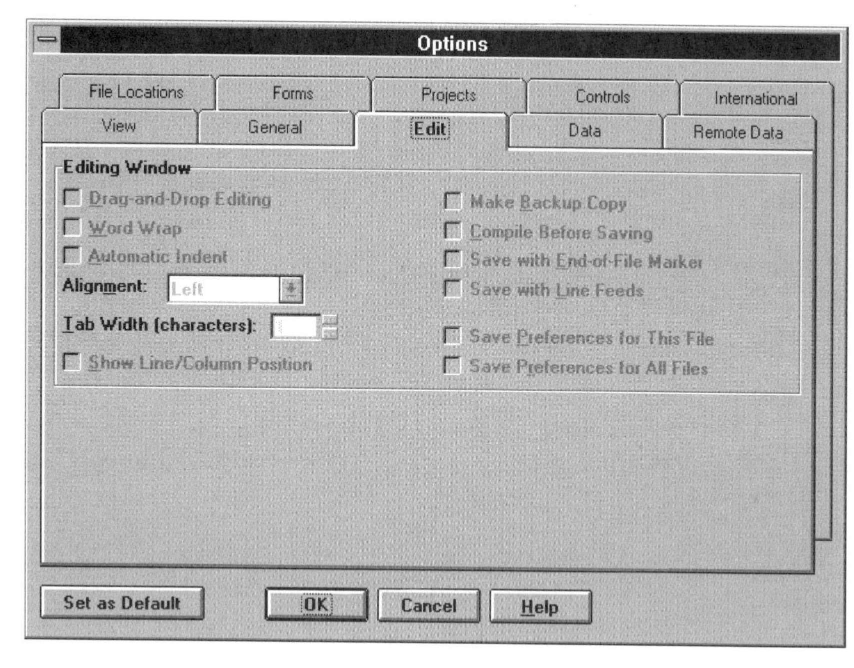

- **Automatic Indent:** Automatically indents each line the same amount as the previous line. This is on by default when you are editing a program file, where it is common to line up commands one below the other to make the program easier to read. It is off by default in text files and memo fields.
- **Alignment:** Controls whether text is left-justified, right-justified, or centered within the editing window.
- **Tab Width:** Determines how many spaces the Tab character is equivalent to. Enter a number in this text box or use the spinner control to select a number.
- **Show Line/Column Position:** Controls whether the line and column of the cursor location is displayed in the status bar.
- **Create Backup Copy:** Automatically makes backup files. When you save a new version of a file, the previous version is saved in a file with the extension BAK.

- **Compile Before Saved:** Automatically compiles a program file when you save it.
- **Save with End-of-File Marker:** Uses the control character Ctrl+Z (ASCII character 26) to mark the end of a file. If this box is checked, the editor treats the first Ctrl+Z in the file as the end of file, even if there is text after it. This option will not let you edit beyond the Ctrl+Z and will not save any text beyond the Ctrl+Z.
- **Save with Line Feeds:** Saves files with a carriage return/linefeed at the end of each line. If this box is not checked, files are saved with a carriage return/linefeed only where you pressed Enter, making it possible to rejustify the text the next time you edit it.
- **Save Preferences for This File:** Saves the preferences you've selected in this panel so that they are used whenever you edit the current file.
- **Save Preferences for All Files:** Saves your preferences so that they are used whenever you edit or create a memo or a file with the same extension as the current file.

▸▸ The Data Panel

The Data panel, shown in Figure 19.5, has a number of options for working with data that are very useful for the average user, and a number of pitfalls to avoid. We'll look in some detail at its more important options.

▸ Networking Options

The Open Exclusive check box controls whether tables are opened exclusively, so that they cannot be accessed by other users on a network when one user opens them. However, if you deselect this check box when using Visual FoxPro on a network, you must use the Locking and Buffering area to implement record locking, in order to avoid possible loss of data.

FIGURE 19.5

The Data panel

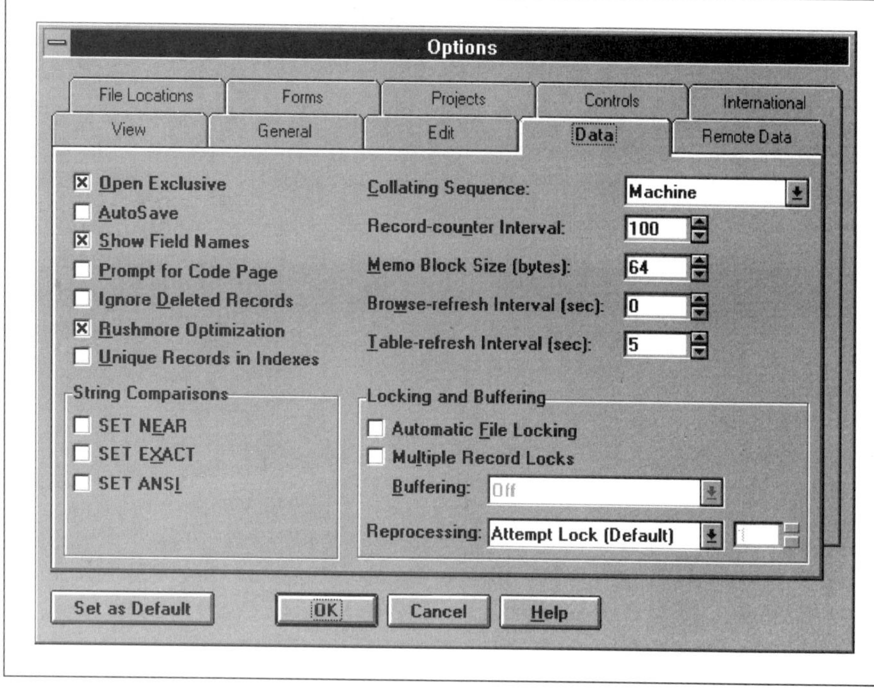

Ignore Deleted Records

As you learned in Chapter 3, records marked for deletion are displayed by default, but you can hide them by using the commands SET DELETED ON (or redisplay them by using the command SET DELETED OFF).

Selecting the Ignore Deleted Records check box in this panel is equivalent to using these commands. The check box is not selected by default, because deleted records are not hidden.

NOTE

Remember that the default setting of the Deleted feature is *off*; the feature does *not* ordinarily screen out records marked for deletion. By selecting the check box, you set it *on*; the feature *does* screen out records marked for deletion.

▸ Rushmore Optimization

The Rushmore Optimization check box (or the SET OPTIMIZE ON ¦ OFF command) can be used to disable and enable the Rushmore technology that Visual FoxPro uses by default to speed up searches. Rushmore optimization was covered in Chapter 11.

When you need to disable Rushmore optimization, it is generally preferable to add a NOOPTIMIZE clause to individual commands instead of using this environment setting. You may have reason to disable Rushmore for a single command, but it is rare to need to disable it for a series of commands.

▸ Unique Indexes

The Unique Records in Indexes check box controls whether indexes include records that have duplicate values in the key field. For example, if you select this check box and create an index based on the State field, the table will include only one record from each state when you use this index as the controlling index. This check box (or the SET UNIQUE ON ¦ OFF command) lets you create a series of unique indexes without including the UNIQUE option in each INDEX command; although it saves a bit of time, it can create serious problems if you leave it on by mistake and then create other indexes that you do not realize are unique. It is generally best to use the UNIQUE clause or select Unique from the Type drop-down list for each individual index, instead of making this change in the working environment.

▸ Settings Affecting Searches

The SET NEAR check box can be very useful in searches. Select it (or enter SET NEAR ON) to place the pointer on the nearest matching record after you use the FIND or SEEK command, if there is no exact match. Then you can browse through nearby records to see if any is the one you want: this usually makes it easy to find the record you want if, for example, you misspelled the field value when you did the search. If this setting is not turned on, the pointer is moved to the end of the file after an unsuccessful search.

If you select the SET EXACT check box, strings must match exactly for Visual FoxPro to find a match in a comparison. For example, if you search for the last name "SMITH" in a table, Visual FoxPro will by default find a match in records with the last name SMITH, SMITHSON, SMITHERS, or any other name that begins with SMITH. If this check box is selected, it will only find a match with SMITH.

The SET ANSI check box also affects how Visual FoxPro does comparisons. If it is selected, Visual FoxPro will pad the shorter string with spaces to make it the same length as the longer string before doing the comparison. Thus, if by default, "SMITH" (with no blanks following it) matches either "SMITHERS" or "SMITH   " (SMITH with three blanks following it). If this check box is selected, however, Visual FoxPro pads "SMITH" with three extra blanks when it performs this comparison, so it matches "SMITH " but not "SMITHERS".

Collating Sequence

The Collating Sequence drop-down control is very important when you are creating indexes. As you learned in Chapter 10, indexes by default organize records in ASCII order, which creates two possible problems. In ASCII order, all uppercase letters come before all lowercase letters; thus, ASCII order may not be the same as alphabetical order if your data is capitalized inconsistently. Also, ASCII order puts all letters with accent marks after all letters without accent marks; thus, foreign words that include accented letters will not be in proper alphabetical order.

Indexes use ASCII order if the default Machine option is selected in the Collating Sequence drop-down list.

If you choose General from this drop-down list or enter the command **SET COLLATE TO GENERAL** in the Command window, indexes will use proper alphabetical order in English, French, German, modern Spanish, Portuguese, and other western European languages.

SET COLLATE TO GENERAL is almost always best, though you do not have to worry about collation order if capitalization is correct and only English-language data is used.

►► The Remote Data Panel

The Remote Data panel, shown in Figure 19.6, lets you control how records are fetched from a server and updated in the server's table; it also contains the default connection settings that are used. Do not make any changes in these defaults without consulting your system administrator.

FIGURE 19.6

The Remote Data panel

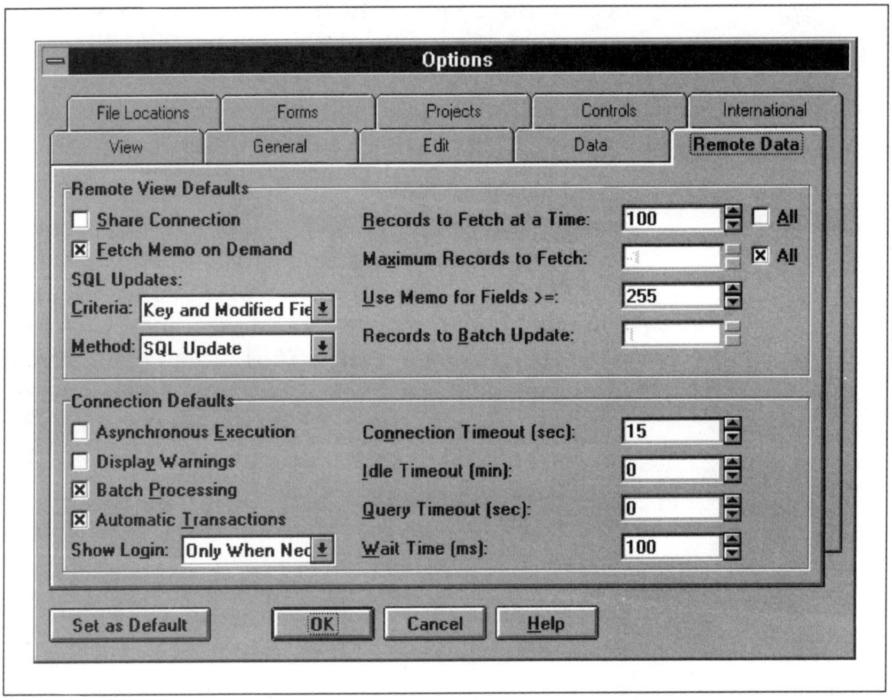

►► The File Locations Panel

The File Locations panel, shown in Figure 19.7, controls environment settings that determine where Visual FoxPro searches for files. All of its features are equivalent to SET … TO commands.

FIGURE 19.7

The File Locations panel

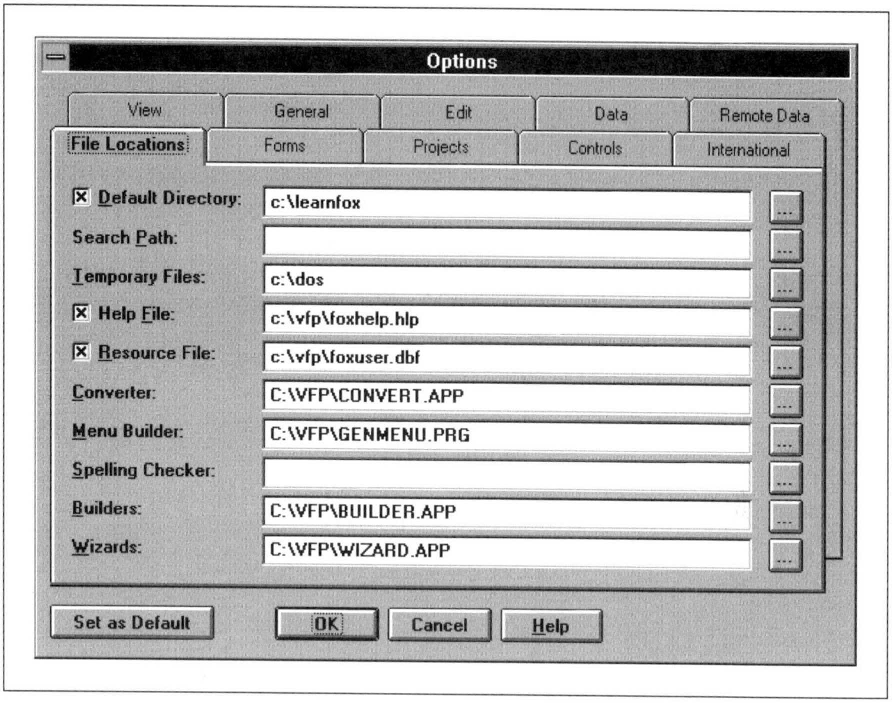

Some of the options in this panel require you to enter the full path name of a directory; you can type the directory name directly in a text box or click its ... button to display a dialog box such as the Select Directory dialog box, shown in Figure 19.8. Use this dialog box to select a drive and directory, as you do in the Open dialog box, and your selection will be entered in the text box.

Other File Location options require that you enter a file name, rather than just a directory; clicking the ... button for one of these options displays the Open dialog box, where you can select the file.

Choosing a Default Drive and Directory

Use the Default Directory control to choose the default drive and directory that will be used for all file input and output. Select the check box and then click the ... button to display the Select Directory dialog box, and use the drop-down list to select a drive and directory, as you do in the Open dialog box.

FIGURE 19.8

The Select Directory dialog box

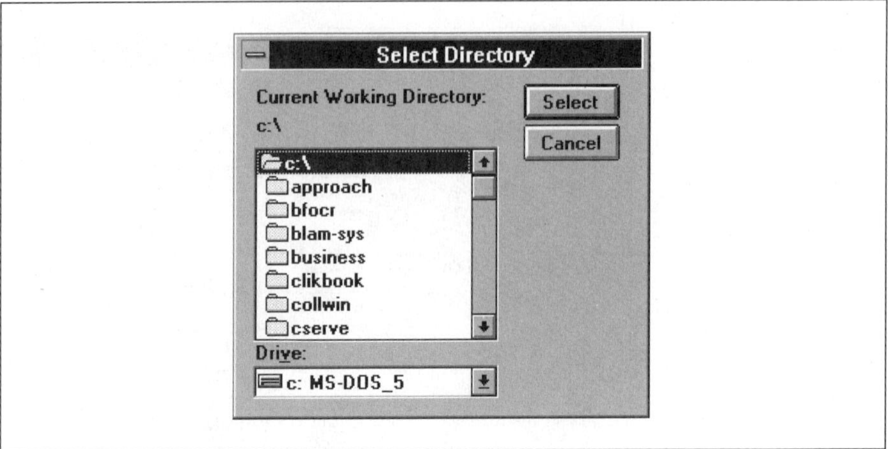

By default, Visual FoxPro will look for files in the directory you specify here. For example, if you select C:\LEARNFOX as your default directory, the files in this directory will be displayed initially when you use the Open or Save As dialog box. You will also be able to use commands that include only a file name instead of the file's entire path name, such as **USE EMPLIST** to open the Emplist table, rather than USE **C:\LEARNFOX\EMPLIST.**

The default directory is also the first place Visual FoxPro looks for commands you execute.

This control is equivalent to the command

```
SET DEFAULT TO <letter of drive>:<directory path>
```

►► **TIP**

This command can save you a considerable amount of typing if you are working from the Command window, by letting you enter file names without typing the full path name.

► *The Search Path*

The Search Path is a list of directory names you specify, where Visual FoxPro searches for files not found in the working directory. Enter the directory names, separated by semicolons, or click the button to the right and select directories repeatedly to add them all to the list in this text box, with semicolons included automatically.

To remove directories from the Search Path, use the usual Windows editing techniques to remove their names from this list.

This option is equivalent to the command:

```
SET PATH TO <list of directory paths>
```

NOTE

Do not confuse this with the DOS search path, where DOS looks for commands that you enter. Visual FoxPro searches this path for all files whose names you use in commands—for example, for table names included in a USE command.

Temporary Files

This option controls the directory where Visual FoxPro stores temporary files. Since these files should be deleted automatically, there is little reason for the user to worry about where they are stored. If the program terminates abnormally, however (for example, because of a power failure), temporary files may be left for you to delete.

Selecting a Help File

The Help File control lets you specify which file is to be used when the user selects System ➤ Help (or presses F1). Use it to display a dialog box that lets you select a help file. It is equivalent to the command SET HELP TO <file name>.

Two help files come with Visual FoxPro: Windows-style help (the default, briefly discussed in Chapter 1) in the file FOXHELP.HLP, and DBF-style help in FOXHELP.DBF. Both files are kept in the VFP directory by default.

Using DBF Help

If you use this button to select FOXHELP.DBF, Visual FoxPro displays the window shown in Figure 19.9 whenever you use the Help system.

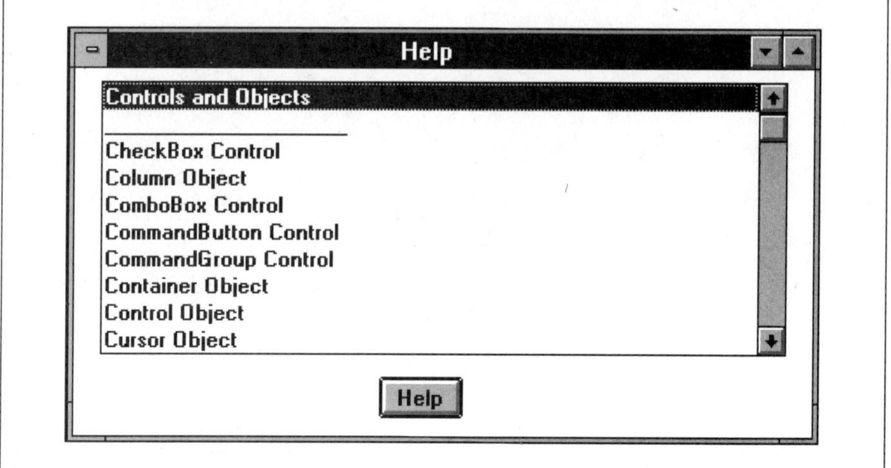

FIGURE 19.9

The DBF-style Help window

This window contains an alphabetical listing of commands, functions, controls and objects, system variables, events, properties, and other features of Visual FoxPro. You can search for one of these topics simply by typing it. The search is incremental; for example, if you type C, it moves the highlight to the first topic beginning with C, and if you type CO, it moves to the first topic beginning with CO, and so on. You can also scroll through the list in this Help window.

Once you have highlighted the topic that you want, simply click the Help button to display information on a topic, as shown in Figure 16.10. Click the Topics button to return to the list of commands and functions. Click the Next or Previous button to display the next command or function in the list. Use the See Also drop-down list to select a related topic and display help on it.

This system is not as versatile as Windows-style help, but it makes looking up topics so easy that you can save time by using it, if you are just searching for help on commands, functions, events, and properties, and not on the Visual FoxPro interface.

FIGURE 19.10

DBF-style help on a topic

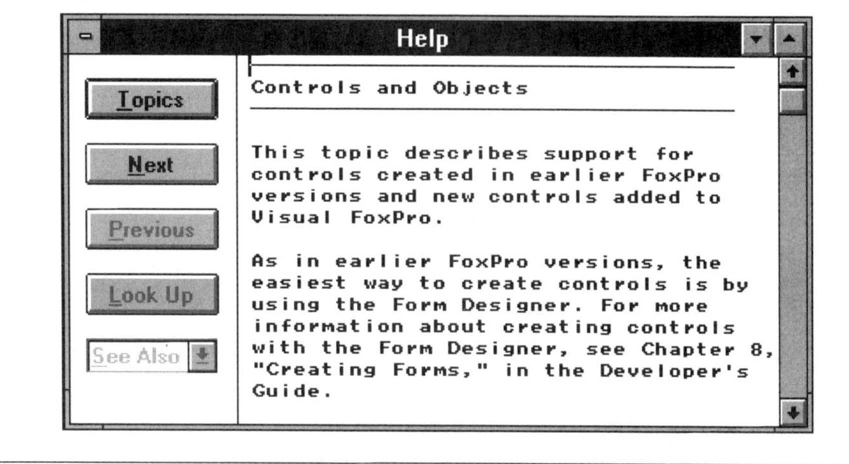

Help System for Applications

You can also create your own help system, based on either Windows or DBF help, and use them instead of Visual FoxPro's help systems, by using the Help File button or the SET HELP TO command. This is useful to provide help for an application you have developed using Visual FoxPro.

The table FOXHELP.DBF is shown in Figure 19.11. You can create a similar DBF file, with a series of topics in the Topic field and help on each in the Details memo field, and use it as DBF help for an application.

To create Windows-style help, you must use the Windows Help compiler (which is included in the Developer's edition of Visual FoxPro and in many other development packages) to create a file with an HLP extension.

You can also SET HELP ON or OFF using the check box to the right of this push button. The default setting for Help is *on*. The only reason you would want to turn it off is if you have developed a simple application that has no help system, and you do not want to confuse users by letting them display the Visual FoxPro Help system.

The Resource File

The Resource File control displays a dialog box to let you specify the resource file that Visual FoxPro uses.

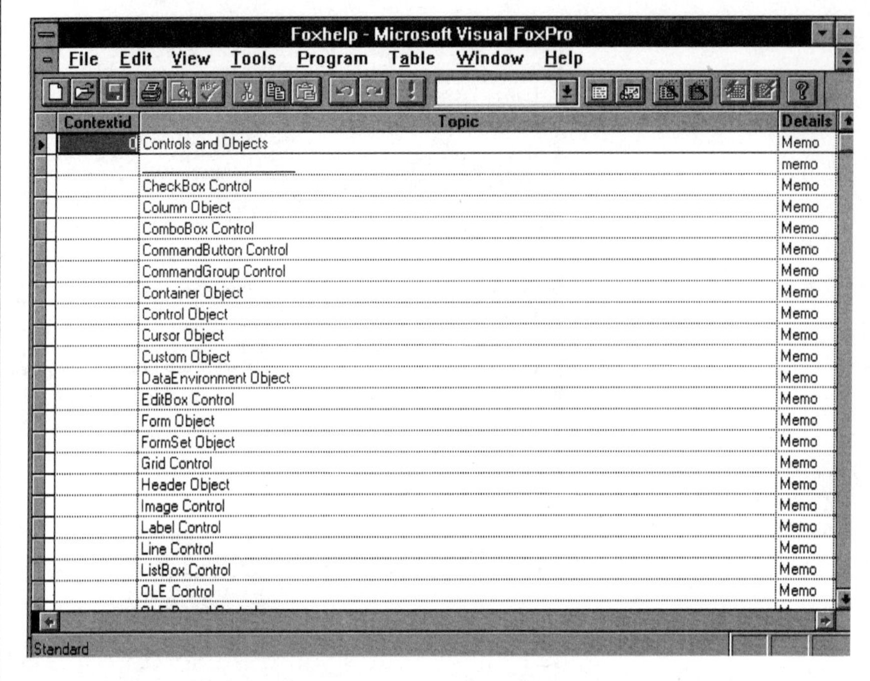

FIGURE 19.11

The Foxhelp.dbf table

The resource file stores information about the location and size of your Browse windows, color selections, and other preferences. By default, Visual FoxPro automatically creates a resource file named FOXUSER.DBF. Then, if you change your Browse window, for example, the program uses this file to set up the Browse window when you use the command BROWSE LAST in a later session.

You can create a variety of resource files with different names and use them for different purposes—for example, if several users who prefer different color schemes and different configurations of the Browse window are sharing Visual FoxPro.

You can also set Resource on or off using the check box to the right of this push button; the default is *on*. If Resource is *off*, Visual FoxPro uses default settings when you start it, rather than settings stored in a resource file.

Other Files

The remaining controls let you specify which file will be used as the Converter, Menu Builder, Spelling tool, Builders, and Wizards. Advanced programmers can write their own programs or applications to use instead of the programs distributed with Visual FoxPro for these purposes.

The Forms Panel

The Forms panel, shown in Figure 19.12, is used to work with custom forms, an advanced feature of Visual FoxPro that is covered briefly in Chapter 17 of this book.

FIGURE 19.12

The Forms panel

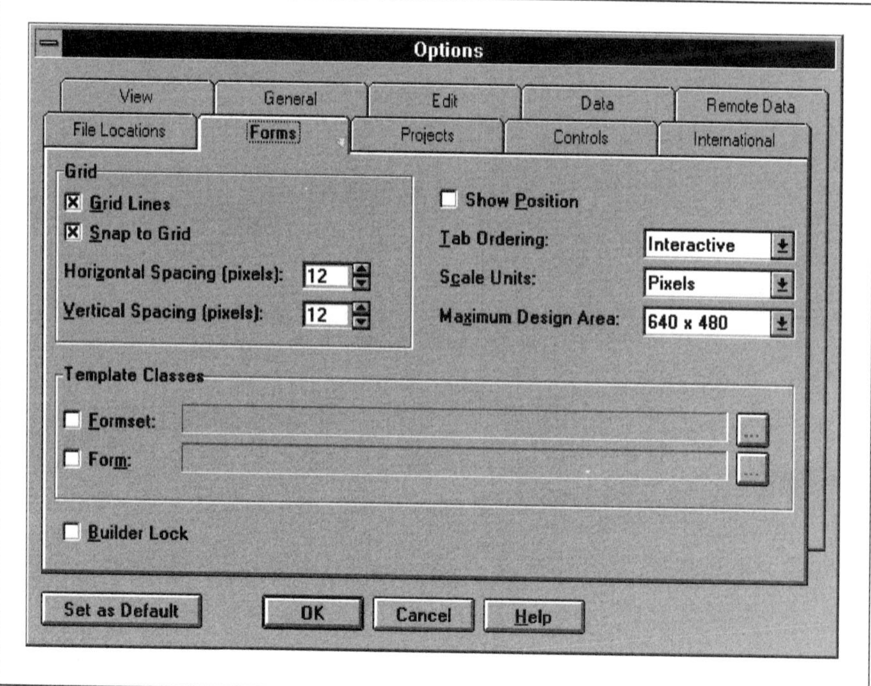

Use the Grid lines check box to specify whether gridlines should be displayed to help you align controls in the form. Use the Snap to Grid check boxes to specify whether controls should automatically be placed on these gridlines. You can also use the Horizontal and Vertical Spacing spinners to control the fineness of this grid. (Other features of this panel are beyond the scope of this book.)

►► The Projects Panel

The Projects panel, shown in Figure 19.13, is used to work with Visual FoxPro projects. Projects are used primarily by developers, to make it easier to organize and work with all the files in an application, and they are covered in Chapter 25.

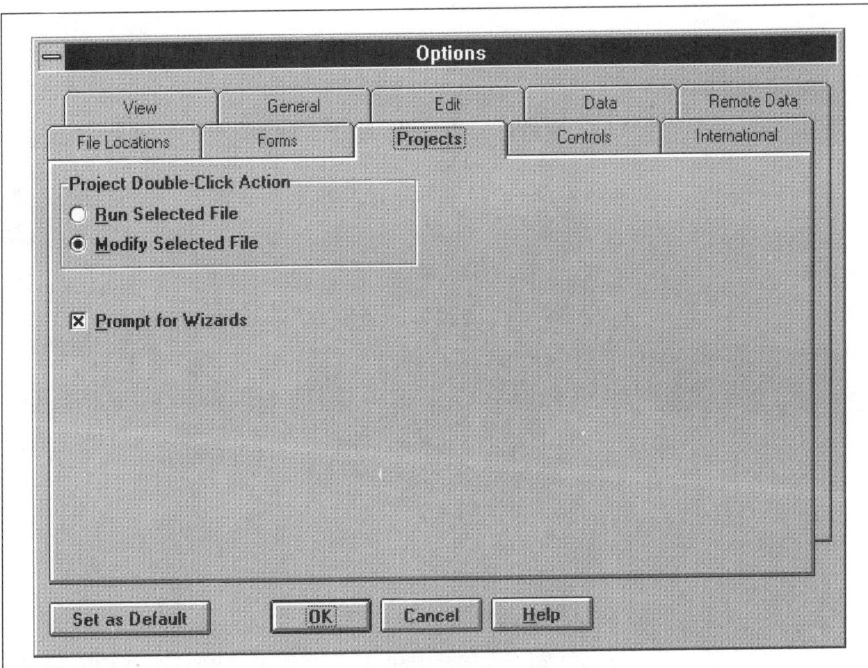

FIGURE 19.13 ►

The Projects panel

►► The Controls Panel

The Controls panel is used to work with custom controls included in forms, an advanced feature of Visual FoxPro that is not covered in this book.

The International Panel

The International panel, shown in Figure 19.14, controls settings for currency and date formats, and other details that differ in various countries.

FIGURE 19.14

The International panel

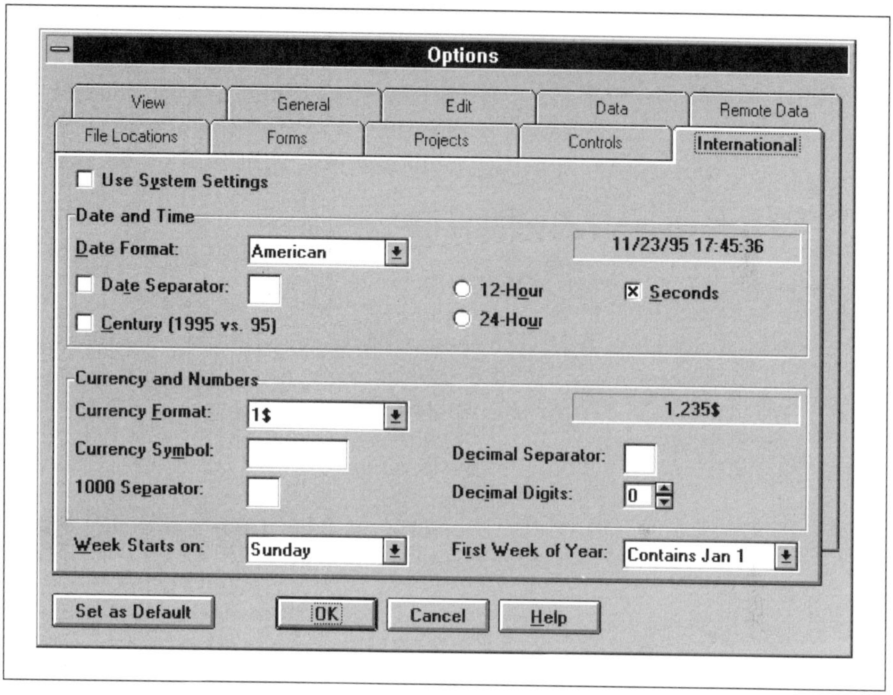

Select the Use System Settings check box to use all the settings from your Windows control panel. This is usually the easiest way of customizing the settings that Visual FoxPro uses, if you do not use its default settings. This check box must be deselected before using the other controls in this panel.

The Date and Time Area

The Date Format drop-down control lets you choose among date formats. The default is American, which lists dates in the order mm/dd/yy. Other date format options are ANSI (yy.mm.dd), British or French (dd/mm/yy), German (dd.mm.yy), Italian (dd-mm-yy), and Japan (yy/mm/dd), as well as USA (mm-dd-yy), MDY (mm/dd/yy), DMY (dd/mm/yy), and YMD (yy/mm/dd).

You can select these formats from the drop-down list or use the format names capitalized with the command SET DATE TO.

Other features of the date format are controlled by the check boxes to the right of this drop-down list:

- **Date Separator:** Lets you change the delimiter used between the numbers for the year, month, and day. Select the check box and type the delimiter you want in the text box to its right.
- **Century:** Lets you display the entire four-digit year, not just the last two digits. The equivalent command is SET CENTURY ON or OFF.
- **12-Hour** and **24-Hour:** Let you control whether the time is displayed using the conventional 12-hour clock or a 24-hour clock—for example, as 3:00 PM or as 15:00.
- **Seconds:** Lets you control whether seconds are displayed.

Notice that a sample of the format you select is always displayed in the upper-right corner of this area.

► Currency and Number Formats

The Currency and Numbers area lets you specify the way currency and other numbers are displayed.

Use the Currency Format control to choose whether the currency symbol (such as the $ symbol) goes before or after the amount of currency.

Enter any character in the Currency Symbol text box to have it replace the default $ sign.

Enter any character in the 1000 Separator text box to have it replace the comma that is used to separate thousands, millions, and so on by default.

Enter any character in the Decimal Separator text box to have it replace the period that is used as a decimal point by default.

Use the Decimal Digits text box or spinner control to specify the number of digits displayed to the right of the decimal point.

Again, a sample of the format you select is always displayed in the upper-right corner of this area.

▶ Beginning of Week and Year

Use the Week Starts On list to select any day as the first day of the week, rather than the default Sunday.

By default, the week that contains January 1 is counted as the first week of the year, even if that date falls on its last day. Instead, you can use the First Week of Year drop-down control to specify that the first week with the majority of its days (at least four days) in the year or that the first week with all its days in the year should be counted as the first week of the year.

You might want to change one or both of these settings if, for example, you were totaling sales for each week of the year. You might want to exclude the first week if it does not have the full seven days, because it cannot be compared with other weeks; or you might want the week to start on the same day as the first day of the year, so that every week is the full seven days.

▶▶ To Sum Up

In this chapter, you learned to use the Options dialog box and SET commands to customize the working environment, altering the way that Visual FoxPro responds in many different commands and menu selections. In the next chapter, you will learn to customize Visual FoxPro's toolbar, giving you even more control over the FoxPro desktop.

CHAPTER 20

Creating Custom Toolbars

▸▸ FAST TRACK

▶ *To display or hide toolbars,* 605

choose View ➤ Toolbars and use the check boxes of the Toolbars dialog box to specify which toolbars are displayed.

▶ *To customize a toolbar,* 606

click the Customize button of the Toolbars dialog box to display the Customize Toolbar dialog box. Click and drag buttons from this dialog box to a toolbar to add the button to it. Click and drag a button off a toolbar to remove the button from it.

▶ *To restore a toolbar to its default form,* 608

select it in the Toolbars list of the Toolbars dialog box and click the Reset button.

▶ ***To create a new toolbar,*** 608

enter a name for the new toolbar in the Toolbar Name text box of the Toolbars dialog box and click the OK button to display an empty toolbar with that name and the Customize dialog box. Then click and drag buttons from the Customize dialog box to the empty toolbar, just as you would if you were customizing an existing toolbar.

▶ ***To delete a new toolbar,*** 608

select it in the Toolbars list of the Toolbars dialog box. The Reset to Default button is replaced by a Delete button.

▸▸ **V***isual FoxPro* lets you control your working environment by customizing toolbars, as other Microsoft applications do. You can specify which buttons are on its toolbars and create new toolbars.

It is very easy to customize Visual FoxPro's toolbars. After you have displayed the Customize Toolbar dialog box, you can generally just drag-and-drop buttons on to or off of toolbars.

▸▸ The Toolbars Dialog Box

Choose View ➤ Toolbars or right-click any toolbar and choose Toolbars from its shortcut menu to display the Toolbars dialog box, shown in Figure 20.1. The Toolbars list here includes names of all the toolbars that are included with Visual FoxPro and of custom toolbars that you create, and the buttons to the right let you work with these toolbars and create new ones.

The dialog box also has three check boxes that control how the toolbars are displayed:

- The Color Toolbars check box controls whether the buttons are displayed in color or black-and-white. Color is the default.
- The Large buttons check box lets you display the buttons in larger than conventional size. This may be useful if you have a high-resolution monitor (in which the same number of pixels takes up a smaller screen area than it would at a lower resolution) and you have set up Windows to display everything in a smaller size, so that the buttons cannot be read if they are their conventional size.

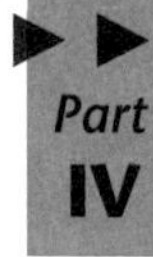

FIGURE 20.1

The Toolbars dialog box

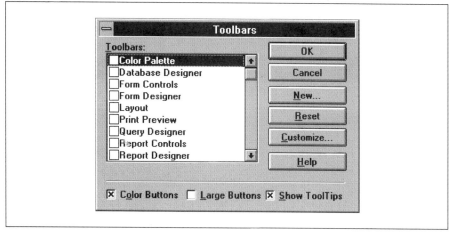

- The Show ToolTips check box controls whether a box with the name of the tool is displayed next to the tool as help after you leave the pointer on the tool for a moment.

▶▶ Displaying and Hiding Toolbars

In general, Visual FoxPro displays the toolbars that you need in any given situation, for example, by automatically displaying the Report toolbar when you use the Report Designer.

If you want to specify which toolbars are displayed, however, you can:

- Select or deselect the check box to the left of any toolbar in the Toolbars list.
- Right-click any toolbar to display its shortcut menu. As you can see in Figure 20.2, this menu includes the names of all available toolbars, with check marks to the left of the ones that are displayed. You can choose any one to display it (if it is not already checked) or to hide it (if it is checked).

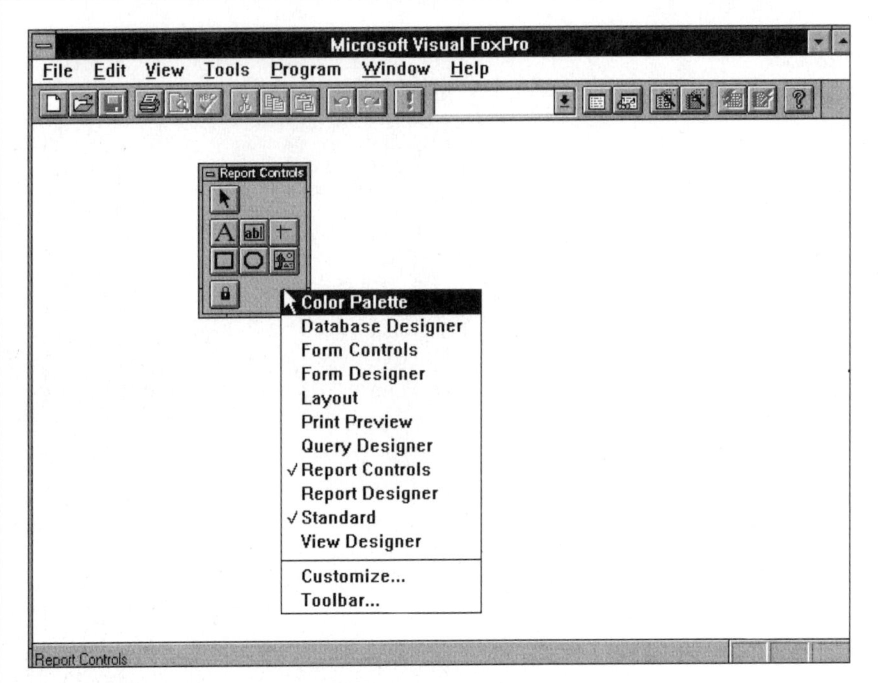

FIGURE 20.2 *A toolbar's shortcut menu*

▸▸ Customizing Toolbars

It is easy to customize toolbars, simply by clicking or dragging buttons on or off them. You can click and drag buttons among toolbars when the Toolbars dialog box is open. You can also choose from a large selection of buttons that you can add to Toolbars, by displaying the Customize dialog box:

- Click the Customize button of the Toolbars dialog box, or
- Right-click any toolbar and choose Customize from its shortcut menu

The Toolbars and Customize dialog boxes do not disable all the controls on the desktop, as most dialog boxes do. Instead, they let you use them differently. When either the Toolbars or Customize dialog box is open, you can customize toolbars in the following ways.

Removing a Button from a Toolbar

Simply click and drag any button from a toolbar to any place on the desktop to remove it from that toolbar.

Moving Buttons among Toolbars

Likewise, simply click and drag any button from one toolbar to another to move it to that toolbar.

Adding Buttons from the Customize Toolbar Dialog Box

As you can see in Figure 20.3, the Customize Toolbar dialog box has a list of Categories, and you can select any one to display a selection of buttons from that Category. Click the button in the Customize Toolbar dialog box to display a description of what it does at the bottom of the dialog box.

Simply click and drag any button from this dialog box to a toolbar to add the button to that toolbar.

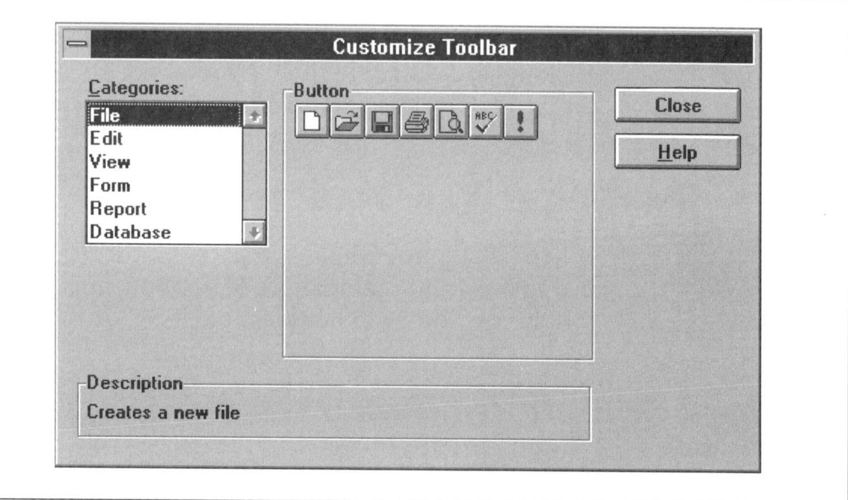

FIGURE 20.3

The Customize Toolbar dialog box

▸ Restoring a Toolbar to Its Default Design

After customizing a toolbar, you can select it in the Toolbars list of the Toolbars dialog box and click Reset to undo all changes you made in it and restore it to its original design.

▸▸ Creating New Toolbars

You might find it convenient to create a new toolbar to hold tools that you use frequently. For example, if you often edit text, you might prefer to add the Cut, Copy, and Paste tools to their own toolbar, rather than keep them on the main toolbar. You can also create new toolbars with entirely new functions, by designing new buttons and attaching macros to them. This is the easiest way to use a set of macros that you work with frequently.

Creating a new toolbar is very much like customizing an existing one. First, however, you must enter a name for the toolbar in the Toolbar Name text box of the Toolbars dialog box; then click its OK button to create a new toolbar. When you do this, Visual FoxPro automatically displays the Customize dialog box.

Visual FoxPro also displays a new toolbar with the name you specified. This toolbar is empty to begin with, and you can add new tools to it by clicking and dragging them from other toolbars or from the Customize dialog box, just as you do when you are modifying an existing toolbar.

▸ Deleting a New Toolbar

When a custom toolbar is selected in the Toolbars list of the Toolbars dialog box, that dialog box's Reset button is replaced by a Delete button, which you can click to delete the new toolbar.

▸ A Sample Toolbar

If you want a bit of experience in customizing toolbars, you can try creating a simple new one. Let's say that you want to put the editing tools

(Cut, Copy, and Paste) on a special floating toolbar, rather than having them on the standard toolbar:

1. Choose View ➤ Toolbars to display the Toolbar dialog box. Click the New button. In the New Toolbar dialog box, enter the toolbar name **Edit**. Then click New to display a small empty floating toolbar.

2. Click and drag the Cut and Copy buttons from the Standard toolbar to the new Edit toolbar.

3. To try the other method of placing toolbar icons, choose Edit from the Categories list of the Customize dialog box. Drag the Paste tool from this dialog box to the Edit toolbar. Then remove the Paste tool from the Standard toolbar by dragging it to the desktop. Close the Customize dialog box. The custom toolbar is shown in Figure 20.4.

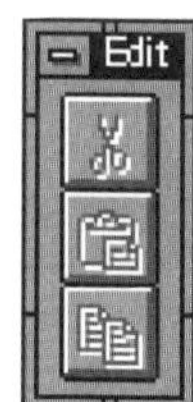

FIGURE 20.4

A custom Edit toolbar

4. Now, to get rid of this custom toolbar, right-click it and choose Toolbars from its shortcut menu. Select it in the Toolbars list; click the Delete button and click yes to delete it.

5. Finally, select Standard in the Toolbars list and click the Reset button to restore the three editing tools to the Standard toolbar.

►► To Sum Up

In this chapter, you learned to customize toolbars. In the next chapter, you will look at how to create macros, another method of customizing Visual FoxPro to make your work easier.

CHAPTER 21

Using Keyboard Macros

▶▶ FAST TRACK

▶ ***To record a new macro,*** **616**

choose Tools ➤ Macros to display the Keyboard Macros dialog box or press Shift+F10. When Visual FoxPro displays the Macro Key dialog box, press the keys that you want to use to activate the macro.

▶ ***To stop recording a macro,*** **619**

press Shift+F10 while you are recording, and click OK in the Stop Recording Macro dialog box.

▶ ***To insert a pause in a macro,*** **619**

click the Insert Pause button in the Stop Recording Macro dialog box. The macro will allow you to type text of any length at this point. If you select the Key to Resume radio button, the macro will continue when you press Shift+F10. If you click the Seconds button, a spinner control is added on the right with the default value of one second; the macro continues executing after the time you enter here has elapsed, even if you do not enter anything.

▶ ***To edit a macro,*** 621

select it in the Keyboard Macros dialog box and click the Edit button.

▶ ***To save a set of macros,*** 623

click the Save button in the Keyboard Macros dialog box and use the Save As dialog box to specify a file where you will save all the macros currently displayed in the Keyboard Macros dialog box.

▶ ***To use a saved set of macros,*** 623

click the Restore button of the Keyboard Macros dialog box and use the Open dialog box to open the file where you saved the macro set.

In the last two chapters, you learned how to set up Visual FoxPro to make it easier to use by customizing the working environment and the toolbars. In this chapter, you will learn to use keyboard macros, a utility that lets you customize Visual FoxPro and saves you a considerable amount of work.

Macros let you record keystrokes. Even simple macros can make your work with Visual FoxPro easier by saving you repetitive data entry. As you become more advanced, you can also use them to automate commands and give yourself extra power.

▶▶ What Are Macros?

Many programs let you create keyboard macros. A macro simply records a series of keystrokes and assigns them to some special key or key combination so you can press one key or a key combination each time you need to use the series of keystrokes you have recorded.

Macros are a convenience to save you time in entering keystrokes you use frequently. Although you can save any sequence of keystrokes in a macro, generally you will use them to save data entry time. For example, if you have to enter a large number of records with addresses in San Francisco, you can create a macro that stores the whole sequence of keystrokes needed to type **SAN FRANCISCO**, move to the State field, and type **CA**. Macros are also useful for customizing the editing key combinations—for example, to make them work as they do in a program you are more familiar with.

Key Combinations Used for Macros

Visual FoxPro lets you assign a macro to any of the function keys and to a large number of key combinations that use Ctrl, Alt, or Shift with function keys or letter keys. Remember that only letter keys and function keys can be used in macros, not numbers, special characters, or editing keys. The permissible combinations of keys are

- Any function key
- Shift plus any function key except F10
- Ctrl plus any single letter or function key
- Shift+Ctrl plus any single letter or function key
- Alt plus any single letter or function key except F10
- Shift+Alt plus any single letter or function key except F10
- Ctrl+Alt plus any single letter or function key except F10
- Ctrl+Shift+Alt plus any single letter or function key except F10

NOTE

Visual FoxPro *does* let you use Alt+F10 (and Shift+Alt+F10, Ctrl+Alt+F10, and Ctrl+Shift+Alt+F10), but only when followed by a letter. This gives you even more combinations of keystrokes that can be assigned macro values.

These keys and key combinations give you hundreds of possible keyboard macros, more than you will ever need, and probably more than you could ever remember. The maximum number of keystrokes you can store in any macro is 1024—again, probably more than you will ever need.

The function keys by themselves are assigned default macro values by Visual FoxPro. F1 is Help, and because this is very useful, it generally should not be assigned another value. The other function keys' default values are left over from the days when dBASE did not have a menu interface; they let you enter the most common commands at the command line. Most people find that these default macros are no longer useful now that it is easier to use the menus. As you will see shortly, you can save new default values for these function keys so they will be set automatically whenever you start Visual FoxPro.

▸▸ TIP

Default macros that you create are saved in a file named DEFAULT.FKY in either your Visual FoxPro home directory or in the current directory. Until you create new defaults, this file does not exist, and Visual FoxPro simply generates the standard defaults when the program is started. If default macros you have saved are not available when you start Visual FoxPro, search for the DEFAULT.FKY file.

▸ The Macros Dialog Box

Choose Tools ➤ Macros to display the Macros dialog box, shown in Figure 21.1.

The pushbuttons on the right let you work with individual macros.

The pushbuttons in the Macro Set box at the bottom of this dialog box let you work with sets of macros—for example, to save all the macros that are currently active as a set or to use a set of macros that you saved earlier. Later in this chapter you'll see how grouping related macros into sets can be useful.

▸▸ Recording and Using a New Macro

You can create a new macro by selecting the Record pushbutton of the Keyboard Macros dialog box. In addition, you can create a new macro

FIGURE 21.1

Macros dialog box

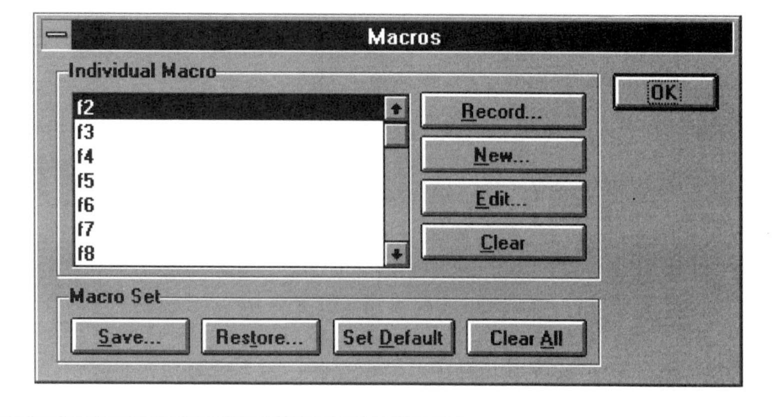

at any time by pressing Shift+F10 (which is why Shift+F10 is one of the combinations you cannot assign to your own macro).

Although it is not necessary, it generally is easier if you create the macro at the same point in Visual FoxPro where you will use it. For example, to create a macro that fills in a city and state name, first open the Browse window and move the cursor to the City field. Then press Shift+F10 to create the macro. You will see that it is often handy to create a macro when you are already in the situation where it will be used.

Assigning the Macro to a Key

When you make any of these choices, Visual FoxPro displays the Macro Key Definition dialog box, shown in Figure 21.2. Enter the key combination you want to use to activate the macro; for example, press F2 or press Ctrl+Alt+A. Visual FoxPro will not let you enter illegal combinations.

FIGURE 21.2

Macro Key Definition dialog box

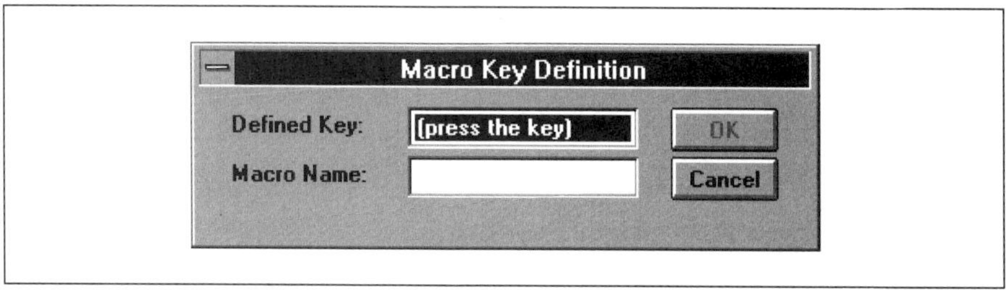

It displays a name for the macro (based on the key combination), as you can see in the illustration. You can change this name if you wish and enter any name up to 20 characters long. When the keystrokes and name are right, choose OK to begin recording the macro.

► Overwriting or Adding to an Existing Macro

If you enter a keystroke combination you have already defined as a macro, FoxPro displays the Overwrite Macro dialog box, shown in Figure 21.3, which gives you these choices:

- **Overwrite:** Replaces the existing macro with the new macro you are defining.
- **Append Keystrokes:** Adds the new keystrokes at the end of the existing macro.
- **Cancel:** Does not replace the existing macro.

FIGURE 21.3 ►

Overwrite Macro dialog box

► Recording the Macro

When Visual FoxPro displays a message saying that it has begun recording, enter any combination of keystrokes you want saved in the macro. These might be just text. For example, type **SAN FRANCISCO**, press Tab, and type **CA** to save yourself time entering that city and state in each record in a database file.

The keystrokes might involve commands. For example, you might create a macro to open the Emplist table, display it in a Browse window, and switch to Append mode.

They might even involve the keystroke versions of menu choices. If you are accustomed to software that lets you delete a line by pressing Ctrl+Y, for example, you can create a Ctrl+Y macro that does just that.

▶▶ WARNING

If you assign Ctrl+key or Alt+key combinations such as this one to macros, they can interfere with your using the keyboard to work with the menu system. If you create an Alt+E macro to help you with data entry, for example, you cannot use Alt+E to pull down the Edit menu when this macro is active. Likewise, Ctrl+C would interfere with the shortcut key combination for Edit ➤ Copy. Be careful to choose combinations for macros that do not interfere with your work.

When you are finished entering the keystrokes you want recorded, press Shift+F10 to stop recording.

The Stop Recording Macro Dialog Box

The Stop Recording Macro dialog box appears, as shown in Figure 18.4. The choices this dialog box gives you are easy to understand:

- **Insert Literal:** Records the literal value of the next keystroke instead of the value assigned to it by an existing macro.
- **Insert Pause:** Stops execution of the macro temporarily and lets the user type text.
- **OK:** Saves the macro as it has been entered.
- **Continue:** Returns to the point where you were when you left off and continues to create and record the macro.
- **Discard:** Does not save the macro.

Inserting a Pause in a Macro

Insert Pause is the most interesting of these choices. It lets the user type text of any length at this point in the macro. Then, when the user presses Shift+F10 or the specified time has elapsed, the macro continues.

For example, you can create a macro that enters your return address at the top of a letter, pauses, and then enters the salutation. First the macro enters the return address; then it pauses to let you enter the address of the

FIGURE 21.4

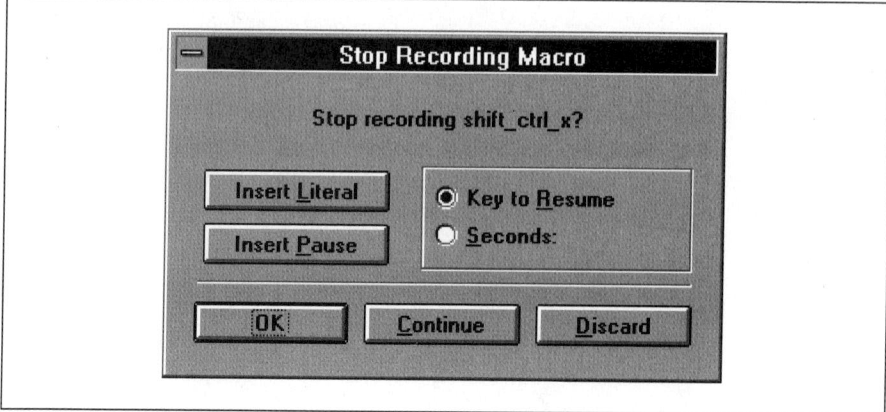

Stop Recording Macro dialog box

person you are writing to. When you press Shift+F10, the macro continues by skipping a line, typing the word *Dear,* and leaving the cursor where you need to type the rest of the salutation and the letter.

The Insert Pause pushbutton has two radio buttons associated with it, which let you control how the pause is ended:

- **Key to Resume:** When the macro pauses, Visual FoxPro prompts you to press the same key you used to start the macro in order to resume execution of the macro.
- **Seconds:** The pause lasts a fixed time before the execution of the macro resumes. The default value is one second; but if you select this radio button, a text box and spinner control are added to its right, to let you enter a different number.

In general, Key to Resume is the better choice since it lets you take as much time as you need to make the entry. Seconds is useful primarily if you want the macro to continue executing after a pause even if no value is entered.

Using the Macro

That's all there is to creating a macro. To summarize the basic steps:

1. To start recording, choose Tools ➤ Macro and click the Record button of the Keyboard Macros dialog box. Alternatively, press Shift+F10 at any time.

2. When the Macro Key Definition dialog box appears, press the key combination you want to assign to the macro, and select OK.

3. Enter all the keystrokes you want to record. After you are done, press Shift+F10 to stop recording, and select OK from the Stop Recording Macro dialog box.

Once the macro has been recorded, use it at any time by pressing the key combination you entered in the Macro Key Definition dialog box.

If a macro does not work properly, the problem is probably that you are in the wrong place when you use it. To give an obvious example, if you saved the keystrokes needed to type San Francisco, you must be in the City field of your table when you use the macro.

Though this is the most common problem associated with macros, other problems could arise if you use a macro after changing environment settings, modify the structure of a table, delete an index tag, or change the way that Visual FoxPro is set up in some other way.

Editing a Macro

When you create a macro, Visual FoxPro stores it in text form so you can edit it if necessary. Special keys are represented by self-explanatory names such as {TAB} for the Tab key, {RIGHTARROW} for the → key, and {LEFTMOUSE} for the left mouse button. Note that these names are in curly brackets.

To edit a macro, select it in the Keyboard Macros dialog box, and then select the Edit pushbutton. Visual FoxPro displays the Macro Edit dialog box shown in Figure 21.5. You can edit the name of the macro and the defined key that plays it, as well as the macro's contents.

The illustration shows a macro meant to speed data entry by typing SAN FRANCISCO, tabbing to the next field, and typing CA when you press Shift+Ctrl+X.

It is useful to edit macros to correct minor errors. For example, if you spelled San Francisco incorrectly when you were recording the macro, it would be easier to edit the macro than to rerecord it.

FIGURE 21.5

Macro Edit dialog box

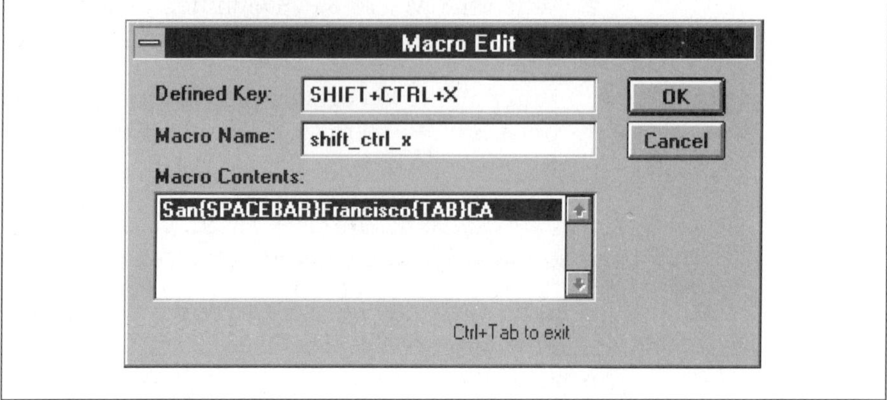

For most errors, though, it is easiest to start from scratch and record the macro again. Give it the same name as the one with the error, and select the Overwrite pushbutton from the alert that Visual FoxPro displays.

Visual FoxPro also lets you use the macro editor to create new macros if you select the New pushbutton of the Keyboard Macros dialog box. Writing anything but the simplest macros in this way, however, is a very difficult and often frustrating exercise in computer programming. It is generally best to record macros rather than write them.

▸▸ Working with Current and Saved Macros

Once you have created a macro using the methods outlined above, it is a *current macro,* which appears in the scrollable list in the Keyboard Macros dialog box. Unless you save it, a current macro exists only until you quit Visual FoxPro.

▸ Working with Macro Sets

Macros you have saved in past sessions are kept in a disk file with the extension FKY. They do not appear in the scrollable list in the Keyboard Macros dialog box and thus are not usable until you restore them and add them to the list of active macros. You can save your macros in several different FKY files, each of which holds a separate *macro set.*

Dividing macros into sets lets you group macros for different applications. For example, there might be one group you use when you are editing programs and others you use when you are entering data in different files. All of the macros that are being used at a given time appear in the scrollable list, and you can save them all as a set with a single name. Then you can recall and use that set whenever you need it.

Saving the Current Macro Set

To save the current set of macros, select Save from the Keyboard Macros dialog box. The familiar Save As dialog box appears, with all of the sets of macros in the current directory in its scrollable list. Select one of these names to overwrite an existing macro set, or enter a new name to create a new macro set.

Using a Macro Set

To use a set of macros that has been saved, select Restore from the Keyboard Macros dialog box. The familiar Open dialog box appears, with the heading Restore Macros From File above a scrollable list of macro set names. Select any one and then select Open to use those macros.

Remember that the macros you restore are added to the macros that are already open, which are in the scrollable list of the dialog box. At some point you might want to get rid of some or all of the current macros before adding new ones.

Clearing Macros

To get rid of a macro, select it from the scrollable list, and then select the Clear pushbutton.

To get rid of all the current macros, select the Clear All button. This option only clears the macros from current memory; it does not erase the file where saved macros are stored on disk.

Creating a Default Macro Set

Finally, to make the current set of macros the *default* set, to be used automatically whenever you start Visual FoxPro, just select the Set

Default pushbutton. Visual FoxPro asks you to confirm this selection. Then it stores the current macros in a file named DEFAULT.FKY, which it automatically uses to set the default whenever it is started.

You can begin by saving one or two macros that you always find useful as the default and add more default macros as you invent more.

▸▸ A Sample Macro

Now you can try creating and working with a macro that you might actually find useful. Let's say that you frequently open your table and add just two or three records to it, and so you often repeat the keystrokes needed to open the table and display it in Append mode. Create a macro to do this for you, and run it using the keys Shift+Ctrl+A (because it is easy to remember that A stands for append).

1. Begin with all tables closed. Choose Tools ➤ Macros to display the Macros dialog box, and click the Record button.
2. When Visual FoxPro displays the Macro Key Definition dialog box, press Shift+Ctrl+A and enter the name **Append**, as shown in Figure 21.6. Click OK. Visual FoxPro indicates that it has begun recording.

FIGURE 21.6 ▸

Naming the macro

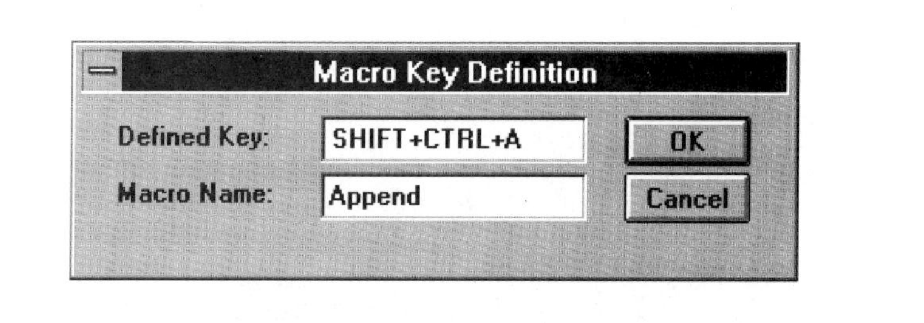

3. Enter the command **USE \LEARNFOX\EMPLIST.** When the status bar shows that the table is open, press Alt+V to display the View menu again, and press A to enter Append mode.
4. This is all you want the macro to do, so press Shift+F10 to stop recording. Click OK in the Stop Recording Macro dialog box.

5. Now, click the Command window to bring it forward, and enter **USE** to close the table and Browse window.

6. To test the macro, press Shift+Ctrl+A to display the table in a Browse window in Append mode. Again, click the Command window to bring it forward, and type **USE** to close the table and Browse window.

7. Choose Tools ➤ Macros. The new macro is listed in the Macros dialog box, as shown in Figure 21.7.

FIGURE 21.7

The new macro is added to the list.

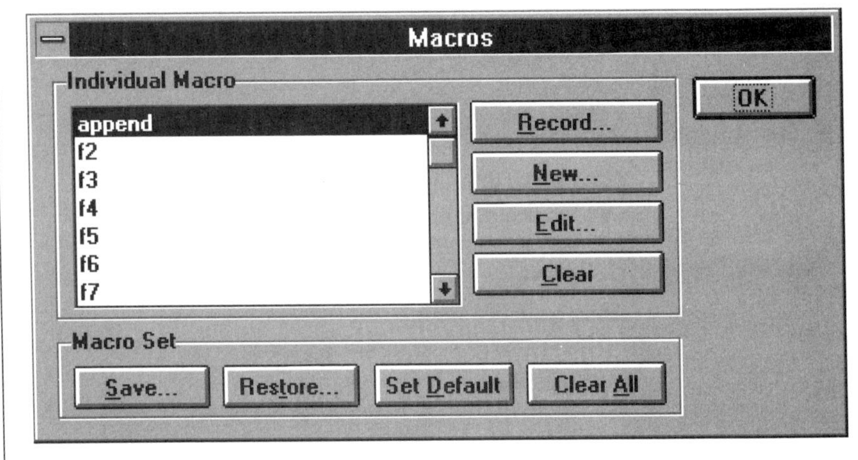

8. Click the Save button. Let's say that you are now using several other macros in addition to the Append macro, all of which are useful in data entry. In the Save Macros dialog box, enter the name **dataentr** and choose Save.

9. In the Macros dialog box, select the Append macro and click the Clear button. Click Yes to discard the macro, and click OK to close the Macros dialog box.

10. Press Shift+Ctrl+A. The macro is not executed. Instead, all the text in the Command window is highlighted, which is the default function of this key combination when you are editing. Press Ctrl+End to unhighlight the text.

11. Choose Tools ➤ Macros. Click the Restore button of the Macros dialog box. In the Restore Macros dialog box, double-click DATAENTR.FKY. The Append macro is restored to the Macros dialog box.

12. Click OK to close the Macros dialog box. Press Shift+Ctrl+A. The Append macro is executed.

Now you have seen how to record a macro and also how to save and restore a macro set. These are the basic features of the Macro Recorder that you need in order to use macros to save yourself work.

▸▸ To Sum Up

The last few chapters covered several major utilities that you can use to display your data in more effective ways and to set up Visual FoxPro to make your work easier. The next chapter covers additional FoxPro utilities.

CHAPTER 22

Getting the Most from Visual FoxPro's Utilities

▸▸ FAST TRACK

▶ ***To import data using the Import Wizard,*** ***633***

in the first step, use the File Type drop-down list to select the type of file the data is being imported from, and then use the ... button next to the Source File box to display the Open dialog box and select the source file. Use the Options step to specify the type of text file being imported or which rows of a spreadsheet file should be excluded. Use the Field Settings step to change the definition of the fields in the new table that FoxPro creates to hold the data.

▶ ***To import simpler data,*** ***637***

choose File ➤ Import and use the Import dialog box to specify the type and name of the source file and the name of the destination file; or use the IMPORT or APPEND FROM command.

▶ ***To export data,*** ***637***

choose File ➤ Export and use the Export dialog box to specify the type and name of the destination file. Click its Options button to add a scope, FOR, WHILE, or FIELDS clause that limits which records and fields are exported. Alternatively, use the EXPORT or COPY TO command.

▶ ***To edit text files,*** 639

choose File ➤ New and use the New dialog box to create a new text or program file. Use the Format menu to format its text. Choose Tools ➤ Spelling to use the Spelling tool to correct spelling.

▶ ***To add an OLE object to a General field,*** 652

cut or Copy the object from the source application and choose Edit ➤ Paste to paste it into the General field, or drag and drop it from another application into the General field. You can also display the General window, choose Edit ➤ Insert Object and use the Insert Object dialog box to select an existing file or to launch an application that you will use to create a new file.

▶▶ **Y**ou have already looked at some of Visual FoxPro's power tools, and this chapter introduces you to additional utilities that can help you work more easily and efficiently. These tools are grouped into three categories:

- **Importing and exporting data:** In the first section you'll learn how to use the Import Wizard and the Visual FoxPro commands for importing and exporting.
- **Advanced editing techniques:** In the second section, you'll learn how to create text and program files and print them. These things will be handy if you write programs or use long Memo fields, although they are not needed for routine data entry and editing.
- **Object Linking and Embedding (OLE):** The third section covers this Microsoft technology which lets you use data from other Windows applications within Visual FoxPro for Windows.

▶▶ *Importing and Exporting Data*

Visual FoxPro gives you several methods of exchanging data with other applications. The most sophisticated is the Import Wizard, which gives you very powerful methods of specifying how to import data from other database and spreadsheet programs or from text files. The Import and Export dialog box and the IMPORT, EXPORT, APPEND FROM, and COPY TO commands also let you import and export data. All of these methods are covered below.

Import Wizard

The Import Wizard can be used to import data that is in a text file, an Excel spreadsheet, a Multiplan spreadsheet, a Lotus 1-2-3 version 1A, 2.x, or 3.x spreadsheet, a Symphony version 1.01 or 1.10 spreadsheet, a Paradox table, or a RapidFile table.

To use this Wizard, choose Tools ➤ Wizards ➤ Import or choose File ➤ Import and click the Import Wizard button of the Import dialog box to display the Import Wizard.

Specify Source and Destination Files

The first step of the Wizard, shown in Figure 22.1, lets you specify the source and destination files.

FIGURE 22.1

Specifying the source and destination files

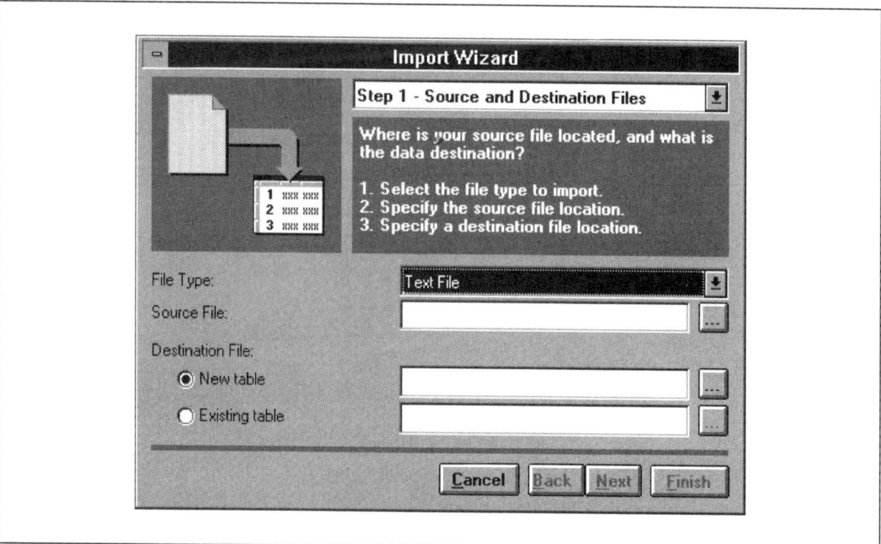

First use the File Type control to select one of the available data types. Then click the button to the right of the Source File text box, and Visual FoxPro will display the Open dialog box to let you select a file of that type.

When you select a file, Visual FoxPro's default is to create a new table of the same name to hold the data: you can edit this name in the New

Table text box. Visual FoxPro will automatically create a table with the structure needed to hold the imported data.

Alternatively, if you want to append the data to an existing Visual FoxPro table, you can select the Existing table radio button and then use the button to its right to select the table, but you must be sure that it has the fields needed to hold the imported data.

Controlling Import Options

The Options step, shown in Figure 22.2, is the most powerful feature of this Wizard. It shows a preview of the data as it will be imported. If the preview is not correct, click the Options button to display the Import Wizard Options dialog box, shown in Figure 22.3.

FIGURE 22.2

The Options step of the Import Wizard

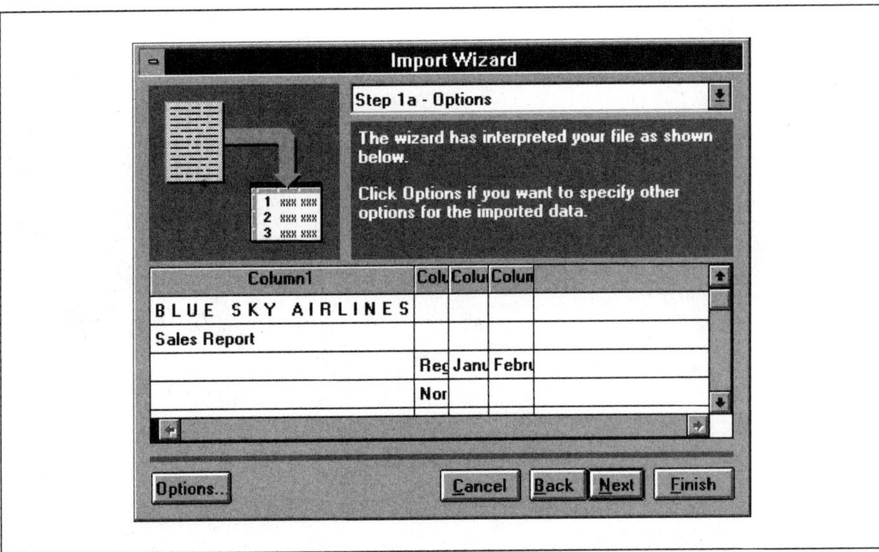

Options for Text Files The controls at the top of this dialog box are used to specify options for text files. The difficulty in importing a text file is to determine where each record and field begins, and there are fundamentally different types of text files that you can import into a table:

- **Fixed Width files:** All fields and records in the table are a fixed width; if the data is not long enough to fill out that width, it is padded with blank spaces. Thus, Visual FoxPro can tell where new

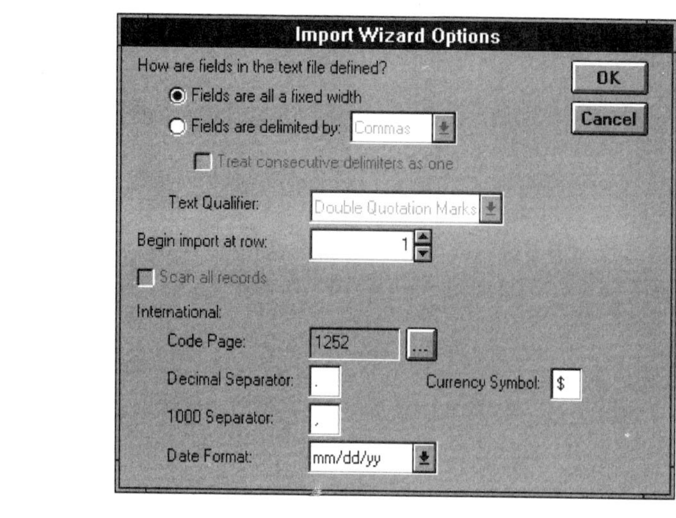

FIGURE 22.3

The Import Wizard Options dialog box

fields and new records begin by counting the number of characters from the beginning of the file.

- **Delimited files:** Fields are separated by some delimiter, such as a comma, and new records begin on a new line, so Visual FoxPro can use these delimiters to tell where new fields and records begin. In addition, text fields are enclosed in some delimiter, such as quotation marks.

Which of these types you are importing depends on the source of the text file, which was probably exported by some other database management program.

By default, Visual FoxPro imports fixed-width text files. To import a delimited file, select the Fields Are Delimited By radio button of the Import Wizard dialog box, use the drop-down list to its right to specify the character that is used as a delimiter between fields (comma is the default), and use the Text Qualifier list to specify the character used to delimit the data in text fields (double quotation mark is the default).

These controls are available only if you are importing a text file, since all other file types are spreadsheets or database tables, which have fixed-width fields.

Options for Database and Spreadsheet Files The Begin Import At Row control of the Import Wizard Options dialog box is particularly useful when you are importing a spreadsheet. Often, a spreadsheet used to hold data will have descriptive names at the top of each column, and will begin listing the data in these columns in its third or fourth row. Use this control to specify the row where the data begins. When it imports data from a spreadsheet, Visual FoxPro always treats the rows as records and the columns as fields.

The controls in the International section of the Import Wizard dialog box are useful if the source file uses formats for numbers, currency, or dates that are different from your standard formats.

When you finish making selections in this dialog box and return to Import Wizard, look at the Preview window to see if there are any problems that need to be corrected.

Controlling Field Settings

The Field Settings step of the Import Wizard, shown in Figure 22.4, lets you control the definition of the table you're importing the data into. Click any column in the preview window to select it, and then use the controls above it to change the name, data type, and (if they apply to that data type) the width and number of decimal places in that field. The options that are available are the same as those available in the Table Designer, described in Chapter 2. This step is most useful to name fields, which are given names such as Column1 and Column 2 by default.

▸▸ **WARNING**

As when you modify the structure of a table that already has data in it, you will lose data if you change specifications in inappropriate ways in the Import Wizard. For example, imported data will be truncated if you make a field too narrow to hold it, and character data in a column will be lost if you change that column to numeric type.

FIGURE 22.4

The Field Settings step

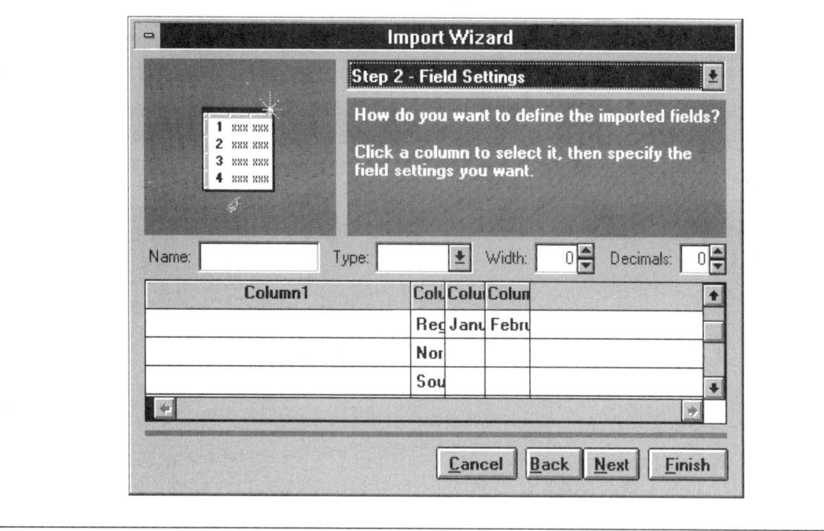

Importing the Data

Click the Finish button in the final step of the Wizard to import the data. After the new table is created, you can use the usual methods to work with it or modify it.

▶ The Import and Export Dialog Boxes

If you do not need to use the Import Wizard to control how data is imported, you can simply use the Import dialog box to specify the file to import and the FoxPro table to import it into. Choose File ➤ Import to display the Import dialog box, shown in Figure 22.5.

Use the Type drop-down list to specify the type of file that you are importing from, such as a FoxPro table, Delimited Text file, Microsoft Excel spreadsheet, and so on; file types were described in the section on the Import Wizard above. Then click the button to the right of the From text box and use the Open dialog box to select the file that the data is being imported from. Click the button to the right of the To text box and use the Save As dialog box to specify the file that the data will be appended to.

To export data, choose File ➤ Export to display the Export dialog box, shown in Figure 22.6. As you can see, this dialog box works like the

FIGURE 22.5

The Import dialog box

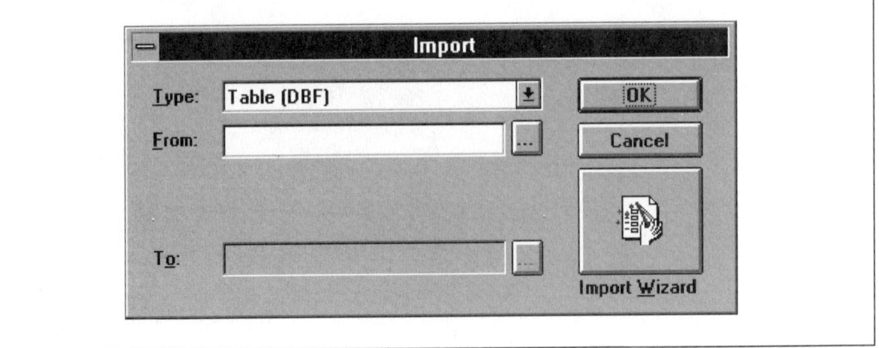

Import dialog box. Use the To control to specify the Excel spreadsheet (for example) where you'll be sending the data, either by typing its drive\directory path in the text box or by clicking the ... button to display a dialog box where you can select the file.

FIGURE 22.6

The Export dialog box

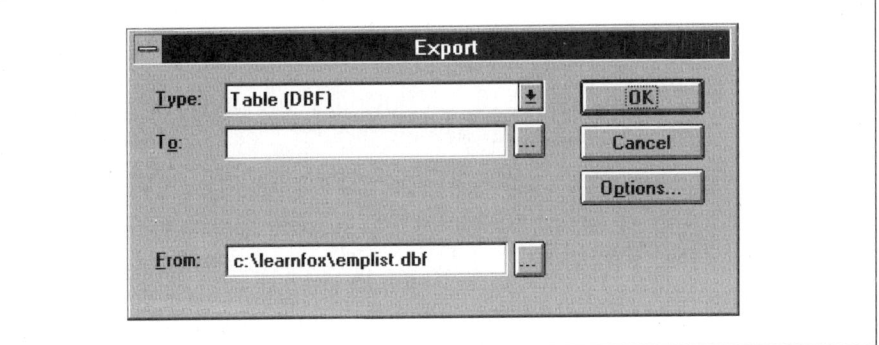

You can also click its Options button to display the Export Options dialog box, shown in Figure 22.7. Use the buttons in this dialog box to add a Scope, FOR, WHILE, or FIELDS clause that determines which records or fields of the FoxPro table are exported. These clauses were covered in Chapter 11.

There is no need for an Export Wizard, because it is easy to create the new files that you specify. There is no need to customize field definitions or to specify which rows of a spreadsheet to use, as there sometimes is when you import data. If you export to a spreadsheet application, for example, Visual FoxPro will create a new spreadsheet to hold the data. Its columns will be equivalent to the fields and its rows will be equivalent to the records of the table whose data you are exporting.

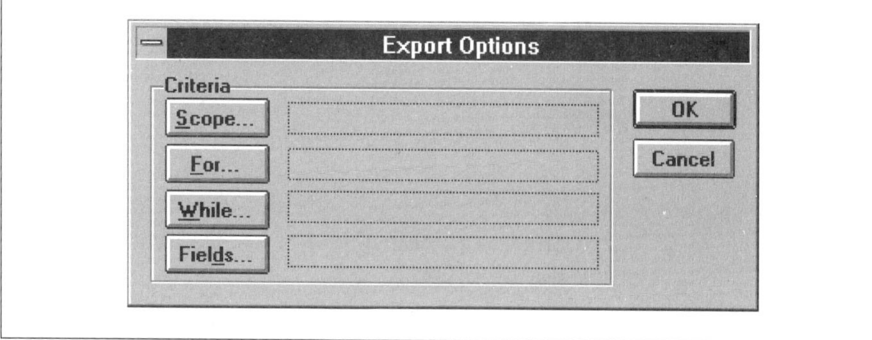

FIGURE 22.7

The Export Options dialog box

▶ Importing and Exporting via the Command Window

Use the following commands to import or export data:

- **IMPORT:** Imports data from a different file type and creates a new Visual FoxPro table.
- **APPEND FROM:** Adds records to an existing Visual FoxPro table, either from another Visual FoxPro table or from a different file type.
- **EXPORT:** Copies data from a Visual FoxPro table to a different file type.
- **COPY TO:** Copies data from a Visual FoxPro table either to a new Visual FoxPro table or to another file type.

These commands are all covered in Appendix B.

▶▶ Editing Text

So far, you have just used the standard Windows editing features to work with text in Visual FoxPro. These techniques are sufficient for most text editing that you need to do–for example, for entering data in tables or adding text to reports. However, Visual FoxPro also has other features that are useful in working with text files, with long memo fields, with reports, and the like. This section covers all the features of Visual FoxPro that you need for editing text.

▸ Creating a Text or Program File

You can choose File ➤ New to create ordinary text files and to create program files, as you use it to create other files in Visual FoxPro. Select the Text File or Program radio buttons of the New dialog box and click the New button. Visual FoxPro opens a window with a name such as File1 or Program1. Simply type the text or the program into the window that is opened. You can use the Save As dialog box to name the file the first time you save it.

You can also create text or program files from the Command window by entering **MODIFY FILE <filename>** or **MODIFY COMMAND <filename>**.

▸▸ NOTE

Unlike most files that you create selecting File ➤ New, text and program files are not created using a command that begins with CREATE. Instead, the command beginning with MODIFY both modifies and creates these files, modifying a file if a file with the name that is specified already exists, or creating a new file if it does not.

The difference between text and program files is in the default editing settings they use. The major difference is that the default setting for text files includes the word-wrap feature, which automatically moves the cursor to the next line when you get to the right margin. Since program files must keep each command on a line of its own, when you're creating a program word wrap is turned off by default. These and other editing preferences are discussed later in the chapter.

▸ The Edit Menu

You should already know the basic features of the Edit menu, which are common to many Windows applications:

- Choose Edit ➤ Undo or click the Undo tool to undo the last change you made.

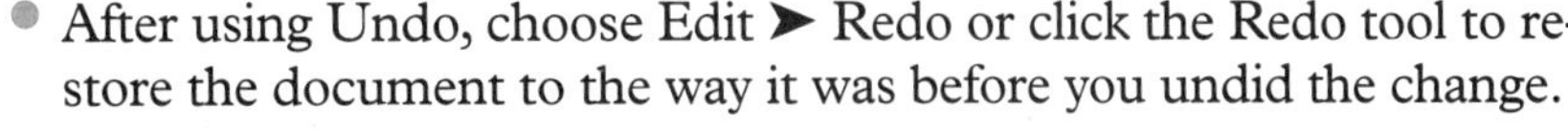

- After using Undo, choose Edit ➤ Redo or click the Redo tool to restore the document to the way it was before you undid the change.

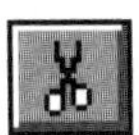

- Choose Edit ➤ Cut or click the Cut tool to remove text (or another control) from its current location and place it on the Clipboard.

- Choose Edit ➤ Copy or click the Copy tool to leave text (or another control) in its current location and place a copy of it on the Clipboard.

- Choose Edit ➤ Paste or click the Paste tool to place the text (or control) that is currently on the Clipboard in the current location of the cursor.

You can also use these commands to cut (or copy) and paste text (and other controls) among different Windows applications.

TIP

if you are moving text a short distance within a document, it is quicker to drag and drop than to cut and paste. After selecting the text you want to move, simply click anywhere on the selected text. Hold down the mouse button and drag the cursor to any other location to place the text at that location.

As a shortcut, you can choose Edit ➤ Select All to mark (or select) all the text in the document.

After these simple features, the Edit menu includes a group of useful features that let you search for specific words, do search-and-replace operations, and move around the document.

The final group of features on the Edit menu is used for working with OLE Objects, so they are covered in the section on Object Linking and Embedding later in this chapter.

Find

Selecting Edit ➤ Find displays the Find dialog box, shown in Figure 22.8. The items in this dialog box let you search for text—a word, several words, or just a few letters—in the current document.

FIGURE 22.8

The Find dialog box

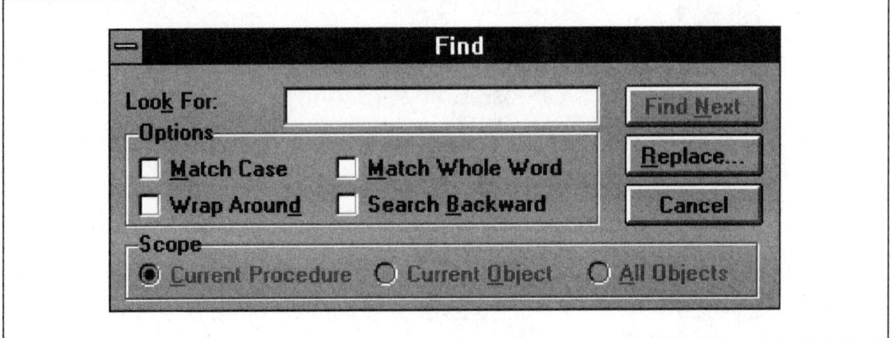

TIP

You can also use Find to search for text in the Browse window, for example, as a quick way to search for a person's name. However, if you are using a large table, Find is slow, and you'll find it is better to use the indexed searches covered in Chapter 11.

Just type the text you are searching for in the Look For text box and click the Find Next button. Continue to click Find Next until you have found the occurrence of the text that you are looking for, and then close the Find dialog box.

You can search for control characters by using the following symbols:

- \r to stand for carriage return
- \t to stand for tab
- \n to search for the new line character
- \\ to search for the backslash

Type these special characters in the Look For text box, along with any other text. For example, type **\n\tThe** to find the word *The* at the beginning of a paragraph (where it follows a new line and a tab).

As you can see, this dialog box includes four check boxes:

- **Match Case:** If you check this, the search takes into account differences in capitalization. By default, the search ignores capitalization: for example, if you search for *HELLO,* it will find not only *HELLO* but also *Hello, hello,* and so on, unless you select this option.
- **Match Whole Word:** If you check this, the search looks for an exact match only. It will not find a word that has the word you are looking for embedded in it. For example, if you search for *top,* it will not find *stop* or *estoppel*.
- **Wrap Around:** If you check this, the search looks from the location of the cursor to the end of the file and then "wraps around" and continues the search at the beginning of the file. This option lets you search through the entire file without first moving to the beginning of the file.
- **Search Backward:** If you check this, the search begins at the current cursor location and continues upward toward the beginning of the file. Use it to find the previous occurrence of the text, rather than the next occurrence, which is found by default.

The Scope options are useful in programming, to restrict the search to a single procedure or control.

Replacing Text

If you want to replace the text you are searching for with some other text, click the Replace button to display the Find dialog box in the expanded form shown in Figure 22.9. Type the new text in the Replace With text box. Then you can either:

- Click Find Next to find the next occurrence of the text; then click Replace to replace it. When you replace text in this way, the editor automatically finds the next occurrence of the same text, so you can simply click Replace again to continue replacing text. You can click Find Next to look for the next occurrence of the text without replacing the currently found occurrence.

- Click Replace All to replace all occurrences of the text in the document. This can lead to unexpected results, and it is best to save the document before doing it. Then, if the replacement does not do what you expected, you can close the file without saving the changes.

FIGURE 22.9

The expanded Find dialog box

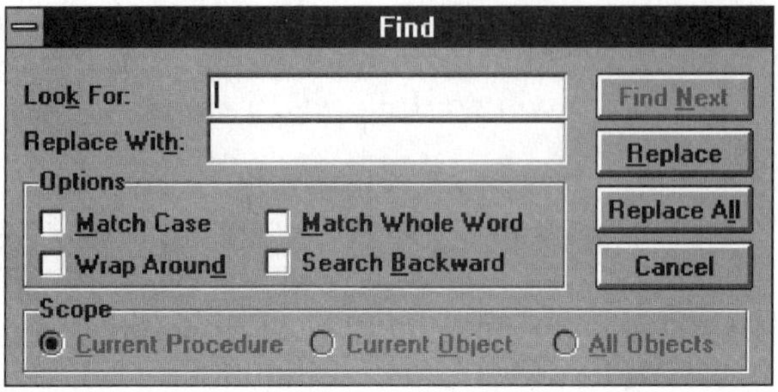

Goto Line

Choose Edit ➤ Goto Line to display the Goto Line dialog box. This dialog box lets you move the cursor to any line in the document if you know its line number. It simply includes a text box and spinner control which you can use to enter the line number.

This option is disabled when word wrap is on because then the number of lines depends on the size of the Edit window. It is most useful if you are editing programs.

▸ The Format Menu

You can also use the Format menu to control the font, spacing, and indentation of a text file.

The Font Dialog Box

Select Format ➤ Font to display the Font dialog box, shown in Figure 22.10, which is common to many Windows applications and is very easy to use. Simply select a typeface from the Font list, a point size from the Size list, and (if desired) Bold, Italic, or Bold Italic from the Font Style list. All text in the file will be displayed in this font.

Choose Format ➤ Enlarge Font or Format ➤ Reduce Font to enlarge or reduce the size of all the text in the file by one point.

FIGURE 22.10

Font dialog box

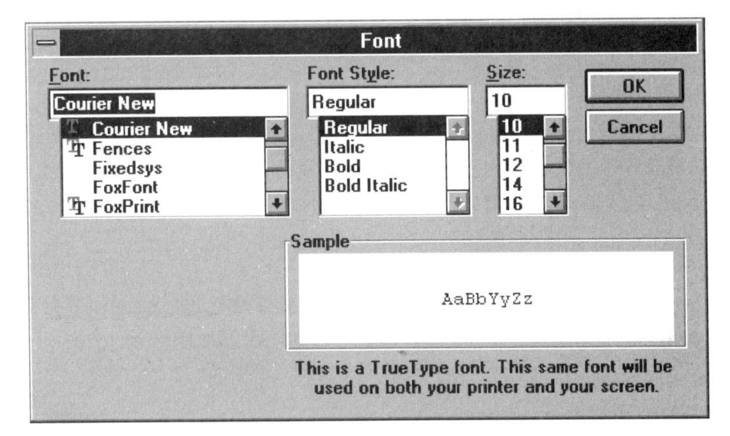

TIP

You can also change the font of the Visual FoxPro main window (application window). If you press Shift when you use the text menu, its first selection will be Screen Font rather than Font. Select Screen Font to display the Font dialog box. Any text that scrolls through the main Visual FoxPro window (for example, the text displayed when you use a LIST command) will be in the font you select. Visual FoxPro comes with fonts of its own, FoxFont and FoxPro Windows Font. These are included to allow FoxPro for DOS applications to run in Visual FoxPro for Windows without any changes.

Line Spacing

Choose Format ➤ Single Space, Format ➤ $1\frac{1}{2}$ Space, or Format ➤ Double Space to specify the line spacing of the text in the document.

Indentation

Choose Format ➤ Indent or Format ➤ Remove Indent to add or remove a Tab character at the beginning of the current line or all selected lines. You can use these menu options repeatedly to add or remove multiple tabs.

These options are useful primarily in programming, where you need to control the indentation of multiple lines of text.

► The Spelling Tool

The Spelling tool can be useful for text files, memo fields, or program files.

To check the spelling of the file in the current window, simply select Tools ➤ Spelling. Visual FoxPro begins checking spelling at the current location of the cursor. When it reaches the end of the document, it asks if it should continue at the beginning until the entire document has been checked.

If Visual FoxPro finds an error—a word that is not in its dictionary—it displays the Spelling dialog box, shown in Figure 22.11. The word it could not find is displayed at the top of the dialog box, with the message Not in Dictionary. A list of suggested corrections for this word is in the Suggestions scrollable list. The item highlighted in this list (the first item in the list by default) is displayed in the Change To text box.

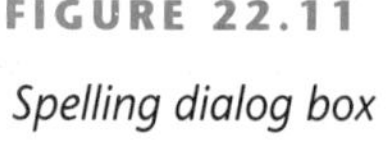

FIGURE 22.11

Spelling dialog box

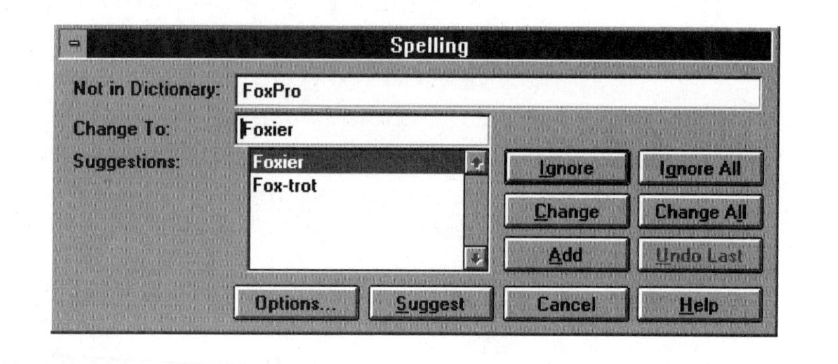

To correct an error, enter the correct spelling in the Change To text box: either select it from the list (if it is not initially selected) or type it in the text box to replace the suggested spelling. Once the correct spelling is in the text box, select the Change pushbutton to correct this occurrence of the error or select the Change All pushbutton to correct every occurrence of the error.

If Visual FoxPro finds a word that is not in its dictionary but is spelled correctly, select the Ignore button to leave this current instance of it unchanged, or select the Ignore All pushbutton to leave all occurrences of this word as they are.

TIP

It is generally best to select Ignore All, so the Spelling tool does not stop for future occurrences of the same word in your current session.

You can also select the Add pushbutton to add the word to your dictionary so that the Spelling tool does not consider it an error in the rest of the session or in future sessions.

After you have used the Spelling tool to make a change, the Undo Last pushbutton is enabled, and you can select it to undo the change.

Click the Options button to display the Spelling Options dialog box, shown in Figure 22.12.

FIGURE 22.12

The Spelling Options dialog box

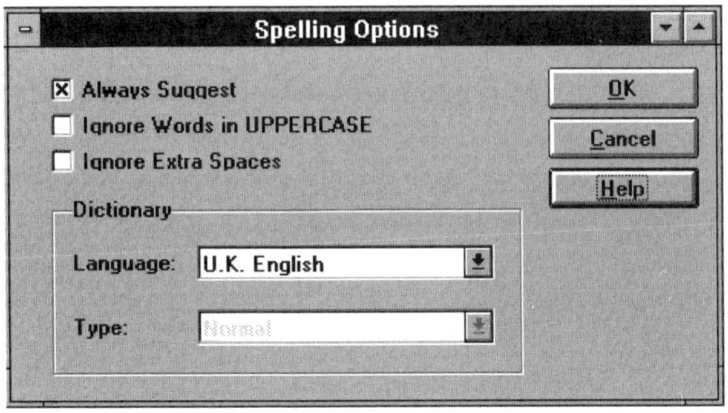

The Always Suggest check box of this dialog box is checked by default, so Visual FoxPro automatically suggests corrections when you make changes. If you remove the check from this box, Visual FoxPro suggests corrections only when you click the Suggest pushbutton; if your computer system is slow, you can save a significant amount of time by not having Visual FoxPro automatically make suggestions.

Select the Ignore Words in UPPERCASE check box to make the Spelling tool skip words that are in all uppercase, and the Ignore Extra Spaces check box to make the Spelling tool ignore multiple spaces. Both options are useful in checking program files. The Dictionary drop-down controls let you choose a dictionary for American or British spelling, and special dictionary types.

► Setting Editing Preferences

You can control many of Visual FoxPro's editing features by choosing Tools ➤ Options to display the Options dialog box and clicking its Edit tab to display the panel shown in Figure 22.13.

The default settings are different for text files, program files, and Memo fields, and are usually the settings you need for the type of text you are editing. Figure 22.13 shows the Edit panel for a program file.

For example, if you are creating a text file, you ordinarily want to have a word-wrap feature so the right margin automatically determines where to break a line without your having to keep track of where the margin is. If you are creating a program file, though, you need to keep each command on its own line and press Enter at the end of each command so Visual FoxPro knows when the command is complete, even if that means going beyond the visible right margin for some commands.

Likewise, if you are creating a text file, you want to press Tab to indent at the beginning of a paragraph without indenting the lines that follow. When you are writing a program, however, as you will learn in Chapter 23, it is common to indent multiple lines of code to align them with each other and make the program easier to read.

Visual FoxPro's defaults are set accordingly. If you create a new text file and use the Options dialog box, you will see that the Word Wrap check box of the Edit Panel is selected and its Automatic Indent check box is deselected. If you display this dialog box when you are editing a

FIGURE 22.13

The Edit panel of the Options dialog box

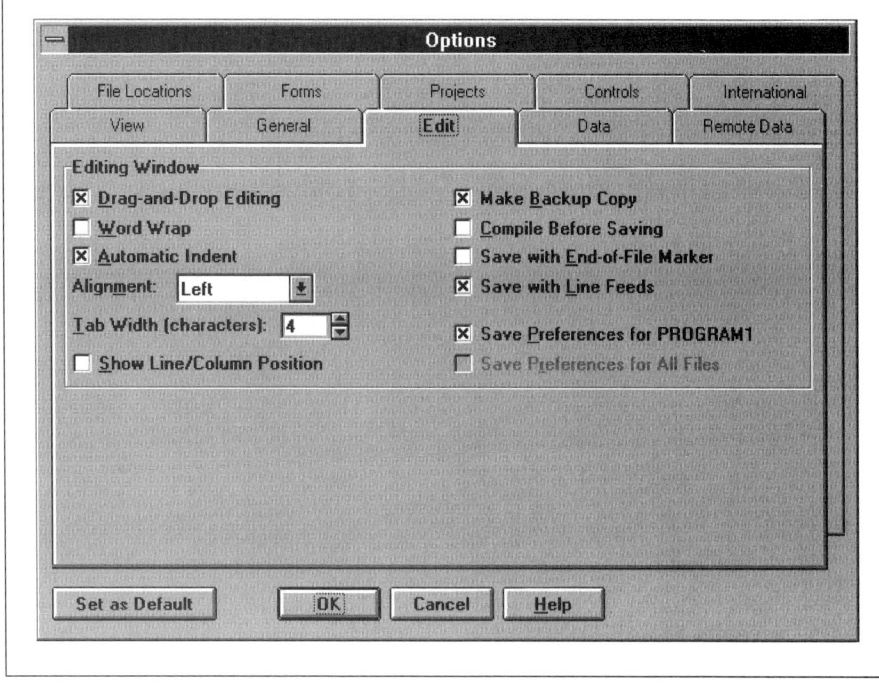

program file, you will find it has the opposite defaults. The options on this panel will not be enabled if you are not editing a file when you display it.

For details on using this panel box to control other editor options, see Chapter 19, which covers the entire Options dialog box.

▶▶ Object Linking and Embedding

Object Linking and Embedding (OLE) lets you include objects from one application in another. Visual FoxPro for Windows supports OLE only as a client; that is, you can include objects from other Windows programs in Visual FoxPro for Windows, but you cannot include objects from Visual FoxPro for Windows in other programs.

You can only add embedded objects from source applications that support OLE as a server. You can add linked objects from source applications that support OLE or dynamic data exchange (DDE).

As you have already learned, you can include OLE objects in a table in a field of the General data type. For example, you can include graphs from a spreadsheet or scanned photographs stored in a graphics program in your table by adding a General field and embedding the other program in it. You can also add OLE objects to report and form designs. For example, if you have your company logo in a drawing program, you can use it in your printed reports or your data entry forms.

► Linking versus Embedding

When you *link* an object, you access the original object through Visual FoxPro. Any changes made in the object in the source application are reflected in Visual FoxPro. If you link a graph from a spreadsheet application to Visual FoxPro for Windows, for example, and the data and graph change in the spreadsheet, the graphs will also change in Visual FoxPro. If you want to make a change, you must open the source application and use it in the usual way.

When you *embed* an object, you create a separate copy of the object, used by Visual FoxPro. Changes made in the source application are not reflected in Visual FoxPro, but you can access the document and change it directly from Visual FoxPro. If you embed a graph from a spreadsheet application, for example, changes you make in the spreadsheet are not reflected in Visual FoxPro. On the other hand, you can simply double-click the object in Visual FoxPro to display the original as a document of the spreadsheet application and change it. The changes you make apply only within Visual FoxPro and are not reflected in the object within the spreadsheet.

Because a linked object is stored by its original application, it can be lost if the table or source document is moved. An embedded object is stored in Visual FoxPro itself, so it can be moved easily with no danger of being lost. (If you move it to another system, however, it can be edited only if the new system also has the application it was created in.)

► Working with the General Data Type

Visual FoxPro for Windows supports OLE through the new General data type. This is similar to the Memo data type, except that it holds linked or embedded objects.

For example, Figure 22.14 shows a table designed to hold the chapters of this book. It consists of only two fields. The first field, Chap_num, is a Character field to hold the number of the chapter. The second, text, is a General field that holds the Word for Windows file with the text for that chapter. Notice that as with Memo fields, the General field has the word *Gen* in it as a place holder, with a capital *G* if data has been entered.

FIGURE 22.14

A table with a General field

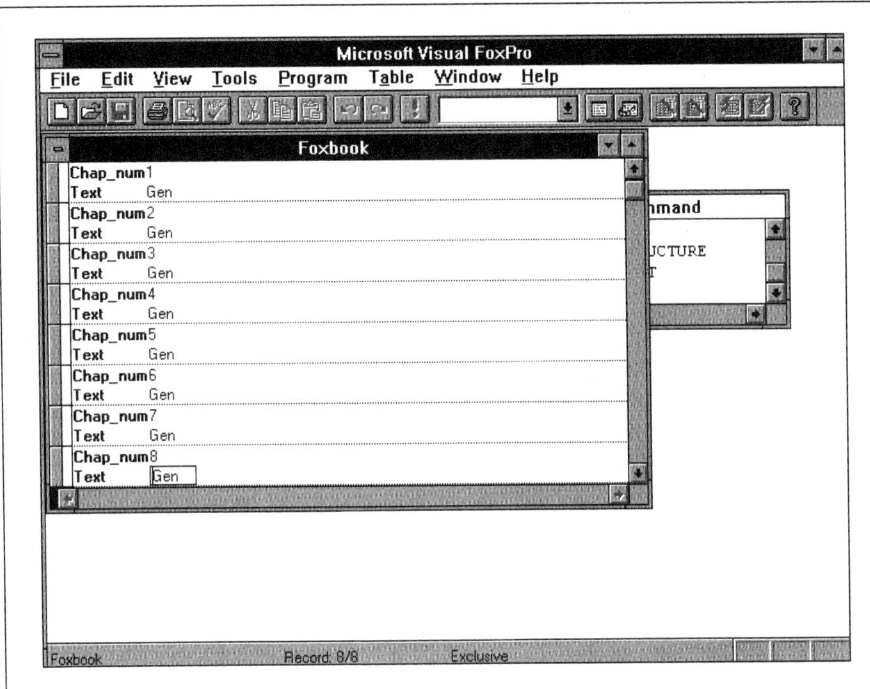

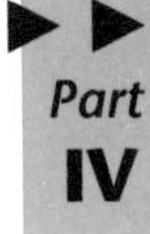

Viewing the Data in a General Field

View the data in the General field just as you do in a Memo field. Double-click it or move the highlight to it and press Ctrl+PgDn, and Visual FoxPro opens a window displaying the data in the General field, as shown in Figure 22.15. In the example, the data is represented by an icon that you can double-click to open Word for Windows and the Word document containing the text for that chapter.

To return to Visual FoxPro, close the window as you would a memo window, by pressing Esc, Ctrl+W, or Ctrl+Q or by selecting Close from the document's Control menu.

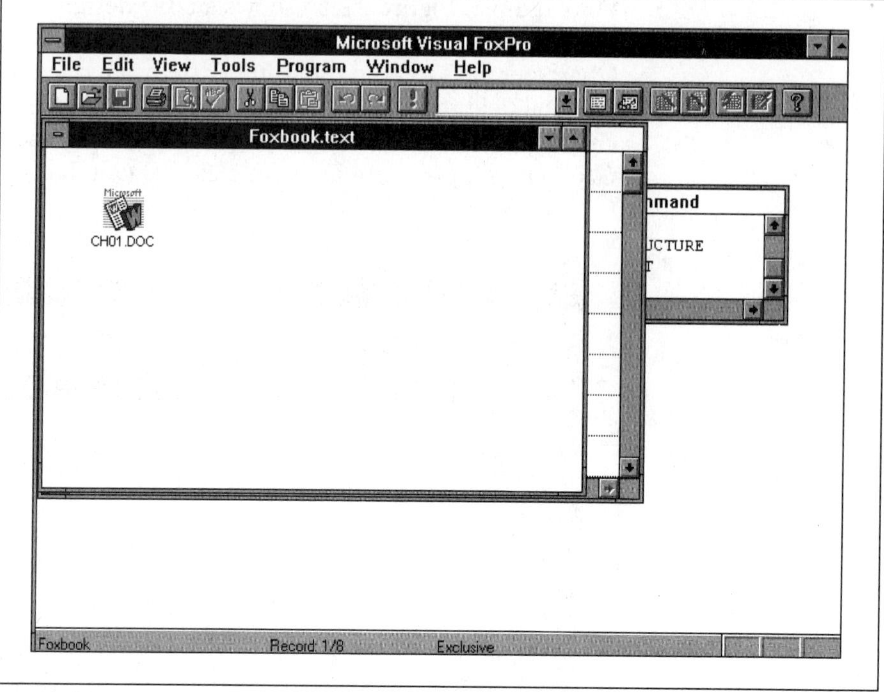

FIGURE 22.15

Viewing the contents of the General field

Editing the Object

If the data is embedded (rather than linked) in the Visual FoxPro General field, then after opening the General window, you can simply double-click it to open the source application and use it to edit the object.

When your other application opens, it displays a dialog box asking whether it should update Visual FoxPro to reflect the changes you made. If you select Yes, the image is displayed in the General window (and stored permanently in the General field) in this altered form.

Using Cut or Copy and Paste

If you have already created an object in another application, you can either link or embed it in a General field by using the Cut or Copy and Paste (or Paste Special) option.

First, select the object in the other application; then select either Cut or Copy from that application's Edit menu to place a copy of the object in the Windows Clipboard. Then switch to Visual FoxPro for Windows, open the General window of the record you want to store the object in, and select either Paste or Paste Special from Visual FoxPro's Edit menu.

- To embed the object, select Paste.
- To link the object, select Paste Special. When Visual FoxPro displays the Paste Special dialog box, select the Paste Link pushbutton.
- To paste the object without linking or embedding, select Paste Special. When Visual FoxPro displays the Paste Special dialog box, select the Paste pushbutton. You might do this if you were archiving data and never wanted the object to change.

Using the Insert Object Option

You can also create a new OLE object from within Visual FoxPro and embed it in a General field, or you can add an existing object to a Visual FoxPro general field, by first opening the General window and then choosing Edit ➤ Insert Object to display the Insert Object dialog box.

By default, the Create New radio button of the Insert Object dialog box is selected, and the dialog box is displayed in the form shown in Figure 22.16. Use this dialog box to select from among the Windows applications you have available. Then select OK to open the application, and use it to create the OLE object.

Select the Create From File radio button of the Insert Object dialog box to display the dialog box in the form shown in Figure 22.17. Enter the name of the existing file that you want to add as an OLE Object, or click the Browse button to display a dialog box that is similar to the Open dialog box, which you can use to select the file. Select the Link check box to add it as a linked rather than an embedded object.

Drag and Drop between Applications

Finally, you can also embed an OLE object in Visual FoxPro simply by dragging it from its source application. You must display both applications on the screen at the same time, before beginning the drag-and-drop operation.

By default, drag-and-drop is equivalent to copy-and-paste. However, you can also hold the Ctrl key while dragging to cut the object out of the source application and paste it into Visual FoxPro. In either case, the object is embedded, not linked.

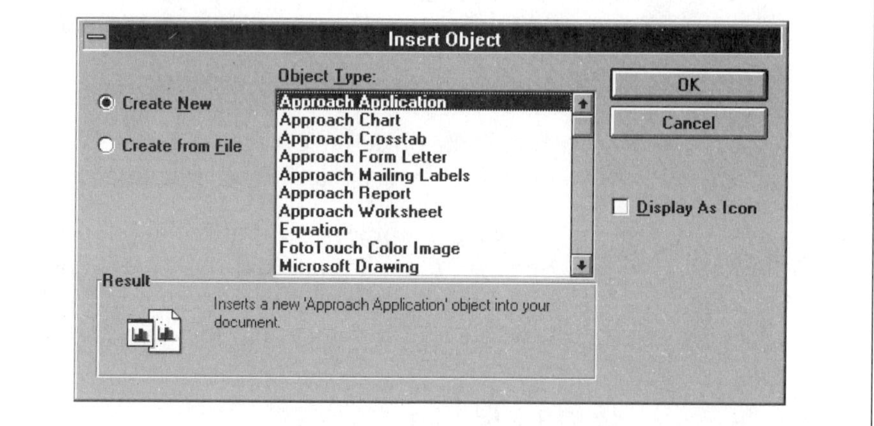

FIGURE 22.16

Using the Insert Object dialog box to create a new object

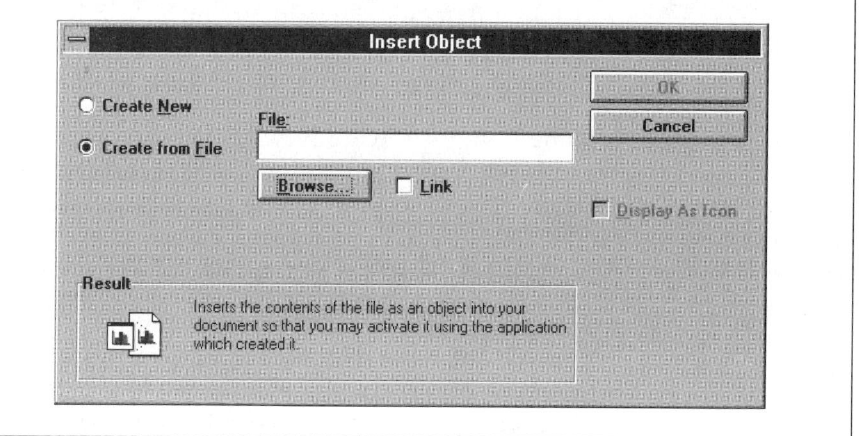

FIGURE 22.17

Using the Insert Object dialog box to add an existing object

▸▸ **WARNING**

Error messages are not always displayed when you drag and drop an OLE object. It is possible to drag an object onto an existing OLE object and overwrite it without Visual FoxPro displaying any warning. To avoid data loss, you must be particularly careful where you place the new OLE object.

Special Features of the Edit Menu

The Edit menu of Visual FoxPro for Windows has a few options designed to help you work with OLE objects. You have already looked at Paste Special and Insert Object, both of which (along with Paste) let you add OLE objects to General fields.

The following options of the Edit menu let you work with objects you have added to General fields:

- **Change Link:** Relinks a General field to the file it comes from. This option can be used if the link is broken because you have renamed or moved the linked file.
- **Convert to Static:** Makes it impossible to edit an embedded or linked object. Using this option converts linked objects to embedded objects, and they cannot be changed back to linked objects.
- **Object:** This option changes to indicate the type of the object when you display a field containing a sound or audio-visual object in a General field; for example, it may change to Sound Object. Select it to activate the object.

To Sum Up

This chapter concludes Part IV of this book, which covers the major Visual FoxPro power tools that you can use to make your work easier or more powerful. Part V is an introduction to programming and developing applications with Visual FoxPro.

Programming and Developing Applications

PART FIVE

CHAPTER 23

Getting Started with Programming

FAST TRACK

To execute one of two blocks of code, 696

use the command **IF <logical exp>** followed by one block of code, followed by the keyword **ELSE**, followed by the second block of code, followed by **ENDIF**. If the logical expression is true, the first block of code is executed. If it is not true, the second block is executed. (You can also use IF <logical exp> followed by a block of code, followed by ENDIF. If the logical expression is true, the code is executed; if it is not true, nothing is done.)

To execute one of many blocks of code, 698

use the **DO CASE** … **ENDCASE** command. Between these two lines of code, you can use the statement **CASE <logical exp>** followed by a block of code any number of times. Visual FoxPro executes the code following the first CASE whose logical expression is true. You can also add OTHERWISE followed by a block of code after the final CASE, and this code will be executed if none of the CASE statements are true.

To pass the value of a variable to a user-defined function, 707

put the value in the parentheses of the function, just as you do when you are using one of Visual FoxPro's ordinary functions. The user-defined function must begin with the command **FUNCTION <function name>** or **PROCEDURE <procedure name>**. The line of code immediately after its name must use the command **PARAMETER <memvar list>**. The expressions you include in its parentheses when you call this function are assigned to the memory variables in order.

This chapter is a general introduction to procedural programming in Visual FoxPro. It will teach you simple commands used to interact with the user and to organize the flow of a program. At the same time, it will use these commands to teach you the basic principles of procedural programming that are useful for people who use Visual FoxPro to manipulate their own data. This chapter begins with a thorough introduction to procedural programming in Visual FoxPro, and then goes on to show you how to develop a utility program that you might actually want to use in working with your own data.

An Overview of Programming and Development

Before you begin programming, you should understand the two major types of programming and development that Visual FoxPro supports. Early versions of FoxPro and of other Xbase languages were *procedural* programming languages. Now, Visual FoxPro still supports procedural programming, as it always has, but it also supports *object-oriented* programming and development.

To understand the difference between these two types of programming, you should look briefly at how programming developed.

Machine Language

The earliest computers were programmed in *machine language*: The programs were lists of binary codes made up of ones and zeros. The central processing unit of every computer has a built-in *instruction set;* that is, it has ways of manipulating data that are wired into the processor.

Each of these circuits is activated by a binary code; and in order to write programs, the earliest programmers actually had to learn all these codes and what they did in a particular type of computer.

▶ Assembly Language

Before long, computer scientists devised the idea of using English-like words to symbolize these codes. You could write programs made up of these words and use a special program to translate each of these words into machine code. A computer can do this sort of translation very easily. When it sees the word ADD or MOV, the computer replaces that word with the binary code that tells the central processing unit to add two numbers or to move data. *Assembly language,* which is still used in some cases to improve performance, is this sort of language, and the program used to translate each word into binary code is called an *assembler.*

Both of these early forms of programming language were based on how the hardware works, not on how people think, and using them required rigorous technical training.

▶ High-Level Languages

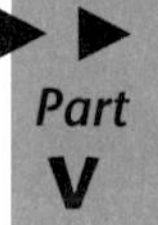

During the 1950s and 1960s, as businesses began to computerize, it became apparent that it would be impossible to get enough programmers with the technical knowledge needed to write programs in assembly language. Computer scientists began to develop what were known as *high-level languages,* which were designed to be easy to learn and understand. It became possible for businesses to hire people who had never used computers, train them for a few months, and then start them working as programmers.

The best known of the early high-level languages were COBOL and BASIC. The earliest versions of these languages, however, often led programmers to create long, unwieldy programs, which were difficult to understand; their complexity made it difficult to debug them (to find and correct errors) and to maintain them (to add new features as the user demanded them).

The next high-level languages, such as Pascal, were designed to encourage *structured programming.* They made it easy to break complicated programs into smaller procedures, each of which was easy to understand, and each of which could be debugged individually.

A bit later, high-level languages were designed for special purposes, such as database development. Rather than requiring the programmer to design and index files to look up records quickly, for example, these languages might have a built-in INDEX command.

Notice that all of these developments were meant to make the programmer's job easier. Early Xbase was a structured programming language with built-in commands for manipulating data, which made it one of the easiest languages to learn and work with.

Today, however, programmers have switched to *event-driven* and *object-oriented* programming in order to develop applications under the Windows or Macintosh interface. Earlier developments were meant to make the programmer's work easier, but these new developments are meant to make the programs easier for their users, and they make programming harder in some ways.

Procedural programming always let users do only one thing at a time. Early DOS Xbase programs, for example, displayed a menu with four or five choices. Once you selected one, the program might have displayed a data entry screen. After you were done entering data, you had to close that screen and return to the menu. There were always a limited number of choices available, and the programmer foresaw every possible situation.

By contrast, a Windows program lets you open several windows and use the menu system at the same time; or it displays a dialog box with a dozen different controls that you can use. The program is *event-driven*, because it waits for an event such as a mouse click or a keystroke, which tells it which of its features should be active.

It is impossible to foresee every possible combination of features that can be used at the same time. Instead, each feature is treated as a separate *object*, and it has code encapsulated in it and is isolated from the rest of the program. Programming is described as object-oriented when it focuses on designing these objects.

Visual FoxPro still has all the older commands that let you do procedural programming, as well as new commands that make it an object-oriented language. This chapter will focus on procedural programming, which makes it easy to write the sort of utility programs that you will need to manipulate your own data. The solid background in procedural programming that you get here will also be a useful foundation if you want to go on to more advanced books that cover object-oriented programming.

▶▶ Some Preliminary Details

In the next section, as you learn FoxPro programming commands, you will write brief sample programs to try them out. First, though, you will look at a few preliminary details you must know before you begin.

▶ Creating Program Files

A program in Visual FoxPro is simply a plain ASCII text file, which you can create with most text editors and word processors.

The easiest way of creating a program is by using the Visual FoxPro editor. Select File ➤ New and then select the Program radio button (or enter the command **MODIFY COMMAND <file name>**) to create a new program file.

Programs you create in this way have the extension PRG, but you will see in later chapters that you can also create programs with other extensions.

▶ Running the Program

As you learned in Chapter 5, you can run the program at any time by selecting Do from the program menu and using the Do dialog box to select a program. This dialog box works just like the Open dialog box.

Alternatively, enter the command **DO <file name>**. If you use this command and do not include the extension with the file name, Visual FoxPro assumes it has a PRG extension. You must include the extension to run a program that has any other extension.

▶ Making the Program More Readable

Look at a few requirements of how the program must be laid out visually, so you can see how to make it most readable.

The New Line Delimiter

Visual FoxPro and other Xbase languages require you to include a new line at the end of each line of programming code. The new line is the delimiter that lets Visual FoxPro know where a single command begins and ends. For this reason, you cannot use an editor with a word-wrap feature that breaks up a line when it reaches the right margin. Instead, you can simply keep typing the code beyond the right margin. If you select File ➤ New and then select the Program radio button (or if you enter the command **MODIFY COMMAND <file name>**), the Visual FoxPro editor will have its word-wrap feature turned off so you can type code beyond the right margin.

If you want to be able to read your code more easily, without its going beyond the right margin, you can break a long line in two by adding a semicolon (;) at the end of the first line. This makes Visual FoxPro ignore the new line and read the two lines as a single command. Of course, the listings in this book use the semicolon to fit the command within the width of the printed page. When you see this character, you can either type the code as it is in the printed listing or leave out the semicolon and continue typing the code on a single line.

▸▸ **NOTE**

You cannot use a semicolon within a character string to divide it between two lines. If you need a line break within a character string, you must break the string into two strings, each enclosed in quotation marks and concatenated using a plus sign (+). Use the semicolon after the first string and place the + and second string on the second line.

Blank Spaces

Visual FoxPro ignores extra blank spaces. You can skip lines and add extra blank spaces or tabs whenever you think doing so will make the program easier to read. When you break a line in two using the ; character, for example, it is a good idea to indent the second line to make it clear that it is a continuation of the same command. Likewise, as you will see, indentation is very important to make programs more readable, particularly when you are using the methods of control flow covered in later sections of this chapter.

Comments

Programs should also contain comments, which are not used by the program itself but are meant to make it easier for people to understand.

Visual FoxPro includes three commands that let you add comments. You can use either an asterisk (*) or the word NOTE at the beginning of a line, and Visual FoxPro will ignore everything on that line. Using an asterisk at the beginning of the line is the most common way of adding comments. It is also a good idea to add a few hyphens after the asterisk; although they are not required, they make the comments stand out so they are easier to follow.

The symbol && is used to add comments to the right of your programming code (rather than on a separate line). You can use this double ampersand anywhere in the line. Visual FoxPro executes the command to its left and ignores only the text that comes to its right.

Why add comments? Programs are often difficult to follow when you come back to one after not working with it for a long time. The logic that seemed so obvious when you were writing the program suddenly seems mysterious; it is hard to figure out what you were doing. For this reason, it is a good idea to write a comment before each major activity the program performs, saying what the program is about to do.

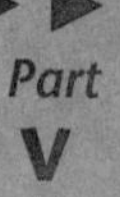

▶ Stopping a Program

You can stop a program from running by pressing Esc. When you do this, Visual FoxPro displays an alert that gives you three choices:

- **Cancel:** Stops execution of the program permanently. This is the default choice.
- **Suspend:** Stops execution of the program temporarily and returns you to the Command window. You can start the program again from the point where you left off by selecting Program ➤ Resume or by entering the command **RESUME**.
- **Ignore:** Ignores the fact that you pressed Esc and continues execution of the program.

▸▸ NOTE

The command SET ESCAPE OFF disables the Esc key so that you cannot use it to stop a program. You can include this command at the beginning of a program you have created, to keep the user under your control at all times, but you should add it at the very end of your own programming and debugging work so you can use the Esc key yourself.

If there is an error in your program, Visual FoxPro displays an alert with the same choices plus an error message. It also displays the line in the code that contains the error and lets you edit it, as you will see when you test the first program.

▸▸ Talking to the User: Input/Output

One basic element of any programming language is input/output—the commands the program uses to communicate with the user. In event-driven programming, much input is handled using the mouse; the user just has to click a button or make a choice from a list. The Visual Fox-Pro Form Designer automatically handles mouse support. Here, you will learn some simpler forms of input/output that are still available and useful in Visual FoxPro.

▸ Variables

Input/output commands are commonly used in connection with variables, which are used to store the user's input so it can be used later in the program.

The names of the fields in a table are variables because their values change as you move from record to record. If you enter the command **? STATE**, for example, the letters that Visual FoxPro prints can change depending on which record the pointer is on.

The values of the fields in your tables are stored permanently when you quit Visual FoxPro. But Visual FoxPro also lets you create temporary variables that are lost when you quit the program. Unlike table files, these variables are not stored on disk. They are just kept in your computer's memory, so they are called memory variables. It is conventional to give memory variables names beginning with the letter *M*. As you will see in later examples, memory variables are used as counters, to store input from the user, and for many other purposes in programming.

Creating Memory Variables

You can create a memory variable from the Command window and assign it a value by using this command:

```
STORE <value> TO <variable name>
```

or this command:

```
<variable name> = <value>
```

The equal sign in the second version of the command should not be confused with the = operator that is used for comparison in logical expressions. In this case it actually creates the variable and assigns the value to it, so it should be read as *let variable name equal value.*

You can use either of these commands to change the value of an existing memory variable as well as to create a new one.

In the following short exercise you will create and print a couple of different variables. When you print the variable, the number includes leading blanks. As you learned in Chapter 9, you can control its width and number of decimal places by using the STR( ) function.

1. If necessary, close open windows and enter **CLEAR** in the Command window to clear the screen.
2. Enter **STORE 20 TO MVAR1**.
3. Enter **? MVAR1**, and Visual FoxPro prints `20`.
4. Enter **MVAR2 = 10**. Then enter **? MVAR2**, and Visual FoxPro prints `10`.
5. Try changing the value of an existing variable. Enter **MVAR1 = 23**. Then enter **? MVAR1**, and Visual FoxPro prints `25`.

6. You can also perform calculations using memory variables. Enter **? MVAR1 – MVAR2**, and Visual FoxPro prints 15. Enter

```
? (MVAR1 * 2) - (MVAR2/2)
```

and Visual FoxPro prints 45.00, as shown in Figure 23.1.

FIGURE 23.1

Using memory variables

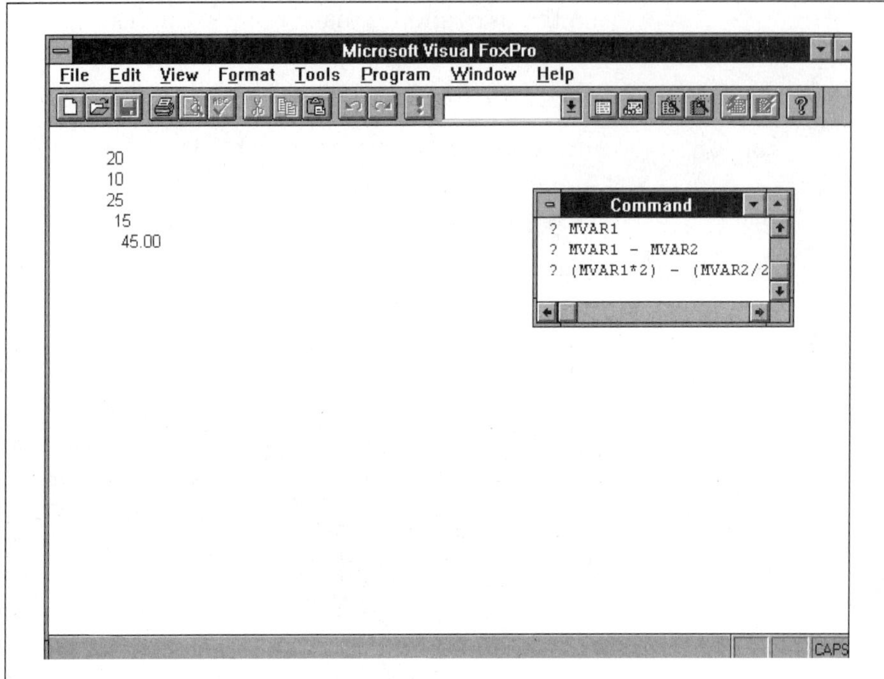

The data type of a memory variable depends on the delimiters you use when you create the variable. For example, the command MVAR3 = "HELLO" would create a memory variable of the Character type with the word *HELLO*. Table 23.1 summarizes which delimiters you can use to create memory variables; notice that not all data types available for fields can be used for variables.

Arrays

Visual FoxPro also lets you create a special type of memory variable called an *array*, which lets you have a number of memory variables that have the same name and are distinguished by an index number.

TABLE 23.1: *Data Types for Memory Variables*

Data Type	Description	Use of Delimiters	Example
Character	text from 1 to 254 characters	"text", 'text', or [text]	m_text = "hello"
Currency	amounts of money	$number	m_money = $500
Date	dates	{date}	m_date = {01/01/96}
DateTime	dates plus times	{date time}	m_datetime = {10/01/96 11:00am}
Logical	true of false	.T. or .F.	m_yesno = .T.
Numeric	numbers	number used with no delimiter	m_num = 100

For example, you might use variables with the names *m_var[1], m_var[2], m_var[3],* and so on. These are often convenient to use because you can refer to them all in just a few lines of code by using a variable as the index number. For example, if you created a numeric variable named *m_cntr,* you could refer to all the variables above as *m_var[m_cntr]* by assigning *m_cntr* the values 1, 2, 3, and so on, making it easy to reference an entire list of items held in the m_var array.

Arrays are not used in the exercises in this book, but they are mentioned here because they are a common feature of programming languages that you may find useful in your work. For more information on arrays, see either DECLARE or DIMENSION in Appendix B; you can use either of these commands to create an array.

NOTE

The index numbers of arrays can be enclosed in either square brackets or parentheses. Visual FoxPro supports both one- and two-dimensional arrays.

▸ Simple Output with the ? Command

You have already used the most important of the simple output commands. The ? command displays text in the Visual FoxPro main window on a new line.

▸▸ NOTE

If your program includes user-defined windows, this command will display output to the currently active user-defined window, if one is active.

If there is no room for the new line on the screen, the text already there scrolls up to make room for it. Thus, ? is sometimes used without any character expression following it, to print a blank line in order to skip a line.

You also learned the ?? command, which prints a line of text to the screen without printing a ↵ first.

Any text that scrolls by in this way is unformatted output. For example, you have seen that the LIST command works in this way.

You can also send unformatted output to the printer, as you know, by adding TO PRINT at the end of certain commands—for example, LIST TO PRINT. If you want to send unformatted output to the printer and the command you are using cannot take the clause TO PRINT, you can use the command SET PRINT ON before entering it.

Making the Computer Beep

One other important use of ? in programming is to make the computer beep in case the user makes an invalid entry or some other error. You can use the command ? to print any ASCII character, and the beep happens to be ASCII character number 7. Thus, the command **? CHR(7)** makes the computer beep.

Suppressing Screen Output

Finally, there are times in programs when you do not want output displayed on the screen. To suppress the screen display, you can use the command **SET CONSOLE OFF**. For example, you can use this in combination with **SET PRINT ON** if you want something sent to the printer but not displayed on the screen. Then, when you are done, use the commands **SET CONSOLE ON** and **SET PRINT OFF** to return to normal.

Other Options of the ? Command

The ? and ?? commands also include options that let you control how the data is displayed. The full syntax of the command is:

```
?¦?? [<exp1>]
     [PICTURE <expC1>]
     [FUNCTION] [<exp2>]
     [AT <expN2> ]
     [FONT <expC2> [,<expN3>] [STYLE <expC3>]]
     [, <exp3>]...
```

In the simple form that you used earlier, the command evaluates the expression and displays it.

In addition, the PICTURE and FUNCTION options allow you to specify the format in which the expression is displayed by including a PICTURE or a FUNCTION clause and a picture template or picture function. For example, the clause PICTURE "@!" displays the expression in all uppercase. Both options are covered in the section "Picture Clauses" later in this chapter.

The AT option lets you specify the column where the expression is displayed. It must be followed by a number or numeric expression. This option lets you line up output in columns.

The [FONT <expC2> [,<expN3>] [STYLE <expC3>]] option lets you specify the typeface, size, and style of the font used to display the output. The character expression and numeric expression should be the name and size of an available font, and if you include the clause but omit the size option, a 10-point font is used. The STYLE clause may be followed by one of the following codes:

- B: boldface
- I: Italic
- N: normal
- O: outline

- Q: opaque
- S: shadow
- –: strikeout
- T: transparent
- U: underline

If this clause is omitted, normal style will be used.

The <exp3> … option is included to show that this command may be used with any number of expressions, separated by commas. Each of these expressions may also use all the previous options.

▸ Getting Input from the User

The commands you have looked at so far just display output to the screen, something you have already done earlier in this book, working from the Command window. You are doing something completely new, though, when you use the Visual FoxPro commands that get input from the user.

The WAIT Command

There is one simple input command you will find useful. If you want to let the user press just one key or click the mouse, use the command

```
WAIT [<char_exp>] [TO <memvar>]
```

The character expression is displayed as a prompt for the user, and the key that the user presses is stored in the memory variable. The program will also proceed if the user clicks the mouse.

For example, if you use the code

```
WAIT "Do you want to continue? (y/n) " TO myesno
```

The program displays the message `Do you want to continue? (y/n)` and waits for the user to press a key. As soon as the user presses any key, its value is stored in the variable *myesno,* and the program continues to execute without waiting for the user to press Enter. What the program did next would depend on the value of *myesno.*

Notice that the clause TO <memvar> is optional in this command. Often, WAIT is just used to stop the program until the user is ready to continue; with other commands, you have to create a variable to store the user's input, even if this variable is never used, but this is not necessary with WAIT.

In addition, you can include a character expression that will be used as the prompt. If you do not, WAIT displays the default prompt, `Press any key to continue ...`. For example, if your program has reached a point where it is ready to print something, you could use the code

```
? "Make sure your printer is ready and"
WAIT
```

This displays the message

```
Make sure your printer is ready and
Press any key to continue...
```

The WAIT WINDOW Command

In Visual FoxPro, the old Xbase command WAIT has been updated with the addition of the optional clause WINDOW. You use this in the same way you always use WAIT:

```
WAIT WINDOW [<char_exp>] [TO <memvar>]
```

As always, you have the option of specifying the prompt or of using the default prompt, `Press any key to continue...`, and you have the option of creating a memory variable to store the user's keystroke. The difference is that the message appears in a small window at the upper right of the screen, as a Visual FoxPro system message.

The command has one other important option: If you add a final clause, NOWAIT, the system window disappears without trapping a keystroke, like a Visual FoxPro system message. As you know, you must press a key to get rid of a Visual FoxPro alert before going on with your work, but you can just go on with your work if Visual FoxPro displays a system message. You can get both of these effects by using WAIT WINDOW with or without the NOWAIT option.

Because it does not trap a keystroke, WAIT WINDOW NOWAIT cannot be used to assign a value to a variable. Visual FoxPro just assigns the null string to this variable if you include the TO <memvar> clause.

Sampling the WAIT Command

To get a feel for commands that get user input, try a few variations on the WAIT and WAIT WINDOW commands:

1. Enter **CLEAR**. Then enter **WAIT** in the Command window. Visual FoxPro displays the message `Press any key to continue...`. Press any key or click the mouse.

2. In the Command window, enter **WAIT "Enter a sample variable " TO mtest**. Visual FoxPro displays the prompt `Enter a sample variable`. Type **a**. Now, to confirm that you have created this variable, enter **? mtest**. Visual FoxPro displays an `a`.

3. Now, enter **WAIT WINDOW** in the Command window. Visual FoxPro displays a system window in the upper right with the message `Press any key to continue ...`. Press any key or click the mouse.

4. Enter **WAIT WINDOW "Enter a sample variable " TO mtest**. Visual FoxPro displays a system window with the prompt `Enter a sample variable`, as shown in Figure 23.2. Type **b**. Again, to confirm that you have stored this value in the variable, enter **? mtest**. Visual FoxPro displays a `b`.

5. Finally, to try the NOWAIT option, enter **WAIT WINDOW "Enter a sample variable " TO mtest NOWAIT**. Again, Visual FoxPro displays a system window with the prompt `Enter a sample variable`. Type **c**. Notice that the `c` appears in the Command window; it is not trapped by the WAIT command. In the Command window, enter **? mtest**. Visual FoxPro does not display a new value for the variable.

You have looked at the most important features of the WAIT command. For other options that it offers, see Appendix B.

► The @ ... SAY ... GET Command

The Visual FoxPro/Xbase language provides one other very versatile command that you can use for input/output. The basic form of this command is

```
@ <row>,<column> [SAY <exp>] [GET <variable>]
READ [CYCLE]
```

FIGURE 23.2

Using WAIT WINDOW

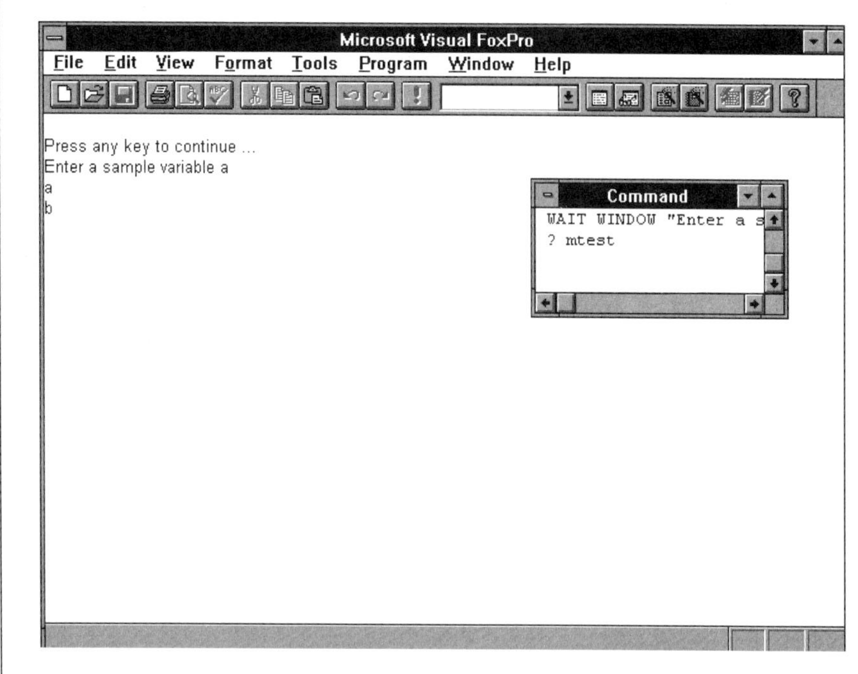

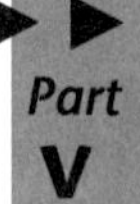

The first clause, @ <row>,<column>, places the cursor; that is, it determines where the input/output will appear.

In Visual FoxPro for Windows, the maximized application window is 80 columns by 36 rows if you use the standard font. Visual FoxPro for Windows also lets you add a FONT clause to this command to specify which font is used. If you use @ … SAY … GET in a window that is not maximized, the row and column are measured from the upper-left corner of the current window rather than the upper-left corner of the screen, and their maximum value depends on the size of the window.

Thus, if you begin this command with **@ 3, 5**, the output will be displayed on the third line of the window and will be indented five spaces from the left.

The second clause, SAY <exp>, determines what the prompt will be.

The third clause, GET <variable>, creates a field for the user's input, which is highlighted. The important thing to remember about this command is that the variable used after GET should be defined in advance.

Although this makes you go through an extra step as a programmer, it also gives you more control. The data type of the variable you create determines the data type of the variable that is entered.

▸▸ TIP

Although it is most common to use numbers, you can also use numeric expressions with this command. For example, you can use variables as the row and column numbers so the location of the cursor changes in the course of the program. You will look at a program that does this later in this chapter.

In addition, the value you give to the variable appears as a default value. It is common to define the variable as a series of blank spaces so that the user has a blank data entry field of the proper length. Programmers often use the function SPACE(<num_exp>) to do so; this function returns a number of blank spaces equal to the expression. Although you can simply use a series of blank spaces in quotation marks to define the variable, it is often easier to use this function. You can also give the variable a useful default value, which the user can confirm by pressing Enter or can type over.

▸▸ TIP

Rather than defining the variable in advance, you can use the optional DEFAULT clause of this command to create and initialize the specified variable if it does not already have a value. For more details, see Appendix B.

Finally, after you use the @ … SAY … GET command, you must use a separate command, READ, to make the program pause to get the user's input. The advantage of this is that you can write a long series of @ … SAY … GET commands and then use READ just once at the end to get the user's input for all of them. Rather than just getting input one line at a time, as you did with unformatted input/output commands, you can present the user with an entire data entry screen before getting any input.

If the command READ is used alone, when the cursor is in the final field, pressing Enter makes the program go on to the next line of code after READ.

If the command READ CYCLE is used and the user presses Enter when the cursor is in the last GET field, the cursor moves back to the first GET field. That is, the cursor cycles through the screen until the user does something (such as select an OK button) to terminate data entry.

Notice that the SAY and GET clauses in this command are both in square brackets, indicating that they are optional. It is most common to use both clauses in a single command. The variable you GET will appear just to the right of the prompt you SAY. It is also possible, though, to leave one of them out and use the command just to print a prompt or just to get input without a prompt.

In general, the user must press Enter or Tab or use the mouse to move the cursor after each input. If the input fills up the entire width of the field, though, Visual FoxPro will beep (assuming that you have not SET BELL OFF) and go on to the next field, just as it does in ordinary data entry.

▶ A Sample Program

As an exercise, try creating a very simple program to get a feel for the basics of this command and the basic mechanics of creating a program.

▶▶ **NOTE**

The program listings in this book follow the common programming convention of writing words of the Visual FoxPro language in uppercase letters and writing variables and comments in lowercase letters. This is merely meant to make the program easier to read. Capitalization does not matter to the program, except in the case of literals, such as "How old are you?", which are printed to the screen with the capitalization they have in the program. You can type the program in all uppercase if you find it easier.

1. To create the program, select File ➤ New. Select the Program radio button and select New. Enter the program shown in Figure 23.3. Then select File ➤ Save As. Notice that the Save As dialog box has many PRG files in its scrollable list: these programs that came with Visual FoxPro are in your Visual FoxPro home directory. Select \LEARNFOX (the directory you created for the Emplist sample table back in Chapter 2) from the list of directories. Enter **TEST1** as the name of the new file; then select the default button, Save. Visual FoxPro automatically adds the PRG extension. Close the Edit window.

FIGURE 23.3

Sample program to test @ ... SAY ... GET

```
************************
*TEST1.PRG
*sample program to illustrate the use of @...SAY...GET
************************

CLEAR

m_age = 0
@ 10, 1 SAY "How old are you?" GET m_age
READ

@ 12, 1 SAY "Sorry. Next year you will be " + LTRIM(STR(m_age +
1))

dummy = SPACE(1)
@ 15,1 SAY "Press any key to continue . . . " GET dummy
READ

CLEAR
```

2. Select Program ➤ Do. The Do Program File dialog box appears. Use the scrollable list to select TEST1.PRG. Select the default pushbutton, Do, to run the program. Visual FoxPro automatically compiles it and runs it, creating the screen shown in Figure 23.4. When you enter the age, try typing a letter first, and notice that Visual FoxPro simply beeps and does not accept the entry. Then type a number.

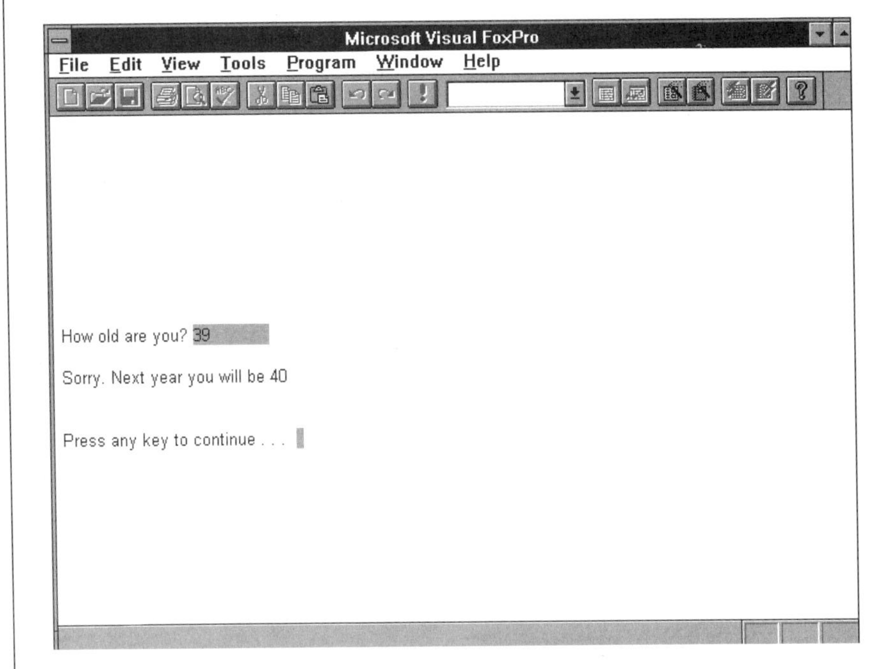

FIGURE 23.4

Screen displayed by the TEST1 sample program

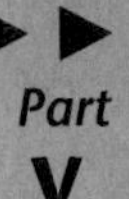

3. If you did not have any errors in the program, try adding one to get a demonstration of Visual FoxPro's debugging capabilities. Enter **MODI COMM TEST1**, and edit TEST1.PRG again to eliminate the final parenthesis following the function that prints the age, so that it now reads LTRIM(STR(m_age + 1), with unbalanced parentheses. Save it in this new form and then run it. When you get to the line with the error, Visual FoxPro displays an error message plus the program code with a highlight on the line that has the error, as shown in Figure 23.5.

4. Click the Cancel button. Visual FoxPro automatically lets you edit the program, with the cursor in the line where the error is. Add the closing parenthesis at the end of the line. Save the file; then close the editing window and run the program again to make sure it is correct.

As you can see when you run the program, the character expression that you included after SAY, "How old are you?" appears as a prompt for the user; and the GET statement displays a data entry area with the

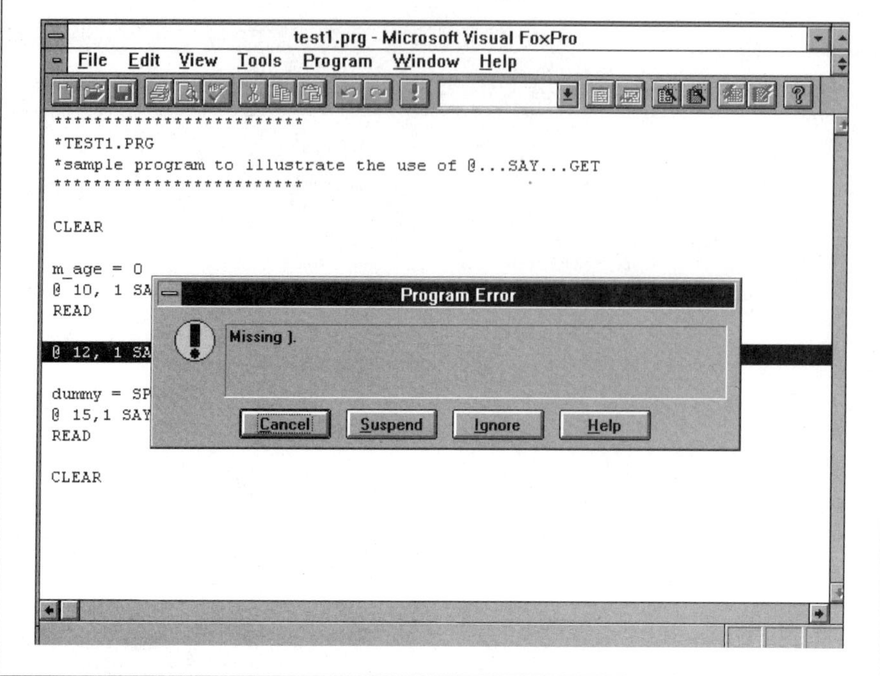

FIGURE 23.5 ► *Visual FoxPro shows you the error.*

initial value of *m_age* as its default value, which you may edit. The user's entry is stored as the new value of *m_age* and then used by the program as part of the next message to the user. A second @ … SAY … GET command is used to make the program pause for the user to read this message. Because the GET clause must always include a variable to hold the user's response (even when no response is expected), this second occurrence of the command uses a memory variable named "dummy" because its value is never actually used.

By defining the initial value of *m_age* as a number, you determine that variable's data type and make it impossible for the user to enter anything but numbers in it.

► Picture Clauses

Both the ? and @ … SAY … GET commands can use a PICTURE or FUNCTION clause. In the ? command, these clauses control the format of the output. In the @ … SAY … GET command, they can be used following the SAY clause to format the output or following the GET clause to format or control the user's input.

For example, the picture template or the picture function ! is used to capitalize both output and input. If you use either with ?? or with a SAY statement, it will display the output in uppercase; if you use either in a GET statement, it will convert the input to uppercase, regardless of how the user enters it.

PICTURE may be followed by either a picture template or a picture function, while FUNCTION must be followed by a picture function. The difference between the two is in the scope of their operations:

- A picture *template* is used to format input or output on a character-by-character basis.
- A picture *function* is used to format all of the input and output.

If you had a five-character variable, you could format it in any of the following ways:

- Use the clause PICTURE "!!!!!" to format it using a picture template. The template must have the picture symbol repeated for each character.
- Use the clause PICTURE "@!" to format it using a picture function. The picture function needs to use the symbol only once.
- Use the clause FUNCTION "!" to format it using a picture function, again using the symbol only once.

Notice that you can use a picture function by using the keyword PICTURE followed by @ and the function's symbol, or by using the keyword FUNCTION followed by the symbol alone. Thus, the clause FUNCTION "!" is equivalent to the clause PICTURE "@!"

NOTE

Notice that the template and function are both delimited by quotation marks. This is because the keyword PICTURE or FUNCTION must be followed by a character expression.

There are different symbols for picture templates and functions. Although ! can be used for both, there are many symbols that can be used only for one or the other. In addition, some templates and functions work differently from others. The symbol ! in a GET clause lets the user enter anything but capitalizes any letters that are entered in lowercase. Most picture templates in GET clauses, though, restrict what the user may enter.

For example, the picture template 9 allows only numbers to be entered in a character field. If the user tries to enter a letter, Visual FoxPro beeps and refuses to accept it, just as it did in the first sample program, where the GET variable was defined as numeric.

Try testing these picture templates:

1. In the Command window, enter **MODI COMM TEST1**.
2. When the edit window appears, edit TEST1 so it looks like the the program shown in Figure 23.6.

FIGURE 23.6

Sample program with a PICTURE clause

```
*************************
*TEST2.PRG
*sample program to illustrate the use of @...SAY...GET
*************************

CLEAR

mname = SPACE(20)
m_age = SPACE(2)
@ 8, 1 SAY "What is your name?" GET mname PICT "@!"
@ 10, 1 SAY "How old are you?" GET m_age PICT "99"
READ

@ 12, 1 SAY "Sorry, " + PROPER(mname)
@ 13, 1 SAY "Next year you will be " + LTRIM(STR(VAL(m_age) + 1))

dummy = SPACE(1)
@ 15,1 SAY "Press any key to continue . . . " GET dummy
READ

CLEAR
```

3. Select File ➤ Save As. Save this program under the name TEST2. Visual FoxPro adds the PRG extension.
4. To run the program, enter **DO TEST2** in the Command window (or edit the command line that Visual FoxPro generated when you ran TEST1).

The output of the program is shown in Figure 23.7.

FIGURE 23.7

Output of the TEST2.PRG program

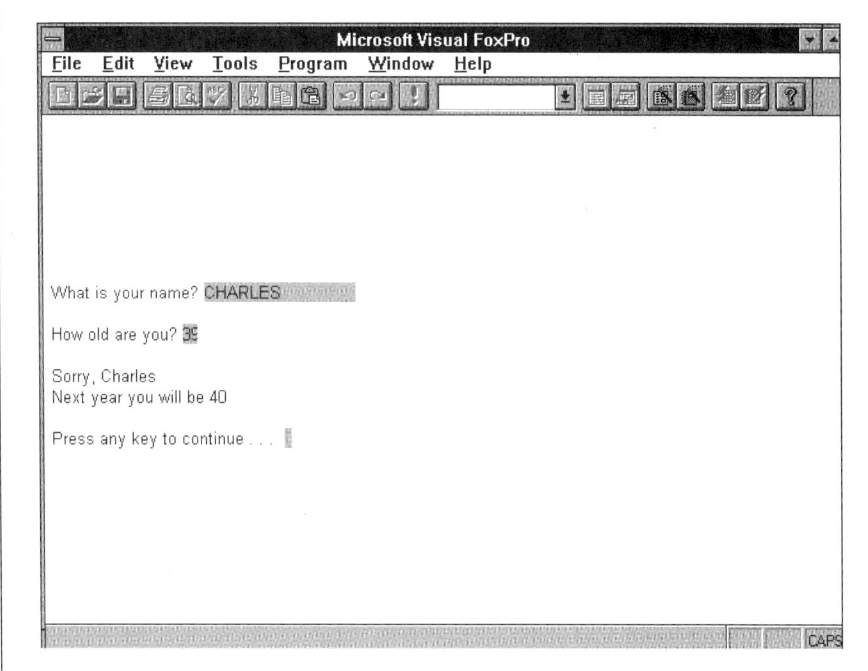

When you try this program, notice that your name is capitalized as you enter it, even if you try to use lowercase, and notice that you can enter only numbers in the m_age field. Finally, notice the sort of control the READ statement gives you over data entry: The user can move back and forth between the name and the age fields until the entry in the age field is complete and the READ command is executed. After the first READ is executed, these two GET fields become totally inaccessible. As you will see in the next section, this is useful when you are redirecting the flow of program control.

▸▸ Control Flow

The simplest program is just a list of commands, executed from beginning to end. What really makes computer programs powerful, though, is the ability to direct the flow of program control.

Programs written in early procedural languages were often very difficult to understand and maintain, because they imitated assembly language and directed control flow by using the command GOTO. Early versions of BASIC, for example, gave each line of programming code a number; whenever a program wanted to use the block of code at line 10200, it would use the command GOTO 10200 or perhaps GOSUB 10200.

Needless to say, a program written this way is very difficult to follow. You need to flip through pages of code to find line 10200 in order to understand what that command actually does. And it is likely that the code you find there will contain another GOTO that sends you flipping through the pages again. Programs written in this way get so twisted up that programmers began referring to them as "spaghetti code." It is possible (but just barely) to keep the logic in your mind when you are writing the program, but it is much more difficult to follow the logic when you are debugging the program or when you go back to the program a year later to modify it. And it is almost impossible to unravel the code if you have to modify a program that someone else wrote.

Structured programming was developed to make it easier to understand and maintain programs. Computer scientists proved that the command GOTO was not necessary. Any program could be written using only three types of control flow:

- **Sequence:** The most basic type of control flow. Sequence simply means that commands are executed one after another, as they appear in the code.
- **Selection:** The use of IF and ELSE to select one out of a group of alternatives. If a condition is true, the program does one thing; otherwise, it does something else.
- **Iteration (or looping):** The use of repetition. The same commands are repeated as long as some condition is true.

Sequence is the only form of control flow used in the sample programs that you have tried so far and is very easy to understand, as commands are simply executed one after another. Now that you have learned about input/output, you are ready to work with more sophisticated forms of control flow.

Looping

The basic command used for iteration in Visual FoxPro/dBASE-compatible languages is the DO WHILE loop, which has the following form:

```
DO WHILE <logical exp>
     ...
ENDDO
```

The ellipsis between the first and last line stands for any number of lines of programming code.

Each time the program reaches this DO WHILE command, it checks to see if the logical expression evaluates as true. If it does, the program executes the commands that follow. When it gets to ENDDO, the program loops back up to the preceding DO WHILE and checks again to see if the logical expression evaluates as true; if so, it executes the same commands. Whenever the program discovers that the logical expression does not evaluate as true, it skips all these commands and instead executes the commands that follow ENDDO.

Infinite Loops

Of course, the lines of code within a loop must do something that ultimately makes the condition untrue. For example, to execute a block of code ten times, you might use the condition DO WHILE MCOUNTER < 10 and include a line of code that increments the counter by 1 each time the code is executed; the examples in the sections that follow make a similar use of counters.

If you do not have some code that makes the condition untrue, the program will continue executing this series of commands forever. This is a common error in programming, called an *infinite loop.* If your program seems to die—to stop doing anything at all—what has probably happened is that it has come to some infinite loop that does not display anything on the screen. It is actually performing some group of instructions over and over and never getting up to the next command that makes it do something you would notice. Alternatively, a program may display the same thing over and over as the result of an infinite loop. If either of these things happens, press Esc to interrupt the program and look through the code to see where and why a loop is executing indefinitely.

TIP

If Esc does not work—for example, because you have SET ESCAPE OFF—remember that you can always get out of an infinite loop by turning off the computer. As you learned earlier, turning off the computer without quitting Visual FoxPro can lose data, so you should do this only if necessary during debugging.

A Sample of Looping

Consider a simple example of looping that makes your screen look a bit like a primitive video game. Enter the listing in Figure 23.8 in a file named TEST3.PRG and run it. The output is shown in Figure 23.9.

FIGURE 23.8

Sample program to demonstrate looping

```
*************************
*TEST3.PRG
*sample program to illustrate looping
*************************/

col_cntr = 0
CLEAR
DO WHILE col_cntr < 100
     @ 10, col_cntr SAY ">"
     col_cntr = col_cntr + 1
ENDDO
WAIT
```

Notice the way this program is indented. Whenever you have a DO WHILE loop, you should indent the code that is within the loop. This does not affect the way Visual FoxPro runs the program, but it does make it much easier for you to understand the code.

FIGURE 23.9

Output of the TEST3.PRG program

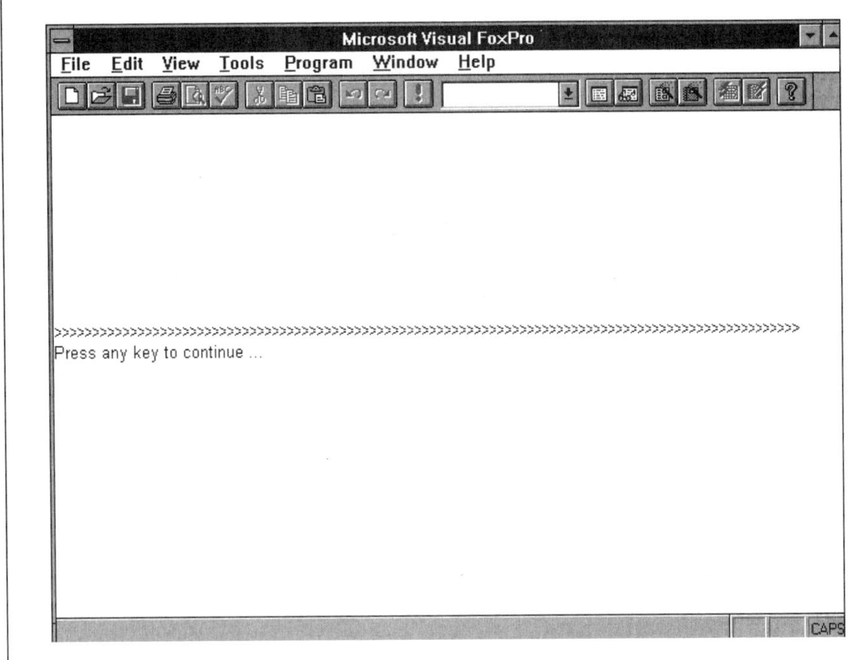

How exactly does this program work?

First, you create a variable named col_cntr, a counter that will hold all the column numbers you use in the program. You must define this variable before the program comes to the DO WHILE command. Because you gave it a value of 0, the logical expression that follows DO WHILE is true, so the code within the DO WHILE loop is executed. This code clears the screen and then uses the @ ... SAY command to display the character > at row 10, column 0 (since the value of 10,col_cntr is 10,0 this time through the loop).

Then the program increments the value of col_cntr by 1. The line of code that does this,

```
col_cntr = col_cntr + 1
```

looks strange to many beginning programmers. People are used to the meaning of the equal sign in arithmetic, where it signifies equality; in arithmetic, of course, the equation

col_cntr = col_cntr + 1

would be absurd, since a number cannot equal 1 more than itself. In Visual FoxPro, though, as in most computer languages, the equal sign represents assignment. This line of code should be read as *make col_cntr equal to col_cntr plus 1* or *let col_cntr = col_cntr plus 1*. Since the value of col_cntr was 0 when the program got to this line, it makes its value equal to 1.

Then the program gets to ENDDO, sending it back up to the top of the loop, where it checks the condition following DO WHILE once again. Since *col_cntr* is now equal to 1, the condition is still true, and the program executes the code in the loop again. It clears the screen and then prints the > at row 10, column 1, so it looks as if the symbol has moved one column to the right. Then it makes the value of col_cntr equal to 2, adding 1 to its current value of 1.

Thus, it continues going through the loop and printing the sign > at column 2, column 3, and so on. When *col_cntr* is equal to 79, though, it prints the sign > at row 10, column 79. Then it adds 1 to col_cntr and makes its value 80. At this point, when the program checks the condition of the DO WHILE loop, it finds that the condition col_cntr < 80 is no longer true, so it does not execute the code in the loop again. Instead, it continues with the next line of code after ENDDO, printing the WAIT statement's familiar prompt.

This program illustrates the basic principle of a DO WHILE loop. The variable used in the loop's condition must change its value so that the condition is ultimately untrue.

Nested DO WHILE Loops: A Simple Example

It is not uncommon to use one DO WHILE loop within another. This is known as *nesting*. Consider a simple example, in which you just use the inner loop as a delay mechanism (since it actually takes the program time to do the counting). On most computers, Visual FoxPro runs the previous program so quickly you cannot see that the > character is printed out one column at a time; it seems to be displayed across the entire width of the screen at once. Let's say you want the user to watch this character move across the screen, so you slow down the program by adding a loop that simply wastes time by counting to 1000.

Edit the previous example to add this loop, as shown in Figure 23.10, and save it in the file TEST4.PRG. Then compile and run it by entering DO TEST4.

FIGURE 23.10

Adding a delaying loop within the main loop

```
************************
*TEST4.PRG
*sample program to illustrate a delaying loop
************************/

col_cntr = 0
CLEAR
DO WHILE col_cntr < 80

     @ 10, col_cntr SAY ">"
     col_cntr = col_cntr + 1

     time_cntr = 0
     DO WHILE time_cntr < 1000
          time_cntr = time_cntr + 1
     ENDDO

ENDDO
WAIT
```


Each time it goes through the main loop, the program makes *time_cntr* equal to 0; then it must add 1 to it a thousand times before it can continue. Although the output is the same, the program runs so much more slowly than it did before you added this extra loop that you can now see the character being displayed on the screen one column at a time.

TIP

If you have a slow computer, you might not want to wait for the symbol to be displayed across the entire width of the screen. Remember that you can always stop the program by pressing Esc. If you have a very fast computer, you may want the *time_cntr* value to equal more than 1000 each time through the loop.

More Sophisticated Nested Loops

Nested loops are more complex if both the inner and outer loops change the value of meaningful variables. For example, let's say you want the > sign to go not just across the columns of row 10, but across the columns of all the rows, one after another. You can add a loop to count the rows outside of the loop that counts the columns. Edit TEST3.PRG to add this extra outer loop, as shown in Figure 23.11. Then save it under the name TEST5.PRG and run it by entering DO TEST5.

FIGURE 23.11

More complex example of nested loops

```
*************************
*TEST5.PRG
*sample program to illustrate nested loops
*************************

CLEAR
row_cntr = 0
DO WHILE row_cntr < 20

     col_cntr = 0
     DO WHILE col_cntr < 100
          @ row_cntr, col_cntr SAY ">"
          col_cntr = col_cntr + 1
     ENDDO

     row_cntr = row_cntr + 1

ENDDO
WAIT
```

The indented lines inside the main loop (the six lines beginning with col_cntr = 0) are essentially the same as the earlier program, TEST4.PRG. These lines display the character > on each column across the screen. The difference is that they do not just go across row 10, as the earlier program did; instead, they are nested in a larger loop that executes them on all the rows, one row after another. To begin with, the row_cntr is 0. The program displays > at 0,0, at 0,1, at 0,2, and so on, until it has gone through all the columns and displayed it at 0,79. Then, it finds that the condition col_cntr < 80 is no longer true, so it stops executing the inner DO WHILE loop and goes to the next line of code following the inner ENDDO, which adds 1 to row_cntr. Then it reaches the final, outer ENDDO, which sends it back up to the first DO WHILE to see if the condition is true. Because row_cntr is still less than 20, it executes this outer loop again. First, it makes col_cntr equal 0. Then it executes the inner loop, displaying > at 1,0, at 1,1, at 1,2, and so on, until it has reached 1,79. Then it makes row_cntr equal to 2 so that the next time through, the inner loop displays > in all the columns of the next row. It keeps doing this until it has displayed > across all the columns of all 20 rows. Finally, when row_cntr equals 20, the condition of the outer loop is no longer true.

This program shows how important it is to indent code properly. When one loop is nested in another, its operation is very difficult to follow unless it is indented in a way that makes the logic clear.

Looping through a Table

Finally, try one example that uses a DO WHILE loop with a table file. It is common in programs to go through an entire file by using the function EOF( ) as the condition of a DO WHILE loop. Remember from Chapter 9 that Visual FoxPro makes this function true after you move the pointer beyond the last record. Thus, you can use EOF() to display all the records in a file by using the code shown in Figure 23.12. Try creating and running this program. The screen output is shown in Figure 23.13.

NOTE

Because this chapter is designed to be used by readers who have just finished Part II of this book, as well as by those who have read the entire book, it assumes that you have not made this table part of a FoxPro database (as you would in Chapter 15's exercises). If you have, you must remove it from the database before you run this program.

FIGURE 23.12

Program to loop through a table

```
************************
*TEST6.PRG
*sample program that loops through the records of a file
************************

USE c:\learnfox\emplist
CLEAR
?
?
DO WHILE .NOT. EOF()
     ? PROPER(TRIM(fname) + " " + lname)
     SKIP
ENDDO
?
USE
WAIT
```

FIGURE 23.13

Output of the TEST6.PRG program

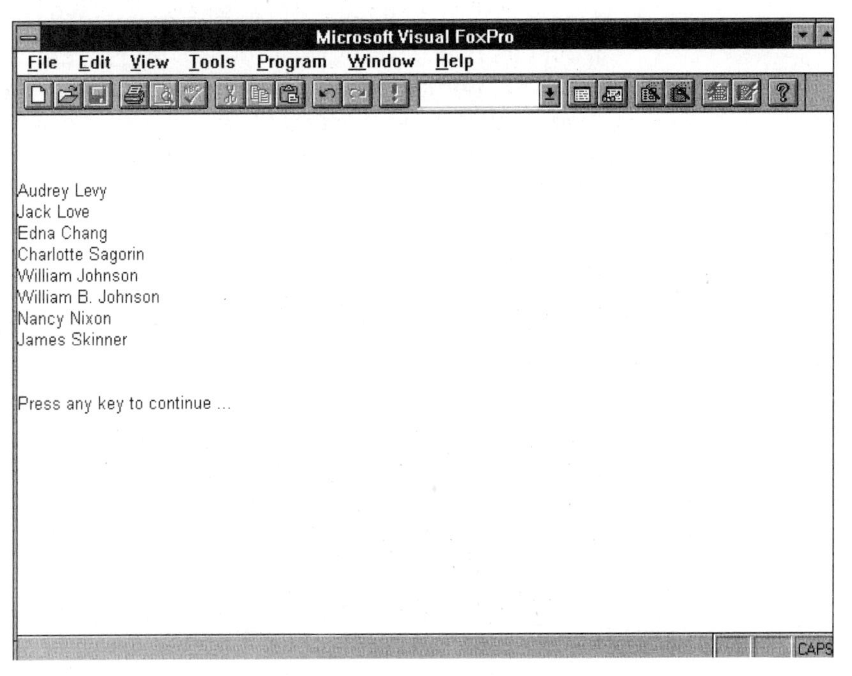

This little program is essentially equivalent to the command LIST PROPER(TRIM(fname)+" "+lname). It simply reads through the entire file and prints the first and last name from each record. When it gets past the last record, the condition of the DO WHILE loop is no longer true, so the program stops. You can begin to appreciate how helpful it is to be using a language that has commands you can use interactively such as LIST, rather than always having to write programs like this.

The SCAN Command

It is instructive to use the DO WHILE loop to read all the records of a program, to learn how looping works. In practice, however, it is better to use the SCAN command, which has the basic form:

```
SCAN
        ...
ENDSCAN
```

This command is designed to go through all the records in a table and perform the statements between SCAN and ENDSCAN on all of them.

It works like DO WHILE .NOT. EOF( ) … ENDDO, except that it is faster. Thus, the program in Figure 23.14 will produce the same output as the program using DO WHILE that you just looked at.

Notice that you do not have to use the SKIP command within the loop or use the WHILE NOT EOF() condition when you use this command, as you would if you used a DO WHILE loop to read the file; these features are built into the SCAN command.

For more details on all the options available with the SCAN command, see Appendix B.

▶ Selection

Now that you have looked at sequence and iteration, *selection* is the last of the three methods of control flow used in structured programming that you need to learn about.

Visual FoxPro includes two basic methods of selection. When there are just one or two choices, it is most convenient to use the IF … ELSE … ENDIF command. When you have a larger number of choices, it is most convenient to use the DO CASE … ENDCASE command.

FIGURE 23.14

Program to loop through a table using scan

```
*************************
*TEST7.PRG
*sample program that loops through the records of a file
*using SCAN
*************************

USE c:\learnfox\emplist
CLEAR
?
?
SCAN
     ? PROPER(TRIM(fname) + " " + lname)
ENDSCAN
?
USE
WAIT
```

IF ... ELSE ... ENDIF

The IF ... ELSE ... ENDIF command is fairly straightforward and easy to understand. It takes the form

```
IF <logical exp>
       ...
[ELSE
       ...]
ENDIF
```

The ellipses represent any number of lines of code. If the logical expression is true, the code following the IF clause is executed. If the expression is not true, the code following the ELSE clause is executed.

As the square brackets indicate, you can also use this command without any ELSE clause, in the form

```
IF <logical exp>
       ...
ENDIF
```

The code is executed if the expression is true.

For example, let's revise the previous program to give the user the choice of whether to get the listing or omit it. Edit TEST6.PRG, the program using a DO loop to read through a table, and nest the loop that prints the names within an IF statement, as shown in Figure 23.15. Save it under the name of TEST8.PRG and run it. The output (if you enter Y to get the listing) is shown in Figure 23.16.

FIGURE 23.15

DO loop nested in an IF statement

```
*************************
*TEST8.PRG
*a sample of a DO loop nested in an IF statement
*************************

USE c:\learnfox\emplist
CLEAR
?
WAIT "Do you want a listing (y/n)? " TO yesno
IF UPPER(yesno) = "Y"
     ?
     DO WHILE .NOT. EOF()
          ? PROPER(TRIM(fname) + " " + lname)
          SKIP
     ENDDO
ENDIF
?
USE
WAIT
```

FIGURE 23.16

Output of the TEST8.PRG program

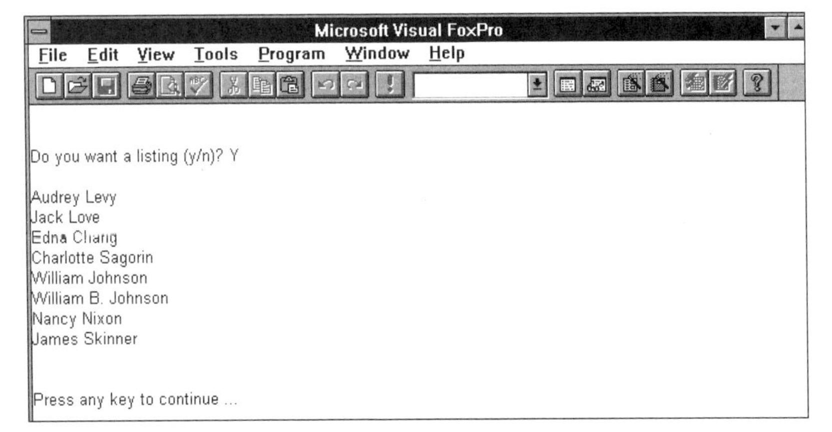

If the user does not press Y, the program will not execute the DO WHILE loop at all.

As an example of a program with both an IF and an ELSE clause, try giving the user a choice of whether to capitalize the names. Edit TEST8.PRG, the program you just wrote, as shown in Figure 23.17. Save it under the name of TEST9.PRG and run it. One of its possible outputs is shown in Figure 23.18.

FIGURE 23.17

Combining a DO loop and an IF/ELSE statement

```
*************************
*TEST9.PRG
*a sample of a DO loop nested in an IF statement
*************************

USE c:\learnfox\emplist
CLEAR
?
WAIT "Do you want the names capitalized (y/n)? " TO yesno
?
DO WHILE .NOT. EOF()
     IF UPPER(yesno) = "Y"
          ? UPPER(TRIM(fname) + " " + lname)
          SKIP
     ELSE
          ? PROPER(TRIM(fname) + " " + lname)
          SKIP
     ENDIF
ENDDO
?
USE
WAIT
```

DO CASE ... ENDCASE

The DO CASE ... ENDCASE command is useful when there is a larger number of choices.

It is possible to use the IF ... ELSE ... ENDIF command to select among multiple choices by nesting one IF ... ELSE ... ENDIF within another. Consider the TEST10 program shown in Figure 23.19, which simply tells the user what number was entered. Figure 23.20 shows one possible output of this program.

FIGURE 23.18

One possible output of the TEST9.PRG program

```
Do you want a the names capitalized (y/n)? y

AUDREY LEVY
JACK LOVE
EDNA CHANG
CHARLOTTE SAGORIN
WILLIAM JOHNSON
WILLIAM B. JOHNSON
NANCY NIXON
JAMES SKINNER

Press any key to continue ...
```

FIGURE 23.19

An IF/ELSE ladder

```
*************************
*TEST10.PRG
*a sample IF/ELSE ladder
*************************

CLEAR
?
?
WAIT "Type a number between 1 and 4 > " TO usr_nmbr
?
IF usr_nmbr = "1"
     ? "You typed one."
ELSE
     IF usr_nmbr = "2"
          ? "You typed two."
     ELSE
          IF usr_nmbr = "3"
               ? "You typed three."
          ELSE
               IF usr_nmbr = "4"
                    ? "You typed four."
               ELSE
                    ? "Error: entry not between 1 and 4."
               ENDIF
          ENDIF
     ENDIF
ENDIF
?
WAIT
```

FIGURE 23.19

One possible output of the TEST10.PRG program

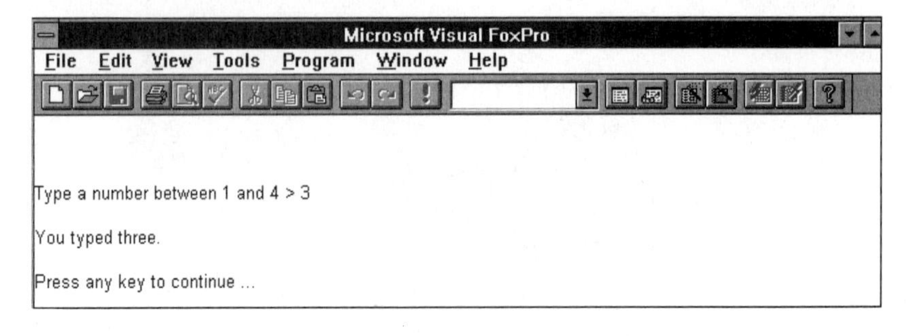

FIGURE 23.21

DO CASE statement

```
*************************
*TEST11.PRG
*a sample DO CASE
*************************

CLEAR
?
?
WAIT "Type a number between 1 and 4 > " TO usr_nmbr
?
DO CASE
     CASE usr_nmbr = "1"
          ? "You typed one."
     CASE usr_nmbr = "2"
          ? "You typed two."
     CASE usr_nmbr = "3"
          ? "You typed three."
     CASE usr_nmbr = "4"
          ? "You typed four."
     OTHERWISE
          ? "Error: entry not between 1 and 4."
ENDCASE
?
WAIT
```

Look carefully at how this program works. All of the other IF … ELSE commands are nested within the first ELSE. Thus, if the user enters 1, the program executes the command under the first IF; then it skips all the lines between the first ELSE and the last ENDIF. If the user does not enter 1, though, the program executes the line under the first ELSE and checks to see if the user entered 2. If the user entered 2, it skips all the lines nested in the second ELSE, but if the user did not enter 2, it executes the line under the second ELSE and checks whether the user entered 3. Likewise, if the user did not enter 3, it checks to see if the user entered 4. Finally, if the user did not enter 4, it prints an error message.

This program is an example of what is called an IF/ELSE ladder, and you do see it in programs on occasion. Needless to say, it is difficult for the programmer to read. Thus, Visual FoxPro gives you another command, DO CASE, which does the same thing. The TEST11 program in Figure 23.21 works just like the previous one and produces identical output.

DO CASE works just like an IF/ELSE ladder. The program looks through the CASE statements to find if one is correct. If it is, the program executes the code following that CASE statement and, after it is done with that block of code, goes on to the code following ENDCASE. OTHERWISE works like the final ELSE of the IF-ELSE ladder: The statements following it are executed if the conditions in all of the CASE statements are untrue. You can also use DO CASE without OTHERWISE; if none of the conditions are true, no code is executed.

EXIT and LOOP

If you use one of these methods of selection within a loop, you can create infinite loops deliberately and use the command EXIT to break out of them.

EXIT and LOOP are two commands that programmers use when they want to make loop control more explicit. EXIT breaks out of the loop and directs control to the statement following ENDDO. LOOP returns control to the DO WHILE statement. This makes it possible to return to the beginning of the loop without some of the commands that are in it.

It is often clearer to put an EXIT command within an infinite loop than to put the condition after DO WHILE. You can create an infinite loop by using some condition that is always true—for example, DO WHILE 1 = 1. You can use a more elegant command, though, if you remember that Visual FoxPro evaluates any condition of this sort and executes the loop if it evaluates as true. To save it the trouble, you can just use the condition DO WHILE .T.

Try rewriting TEST11.PRG to add an infinite loop using the EXIT and LOOP commands, as in Figure 23.22. Save this program in a file named TEST12.PRG and run it. Its output is shown in Figure 23.23.

FIGURE 23.22

Using EXIT and LOOP to control a loop

```
*************************
*TEST12.PRG
*a sample of EXIT and LOOP
*************************

DO WHILE .T.
     CLEAR
     ?
     ?
     WAIT "Type a number between 1 and 4 > " TO usr_nmbr
     ?
     DO CASE
          CASE usr_nmbr = "1"
               ? "You typed one."
          CASE usr_nmbr = "2"
               ? "You typed two."
          CASE usr_nmbr = "3"
               ? "You typed three."
          CASE usr_nmbr = "4"
               ? "You typed four."
          OTHERWISE
               ? "Error: entry not between 1 and 4."
     ENDCASE
     ?
     WAIT "Do you want to try again? (y/n) " TO yesno
     IF UPPER(yesno) = "Y"
          LOOP
     ELSE
          EXIT
     ENDIF
ENDDO
```

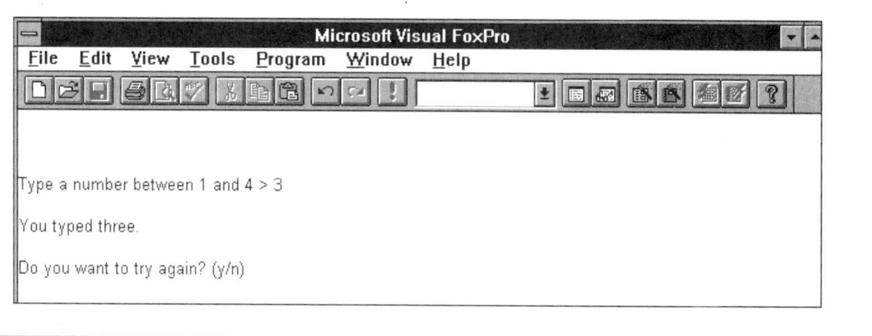

FIGURE 23.23

Output of the TEST12.PRG program

Notice that the command LOOP is not actually needed in this case; the program would loop up anyway when it reached the final ENDDO. You could rewrite the condition at the end of the program as

```
WAIT "Do you want to try again? (y/n)" TO yesno
IF UPPER(yesno) <> "Y"
     EXIT
ENDIF
```

and the program would run in exactly the same way. In this case, adding LOOP is merely a stylistic convenience, to make the program easier to understand. In other cases, LOOP is used to bypass some of the commands within a DO WHILE loop.

►► Procedures and Parameters

Structured programming also involves breaking down a program into *modules* or *procedures*. Rather than a single long listing, with GOTO twisted all through it, structured programs are broken down into parts that are easier to understand. Although the utility programs you will write as a Visual FoxPro user usually will not be complex enough to require multiple modules, you should glance at how to do so in this section.

In early versions of the dBASE language, each module had to be kept in a separate PRG file, and it is still possible to write programs in this way.

To call a program in another file, you simply use the command DO <filename> within a program, just as you have been doing from the Command window. Control of the program passes to the program you have called. When that program is done, control returns to the following line in the calling program.

Control returns to the calling program automatically when it reaches the end of the called program. You can also use the command RETURN anywhere in the called program to return control to the calling program (or, if you used the program directly from the Command window, to return to Visual FoxPro).

One principle of structured programming, though, is that it is best for control to flow to the bottom of each procedure, so it is not good style to use RETURN in the middle of a module. Many programmers put RETURN at the end of each module, even though it is not needed, to make the flow of the program explicit.

▸▸ NOTE

RETURN TO MASTER is a variation on the command RETURN. It returns control to the first PRG file executed rather than to the file that called the current one.

▸ The Scope of Variables and Passing Parameters

If a procedural program is complex, dividing it into separate modules makes it much easier to develop, debug, and maintain. The modules are truly separated from one another, though, only if the variables in one module can be independent of the variables used in other modules.

For example, if you create a general-purpose procedure to be reused many times, you should be able to use it without having to worry that a statement assigning a value to a variable in that procedure might change the value of a variable somewhere else in the program. When you create a variable named *m_counter* in the main program, you should not have to worry about whether the program calls another procedure that also happens to contain a variable named *m_counter.*

To develop modules of a program independently, then, you should be able to control whether a memory variable is accessible to all the modules of the program. This is called the *scope* of the variable.

By default, a memory variable initialized in any module remains active until program control returns to the code that called that module—either because it reaches a RETURN command or because it reaches the end of that module. In other words, the variable is accessible to any module called by that module directly or indirectly.

You can change the default scope of variables by using two simple commands at the beginning of any PRG file or procedure:

- **PRIVATE <memvar list>** limits the availability of the specified memory variables to the active PRG file or procedure and to modules called by it directly or indirectly. If a module that calls the PRG or procedure happens to have a variable with the same name, Visual FoxPro considers it a different variable from the one that is declared private.
- **PUBLIC <memvar list>** makes the specified memory variables available to all programs and procedures. (Although you can use this command at the beginning of any module, it is best to use it in the highest-level module where the variables are used.)

PRIVATE is useful if you are writing a minor module that is called by many other modules and you do not want to worry about whether the other modules use variables of the same name. PUBLIC is useful if you *want* the value assigned to the variable in one module to be available to all the other modules of the program.

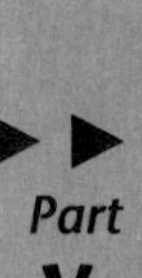

Apart from these two alternatives, though, there are also many cases in which you want the values of variables to be available to only two modules. To let the calling module pass the value of a variable to the module it calls, you use the command PARAMETER <memvar list> as the first command in the module that is called. Then, the simplest way of passing a parameter to that module when you call it is to use the command DO … WITH <expr list>. The expressions in the list following DO … WITH are assigned in order to the memory variables in the list following PARAMETER and thus are passed to the module that is called.

As you will see in a moment, you can also pass parameters from the Command window.

Try writing a procedure that uses the PARAMETER command to capitalize the initial letter of a string. As you know, Visual FoxPro has the function PROPER( ) to capitalize the first letter of each word of a string—as well as the functions UPPER( ) and LOWER( ) to make all the letters of a string uppercase or lowercase—but it does not have a function to capitalize just the first letter of a *string*. The procedure shown in Figure 23.24 will print the string in this form. Try it out:

1. Enter the listing in Figure 23.24 in a file with the name \LEARNFOX\MYPROCS.PRG.

FIGURE 23.24 ▸

Procedure to capitalize the first letter of a string

```
*************************
*PROCEDURE INITCAP
*a procedure to capitalize the first letter of a
*character string and make all the others lowercase
*************************

PROCEDURE initcap
PARAMETER mstring

? UPPER(SUBSTR(mstring,1,1)) + LOWER(SUBSTR(mstring,2))
```

▸▸ **TIP**

If there is a typographical error in your program code that you must correct, the procedure file will automatically be closed when you edit it. You must use the command SET PROCEDURE TO MYPROCS again before retesting it.

2. After saving the file in the \LEARNFOX subdirectory and returning to the Command window, enter the command **SET PROCEDURE TO \LEARNFOX\MYPROCS**.
3. Enter **CLEAR** to clear the screen and enter **?** to skip a line. Then enter the command **DO INITCAP WITH "KNOW THYSELF!"**

As you can see from Figure 23.25, the program prints the string you entered with only the first letter capitalized.

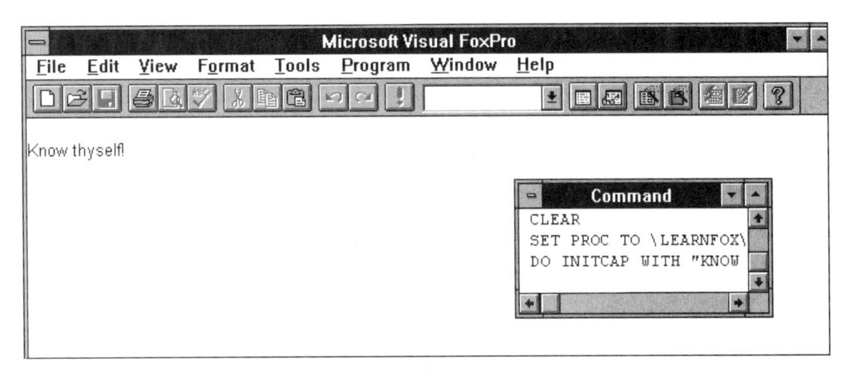

FIGURE 23.25

Using the capitalization procedure

It is easy to see how this program works. The expression following WITH in the DO command is passed to the INITCAP procedure as a parameter, so it is assigned to the variable *mstring*, used in the PARAMETER command of that procedure. Notice that the first use of SUBSTR() returns a substring that begins with the first letter and is one letter long; the second SUBSTR() begins with the second letter and, since no length is specified, continues to the end of the string.

Things become a bit trickier when you want to pass a parameter to the called procedure and then pass a new value back to the calling procedure. As you can see in the program in Figure 23.26, you assign the variable a value in the calling module. That variable is assigned to the parameter and is altered in the called module. As a result, the value is changed in the calling module as well. In this way, you can pass the values of variables back and forth between two modules without worrying about whether the variables have the same name in both modules. This makes the modules much more independent of each other and makes the program more structured. Try entering and running this program in the usual way.

User-Defined Functions

You are not limited to the functions that are provided as part of the Visual FoxPro language. If they are inadequate for your purposes, you can create functions of your own, which you can use just like the program's built-in functions.

FIGURE 23.26

Program to test passing parameters

```
************************************
*TEST13.PRG
*a program to test passing parameters
************************************

CLEAR
mproverb = "KNOW THYSELF!"
DO initcap WITH mproverb
? mproverb

**************************************************
*PROCEDURE INITCAP
*a procedure to capitalize the first letter of a
*character string and make all the others lowercase
**************************************************

PROCEDURE initcap
PARAMETER mstring

mstring = UPPER(SUBSTR(mstring,1,1)) + LOWER(SUBSTR(mstring,2))
```

Visual FoxPro lets you use the command FUNCTION just as you use the command PROCEDURE. In fact, the way these two commands work is identical, but as a matter of programming style it makes sense to use FUNCTION at the beginning of a user-defined function and PROCEDURE at the beginning of a procedure, in order to make the program easier to understand when you are modifying or debugging it.

The real difference between procedures and user-defined functions is the way you pass parameters and return a value. So far, you have used the word RETURN by itself to return control to the calling program. Remember, though, that by definition a function returns a value. If you end a user-defined function with the command RETURN <exp>, the expression is returned to the calling program as the value of that function.

User-defined functions are just like ordinary functions. Rather than passing a value to the user-defined function by using the command DO… WITH, you simply put the value (or values) being passed to the function in the parentheses following it. The function itself begins with FUNCTION… followed by the PARAMETER <parameter list> command, and the value or values passed to it are assigned to the variables in the parameter list in order, just as they are with ordinary procedures. When the function reaches the command RETURN <expr>, the expression returned is used as the value of the function, just as it is with one of the built-in functions of Visual FoxPro.

This sounds complicated, but it will be very easy to understand when you create a user-defined INITCAP() function to do the same thing as the procedure you just wrote.

1. If you want, enter **CLEAR** in the Command window to clear the screen. Then enter **MODI COMM \LEARNFOX\MYFUNCTS** to edit a new program file that will hold the user-defined functions you are about to create, and enter the code shown in Figure 23.27.

FIGURE 23.27

Code for the user-defined function

```
*************************
*INITCAP()
*a user defined function to capitalize the first letter of
*a character string and make all the others lowercase
*************************

FUNCTION initcap
PARAMETER mstring

RETURN UPPER(SUBSTR(mstring,1,1)) + LOWER(SUBSTR(mstring,2)
```

2. After you have saved the file and returned to the Command window, enter the command **SET PROCEDURE TO \LEARNFOX\MYFUNCTS** to make this new file the active procedure file. Then enter **?** to skip a line and enter **? INITCAP("KNOW THYSELF!")**.

Visual FoxPro displays `Know thyself!`

As you see, the new value is returned as the value of the INITCAP( ) function itself. You use this function that you created yourself in the same way you use built-in functions such as UPPER( ) and PROPER( ). Just place the parameter that you pass to the function in the parentheses following the function's name, and the result is returned as the value of that function. You can use user-defined functions, like any functions, in programs in the same way you use them in the Command window.

User-defined functions, though, can be much more powerful than most of Visual FoxPro's built-in functions because they can do much more than return a value. They can contain virtually any command that a program or procedure can, and they execute all these commands—as any procedure does—before they get to the RETURN command and return a value. The other commands they execute need not have anything to do with the value that is returned.

▸▸ A Sample Utility Program

To complete our discussion of procedural programming, let's look at a procedural program that you might actually use to work with your own data.

▸ Defining the Problem

The program listed in Figure 23.28 is designed to look up telephone numbers in other tables and add them to your Emplist table. In practice, of course, you would already know the telephone numbers of all your employees, and the Emplist table is used as an example only because you already have it available.

You might actually want to use this program to look up telephone numbers, for a mailing list with just names and addresses, for example, so you can telephone prospects on it, or to look up telephone numbers for a list of registered voters, so you can call them on behalf of your candidate.

You can get the other tables, which include the telephone number, from a variety of sources. The program assumes that the other tables have FNAME, LNAME, and ADDRESS fields, like the Emplist table; if these fields have different names, you can use the Table Designer to rename them.

FIGURE 23.28

Using the capitalization procedure

```
**********************************************
*PHONENTR.PRG
*A program to look up telephone numbers
*in PHONLIST.DBF and enter them in EMPLIST.DBF.
*Both tables must be in default directory
**********************************************

**open tables
CLOSE ALL
USE emplist
SELECT B
USE phonlist
SELECT A

**create a memory variable to count
**how many phone numbers are entered
**and clear screen
mctr = 0
CLEAR

DO WHILE .NOT. EOF()
     **If records in Emplist.dbf already have phone numbers,
     **skip them.
     DO WHILE phone <> " "
          SKIP
     ENDDO

     **exit from the loop and end the program if it reaches
     **EOF()
     IF EOF()
          EXIT
     ENDIF

     **If a record in Emplist.dbf does not have a phone
     **number, look for a record in Phonlist.dbf with the
     **same name and address.
     SELECT B
     LOCATE FOR UPPER(lname) = UPPER(TRIM(A.lname));
          .AND. UPPER(fname) =
UPPER(TRIM(SUBSTR(A.fname,1)));
          .AND. UPPER(address) = UPPER(TRIM(A.address))
```

FIGURE 23.28

Using the capitalization procedure (continued)

```
     **If the record if found in Phonlist.dbf, enter its
     **phone number in Emplist.dbf and display a message
     **for the user.
     IF .NOT. EOF()
          REPLACE A.phone WITH B.phone
          ? "Entered the phone number " + b.phone + " for "
             + a.lname
          mctr = mctr + 1
     ENDIF

     **Display a message reporting on progress for user.
     SELECT A
     SKIP
     ? "In Emplist, up to record number "
     ?? RECNO()
ENDDO

**After the program has read through Emplist.dbf,
**tell the user how many phone numbers were entered,
**and give the option of closing the tables
?
? mctr
?? " phone numbers entered in total."
?
WAIT "Do you want to close the tables? (y/n) " to myesno
IF UPPER(myesno) = "Y"
     CLOSE ALL
     ? "Tables closed."
ENDIF
```

The program also uses the name PHONLIST for the table in which you are looking up telephone numbers. As you get different tables to use as sources, you can either change this name in the program or use File ➤ Save As to rename each table PHONLIST.

Assume that some of the matches are inexact, both because of capitalization and because the source lists sometimes have just a first initial, rather than a complete first name.

Writing the Program

You can use the program shown in Figure 23.28 to look up telephone numbers in the PHONLIST table and automatically enter them in the EMPLIST table. Look carefully at how this program works.

First, it uses the commands

```
CLOSE ALL
USE emplist
SELECT B
USE phonlist
SELECT A
```

to close any tables that are already open and open the Emplist table, where you want to enter telephone numbers, in Work Area A, and to open the Phonlist table, where you are looking up the numbers, in Work Area B.

NOTE

Although Part V of this book does not require that you use a relational database, this program does open two tables simultaneously, using the methods described in Chapter 14. If you have not already read that chapter, you should look at the section "Using Work Areas" to learn how to open and work with two tables simultaneously.

Remember that CLOSE ALL not only closes all tables but also selects Work Area A, so that you are controlling the work area where Emplist is open, even though you do not do so explicitly.

The USE commands assume that the Emplist and Phonlist tables are both in the same directory, and that you have already made this the default directory before running the program by using the command SET DEFAULT TO.

Then, the program uses the command:

```
mctr = 0
```

to create a memory variable that will be used to count how many telephone numbers are entered in Emplist. Though this is not absolutely necessary, it might be useful to know how successful you are with phone lists from various sources.

It is also useful when you are writing and debugging the program, to make sure that it is actually entering data in Emplist, rather than just reading through it.

The next command, **DO WHILE .NOT. EOF( )**, begins the program's main loop. The commands between it and **ENDDO** will be executed for each record in the Emplist table. Remember that you used the command SELECT A before beginning this loop, so Emplist is the current table the first time it is executed. You will also have to use the command SELECT A again, near the bottom of the loop, so Emplist is the current table again each time you move through the table.

The next set of commands

```
DO WHILE phone <> " "
     SKIP
ENDDO
```

simply looks to see if the current record of the Emplist table has data in the Phone field, which holds the telephone number. If you already found a phone number for this record while searching a previous phone list, there is no need to search for its phone number again.

If there is data in the field, the SKIP command moves the pointer to the next record. Because SKIP is in a DO loop, the program continues to move to the next record until it finds a record in Emplist that is blank.

Following this DO loop is the code

```
IF EOF()
     EXIT
ENDIF
```

This is needed so that the program does not execute the next SKIP command if it has already reached EOF( ), which would cause an error.

Then it goes on to look for a matching record in Phonlist, using the code:

```
SELECT B
LOCATE FOR UPPER(lname) = UPPER(TRIM(A.lname) ;
     .AND. UPPER(fname) = UPPER(TRIM(SUBSTR
           (A.fname,1));
     .AND. UPPER(address) = UPPER(TRIM(A.address)
```

This code finds a match as long as the last name, address, and the first letter of the first name are the same, regardless of capitalization.

It does not use just Lname and Address, because people in the same apartment building might have the same last name and address, though they live in different apartments. It does not match the entire first name, because some entries may have only the first initial entered rather than the entire name.

These are just assumptions about the data in the tables you are using, and you might use a different rule for finding a match if you were sure that all addresses included the apartment number or that all first names were spelled out in full.

This search can be time-consuming, and you might improve performance of the program in two ways:

- Index the Phonlist table on UPPER(lname), on UPPER(fname), and on UPPER(address) before running the program, so Visual FoxPro can use Rushmore to optimize the search.
- Make the proper choice of which table to search. The program reads through every record of the Emplist table and searches for an equivalent record in the Phonlist table, because it assumes that Phonlist is longer than Emplist. If Emplist were longer, you could save time by reading through every record of Phonlist and searching for an equivalent record in Emplist.

The code that follows:

```
IF .NOT. EOF()
     REPLACE A.phone WITH B.phone
     ? "Entered the phone number " + b.phone + "for
             " + a.last
     mctr = mctr + 1
ENDIF
```

begins by using the EOF( ) function to see if a matching record was found.

If one was found, the program uses the REPLACE command to copy the phone number from Phonlist (the current value of B.phone) into the current record of Emplist (A.phone).

It also adds 1 to the variable *mctr* only if a match was found. Thus, *mctr* keeps track of how many new phone numbers were entered in Emplist.

Finally, the code

```
        SELECT A
        SKIP
        ? "In Emplist, up to record number "
        ?? RECNO()
    ENDDO
```

comes at the end of the DO loop. The SELECT command makes Emplist the current table again, and it moves the pointer to the next record.

Then, when control returns to the DO loop, the WHILE condition will check to see if it has reached the EOF( ) of the Emplist table. If EOF( ) is true, it skips the DO loop and goes to the end of the program. If EOF( ) is not true, it executes the DO loop again, searching for a match to more records in Emplist.

Before returning to the beginning of the DO loop, the program prints a message saying which record of Emplist it has reached. Although displaying this sort of message is not necessary, it is very helpful in a program that takes a significant amount of time to execute, so that the user has some idea of how the program is progressing. It is very annoying to stare at a blank screen while you wait.

When you are writing this sort of quick utility program, it is easier to use ? and ?? to print a line of output made up of two data types, as this program does, than to use a function to convert data types so you can print them out with a single line of code.

Finally, after the DO loop is executed, the program uses the code

```
?
? mctr
?? "phone numbers entered in total."
```

which uses the *mctr* variable to tell you the total number of phone numbers entered in Emplist. Then it uses the following code:

```
? WAIT "Do you want to close the tables? (y/n)" to
          myesno
```

```
IF UPPER(myesno) = "Y"
     CLOSE ALL
     ? "Tables closed."
ENDIF
```

to ask the user whether to close the tables, and then to close them if a Y is entered.

▶ Using the Program

▶▶ NOTE

As mentioned earlier, this chapter assumes that you have not made the Emplist table part of a FoxPro database. If you have, you must remove it from the database, before you run this program.

To try the sample program:

1. If you have not already done so, enter **SET DEFAULT TO C:\LEARNFOX**.

2. USE the Emplist table. Enter **MODI STRU**, and use the Table Designer to add a Phone field to it, as shown in Figure 23.29. Close the Table Designer, saving the change.

3. Enter **COPY TO PHONLIST FOR STATE = "CA"** to create the Phonlist table and add sample records to it in an easy way, by including all records from Emplist that are from California. Then USE the Phonlist table, BROWSE it, and enter the telephone numbers in it, as shown in Figure 23.30. (The phone column in the illustration has been moved, so you can see which name goes with which phone number.)

4. Choose File ➤ New to create a new program file. Enter the program shown above in Figure 23.28. Close the window, saving the program with the name PHONENTR.PRG.

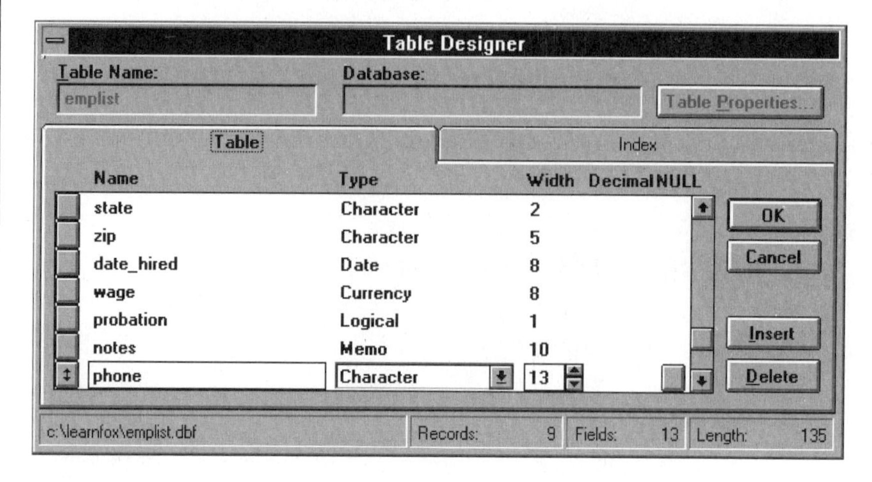

FIGURE 23.29

Modifying the Emplist table

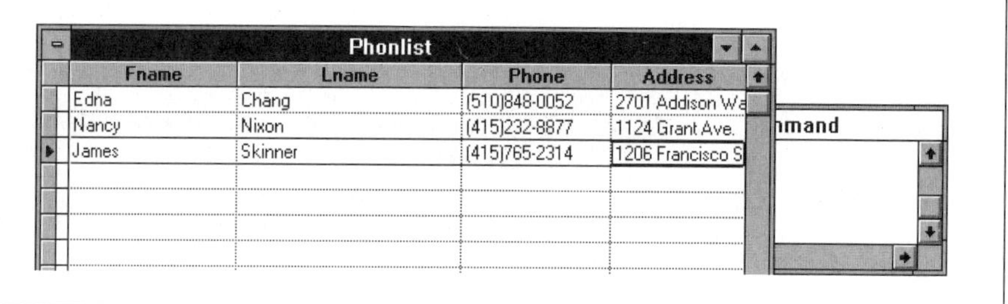

FIGURE 23.30

Sample data in the Phonlist table

5. Finally, enter **DO PHONENTR** to run the program. If Visual FoxPro identifies bugs because of typographical errors in copying the program, correct them and run the program again. It should display the messages shown in Figure 23.31. When it is done, open the Emplist table and browse it to verify that the phone numbers from Phonlist have all been added to it.

This is the sort of problem in data manipulation that Visual FoxPro users generally go to consultants to solve, but it is not difficult to write programs to solve this sort of problem yourself, using the techniques that you learned in this chapter.

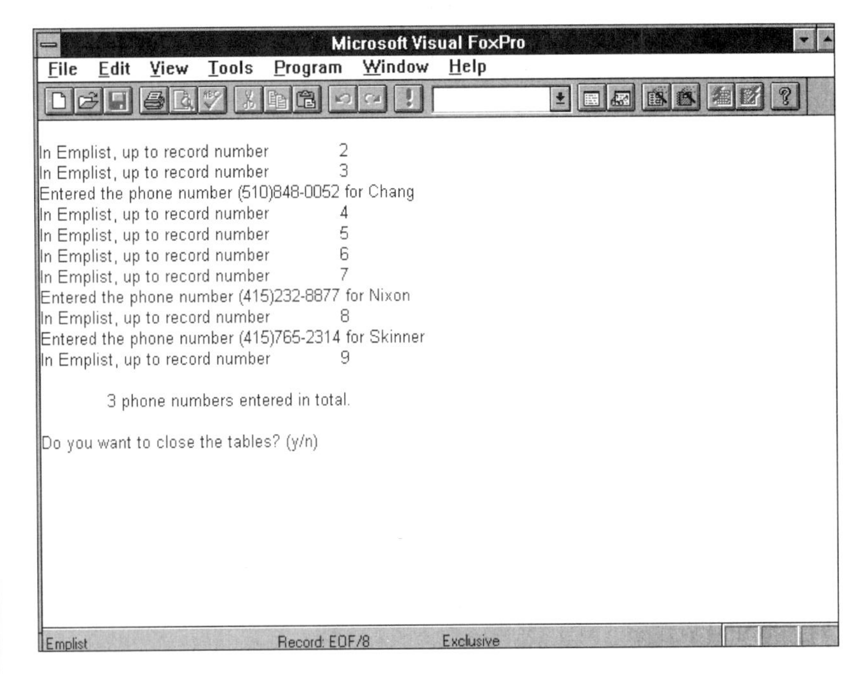
Microsoft Visual FoxPro
File Edit View Tools Program Window Help
In Emplist, up to record number 2
In Emplist, up to record number 3
Entered the phone number (510)848-0052 for Chang
In Emplist, up to record number 4
In Emplist, up to record number 5
In Emplist, up to record number 6
In Emplist, up to record number 7
Entered the phone number (415)232-8877 for Nixon
In Emplist, up to record number 8
Entered the phone number (415)765-2314 for Skinner
In Emplist, up to record number 9
3 phone numbers entered in total.
Do you want to close the tables? (y/n)
Emplist
Record: EOF/8
Exclusive

FIGURE 23.31 *The messages indicate which phone numbers have been added to Emplist.*

►► To Sum Up

In this chapter, you got a thorough grounding in the basics of procedural programming in Visual FoxPro, which you can use to write your own utility programs and which will be useful background if you go on to learn more advanced object-oriented programming. In the next chapter, you will look at the Menu Builder, which you can use to set up turnkey applications for beginners.

CHAPTER 24

Using the Menu Designer

FAST TRACK

▶ *To use the Menu Designer to create a new menu,* **724**

select File ➤ New and select the Menu radio button; name the menu later by selecting File ➤ Save As. Alternatively, enter the command **CREATE MENU <menu name>**.

▶ *To add a menu item to the main menu bar,* **726**

enter the prompt. Use the Result drop-down control to specify whether its result will be a command, an item on the Visual FoxPro main menu, a submenu, or a procedure. If it is a command or a menu item, simply enter the result in the editing area to its right. If it is a procedure, select the Create button to display an editing area where you enter it. If it is a submenu, select the Create button to display a panel where you can enter its prompts and their results. Use the Insert and Delete buttons to insert a new item or delete an existing one.

▶ *To add a menu item to a submenu,* **728**

enter the prompt and use the Result control to specify its result, just as you do with the main menu. The options are the same, except that you can assign one of the menu bars of the Visual FoxPro system menu instead of one of its menu pads. When you are done, use the Menu Level drop-down control to move back up to the main menu bar.

▶ *To define hot keys,* **731**

add the characters \< before the letter of the prompt you want to use as the hot key. You can use hot keys on menu pads only when the menu is already activated. You can use hot keys on the bars of submenus only when the submenu is already popped up.

▶ ***To define shortcut keys,*** *732*

select the Options button to the right of the prompt in the Menu Designer to display the Prompt Options dialog box. Select the Shortcut check box to display the Menu Shortcut dialog box. Press the shortcut key combination, and it is automatically entered in this dialog box.

▶ ***To add code before or after the menu code that is generated,*** *735*

select Menu ➤ General Options. In the General Options dialog box, select the Setup or Cleanup check box. The code you enter in the Setup editing area will be included before the menu code the Menu Designer generates. The code you enter in the Cleanup editing area will be included after the menu code the Menu Designer generates; this is the place to put general-purpose procedures that will be called by several of the menu options.

▶ ***To create a quick menu,*** *738*

select Menu ➤ Quick Menu. The quick menu has all the features of the Visual FoxPro system menu. You can remove features or add extra ones. The Menu Designer generates code to create a Visual FoxPro system menu, which has the name _MSYSMENU.

▶ ***To use a menu instead of the system menu,*** *741*

use the command READ EVENTS immediately after the DO command that displays the menu. Include the command CLEAR EVENTS as the result of File ➤ Exit or of one of the other menu options.

In the last chapter, you learned to use procedural programming to create a utility program. To run this program, you had to choose Program ➤ Do or use the DO command.

Now you will look at how to give a program a more user-friendly interface by using the Menu Designer. To help users run your programs, you can create new menu options and add them to the Visual FoxPro system menu, or you can create an entirely new menu system and use it instead of the default system menu.

After learning how to use the Menu Designer, you will create a sample menu, which will let a novice use the sample application that you have been working with all through this book.

The Menu Designer

You use the Menu Designer, shown in Figure 24.1, in much the same way you use other features of Visual FoxPro. To use the Menu Designer to create a new menu, select File ➤ New, select the Menu radio button, and click the New button; name the menu later by selecting File ➤ Save As.

Alternatively, simply enter the command **CREATE MENU <menu name>**.

NOTE

Because the Menu Designer is an advanced feature of Visual FoxPro, there is no Menu Wizard; you must use the Menu Designer window directly.

FIGURE 24.1

The Menu Designer

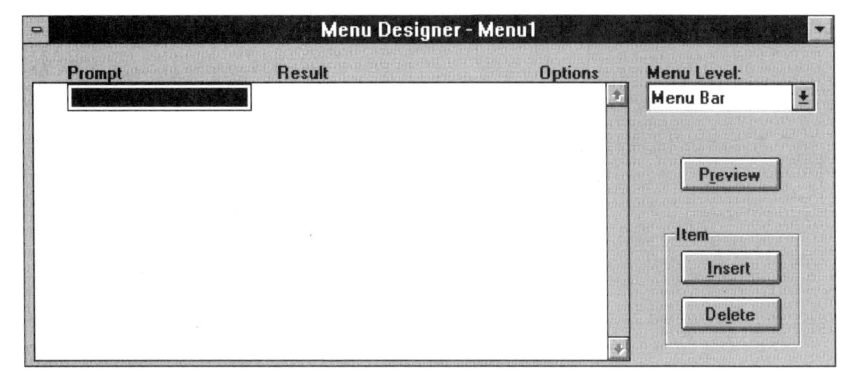

To use the Menu Designer to modify an existing menu, select File ➤ Open and use the Open dialog box in the usual way to open the menu file you want. Alternatively, enter the command **MODIFY MENU <menu name>.**

When you use the Menu Designer, a Menu item is added to the Visual FoxPro main menu, which lets you create a quick menu, preview the menu, or insert and delete menu items.

Generating Menu Code

The specifications for the menu are kept in an ordinary database table with the extension MNX. You open this MNX file to display these specifications in the Menu Designer, in order to modify a menu.

After you have entered the options you want in the Menu Designer, you must generate menu code, by selecting Menu ➤ Generate.

The code that is generated is kept in a program with the extension MPR, so you must use the entire name of the program, including its extension, when you run the program using a DO command. If you use the command **DO <file name>** without including an extension, Visual FoxPro assumes that the file has the extension PRG.

► The Basics of Designing Menus

The Menu Designer is easy to use. You begin with the main menu bar as the uppermost level of your menu system and type the prompts for it in the left column. When you enter a prompt, a drop-down control is displayed in the Result column. For the main menu bar, as you can see in Figure 24.2, the options on the drop-down control are Command, Pad Name, Submenu, and Procedure.

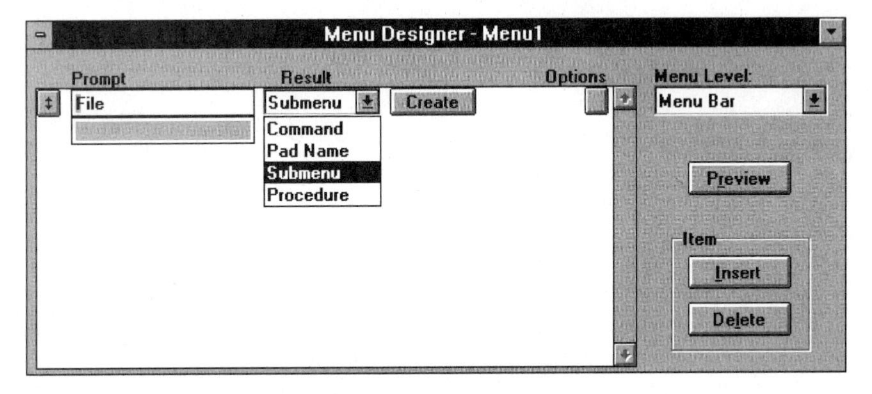

FIGURE 24.2 ►

Adding a menu item

Assigning a Command to a Menu Option

If you select Command, a text box is displayed to the right of the Result drop-down list. You must enter a single command that will be executed when the user selects this menu pad, for example **QUIT** or **PACK**.

Assigning a Pad to a Menu Option

If you selected Pad Name, a text box is displayed to the right of this drop-down list. As shown in Figure 24.3, you must enter the name of a menu pad—either one you defined yourself or one of the Visual FoxPro system menu pads—to assign all of its features to this menu.

To assign Visual FoxPro system menu pads to the pads you are defining, use the internal names of the pads shown in Table 24.1.

FIGURE 24.3

Assigning a pad to a menu option

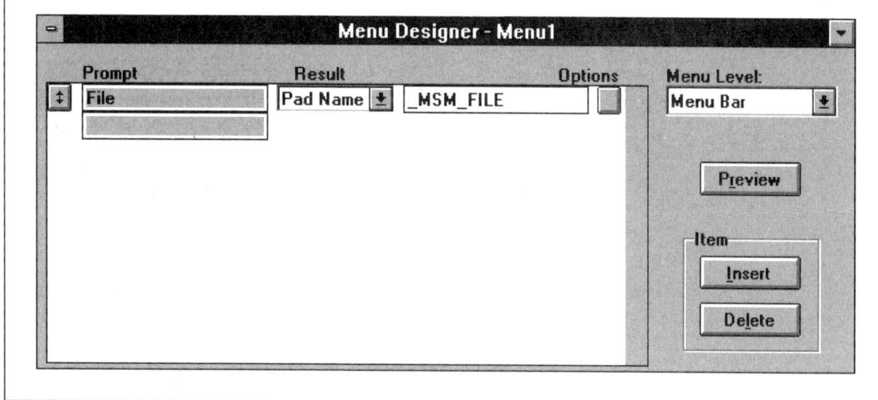

TABLE 24.1: *Names of Visual FoxPro Menu Pads*

Menu Pad	Internal Name
File	_MSM_FILE
Edit	_MSM_EDIT
View	_MSM_VIEW
Tools	_MSM_TOOLS
Program	_MSM_PROG
Format	_MSM_TEXT
Window	_MSM_WINDO
Help	_MSM_SYSTM

Assigning a Procedure to a Menu Option

If you select Procedure, a Create button is displayed to the right of the Result control. Clicking this button opens an editing window, as shown in Figure 24.4, where you can enter a procedure to be executed whenever this menu option is selected.

You should *not* use the PROCEDURE command (covered in Chapter 23) to name this procedure, since Visual FoxPro will generate the procedure name when it generates the program.

FIGURE 24.4

Entering a procedure to execute when the option is selected

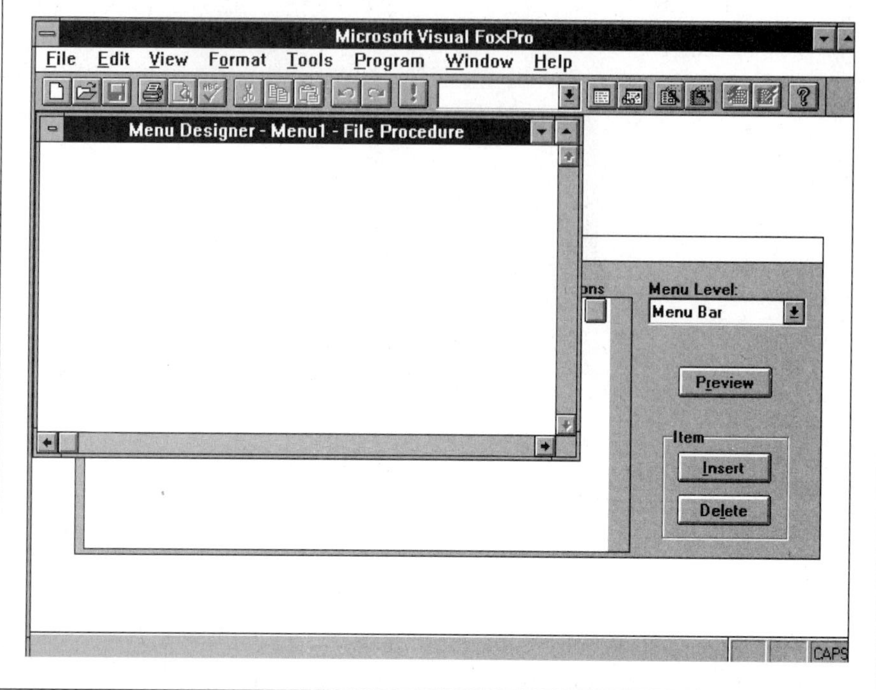

Once you create the procedure, this button changes from Create to Edit, and you can select it to modify the submenu or procedure you created earlier.

Assigning a Submenu to a Menu Option

If you select Submenu, a Create button is displayed to the right of the Result control. Clicking this button lets you create a submenu. Once you create the submenu, this button changes from Create to Edit, and you can select it to modify the submenu you created earlier.

When you are working on the main menu bar, the default Result setting is Submenu since you most often want to display a drop-down submenu when the user clicks a pad of the main menu bar. As soon as you enter a prompt name, Submenu is selected, and you just need to select the Create button to create a drop-down menu that will be displayed whenever you select the menu option.

When you create a submenu, you use a panel that is just like the panel you use to enter selections for defining the main menu bar. Simply enter the prompts to be displayed by the drop-down in the left column, and enter the result for each in the Result column. The difference, as you can see in Figure 24.5, is that when you are working on submenus, the options on the Result drop-down are Command, Bar #, Submenu, and Procedure.

FIGURE 24.5

Adding a submenu item

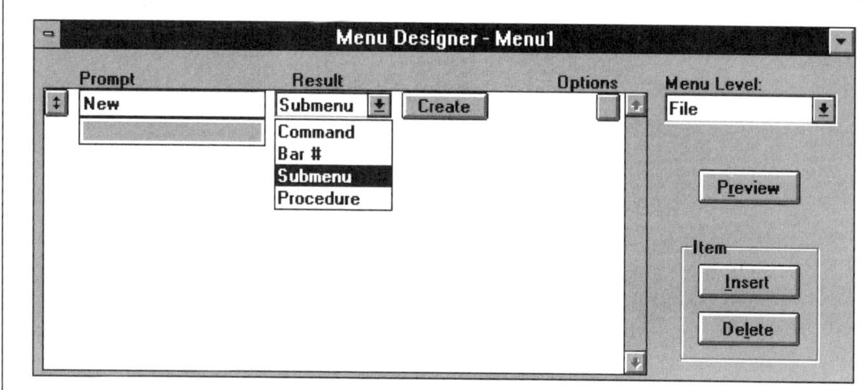

These are the same options available for the main menu, except that Pad Name is replaced by Bar #. Rather than assigning an item a pad as its result, you can assign it a bar number of your own or the name of one of the bars of the Visual FoxPro system menu.

To see the names of all the menu bars of the Visual FoxPro system menu, select Menu ➤ Quick Menu. This option creates a menu with pads and drop-down options that are the same as the Visual FoxPro main menu. Each drop-down submenu item uses Bar # to assign it the same action as the equivalent item on the Visual FoxPro menu, as discussed below in the section "Quick Menus." Alternatively, look under the Help topic "Menu—System Menu Names" for more information.

NOTE

As with the main menu, do not use the PROCEDURE command to name procedures you assign to submenu options. Visual FoxPro will name the procedure when it generates the code for the menu program.

You can see how easy it is to create a main menu bar and submenu drop-down lists. Notice that you can create a submenu under a submenu—that is, a second drop-down that is displayed when one of the bars on a menu drop-down is selected—with no extra effort.

Moving through the Menu Tree

To work on a submenu, as you know, you display its parent menu and select the Create or Edit button to the right of its prompt.

To move back up to the parent menu from a submenu, select the Menu Level control in the upper-right corner of the Menu Designer, shown in Figure 24.6. This drop-down list shows the name of the current menu, whether it is the main menu bar or a submenu. To move up the menu system, select the name of the parent menu you want to work on from this list.

FIGURE 24.6

Moving up the menu tree

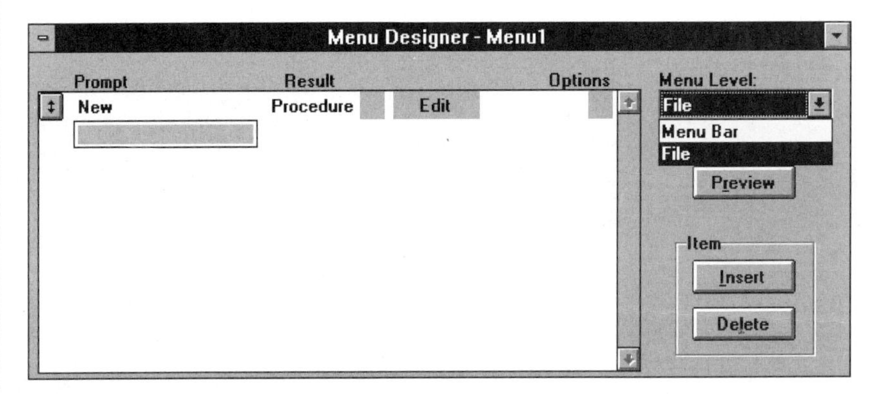

Deleting, Inserting, and Changing the Order of Menu Items

Select the Delete button or choose Menu ➤ Delete Item to delete the currently selected menu item.

Select the Insert button or choose Menu ➤ Insert Item to insert a new menu item above the currently selected menu item.

To change the order of items, simply click and drag the button to its left.

Testing the Menu

Click the Try It button or choose Menu ➤ Preview to try using the menu system without taking time for code generation.

When you do either of these, the menu bar you have defined in the Menu Designer is displayed at the top of the screen, and the drop-down submenus that you specified are displayed when you select their pads from the main menu.

When you choose an option that executes code, however, Visual Fox-Pro just displays a dialog box with the code that would be executed by that option.

▶ Menu Shortcuts

The Menu Designer lets you create two kinds of shortcuts, hot keys and shortcut key combinations.

Hot Keys

The term *hot keys* is used in a very precise sense when you are defining menus: A hot key is a single key you can press in a particular situation to select a menu option. For example, F is the hot key for the File menu pad; if any menu pad is already highlighted, you can pull down the File menu by pressing F. Likewise, S is the hot key for the Save option on the File menu; if the File menu is already displayed, you can select Save by pressing S.

It is easy to specify hot keys for menu options: Add the characters **\<** before the character you want to use as the hot key.

NOTE

Many Visual FoxPro menus have their options grouped, with groups separated by lines. If you want to group choices in this way, you can add this sort of line by using the characters \- as a prompt.

When you define a hot key using \< before a character, it only creates this sort of single-key hot key.

Shortcut Key Combinations

In addition to these hot keys, Visual FoxPro also has shortcut key combinations for many menu choices, which can be used to make a selection immediately, regardless of where you are in the program.

In Visual FoxPro and other Windows applications, these shortcut key combinations are different for main menu pads and for their drop-down menu options:

- **Menu pads:** The shortcut key combination for any pad on the main menu is generally Alt plus the hot key. For example, if one of the menu pads is already highlighted, you can display the File menu by pressing the hot key F. At any other time, you can display the File menu by pressing the shortcut key combination Alt+F.
- **Menu commands:** The shortcut key for a menu command is generally Ctrl plus some key. For example, you can select Edit ➤ Paste at any time by pressing Ctrl+V.

You must keep this distinction between hot keys and shortcut keys in mind when you are designing menus. The symbol \< lets you create only hot keys. If you also want to implement a shortcut key combination, you must use the Options button to the right of the relevant item in the Menu Designer, as described below in the section "Prompt Options."

►► NOTE

If you want your main menu to work like most Windows applications—for example, if you want F to be the hot key and Alt+F the shortcut key combination for the File menu pad—you must define both a hot key and a shortcut key combination.

► Prompt Options

Selecting the Options button for any menu item displays the Prompt Options dialog box, shown in Figure 24.7.

FIGURE 24.7

Prompt Options dialog box

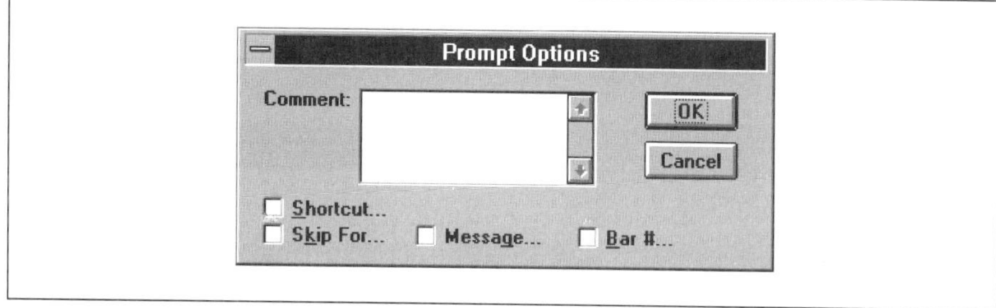

Specifying a Shortcut Key

Select the Shortcut check box of the Prompt Options dialog box to specify a key combination shortcut (as described above) for that menu item. Visual FoxPro displays the Key Definition dialog box, shown in Figure 24.8.

FIGURE 24.8

The Key Definition dialog box

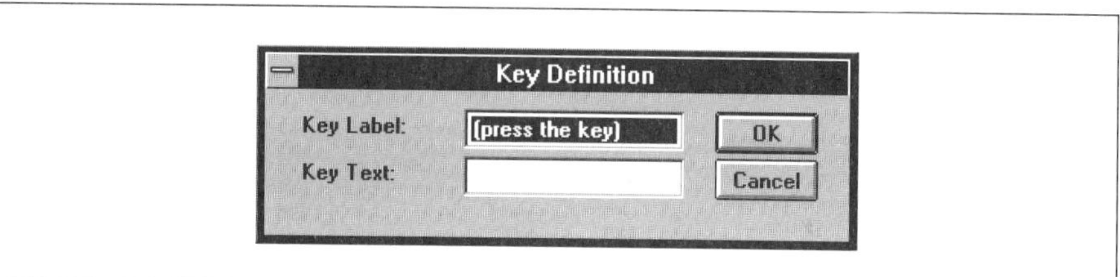

This dialog box prompts you to press the key you want to use as the shortcut in order to enter it in the Key Label text box.

If you want to follow the same conventions as the Visual FoxPro system menu, press Alt plus the hot key as the shortcut for main menu pads.

In addition, you should enter any text that you want displayed as part of the option in the Key Text text box. For example, enter **Ctrl+V** here if you are making that key combination the shortcut for the Edit ➤ Paste command, and you want that prompt displayed at the right of the Edit menu bar.

Skipping a Menu Option

Select the Skip For check box to disable the current menu item under certain conditions. Visual FoxPro displays the Expression Builder, and you must create or enter a logical expression. The menu option will be disabled when this expression evaluates to .F.

When you are developing applications, it is important to disable certain options at some times, to avoid conflicts.

Displaying a Help Message in the Status Bar

Selecting Message displays the Expression Builder, where you can specify a Help message that will be displayed when the option is highlighted, like the messages that are displayed in the Visual FoxPro status bar when you move through the menu pads or options.

Ordinarily, you simply enter a text expression to use as the help message.

Naming a Pad

Select Pad Name to display the Pad Name dialog box, if you are working on the main menu bar; or select Bar # to display the Bar Number dialog box, shown in Figure 24.9, if you are working on a submenu. These let you specify the name for a menu pad or menu option.

FIGURE 24.9

The Bar Number dialog box

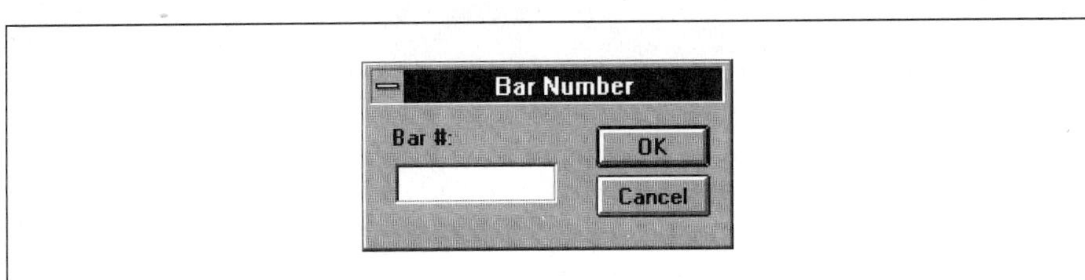

If you want to work with the menuing code that the Menu Designer generates, you should use these dialog boxes to enter meaningful names for menu items.

Entering Comments

The Prompt Options dialog box also includes a Comment area, where you can enter comments for your own use.

The View Menu

When you use the Menu Designer, the following commands are added to the Visual FoxPro View menu:

- **General Options** lets you enter options that apply to the entire menu system.
- **Menu Options** lets you enter options that apply to the main menu bar or a specific submenu.

General Options

Selecting Menu ➤ General Options displays the dialog box shown in Figure 24.10.

FIGURE 24.10

The General Options dialog box

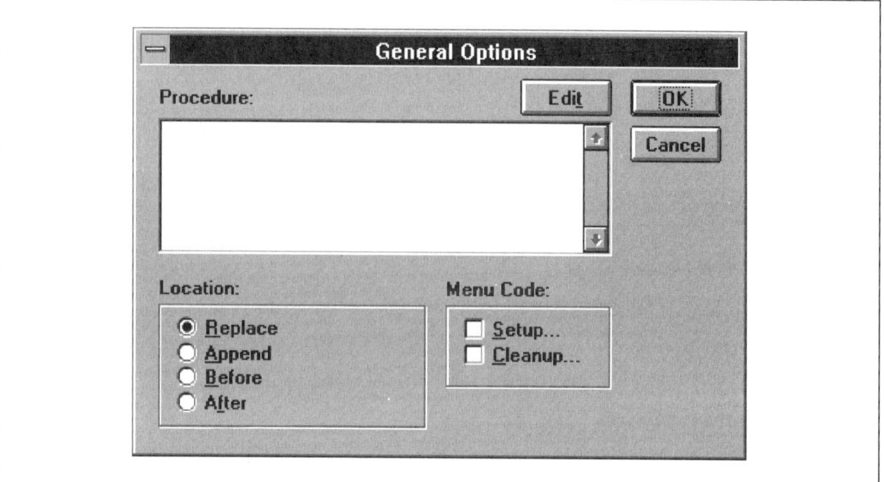

Entering Setup and Cleanup Code

The most important features of this dialog box are the Setup and Cleanup check boxes (in the Menu Code area). Select these to display text-editing windows where you can enter setup code to be executed before executing the code that displays the menu and Cleanup code to be executed after the code that displays the menu.

For example, if you create a menu system to let a user work with a relational database, you can enter setup code to open and relate the tables.

If you are using the menu as a system menu, you must remember that the entire program, including the cleanup code, is executed before the user works with the menu system. In this case, for example, you cannot use the cleanup code to close tables, or they will be closed before the user works with the menu system. Instead, you can attach cleanup code to the File ➤ Exit command. For more information, see the section "Using the Default System Menu" below.

TIP

You can also use the Cleanup text-editing window to enter general-purpose procedures that are called by various options of the menu system. Unlike procedures entered as the result of menu items, these procedures must include the PROCEDURE command to name them. Since you call them elsewhere in the program, you need to know their names, and so their names cannot be generated by Visual FoxPro. Simply type the procedure after the cleanup code. When the program is generated, cleanup code will be at the end of the main module, and the procedure will appear immediately after it, just where you would put it if you were writing out the program by hand.

Specifying the Location of the Menu

Select one of the Location radio buttons of the General Options dialog box to specify how the menu system you are defining is placed with respect to the active menu.

By default, Replace is selected, so that the new menu system replaces the active menu.

You can select Append to add the new menu system to the right of the active menu.

If you select Before or After, a drop-down control appears so that you can select among the prompts of the active menu; the new menu system will be inserted before or after the prompt you select.

You have noticed that, when you choose certain options from FoxPro, a new menu pad is added to the system menu. The Replace, Before, and After options let you add new pads that are displayed this way.

Entering a General Procedure

Use the Procedure text-editing area to enter a procedure for the entire menu system—or, to enter a longer procedure, select the Edit button to open an editing window.

This procedure will be executed when any menu pad is selected. If you have created a procedure for a specific menu pad, however, it will be executed instead.

The procedure entered in this text-editing area is executed only if no other procedure exists for the menu pad, and it is useful primarily for testing a menu as you are developing it.

▶ Menu Options

Choosing View ➤ Menu Options displays the dialog box shown in Figure 24.11, which lets you add options for just the main menu bar or just a specific submenu.

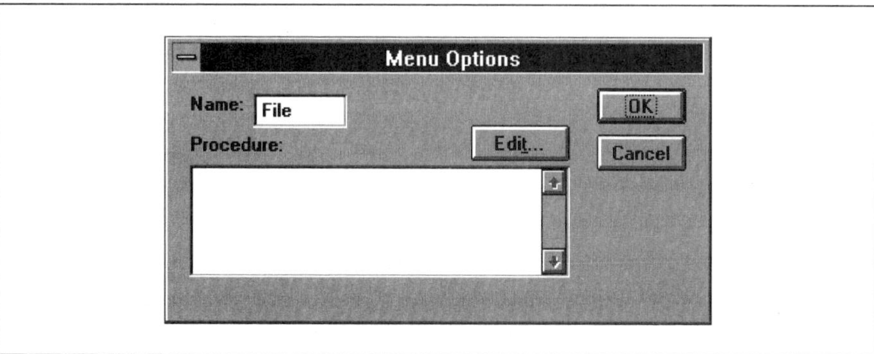

FIGURE 24.11

The Menu Options dialog box

Use the Procedure text-editing area or select the Edit button to enter a procedure to be used by all the menu options of the main menu bar or of the drop-down control for which you are defining the menu options.

When you define multiple procedures, the procedure at the lowest level takes precedence. Thus, if you define a procedure as a General option and then use this dialog box to define a procedure for a submenu, this submenu procedure takes precedence. But if you define procedures or other options for individual bars of that submenu, they take precedence over the procedure defined here.

The Menu Options dialog box is usually used to define a default option for all the items on a menu bar or drop-down to be used for testing while you are developing a program. The default option is executed only until you add specific results for all menu pads and drop-down menus.

►► Quick Menus

The Menu ➤ Quick Menu option is active only if nothing has been entered in the Menu Definition window. Choose it to create a quick menu that works identically to the Visual FoxPro system menu. You can then use the Menu Designer to customize this menu as needed.

As you can see in Figure 24.12, the Quick Menu main menu bar has the same options as the Visual FoxPro main menu, and each calls a submenu. Figure 24.13 shows the Edit submenu, which has the same items as Visual FoxPro's Edit menu. Each of these items uses the Bar # option of the Result menu to assign it the same result as the equivalent item in the Visual FoxPro main menu.

Note the names used to refer to the items of the Visual FoxPro Edit menu. Each begins with _MED_. Results are assigned to all the submenus of the quick menu in the same way. As you know, you can use the Bar # option of the Result drop-down list plus one of these names to define the result of any submenu item on any menu you create.

You can begin with this quick menu and alter it in any way you want to create variations on the Visual FoxPro system menu. For example, if you want to be able to execute the phone lookup program that you created in Chapter 23 from your Visual FoxPro system menu, just add a prompt for it to one of these submenus, and enter the command **DO PHONENTR** as its result.

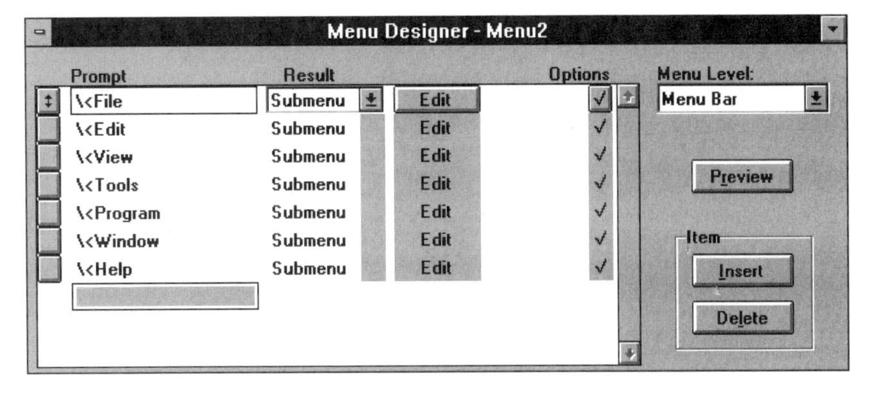

FIGURE 24.12 The Quick Menu main menu bar

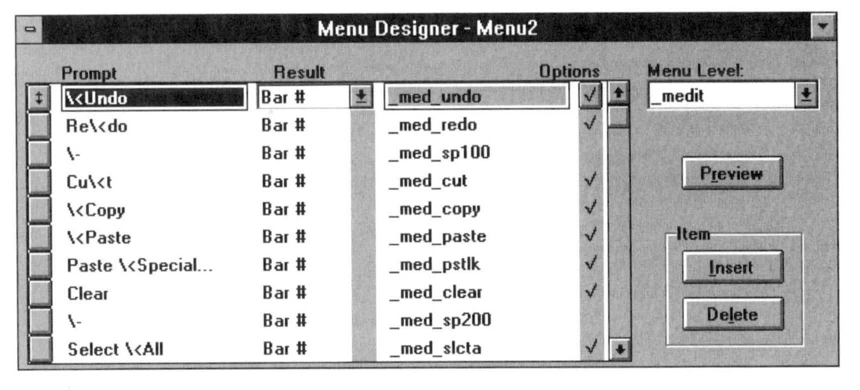

FIGURE 24.13 The Edit submenu of the Quick Menu menubar

▶▶ Generating Code

Once you have finished designing the menu system, you can produce the code by selecting Menu ➤ Generate to call up the dialog box shown in Figure 24.14. Visual FoxPro will prompt you to save changes and to name the menu you are creating before displaying this dialog box, if you have not yet done so.

In the Output File text box, enter the name of the program file that will hold the generated code. Alternatively, select the button to its right to display the Save As dialog box, which you can use to name the file.

FIGURE 24.14

Generating the code

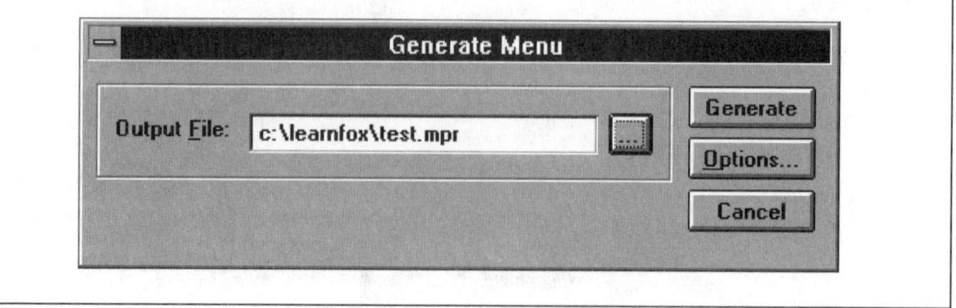

As a default, Visual FoxPro suggests the same name as the menu design, with the extension MPR.

Click the Comment Options button to display the Options dialog box, shown in Figure 24.15. Here you can enter your name and company name to be included in the header of the generated program as comments, choose whether comments should be surrounded by boxes or asterisks, specify the location of program files, and choose project options.

FIGURE 24.15

The options dialog box

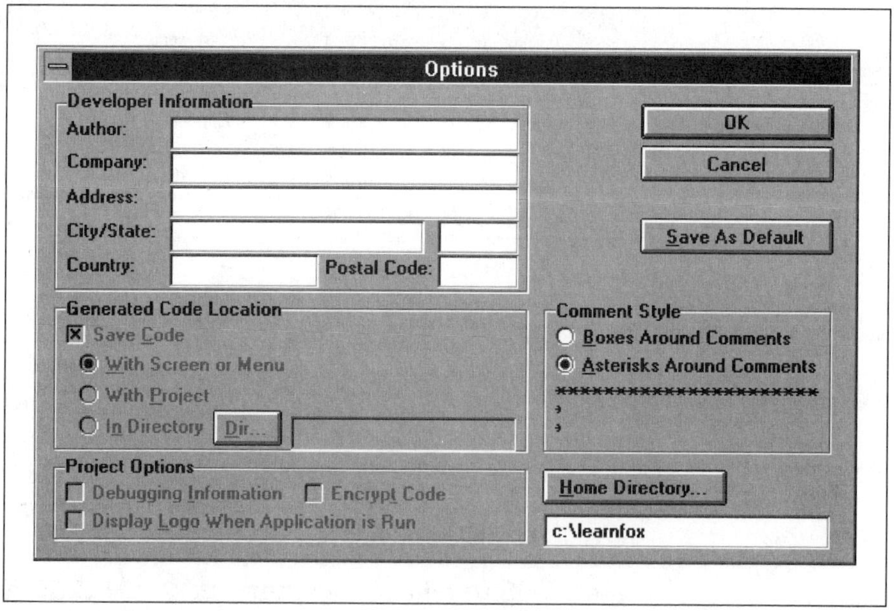

Menuing Commands

It might seem strange that the Quick Menu option lets you create menus that are variations of the Visual FoxPro system menu, since it is unlikely that any program you ever write will have a menu like Visual FoxPro's menu. However, the Visual FoxPro language actually lets you use menus in two different ways:

- You can define menus to use as substitutes for the Visual FoxPro system menu. After you run the program that defines this menu, by using the command DO MENU <menu name>, Visual FoxPro returns to its usual Command Window interface, but displays the new menu that you defined instead of its usual system menu. By altering the system menu in this way, you can make Visual FoxPro easier to use for beginners.
- You can define menus to use in your own applications. You must use the menu by running a program that includes the command DO MENU <menu name> followed by the command READ EVENTS. Once the READ EVENTS command is issued, Visual FoxPro will not display its usual interface until you issue the command CLEAR EVENTS. Thus, this method lets you use Visual FoxPro to create entire new applications.

NOTE

Knowing these menuing commands will help you find errors as you look through generated programs while debugging. For example, if you entered an invalid command as the command to be executed when one of the menu options is chosen, the debugger will place you on the line of code with that command. Then you might want to scroll back through the program to look for the earlier line that makes this later line invalid. You should know enough to skip through the menuing commands themselves looking for the bits of code you added. For more details about the commands, see the individual commands and cross-references in Appendix B.

Both of these methods are discussed at greater length below. Both use the same commands to define the menu system, and you should glance at these before looking at the different ways of using the menu.

▶ Defining a Menu

Before the Menu Designer was added to Visual FoxPro, you had to type a tedious and repetitive set of commands to define a menu system. The brief descriptions that follow are intended to give you a quick overview of the menu-definition code that the Menu Designer generates, which will help you understand this code; they are not intended to get you started writing menu code.

First, you had to use the command DEFINE MENU <menu name> to specify the name of the main menu bar. Then you had to use a series of commands in the form DEFINE PAD <pad name> OF <menu name> PROMPT <char exp> to specify the names and prompts of all the pads of this menu bar.

You also had to use a series of commands in the form DEFINE POPUP <control name> to specify the names and locations of the drop-down controls. And for each control, you had to use a series of commands in the form DEFINE BAR <num exp> OF <drop-down name> PROMPT <char exp> to specify all of its options.

For each pad, you also had to use the command ON PAD <pad name> OF <menu name> ACTIVATE POPUP <drop-down name> to "install" the drop-downs in the appropriate pads so that a drop-down is activated when its pad is selected.

You also had to write a series of commands in the form ON SELECTION BAR <num exp> OF <drop-down name> <command> to specify the command that would be executed when each menu option was chosen. Alternatively, you could use the command ON BAR <num exp> OF <drop-down name 1> ACTIVATE POPUP <drop-down name 2> ¦ ACTIVATE MENU <menu name> to display a submenu when a menu option is chosen. Notice that the menu options are referred to as numbered bars of their drop-down lists; BAR 1 is the first option on the drop-down, and so on.

This is just an outline of the commands used for defining a menu, but it is enough to let you look through the code generated by the Menu Designer without being totally lost while you are debugging a menu program, and it is enough to let you see how unwieldy these commands are and how much easier it is to use the Menu Designer than to type them by hand.

▶ Customizing the System Menu

It is relatively easy to design a menu program to modify the Visual FoxPro system menu.

Create the new menu that you want to substitute for the default system menu in one of two ways:

- Begin by opening the Menu Designer and choosing Menu ➤ Quick Menu to create a custom menu with all the options of the usual Visual FoxPro system menu. Then modify these options as needed.
- Use the Menu Designer to create new pads and submenus that you want to add to the system menu. Then choose Tools ➤ General Options and use the Location area of the General Options dialog box to add this menu to the default system menu, rather than replacing the default system menu with it.

In either case, after generating the code, simply use the command **DO <menu name>**. Visual FoxPro will run the program and return to its usual interface with the new menu as its system menu. You will be able to use the Command window and other features of the interface as well as using the new menu you created.

▶ Creating an Application

If you are using Visual FoxPro to develop an entire application, though, you obviously do not want to return to the usual Visual FoxPro interface. If you are creating an accounting application, for example, you do not want to display the Visual FoxPro Command window, which could only confuse the user by adding capabilities that are irrelevant to your new application.

The way to prevent Visual FoxPro from running the entire program is to use the READ EVENTS commands. This command suspends execution of the program and waits for user input, rather than executing the entire program and displaying irrelevant features of the Visual FoxPro interface, such as the Command window, so that the user can make selections from the interface that the program creates. The program does not continue executing until the command CLEAR EVENTS is issued.

Typically, to create an application, you use a main program, similar to the one shown below:

```
* MAIN.PRG
* Sample main program for a menu driven application
*************************************************

DO setup
DO mainmenu.mpr
READ EVENTS
DO cleanup
```

The first line of code runs a program named SETUP.PRG, which does things like control the working environment and open tables. The second line of code displays your menu.

Then, the READ EVENTS command suspends execution of this program and waits for user input. The custom menu is displayed, but the program does not return to the Visual FoxPro interface, so the user can make selections from your menu without being distracted by the Command window or any other irrelevant features of Visual FoxPro.

Some feature of the custom menu must execute the command CLEAR EVENTS. Typically, you would attach this command to the menu option File ➤ Exit. Alternatively, you could create a form with a button that executes this command.

Once the user executes CLEAR EVENTS from the custom interface you created, the execution of the MAIN program continues. Its final line of code runs a program named CLEANUP.PRG, which might reset the working environment to its default settings and return to Visual FoxPro or might simply QUIT Visual FoxPro and return to Windows.

▶▶ NOTE

As you learned earlier, the General Options dialog box lets you enter Setup and Cleanup code for a menu system. This Setup code could be used in place of SETUP.PRG, described above, but the Cleanup code cannot be used in place of CLEANUP.PRG, because the entire menu program, including this Cleanup code, is executed before you reach the command READ EVENTS. Thus, if you included the command QUIT in CLEANUP.PRG, which is run by MAIN.PRG, the READ EVENTS command would let the user work with the menu, and the program would QUIT and return to Windows only after the user chose some option that executed the CLEAR EVENTS command. On the other hand, if you included the command QUIT in the Cleanup code of the menu system, this command would be part of the menu program that was run before the READ EVENTS command. The menu program would display the menu momentarily and then QUIT Visual FoxPro and return to Windows before the user could make any menu selections.

▶ Using the Default System Menu

Whichever method you use to display a custom menu, you may want to return to using the default system menu at some point. You can do this by using the command:

```
SET SYSMENU TO DEFAULT
```

For example, you would include this command in the cleanup code in CLEANUP.PRG, as described above, if you wanted to return the user to Visual FoxPro after exiting the application.

This command has one other option that you may find useful. SET SYSMENU TO <menu list> limits the system menu to the menus in the list; the list can include the internal menu names listed in Table 24.1, earlier in this chapter. To set up Visual FoxPro so it is easy for a beginner to use, for example, you might enter

```
SET SYSMENU TO _MSM_FILE, _MSM_EDIT, MST_VIEW,
_MSM_WINDO,_MSM_HELP
```

to eliminate the Tools and Program menus from the System menu. (Of course, you should enter the command on a single line even though it occupies two lines on the printed page.)

SET SYSMENU TO by itself displays a System menu bar with no pads. For other options, see Appendix B.

▸▸ TIP

If a program that includes a menu is interrupted—for example, because it includes an error—the program's menu will still be the system menu. Remember that you can enter SET SYSMENU TO DEFAULT to return to the ordinary Visual FoxPro menu.

▸▸ Event-Driven Programming

There is one other fundamental point to bear in mind when you create applications with custom menus.

The sort of procedural programming that you looked at in the last chapter is linear. The user can do only one thing at a time. On the other hand, as you learned in that chapter, a modern interface of windows and drop-down menus is *event-driven.* There are a number of possibilities open for the user at any time, and what the program does next depends on what the user does.

For example, if a Browse window is open, the main menu bar also remains accessible. In the midst of browsing a table, without closing the Browse window, the user can select one of the other menu options to export records or produce a report or mailing labels.

Needless to say, this makes programming much more complex. Rather than just following one train of logic from beginning to end, as you do with procedural programming, you must think about every combination of selections the user can make to see if any interferes with any other; you must prevent the user from simultaneously performing two actions that might conflict with each other.

You can avoid this sort of conflict by using dialog boxes and menu skip conditions.

The Modal Read

The usual convention is that while a dialog box is being used, no other control is accessible. Thus, the dialog box is effectively isolated from the rest of the program, simplifying program design.

If you go on to use the Visual FoxPro Form Designer to do object-oriented development, you will see that it is easy to create dialog boxes that behave in this way. It involves generating a MODAL clause in the READ command; a *modal read* makes it impossible to use other features of the interface until the dialog box is closed and the READ is terminated.

The SKIP FOR Clause

You can handle conflicts among windows that are not dialog boxes by creating SKIP conditions for menus or commands. For example, the menu system of Visual FoxPro itself disables menu options when dialog boxes are displayed rather than using modal reads, so that you can still use its Control menu, even when a dialog box is displayed.

You learned earlier that when you select the Options box for any menu prompt (either of the main menu bar or of a submenu), Visual FoxPro displays the Prompt Options dialog box, which includes (among other features) a Skip For check box. If you select this check box, Visual FoxPro displays the Expression Builder to let you enter a logical expression, and that menu pad or option will be disabled when the condition is true.

Using this check box generates the optional clause SKIP FOR <log exp> in the DEFINE PAD or the DEFINE BAR command used to define that menu item. The menu item is disabled whenever the logical condition is true.

► The SET SKIP OF Command

You can also disable and enable menu items by using a separate SET SKIP OF command. In their simplest form, these commands are

```
SET SKIP OF MENU <menu name> .T.¦.F.
SET SKIP OF PAD <pad name> .T.¦.F.
SET SKIP OF POPUP <drop-down name> .T.¦.F.
SET SKIP OF BAR <bar name> .T.¦.F.
```

For example, if your menu has a pad named TESTPAD, it will be disabled when you use the command SET SKIP OF PAD TESTPAD .T.; the user will not be able to use it. It will be reenabled when the command SET SKIP OF PAD TESTPAD .F. is executed. You can also use this command in more sophisticated ways by using a logical expression rather than .T. or .F.

►► NOTE

Do not confuse the SET SKIP OF command, used to disable menu items, with the SET SKIP TO command, covered in Chapter 14, which is used to create a one-to-many relation.

►► Sample Menu

These advanced features are covered in books on using Visual FoxPro for object-oriented development. For now, you should solidify your understanding of how to create a menu system by setting up a simple custom menu, to make it easier to use the sample Emplist application that you have been working with throughout this book. In this exercise you'll add an extra menu pad to the Visual FoxPro system menu that gives you instant access to the data of the Emplist table and the reports and mailing labels you created for it.

You will create a new menu pad, named Employees, with a submenu that has four options:

- **Data:** displays the form EMPLIST.SPR, which you created in Chapter 5 using the Form Wizard. This form gives the user an easy way of looking up records and maintaining the table.
- **Reports:** displays a submenu that lets the user produce any of the reports on the Emplist table that you created in Chapter 6. The user can display each of these reports in the Print Preview window, or can print each.
- **Labels:** lets the user print or preview the mailing labels you created in Chapter 7.
- **Remove this menu:** removes this extra menu pad from the system menu.

This is a use of the Menu Designer that's practical for typical Visual FoxPro users. You might want to add a pad with options like these to the system menu to make it easy for a user who knows nothing about Visual FoxPro to work with the Emplist table.

NOTE

As mentioned in Chapter 23, this part of the book is designed so it can be used immediately after Part II. Thus, it assumes that you have not made the Emplist table part of a FoxPro database. If you have, you must remove it from the database before you run this program.

To create the sample menu, follow these steps:

1. Choose File ➤ New. In the New dialog box, select the Menu radio button and click the New File button to display the Menu Designer.
2. As the first prompt, enter **Emplo\<yes**. Remember that you include **\<** to make the Y a hot key, but to make this behave like other menu options, you must also make Alt+Y a shortcut combination. To do this, first click the Options button at the right edge

of this line. In the Prompt Options dialog box, click the Shortcut check box. When Visual FoxPro displays the Key Definition dialog box, press Alt+Y to display it in that dialog box, as shown in Figure 24.16. Then click OK to return to the Prompt Options dialog box, and OK to return to the Menu Designer.

FIGURE 24.16

Creating a shortcut key combination

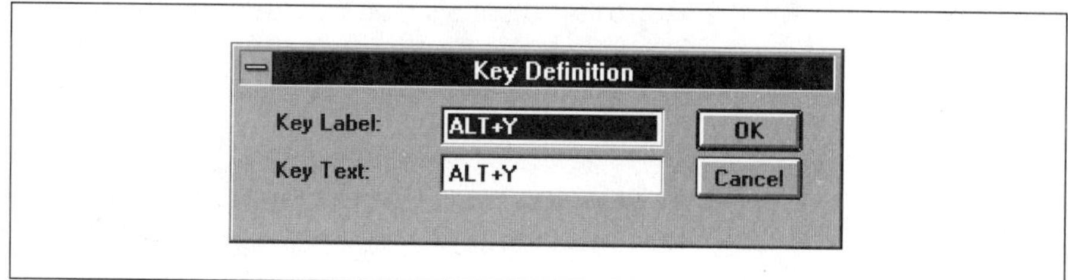

3. Now, to create the submenu for this menu pad, leave Submenu in the Result column, and click the Create button to its right. As the first prompt of the submenu, enter **\<Data.** Choose Command from the Result drop-down list. In the text box to its right, enter **DO \learnfox\emplist.scx**, as shown in Figure 24.17.

FIGURE 24.17

A menu option to display a form

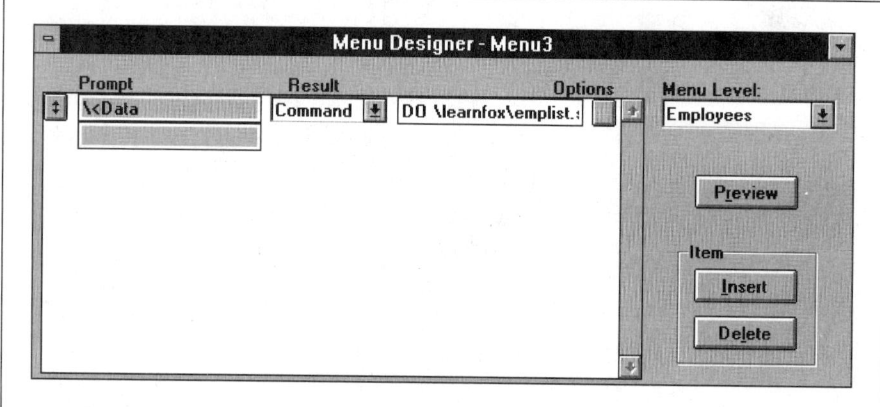

4. As the second prompt, enter **\<Reports**. Leave Submenu as the result. Click Create to create the submenu.

5. Enter three prompts for this submenu: **\<Data**, **\<Wages**, and **By \<State**, as shown in Figure 24. 18.

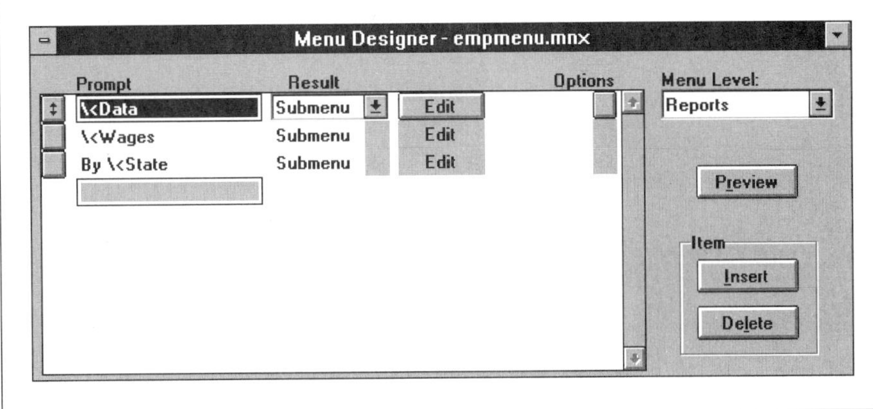

FIGURE 24.18

The Reports submenu

6. Leave Submenu selected as the result of the first prompt, and click its Create button. As the first submenu prompt, enter **Pre\<view**. Select Command as its result. In the text box to its right, enter **REPORT FORM \LEARNFOX\EMPDATA PREVIEW**.

7. As the prompt for the second submenu option, enter **\<Print**. From the Result drop-down list, select Command. In the text box to its right, enter **REPORT FORM \LEARNFOX\EMPLIST TO PRINTER PROMPT**. This submenu is shown in Figure 24.19.

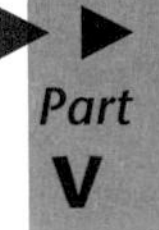

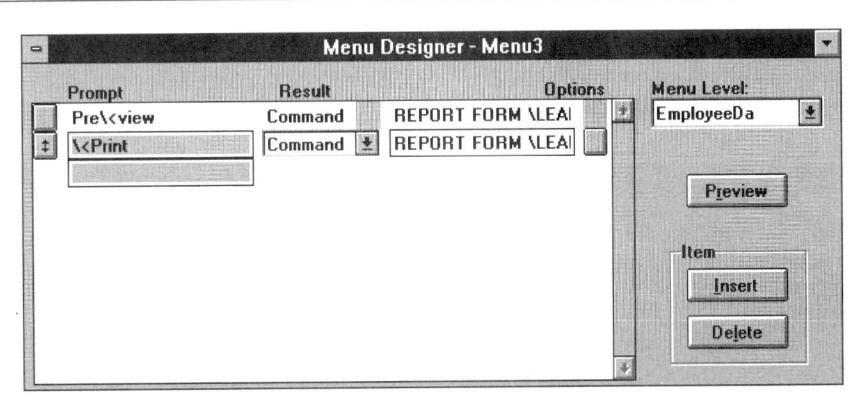

FIGURE 24.19

A submenu to let the user print or preview a report

Select Reports from the Menu Level control to go back to the Reports submenu. Click the Create button on the second line to create the Wages submenu. As you did above, enter **Pre\<view** as the first prompt, select Command as its result, and enter **REPORT FORM \LEARNFOX\EMPWAGES PREVIEW** in the text box to its right. Enter **\<Print** as the second prompt, select Command as its result, and enter **REPORT FORM \LEARNFOX\EMP-WAGES TO PRINTER PROMPT** in the text box to its right.

9. Select Reports from the Menu Level drop-down list to go back to the reports submenu. Click the Create button on the third line to create the Wages submenu. Again, enter **Pre\<view** as the first prompt, select Command as its result, and enter **REPORT FORM\LEARNFOX\ST_WAGES PREVIEW** in the text box to its right. Enter **\<Print** as the second prompt, select Command as its result, and enter **REPORT FORM \LEARNFOX\ST_ WAGES TO PRINTER PROMPT** in the text box to its right.

10. Now, to add an option for labels, select Employees from the Menu Label drop-down list. As the third prompt, enter **\<Labels**. Click the Create button to its right to create a submenu. As you did for reports, enter **Pre\<view** as the first prompt, select Command as its result, and enter **LABEL FORM \LEARNFOX \STANDARD PREVIEW** in the text box to its right. Enter **\<Print** as the second prompt, select Command as its result, and enter **REPORT FORM \LEARNFOX\STANDARD TO PRINTER PROMPT** in the text box to its right.

11. Now, to add an option to remove this menu, select Employees from the Menu Label drop-down list. As the fourth prompt, enter **Remove \<Menu**. Select Command as the result. In the text box to the right, enter **SET SYSMENU TO DEFAULT**.

12. To place the new menu within the system menu, choose View ➤ General Options. In the General Options dialog box, select the Before radio button, and select Window from the drop-down list to its right, as shown in Figure 24.20. Then click OK.

13. Choose File ➤ Save. As the name of the menu, enter **EMP-MENU**. Be sure the LEARNFOX directory is selected, and click the Save button.

14. The final menu design is shown in Figure 24.21. Choose Menu ➤ Generate to display the Generate dialog box. (If you want, you can click the Options button and enter your name and address in

FIGURE 24.20

Placing the new menu within the system menu

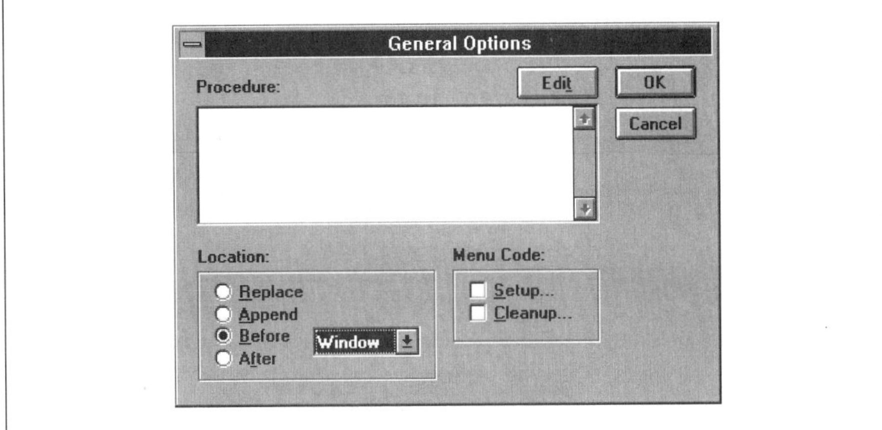

FIGURE 24.21

The final design of the menu

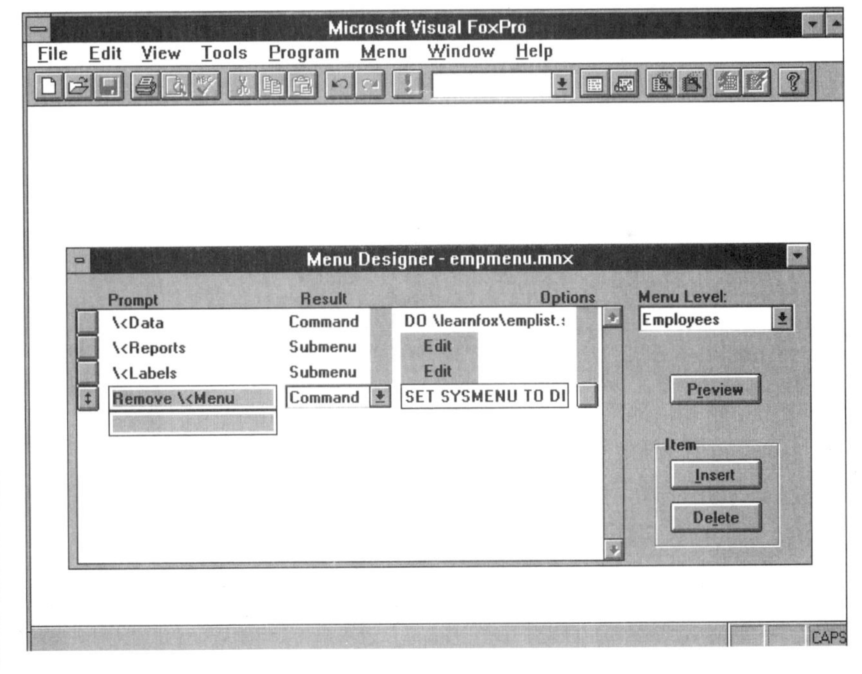

the Developer Information area of the Options dialog box, so they will be added to the code as comments; then click OK to return to the Generate dialog box.) Leave the default name for the output file, \learnfox\empmenu.mpr. Click the Generate button.

15. When Visual FoxPro is finished generating the code, close the Menu Designer. In the Command window, enter **DO\LEARN-FOX\EMPMENU.MPR** to add the new menu to the main menu bar. Press Alt+Y to display the submenu, and try displaying some of the other submenus under it, as shown in Figure 24.22. (The Command window is closed in the illustration, so you can see the menu more clearly.)

FIGURE 24.22

Using the new menu

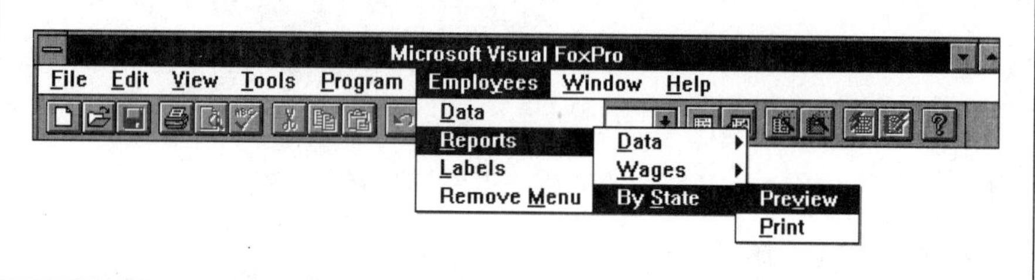

16. Try some of the options on this menu, and when you are done, choose Employees ➤ Remove Menu to remove this new menu from the menu bar.

▸▸ To Sum Up

In this chapter, you learned to use the Menu Designer to create drop-down menus, like the main menu of Visual FoxPro for Windows, and you developed a menu system to let novices work with your Emplist table, even if they know nothing about Visual FoxPro. In the next chapter, you will learn to use the Project Manager to organize all the files that are used by this menu system and to create an application based on them.

CHAPTER 25

Using the Project Manager

▸▸ FAST TRACK

▶ ***To create a project,*** **761**

select File ➤ New, select the Project radio button, and select the New button. Name the project later by selecting File ➤ Save As. Alternatively, enter the command **CREATE PROJECT <project name>**.

▶ ***To add files to the Project Manager window,*** **764**

select the Add button to display the Add File dialog box, and select the file you want to add. By default, the first file you add is the main module of the application, executed when the application starts.

▶ ***To modify the files in a project,*** **764**

highlight a file in the list in the Project Manager and select the Modify button (or simply double-click the file) to display the window you use to edit or lay out that file.

▶ ***To display summary information on the project,*** **765**

select Project ➤ Project Info to display the Project Information dialog box, which includes summary information on the files of the project.

▶ ***To create an application,*** **767**

select the Build button of the Project Manager window to display the Build Options dialog box. Select Build Application to create an APP file that incorporates all the files in the project. Select Build Executable to create a standalone EXE file that incorporates all these files. (This radio button is accessible only in the Professional Edition of Visual FoxPro.)

To add related files automatically to the Project Manager window, ***768***

select the Build button to display the Build Options dialog box. Select Rebuild Project, and FoxPro automatically adds every file called by the files already listed in the Project Manager to its list of files. When you make this selection, FoxPro also regenerates the code for these files.

To exclude a file in the Project Manager from an application, ***769***

highlight the file and select Project ➤ Exclude. This allows you to use the Project Manager to keep track of files, such as most database and index files, that are related to the application but should not be included in the APP or EXE file that is generated.

To make a different file the main file, executed when the application begins, ***770***

highlight the file you want to be the main file, and select Project ➤ Set Main.

The Project Manager lets developers combine all the files of an application into a single file: either an APP file, which you can run using a Visual FoxPro DO command, or a stand-alone EXE file (the type of file used for most commercial programs). To create EXE files, however, you must use the Professional Edition of Visual FoxPro, rather than the Standard Edition.

The Project Manager is also useful for keeping track of all the files involved when developing a complex application that you plan to use within Visual FoxPro. Ordinarily, the best way of developing an application is to include the files in the Project Manager as you create them. Then, all the files will be listed in one place, and it is easy to work on any one by pointing and clicking with your mouse.

When you use the Project Manager to build an APP or EXE file, all of the files used in the application—including, for example, programs, report forms, and label forms—can be combined in this single file. Even database tables and indexes can be included in this file, but only if they are read-only.

NOTE

If the program simply uses the database table and its index as a lookup table, they can be included in the APP or EXE file, but if the user modifies a database table, that file (including both the DBF and the Memo file) and its indexes must be kept separate. For example, a table that lets the user look up city and state on the basis of ZIP code could be included in the APP file, because it is created by the developer and never changed by the user. The table where the user enters names and addresses, however, must be excluded from the APP file.

►► *The Project Manager*

You create a project in the familiar way: Select File ➤ New, select the Project radio button, and select New to use the Project window; Visual FoxPro displays the Create dialog box to let you name the project. Alternatively, enter the command **CREATE PROJECT <project name>**.

►► NOTE

If you are creating a project that includes existing files, you can create the project and specify the files to be included in it by using the command BUILD PROJECT <project file> FROM <file list>. For more details, see this command in Appendix B.

Once you've created a project, you can display the Project Manager to modify it in the familiar ways: Select File ➤ Open, select Project from the popup control, select the name of the project you want to modify from the scrollable list, and select Open. Alternatively, just enter the command **MODIFY PROJECT <project name>**. The names of projects you have used recently are added to the end of the File menu, and you can simply choose them to open them.

FoxPro keeps the information about a project in a database table with the extension PJX and an associated memo file with the extension PJT.

When you work on a project in any of these ways, FoxPro opens the Project Manager window and adds a Project pad to the menu, as shown in Figure 25.1.

You may find that collapsing the Project Manager window, as shown in Figure 25.2, makes it easier to work with. To do so, click the ↑ button in its upper-right corner. As you can see in the figure, when the window is collapsed, this button has a ↓ symbol on it, and clicking it expands the window to its original size.

FIGURE 25.1

The Project Manager window

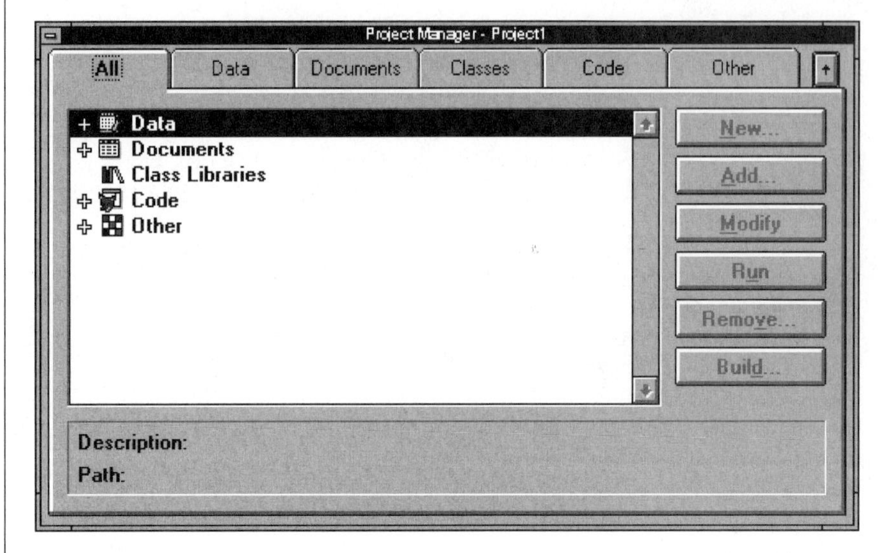

FIGURE 25.2

Collapsing the Project Manager window

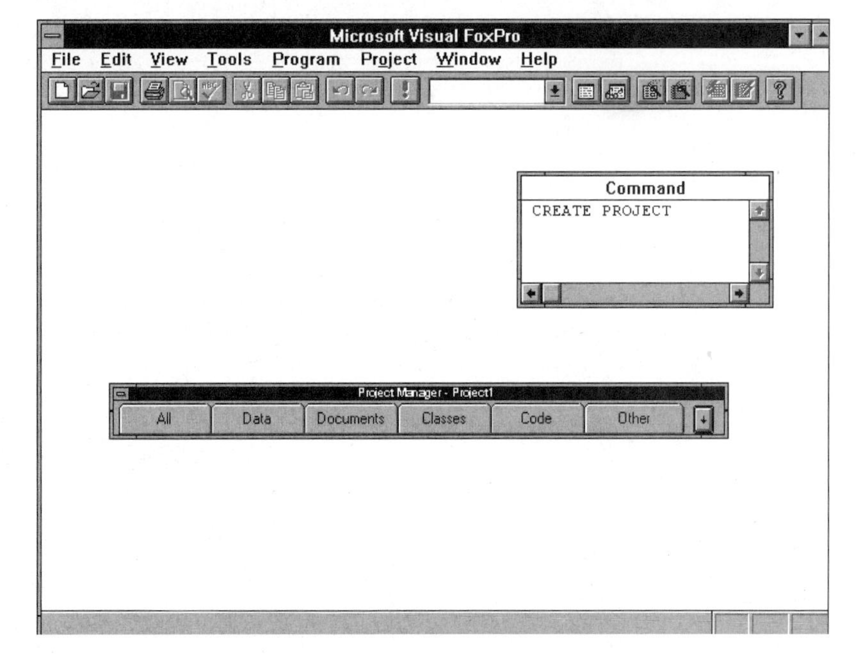

Using the Project Manager

As you can see from Figure 25.1, the Project Manager window includes tabbed panels that let you display the following elements in the project:

- **Data:** The Data panel displays databases, free tables, and queries.
- **Documents:** The Documents panel displays forms, reports, and labels.
- **Classes:** The Classes panel displays class libraries, which are used in object-oriented programming and are not covered in this book.
- **Code:** The Code panel displays programs, API libraries (libraries created using other programming languages, which can be used in Visual FoxPro programs), and applications.
- **Other:** The Other panel displays menus, text files, and other files.

In addition, the All panel, which is displayed by default, displays all of the files in the application. You can use it instead of the other panels when you don't want to display different types of files separately.

Displaying and Hiding Items

The lists in these panels are displayed in collapsible outline form. If an item in the list has a plus sign to its left, you can double-click it to display the items under it in outline form. If it's marked with a minus sign, you can double-click it to hide the items under it.

In Figure 25.1, for example, the Data item in the All panel had a plus sign to its left. If you double-click the item or the plus sign, it is displayed in the expanded form shown in Figure 25.3, with the three types of data files shown under it. The plus mark to the left of Data has been replaced by a minus, indicating that you can double-click it to hide all the items under it.

You can expand the list completely to display all its items by right-clicking the Project Manager and choosing Expand All from its shortcut menu.

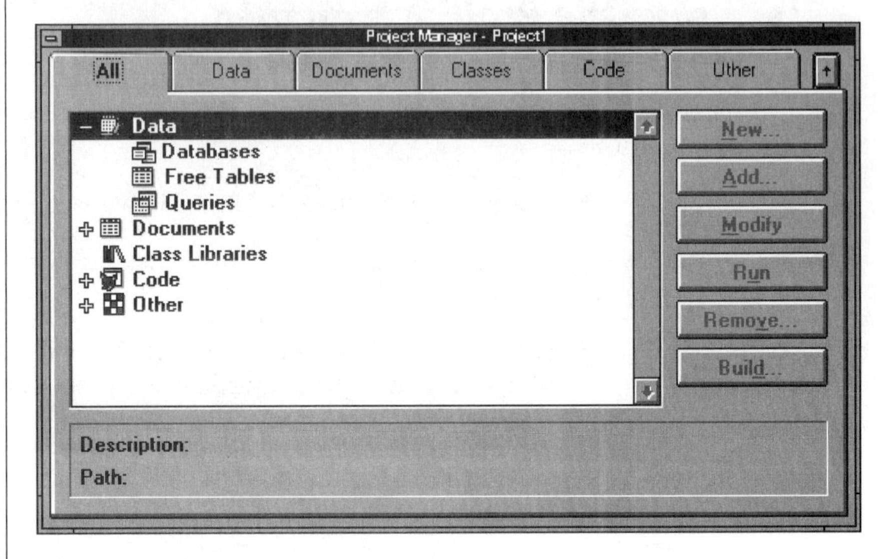

FIGURE 25.3

Expanding the Data item in the All panel

Working with Files

You can use the buttons to the right of the file list or the equivalent menu choices to create and work with files, as follows:

- Click New or choose Project ➤ New File to create a new file of the type that is selected in the list: Visual FoxPro lets you create the file in the same way that you ordinarily do. For example, if you have selected Free Tables or an individual table in the Data list, and then click New, FoxPro displays the Create dialog box and Table Designer to let you name and define the structure of the table. When you have designed the table, it will be added to the project.
- Click Add or choose Project ➤ Add File to add an existing file to the list. Visual FoxPro displays the Open dialog box to let you select the file to be added.
- Click Modify or choose Project ➤ Modify File to use the appropriate Designer to modify the file that is selected in the list.
- Click Open or choose Project ➤ Open File to open the file that is selected in the list.

- Click Browse or choose Project ➤ Browse File to open and browse the table that is selected in the list. This option is available instead of Open when a table is selected.
- Click Run or choose Project ➤ Run File to run the program that is selected in the list. This option is available instead of Open when you've selected a query, document, or menu, or the Code option. As you know, all of these file types are actually programs.
- Click Remove or choose Project ➤ Remove File to remove the currently selected file from the list. Visual FoxPro displays the dialog box shown in Figure 25.4, which gives you the option of just removing the file from the application or removing it and also deleting it permanently from your disk.

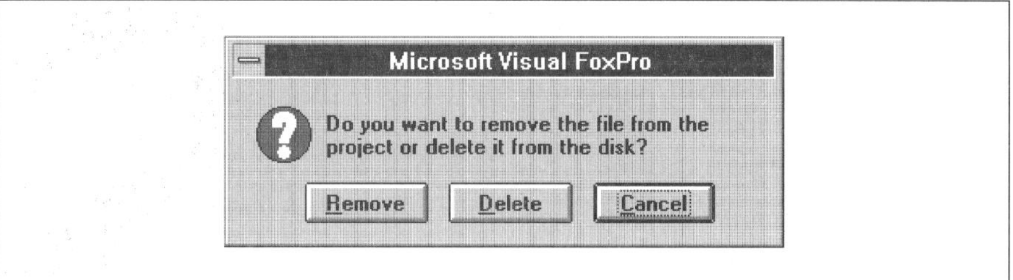

FIGURE 25.4

Removing a file from the application

You can also rename a file by selecting it and choosing Project ➤ Rename File or right-clicking the Project Manager and choosing Rename from its shortcut menu.

To add a description of a file for your own use, select the file and choose Project ➤ Edit Description to display the Description dialog box, shown in Figure 25.5. In the text box, enter a description or edit one you entered earlier. When the file is selected, this description and the file's full path name are displayed below the Project Manager's file list.

Displaying Project Information

Select Project ➤ Project Info to use the Project Information dialog box. The Project panel, shown in Figure 25.6 lets you enter information on the developer, specify the home directory, and choose an ICO file that will be used as the icon to run the project. The Files panel, shown in

FIGURE 25.5

The Description dialog box

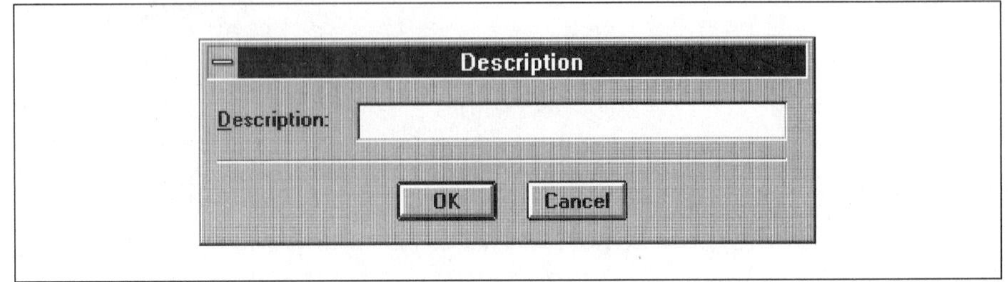

FIGURE 25.6

The Project panel of the Project Information dialog box

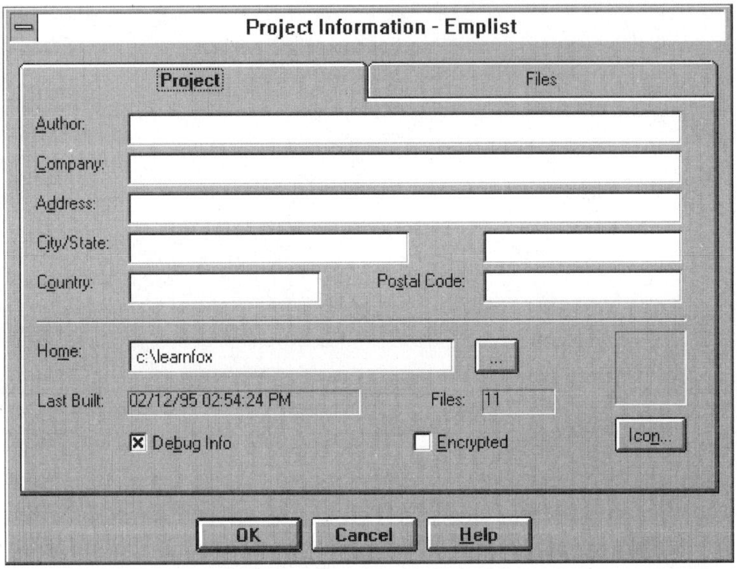

Figure 25.7, gives a general overview of all the files in the project—the type and name or each file in the project, when each was last modified, and which files are included in the current build of the project.

Packing the Project

Select Project ➤ Cleanup Project to pack the table that contains the project. Remember that the project is stored in an ordinary database table with the extension PJX. When you remove a file from the project, the associated record in the PJX file is marked for deletion. Selecting Cleanup Project removes this record permanently.

FIGURE 25.7

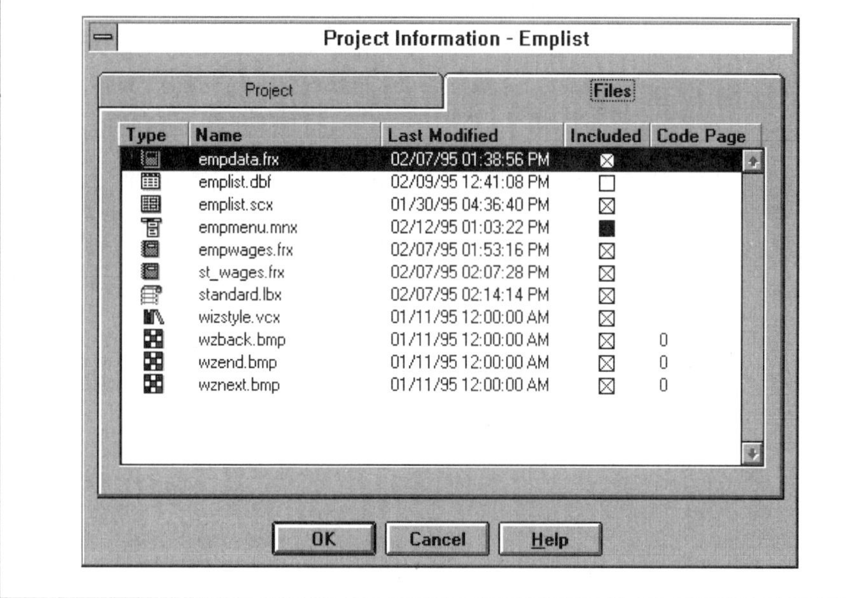

The Files panel of the Project Information dialog box

Building a Project or Application

Click the final button, Build, or choose Project ➤ Build to display the Build Option dialog box, shown in Figure 25.8, which is the key to using the Project Manager. As you can see, the three radio buttons give you these options:

- **Rebuild Project:** Update the project. Add any new files that are called by the programs in the project, and generate new code if the screen or menu design has been altered since the last build.
- **Build Application:** Update the project and create an APP file.
- **Build Executable:** Update the project and create an EXE file. (This radio button is dimmed in the Standard edition of Visual FoxPro and available in the Professional edition.)

By default, these options update the project by refreshing only those components whose source file has a time stamp that is more recent than that in the project file. If the Recompile All Files check box is checked, however, it will rebuild all files in the project.

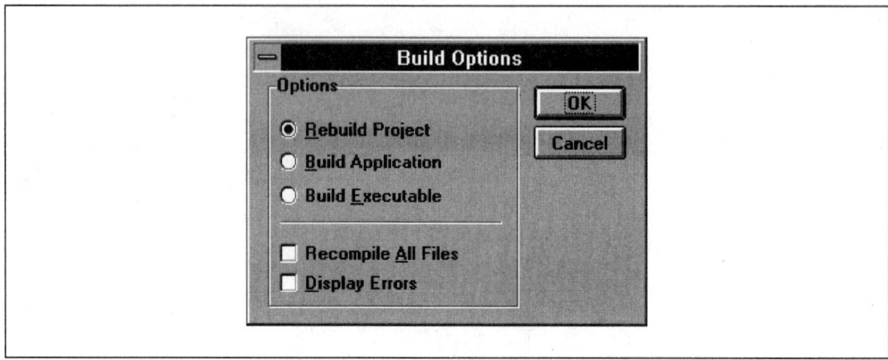

FIGURE 25.8

The Build Options dialog box

Displaying Errors

If the Display Errors check box of the Build Option dialog box is checked when you build the application, FoxPro automatically displays the error file over the Project Manager window when the build is complete.

An error occurs, for example, if a file referred to in a program cannot be found. Errors are listed in a file with the same name as the project and with the extension ERR. You can also look at this file by selecting Project ➤ Errors (or, since it is an ordinary text file, by entering the command **MODI FILE <project name>.ERR**).

▸▸ TIP

You can save time by choosing Rebuild Project in the Build Option dialog box to see whether there are errors before you build an application or executable. Correct the errors and rebuild the project again, until you can do so with no errors. Then create the APP or EXE.

Adding Files Automatically

One of the most convenient features of the Project Manager is that if you add a file to the list, selecting any of the Build options automatically adds all the files that are called by that file.

Rather than adding files individually, for example, you can simply add a menu to the Project Manager and then rebuild the project to add all the files it calls.

If FoxPro cannot find files although there are references to them in the code, it displays a dialog box that gives you these options:

- **Locate:** Displays a dialog box you can use to search through other subdirectories to find the missing file.
- **Ignore:** Ignores the fact that this file is missing and continues the build.
- **Ignore All:** Ignores all files that are missing and continues the build.
- **Cancel:** Cancels the build.

The Ignore and Ignore All buttons are useful if one or more files that are referred to by other programs are not yet available.

Including and Excluding Files

You learned earlier that when you use the Project Manager to build an APP or EXE file, you can include all of the files in the application except database tables and indexes that the user will modify. The APP or EXE file cannot be changed by the user, and so tables and indexes used to hold the user's data must be excluded from it.

Files in the Project Manager that will be excluded from the APP have the "slash" symbol to their left as shown in Figure 25.9.

By default, Visual FoxPro excludes tables in the Project Manager from the APP file. However, there are some cases where you might want to include tables in the APP, if they are not meant to be altered by the user and are only used by the program to look up data. For example, if you have a table that lets the program look up city and state on the basis of ZIP code, including this table in the APP file will ensure that the user cannot modify it.

Likewise, it is useful to add tables to the Project Manager during the development stages, even if you do not want to include them in the APP, to make it easier to keep track of them and work with them.

You can specify whether any file will be included in the APP or EXE file by selecting it in the Project Manager and choosing Project ➤ Exclude (or Exclude from the shortcut menu) or choosing Project ➤ Include (or Include from the shortcut menu).

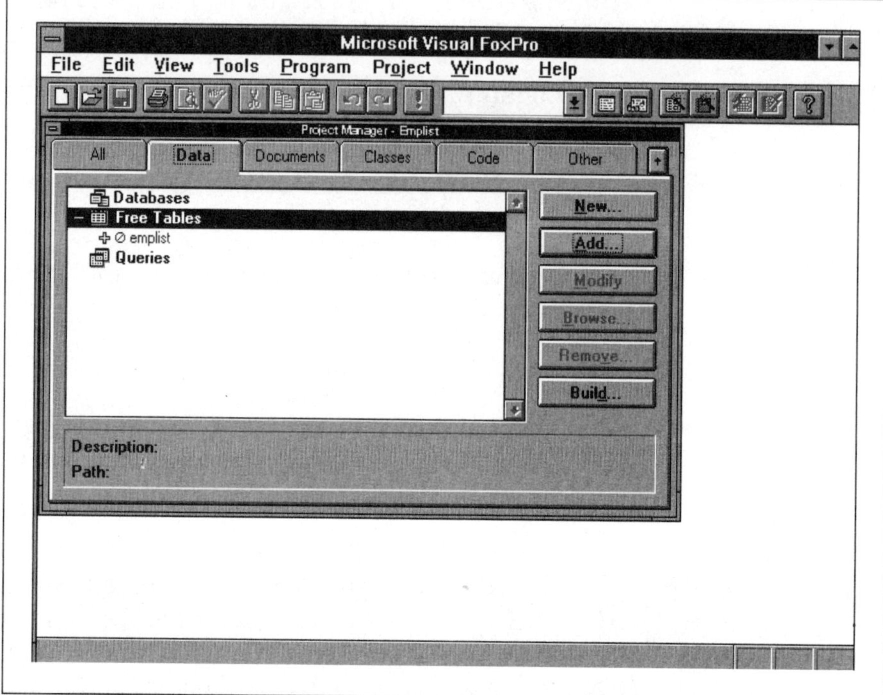

FIGURE 25.9

The symbol next to the Emplist table means it will be excluded from the APP.

This option is a toggle; if the selected file is already included, it will be displayed as Exclude, and if the selected file is excluded, it will be displayed as Include.

Choosing the Main Module

When you run an application, its main module is executed first. The Project's main module is indicated by a bullet to its left in the Project Manager.

In Figure 25.10, for example, the menu program that you created in the last chapter is the main module of the APP. When you run the APP, it begins by running this program, just as you ran it in the last chapter.

The first file you add to the project is its main module by default. Choose Project ➤ Set Main (or choose Set Main from the Project Manager's shortcut menu) to make the currently selected file the main module of the generated program.

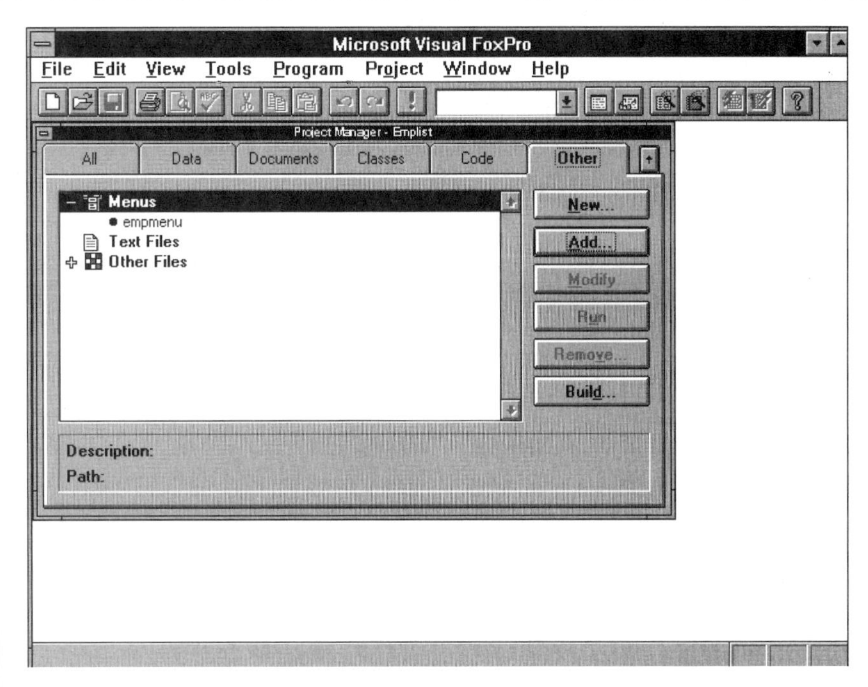

FIGURE 25.10 *The bullet indicates the main module.*

NOTE

The Set Main option is disabled if the file selected in the Project Manager window cannot be the main module of a program—for example, if it is a label or report form.

Creating a Sample Application

It is easy to create a project that includes all the files used in the menu system that you developed in the previous chapter. Begin by adding the menu file itself. Then select Build to add all the other files that it calls.

1. Choose File ➤ New. Be sure the Project radio button is selected, and click the New File button. When Visual FoxPro displays the

Create dialog box, enter the name **Emplist**, make sure that \LEARNFOX is the current directory, and click Create.

2. Click the Other tab of the Project Manager. Be sure Menus is selected and click the Add button. Use the Open dialog box to select the file EMPMENU.MNX, which you created in the previous chapter. Click the plus sign to the left of Menus, so you can see that the file was added with a bullet to its left; it is automatically the main file of the application, because you added it first.

3. Click the Build button. When Visual FoxPro displays the Build Options dialog box, leave the Rebuild Project Radio button selected, and click OK.

4. Click the Documents tab and click the plus signs to the left of Forms, Reports, and Labels, to verify that the form, reports, and labels used by the menu have been added to the project.

5. Even though the Emplist table should not be included in the APP file, you can add it to the Project Manager as a convenience. Click the Data tab. Select Free Tables and then click the Add button. Use the Open dialog box to add \LEARNFOX\EMPLIST.DBF to the project. Click the plus sign to the left of Free Tables to verify that it has been added and is excluded from the project by default, because it is a table.

6. To create the APP file, click the Build button, select the Build Application radio button of the Build Options dialog box, and click OK. When Visual FoxPro displays the Save As dialog box, keep the default name EMPLIST.APP and click Build. After a moment, the application is complete.

7. In the Command window, enter **DO\LEARNFOX\EMPLIST.APP**. Visual FoxPro displays the Employees menu that you created in the last chapter. Try it to see that it works, as you did in the previous chapter. When you are done, choose Employees ➤ Remove Menu.

Now, if you want to modify this application, you can easily access all its files using the Project Manager. If you want to move it to another computer, the only files that you need to move are EMPLIST.APP, the application file, and EMPLIST.DBF and EMPLIST.FPT, the table and memo files; all the screen, report, and label files used by the application have been bundled into the APP file.

►► To Sum Up

In this chapter, you learned to use the Project Manager to manage all the files used in an application and to build them into a single APP file. This chapter has brought you to the edge of professional application development. You have learned all you need to know to manage your own data, to write utility programs to manipulate your data, and to create simple applications that customize the Visual FoxPro menu system to make it easy for beginners to manage your data.

Now, you should be able to do everything you need to work with Visual FoxPro on your own. If you want to, you can also go on to learn how to develop professional applications with Visual FoxPro.

APPENDICES

APPENDIX A

Installing Visual FoxPro on Your Computer

▶▶ *Installing* FoxPro is a very simple process. After you enter the SETUP command, it is essentially done for you. After the main program is installed, you are asked to decide which of FoxPro's optional features you want to install.

This appendix covers installation of FoxPro for Windows on a stand-alone computer using Windows 3.1. If you are working on a network, consult your network administrator for more detailed instructions.

▶▶ System Requirements

Visual FoxPro for Windows runs on any computer with at least an 80386 processor, a mouse, 8 megabytes of RAM, and Microsoft Windows 3.0 or higher.

The base Visual FoxPro program and the Wizards require over 20 megabytes of free disk space. Help files require about 10 megabytes of disk space. It is best to install at least these files, using over 30 megabytes of disk space, though you can get by without help files if it is necessary to save disk space.

If you must share data with other database management systems, you will also need ODBC support, which requires over 25 megabytes of disk space.

The full Professional Edition of Visual FoxPro requires over 100 megabytes of disk space. The full Standard Edition, including sample files and tools, requires over 75 megabytes of disk space.

If you have enough free space and want to install the entire product, you can select Complete Installation in step 5 below. If you must economize on hard disk space, you may select Custom Installation in order to specify which parts of FoxPro you want to install.

►► Running the Setup Program

The installation program copies the files to your hard disk and creates a program icon for FoxPro in the Windows Program Manager.

To install FoxPro, follow these instructions:

1. If necessary, start Windows. If you are already using Windows, close all open applications. Then insert disk 1 of FoxPro into drive A. Select File ➤ Run from the Program Manager menu system. Windows displays the Run dialog box. In the Command Line text box, type **A:\SETUP**. Then select the OK button.

2. After taking a moment to initialize the Setup program, Visual FoxPro displays a Welcome screen. Select OK to proceed. The Setup program takes a moment to check your system configuration, and displays a dialog box that lets you enter your name and organization. After entering these, click OK, and click OK again to confirm your entry.

3. The next dialog box includes a Product Identification number. Write this number down for your records, as you will need it if you call Microsoft for technical support, and then click OK.

4. Setup suggests that it should create the directory C:\VFP to install Visual FoxPro files. Keep the suggested directory name unless you have some reason to change it. Click OK to proceed.

5. Now you must choose Complete Installation, Custom Installation, or Laptop (Minimum) Installation. If you have enough space on your hard disk, you can select Complete Installation. Otherwise, select Custom Installation to display the Setup Options dialog box with a list of the program's components and the hard disk space each requires. Select the check boxes to install only the components you need.

6. If you choose Custom Installation, Setup displays a dialog box that lets you click check boxes to select the features you want to install. When you select a file, a description of it is displayed to its right. You should install at least Microsoft Visual FoxPro and the Wizard and Builder files. If possible, you should also install Help files. If you need to work with data from other applications, you

must also install ODBC support. Note that the total free space on your hard disk and the disk space required for all the options you have checked are displayed at the bottom of this dialog box. When you have checked the options you want, select Continue.

7. Setup suggests that it should create a FoxPro for Windows group within the Windows Program Manager to hold the FoxPro icon. You might prefer not to create a separate FoxPro for Windows group with just the icon for this program, as it would clutter up your Program Manager. In that case, you will probably find it most convenient to select Applications from the Program Manager group drop-down list. Then select Continue. Any other icons FoxPro installs, such as FoxPro README, can be deleted after they are used. Click OK to proceed.

8. The next dialog box lets you choose whether existing graphs are automatically updated to Microsoft Graph 5.0 when you edit them. If you must share graphs with users of older versions of Microsoft Graph, select No; otherwise, select Yes.

9. After checking to make sure you have the necessary disk space, setup begins copying files to your hard disk. Follow its instructions when it tells you to insert new disks in the drive.

10. After it is done copying files, Setup must restart Windows to complete the installation procedure. You should have already closed all applications before beginning installation, so click Restart Windows.

If you did not install all options, you can add others at a later time by running Setup again. Either click the Microsoft Visual FoxPro Setup icon that has been installed, or run Setup from the installation disks, as you did above. Before it lets you proceed, the Setup program displays a warning saying that Visual FoxPro has already been installed and informing you of your rights under the copyright laws; select Continue to perform the installation. When you reach the appropriate dialog box, Select Custom Installation to choose which options you want to add.

APPENDIX B

The Essential Reference

▶▶ **T**his appendix is a reference to Visual FoxPro for Windows commands, functions, operators, and system variables. It is designed specifically for the intermediate user—someone who is studying this book or who has finished it recently.

In the discussions of commands and other language elements in the preceding chapters, many details were omitted for the sake of readability. For example, if you look at the entry on BROWSE in this appendix, you will see that this command has a very large number of options, many of which are used only in programming. Including this information in the main text of this book would have made it difficult to follow. Also, some commands that are fairly common in programming were not discussed in the main text.

Once you have learned all the basics of using and programming Visual FoxPro, one of the best ways to become a more advanced user or programmer is by browsing through references that discuss commands and functions.

Yet most reference works, including the *Language Reference* that is included as one of Visual FoxPro's manuals, contain more than an intermediate user wants to wade through. They have many commands and functions (such as low-level file I/O commands and commands for working with classes) that only advanced programmers would want to use, and even some essential commands are explained with more technical details than you need at this stage.

This appendix is meant as a bridge to take you from what you have learned in the main text of this book to the point where you will profit from browsing through more advanced reference books. You can use it to look up commands and functions you have learned. And you can browse through it to expand your knowledge of the Visual FoxPro commands you need most without being swamped by entries for commands and functions you do not need at this point.

▶▶ What You Will Find Here

This appendix contains most of the commands and functions used in this book, plus a selection of the operators, system variables, and other commands and functions that intermediate programmers will find most useful, including

- Virtually all the capabilities of the commands and functions (such as BROWSE) that you have already been introduced to in the main text in an abbreviated way—although in some cases this appendix leaves out very technical issues.
- The most useful of the commands and functions that were not discussed in the text, such as the commands DECLARE and DIMENSION, which are used for creating arrays.
- The FoxPro/Xbase file management commands, such as DELETE FILE, which are similar to commands entered at the DOS prompt. This book uses RUN plus a DOS command so you don't have to spend time learning these extra Visual FoxPro commands. But these commands are found rather frequently in Xbase-compatible programs, and it is a good idea to be familiar with them.
- Menuing commands. The text discusses the general sequence of commands used for defining, activating, deactivating, hiding, and showing menu systems, but it does not go into these commands in detail.

▶ Conventions

This appendix uses the following conventions to illustrate the syntax of Visual FoxPro commands and functions:

- Uppercase letters are used for keywords. If a word is capitalized, you type it just as it appears in this book when you are actually using the command.
- Optional clauses are put in square brackets. Any part of the command that is enclosed in square brackets may be included or not when you are actually using the command.
- Alternatives are separated by broken vertical lines (¦). If two clauses are separated by a vertical line, you may use one or the other, but not both, when you are actually using the command. Likewise, if several clauses are separated by vertical lines, you may use only one.

- Words whose value you must fill in are written in lowercase letters in angle brackets. For example, if a command includes <file name>, it indicates that you must fill in a real file name in that place when you use the command.

In addition, this appendix uses the following abbreviations for many expressions that can be used with commands:

- <expC> indicates that the command requires you to fill in a character expression.
- <expN> indicates that the command requires a numeric expression.
- <expL> indicates that the command requires a logical expression.
- <expD> indicates that the command requires a date expression.
- <expT> indicates that the command requires a datetime expression.

In cases in which several expressions of a given type can be used in the same command, these are designated by numbers—for example, <expN1>, <expN2>, and so on.

►► Commands, Functions, Operators, and System Variables

Following is an alphabetical listing of commands, functions, operators and system variables.

► The $ Operator

Syntax

```
<search_for expC> $ <search_in expC>
```

Usage This operator returns .T. if <search_for expC> is contained in <search_in expC>. Used only with character expressions.

See Also !, !=, #, <, <=, <>, =, ==, >, >=, .AND., EXACTLY LIKE, GREATER THAN, GREATER THAN OR EQUAL TO, LESS THAN, LESS THAN OR EQUAL TO, LIKE, .NOT., NOT LIKE

► The != Operator

Syntax

```
<search_in exp> != <search_for exp>
```

Usage This operator returns .T. if <search_in exp> (the expression being searched in) is not equal to <search_for exp>.

See Also #, $, <, <=, <>, =, ==, >, >=, EXACTLY LIKE, GREATER THAN, GREATER THAN OR EQUAL TO, LESS THAN, LESS THAN OR EQUAL TO, LIKE, NOT LIKE

The # Operator

Syntax

```
<search_in exp> # <search_for exp>
```

Usage This operator returns .T. if <search_in exp> (the expression being searched in) is not equal to <search_for exp>.

See Also !=, $, <, <=, <>, =, ==, >, >=, EXACTLY LIKE, GREATER THAN, GREATER THAN OR EQUAL TO, LESS THAN, LESS THAN OR EQUAL TO, LIKE, NOT LIKE

The & Command

Syntax

```
& <mem var> [.<expC>]
```

Usage This command performs a macro substitution. A command uses the value of the memory variable that is specified, as if that value were literally typed in the location of the & command.

Options The .<expC> option appends the characters in a character expression at the end of the macro.

The && Command

Syntax

```
<programming code> && <text>
```

Usage This command allows you to place in-line comments in a program file to help others understand what the program is doing when looking at the program code. It is used after a line of code to tell Visual FoxPro that everything else on that line is a note. Visual FoxPro ignores everything to the right of the && when running the program.

See Also *, NOTE

▶ The * Command

Syntax

```
* ¦ NOTE
```

Usage These commands allow you to place comments in the programs you write. Any subsequent text on the same line is ignored by Visual FoxPro. Comments help make programs easier for the programmer and others to understand. If * or NOTE is at the far left of a line in a program, Visual FoxPro ignores this line when it executes the program. Nothing else may be on the line except these commands and comments.

See Also NOTE, &&

▶ The * Operator

Syntax

```
<expN> * <expN>
```

Usage This operator is used to multiply numeric expressions.

See Also +, –, /, **, ^

▶ The ** Operator

Syntax

```
<expN> ** <expN>
```

Usage This operator is used to raise the first numeric expression to the power of the second. It is identical to the ^ operator.

See Also +, –, *, /, ^

▶ The + Operator

Syntax

```
<expr> + <expr>
```

Usage This operator is used to add numeric or date expressions and to concatenate character expressions.

See Also –, *, /, **, ^

The .AND. Operator

Syntax
```
<expL> .AND. <expL> ¦ <expL> AND <expL>
```

Usage This operator returns .T. if both logical expressions return .T.

See Also !, .NOT., .OR.

The .NOT. Operator

Syntax
```
.NOT. <expL> ¦ NOT <expL> ¦ ! <expL>
```

Usage This operator returns .T. if the logical expression returns .F.

See Also !, .AND., .OR.

The .OR. Operator

Syntax
```
<expL> .OR. <expL> ¦ <expL> OR <expL>
```

Usage This operator returns .T. if either logical expression returns .T.

See Also !, .AND., .NOT.

The / Operator

Syntax
```
<expN> / <expN>
```

Usage This operator is used to divide the first numeric expression by the second.

See Also +, –, *, **, ^

The < Operator

Syntax
```
<search_in exp> < <search_for exp>
```

Usage This operator returns .T. if <search_in exp> (the expression being searched in) is less than <search_for exp>.

See Also !=, #, $, <=, <>, =, ==, >, >=, EXACTLY LIKE, GREATER THAN, GREATER THAN OR EQUAL TO, LESS THAN, LESS THAN OR EQUAL TO, LIKE, NOT LIKE

The <= Operator

Syntax

```
<search_in exp> <= <search_for exp>
```

Usage This operator returns .T. if <search_in exp> (the expression being searched in) is less than or equal to <search_for exp>.

See Also !=, #, $, <, <>, =, ==, >, >=, EXACTLY LIKE, GREATER THAN, GREATER THAN OR EQUAL TO, LESS THAN, LESS THAN OR EQUAL TO, LIKE, NOT LIKE

The <> Operator

Syntax

```
<search_in exp> <> <search_for exp>
```

Usage This operator returns .T. if <search_in exp> (the expression being searched in) is not equal to <search_for exp>.

See Also !=, #, $, <, <=, =, ==, >, >=, EXACTLY LIKE, GREATER THAN, GREATER THAN OR EQUAL TO, LESS THAN, LESS THAN OR EQUAL TO, LIKE, NOT LIKE

The = Operator

Syntax

```
<search_in exp> = <search_for exp>
```

Usage This operator returns .T. if <search_in exp> (the expression being searched in) is equal to <search_for exp>.

For character expressions, by default, there is a match if <search_in exp> begins with <search_for exp>, even if it also contains additional characters. However, if the command SET EXACT ON has been used, character expressions must be identical for there to be a match.

See Also !=, #, $, <, <=, <>, ==, >, >=, EXACTLY LIKE, GREATER THAN, GREATER THAN OR EQUAL TO, LESS THAN, LESS THAN OR EQUAL TO, LIKE, NOT LIKE

The == Operator

Syntax

```
<search_in expC> == <search_for expC>
```

Usage This operator returns .T. if <search_in expC> (the expression being searched in) is identical to <search_for expC>. Unlike the = operator, it does not find a match if <search_in expC> has additional characters following those that match <search_for expC>. Used only with character expressions.

See Also !=, #, $, <, <=, <>, =, >, >=, EXACTLY LIKE, GREATER THAN, GREATER THAN OR EQUAL TO, LESS THAN, LESS THAN OR EQUAL TO, LIKE, NOT LIKE

The > Operator

Syntax

```
<search_in exp> > <search_for exp>
```

Usage This operator returns .T. if <search_in exp> (the expression being searched in) is greater than <search_for exp>.

See Also !=, #, $, <, <=, <>, =, ==, >=, EXACTLY LIKE, GREATER THAN, GREATER THAN OR EQUAL TO, LESS THAN, LESS THAN OR EQUAL TO, LIKE, NOT LIKE

The >= Operator

Syntax

```
<search_in exp> > <search_for exp>
```

Usage This operator returns .T. if <search_in exp> (the expression being searched in) is greater than or equal to <search_for exp>.

See Also !=, #, $, <, <=, <>, =, ==, >, EXACTLY LIKE, GREATER THAN, GREATER THAN OR EQUAL TO, LESS THAN, LESS THAN OR EQUAL TO, LIKE, NOT LIKE

The ? Command

Syntax

```
?¦?? [<exp1>]
     [PICTURE <expC1>]
```

```
[FUNCTION] <exp2>]
[AT <expN2> ]
[FONT <expC2> [,<expN3] [STYLE <expC3>]
[, <exp3>]...
```

Usage This command evaluates and displays an expression. In the basic form of the command, ? <exp1> displays the value of the expression on a new line, one line below the current location of the cursor. The form ?? <exp1> displays the expression at the current location of the cursor, without moving to a new line. When ? is used without an expression, it simply moves the cursor to the new line.

Notice also that in the full command, another expression can be used following the first and separated from it by a comma. The ellipsis (...) indicates that the second expression can be followed by any of the optional clauses and by more expressions and optional clauses.

If CONSOLE is SET ON and PRINT is SET OFF (the default environment settings), the evaluated expression is displayed on the screen. If PRINT has been SET ON, it is sent to the printer. If CONSOLE has been SET OFF, it is not displayed on the screen. (For more information, see SET CONSOLE and SET PRINTER.)

Options The PICTURE option allows you to specify the format in which the expression is displayed by including a PICTURE clause and a picture template or picture function. For example, the clause PICTURE "@!" displays the expression in all uppercase letters.

The FUNCTION option lets you use the picture functions that are used in a PICTURE clause following an @ without including the @ symbol. For example, FUNCTION "!" after the SAY clause causes the expression to be displayed in all uppercase; and FUNCTION "!" after the GET clause causes the variable you enter to be read as uppercase.

The AT option lets you specify the column where the expression is displayed. It must be followed by a number or numeric expression. The row where the expression is displayed, of course, is either the row where the cursor is (if you use ??) or the following row (if you use ?). This is useful if you are producing a tabular report, where columns need to be lined up.

The [FONT <expC> [,<expN] [STYLE <expC3>] option lets you specify the typeface, size, and style of the font. <expC> and <expN> should be the name and size of an available font. If the font you specify is not available, Visual FoxPro trics to substitute a similar font. If you omit the FONT clause, the main Visual FoxPro window font is used, and if you include the clause but omit the size option, a 10-point font is used. The STYLE clause may be followed by one of the following codes:

- B: boldface
- I: italic
- N: normal
- O: outline
- Q: opaque
- S: shadow
- -: strikeout
- T: transparent
- U: underline

If this clause is omitted, normal style will be used.

The <exp3> ... option indicates that this command may be used with any number of expressions, separated by commas, and that each may use all the previous options.

See Also @ ... SAY, SET PRINTER

The ??? Command

Syntax

```
??? <expC>
```

Usage This command sends characters directly to the printer. It can be used to print a line of ordinary text characters, but it is most powerful when it is used with printer codes. Because it sends characters directly to the printer, without going through the printer driver, it lets you use printer control codes that are not supported by the printer driver. Printer control codes let you change type sizes and styles, for example. When you use them with ???, enclose control codes in curly brackets: {}.

Using printer control codes is a rather exacting technical task. Codes are listed in your printer's manual.

See Also SET PRINTER

▶ The @ ... CLEAR Command

Syntax

```
@ <row1>,<col1> CLEAR [TO <row2>,<col2>]
```

Usage This command is used to clear part of the screen or active window. <row1>, <col1> is the upper-left corner of the rectangle that is cleared.

Options If the optional TO clause is included, <row2>,<col2> define the lower-right corner of the rectangular area that is cleared. If not, the rectangle that is cleared extends to the lower-right corner of the screen or active window.

See Also @ ... TO

▶ The @ ... SAY ... GET Command

Syntax

```
@ <row,col>
     [SAY <exp1>
          [PICTURE <expC1>]
          [FUNCTION <expC2>]
          <file name> [BITMAP] ¦ <general field name>
          [SIZE <expN1>,<expN2>]
          [CENTER]
          [ISOMETRIC ¦ STRETCH]
          [FONT <expC3> [,<expN3>]] [STYLE <expC4>]
          [VERB <expN4>]
          [COLOR SCHEME <expN5> ¦ COLOR <color pair
                 list>]]
     [GET <variable>
          [PICTURE <expC5>]
          [FUNCTION <expC6>]
          [DEFAULT <exp2>]
          [ENABLE ¦ DISABLE]
          [MESSAGE <expC7>]
          [[OPEN] WINDOW <window name>]
          [RANGE [<exp3>] [,<exp4>]]
          [SIZE <expN6>,<expN7>]
          [VALID <expL1> ¦ <expN8> [ERROR <expC8>]]
```

```
[WHEN <expL2>]
[FONT <expC9> [,<expN9>]] [STYLE <expC10>]
     | COLOR SCHEME <expN10>
     | COLOR <color value list>]]
```

Usage In its basic form, @ <row,col> [SAY <exp>] [GET <variable>], this command is used for formatted input/output. The cursor is placed on the row and column of the screen or active window defined by the <row> and <col> numbers following the @ sign. (Rows are numbered from 0 at the top of the screen to 35 at the bottom. Columns are numbered from 0 at the left edge of the screen to 79 at the right, although results might vary depending on your display.) The expression following SAY is displayed on the screen in this location, and the variable following GET is displayed immediately after it. The READ command is generally used later in the program to let you edit this variable.

Notice that both the SAY and GET clauses are optional. If the command is used without either, it simply places the cursor at the specified location.

If the command SET DEVICE TO PRINT has been used previously, the output is sent to the printer; then the maximum row and column lengths depend on the size of the paper. SET DEVICE TO SCREEN returns to the default setting, with output sent to the screen.

The value of the variable must be defined before this command is used unless you use the default option described below. If this command (or a series of these commands) is followed by the command READ, the user can change the value of the variable.

In general, the expression following SAY is used to prompt the user about what to enter in the GET clause. The command can be used with just a SAY or a GET clause to display just a message or a variable.

Options As you can see from the full form of the command, either the expression following SAY or the variable following GET can be formatted using a picture template or function code. For example, PICTURE "@!" after the SAY clause causes the expression to be displayed in all uppercase; and PICTURE @! after the GET clause causes the variable the user enters to be read as uppercase.

You can use the following symbols in PICTURE templates:

A	Allows only alphabetic characters
L	Allows only logical data (.T. or .F.)

N	Allows only letters and numbers
X	Allows any character
Y	Logical data only; converts to uppercase Y and N
9	Allows numeric data only
#	Accepts numbers, blanks, and signs
!	Converts alphabetic characters to uppercase
$	Displays currency symbol
*	Displays asterisks in front of numbers
.	Specifies decimal-point position
,	Separates digits left of the decimal point

The FUNCTION option lets you omit the @ symbol. For example, FUNCTION "!" after the SAY clause causes the expression to be displayed in all uppercase; and FUNCTION "!" after the GET clause causes the variable you enter to be read as uppercase.

You can use the following symbols in picture functions:

A	Allows only alphabetic characters
B	Left justifies numeric data
C	Displays a CR after positive numeric data
D	Uses current SET DATE format
E	Uses European-style date format
I	Centers text within field
J	Right justifies text
K	Allows entire field to be edited
L	Displays leading zeros before numeric data
M <list>D	Defines list of pre-set choices for the user, separated by commas
R	Displays but does not store formatting characters
S <n>	Limits display width to <n> characters

T	Trims leading and trailing blanks
V <expN>	Stretches text so it fills the space indicated by the numeric expression
X	Displays a DB after negative numeric data
Z	Displays blanks instead of 0 in Numeric fields
(	Encloses negative numbers in parentheses
!	Converts alphabetic characters to uppercase
	Displays numbers with scientific notation
$	Displays data in currency format

The @ ... SAY <file name> [BITMAP] ¦ <general field name> option lets you display a BMP (bitmapped) picture or an OLE (object linking and embedding) object stored in a General field at a specified location on the screen. This option gives you sophisticated abilities to display graphics and data from outside Visual FoxPro. You can determine the height and width of the imported image with the SIZE clause, and you can center it within the area specified with the CENTER clause. The ISOMETRIC clause scales down the image to fit the available space so the proportions of the image are maintained, while the STRETCH clause scales the image to fit available space without maintaining proportions. Finally, the VERB option applies a specified command verb to the imported object.

The DEFAULT option can be used to specify a value that appears in the GET field by default. If the variable that follows GET has already been defined, its value overrides the value specified in the DEFAULT clause. If the variable has not been defined, the DEFAULT clause creates it and initializes it with the specified value so it appears in the field as the DEFAULT choice for the user.

The DISABLE option prevents a user from editing a GET field and shows that field in disabled colors. The default for GET is ENABLE.

The MESSAGE option displays a message on the status bar or the last line of the window when the user puts the cursor in that GET field.

The [OPEN] WINDOW option lets the user edit a Memo field in a window. The window must be defined first, and you must specify the name of the window. If the optional OPEN is included, the window is opened automatically, but the user must double-click or press Ctrl+Home to enter it and press Ctrl+End to leave it. If OPEN is omitted, the user must press Ctrl+Home to open it.

The RANGE option can be used to specify a range of values within which character, numeric, or date input must fall. The data type of the expressions used here depends on the data type of the variable following GET. If the user enters a value that does not fall between the two values in the RANGE clause, an alert is displayed that includes the required range. Either of the two expressions following RANGE may be omitted and the clause will check only for values that are too low or high; if the single expression following it is preceded by a comma, it is read as the upper bound of the range.

The SIZE option allows you to specify the size of a GET field by supplying a new length and height.

The VALID option can be used to validate input. It generally must be used with expressions based on user-defined functions that were designed specifically to test this input. If VALID is used with a logical expression, the input is considered valid if the expression is true; the ERROR clause can be used to display a custom error message if the expression is false. If VALID is used with a numeric expression, then a 0 indicates an error, a positive number indicates how many GET fields the cursor should move forward before the next input, and a negative number indicates how many GET fields the cursor should move backward before the next input. In addition to validating data, VALID clauses often include other commands to be executed when the field is read.

The WHEN option allows or prevents editing of the field, depending on the value of the logical function. If the WHEN clause evaluates as a logical false (.F.), the cursor skips to the next GET field. Like VALID clauses, WHEN clauses are often used with user-defined functions including other commands, which are executed when the field is displayed.

The [FONT <expC> [,<expN] [STYLE <expC>] option lets you specify the typeface, size, and style of the font used. <expC> and <expN> should be the name and size of an available font; if the font you specify is not available, Visual FoxPro tries to substitute a similar font. If you omit the FONT clause, the main Visual FoxPro window font is used, and if you include the clause but omit the size option, a 10-point font is used. The STYLE clause may be followed by one of the following codes:

- B: boldface
- I: italic

- N: normal
- O: outline
- Q: opaque
- S: shadow
- -: strikeout
- T: transparent
- U: underline

If this clause is omitted, normal style will be used.

Either the COLOR or the COLOR SCHEME option changes the color attributes used by both the SAY and GET clauses. If you use COLOR, the standard color is used following SAY and the enhanced color following GET; both are defined by using a pair of color codes separated by a slash. If you use COLOR SCHEME instead, you can use a predefined color scheme you refer to by specifying a number between 1 and 24.

See Also @ … EDIT, READ, SHOW GETS

▶ The ^ Operator

Syntax

```
<expN> ^ <expN>
```

Usage This operator is used to raise the first numeric expression to the power of the second. It is identical to the ** operator.

See Also +, –, *, /, **

▶ The – Operator

Syntax

```
<expr> - <expr>
```

Usage This operator is used to subtract numeric or date expressions and to concatenate character expressions with all embedded blanks removed and added to the end of the expression.

See Also +, *, /, **, ^

► The ! Operator

Syntax

```
! <expL> ¦ .NOT. <expL> ¦ NOT <expL>
```

Usage This operator returns .T. if the logical expression returns .F.

See Also .AND., .NOT., .OR.

► The ABS( ) Function

Syntax

```
ABS(<expN>)
```

Usage This function returns the absolute value of a numeric expression—the value disregarding its positive or negative sign.

See Also SIGN( )

► The ACOS( ) Function

Syntax

```
ACOS(<expN>)
```

Usage This function returns the arc cosine of a numeric expression in radians. You can use the RTOD( ) function to convert this result to degrees.

See Also ASIN( ), ATAN, COS( ), DTOR( ), RTOD( ), SIN( ), TAN( )

► The ACCEPT Command

Syntax

```
ACCEPT [<expC>] TO <memvar>
```

Usage This command gets character input from the keyboard without requiring you to use quotation marks or any of the other character-string delimiters, as the INPUT command does. When this command is executed, the program pauses until you press Enter. Any keystrokes typed before Enter is pressed are assigned to the memory variable following the word TO. This command can create the memory variable; it does not have to be defined in advance.

This unformatted input/output command is included for compatibility with earlier versions of the Xbase language. The Form Designer or formatted input/output using @ … SAY … GET is now used instead.

Options The optional character expression displays a prompt for the user.

See Also @ … SAY … GET, INPUT

The ACTIVATE MENU Command

Syntax

```
ACTIVATE MENU <menu name>
     [NOWAIT]
     [PAD <pad name>]
```

Usage This command, used in programming, causes a previously defined menu bar to be activated and displayed on the screen. The user can then select choices from this menu to perform various tasks. A menu remains activated until the system receives a DEACTIVATE MENU command or another menu is activated.

Options The NOWAIT option lets your program keep running while the menu is displayed.

The PAD option lets you designate a particular menu pad as the default choice.

See Also CLEAR MENU, CREATE MENU, DEACTIVATE MENU, DEFINE MENU, HIDE MENU, MODIFY MENU, SHOW MENU

The ACTIVATE POPUP Command

Syntax

```
ACTIVATE POPUP <popup name>
     [AT <row>,<col>]
     [BAR <expN>]
     [NOWAIT]
     [REST]
```

Usage This command, used in programs, activates a menu popup to present a list of choices to the user. The popup must have been previously defined with commands such as DEFINE POPUP and DEFINE BAR.

Options The AT option lets you specify where the popup is to appear on the screen.

The BAR option lets you select a certain bar of the popup as the default menu option.

The NOWAIT option lets the program keep running while the popup is displayed.

The REST option is used with menus created using the PROMPT FIELD option of the DEFINE POPUP command, which creates a menu whose options depend on the content of a field. By default, the first item in the menu popup is highlighted when the menu pad is selected, regardless of which field the pointer is on in the table. If you use the REST option, the current field of the table is highlighted when you first display the popup.

See Also DEACTIVATE POPUP, DEFINE BAR, DEFINE POPUP, HIDE POPUP, ON SELECTION

► The ACTIVATE WINDOW Command

Syntax

```
ACTIVATE WINDOW [<window name1>,<window name2> ...]
           ¦ ALL
     [IN [WINDOW] <window name3> ¦ IN SCREEN]
     [BOTTOM ¦ TOP ¦ SAME]
     [NOSHOW]
```

Usage This command activates a window (or windows) that you have previously initialized with the DEFINE WINDOW command. All subsequent screen output will be directed to this window unless you activate another window on top of it.

Once you have activated a window, @ ... SAY ... GET commands display information within that window, rather than at a position relative to the overall screen. For example, @ 0,0 SAY ... displays output in the upper-left corner of the current window, not in the upper-left corner of the screen.

The window(s) you activate may be removed from active use with the DEACTIVATE WINDOW command.

Options If you specify the ALL option, all previously defined windows will be activated.

The IN [WINDOW] <window name> option activates the specified window(s) within a parent window. Conversely, the default IN SCREEN option specifically places the new window(s) on the screen instead of inside another window.

The TOP option places the new window(s) on top of other previously displayed windows, while the BOTTOM option puts them behind these other windows.

The SAME option puts a specified window that was previously deactivated with the DEACTIVATE WINDOWS command back on the screen in the same place that it was before it was deactivated.

The NOSHOW option directs output to the designated windows without showing it on the screen.

See Also CLEAR WINDOWS, DEFINE WINDOW, HIDE WINDOW, RELEASE WINDOWS, RESTORE WINDOW, SAVE WINDOW, SHOW WINDOW

▶ *The ADD TABLE Command*

Syntax

```
ADD TABLE <name> ¦ ?
     [NAME <long table name>]
```

Usage This command adds a table to the currently open database. Only an existing free table may be added.

Options The <name> option lets you specify the name of the table to add.

The ? option displays the Open dialog box, which you can use to select a table to add.

The NAME <long table name> option lets you specify a long name for the table, which can be used instead of its file name.

See Also ALTER TABLE, CLOSE, CREATE, CREATE TABLE, DISPLAY TABLES, FREE TABLE, LIST TABLES, MODIFY STRUCTURE, REMOVE TABLE, USE

▶ *The ALIAS( ) Function*

Syntax

```
ALIAS([<work area> ¦ <table name>])
```

Usage This function returns the alias of the table that you specify or of the table in the current work area. If no table is open in the specified or current work area, the function returns an empty string.

Options The <work area> argument must be a numeric expression specifying the number of a work area. The function returns the name of the table open in this area.

The <table name> argument represents a table name or alias. The function returns the alias of this table.

If neither of these optional arguments is included, the function returns the alias of the table in the current work area.

See Also USE

▶ The ALLTRIM( ) Function

Syntax

```
ALLTRIM(<expC>)
```

Usage This function returns the character expression with all leading and trailing blanks removed. Three other functions perform similar tasks: LTRIM( ) removes leading blank spaces, and TRIM( ) or RTRIM( ) removes trailing blank spaces.

See Also LTRIM( ), RTRIM( ), TRIM( )

▶ The ALTER TABLE Command

Syntax

```
ALTER TABLE <Table Name>
     [ADD ¦ ALTER [COLUMN] <Field Name>
          <Field Type> [(<Field Width>
              [, <Precision>])]
          [NULL ¦ NOT NULL]
          [CHECK <expL1> [ERROR <expC1>]]
          [DEFAULT <expr>]
          [PRIMARY KEY ¦ UNIQUE]
          [REFERENCES <Table Name 2> [TAG Tag Name>]]
          [NOCPTRANS]]
     ¦
     [ALTER [COLUMN <field name>]
```

```
     [SET DEFAULT <expr>] ¦ [DROP DEFAULT]
     [SET CHECK <expL2> [ERROR expC2>]] ¦
     [DROP CHECK]]
¦
[RENAME COLUMN <field name> TO <field name>]
¦
[DROP [COLUMN] <field name>]

[SET CHECK <expL3> [ERROR <expC3>]]
[DROP CHECK]
[ADD PRIMARY KEY <expr> TAG <tag name>]
[DROP PRIMARY KEY]
[ADD UNIQUE <expr> TAG <tag name>]
[DROP UNIQUE TAG <tag name>]
[ADD FOREIGN KEY <expr> TAG <tag name>
     REFERENCES <table name> [TAG <tag name>]]
[DROP FOREIGN KEY TAG <tag name> [SAVE]]
[NOVALIDATE]
```

Usage This complex command lets you modify the structure of a table. (It is generally easier to modify the structure of a table using the Table Designer.)

Options The ALTER TABLE <Table Name> option lets you specify the name of the table being modified.

The ADD ¦ ALTER COLUMN Clause The ADD ¦ ALTER [COLUMN] <Field Name> <Field Type> [(<Field Width> [, <Precision>])] option lets you specify the name of a new field to add or the name of an existing field whose definition will be changed.

Field name and field type are needed for all fields. Field width is needed for character, float, and numeric fields. Precision is needed for float, numeric, and double fields.

Field types are entered using the following letters: C for Character, D for Date, T for DateTime, N for Numeric, F for Float, B for Double, Y for Currency, L for Logical, M for Memo, G for General, P for Picture. Field width and precision are entered using integers.

The NULL ¦ NOT NULL option lets you specify whether the null value can be entered in this field.

The CHECK <expL1> [ERROR <expC1>] options let you enter a logical expression used as a validity check for the field and specify an error message that will be displayed if this expression evaluates as false.

The DEFAULT <expr> option lets you specify a default value for the field, which is entered in it automatically whenever you add a new record to the table. The expression must be the same data type as the field.

The PRIMARY KEY ¦ UNIQUE option lets you create a primary or candidate index. Either has the same name as the field.

The REFERENCES <Table Name 2> [TAG Tag Name>] option establishes a persistent relationship to another table and specifies the name of the index tag that the relationship is based on.

The NOCPTRANS option prevents character and memo fields from being translated to a different code page.

The ALTER COLUMN Clause The ALTER [COLUMN] <field name> option specifies the name of a field to be modified.

The SET DEFAULT <expr> option specifies a new default value for this field.

The DROP DEFAULT option removes the current default value for this field.

The SET CHECK <expL2> [ERROR expC2>] options let you enter a logical expression used as a validity check for the field and specify an error message that will be displayed if this expression evaluates as false.

The DROP CHECK option removes the current validity check for this field.

The RENAME COLUMN Clause The RENAME COLUMN <field name> TO <field name> lets you change the name of an existing field.

▸▸ **WARNING**

If you rename a field in this way, existing expressions that include its old field name become invalid. Indexes, validation rules, and other features based on Visual FoxPro expressions may no longer work.

The DROP COLUMN Clause The DROP [COLUMN] <field name> option lets you remove an existing field from the table.

Other Clauses The SET CHECK <expL3> [ERROR <expC3>] options let you enter a logical expression used as a table validation rule and specify an error message that will be displayed if this expression evaluates as false.

The DROP CHECK option removes the existing table validation rule.

The ADD PRIMARY KEY <expr> TAG <tag name> option lets you add a Primary Key index to the table. The index tag is based on the expression specified and has the tag name specified.

The DROP PRIMARY KEY option removes the existing Primary Key index.

The ADD UNIQUE <expr> TAG <tag name> option lets you add a candidate index to the table. The index tag is based on the expression specified and has the tag name specified.

DROP UNIQUE TAG <tag name> option removes the existing candidate index whose name is specified.

The ADD FOREIGN KEY <expr> TAG <tag name> lets you create an index that can be used to create a persistent one-to-many relationship between this table and another table in the database.

The REFERENCES <table name> [TAG <tag name>] establishes the persistent relationship with the other table. If you omit the TAG <tag name> option, the relationship is established between the foreign key specified in the previous option and the primary key of the other table.

The DROP FOREIGN KEY TAG <tag name> [SAVE] option removes an existing Foreign Key index. If you include SAVE, this index tag is not deleted from the structural compound index file.

The NOVALIDATE option lets Visual FoxPro make changes to the table that may validate the integrity of the data in a relational database, such as deleting a field used as the primary key. By default, Visual FoxPro will not allow these changes.

See Also ADD TABLE, CLOSE, CREATE, CREATE TABLE, DISPLAY TABLES, FREE TABLE, LIST TABLES, MODIFY STRUCTURE, REMOVE TABLE, USE

▶ The APPEND Command

Syntax

```
APPEND
      [BLANK]
      [NOMENU]
```

Usage This command lets you add data to the end of the current table. First, you must open the file with the command USE <file name>. If you use this command when no file is open, the Open File dialog box is displayed to let you choose a table.

APPEND by itself opens a Browse/Edit window in Edit mode, displaying a blank record added at the end of the table that is open in the current work area and moving the pointer to that record. If data is entered in the record, that record becomes permanent and a new blank record is added. An indefinite number of records is added as needed.

Options APPEND BLANK adds a single blank record to the end of the table open in the current work area and moves the pointer to that record. Character fields are initialized with spaces. Numeric fields are initialized with 0. Date fields are initialized with " / / ". Logical fields are initialized with .F.

APPEND BLANK does not open a Browse/Edit window. Because the field values are initialized, they can be used in programs as the basis of the variables in a series of @ <row>,<col> SAY <exp> GET <variable> commands and can be filled using a series of REPLACE commands.

(It is possible to open a Browse/Edit window and edit these fields directly by using the command BROWSE, CHANGE, or EDIT immediately after the command APPEND BLANK, but this procedure has no advantage over simply using the command APPEND.)

The NOMENU option removes the Browse command and all commands used for formatting the Browse window from the View menu, so that the user cannot alter the Browse window.

See Also APPEND FROM, BROWSE, CHANGE, EDIT

▶ The APPEND FROM Command

Syntax

```
APPEND FROM <file> ¦ ?
      [FIELDS <field list>]
```

```
[FOR <expL>]
[TYPE] [DELIMITED [WITH <character> ¦ BLANK ¦
      TAB]
     ¦ DIF ¦ FW2 ¦ MOD ¦ PDOX ¦ RPD ¦ SDF ¦ SYLK
     ¦ WK1 ¦ WK3 ¦ WKS ¦ WR1 ¦ WRK ¦ XLS]
[AS <code page>]
```

Usage This command lets you add data from another file to the end of the table that is open in the currently selected work area.

In the simplest form of the command, the data is appended from another table with a DBF extension. You can specify the name of the data file; Visual FoxPro assumes a DBF extension if none is entered (unless a TYPE clause is included). Or you can use the ? option, and Visual FoxPro displays the Open File dialog box and lets the user select the file to append from.

Options The FIELDS option lets you select which fields in the table will have data appended to them.

The FOR option allows you to select which records in the other file will be added to the table that is currently open. Only records for which the logical expression is evaluated as true (.T.) are added.

A number of other options let you append data to the current table from files that are not Visual FoxPro tables. The types of files you can append data from are:

- **SDF files:** ASCII text files in which records have fixed-length fields and a ↵/linefeed at the end.
- **DELIMITED files:** ASCII text files in which fields are separated by some delimiter (usually a comma). Character fields are also delimited by quotation marks, and there is a ↵/linefeed at the end of each record.
- **DIF files:** From VisiCalc.
- **FW2 files:** From Framework II.
- **MOD files:** From Multiplan version 4.01.
- **PDOX files:** From Paradox version 3.5.
- **RPD files:** From Rapidfile version 1.2.
- **SYLK files:** Symbolic Link files from Multiplan.
- **WK1 files:** From Lotus 1-2-3 version 2.0.

- **WK3 files:** From Lotus 1-2-3 version 3.0.
- **WKS files:** From Lotus 1-2-3 version 1-A.
- **WR1 files:** From Lotus Symphony versions 1.1 and 1.2.
- **WRK files:** From Lotus Symphony version 1.0.
- **XLS files:** From Excel.

With the DELIMITED option, you can specify delimiters other than commas to tell Visual FoxPro that the new file has a blank, a tab, or any other character placed between each field.

The AS <code page> option lets you specify the code page of the appended file. FoxPro copies the data and converts it to the code page you specify.

See Also APPEND, COPY FILE, COPY TO

▸ The APPEND GENERAL Command

Syntax

```
APPEND GENERAL <general field name>
     FROM <file name>
     [LINK]
     [CLASS <OLE class>]
```

Usage This command allows you to import data from another window or another program such as Lotus or Excel into a Visual FoxPro table.

The new data (or object) is imported through a process known as object linking and embedding (OLE). The OLE object is placed in a General field in the current table. You must specify the name of this General field and the name of the file (including its extension) from which the object is being appended.

Options The LINK option allows you to create a link between the OLE object and the file that contains it. The object's data will then be updated if the source file is changed.

The CLASS option lets you specify different classes of OLE objects.

See Also APPEND FROM, MODIFY GENERAL

The APPEND MEMO Command

Syntax

```
APPEND MEMO <memo field name> FROM <text file name>
[OVERWRITE]
```

Usage This command adds data from an existing text file to a memo field. The command must include the memo field name and the text file name, including its extension.

Options If you use the OVERWRITE option, the command replaces any text already in the memo field with the contents of the text file.

The ASC( ) Function

Syntax

```
ASC(<expC>)
```

Usage This function returns the ASCII number of the first character in any character expression. For example, either ASC("A") or ASC ("ABCDEFG") returns 65, since uppercase *A* is ASCII character 65. This function is normally used with a single character as an argument.

You can use this function in combination with ? to look up the ASCII value of characters. For example, if you enter the command **? ASC("A")**, Visual FoxPro displays 65.

See Also CHR( )

The _ASCIICOLS System Variable

Syntax

```
_ASCIICOLS = <expN>
```

Usage This system variable specifies the number of columns in the text file if you use the REPORT command with the TO FILE ASCII option. The default is 80 columns.

See Also ASCIIROWS, REPORT

The _ASCIIROWS System Variable

Syntax

```
_ASCIIROWS = <expN>
```

Usage This system variable specifies the number of rows in the text file if you use the REPORT command with the TO FILE ASCII option. The default is 80 columns.

See Also ASCIICOLS, REPORT

► The ASIN( ) Function

Syntax

```
ASIN(<expN>)
```

Usage This function returns the arc sine of a numeric expression in radians. You can use the RTOD( ) function to convert this result to degrees.

See Also ACOS( ), ATAN, COS( ), DTOR( ), RTOD( ), SIN( ), TAN( )

► The ASSIST Command

Syntax

```
ASSIST
```

Usage This command runs the program represented by the _ASSIST system memory variable.

This command ran the Catalog Managers of dBASE IV and FoxPro 2.6. It is included in Visual FoxPro 3.0 for compatibility.

See Also _ASSIST

► The _ASSIST System Variable

Syntax

```
_ASSIST = <expC>
```

Usage This system variable specifies the program that is executed when the ASSIST command is executed. This command displayed the Catalog Manager in dBASE IV and in FoxPro 2.6. It is included in Visual FoxPro 3.0 for compatibility.

► The AT( ) Function

Syntax

```
AT(<search_for exp>, <search_in exp>)
[, <occurrence>]
```

Usage This function returns the position of a character expressing within another character expression or memo field as a number, counting from the beginning of the string you are searching in.

For example, **AT("a","axe")** would return 1, and **AT("x" "axe")** would return 2.

Options By default, this function returns the location of the first occurrence of the string. Enter a numeric expression as the <occurrence> option to search for a later occurrence; for example, use 2 to search for the second occurrence.

See Also ATLINE( ), ATCLINE( ), LEFT( ), RAT( ),RATLINE( ), RIGHT( ), SUBSTR( )

The ATAN( ) Function

Syntax

```
ATAN(<expN>)
```

Usage This function returns the arc tangent of a numeric expression in radians. You can use the RTOD( ) function to convert this result to degrees.

See Also ACOS( ), ASIN( ), COS( ), DTOR( ), RTOD( ), SIN( ), TAN( )

The ATCLINE( ) Function

Syntax

```
ACTLINE(<search_for exp>, <search_in exp>)
```

Usage This function returns the line number of the first occurrence of a character expression within another character expression or memo field, without regard to case. This function is similar to ATLINE( ), but it ignores capitalization.

See Also AT( ), ATLINE( ), LEFT( ), RATLINE( ) , RIGHT( ), SUBSTR( )

The ATLINE() Function

Syntax

```
ATLINE(<search_for exp>, <search_in exp>)
```

Usage This function returns the line number of the first occurrence of a character expression within another character expression or memo field. This function is similar to AT( ), but it returns the line number of the expression, rather than its position.

See Also AT( ), ATCLINE( ), LEFT( ), RATLINE( ) , RIGHT( ), SUBSTR( )

▶ The AVERAGE Command

Syntax

```
AVERAGE
      [<expN list>]
      [<scope>]
      [FOR <expL1>]
      [WHILE <expL2>]
      [TO <memvar list> ¦ TO ARRAY <array>]
      [NOOPTIMIZE]
```

Usage This command computes the average (arithmetic mean) of numeric expressions. By default, all the Numeric fields in the table that is open in the current work area are averaged.

Options If an expression list is included, only the numeric expressions that are listed are averaged.

All records are included in the average unless a Scope, FOR, or WHILE clause is included to restrict the records that are considered. (See Chapter 11 for a discussion of how these clauses are used.)

If the optional TO clause is included, the results are stored in the specified list of memory variables. Alternately, if a TO ARRAY clause is included, the results are stored in the array that is specified. (Arrays are discussed in the entries on DECLARE and DIMENSION in this appendix.)

The NOOPTIMIZE option for this command disables the Rushmore technology, which normally speeds up data access when you use a FOR statement containing fields in existing indexes. You can disable Rushmore with the NOOPTIMIZE option on a number of Visual FoxPro commands, but in this case there is little reason to do so.

See Also CALCULATE, SUM

The BAR( ) Function

Syntax

```
BAR()
```

Usage This function conveys the number of the last option chosen on a menu. It is particularly useful in programming, when a particular program must carry out different functions depending on the user's choice on a previous menu. The default value of BAR( ) is 0.

See Also DEFINE BAR, DEFINE POPUP, ON BAR

The BETWEEN( ) Function

Syntax

```
BETWEEN(<exp1>,<exp2>,<exp3>)
```

Usage This function returns a logical true (.T.) if the value of <exp1> falls between the values of <exp2> and <exp3> or, more precisely, if <exp1> is greater than or equal to <exp2> and <exp1> is less than or equal to <exp3>. Otherwise, it returns a logical false (.F.). It can be used with numeric, character, or date or datetime expressions.

See Also MAX( ), MIN( )

The BLANK Command

Syntax

```
BLANK
        [<scope>]
        [FOR <expL1>]
        [WHILE <expL2>]
        [NOOPTIMIZE]
```

Usage This command removes data from records but does not delete the records; instead, it leaves their fields blank. By default, it applies only to the current record (the record, in the table that's open in the current work area, when the pointer appears).

Options If an optional Scope, FOR, or WHILE clause is used, all the records included in the specified scope or all the records for which the logical expression following the FOR or WHILE is evaluated as true are emptied of data. For more information on how these clauses work, see Chapter 11.

The NOOPTIMIZE option for this command disables the Rushmore technology, which normally speeds up data access when you use a FOR statement containing fields in existing indexes. You can disable Rushmore with the NOOPTIMIZE option on a number of Visual FoxPro for Windows commands. The only time you need to do this is when your command changes data in the field(s) that make up the index key, since the version of the file used by Rushmore may then become outdated, and incorrect answers may result.

See Also DELETE

▶ The BOF( ) Function

Syntax

```
BOF([<exp>])
```

Usage This function indicates the beginning of the file. It returns a logical true (.T.) if you attempt to move the pointer to a position before the first record of the table.

Options Ordinarily, this function applies to the file that is open in the current work area. If the <exp> option is used, though, it applies to the file that is open in the work area whose letter, number, or alias name is specified.

See Also EOF( )

▶ The BROWSE Command

Syntax

```
BROWSE
    [FIELDS <field list>]
    [FONT <expC> [,<expN] [STYLE <expC2>]
    [FOR <expL1> [REST] ]
    [FORMAT]
    [FREEZE <field name>]
    [KEY <exp1> [,<exp2>]]
    [LAST ¦ NOINIT]
    [LEDIT]
    [LOCK <expN2>]
    [LPARTITION]
    [NOAPPEND]
```

```
[NOCLEAR]
[NODELETE]
[NOEDIT ¦ NOMODIFY]
[NOFOLLOW]
[NOLGRID][NORGRID]
[NOLINK]
[NOMENU]
[NOOPTIMIZE]
[NOREFRESH]
[NORMAL]
[NOWAIT]
[PARTITION <expN3>]
[PREFERENCE <expC3>]
[REDIT]
[SAVE]
[TIMEOUT <expN4>]
[TITLE <expC4>]
[VALID [:F] <expL2> [ERROR <expC5>]]
[WHEN <expL3>]
[WIDTH <expN5>]
[[WINDOW <window name1>]
[IN [WINDOW] <window name2> ¦ IN SCREEN]]
[COLOR [<color pair list>] ¦ COLOR SCHEME
        <expN5>
```

Usage Used by itself, BROWSE opens the Browse/Edit window in its standard Browse configuration, with each record on one line and its fields arranged from right to left.

You can edit existing records or use the Browse menu to add a new record. If you choose Close from the window's Control menu, press Ctrl+W or Ctrl+End, or choose File ➤ Close, you can close the Browse window and save any changes you made. If you press Ctrl+Q or Esc, you can close the Browse window and discard any changes you made. To edit Memo fields, double-click the field with the mouse or move the cursor to it and press Ctrl+PgDn to open the Memo window. When you enter the command BROWSE, a Browse pad is added to the menu bar, which lets you partition the window, toggle the window to Edit mode, delete or recall a record, and otherwise alter the window.

Choosing View ➤ Browse generates the command BROWSE LAST, which opens the Browse/Edit window in its last configuration rather than in the default configuration described in the first paragraph.

Options Many of the options that can be used with BROWSE are useful primarily in programming, where you want to limit what the user can do.

The FIELDS option makes the Browse window contain only the fields mentioned in the field list. It may also include calculated fields (which are read-only), and it includes other options that may be used to control properties of how fields are displayed, such as their heading and their width. The fields in the list must be separated by commas, and each of the fields may be followed by these options:

- [:R] makes the field read-only, so its data can be viewed but not edited.
- [: <expN>] specifies the width of the field.
- [: V <expL> [:F] [:E = <expC>]] creates a validity check, which does not let you leave the field if the logical expression evaluates as false. By default, this expression is evaluated only if the field is modified, but the :F option forces the evaluation, even if the data was not changed. If you use the :E = <expC> option, the character expression will be used as an error message if the logical expression evaluates as false.
- [: P = <expC>] creates a picture template. The character expression must be made up of the same symbols that can be used in a PICTURE clause of an @ … SAY … GET Command, which are listed in the entry on that command. All of the symbols except @M may be used here.
- [: B = <exp>, <exp> [:F]] specifies boundaries. The two expressions are a minimum and maximum value for the data. By default, the boundaries are checked only if the field is modified, but the :F option forces the evaluation, even if the data was not changed.
- [: H = <expC>] lets you specify a character expression to be used as the heading for the field.
- [:W = <expL>] lets you specify a WHEN option that prevents the cursor from moving to the field if the logical expression evaluates as false. The logical expression may be a user-defined function.

The [FONT <expC> [,<expN] [STYLE <expC3>] option lets you specify the typeface, size, and style of the font used. <expC> and <expN> should be the name and size of an available font; if the font you specify is not available, Visual FoxPro tries to substitute a similar font. If you omit the FONT clause, the main Visual FoxPro window font is used, and if you include the clause but omit the size option, a 10-point font is used. The STYLE clause may be followed by one of the following codes:

- B: boldface
- I: italic
- N: normal
- O: outline
- Q: opaque
- S: shadow
- -: strikeout
- T: transparent
- U: underline

If this clause is omitted, normal style will be used.

The FOR option includes only those records for which a logical expression that you specify is true. By default, the pointer is moved to the top of the table when a FOR clause is included, but if the REST option is also used, the pointer remains in its current position.

The FORMAT option lets you use a format file (with an FMT extension) to control the way the fields are displayed. The format file must first be made active with the command SET FORMAT TO <file name>.

The FREEZE option allows changes to be made only to the one field that is mentioned, although all the fields are displayed.

The KEY option lets you select a particular subset of records to browse by specifying one particular field value or a range of field values to be matched. The table must be indexed on the field you select and that index must currently be in usc. For example, **BROWSE KEY '94704,' '94709'** allows you to browse records with a ZIP code between 94704 and 94709 if your table includes a ZIP code field and if the ZIP code index is the controlling index.

The LAST | NOINIT option opens the Browse/Edit window in the same configuration in which it was last used. These options are identical, and NOINIT is included to provide dBASE compatibility.

The LOCK option lets you specify the number of fields to be "locked" in the left partition.

The LPARTITION option places the cursor in the first field in the left partition of a partitioned Browse window. By default, the cursor is placed in the first field of the right partition.

The LEDIT option displays the left partition of a partitioned Browse window in Edit mode.

The NOLINK option removes the normal linkage between left and right partitions, which causes both to scroll together.

The NOAPPEND option makes it impossible to add new records to the file.

The NOCLEAR option leaves the Browse/Edit window visible on the screen after you are done using it. By default, the window disappears when you are done.

The NODELETE option makes it impossible to mark records for deletion. The NOEDIT | NOMODIFY option makes it impossible to make any changes in the data.

The NOFOLLOW option makes the pointer stay where it is in the table when you modify the field the table is indexed on. By default, the pointer stays on the record, following it to the new position that it moves to because its key field was modified.

The NOLGRID and NORGRID options let you remove the vertical lines that normally separate fields in the left and right partitions, respectively.

The NOMENU option makes the Browse/Edit window open without the Browse menu pad being added to the menu bar, so the user cannot access the Browse menu popup.

The NOOPTIMIZE option disables the Rushmore technology, which normally speeds up data access when you use a FOR statement containing fields in existing indexes. You may want to do this if you will be changing data in the same field that is specified in the FOR statement and if the table is indexed on that field. Otherwise, the version of the file used by Rushmore may become outdated, and the Browse display may not be up to date.

The NOREFRESH clause prevents the Browse window from being refreshed, and can be used to improve performance with read-only tables.

The NORMAL option makes the Browse/Edit window open with its normal attributes even if it is opened in a user window. If this option is not used, the Browse window takes its colors and other attributes from the user window it is opened in.

The NOWAIT option makes a program continue without any pause after the Browse/Edit window is opened. If BROWSE is used in a program without this option, the Browse/Edit window is opened and the program is suspended until the window is closed.

The PARTITION option splits the screen into left and right partitions; the numeric expression following it determines the size of the left partition by specifying the column number of the split bar. You can use this clause to lock one set of fields in the left portion of the screen while browsing others in the right portion. If you use a PARTITION clause, the cursor is normally placed in the right partition unless you also include an LPARTITION clause.

The PREFERENCE option lets you save and reuse the attributes of Browse windows. Unlike the LAST option, which reuses only the previous configuration, this option can reuse any configuration used in the past. The first time BROWSE is used with this option followed by a character expression, the PREFERENCE referred to by that name is created. When the Browse window is closed, that PREFERENCE is updated. Anytime in the future that the Browse/Edit window is opened with that PREFERENCE, it will keep the same configuration.

The REDIT option displays the right partition of a partitioned Browse window in Edit mode.

The SAVE option keeps the Browse/Edit window (and an associated Memo window, if one is open) on the screen after the user has exited from it. This option can be used only in programs.

The TIMEOUT option allows you to specify how many seconds the Browse window will remain open without the user making any input. This clause can be used only within a program.

The TITLE option lets you specify a title to appear in the top border of the editing window. The table alias is the default title.

The VALID option lets you check new data entered into each record before BROWSE moves on to the next record. For BROWSE to move on, the logical expression you specify must be true. If it is not, an error message that you set up with an ERROR clause is displayed. If you include :F after the word VALID, you can force the validation check to occur whether or not the user has actually entered new data in that record.

The WHEN option allows the user to make changes only to the current record when a certain logical condition you specify is true.

The WIDTH option limits the width of the display of all fields. Only the display is affected, not the actual data. You can use the arrow keys to scroll through a field and see all its data.

The WINDOW option lets the Browse/Edit window take on the characteristics of another window you specify. That window must first be defined using the DEFINE WINDOW command. The IN WINDOW option actually opens the Browse window within another window, although the Browse window will not necessarily have the characteristics of this parent window unless you also use a WINDOW clause. The default is IN SCREEN.

The COLOR option allows you to specify the color attributes of the Browse window. You can do this by means of a color pair list (for example, COLOR 'B/R') or a COLOR SCHEME (a number between 1 and 24 that lets you choose any of 24 preset color schemes).

See Also CHANGE, EDIT

▸ The BUILD APP Command

Syntax

```
BUILD APP <file name> FROM <project name>
```

Usage This command creates a program file with an APP extension based on the project whose name is specified. The APP file combines the files in the project into a single file; you should use the Project Manager to exclude tables that can be modified and their indexes.

See Also BUILD EXE, BUILD PROJECT, CREATE PROJECT, MODIFY PROJECT

▸ The BUILD EXE Command

Syntax

```
BUILD EXE <file name> FROM <project name>
```

Usage This command creates a program file with an EXE extension based on the project whose name is specified. The EXE file combines the files in the project into a single file; you should use the Project Manager to exclude tables that can be modified and their indexes.

This EXE file can be run by users who do not have Visual FoxPro. This feature is available only in the Professional Edition of Visual FoxPro.

See Also BUILD APP, BUILD PROJECT, CREATE PROJECT, MODIFY PROJECT

The BUILD PROJECT Command

Syntax

```
BUILD PROJECT <file name> FROM <file name> [<file
        name2> . . .]
```

Usage This command creates a project (PJX) file that includes the files you list. The list can include one or more program, menu, report, label, form, or library files. The project file will include not only the files that are listed but all the files they call. For example, if you use only a menu file name in the list, the project will also include all the files that are used when any of the menu options is selected.

See Also BUILD APP, BUILD EXE, CREATE PROJECT, MODIFY PROJECT

The CALCULATE Command

Syntax

```
CALCULATE <math exp list>
     [<scope>]
     [FOR <expL1>]
     [WHILE <expL2>]
     [TO <memvar list> ¦ TO ARRAY <array>]
     [NOOPTIMIZE]
```

Usage This command lets you perform a variety of mathematical operations on table fields or field expressions. You can include one or more other Visual FoxPro financial or statistical functions within this command.

The functions that can be used within CALCULATE are:

- **AVG(<expN>):** Computes the average (arithmetic mean) value for a Numeric field or field expression.

- **CNT( ):** Computes the total number of records (and so does not require you to place a field name or expression within the parentheses).
- **MAX(<exp>):** Finds the maximum value for a field or field expression.
- **MIN(<exp>):** Finds the minimum value for a field or field expression.
- **NPV(<expN1>,<exp> [,<expN2>]):** Calculates the Net Present Value of a series of payments over time discounted at some constant interest rate. The interest rate, expressed as a decimal, is entered as <expN1>. The series of payments is represented by <exp>, which must be the name of a field, a field expression, or a numeric expression. Optionally, an initial investment can be represented by <expN2>.
- **STD(<expN>):** Calculates the standard deviation for the values in a Numeric field or field expression.
- **SUM(<expN>):** Calculates the sum of the values in a Numeric field or field expression.
- **VAR(<expN>):** Calculates the variance from the average for a Numeric field or field expression.

Options If an optional scope, FOR, or WHILE clause is used, only the records included in the specified scope or only the records for which the logical expression following the FOR or WHILE is evaluated as true are included in the calculation. For more information on how these clauses work, see Chapter 11.

Records that are marked for deletion are included in the calculation unless the command SET DELETED ON has been used.

If the optional TO clause is included, the results are stored in the specified list of memory variables. Alternately, if a TO ARRAY clause is included, the results are stored in the array that is specified. (Arrays are not covered in this book, but they are discussed in the entries on DECLARE and DIMENSION in this appendix.)

The NOOPTIMIZE option for this command disables the Rushmore technology, which normally speeds up data access when you use a FOR statement containing fields in existing indexes. You can disable

Rushmore with the NOOPTIMIZE option on a number of Visual Fox-Pro commands, but in this case there is little reason to do so.

See Also AVERAGE, COUNT, SUM

▶ The _CALCMEM System Variable

Syntax

```
_CALCMEM = <expN>
```

Usage This system variable specifies the number that is stored in the memory of the Calculator. Your program can store a value to this location, so that it becomes the default for the user, or it can test the variable for a value before doing something else.

See Also _CALCVALUE

▶ The _CALCVALUE System Variable

Syntax

```
_CALCVALUE = <expN>
```

Usage This system variable specifies the number that is displayed in the Calculator. Your program can store a value to this location, so that it becomes the default for the user, or it can test the variable for a value before doing something else.

See Also _CALCMEM

▶ The CANCEL Command

Syntax

```
CANCEL
```

Usage This command terminates execution of a program, releases all private memory variables, and returns control to the Visual FoxPro Command window.

It can be used, for example, to exclude users who do not enter the proper password. If the user's entry does not match the designated password embedded in the program code, a CANCEL statement returns the user to the Command window.

See Also QUIT, RETURN, SUSPEND

▸ The CANDIDATE( ) Function

Syntax

```
CANDIDATE([<index number>]
     [, <work area num> | <table alias>]
```

Usage This function returns .T. if the index tag specified is a candidate index. By default, it applies to the index currently used as the controlling index.

Options Use the <index number> argument to specify the index, with all open indexes numbered as follows. All single-file indexes are numbered first, in the order that they were opened. All tags in the structural compound index file are numbered next, in the order in which they were created. All tags in open independent compound index files are numbered next, in the order in which the files were opened, and in the order in which the tags were created within each file.

If you specify a number larger than all open indexes, the function returns the empty string.

The <work area num> option specifies the number of the work area that the table is open in; and the <table alias> option specifies the name or alias of the table. If neither option is used, the function applies to the current table.

See Also ALTER TABLE, CREATE TABLE, INDEX, PRIMARY( )

▸ The CD | CHDIR Command

Syntax

```
CD <path> | CHDIR <path>
```

Usage This command changes the current drive and current directory, in which Visual FoxPro searches for files if you specify a file name without using a path name.

The <path> is specified in the same way as in MS-DOS. It may be a drive, such as **c:** or **d:**, a drive and directory, the full path name of a directory in the current drive, a child directory of the current directory, or any other valid specification for a DOS directory.

See Also MD | MKDIR, RD | RMDIR

▶ The CDOW( ) Function

Syntax

```
CDOW(<date exp>)
```

Usage This function returns the day of the week in character form. For example, **? CDOW({11/6/92})** returns `Friday`.

See Also CMONTH( ), CTOD( ), DTOC( )

▶ The CEILING( ) Function

Syntax

```
CEILING(<expN>)
```

Usage This function returns the next integer that is greater than or equal to the numeric expression that is specified.

See Also FLOOR( ), INT( ), ROUND( )

▶ The CHANGE Command

Syntax

```
CHANGE
      [FIELDS <field list>]
      [<scope>]
      [FOR <expL1>]
      [WHILE <expL2>]
      [FONT <expC> [,<expN] [STYLE <expC2>]]
      [FREEZE <field name>]
      [KEY <exp1> [,<exp2>]]
      [LAST ¦ NOINIT]
      [LEDIT][REDIT]
      [LPARTITION]
      [NOAPPEND]
      [NOCLEAR]
      [NODELETE]
      [NOEDIT ¦ NOMODIFY]
      [NOFOLLOW]
      [NOLINK]
      [NOMENU]
```

```
[NOOPTIMIZE]
[NORMAL]
[NOWAIT]
[PARTITION <expN2>]
[PREFERENCE <expC3>]
[REST]
[SAVE]
[TIMEOUT <expN3>]
[TITLE <expC4>]
[VALID [:F] <expL3> [ERROR <expC5>]]
[WHEN <expL4>]
[WIDTH <expN4>]
[[WINDOW <window name1>]
[IN [WINDOW] <window name2> ¦ IN SCREEN]]
[COLOR [<color pair list>] ¦ COLOR SCHEME
     <expN4>
```

Usage CHANGE opens the Browse window in its Edit configuration, with each field on one line. The commands CHANGE and EDIT are identical; EDIT was more common in earlier Xbase-compatible programs.

You can edit existing records or use the Browse menu to add a new record. If you click the close box, press Ctrl+W or Ctrl+End, or choose File – Close, you can close the Browse/Edit window and save any changes you made. If you press Ctrl+Q, you can close the Browse/Edit window and discard any changes you made. To edit Memo fields, double-click the field with the mouse or move the cursor to it and press Ctrl+PgDn to open the Memo window.

Options Many of the options that can be used with CHANGE are useful primarily in programming, where you want to limit what the user can do.

The FIELDS option makes the Browse window contain only the fields mentioned in the field list. It may also include calculated fields (which are read-only), and it includes other options that may be used to control properties of how fields are displayed, such as their heading and their width. The fields in the list must be separated by commas, and each of the fields may be followed by the following options:

- [:R] makes the field read-only, so its data can be viewed but not edited.

- [: <expN>] specifies the width of the field.
- [: V <expL> [:F] [:E = <expC>] creates a validity check, which does not let you leave the field if the logical expression evaluates as false. By default, this expression is evaluated only if the field is modified, but the :F option forces the evaluation, even if the data was not changed. If you use the :E = <expC> option, the character expression will be used as an error message if the logical expression evaluates as false.
- [: P = <expC>] creates a picture template. The character expression must be made up of the same symbols that can be used in a PICTURE clause of an @ ... SAY ... GET Command, which are listed in the entry on that command. All of the symbols except @M may be used here.
- [: B = <exp>, <exp> [:F]] specifies boundaries. The two expressions are a minimum and maximum value for the data. By default, the boundaries are checked only if the field is modified, but the :F option forces the evaluation, even if the data was not changed.
- [: H = <expC>] lets you specify a character expression to be used as the heading for the field.
- [:W = <expL>] lets you specify a WHEN option that prevents the cursor from moving to the field if the logical expression evaluates as false. The logical expression may be a user-defined function.

The <scope> option limits the number of records that the Edit window includes, and the FOR and WHILE options include only those records for which a logical expression you specify is true. FOR and WHILE clauses are explained in Chapter 11.

The FONT <expC> [,<expN] [STYLE <expC3>] option lets you specify the typeface, size, and style of the font used. <expC> and <expN> should be the name and size of an available font; if the font you specify is not available, Visual FoxPro tries to substitute a similar font. If you omit the FONT clause, the main Visual FoxPro window font is used, and if you include the clause but omit the size option, a 10-point font is used. The STYLE clause may be followed by one of the following codes:

- B: boldface
- I: italic
- N: normal

- O: outline
- Q: opaque
- S: shadow
- -: strikeout
- T: transparent
- U: underline

If this clause is omitted, normal style will be used.

The FREEZE option allows changes to be made only to the one field that is mentioned, although all the fields are displayed.

The KEY option lets you select a particular subset of records to change by specifying one particular field value or a range of field values to be matched. The table must be indexed on the field you select and that index must currently be in use. For example, **CHANGE KEY '94704', '94709'** allows you to change records with a ZIP code between 94704 and 94709 if your table includes a ZIP code field and if the ZIP code index is in use.

The LAST ¦ NOINIT option opens the Browse/Edit window in the same configuration in which it was last used. These options are identical, and NOINIT is included to provide dBASE compatibility.
The LEDIT option displays the left partition of the Edit window in Browse mode rather than Edit mode, while the REDIT option displays the right partition in Browse mode.

The LOCK option lets you specify the number of fields to be "locked" in the left partition.

The LPARTITION option places the cursor in the first field in the left partition of a partitioned Browse window. By default, the cursor is placed in the first field of the right partition.

The NOLINK option removes the normal linkage between left and right partitions, which causes both to scroll together.

The NOAPPEND option makes it impossible to add new records to the file.

The NOCLEAR option leaves the Browse/Edit window visible on the screen after you are done using it. By default, the window disappears when you are done.

The NODELETE option makes it impossible to mark records for deletion. The NOEDIT ¦ NOMODIFY option makes it impossible to make any changes in the data.

The NOFOLLOW option makes the pointer stay where it is in the table when you modify the field the table is indexed on. By default, the pointer stays on the record, following it to the new position it moves to because its key field was modified.

The NOMENU option makes the Browse/Edit window open without the Browse menu pad being added to the menu bar, so the user cannot access the Browse menu.

The NOOPTIMIZE option disables the Rushmore technology, which normally speeds up data access when you use a FOR statement containing fields in existing indexes. You may want to do this if you will be changing data in the same field that is specified in the FOR statement and if the table is indexed on that field. Otherwise, the version of the file used by Rushmore may become outdated, and the Edit display may not be up to date.

The NORMAL option makes the Browse/Edit window open with its normal attributes even if it is opened in a user window. If this option is not used, the Browse window takes its colors and other attributes from the user window it is opened in.

The NOWAIT option makes a program continue without any pause after the Browse/Edit window is opened. If CHANGE is used in a program without this option, the Browse/Edit window is opened and the program is suspended until it is closed.

The PARTITION option splits the screen into left and right partitions. The numeric expression following it determines the size of the left partition by specifying the column number of the split bar. You can use this clause to lock one set of fields in the left portion of the screen while browsing others in the right portion. If you use a PARTITION clause, the cursor is normally placed in the right partition unless you also include an LPARTITION clause.

The PREFERENCE option lets you save and reuse the attributes of Browse windows. Unlike the LAST option, which reuses only the previous configuration, this option can reuse any configuration used in the past. The first time CHANGE is used with this option followed by a character expression, the PREFERENCE referred to by that name is created. When the Browse window is closed, that PREFERENCE is updated. Anytime in the future that the Browse/Edit window is opened with that PREFERENCE, it will keep the same configuration.

By default, the pointer is moved to the top of the table when a FOR clause is included, but if the REST option is also used, the pointer remains in its current position.

The SAVE option keeps the Browse/Edit window (and an associated Memo window, if one is open) on the screen after the user has exited from it. This option can be used only in programs.

The TIMEOUT option allows you to specify how many seconds the Browse window will remain open without the user making any input. This clause can be used only within a program.

The TITLE option lets you specify a title to appear in the top border of the editing window.

The VALID option lets you check new data entered into each record before CHANGE moves on to the next record. For CHANGE to move on, the logical expression you specify must be true. If not, an error message that you set up with an ERROR clause is displayed. If you include :F after the word VALID, you can force the validation check to occur whether or not the user has actually entered new data in that record.

The WHEN option allows the user to make changes only to the current record when a certain logical condition you specify is true.

The WIDTH option limits the width of the display of all fields. Only the display is affected, not the actual data. You may use the arrow keys to scroll through a field and see all its data.

The WINDOW option lets the Browse/Edit window take on the characteristics of another window you specify. That window must first be defined using the DEFINE WINDOW command. The IN WINDOW option actually opens the Browse window within another window, although the Browse window will not necessarily have the characteristics of this parent window unless you also use a WINDOW clause. The default is IN SCREEN.

The COLOR option allows you to specify the color attributes of the Browse window. You can do this by means of a color pair list (for example, COLOR 'B/R') or a COLOR SCHEME clause (including a number between 1 and 24 that lets you choose any of 24 preset color schemes).

See Also BROWSE, EDIT

The CHR( ) Function

Syntax

```
CHR(<expN>)
```

Usage This function returns the character corresponding to any ASCII number. For example, CHR(65) returns A; uppercase *A* is ASCII character 65.

The numeric expression used in the argument must evaluate to a number between 0 and 255.

See Also ASC( )

The CLEAR Command

Syntax

```
CLEAR
      ALL ¦ FIELDS ¦ GETS ¦ MACROS ¦ MEMORY
      ¦ MENUS ¦ POPUPS ¦ PROGRAM ¦ PROMPT
      ¦ READ [ALL] ¦ TYPEAHEAD ¦ WINDOWS
```

Usage The CLEAR command by itself clears the screen or the current output window, leaving it blank. The options let you specify a number of other items to be cleared from the screen or memory.

Options The ALL option performs a number of different tasks. It

- Releases all memory variables and arrays
- Closes any open tables, index files, format files, and memo files
- Selects Work Area 1 as the current work area
- Releases active menus, popups, or windows

This option does not have any effect on system memory variables.

The FIELDS option releases the field display that was created using the SET FIELDS TO <field list> command. The command SET FIELDS OFF is then automatically executed. This option differs from SET FIELDS TO because it releases the field lists in all work areas, while SET FIELDS TO works just in the current work area.

The GETS option releases pending GETs, so the user cannot make any entries in them. In programs, this can be used instead of a READ statement if you want to display field or memory variables using the @ ... SAY ... GET command but you do not want the user to be able to edit them.

The MACROS option releases keyboard macros, including function key assignments, from memory.

The MEMORY option clears all public and private memory variables and arrays but does not clear system memory variables.

The MENU option clears all user-defined menus from the screen and releases them from memory.

The POPUPS option clears all menu popups from memory and from the screen.

The PROGRAM option clears the compiled program buffer.

The PROMPT option clears any prompts that were previously displayed on the screen with the @ ... PROMPT command.

The READ option ends the current READ and returns control to the previous READ level, if any exists. If the ALL option is added, it ends all reads.

The TYPEAHEAD option allows you to clear any keystrokes stored in the keyboard typeahead buffer. In programs, it is often useful to CLEAR TYPEAHEAD before presenting the user with a new @ ... GET ... READ statement, to make sure that stray keystrokes or extra carriage returns do not cause the program to jump forward over this READ.

The WINDOWS option removes all user-defined windows from the screen and releases them from memory. Windows definitions you have saved as disk files with the SAVE WINDOW command will remain for later use.

See Also @ ... CLEAR

▸ The CLEAR EVENTS Command

Syntax

```
CLEAR EVENTS
```

Usage This command must be used after a READ EVENTS command, which stops the execution of a program and instead waits for events such as mouse clicks and keystrokes. CLEAR EVENTS continues the execution of the program on the next line after the READ EVENTS command.

Before READ EVENTS can be used, the menu system or dialog boxes must be set up so that at least one choice issues the CLEAR EVENTS command. For example, after running a menu program, a program could include the command READ EVENTS, which makes the program wait for the user's menu choices. If the user chooses File ➤ Exit, it would execute the command CLEAR EVENTS.

See Also READ EVENTS

▶ The _CLIPTEXT System Variable

Syntax

```
_CLIPTEXT = <expC>
```

Usage This system variable specifies the text that is stored in the Clipboard. Your program can store a value to this location, so that it becomes the default for the user, or it can test the variable for a value before doing something else.

▶ The CLOSE Command

Syntax

```
CLOSE
     ALL
     ¦ ALTERNATE
     ¦ DATABASES
     ¦ FORMAT
     ¦ INDEX
     ¦ MEMO <memo field list> ¦ MEMO ALL
     ¦ PROCEDURE
     ¦ TABLES [ALL]
```

Usage This command closes various types of files. It must be used with one of the alternatives listed after it.

Options The ALL option closes all file types and selects Work Area 1.

The ALTERNATE option closes an alternate file used to capture output in a text file. For more information on this type of file, see SET ALTERNATE TO.

The DATABASES option closes all open database, table, index, and format files and selects Work Area 1.

The FORMAT option closes a format file that is open in the current work area.

The INDEX option closes all index files in the current work area, except the structural compound index file.

The MEMO <memo field list> option closes editing windows that were opened for the Memo fields that are listed. The names in the Memo field list must be separated by commas if this list contains more than one name.

The MEMO ALL option closes all Memo fields in all work areas.

The PROCEDURE option closes procedure files.

The TABLES option closes all tables in the current database, and the TABLES ALL option closes all tables in all databases. If no database is open, CLOSE TABLES closes all free tables that are open.

▶ The CMONTH( ) Function

Syntax

```
CMONTH(<expD> | <expT>)
```

Usage This function returns the name of the month in character form. For example, ? CMONTH({11/6/92}) returns `November`.

See Also CDOW( )

▶ The COL( ) Function

Syntax

```
COL()
```

Usage This function returns the column number of the current position of the cursor. This function can be used in combination with @ … SAY … GET to direct screen output to a position that you specify as offset from the current column position of the cursor.

See Also @ … SAY … GET, PCOL( ), PROW( ), ROW( ), SCOLS( ), SROWS( ),WCOLS( ), WROWS( )

▶ The COMPILE Command

Syntax

```
COMPILE <file name> | <skeleton>
     [ENCRYPT]
     [NODEBUG]
```

Usage This command allows you to compile the source code in a program file you have written in order to create an object file. If the source code has a PRG extension, the object file will be given an FXP extension.

The compiler assumes a PRG extension; if you specify the extension, you may compile any program in a text file.

You can compile a number of files at once by using a skeleton file name, such as FILE*.PRG.

Options The ENCRYPT option encrypts your compiled programs to prevent users from obtaining access to your original source code.

The NODEBUG option removes line numbers from your code, disabling the use of the Trace window. By doing so, it reduces your program size by 2 bytes per line of source code (the bytes that are used to designate line numbers).

See Also MODIFY COMMAND

The CONTINUE Command

Syntax

```
CONTINUE
```

Usage This command finds the next record that matches the criterion of a LOCATE FOR <expL> command that has been used previously—that is, the next record in the table for which the logical expression in the LOCATE FOR command is evaluated as true. If a record is not found, the cursor is left at the end of the file, and the end-of-file marker EOF( ) is given the value of .T.

CONTINUE can be used repeatedly until you reach the end of the table (or the end of the Locate scope, if a scope clause was used with the original LOCATE command).

See Also FIND, SEEK

The COPY FILE Command

Syntax

```
COPY FILE <filename1> TO <filename2>
```

Usage This command makes an exact copy of the first file named. If the second file does not exist, it creates it. If the second file exists, it gives a warning before overwriting it if SAFETY is ON or overwrites it without giving a warning if SAFETY is OFF. You must use both the name and extension of both files.

This Visual FoxPro command is similar to the DOS command COPY, but it has the advantage of giving a warning before overwriting a file.

See Also DELETE FILE, SET SAFETY

► The COPY INDEXES Command

Syntax

```
COPY INDEXES <index file list> | ALL
     [TO <.cdx file>]
```

Usage This command allows you to copy individual index files to a compound index file containing many different index keys. Compound index files are more compact than single-entry index files. In addition, structural compound index files are always opened whenever the cor responding table is opened.

Options The ALL option copies all open index files into the specified compound index file.

The TO option lets you specify a compound index file other than the structural compound index file. If no file with this name exists, Visual FoxPro creates one.

See Also INDEX, REINDEX, SET INDEX

► The COPY MEMO Command

Syntax

```
COPY MEMO <memo field name> TO <file name> [ADDITIVE]
```

Usage This command copies the contents of the memo field in the current record to a text file. If no extension is included with the file name, TXT is assumed.

If the text file does not exist, it is created. If it does exist, it is overwritten, unless the ADDITIVE option is used.

Options If the ADDITIVE option is used, the contents of the memo field are added to the current contents of the text file, if it already exists.

See Also COPY FILE

▶ The COPY STRUCTURE Command

Syntax

```
COPY STRUCTURE TO <file name>
     [FIELDS <field list>]
     [[WITH] CDX ¦ [WITH] PRODUCTION]]
```

Usage This command creates a new table with the file name that is specified. This new file will have the same structure as the table that is open in the current work area.

Options If a FIELDS clause is included, the new file has only the fields that are listed.

The CDX and PRODUCTION options both create a structural index for the new table if the table you are currently using has a structural index file associated with it.

▶ The COPY STRUCTURE EXTENDED Command

Syntax

```
COPY STRUCTURE EXTENDED TO <file name>
     [FIELDS <field list>]
```

Usage This command creates a new table that holds a description of the fields in the current table. This new table includes the following fields:

- FIELD_NAME: This character field holds the names of the fields from the original table.
- FIELD_TYPE: This character field holds a one-letter code representing the data type of the fields in the original table. It uses the codes **C** (Character), **Y** (Currency), **N** (numeric), **F** (float), **I** (integer), **B** (double), **D** (date), **T** (datetime), **L** (logical), **M** (memo), and **G** (general).
- FIELD_LEN: This numeric field holds the width of the field.
- FIELD_DEC: This numeric field holds the number of decimal places in the field.
- FIELD_NUL: This logical field indicates whether the field can accept a null value.

- FIELD_NOCP: This logical field indicates whether code page translation is allowed for character and memo fields.
- FIELD_RULE: This memo field holds field validation rules.
- FIELD_ERR: This memo field holds field validation text.
- TABLE_RULE: This memo field holds table validation rules.
- TABLE_ERR: This memo field holds table validation text.

You can modify this new table and use the CREATE FROM command to create a new table.

Options If the FIELDS <field list> option is included, only the fields of the current table that are listed are specified in the new table.

See Also CREATE FROM

▶ The COPY TO Command

Syntax

```
COPY TO <file name>
     [FIELDS <field list>]
     [<scope>]
     [FOR <expL1>]
     [WHILE <expL2>]
     [[WITH] CDX] ¦ [[WITH] PRODUCTION]
     [TYPE] [SDF ¦ FOXPLUS ¦ DIF ¦ MOD ¦ SYLK
          ¦ WK1 ¦ WKS ¦ WR1 ¦ WRK ¦ XLS
          ¦ DELIMITED [WITH <character> ¦ WITH BLANK
               ¦ WITH TAB]]
     [NOOPTIMIZE]
     [AS <code page>]
```

Usage This command copies the records in the table that is open in the current work area to the file whose name is specified.

In the simplest form of the command, the data is copied to another table with a DBF extension. You can specify the name of the data file; Visual FoxPro assumes a DBF extension if none is entered (unless a TYPE clause is included).

Options The <scope> option lets you select which records will be copied; only records in the specified scope will be copied. Scope options include ALL, NEXT <expN>, RECORD <expN>, and REST. If this clause is omitted, the default scope is ALL.

The FIELDS option lets you select which fields in the table will be copied.

The FOR and WHILE options let you select which records will be copied. Only records for which the logical expression is evaluated as true are copied.

For more information on how scope, FIELDS, FOR, and WHILE clauses work, see Chapter 11.

Either the [WITH] CDX or the [WITH] PRODUCTION option copies the structural compound index file as well as the table. It can be used only if you are copying the file to a new Visual FoxPro table.

The TYPE option lets you copy data to files that are not Visual FoxPro-compatible tables. The types of files you can copy data to are:

- **SDF files:** ASCII text files in which records have fixed-length fields and a ↵/linefeed at the end
- **DELIMITED files:** ASCII text files in which fields are separated by some delimiter (usually a comma). Character fields are also delimited by quotation marks, and there is a ↵/linefeed at the end of each record.
- **DIF files:** Used by VisiCalc
- **MOD files:** Used by Multiplan version 4.01
- **SYLK files:** Symbolic Link files used by Multiplan
- **WK1 files:** Used by Lotus 1-2-3 version 2.0
- **WKS files:** Used by Lotus 1-2-3 version 1-A
- **WR1 files:** Used by Lotus Symphony versions 1.1 and 1.2
- **WRK files:** Used by Lotus Symphony version 1.0
- **XLS files:** Used by Excel
- **FOXPLUS files:** Used by FoxBASE+

The NOOPTIMIZE option for this command disables the Rushmore technology, which normally speeds up data access when you use a FOR statement containing fields in existing indexes. You can disable Rushmore with the NOOPTIMIZE option on a number of Visual FoxPro commands, but in this case there is little reason to do so.

The AS <code page> option specifies the code page for the file this command creates.

See Also APPEND FROM, COPY FILE

The COS( ) Function

Syntax

```
COS(<expN>)
```

Usage This function returns the cosine of an angle. The numeric expression represents the size of the angle in radians. You can use the DTOR( ) function to convert angles from degrees to radians.

See Also ACOS( ), ASIN( ), ATAN, DTOR( ), RTOD( ), SIN( ), TAN( )

The COUNT Command

Syntax

```
COUNT
     [<scope>]
     [FOR <expL1>]
     [WHILE <expL2>]
     [TO <memvar>]
     [NOOPTIMIZE]
```

Usage This command counts the total number of records in the table that is open in the current work area.

Options If an optional scope, FOR, or WHILE clause is used, only the records included in the specified scope or only the records for which the logical expression following the FOR or WHILE is evaluated as true are included in the count. For more information on how these clauses work, see Chapter 11.

Records that are marked for deletion are included in the count unless the command SET DELETED ON has been used.

If the optional TO clause is included, the result is stored in the specified memory variable.

The NOOPTIMIZE option for this command disables the Rushmore technology, which normally speeds up data access when you use a FOR statement containing fields in existing indexes. You can disable

Rushmore with the NOOPTIMIZE option on a number of Visual FoxPro commands, but in this case there is little reason to do so.

See Also RECCOUNT( )

▶ The CREATE Command

Syntax

```
CREATE [<file name> ¦ ?]
```

Usage This command displays the Table Designer to let you define the structure of a new table.

Options If you specify a file name, the new table is given that name immediately. If you specify a name but no extension, Visual FoxPro assumes a DBF extension.

If you do not specify a file name or if you use the ? option, Visual FoxPro for Windows immediately displays the Create dialog box so you can name the new table.

See Also ADD TABLE, ALTER TABLE, CLOSE, CREATE TABLE, DISPLAY TABLES, FREE TABLE, LIST TABLES, MODIFY STRUCTURE, REMOVE TABLE, USE

▶ The CREATE CONNECTION Command

Syntax

```
CREATE CONNECTION [<connection name> ¦ ?]
     [DATASOURCE <data source name>
     [, USERID <user ID>] [, PASSWORD <password>]
     ¦ CONNSTRING <connection string>]
```

Usage This command creates a named connection to an ODBC data source. A database must be open before you can use this command.

Options The <connection name> gives a name to the connection you are designing.

The ? option displays the Connection Designer, which you can use to create a named connection. This is used instead of all of the following options.

The DATASOURCE <data source name> option specifies an ODBC data source.

The USERID <user ID> specifies your user identification for this data source.

The PASSWORD <password> option specifies your password for this data source.

The CONNSTRING <connection string> option specifies a connection string that can be used instead of the data source name, user identification, and password.

See Also DELETE CONNECTION, DISPLAY CONNECTIONS, LIST CONNECTIONS, MODIFY CONNECTION

▸ The CREATE CURSOR Command

Syntax

```
CREATE CURSOR <cursor name>
     >(<field name1> <field type> [<field width> [,
<precision] ] )
     [(<field name2> ...) ]
         ...
     ¦ FROM ARRAY <array name>
```

Usage This command creates a cursor, a temporarily table that is accessible as long as it remains open but is discarded as soon as it is closed.

▸▸ **NOTE**

You can also create a cursor by using the INTO CURSOR option of the SELECT—SQL command.

Options The (<field name1>< field type> [<field width> [, <precision>]]) clause defines the first field of the cursor. Field name and field type are needed for all fields. Field width is needed for character, float, and numeric fields. Precision is needed for float, numeric, and double fields.

Field types are entered using the following letters: **C** for Character, **D** for Date, **T** for DateTime, **N** for Numeric, **F** for Float, **B** for Double, **Y** for Currency, **L** for Logical, **M** for Memo, **G** for General, **P** for Picture.

Field width and precision is entered using integers. If precision is not entered for a Numeric, Float, or Double field, the default is zero decimal places.

The ellipses indicate that all of the above options can be repeated for each field in the cursor.

The FROM ARRAY <array name> option lets you create a table from an array, rather than defining the fields as described above. You must specify the name of an array that contains the name, type, precision, and scale for each field in the table.

See Also CREATE TABLE, SELECT—SQL

▶ The CREATE DATABASE Command

Syntax

```
CREATE DATABASE [<database name> ¦ ?]
```

Usage This command creates a new database and makes it the current database.

Options The <database name> option lets you specify a name for the database.

The ? option lets you use the Save As dialog box to name the database.

See Also DELETE DATABASE, DISPLAY DATABASE, LIST DATABASE, MODIFY DATABASE, OPEN DATABASE, PACK DATABASE

▶ The CREATE FROM Command

Syntax

```
CREATE <table name1> FROM <table name2>
```

Usage This command creates a new table from a file of the sort that is created using the COPY STRUCTURE EXTENDED command. <table name1> is the newly created table. <table name2> is a table with the field specifications that are created when you use COPY STRUCTURE EXTENDED.

See Also COPY STRUCTURE EXTENDED

▶ The CREATE LABEL Command

Syntax

```
CREATE LABEL [<file name> ¦ ?]
     [[WINDOW <window name1>]
     [IN [WINDOW] <window name2> ¦ IN SCREEN]
```

```
[NOWAIT]
[SAVE]
```

Usage This command opens the Label Designer window, allowing you to create a new label form.

If you specify a file name, Visual FoxPro assumes an LBX extension.

Options If you use the ? option, Visual FoxPro displays a dialog box that lets the user select or enter the name of the new file to be created.

The WINDOW option allows you to give the Label Designer window the characteristics of another window you specify.

The IN WINDOW option allows you to open the Label Designer window within a parent window you specify, although it will not necessarily have the characteristics of the parent window unless you also use a WINDOW clause.

The IN SCREEN option allows you to open the Label Designer window in the main Visual FoxPro window.

The NOWAIT option allows programs to keep running after the Label Designer window is opened.

The SAVE option keeps the Label Designer window open while you temporarily open another window on top of it.

See Also LABEL, MODIFY LABEL

► The CREATE MENU Command

Syntax

```
CREATE MENU [<menu name> ¦ ?]
      [WINDOW <window name1>]
      [IN [WINDOW] <window name2> ¦ IN SCREEN]
      [NOWAIT]
      [SAVE]
```

Usage This command activates the Menu Builder window, which you can use to create menus to go with programs you create. This interactive utility lets you define a menu system without typing a long list of individual commands such as DEFINE MENU, DEFINE PAD, DEFINE POPUP, DEFINE BAR, ON PAD, and ON SELECTION. You can then generate the code.

If you specify a <menu name>, the menu builder creates a menu table with that name, followed by the MNX extension.

If you use the ? option, Visual FoxPro displays a dialog box that lets the user select or enter the menu file name.

Options You can use the WINDOW option to give the Menu Designer window the characteristics of another window you specify.

Likewise, you can use the IN WINDOW option to open the Menu Designer window within another specified window, although this layout window will not necessarily take on the characteristics of the parent window unless you also use the WINDOW option. The default IN SCREEN option displays the Menu Designer window in the Visual FoxPro main window.

The NOWAIT option allows programs to keep running after the Menu Designer window is opened.

The SAVE option keeps the Menu Designer window open while you temporarily open another window on top of it.

See Also ACTIVATE MENU, DEFINE MENU, MODIFY MENU

The CREATE PROJECT Command

Syntax

```
CREATE PROJECT [<file> ¦ ?]
      [NOWAIT]
      [SAVE]
      [WINDOW <window name1>
      [IN [WINDOW] <window name2> ¦ IN SCREEN]
```

Usage This command opens the Project Manager window to let you create a project, allowing you to keep track of all the files in an application and to compile them into a single APP or EXE file.

If you do not specify the project name, it will be named Untitled until you save it under a name. If you specify a project name, it is given that name initially.

If you use the ? instead of a name, Visual FoxPro displays a dialog box that lets you enter or select the name.

Options The NOWAIT option can be used in programs to allow program execution to continue without pausing for the Project Manager window to be closed.

The SAVE option can be used in programs to keep the Project Manager window open after another window becomes active. Neither of these options has any effect if it is used from the Command window.

The WINDOW <window name1> option gives the Project Manager window the features of the window specified.

The IN [WINDOW] <window name2> option opens the Project Manager window in the window specified.

The IN SCREEN option opens the Project Manager window in the screen.

▸ The CREATE QUERY Command

Syntax

```
CREATE QUERY [<file name> ¦ ?]
```

Usage This command opens the Query Designer window so you can interactively create a SQL (Structured Query Language) query. SQL queries are a flexible, powerful way to retrieve information from tables. A single SQL query can take the place of many other individual Visual FoxPro commands.

You can save your query command as a Visual FoxPro program file, which will be given a QPR extension. You can then run the query again later by typing DO plus the name of the program (including the QPR extension). To name your program, type a file name <file name> after CREATE QUERY.

If you use the ? option, Visual FoxPro displays a dialog box to let the user select or enter the query name.

See Also MODIFY QUERY, SELECT

▸ The CREATE REPORT Command

Syntax

```
CREATE REPORT [<file name> ¦ ?]

        [[WINDOW <window name1>]
        [IN [WINDOW] <window name2> ¦ IN SCREEN]]
        [NOWAIT]
        [SAVE]
```

```
    ¦
    FROM <file name 2>
    [FORM ¦ COLUMN]
    [FIELDS <field list>]
    [ALIAS]
    [NOOVERWRITE]
    [WIDTH <expN>]
```

Usage This command opens the Report Designer window to let you create a new report form, or creates a Quick Report.

Options The <file name> option lets you name the file. If you specify a file name, Visual FoxPro assumes an FRX extension.

If you use the ? option, Visual FoxPro displays a dialog box that lets the user enter the name of the new file to be created.

The first group of options that follows is used to specify how the Report designer is opened.

You can use the WINDOW option to give the Report Designer window the characteristics of another window you specify.

Likewise, you can use the IN WINDOW option to open the Report Designer window within another specified window, although this layout window will not necessarily take on the characteristics of the parent window unless you also use the WINDOW option. The default IN SCREEN option displays the Report Designer window on the screen.

The NOWAIT option allows programs to keep running after the Report Designer window is opened.

The SAVE option keeps the Report Designer window open while you temporarily open another window on top of it. This applies only in programs and has no effect from the Command window.

The second group of options that follows is used to define the Quick Report that is created.

The FROM <file name2> option specifies the table that is used as the basis of the report. The file must be a table; queries cannot be used.

The FORM ¦ COLUMN options specify whether the fields are in Form layout, with one field above another and the name to the left of each, or in Column layout, with the fields of each record arranged from left to right and the name of the field at the top of each column.

The FIELDS <field list> option lets you specify the fields of the table named in the FROM clause that are included in the report. List the fields with commas separating them. Only fields may be used, not expressions.

If you use the ALIAS option, the report includes the table name as part of the field names used as labels.

If you use the NOOVERWRITE option, the report will not be created if a report already exists with the same name. Without this option, the command will overwrite a report with the same name.

The WIDTH <expN> option specifies the width of the report page, with the numeric expression used to specify the number of columns in the page.

See Also MODIFY REPORT, REPORT

▸ The CREATE SCREEN Command

Syntax

```
CREATE SCREEN [ <file name> ¦ ?]
     [WINDOW <window name1>]
     [IN [WINDOW] <window name2> ¦ IN SCREEN]
     [NOWAIT]
     [SAVE]

     ¦
     [ROW ¦ COLUMN]
     [FIELDS <field list>]
     [ALIAS]
     [NOOVERWRITE]
     [SIZE <expN1>, <expN2>]
     [SCREEN]
```

Usage This command opens the Form Designer window to let you create a new form, or creates a Quick Form.

Options The <file name> option lets you name the file. If you specify a file name, Visual FoxPro assumes an SCX extension.

If you use the ? option, Visual FoxPro displays a dialog box that lets the user enter the name of the new file to be created.

The first group of options that follows is used to specify how the Form Designer is opened.

If you use the WINDOW <window name1> option, the Screen Designer window assumes the attributes of <window name1>—for example, borders, size, title, and color.

If you use the IN [WINDOW] <window name2> option, the Screen Designer window will be opened within another window you specify, although it will not take on the attributes of that other window.

The IN SCREEN option allows you to explicitly place the new window on the screen rather than in another window. This is the default setting.

The NOWAIT option allows programs to keep running after the Screen Designer window is opened.

The SAVE option keeps the Screen Designer window open while you temporarily open another window on top of it. This option is used only in programming and has no effect from the Command window.

The second group of options lets you create a quick screen without opening the Form Designer window.

The FROM <file name 2> option specifies the table that is used as the basis of the form.

The ROW option arranges the table's fields from top to bottom on the screen. This is the default. In contrast, the COLUMN option arranges fields from left to right across the screen.

The FIELDS option lets you choose only certain fields to be displayed while you design the screen.

The ALIAS option includes the table alias name with the field names as the labels of the form.

The NOOVERWRITE option protects any existing screen with the same name as <file name 1> from being overwritten.

The SIZE option allows you to specify the height and width of the window in which you are creating the new screen.

The SCREEN option places the Screen Designer window in the main Visual FoxPro window.

See Also MODIFY SCREEN

► The CREATE SQL VIEW Command

Syntax

```
CREATE SQL VIEW [<name>]
     [REMOTE]
     [CONNECTION < connection name> [SHARE] ¦
          CONNECTION <data source name>]
```

Usage This command displays the View Designer, which is used to create SQL views.

Options The <name> option names the view.

The REMOTE option allows you to include remote tables in the view. Without this option, only local tables may be used.

CONNECTION < connection name> [SHARE] lets you specify a named connection to a remote data source. If you include SHARE, Visual FoxPro will use a shared connection if available.

CONNECTION <data source name> lets you specify a connection to a remote data source.

See Also DELETE VIEW, DISPLAY VIEWS, LIST VIEWS, MODIFY VIEW

► The CREATE TABLE—SQL Command

Syntax

```
CREATE TABLE ¦ DBF <table name>
[NAME <long table name> [FREE]
     (<field name1><field type>[<field width>
              [,<precision>] ] )
          [NULL ¦ NOT NULL]
          [CHECK <expL> [ERROR <message]]
          [DEFAULT <exp>]
          [PRIMARY KEY [<expr> TAG <tag name>]
          ¦ UNIQUE [<expr> TAG <tag name>]]
          [FOREIGN KEY <expr> TAG <tag name>
               [REFERENCES <table name>
                   [TAG <tag name1> ]]
          [NOCPTRANS]
```

```
[(field name2 ...)]
     ...
| FROM ARRAY <array name>
```

Usage This command lets you create a table without using the Table Designer. The table is created and is opened exclusively in the lowest available work area.

Options The command can use either the CREATE TABLE <table name> clause or the CREATE DBF <table name> clause to specify the name of the table—the two clauses are identical.

The NAME <long table name> option lets you give the table a long name of up to 128 characters if it is part of a database.

The FREE option specifies that the table is not part of the currently open database. This option is not needed if no database is open when this command is used.

The (<field name1> <field type> [<field width> [, <precision>]]) clause defines the first field of the table. Field name and field type are needed for all fields. Field width is needed for character, float, and numeric fields. Precision is needed for float, numeric, and double fields.

Field types are entered using the following letters: **C** for Character, **D** for Date, **T** for DateTime, **N** for Numeric, **F** for Float, **B** for Double, **Y** for Currency, **L** for Logical, **M** for Memo, **G** for General, **P** for Picture.

Field width and precision is entered using integers. If precision is not entered for a Numeric, Float, or Double field, the default is zero decimal places.

The NULL and NOT NULL options allow or disallow null values in the field.

The CHECK <expL> option creates a validity check: Data will be accepted only if the expression evaluates to true. If you use this option, you can also use the ERROR <message> option to specify the error message that is displayed if the expression evaluates to false.

The DEFAULT <expr> option specifies a default value for the field.

The PRIMARY KEY [<expr> TAG <tag name>] option creates a primary index. If you do not include the expression and tab name, the index is based on the field and has the same name as the field. A table may have only one primary index.

The UNIQUE [<expr> TAG <tag name>] option creates a candidate index. If you do not include the expression and tab name, the index is based on the field and has the same name as the field.

The FOREIGN KEY <expr> TAG <tag name> option creates a foreign key index and relates the table to a parent table.

The REFERENCES <table name> [TAG <tag name>] option specifies the parent table that is related to this table using the foreign key. If the TAG <tag name> clause is included, it specifies the name of the index in the parent table that this foreign key is related to. If this clause is omitted, the Foreign key is related to the Primary key of the parent table.

The NOCPTRANS option prevents translation of character or memo fields to a different code page.

The ellipses options indicate that each of the above options can be repeated for each field in the table.

The FROM ARRAY <array name> option lets you create a table from an array, rather than defining the fields as described above. You must specify the name of an array that contains the name, type, precision, and scale for each field in the table.

See Also ADD TABLE, ALTER TABLE, CLOSE, CREATE, DISPLAY TABLES, FREE TABLE, LIST TABLES, MODIFY STRUCTURE, REMOVE TABLE, USE

▸ The CREATE TRIGGER Command

Syntax

```
CREATE TRIGGER ON <table name>
     FOR DELETE ¦ INSERT ¦ UPDATE
     AS <expL>
```

Usage This command creates a trigger, which includes a logical expression that is evaluated when a record is deleted, inserted, or updated, and which prevents the change if the expression evaluates as false.

Options The <table name> option specifies the table that the trigger applies to. It must be in the current database.

The FOR DELETE ¦ INSERT ¦ UPDATE option specifies when the logical expression is evaluated.

The AS <expL> option specifies the logical expression that is evaluated.

See Also DELETE TRIGGER

The CREATE VIEW Command

Syntax

```
CREATE VIEW <file name>
```

Usage This command opens the View window to let you create a view file containing information about the Visual FoxPro environment. This file will be saved with the extension VUE and can then be used at any time by entering the command SET VIEW TO <file name> or by choosing File ➤ Open.

See Also SET VIEW

The CTOD( ) Function

Syntax

```
CTOD(<expC>)
```

Usage This function returns a character expression in the Date data type. The character expression used must be a valid date between the year 100 and the year 9999.

For example, CTOD("01/01/94") returns January 1, 1994 as Date data, so it is identical to {01/01/94}. This function was commonly used in the earliest implementations of the Xbase language, which did not include the curly bracket delimiters to indicate the Date data type.

By default, the character expression used for the date must be in the format mm/dd/yy, and it is assumed that the date is in the twentieth century. If you have used the SET DATE or SET CENTURY command, the format of the character expression changes.

See Also DTOC( ), SET CENTURY, SET DATE

The DATE( ) Function

Syntax

```
DATE()
```

Usage This function returns the current system date—the date on your computer's clock/calendar or the date you entered when you started your computer.

See Also SET DATE, TIME( )

▶ The DAY( ) Function

Syntax

DAY(<expD> ¦ <expT>)

Usage This function returns the day of the month of the specified date or datetime expression in number form. If the date expression is 12/10/90, for example, the function returns 10.

See Also CDOW( )

▶ The DEACTIVATE MENU Command

Syntax

DEACTIVATE MENU

Usage This command removes a previously activated menu from the screen. The menu remains in memory until you remove it with CLEAR MENUS or RELEASE MENU and can be reactivated when needed with ACTIVATE MENU.

You don't need to type the menu name, because only one menu can be active at once.

See Also ACTIVATE MENU, CLEAR MENUS, CREATE MENU, DEFINE MENU, HIDE MENU, MODIFY MENU, SHOW MENU

▶ The DEACTIVATE POPUP Command

Syntax

DEACTIVATE POPUP

Usage This command removes a previously activated popup menu from the screen. The popup menu remains in memory until you remove it with CLEAR POPUPS or RELEASE POPUPS and can be reactivated when needed with ACTIVATE POPUP.

You don't need to type the popup name, since only one popup menu can be active at once.

See Also ACTIVATE POPUP, CLEAR POPUPS, DEFINE POPUP, HIDE POPUP, RELEASE POPUPS, SHOW POPUP

▶ The DEACTIVATE WINDOW Command

Syntax

```
DEACTIVATE
     WINDOW <window name1> [,<window name2> ...]
     | ALL
```

Usage This command removes a previously activated window or windows from the screen. The windows remain in memory until you remove them with CLEAR WINDOWS or RELEASE WINDOWS.

Options The WINDOW <window name1> [,<window name2> ...] options let you specify the names of one or more windows to deactivate.

The ALL option causes all previously activated windows to be deactivated.

See Also ACTIVATE WINDOW, CLEAR WINDOWS, DEFINE WINDOW, HIDE WINDOW, RELEASE WINDOWS, RESTORE WINDOW, SAVE WINDOW, SHOW WINDOW

▶ The DECLARE Command

Syntax

```
DECLARE <array1> (<expN1> [,<expN2>])
     [,<array2> (<expN3> [,<expN4>])]
     [...]
```

Usage This command is used to create an array. It is identical to the DIMENSION command.

An array is a series of memory variables that have the same name but are distinguished by their index numbers (also called their subscripts).

For example, if you have 10 different interest rates that you need to use in a program, it could be confusing to give each a separate name. You might find it easier to create an array to hold them. The command

```
DECLARE int_rate(10)
```

creates 10 memory variables, named int_rate(1), int_rate(2), int_rate(3), and so on. You can then initialize these variables as you do any memory variable—for example,

```
int_rate(1) = .1
```

to use 10 percent as the first interest rate.

The data type of each variable in the array is determined when it is initialized.

If you add the optional second numeric expression following the array, you will create a two-dimensional array that is referred to by two index numbers. Let's say you have 10 different interest rates for each month. You could use the command

```
DECLARE int_rate(12,10)
```

to create 120 memory variables. Then you could use the variable int_rate(1,1) to hold the lowest interest rate for January, the variable int_rate(1,2) to hold the second interest rate for January, and so on through int_rate(1,10), which holds the highest interest rate for January. Likewise, you could use the variable int_rate(2,1) to hold the lowest interest rate for February, the variable int_rate(2,2) to hold the second interest rate for February, and so on through int_rate(2,10), which holds the highest interest rate for February.

Arrays are particularly powerful because you can use a variable as the index number and access the entire array by altering the value of the variable. If you use a DO WHILE loop to change the value of the index number, you can print out hundreds of variables using just a few lines of code.

See Also DIMENSION

► The DEFINE BAR Command

Syntax

```
DEFINE BAR <expN1> OF <popup name> PROMPT <expC1>
     [BEFORE <expN2> ¦ AFTER <expN3>]
     [KEY <key label> [, <expC2>]]
     [MARK <expC3>]
     [MESSAGE <expC4>]
     [SKIP [FOR <expL>]]
     [COLOR <color pair list> ¦ COLOR SCHEME <expN4>]
```

Usage This command, used in programming, lets you define bars (choices) on a menu popup you have previously defined with DEFINE POPUP. You must specify a number for each bar, the name of the popup in which the bar is to appear, and a prompt that will appear on the screen for the user.

Options The BEFORE and AFTER options allow you to determine the order in which bars are displayed.

The KEY option allows you to designate a particular key or combination of keys that will activate a bar.

The MARK option lets you designate a mark character to be placed before a particular bar instead of the default checkmark. However, this clause is ignored if the menu is integrated into the Visual FoxPro system menu or if FoxFont is not the font for the main Visual FoxPro window or for the user-defined window where this menu is displayed.

The SKIP option lets your menu popup skip a certain bar if a condition you specify is true.

The MESSAGE option displays a message you specify when the user selects the current bar. The message appears in the status bar or in a location specified by the SET MESSAGE command.

The COLOR option lets you determine the color of an individual bar. You can do this by means of a color pair list (for example, COLOR 'B/R'), or a COLOR SCHEME (a number between 1 and 24 that lets you choose any of 24 preset color schemes).

See Also DEFINE POPUP, ON BAR

The DEFINE MENU Command

Syntax

```
DEFINE MENU <menu name>
     [BAR [AT LINE <expN1>]]
     [IN [WINDOW] <window name> ¦ IN SCREEN]
     [KEY <key label>]
     [MARK [<expC1>]
     [MESSAGE <expC2>]
     [NOMARGIN]
     [COLOR <color pair list> ¦ COLOR SCHEME <expN2>]
```

Usage This command defines a menu to control a system of programs you create. In many cases, it is better to use the Menu Designer (which you can display using the command CREATE MENU), which lets you generate the program code for menus, as discussed in Chapter 24.

DEFINE MENU creates the menu bar for your menu system, creating a file with the <menu name> you specify. You must then define each of the pads on the menu bar with the DEFINE PAD command. To use the menu, your program must contain an ACTIVATE MENU command.

Options The BAR option gives your menu bar the characteristics of the Visual FoxPro main menu bar. The BAR AT LINE option then places this menu at a screen or window row number you specify.

The IN WINDOW option places menu bars within another specified window. The default IN SCREEN option displays the menu bar on the screen.

The KEY option allows you to designate a key or key combination as a way to activate the menu bar. This is similar to the ON KEY LABEL command.

The MARK option lets you designate a mark character to be placed before a particular bar instead of the default check mark. However, this clause is ignored if the menu is integrated into the Visual FoxPro system menu or if FoxFont is not the font for the main Visual FoxPro window or for the user-defined window where this menu is displayed.

The MESSAGE option lets you display a message whenever the user selects a particular option on the menu.

The NOMARGIN option eliminates the spaces that are usually placed between each menu pad.

The COLOR option allows you to specify the color attributes of the menu. You can do this by means of a color pair list (for example, COLOR 'B/R'), or a COLOR SCHEME (a number between 1 and 24 that lets you choose any of 24 preset color schemes).

See Also ACTIVATE MENU, CREATE MENU, DEFINE PAD, HIDE MENU, MODIFY MENU, ON PAD, ON SELECTION, SET MESSAGE, SHOW MENU

▸ The DEFINE PAD Command

Syntax

```
DEFINE PAD <pad name> OF <menu name> PROMPT <expC1>
     [AT <row>,<col>]
     [BEFORE <pad name> | AFTER <pad name>]
     [KEY <key label> [,<expC2>]]
     [MARK <expC3>]
```

```
[SKIP [FOR <expL>]]
[MESSAGE <expC4>]
[COLOR <color pad list> ¦ COLOR SCHEME <expN>)]
```

Usage This command, used in programming, allows you to define particular pads (choices) on a menu bar you have created with the DEFINE MENU command. When the user of your program selects a particular pad, the program performs a particular function or presents a menu with further choices.

You can also create menus with the Visual FoxPro menu builder (accessed through the commands CREATE MENU and MODIFY MENU). This automatically generates the program code for your menu so you don't need to enter a long series of commands like DEFINE MENU, DEFINE PAD, and ON PAD.

Each DEFINE PAD command must be followed by a pad name, menu name, and user prompt. You will need to have previously defined a menu with the DEFINE MENU command. After you have defined each pad of the menu with DEFINE PAD, you will need to direct your program toward another procedure or program that will carry out the functions the user chooses. These choices are usually passed to this other program by means of PAD( ) and MENU( ). For example:

```
DEFINE MENU maillist
DEFINE PAD renewal OF maillist PROMPT "Renewals"
DEFINE PAD new OF maillist PROMPT "Additions"
DEFINE PAD delete OF maillist PROMPT "Deletions"
DEFINE PAD quit OF maillist PROMPT "Quit"
ON SELECTION MENU maillist;
     DO mailproc WITH PAD(), MENU()
ACTIVATE MENU maillist
```

In this case, the program defines four menu pads and then includes an ON SELECTION statement that will call up a program, Mailproc, after the user makes a choice on the menu. Mailproc will perform the task chosen by the user.

Options The AT option, used with DEFINE PAD, allows you to place the pad at a particular location on the screen.

The BEFORE and AFTER options allow you to determine the order in which pads are displayed.

The KEY option allows you to designate a particular key or combination of keys that will activate a pad.

The MARK option lets you designate a mark character to be placed before a particular bar instead of the default check mark. However, this clause is ignored if the menu is integrated into the Visual FoxPro system menu or if FoxFont is not the font for the main Visual FoxPro window or for the user-defined window where this menu is displayed.

The SKIP option lets your menu skip a certain pad if a certain condition you specify is true.

The MESSAGE option displays a message you specify when the user selects the current pad.

The COLOR option lets you determine the color of an individual pad. You can do this by means of a color pair list (for example, COLOR 'B/R'), or a COLOR SCHEME (a number between 1 and 24 that lets you choose any of 24 preset color schemes).

See Also ACTIVATE MENU, CREATE MENU, DEFINE MENU, MODIFY MENU, RELEASE PAD, SET MESSAGE

▶ The DEFINE POPUP Command

Syntax

```
DEFINE POPUP <popup name>
     [FROM <row1>,<col2>] [TO <row2>,<col2>]
     [IN [WINDOW] <window name> ¦ IN SCREEN]
     [FOOTER <expC1>]
     [KEY <key label>]
     [MARGIN]
     [MARK <expC2>]
     [MESSAGE <expC3>]
     [MOVER]
     [MULTI]
     [PROMPT FIELD <exp>] ¦ [PROMPT FILES]
     [SCROLL]
     [SHADOW]
     [TITLE <expC4>]
     [COLOR <color pair list> ¦ COLOR SCHEME <expN>]
```

Usage This command, used in programming, lets you create a popup menu. Popups appear on the screen to present a list of options to the user, often in response to the user's selection from a previous menu or popup. They can be used as the popups of a menu bar or elsewhere.

Options The FROM and TO options let you specify the dimensions and location of the popup. The default is for it to appear at the upper-left corner of the screen.

The IN WINDOW option lets you place your popup within another window. The default is IN SCREEN.

The FOOTER option allows you to place a certain expression <expC1> at the bottom of the window as a footer. The MESSAGE option displays a message when the popup is activated.

The KEY option lets you designate a particular key or combination of keys as a way to activate the popup menu.

The MARGIN option puts an extra space on either side of each popup option bar. The SHADOW option places a shadow behind the popup. The TITLE option lets you place a title in the top border of the popup.

The MARK option lets you designate a mark character to be placed before a particular bar instead of the default check mark. However, this clause is ignored if the menu is integrated into the Visual FoxPro system menu or if FoxFont is not the font for the main Visual FoxPro window or for the user defined window where this menu is displayed.

The MOVER option allows the user to rearrange options within the popup, using a mouse.

The MULTI option lets the user choose multiple options from the popup.

The PROMPT FIELD option lets you display fields from a specified table as the options in the popup. The PROMPT FILES option lets you display disk files as options in the popup.

The SCROLL option puts a scroll bar to the right of the popup to assist users in scrolling through the popup menu with a mouse.

The COLOR option lets you determine the colors of the popup. You can do this by means of a color pair list (for example, COLOR 'B/R'), or a COLOR SCHEME (a number between 1 and 24 that lets you choose any of 24 preset color schemes).

See Also ACTIVATE POPUP, DEACTIVATE POPUP, DEFINE BAR, HIDE POPUP, MOVE POPUP, ON SELECTION, SHOW POPUP

▸ The DEFINE WINDOW Command

Syntax

```
DEFINE WINDOW <window name1> FROM <row1>,<col1> TO
<row2>,<col2>
     [AT <row1>,<column1>]
     [SIZE <row2>,<column2>]
     [IN [WINDOW] <window name2> ¦ IN SCREEN ¦ IN
            DESKTOP]
     [FONT <expC1> [,<expN>]] [STYLE <expC2>]
     [FILL FILE <expC3>]
     [ICON FILE <expC4>]
     [HALFHEIGHT]
     [MDI ¦ NOMDI]
     [FOOTER <expC1>]
     [TITLE <expC2>]
     [DOUBLE ¦ PANEL ¦ NONE ¦ SYSTEM ¦ <border
           string>]
     [CLOSE ¦ NOCLOSE]
     [FLOAT ¦ NOFLOAT]
     [GROW ¦ NOGROW]
     [MINIMIZE]
     [SHADOW]
     [ZOOM ¦ NOZOOM]
     [FILL <expC3>]
     [COLOR <color pair list> ¦ COLOR SCHEME <expN>]
```

Usage This command, used in programming, allows you to define a window for later use. You can define the upper-left and lower-right corners of the window by specifying FROM and TO coordinates.

Options The AT option also allows you to specify the upper-left corner of the window. If this is used in conjunction with the SIZE option, Visual FoxPro adjusts the size of the window to accommodate the amount and font of text in the window.

The IN [WINDOW] <window name2> option allows you to define a window within another window. The IN SCREEN option, which is the default, specifies that the new window will be defined within the overall screen. The IN DESKTOP option allows you to place your window on the Windows desktop, outside the main Visual FoxPro window.

The [FONT <expC> [,<expN] [STYLE <expC>] option lets you specify the typeface, size, and style of the font used. <expC> and <expN> should be the name and size of an available font; if the font you specify is not available, Visual FoxPro tries to substitute a similar font. If you omit the FONT clause, the main Visual FoxPro window font is used, and if you include the clause but omit the size option, a ten point font is used. The STYLE clause may be followed by one of the following codes:

- B: boldface
- I: italic
- N: normal
- O: outline
- Q: opaque
- S: shadow
- -: strikeout
- T: transparent
- U: underline

If this clause is omitted, normal style will be used.

The HALFHEIGHT option lets you create windows with half-height title bars. This lets you create windows in Visual FoxPro for Windows with title bars the same size as the title bars in FoxPro for DOS so programs can be used in both environments without change.

The TITLE option lets you create a title at the top of the window. The MDI and NOMDI options allow you to specify whether or not windows are Multiple Document Interface compliant. MDI is the default, which is used if no option is specified.

The DOUBLE ¦ PANEL ¦ NONE ¦ SYSTEM ¦ <border string> options let you define the border around the window with a double line, a wide solid panel, no line, or the window border currently used by the system. The default is a single line. You can customize your windows with the <border string> option.

The CLOSE option makes it possible for a user to remove the window from memory later on by using the File menu popup. The default option is NOCLOSE, which requires an activated window to be closed by means of a DEACTIVATE WINDOW, CLEAR WINDOWS, HIDE WINDOW, or RELEASE WINDOWS command.

The FLOAT option allows later users to move a window to other locations on the screen by using the File menu popup, pressing Ctrl+F7, or clicking the mouse on the window's top border and moving the window while holding down the mouse button. The default is NOFLOAT, which does not allow windows to be moved.

The GROW option allows later users to change the size of a window by using the Window menu popup, pressing Ctrl+F8, or clicking the mouse on the window's lower-right corner and adjusting the size while holding down the mouse button. The default is NOGROW, which does not allow the window's size to be adjusted.

The MINIMIZE option lets you reduce a window to an icon. The ICON FILE option lets you specify the icon displayed when the window is minimized.

The SHADOW option adds a shadow behind the window.

The ZOOM option lets you maximize a window to cover the entire screen (or Visual FoxPro for Windows document window) and restore it to its original size.

The FILL option lets you fill the background of a window with a character string you specify, contained within quotation marks, or with other ASCII characters specified by the CHR( ) function. For example, FILL CHR(176) creates a solid gray background.

The COLOR option lets you specify color pairs for various parts of the window. You can do this by means of a color pair list (for example, COLOR 'B/R'), or a COLOR SCHEME (a number between 1 and 24 that lets you choose any of 24 preset color schemes).

After a window has been defined, you can modify it with MODIFY WINDOW, activate it for use with ACTIVATE WINDOW <window name list>, or display it without letting it be used with the command SHOW WINDOW <window name list>. The command HIDE WINDOW <window name list> lets you stop displaying one or more windows without deactivating them, while DEACTIVATE WINDOW <window name list> lets you deactivate them. SAVE WINDOW lets you save your window definitions to a disk file or a Memo field. Finally, you can clear windows from the screen and from memory by means of the command CLEAR WINDOWS or RELEASE WINDOWS <window name list>.

See Also ACTIVATE WINDOW, CLEAR WINDOWS, DEACTIVATE WINDOW, HIDE WINDOW, MODIFY WINDOW, MOVE WINDOW, RELEASE WINDOWS, SAVE WINDOW, SHOW WINDOW

The DELETE Command

Syntax

```
DELETE
     [<scope>]
     [FOR <log exp1>]
     [WHILE <log exp2>]
     [NOOPTIMIZE]
```

Usage This command marks records for deletion. In its simplest form, it marks only the current record (the record where the pointer is in the table open in the current work area) for deletion.

Records that are marked for deletion are not removed from the table until the command PACK is used, and they are treated like other records, although a solid rectangle or a bullet will appear next to them in screen displays. The command SET DELETED ON causes deleted records to become invisible to most Visual FoxPro commands.

Options If an optional scope, FOR, or WHILE clause is used, all the records included in the specified scope or all the records for which the logical expression following the FOR or WHILE is evaluated as true are marked for deletion. For more information on how these clauses work, see Chapter 11.

The NOOPTIMIZE option for this command disables the Rushmore technology, which normally speeds up data access when you use a FOR statement containing fields in existing indexes. You can disable Rushmore with the NOOPTIMIZE option on a number of Visual FoxPro commands. The only time you need to do this is when your command changes data in the field(s) that make up the index key, since the version of the file used by Rushmore may then become outdated, and incorrect answers may result.

See Also PACK, RECALL, SET DELETED

▸ The DELETE CONNECTION Command

Syntax

```
DELETE CONNECTION <connection name>
```

Usage This command deletes a named connection.

Options The <connection name> option specifies the name of the connection to be deleted. This connection must be part of the current database.

See Also CREATE CONNECTION, DISPLAY CONNECTIONS, LIST CONNECTIONS, MODIFY CONNECTION

▸ The DELETE DATABASE Command

Syntax

```
DELETE DATABASE <database name> ¦ ?
     [DELETETABLES]
```

Usage This command lets you delete a database and either convert all its tables to free tables or delete them.

Options The <database name> option lets you specify the database to be deleted.

The ? option lets you use the Open dialog box to select the database to be deleted.

The DELETETABLES option deletes all tables in the database. If this option is not used, these tables become free tables.

See Also CREATE DATABASE, DISPLAY DATABASE, LIST DATABASE, MODIFY DATABASE, OPEN DATABASE, PACK DATABASE

▸ The DELETE FILE Command

Syntax

```
DELETE FILE [<file name> ¦ ?]
```

Usage This command deletes the file whose name is specified or, if the ? option is used, displays a dialog box that lets the user choose which file to delete. The file name must include an extension, and it may include a drive letter and path name, as in DOS.

Use extreme caution when using this command. Even if SAFETY is ON, the file will be deleted without any warning.

This command is identical to the Visual FoxPro ERASE command. It is similar to the DOS commands DEL and ERASE, but it does not support wildcard characters.

See Also ERASE, ZAP

The DELETE TAG Command

Syntax

```
DELETE TAG
     <tag name1> [OF <CDX file name1>]
          [,<tag name2> [OF <CDX file name2>] ]
          [ ... ]

     ¦

     ALL [OF <CDX file name>]
```

Usage This command is used to delete a tag of a compound index file.

Options The <tag name1> [OF <CDX file name1>] option is used to specify the name of the tag to delete. If <CDX file name1> is not included, Visual FoxPro looks for the tag name first in the Structural compound index file and then in other compound index files that are open.

The <tag name2> [OF <CDX file name2>] … option indicates that the command can be used to delete an indefinite number of index files, whose names are separated by commas.

Instead of listing tag names, you can use the ALL option to removes every tag from a compound index file. The OF <CDX file name> option is used to specify the compound index file that has all its tags removed; if it is omitted, all tags are removed from the structural compound index file.

See Also INDEX

The DELETE TRIGGER Command

Syntax

```
DELETE TRIGGER ON <table name>
     FOR DELETE ¦ INSERT ¦ UPDATE
```

Usage This command removes a trigger that is evaluated when a record is deleted, inserted, or modified.

Options The <table name> option specifies the table that the trigger applies to. It must be in the current database.

The FOR DELETE ¦ INSERT ¦ UPDATE option specifies which trigger to remove from the table, its delete, insert, or update trigger.

See Also CREATE TRIGGER

► The DELETE VIEW Command

Syntax

```
DELETE VIEW <view name>
```

Usage This command deletes a SQL view from the current database and from disk.

Options The <view name> option lets you specify the name of the SQL view to be deleted.

See Also CREATE SQL VIEW, DISPLAY VIEWS, LIST VIEWS, MODIFY VIEW

► The DELETED( ) Function

Syntax

```
DELETED([<alias> ¦ <expN>])
```

Usage This function indicates whether the current record is marked for deletion. If it is, DELETED( ) returns .T.; if not, it returns .F.

Options By default, this function applies to the record where the pointer is in the table that is open in the current work area. If the <alias> or <expN> option is used, though, it applies to the current record in the work area indicated by the number, letter, or alias name that is specified.

See Also DELETE, PACK, RECALL, SET DELETED

► The _DIARYDATE System Variable

Syntax

```
_DIARYDATE = <expD>
```

Usage This system variable specifies the current date of the Calendar/Diary. Your program can store a value to this location, so that it becomes the default for the user, or it can test the variable for a value before doing something else.

▶ The DIMENSION Command

Syntax

```
DIMENSION <array1> (<expN1> [,<expN2>])
     [<array2> (<expN3> [,<expN4>])]
     [...]
```

Usage This command is used to create an array. It is identical to the DECLARE command.

An array is a series of memory variables that have the same name but are distinguished by their index numbers (also called their subscripts).

For example, if you have 10 different interest rates that you need to use in a program, it could be confusing to give each a separate name. You might find it easier to create an array to hold them. The command

```
DIMENSION int_rate(10)
```

creates 10 memory variables, named int_rate(1), int_rate(2), int_rate(3), and so on. You can then initialize these variables as you do any memory variable—for example,

```
int_rate(1) = .1
```

to use 10 percent as the first interest rate. The data type of each variable in the array is determined when it is initialized.

If you add the optional second numeric expression following the array, you will create a two-dimensional array that is referred to by two index numbers. Let's say you have 10 different interest rates for each month. You could use the command

```
DIMENSION int_rate(12,10)
```

to create 120 memory variables. Then you could use the variable int_rate(1,1) to hold the lowest interest rate for January, the variable int_rate(1,2) to hold the second interest rate for January, and so on through int_rate(1,10), which holds the highest interest rate for January. Likewise, you could use the variable int_rate(2,1) to hold the lowest interest rate for February, the variable int_rate(2,2) to hold the second interest rate for February, and so on through int_rate(2,10), which holds the highest interest rate for February.

Arrays are particularly powerful because you can use variables as the index number and access the entire array by altering the value of the variable. If you use a DO WHILE loop to change the value of the index number, you can print out hundreds of variables using just a few lines of code.

See Also DECLARE

▸ The DIR Command

Syntax

```
DIR ¦ DIRECTORY
      [ [ON] <drive:>]
      [ [LIKE] [<path>] [<skeleton>]]
      [TO PRINTER [PROMPT] ¦ TO FILE <file name>]
```

Usage In its simplest form, this command displays the names of all tables in the current directory, the number of records in each, the date each was last modified, and the size of each in bytes.

If the command is used with a skeleton, though, it is more like the DOS command DIR, displaying all the files specified by the skeleton. A skeleton can be made up of literals and the two wildcard characters (*, which stands for any word, and ?, which stands for any character). For example, DIR *.* will list a directory of all files in the current subdirectory, and DIR *.TXT will list a directory of all files in the current directory that have the TXT extension.

Options The optional ON clause lets you specify the drive, and the LIKE clause lets you specify the path name and file skeleton, so you can get a directory that is not for the current drive and subdirectory and restrict the files displayed. The words ON and LIKE themselves are optional in these clauses.

The optional TO PRINTER or TO FILE <file name> clause lets you send the directory listing to the printer or to the text file whose name is specified. If the PROMPT option is included, Visual FoxPro will display the Print dialog box before printing. This option must come immediately after the TO PRINTER option.

▶ The DISPLAY Command

Syntax

```
DISPLAY
     [FIELDS <field list>]
     [<scope>]
     [FOR <expL1>]
     [WHILE <expL2>]
     [OFF]
     [TO PRINTER [PROMPT] ¦ TO FILE <file name>]
     [NOCONSOLE]
     [NOOPTIMIZE]
```

Usage In its simplest form, this command displays the contents of the current record on the screen.

Options If an optional FIELDS clause is used, only the fields (or field expressions) listed are displayed on the screen.

If an optional scope clause is used, such as NEXT <expN>, RECORD <expN>, or REST, all the records included in the specified scope will be displayed on the screen. If they require more than one screen, they will be displayed one screen at a time, and the user will be told to press any key to see the next screen. This use of the DISPLAY command is similar to the LIST command; however, DISPLAY pauses whenever the screen becomes full, whereas LIST scrolls information continuously.

If a FOR or WHILE clause is used, all the records included in the specified scope for which the logical expression following the FOR or WHILE is evaluated as true are displayed on the screen.

For more information on how FIELDS, scope, FOR, and WHILE clauses work, see Chapter 11.

If the optional OFF clause is used, the record number is not displayed.

The optional TO PRINTER or TO FILE <file name> clause lets you send the display to the printer or to the text file whose name is specified. If the PROMPT option is included, Visual FoxPro will display the Print dialog box before printing. This option must come immediately after the TO PRINTER option.

The NOCONSOLE option prevents the command from displaying output on the screen, and should be used in combination with either the TO PRINTER or the TO FILE option.

The NOOPTIMIZE option for this command disables the Rushmore technology, which normally speeds up data access when you use a FOR statement containing fields in existing indexes. You can disable Rushmore with the NOOPTIMIZE option on a number of Visual FoxPro for Windows commands, but in this case there is little reason to do so.

See Also LIST

► The DISPLAY CONNECTIONS Command

Syntax

```
DISPLAY CONNECTIONS
      [TO PRINTER [PROMPT] | TO FILE <file name>]
      [NOCONSOLE]
```

Usage This command displays the names, data sources, and connection strings of the named connections in the current database. It displays one window of information at a time and prompts the user to press a key to continue.

Options The TO PRINTER option sends the output of the command to the printer.

The PROMPT option displays the Print dialog box before printing. This clause is available only when you use the TO PRINTER option in Visual FoxPro for Windows, and it must be placed immediately after TO PRINTER.

The TO FILE <file name> option sends the output of the command to the file whose name you specify.

The NOCONSOLE option prevents the command from displaying output on the screen, and should be used in combination with either the TO PRINTER or the TO FILE option.

See Also CREATE CONNECTION, DELETE CONNECTION, MODIFY CONNECTION, LIST CONNECTIONS

► The DISPLAY DATABASE Command

Syntax

```
DISPLAY DATABASE
      [TO PRINTER [PROMPT] | TO FILE <file name>]
      [NOCONSOLE]
```

Usage This command displays information about the current database one window at a time, and it prompts the user to press a key to see additional information.

Options The TO PRINTER option sends the output of the command to the printer.

The PROMPT option displays the Print dialog box before printing. This clause is available only when you use the TO PRINTER option in Visual FoxPro for Windows, and it must be placed immediately after TO PRINTER.

The TO FILE <file name> option sends the output of the command to the file whose name you specify.

The NOCONSOLE option prevents the command from displaying output on the screen, and should be used in combination with either the TO PRINTER or the TO FILE option.

See Also CREATE DATABASE, DELETE DATABASE, LIST DATABASE, MODIFY DATABASE, OPEN DATABASE, PACK DATABASE

The DISPLAY FILES Command

Syntax

```
LIST FILES
    [ON <drive ¦ dir>]
    [LIKE <skeleton>]
    [TO PRINTER [PROMPT] ¦ TO FILE <file name>]
```

Usage This command displays information about disk files.

Options The ON <drive ¦ dir> option lets you specify the disk drive and directory whose files should be listed. If it is omitted, the default drive and directory are listed.

The LIKE <skeleton> option lets you specify which files are listed by using a file skeleton including the symbols **?**, which represents any character, and *, which represents any series of characters. For example, LIST FILES LIKE A*.* will include only files whose names begin with the letter *A* in the listing.

The TO PRINTER and TO FILE options let you send the display to the printer or to a text file you specify. If the PROMPT option is included, Visual FoxPro will display the Print dialog box before printing. This option must come immediately after the TO PRINTER option.

See Also DIR, LIST FILES

► The DISPLAY MEMORY Command

Syntax

```
DISPLAY MEMORY [LIKE <skeleton>]
     [TO PRINTER [PROMPT] ¦ TO FILE <file name>]
     [NOCONSOLE]
```

Usage This command tells you the name, type, contents, and status of all current memory variables. It is particularly useful in developing programs, when you want to see the status of memory variables that may have been altered during the running of a program. The DISPLAY MEMORY and LIST MEMORY commands are similar; however, DISPLAY pauses when the screen becomes full, whereas LIST scrolls information continuously.

Options The LIKE option allows you to display a subset of current memory variables, using a wildcard expression—for example, DISPLAY MEMORY LIKE M*.

The TO PRINTER and TO FILE options allow you to direct output to your printer or to a disk file. If the PROMPT option is included, Visual FoxPro will display the Print dialog box before printing. This option must come immediately after the TO PRINTER option.

The NOCONSOLE option prevents the command from displaying output on the screen, and should be used in combination with either the TO PRINTER or the TO FILE option.

See Also DISPLAY STATUS, LIST MEMORY

► The DISPLAY STATUS Command

Syntax

```
DISPLAY STATUS
     [TO PRINTER [PROMPT] ¦ TO FILE <file name>]
     [NOCONSOLE]
```

Usage This useful command tells you everything you might want to know about current tables, files, network status, SET command settings, and other aspects of the Visual FoxPro environment. The DISPLAY STATUS and LIST STATUS commands are similar; however, DISPLAY pauses when the screen becomes full, whereas LIST scrolls information continuously.

Options The TO PRINTER and TO FILE options direct output to your printer and a disk file, respectively. If the PROMPT option is included, Visual FoxPro will display the Print dialog box before printing. This option must come immediately after the TO PRINTER option.

The NOCONSOLE option prevents the command from displaying output on the screen, and should be used in combination with either the TO PRINTER or the TO FILE option.

See Also DISPLAY MEMORY

▶ The DISPLAY STRUCTURE Command

Syntax

```
DISPLAY STRUCTURE
     [IN <alias> ¦ <expN>]
     [TO PRINTER [PROMPT] ¦ TO FILE <file name>]
     [NOCONSOLE]
```

Usage This command displays the structure of a table on the screen, along with the number of records in that table and the date it was last modified. The DISPLAY STRUCTURE and LIST STRUCTURE commands are similar; however, DISPLAY pauses when the screen becomes full, whereas LIST scrolls information continuously.

Options Ordinarily this command displays the structure of the table that is open in the current work area. The optional IN <alias> ¦ <expN> clause can be used to make it display the structure of a table in another work area. Specify the table's alias or the number of the work area.

The optional TO PRINTER or TO FILE <file name> clause lets you send the display of the structure to the printer or to the text file whose name is specified. If the PROMPT option is included, Visual FoxPro will display the Print dialog box before printing. This option must come immediately after the TO PRINTER option.

The NOCONSOLE option prevents the command from displaying output on the screen, and should be used in combination with either the TO PRINTER or the TO FILE option.

See Also LIST STRUCTURE

▸ The DISPLAY TABLES Command

Syntax

```
DISPLAY TABLES
     [TO PRINTER [PROMPT] ¦ TO FILE <file name>]
     [NOCONSOLE]
```

Usage This command displays information about the tables in the current database one window at a time, and prompts the user to press a key to see additional information.

Options The TO PRINTER option sends the output of the command to the printer.

The PROMPT option displays the Print dialog box before printing. This clause is available only when you use the TO PRINTER option in Visual FoxPro, and it must be placed immediately after TO PRINTER.

The TO FILE <file name> option sends the output of the command to the file whose name you specify.

The NOCONSOLE option prevents the command from displaying output on the screen, and should be used in combination with either the TO PRINTER or the TO FILE option.

See Also ADD TABLE, ALTER TABLE, CLOSE, CREATE, CREATE TABLE, FREE TABLE, LIST TABLES, MODIFY STRUCTURE, REMOVE TABLE, USE

▸ The DISPLAY VIEWS Command

Syntax

```
DISPLAY VIEWS
     [TO PRINTER [PROMPT] ¦ TO FILE <file name>]
     [NOCONSOLE]
```

Usage This command displays information about SQL views in the current database one window at a time, and prompts the user to press a key to see additional information.

Options The TO PRINTER option sends the output of the command to the printer.

The PROMPT option displays the Print dialog box before printing. This clause is available only when you use the TO PRINTER option in Visual FoxPro, and it must be placed immediately after TO PRINTER.

The TO FILE <file name> option sends the output of the command to the file whose name you specify.

The NOCONSOLE option prevents the command from displaying output on the screen, and should be used in combination with either the TO PRINTER or the TO FILE option.

See Also CREATE SQL VIEW, DELETE VIEW, LIST VIEWS, MODIFY VIEW

▶ The DO CASE Command

Syntax

```
DO CASE
     CASE <expL1>
          ...
     CASE <expLN>
          ...
          ...
     [OTHERWISE
          ...]
ENDCASE
```

Usage This command lets a program select among a number of possible courses of action. If the logical expression following the first CASE is evaluated as true, the program executes the commands following it and then proceeds to execute the commands following ENDCASE. Likewise, if the logical expression following any succeeding CASE is evaluated as true, the program executes the commands following it and then moves to the commands following ENDCASE. The command can include any number of CASEs, but it will execute only the first one for which the logical expression is true. Commands following the optional OTHERWISE statement are executed if none of the logical expressions in the CASE statements are true.

See Also DO WHILE, IF ... ENDIF

▶ The DO Command

Syntax

```
DO <program filename>
     [WITH <parameter list>]
     [IN <file name>]
```

Usage This command executes a program. If the program is not yet compiled or if the source code has been modified since it was last compiled, this command automatically compiles the program before running it.

Options The optional parameter list can be used to pass parameters to the program that is being executed. The program must include a PARAMETER command that lists the variables that are parameters. These variables are assigned the values in the parameter list of the DO command. For more information, see PARAMETER.

The IN option runs a procedure that is in a file you specify. It can be used instead of using SET PROCEDURE before the DO command.

See Also PROCEDURE, RUN

▸ The DO WHILE Command

Syntax

```
DO WHILE <expL>
     ...
     ...
     [LOOP]
     [EXIT]
ENDDO
```

Usage This command, used in programming, lets you repeatedly execute a block of program code. The code between DO WHILE and ENDDO will be processed as long as the logical expression is true. This is called a loop.

If the logical expression is untrue when the program first reaches the DO WHILE statement, the program simply skips the entire DO WHILE loop and continues with the line that follows the ENDDO.

If the expression is true, the program executes all these lines of code. When it reaches ENDDO, it goes back to the DO WHILE statement and checks again to see if the condition is true. If not, it continues with the line following ENDDO; if so, it executes the code again.

There normally is some code within the loop that ultimately makes the logical expression false, so the code is executed a finite number of times. Alternately, you can use the command EXIT to break out of the loop. An infinite loop is a common programming error.

One common programming construction is to begin with a DO WHILE .NOT. EOF( ) statement. If a SKIP statement is included before the ENDDO statement, this forms a loop that proceeds record-by-record through the entire file, performing a specified operation or displaying specified information on the screen or printer.

The command EXIT or LOOP can be used at any point within the DO WHILE ... ENDDO command. EXIT causes the program to proceed with the next line following ENDDO, and LOOP causes the program to return immediately to the DO WHILE statement and to evaluate the logical condition there to determine whether or not to go through the loop again.

See Also DO CASE, SCAN

▶ The DOW( ) Function

Syntax

```
DOW(<expD> ¦ <expT>)
```

Usage This function returns a number corresponding to the day of the week of a specified date or datetime expression. For example, if the date expression is a Sunday, this function returns 1, if it is a Monday, this function returns 2, and so on.

You can use this function in combination with ? to look up the day of the week of a specified date. For example, if you enter the command **? DOW({09/26/92})**, Visual FoxPro displays 2 to indicate that that date is a Sunday.

See Also CDOW( )

▶ The DTOC( ) Function

Syntax

```
DTOC(<expD> ¦ <expT> [,1])
```

Usage This function returns the date from the specified date or datetime expression as a character string.

Options The optional ,1 returns the character string in a form that can be used directly in an index—the same ASCII format returned by DTOS( ).

See Also TOD( ), DTOS( )

▸ The DTOR( ) Function

Syntax

```
DTOR(<expN>)
```

Usage Converts degrees to radians. The numeric expression represents the size of an angle in degrees, and the function returns a numeric expression that represents the size of the same angle in radians.

See Also ACOS( ), ASIN( ), ATAN( ), COS( ), RTOD( ), SIN( ), TAN( )

▸ The DTOS( ) Function

Syntax

```
DTOS(<expD> ¦ <expT>)
```

Usage This function returns the date from the date or datetime expression as a character string in ASCII format, yyyymmdd, for use in indexes. This function lets you use an expression that combines a date with other character data as the basis of an index. Because the date is returned in ASCII format, the records will be arranged in proper chronological order.

See Also CTOD( ), DTOC( )

▸ The EDIT Command

Syntax

```
EDIT
     [FIELDS <field list>]
     [<scope>]
     [FOR <expL1>]
     [WHILE <expL2>]
     [FONT <expC> [,<expN] [STYLE <expC2>]]
     [FREEZE <field name>]
     [KEY <exp1> [,<exp2>]]
     [LAST ¦ NOINIT]
     [LEDIT][REDIT]
     [LPARTITION]
     [NOAPPEND]
```

```
[NOCLEAR]
[NODELETE]
[NOEDIT ¦ NOMODIFY]
[NOFOLLOW]
[NOLINK]
[NOMENU]
[NOOPTIMIZE]
[NORMAL]
[NOWAIT]
[PARTITION <expN2>]
[PREFERENCE <expC3>]
[REST]
[SAVE]
[TIMEOUT <expN3>]
[TITLE <expC4>]
[VALID [:F] <expL3> [ERROR <expC5>]]
[WHEN <expL4>]
[WIDTH <expN4>]
[[WINDOW <window name1>]
[IN [WINDOW] <window name2> ¦ IN SCREEN]]
[COLOR <color pair list> ¦ COLOR SCHEME
     <expN4>]
```

Usage EDIT opens the Browse window in its Edit configuration, with each field on one line. The commands EDIT and CHANGE are identical.

You can edit existing records or use the Browse menu to add a new record. If you click the Close box, press Ctrl+W or Ctrl+End, or choose File ➤ Close, you can close the Browse/Edit window and save any changes you made. If you press Ctrl+Q, you can close the Browse/Edit window and discard any changes you made. To edit Memo fields, double-click the field with the mouse or move the cursor to it and press Ctrl+PgDn to open the Memo window.

Options Many of the options that can be used with EDIT are useful primarily in programming, where you want to limit what the user can do.

The FIELDS option makes the Browse window contain only the fields mentioned in the field list. It may also include calculated fields (which are read-only), and it includes other options that may be used to control properties of how fields are displayed, such as their heading and their width. The fields in the list must be separated by commas, and each of the fields may be followed by the following options:

- [:R] makes the field read-only, so its data can be viewed but not edited.
- [: <expN>] specifies the width of the field
- [: V <expL> [:F] [:E = <expC>]] creates a validity check, which does not let you leave the field if the logical expression evaluates as false. By default, this expression is evaluated only if the field is modified, but the :F option forces the evaluation, even if the data was not changed. If you use the :E = <expC> option, the character expression will be used as an error message if the logical expression evaluates as false.
- [: P = <expC>] creates a picture template. The character expression must be made up of the same symbols that can be used in a PICTURE clause of an @ … SAY … GET command, which are listed in the entry on that command. All of the symbols except @M may be used here.
- [: B = <exp>, <exp> [:F]] specifies boundaries. The two expressions are a minimum and maximum value for the data. By default, the boundaries are checked only if the field is modified, but the :F option forces the evaluation, even if the data was not changed.
- [: H = <expC>] lets you specify a character expression to be used as the heading for the field.
- [:W = <expL>] lets you specify a WHEN option that prevents the cursor from moving to the field if the logical expression evaluates as false. The logical expression may be a user-defined function.

The <scope> option limits the number of records that the Edit Window includes, and the FOR and WHILE options include only those records for which a logical expression you specify is true. FOR and WHILE clauses are explained in Chapter 11.

The FONT <expC> [,<expN] [STYLE <expC3>] option lets you specify the typeface, size, and style of the font used. <expC> and <expN> should be the name and size of an available font. If the font you specify is not available, Visual FoxPro tries to substitute a similar font. If you omit the FONT clause, the main Visual FoxPro window font is used, and if you include the clause but omit the size option, a 10-point font is used. The STYLE clause may be followed by one of the following codes:

- B: boldface
- I: italic
- N: normal
- O: outline
- Q: opaque
- S: shadow
- -: strikeout
- T: transparent
- U: underline

If this clause is omitted, normal style will be used.

The FREEZE option allows changes to be made only to the one field that is mentioned, although all the fields are displayed.

The KEY option lets you select a particular subset of records to change by specifying one particular field value or a range of field values to be matched. The table must be indexed on the field you select and that index must currently be in use. For example, EDIT KEY '94704', '94709' allows you to change records with a ZIP code between 94704 and 94709 if your table includes a ZIP code field and if the ZIP code index is in use.

The LAST ¦ NOINIT option opens the Browse/Edit window in the same configuration in which it was last used. These options are identical, and NOINIT is included to provide dBASE compatibility.

The LEDIT option displays the left partition of the Edit window in Browse mode rather than Edit mode, while the REDIT option displays the right partition in Browse mode.

The LOCK option lets you specify the number of fields to be "locked" in the left partition.

The LPARTITION option places the cursor in the first field in the left partition of a partitioned Browse window. By default, the cursor is placed in the first field of the right partition.

The NOLINK option removes the normal linkage between left and right partitions, which causes both to scroll together.

The NOAPPEND option makes it impossible to add new records to the file.

The NOCLEAR option leaves the Browse/Edit window visible on the screen after you are done using it. By default, the window disappears when you are done.

The NODELETE option makes it impossible to mark records for de letion. The NOEDIT ¦ NOMODIFY option makes it impossible to make any changes in the data.

The NOFOLLOW option makes the pointer stay where it is in the table when you modify the field the table is indexed on. By default, the pointer stays on the record, following it to the new position it moves to because its key field was modified.

The NOMENU option makes the Browse/Edit window open without the Browse menu pad being added to the menu bar, so the user cannot access the Browse menu.

The NOOPTIMIZE option disables the Rushmore technology, which normally speeds up data access when you use a FOR statement containing fields in existing indexes. You may want to do this if you will be changing data in the same field that is specified in the FOR statement and if the table is indexed on that field. Otherwise, the version of the file used by Rushmore may become outdated, and the Edit display may not be up to date.

The NORMAL option opens the Browse/Edit window with its normal attributes even if it is opened in a user window. If this option is not used, the Browse window takes its colors and other attributes from the user window it is opened in.

The NOWAIT option makes a program continue without any pause after the Browse/Edit window is opened. If EDIT is used in a program without this option, the Browse/Edit window is opened and the program is suspended until it is closed.

The PARTITION option splits the screen into left and right partitions; the numeric expression following it determines the size of the left partition by specifying the column number of the split bar. You can use this clause to lock one set of fields in the left portion of the screen while browsing others in the right portion. If you use a PARTITION clause, the cursor is normally placed in the right partition unless you also include an LPARTITION clause.

The PREFERENCE option lets you save and reuse the attributes of Browse windows. Unlike the LAST option, which reuses only the previous configuration, this option can reuse any configuration used in the past. The first time EDIT is used with this option followed by a character expression, the PREFERENCE referred to by that name is created. When the Browse window is closed, that PREFERENCE is updated. Anytime in the future that the Browse/Edit window is opened with that PREFERENCE, it will keep the same configuration.

By default, the pointer is moved to the top of the table when a FOR clause is included, but if the REST option is also used, the pointer remains in its current position.

The SAVE option keeps the Browse/Edit window (and an associated Memo window, if one is open) on the screen after the user has exited from it. This option can be used only in programs.

The TIMEOUT option allows you to specify how many seconds the Browse window will remain open without the user making any input. This clause can be used only within a program.

The TITLE option lets you specify a title to appear in the top border of the editing window.

The VALID option lets you check new data entered into each record before EDIT moves on to the next record. For EDIT to move on, the logical expression you specify must be true. If not, an error message that you set up with an ERROR clause is displayed. If you include :F after the word VALID, you can force the validation check to occur whether or not the user has actually entered new data in that record.

The WHEN option allows the user to make changes only to the current record when a certain logical condition you specify is true.

The WIDTH option limits the width of the display of all fields. Only the display is affected, not the actual data. You may use the arrow keys to scroll through a field and see all its data.

The WINDOW option lets the Browse/Edit window take on the characteristics of another window you specify. That window must first be defined using the DEFINE WINDOW command. The IN WINDOW option actually opens the Browse window within another window, although the Browse window will not necessarily have the characteristics of this parent window unless you also use a WINDOW clause. The default is IN SCREEN.

The COLOR option allows you to specify the color attributes of the Browse window. You can do this by means of a color pair list (for example, COLOR 'B/R'), or a COLOR SCHEME (a number between 1 and 24 that lets you choose any of 24 preset color schemes) clause.

See Also BROWSE, CHANGE

▸ The EJECT Command

Syntax

```
EJECT
```

Usage This command sends a form-feed to your printer to move the printer to the top of the next page. It can be used within programs that produce printed output to move to the next page whenever the current line number exceeds a certain limit, such as 55.

▸ The EOF( ) Function

Syntax

```
EOF([<alias> ¦ <exp>]
```

Usage This function returns .T. if the end-of-file is reached. This condition occurs if a table has no records in it, if you try to move the pointer to a record beyond the end of the file, or if the command SEEK, LOCATE, CONTINUE, or FIND was unsuccessful.

By default, this function applies to the table open in the current work area, but the <alias> option lets you specify another work area; use the letter or number of the work area or the name or alias of the file open there.

See Also BOF( )

▸ The ERASE Command

Syntax

```
ERASE <file name> ¦ ?
```

Usage This command deletes the file whose name is specified or, if the ? option is used, displays a dialog box that lets the user choose which file to delete. The file name must include an extension, and it may include a drive letter and path name, as in DOS. Even if SAFETY is ON, the file will be deleted without any warning.

This command is identical to the Visual FoxPro DELETE FILE command. It is similar to the DOS commands DEL and ERASE, but it does not support wildcard characters.

See Also DELETE, DELETE FILE

The EVALUATE( ) Function

Syntax

```
EVALUATE(<expC>)
```

Usage This function evaluates a character expression that is the name of a field or variable and returns the result. For example, EVALUATE (WAGE) would return the value of the wage field in the current record. The value returned by this function has the same data type as the original value.

This function can often be used instead of the & command for macro substitution and runs more quickly.

See Also &, TYPE( )

The EXACTLY LIKE Operator

Syntax

```
<search_in expC> EXACTLY LIKE <search_for expC>
```

Usage This operator returns .T. if <search_in expC> (the expression being searched in) is identical to <search_for expC>. Unlike the LIKE operator, it does not find a match if <search_in expC> has additional characters following those that match <search_for expC>. Used only with character expressions.

See Also !=, #, $, <, <=, <>, =, ==, >, >=, GREATER THAN, GREATER THAN OR EQUAL TO, LESS THAN, LESS THAN OR EQUAL TO, LIKE, NOT LIKE

The EXIT Command

Syntax

```
EXIT
```

Usage This command can be used only within a DO WHILE loop, a FOR loop, or a SCAN WHILE loop. It makes the program continue by executing the code that immediately follows ENDDO, ENDFOR or NEXT, or ENDSCAN, any of which indicates the ends of these loops.

See Also DO WHILE, FOR, SCAN

▸ The EXP( ) Function

Syntax

```
EXP(<expN>)
```

Usage This function returns the value of **e** (the base of natural logarithms) raised to the power specified by the numeric expression.

See Also LOG( )

▸ The EXPORT Command

Syntax

```
EXPORT TO <file name>
     [<scope>]
     [FIELDS <field list>]
     [FOR <expL1>]
     [WHILE <expL2>]
     [TYPE] DIF ¦ MOD ¦ SYLK ¦ WK1 ¦ WKS ¦ WR1 ¦ WRK
            ¦ XLS
     [NOOPTIMIZE]
     [AS <code page>]
```

Usage This command copies the records in the table that is open in the current work area to a file that can be used by another software package.

Options The <scope> option lets you select which records will be copied; only records in the specified scope will be copied. Scope options include ALL, NEXT <expN>, RECORD <expN>, and REST. If this clause is omitted, the default scope is ALL.

The FIELDS option lets you select which fields in the table will be copied.

The FOR and WHILE options let you select which records will be copied. Only records for which the logical expression is evaluated as true are copied.

The TYPE option lets you specify the type of file to copy the data to. The choices are:

- **DIF files:** Used by VisiCalc
- **MOD files:** Used by Multiplan version 4.01
- **SYLK files:** Symbolic Link files used by Multiplan
- **WK1 files:** Used by Lotus 1-2-3 version 2.0
- **WKS files:** Used by Lotus 1-2-3 version 1-A
- **WR1 files:** Used by Lotus Symphony versions 1.1 and 1.2
- **WRK files:** Used by Lotus Symphony version 1.0
- **XLS files:** Used by Excel

You must specify one of these type options, although you do not need to include the word TYPE.

The NOOPTIMIZE option for this command disables the Rushmore technology, which normally speeds up data access when you use a FOR statement containing fields in existing indexes. You can disable Rushmore with the NOOPTIMIZE option on a number of Visual FoxPro for Windows commands, but in this case there is little reason to do so.

The AS <code page> option lets you specify the code page for the new file that the EXPORT command creates.

▶ The FILER Command

Syntax

```
FILER
      [LIKE <skeleton>]
      [NOWAIT]
      IN [WINDOW] <window name> ¦ SCREEN]
```

Usage This command displays the Filer utility, which can be used to manage and maintain files.

Options If you use the LIKE <skeleton> option, the Filer is displayed initially with only the files that match the skeleton. The skeleton uses the wildcard symbols ? to represent any character and * to represent any series of characters.

If you add the NOWAIT option, program execution continues after the Filer is opened. Without this option, the program waits for the user to close the Filer.

The option IN [WINDOW] <window name> opens the Filer in the user defined window whose name is specified.

The option IN [WINDOW] SCREEN opens the filer in the main Visual FoxPro window.

▸ The FILTER( ) Function

Syntax

```
FILTER([<work area num> | <table alias>]
```

Usage This function returns the expression used by the SET FILTER command. If the SET FILTER command is not being used, it returns the empty string.

Options By default, this function returns the filter expression for the table in the current work area.

If you use a numeric expression as the <work area num>, it returns the filter expression for the table open in the work area you specify.

If you use a character expression as the <table alias>, it returns the filter expression of the table whose name or alias you specify.

See Also SET FILTER TO

▸ The FIND Command

Syntax

```
FIND <expC>
```

Usage This command finds the first record that matches the character string you specify. The table must be indexed on the corresponding field and that index must be the current major index. FIND attempts to find a match for the specified character string using the indexed field.

When the specified character string is found, the FOUND( ) function returns a logical true (.T.), the RECNO( ) function returns the number of the matching record, and the record pointer is placed at that record. If no match is found, the pointer is left at the end of the file, EOF( ) returns a logical true (.T.), and FOUND( ) returns a logical false (.F.).

If SET NEAR is ON, the FIND command leaves the pointer after the nearest matching record.

FIND is similar to the SEEK command, except that it requires a literal as the basis of its search and cannot search for expressions that use functions or variables. (It can search for a variable if the macro substitution character, &, is used before the variable name so it reads it as the contents of the variable rather than searching for the letters in the variable's name.) If the literal is a character string, it does not have to be enclosed in quotation marks unless it includes leading blanks.

SEEK is now generally used instead of FIND.

See Also LOCATE, SEEK

▶ The FLOCK( ) Function

Syntax

```
FLOCK([<work area num> ¦ <table alias>])
```

Usage This function attempts to lock a table. It returns .T. if it succeeds in locking the table, and .F. if it fails.

Options By default, this function attempts to lock the table in the current work area.

If you use a numeric expression as the <work area num>, it attempts to lock the table that is open in the work area you specify.

If you use a character expression as the <table alias>, it attempts to lock the table whose name or alias you specify.

See Also LOCK( ), RLOCK, SET REPROCESS

▶ The FLOOR( ) Function

Syntax

```
FLOOR(<expN>)
```

Usage This function returns the next integer that is less than or equal to the specified numeric expression.

See Also CEILING( ), INT( ), ROUND( )

▸ The FOR Command

Syntax

```
FOR <memvar> = <expN1> TO <expN2> [STEP <expN3>]
    ...
    [EXIT]
    [LOOP]
ENDFOR ¦ NEXT
```

Usage This command lets you repeatedly execute a series of lines in a program. The code between FOR and ENDFOR will be executed until the memory variable is equal to the second numeric expression.

When the FOR statement is first encountered, Visual FoxPro creates a memory variable with the name of <memvar> and assigns it the initial value <expN1>. Then it executes the program until it reaches ENDFOR. It then increments the value of <memvar> by 1 and loops back to the FOR statement to check again whether <memvar> is equal to <expN2>. It executes the code in the loop repeatedly until <memvar> is equal to <expN2>, and then it continues with the code following ENDFOR.

Options If the optional STEP clause is included in the command, <memvar> is incremented by the number it specifies each time through the loop—instead of being incremented by 1. It can also be used with a negative number to decrement the variable.

The optional command EXIT or LOOP may be used at any point within the FOR … ENDFOR command. EXIT causes the program to proceed with the next line following ENDFOR, and LOOP causes the program to return immediately to the FOR statement.

See Also DO CASE, DO WHILE, SCAN

▸ The FOUND( ) Function

Syntax

```
FOUND([<alias> ¦ <exp>])
```

Usage This function returns a logical true (.T.) if a record is found by the command SEEK, LOCATE, CONTINUE, or FIND or a logical false (.F.) if the search is unsuccessful. Thus, its value after a search is generally the opposite of the value of EOF( ). The two may be different if NEAR is ON.

By default, this function applies to the table open in the current work area, but the <alias> ¦ <exp> option lets you specify another work area. Use the name or alias of the file or the letter or number of the work area.

See Also EOF( ), FIND, LOCATE, SEEK, SET NEAR

▶ The FREE TABLE Command

Syntax

```
FREE TABLE <table name>
```

Usage This command allows a table to be used without a database being used first. This command is used if a database was deleted accidentally, rather than by using the DELETE DATABASE command, which automatically frees its tables; if the database was not deleted, use the REMOVE TABLE command to free a table from it. No database may be open when it is used.

Options If you enter the command without a <table name>, Visual FoxPro for Windows displays the Free Table dialog box, which you use like the Open dialog box to select a table to free.

See Also ADD TABLE, ALTER TABLE, CLOSE, CREATE, CREATE TABLE, DISPLAY TABLES, LIST TABLES, MODIFY STRUCTURE, REMOVE TABLE, USE

▶ The FUNCTION Command

Syntax

```
FUNCTION <name>
```

Usage This command is used within a program or a procedure file to mark the beginning of a procedure or a user-defined function. If it is in a program file, the program may call it by using the DO command followed by its name. If it is in a procedure file, you may call it by using the DO command from a program or from the Command window only after you have used the SET PROCEDURE command. The procedure or function can receive parameters from the DO command that calls it. For more information, see PARAMETERS.

After all the code in a procedure is executed, control returns to the line following the line that called it (or to the Command window). Alternately, control can be returned to that point by using the command RETURN. A user-defined function must use RETURN followed by an expression to return a value.

The command FUNCTION is identical to the command PROCEDURE, but stylistically it is best to use FUNCTION for user-defined functions and PROCEDURE for procedures that do not return a value.

See Also PARAMETERS, PROCEDURE

▶ The _GENMENU System Variable

Syntax

```
_GENMENU = <expC>
```

Usage This system variable specifies the name of the program that is used as the menu generator to generate code from an MNX file. By default, its value is GENMENU.PRG, the menu-generating program that comes with Visual FoxPro. Change it if you create a custom menu-generating program.

See Also CREATE MENU

▶ The GO Command

Syntax

```
GO ¦ GOTO
    [RECORD] <expN1> ¦ TOP ¦ BOTTOM
    [IN <expN2> ¦ <alias>]
```

Usage This command lets you move the pointer within a table.

If it is used with a record number, it moves the pointer to that record; the word RECORD is optional before the number.

If it is used with TOP or BOTTOM, it moves the pointer to the first or last record of the table.

Options By default, this command works on the table that is open in the current work area, but the optional IN <alias> clause can be used to specify another work area.

See Also RECNO( ), SKIP

▶ The GREATER THAN Operator

Syntax

```
<search_in exp> GREATER THAN <search_for exp>
```

Usage This operator returns .T. if <search_in exp> (the expression being searched in) is greater than <search_for exp>.

See Also !=, #, $, <, <=, <>, =, ==, >, >=, EXACTLY LIKE, GREATER THAN OR EQUAL TO, LESS THAN, LESS THAN OR EQUAL TO, LIKE, NOT LIKE

The GREATER THAN OR EQUAL TO Operator

Syntax

```
<search_in exp> GREATER THAN OR EQUAL TO <search_for
           exp>
```

Usage This operator returns .T. if <search_in exp> (the expression being searched in) is greater than or equal to <search_for exp>.

See Also !=, #, $, <, <=, <>, =, ==, >, >=, EXACTLY LIKE, GREATER THAN, LESS THAN, LESS THAN OR EQUAL TO, LIKE, NOT LIKE

The HELP Command

Syntax

```
HELP
     [<topic>]
     [IN [WINDOW] <window name> ¦ IN [WINDOW] SCREEN]
     [NOWAIT]
```

Usage This command displays the Visual FoxPro Help system.

Options The <topic> option lets you specify the topic displayed in the Help window. Use the same names displayed in the topics list in the bottom half of the Search dialog box of the help system. If you do not use the name of a topic, FoxPro displays the topic whose spelling is closest to the one you used.

The IN [WINDOW] <window name> option lets you display the Help window within a parent window.

The IN [WINDOW] SCREEN option lets you display the Help window within the Visual FoxPro main window.

The NOWAIT lets the program continue executing after the Help window is opened. If this option is omitted, the program continues after the user closes the Help Window.

See Also SET HELP, SET HELP TO

▶ The HIDE MENU Command

Syntax

```
HIDE MENU <menu name1> [,<menu name2>...] ¦ ALL
     [SAVE]
```

Usage This command removes one or more specified menus from the screen while keeping them activated and resident in memory. The ALL option hides all previously activated menus.

Options The SAVE option lets you keep the image of the hidden menu on the screen even though the menu is no longer available for use.

See Also ACTIVATE MENU, CLEAR MENUS, CREATE MENU, DEACTIVATE MENU, DEFINE MENU, MODIFY MENU, SHOW MENU

▶ The HIDE POPUP Command

Syntax

```
HIDE POPUP <popup name1> [,<popup name2>...] ¦ ALL
     [SAVE]
```

Usage This command removes one or more specified menu popups from the screen while keeping them resident in memory. The ALL option hides all previously activated popups.

Options The SAVE option lets you keep the image of the hidden popup on the screen even though it has technically been hidden and is not accessible to the user.

See Also ACTIVATE POPUP, CREATE MENU, DEFINE BAR, DEFINE POPUP

▶ The HIDE WINDOW Command

Syntax

```
HIDE WINDOW <window name1> [[,<window name2>] ...] ¦
         ALL
     [IN [WINDOW] <window name> ¦ SCREEN]
     [SAVE]
```

Usage This command removes one or more specified windows from the screen while keeping them resident in memory. The ALL option hides all previously activated windows.

Options The IN [WINDOW] option hides the specified window within another window, where it can continue to receive output until shown again with the SHOW WINDOW or ACTIVATE WINDOW command. The SCREEN option, which is the default, keeps the hidden window in the Visual FoxPro main window.

The SAVE option lets you keep the image of the hidden window on the screen even though the window has technically been hidden and is not accessible to the user.

See Also ACTIVATE WINDOW, CLEAR WINDOWS, DEACTIVATE WINDOW, DEFINE WINDOW, RELEASE WINDOWS, RESTORE WINDOW, SAVE WINDOW, SHOW WINDOW

▶ The HOUR( ) Function

Syntax

```
HOUR(<expT>
```

Usage This function returns the hour from the specified time expression. Whether it returns it in 12- or 24-hour format depends on the setting of the SET HOURS command.

See Also MINUTE( ), SEC( ), SET HOURS

▶ The IDXCOLLATE( ) Function

Syntax

```
IDXCOLLATE([<cdx file name>] <index number>
     [, <work area num> ¦ <table alias>
```

Usage This function returns the collation sequence for the index or index tag that is specified.

Use the <index number> argument to specify the index, with all open indexes numbered as follows. All single-file indexes are numbered first, in the order that they were opened. All tags in the structural compound index file are numbered next, in the order in which they were created. All tags in open independent compound index files are numbered next, in the order in which the files were opened, and in the order in which the tags were created within each file.

If you specify a number larger than all open indexes, the function returns an empty string.

Options The <cdx file name> option specifies the name of the compound index file.

The <work area num> option specifies the number of the work area in which the table is open; and the <table alias> option specifies the name or alias of the table. If neither option is used, the function applies to the current table.

See Also SET COLLATE

► The IF Command

Syntax

```
IF <expL>
      ...
      [ELSE
      ...]
ENDIF
```

Usage This command determines whether or not program code is executed on the basis of some logical expression. If the logical expression of the IF statement is true, the code following it is executed.

Options An optional ELSE statement can include code that is executed if the logical expression of the IF is evaluated as false. If no ELSE statement is included, the program simply proceeds with the code following ENDIF if this logical expression is evaluated as false.

See Also DO CASE, DO WHILE, FOR, IIF( )

► The IIF( ) Function

Syntax

```
IIF(<expL>,<exp1>,<exp2>)
```

Usage This function, the "immediate if," returns the value of the first expression if the logical expression is true or returns the value of the second expression if the logical expression is false.

Thus, it lets you build an IF into expressions. For example, you could use an IIF( ) on a mailing label to print one string expression for people who have paid their membership dues and another expression for those who have not.

See Also IF ... ENDIF

▶ The IMPORT Command

Syntax

```
IMPORT FROM <file name>
     [TYPE] DIF ¦ MOD ¦ SYLK ¦ WK1 ¦ WK3 ¦ WKS ¦ WR1
            ¦ WRK ¦ XLS ¦ PDOX ¦ RPD ¦ FW2
     [AS <code page>]
```

Usage This command creates a new Visual FoxPro table with data from a non-Visual FoxPro file you specify. The new table will have the same name as this other file.

Options The TYPE option lets you specify the type of file the data is to be imported from. The choices are

- **DIF files:** Used by VisiCalc
- **MOD files:** Used by Multiplan version 4.01
- **SYLK files:** Symbolic Link files used by Multiplan
- **WK1 files:** Used by Lotus 1-2-3 version 2.0
- **WK3 files:** Used by Lotus 1-2-3 version 3.0
- **WKS files:** Used by Lotus 1-2-3 version 1-A
- **WR1 files:** Used by Lotus Symphony versions 1.1 and 1.2
- **WRK files:** Used by Lotus Symphony version 1.0
- **XLS files:** Used by Excel
- **PDOX files:** Used by Paradox
- **RPD files:** Used by RapidFile
- **FW2 files:** Used by Framework II

The command must include one of these options, although the word TYPE need not be included.

The AS <code page> option lets you specify the code page of the new file created by this command.

See Also APPEND FROM, EXPORT

▸ The INDEX Command

Syntax

```
INDEX ON <field exp>
      TO <.IDX file> ¦ TAG <tag name> [OF <.CDX file>]
      [FOR <expL>]
      [COMPACT]
      [ASCENDING ¦ DESCENDING]
      [UNIQUE]
      [ADDITIVE]
      [NOOPTIMIZE]
```

Usage This command creates an index file for the table that is open in the current work area. The index arranges records in an apparent order based on the field expression; the actual order of the records in the table does not change. The field expression may not use Memo or General fields.

INDEX TO <file name> creates a single-index file in a file with the name that is specified that holds only one index. Visual FoxPro assumes an IDX extension for the index file, but this default can be overridden by specifying a name that includes a different extension.

INDEX TAG <tag name> creates a tag of a compound index file. CDX (compound index) files contain multiple index tags within one file. If you do not specify a file name, Visual FoxPro makes this a tag of the structural compound index file, which has the same name as the table and is automatically opened whenever the table is opened. If you specify OF <CDX filename>, Visual FoxPro makes this a tag of some other compound index file.

After this command is used, the index that has just been created is open and sets the order of the records in the file.

Indexes are updated automatically if they are open when the table is modified, or they may be updated using the REINDEX command.

Options The optional FOR clause makes the index include only records for which the logical expression is true. When the file is modified, the index is updated so it always includes all records in the file for which the logical expression is true.

The COMPACT option directs Visual FoxPro to create compact IDX index files; these are desirable but can't be used if you are sharing tables with FoxBASE+ or FoxBASE+/Mac.

The ASCENDING and DESCENDING options allow you to tell Visual FoxPro whether to index the file according to ascending or descending values of a certain field. ASCENDING is the default. DESCENDING cannot be used when creating IDX files. By default, character fields are sorted in ascending or descending ASCII order, but other sort orders can be specified by using the SET COLLATE command before you use the INDEX command.

The UNIQUE option makes the index include only the record with the first occurrence of a given value for the field expression the index is based on. If this expression has the same value for more than one record, all but the first will not be included in the index and will not be accessible when the table is used with this index as the controlling index that sets the order of the records.

The ADDITIVE option allows previously opened index files to remain open while you create a new index.

The NOOPTIMIZE option for this command disables the Rushmore technology, which normally speeds up data access when you use a FOR statement containing fields in existing indexes. You can disable Rushmore with the NOOPTIMIZE option on a number of Visual FoxPro for Windows commands, but in this case there is little reason to do so.

See Also REINDEX, SET COLLATE, USE

▶ The INPUT Command

Syntax

```
INPUT [<expC>] TO <memvar>
```

Usage This command lets a program get input from the user and stores this input in the memory variable that is specified. The data type of the user's input determines the data type of the memory variable that is created; for this reason, it is often preferable to use ACCEPT to get data that is not numeric.

This unformatted input/output command is included for compatibility with earlier versions of the Xbase language. The Form Designer or formatted input/output using @ … SAY … GET is now used instead.

Options If the optional character expression is included, it is displayed as a prompt for the user.

See Also ACCEPT, WAIT

▸ The INSERT—SQL Command

Syntax

```
INSERT INTO <DBF name>
     [<fname1> [, <fname2> ...]]
     VALUES (<exp1> [, <exp2> [,...]])
INSERT INTO <DBF name>
     FROM ARRAY <array>
     FROM MEMVAR
```

▸▸ **NOTE**

There is also an obsolete Xbase INSERT command, with a different syntax, that works very slowly if you are adding data to a large table. It is included in Visual FoxPro for backward compatibility but should not be used. The work INSERT should always be followed immediately by INTO, so that the SQL command is used.

Usage This SQL (Structured Query Language) command lets you add to a specified table a record containing information from memory variables, from an array, or from values you type from the keyboard.

You must specify the name of the table and certain data values—<exp1>,<exp2> ...—that you want placed in the fields of the new record. These values must be in the same order as the fields of the table unless you specifically list the field names (<fname1>,<fname2> ...) in some different order.

You can direct Visual FoxPro to input data into the new record from an array of memory variables with the optional clause FROM ARRAY <array>. You can also input data into the new record from memory variables with the clause FROM MEMVAR.

See Also APPEND, EDIT, REPLACE

▶ The INT( ) Function

Syntax

```
INT(<expN>)
```

Usage This function returns the integer portion of the numeric expression that is specified, with its decimal portion removed.

See Also CEILING( ), FLOOR( ), ROUND( )

▶ The ISALPHA( ) Function

Syntax

```
ISALPHA(<expC>)
```

Usage This function returns .T. if the first character of the expression is a letter of the alphabet.

See Also ISBLANK( ), ISDIGIT( ), ISLOWER( ), ISNULL( ), ISUPPER( )

▶ The ISBLANK( ) Function

Syntax

```
ISBLANK(<expr>)
```

Usage This function returns .T. if the first character of the expression is blank.

For character fields, it returns .T. if the field has no value because it is newly appended or has been emptied using the BLANK command or if it has the empty string or spaces entered in it.

For numeric, currency, float, integer, or double fields, it returns .T. if the field has no value because it is newly appended or has been emptied using the BLANK command.

For date or datetime fields, it returns .T. if the field has no value because it is newly appended or has been emptied using the BLANK command or if it has a blank date { / / } or a blank datetime { / / : : }.

For memo or general fields, it returns true if the field is empty (with no text or OLE object in it).

See Also ISALPHA( ), ISDIGIT( ), ISLOWER( ), ISNULL( ), ISUPPER( )

▶ The ISDIGIT( ) Function

Syntax

```
ISDIGIT(<expC>)
```

Usage This function returns .T. if the first character of the expression is a digit (from 0 through 9).

See Also ISALPHA( ), ISBLANK( ), ISLOWER( ), ISNULL( ), ISUPPER( )

▶ The ISLOWER( ) Function

Syntax

```
ISLOWER(<expC>)
```

Usage This function returns .T. if the first character of the expression is a lowercase letter of the alphabet.

See Also ISALPHA( ), ISBLANK( ), ISDIGIT( ), ISNULL( ), ISUPPER( )

▶ The ISNULL( ) Function

Syntax

```
ISNULL(<expr>)
```

Usage This function returns .T. if the expression evaluates to the null value.

See Also ISALPHA( ), ISBLANK( ), ISDIGIT( ), ISLOWER( ), ISUPPER( )

▶ The ISUPPER() Function

Syntax

```
ISUPPER(<expC>)
```

Usage This function returns .T. if the first character of the expression is an uppercase letter of the alphabet.

See Also ISALPHA( ), ISBLANK( ), ISDIGIT( ), ISLOWER( ), ISNULL( ), ISUPPER( )

The LABEL Command

Syntax

```
LABEL FORM <file name 1> ¦ ?
     [ENVIRONMENT]
     [<scope>]
     [WHILE <expL1>]
     [FOR <expL2>]
     [NOCONSOLE]
     [PREVIEW]
     [SAMPLE]
     [TO PRINTER [PROMPT] ¦ TO FILE <file name 2>]
     [NOOPTIMIZE]
```

Usage This command produces mailing labels for the table that is open in the currently selected work area. If CONSOLE has not been SET OFF, the labels are displayed on the screen. They can also be sent to the printer or to a text file.

Before this command is used, the label form must have been created and saved in a file. The command CREATE LABEL lets you design these mailing label forms using the Label Designer window. The default extension for these files is LBX.

Options An existing form can be specified as <file name 1> of the command, or if the ? option is used, Visual FoxPro displays a scrollable list allowing you to choose among available label forms.

The ENVIRONMENT option may be used if the environment was saved when the label form was created. It automatically uses the same environment—including, for example, an index file to set the order in which labels are printed.

By default, labels are produced for all records in the table. A scope clause makes the command produce labels only for the records that fall in the specified scope. A FOR or WHILE clause makes the command produce labels only for the records that meet some logical criterion. See Chapter 11 for more discussion of how these clauses work.

The PREVIEW option sends a sample of your labels to the screen for your review, rather than printing them. To print the labels, issue another LABEL command without the PREVIEW option.

The optional word SAMPLE makes the command produce a single label as a sample so you can test the alignment of the labels in the printer. Visual FoxPro asks if you want another sample printed, so you can do repeated tests until the alignment is right.

The NOCONSOLE option prevents labels from being shown on the screen while they are being printed or sent to a file.

The TO PRINTER and TO FILE options let you send the labels to the printer or to the text file whose name is specified. If the PROMPT option is included, Visual FoxPro will display the Print dialog box before printing. This option must come immediately after the TO PRINTER option.

The NOOPTIMIZE option for this command disables the Rushmore technology, which normally speeds up data access when you use a FOR statement containing fields in existing indexes. You can disable Rushmore with the NOOPTIMIZE option in a number of Visual Fox-Pro commands, but in this case there is little reason to do so.

See Also CREATE LABEL, MODIFY LABEL

▸ The LEFT( ) Function

Syntax

```
LEFT(<expC>, <expN>)
```

Usage This function returns the number of characters specified from the beginning of the character expression. For example, LEFT("abcdefg", 3) would return `abc`.

See Also AT( ), ATLINE( ), ATCLINE( ), RAT( ),RATLINE( ), RIGHT( ), SUBSTR( )

▸ The LEN( ) Function

Syntax

```
LEN(<expC>)
```

Usage This function returns the length of the specified character expression. The expression may be a literal, a memory variable, the name of a Character field, or the name of a Memo field.

▸ The LESS THAN Operator

Syntax

```
<search_in exp> LESS THAN <search_for exp>
```

Usage This operator returns .T. if <search_in exp> (the expression being searched in) is less than <search_for exp>.

See Also !=, #, $, <, <=, <>, =, ==, >, >=, EXACTLY LIKE, GREATER THAN, GREATER THAN OR EQUAL TO, LESS THAN OR EQUAL TO, LIKE, NOT LIKE

The LESS THAN OR EQUAL TO Operator

Syntax

```
<search_in exp> LESS THAN OR EQUAL TO <search_for
        exp>
```

Usage This operator returns .T. if <search_in exp> (the expression being searched in) is less than or equal to <search_for exp>.

See Also !=, #, $, <, <=, <>, =, ==, >, >=, EXACTLY LIKE, GREATER THAN, GREATER THAN OR EQUAL TO, LESS THAN, LIKE, NOT LIKE

The LIKE Operator

Syntax

```
<search_in exp> LIKE <search_for exp>
```

Usage This operator returns .T. if <search_in exp> (the expression being searched in) is equal to <search_for exp>. For character expressions, there is a match if <search_in exp> begins with <search_for exp>, even if it also contains additional characters.

See Also !=, #, $, <, <=, <>, =, ==, >, >=, EXACTLY LIKE, GREATER THAN, GREATER THAN OR EQUAL TO, LESS THAN, LESS THAN OR EQUAL TO, NOT LIKE

The LIST Command

Syntax

```
LIST
    [<scope>]
    [FIELDS <field exp list>]
    [FOR <expL1>]
    [WHILE <expL2>]
    [OFF]
    [TO PRINTER [PROMPT] | TO FILE <file name>]
```

```
[NOCONSOLE]
[NOOPTIMIZE]
```

Usage This command displays the contents of all records in the current table on the screen. The LIST command is very similar to the DISPLAY command. The main difference is that DISPLAY pauses whenever the screen becomes full, while LIST scrolls information continuously on the screen.

Options If an optional scope clause is used, all the records included in the specified scope are displayed on the screen. If a FOR or WHILE clause is used, all the records included in the specified scope for which the logical expression following the FOR or WHILE is evaluated as true are displayed on the screen. If an optional FIELDS clause is used, only the fields (or field expressions) listed are displayed on the screen. For more information on how these clauses work, see Chapter 11.

If the optional OFF clause is used, the record number is not displayed.

The TO PRINTER and TO FILE options let you send the display to the printer or to a text file you specify. If the PROMPT option is included, Visual FoxPro will display the Print dialog box before printing. This option must come immediately after the TO PRINTER option.

The NOCONSOLE option prevents the command from displaying output on the screen, and should be used in combination with either the TO PRINTER or the TO FILE option.

The NOOPTIMIZE option for this command disables the Rushmore technology, which normally speeds up data access when you use a FOR statement containing fields in existing indexes. You can disable Rushmore with the NOOPTIMIZE option on a number of Visual FoxPro commands, but in this case there is little reason to do so.

See Also DISPLAY

▸ The LIST CONNECTIONS Command

Syntax

```
LIST CONNECTIONS
     [TO PRINTER [PROMPT] | TO FILE <file name>]
     [NOCONSOLE]
```

Usage This command displays the names, data sources, and connection strings of the named connections in the current database, displaying all the information without interruption. The DISPLAY CONNECTION command, which displays one window of information at a time, and prompts the user to press a key to continue, is better for viewing this information on the screen.

Options The TO PRINTER option sends the output of the command to the printer.

The PROMPT option displays the Print Dialog box before printing. This clause is available only when you use the TO PRINTER option, and it must be placed immediately after TO PRINTER.

The TO FILE <file name> option sends the output of the command to the file whose name you specify.

The NOCONSOLE option prevents the command from displaying output on the screen, and should be used in combination with either the TO PRINTER or the TO FILE option.

See Also CREATE CONNECTION, DELETE CONNECTION, MODIFY CONNECTION, DISPLAY CONNECTIONS

The LIST DATABASE Command

Syntax

```
LIST DATABASE
     [TO PRINTER [PROMPT] ¦ TO FILE <file name>]
     [NOCONSOLE]
```

Usage This command displays information about the current database without interruption. The DISPLAY DATABASE command, which displays one window of information at a time, and prompts the user to press a key to continue, is better for viewing this information on the screen.

Options The TO PRINTER option sends the output of the command to the printer.

The PROMPT option displays the Print dialog box before printing. This clause is available only when you use the TO PRINTER option, and it must be placed immediately after TO PRINTER.

The TO FILE <file name> option sends the output of the command to the file whose name you specify.

The NOCONSOLE option prevents the command from displaying output on the screen, and should be used in combination with either the TO PRINTER or the TO FILE option.

See Also CREATE DATABASE, DELETE DATABASE, DISPLAY DATABASE, MODIFY DATABASE, OPEN DATABASE, PACK DATABASE

▸ The LIST FILES Command

Syntax

```
LIST FILES
     [ON <drive | dir>]
     [LIKE <skeleton>]
     [TO PRINTER [PROMPT] | TO FILE <file name>]
```

Usage This command lists information about disk files.

Options The ON <drive | dir> option lets you specify the disk drive and directory whose files should be listed. If it is omitted, the default drive and directory are listed.

The LIKE <skeleton> option lets you specify which files are listed by using a file skeleton including the symbols **?**, which represents any character, and *, which represents any series of characters. For example, LIST FILES LIKE A*.* will include only files whose names begin with the letter *A* in the listing.

The TO PRINTER and TO FILE options let you send the display to the printer or to a text file you specify. If the PROMPT option is included, Visual FoxPro will display the Print dialog box before printing. This option must come immediately after the TO PRINTER option.

The NOCONSOLE option prevents the command from displaying output on the screen, and should be used in combination with either the TO PRINTER or the TO FILE option.

See Also DIR, DISPLAY FILES

▸ The LIST MEMORY Command

Syntax

```
LIST MEMORY
     [LIKE <skeleton>]
     [TO PRINTER [PROMPT] | TO FILE <file name>]
     [NOCONSOLE]
```

Usage This command lists information about memory variables and arrays.

Options The LIKE <skeleton> option lets you specify which memory variables and arrays are listed by using a skeleton including the symbols ?, which represents any character, and *, which represents any series of characters. For example, LIST MEMORY LIKE A* will include only memory variables and arrays whose names begin with the letter *A* in the listing.

The TO PRINTER and TO FILE options let you send the display to the printer or to a text file you specify. If the PROMPT option is included, Visual FoxPro will display the Print dialog box before printing. This option must come immediately after the TO PRINTER option.

The NOCONSOLE option prevents the command from displaying output on the screen, and should be used in combination with either the TO PRINTER or the TO FILE option.

See Also DISPLAY MEMORY

The LIST STATUS Command

Syntax

```
LIST STATUS
[TO PRINTER [PROMPT] ¦ TO FILE <file name>]
[NOCONSOLE]
```

Usage This command lists information about the Visual FoxPro environment.

Options The TO PRINTER and TO FILE options let you send the display to the printer or to a text file you specify. If the PROMPT option is included, Visual FoxPro will display the Print dialog box before printing. This option must come immediately after the TO PRINTER option.

The NOCONSOLE option prevents the command from displaying output on the screen, and should be used in combination with either the TO PRINTER or the TO FILE option.

See Also DISPLAY STATUS

The LIST STRUCTURE Command

Syntax

```
LIST STRUCTURE
     [TO PRINTER [PROMPT] ¦ TO FILE <file name>]
     [NOCONSOLE]
```

Usage This command lists the structure of the current table.

Options The TO PRINTER and TO FILE options let you send the display to the printer or to a text file you specify. If the PROMPT option is included, Visual FoxPro will display the Print dialog box before printing. This option must come immediately after the TO PRINTER option.

The NOCONSOLE option prevents the command from displaying output on the screen, and should be used in combination with either the TO PRINTER or the TO FILE option.

See Also DISPLAY STRUCTURE, MODIFY STRUCTURE

▸ The LIST TABLES Command

Syntax

```
LIST TABLES
     [TO PRINTER [PROMPT] ¦ TO FILE <file name>]
     [NOCONSOLE]
```

Usage This command displays information about tables in the current database without interruption. The DISPLAY TABLES command, which displays one window of information at a time, and prompts the user to press a key to continue, is better for viewing this information on the screen.

Options The TO PRINTER option sends the output of the command to the printer.

The PROMPT option displays the Print dialog box before printing. This clause is available only when you use the TO PRINTER option in Visual FoxPro for Windows, and it must be placed immediately after TO PRINTER.

The TO FILE <file name> option sends the output of the command to the file whose name you specify.

The NOCONSOLE option prevents the command from displaying output on the screen, and should be used in combination with either the TO PRINTER or the TO FILE option.

See Also ADD TABLE, ALTER TABLE, CLOSE, CREATE, CREATE TABLE, DISPLAY TABLES, FREE TABLE, MODIFY STRUCTURE, REMOVE TABLE, USE

▶ The LIST VIEWS Command

Syntax

```
LIST VIEWS
     [TO PRINTER [PROMPT] ¦ TO FILE <file name>]
     [NOCONSOLE]
```

Usage This command displays information about SQL views in the current database without interruption. The DISPLAY VIEWS command, which displays one window of information at a time, and prompts the user to press a key to continue, is better for viewing this information on the screen.

Options The TO PRINTER option sends the output of the command to the printer.

The PROMPT option displays the Print dialog box before printing. This clause is available only when you use the TO PRINTER option in Visual FoxPro for Windows, and it must be placed immediately after TO PRINTER.

The TO FILE <file name> option sends the output of the command to the file whose name you specify.

The NOCONSOLE option prevents the command from displaying output on the screen, and should be used in combination with either the TO PRINTER or the TO FILE option.

See Also CREATE SQL VIEW, DELETE VIEW, DISPLAY VIEWS, MODIFY VIEW

▶ The LOCATE Command

Syntax

```
LOCATE FOR <expL1>
     [<scope>]
     [WHILE <expL2>]
     [NOOPTIMIZE]
```

Usage This command searches the current table until it finds the first record in which the logical expression following FOR is evaluated as true. The logical expression can make use of any field of the table, and the table does not need to be indexed. If the file is indexed, Visual FoxPro will automatically use Rushmore technology to speed the search, if possible.

If LOCATE finds a matching record, it places the pointer on that record, and the FOUND( ) function returns a logical true (.T.). You can then continue the search with the command CONTINUE, which finds the next record for which the logical expression is true.

If LOCATE does not find a matching record, the record pointer is left at the end of the file, the FOUND( ) function remains false, and the function EOF( ) is made true.

Options If you add an optional Scope or WHILE clause, the search continues only until the end of the scope is reached or until the logical expression following WHILE is no longer true.

The NOOPTIMIZE option for this command disables the Rushmore technology, which normally speeds up data access when you use a FOR statement containing fields in existing indexes. You can disable Rushmore with the NOOPTIMIZE option on a number of Visual FoxPro commands, but in this case there is little reason to do so.

See Also CONTINUE, EOF( ), FIND, FOUND( ), SEEK

▸ The LOCK( ) Function

Syntax

```
LOCK([<work area num> ¦ <table alias>]
     ¦ [<record num list>, <work area num> ¦ <table
          alias>])
```

Usage This function attempts to lock a record or multiple records. It returns .T. if it succeeds in locking all records specified, and .F. if it fails.

Options By default, this function attempts to lock the current record in the table in the current work area.

If you use a numeric expression as the <work area num>, it attempts to lock the current record in the table open in the work area you specify. If you use a character expression as the <table alias>, it attempts to lock the current record in the table whose name or alias you specify.

If you use a <record num list> followed by either a <work area num> or a <table alias>, it attempts to lock all the records specified in the table specified.

See Also FLOCK( ), RLOCK, SET REPROCESS

The LOG( ) Function

Syntax

```
LOG(<expN>)
```

Usage This function returns the natural logarithm of the numeric expression that is specified.

See Also EXP( ), LOG10( )

The LOG10( ) Function

Syntax

```
LOG10(<expN>)
```

Usage This function returns the common logarithm of the numeric expression that is specified.

See Also LOG( )

The LOOP Command

Syntax

```
LOOP
```

Usage This command can be used only within a DO WHILE loop, a FOR loop, or a SCAN WHILE loop. It makes the program return directly to the beginning of the loop. If the condition there is true, it executes code in the loop again; if not, Visual FoxPro continues by executing the code that immediately follows ENDDO, ENDFOR or NEXT, or ENDSCAN.

See Also DO WHILE, FOR, SCAN

The LOWER( ) Function

Syntax

```
LOWER(<expC>)
```

Usage This function returns the specified character expression with all its letters converted to lowercase. It does not affect nonalphabetic characters.

See Also PROPER( ), UPPER( )

▸ The LTRIM( ) Function

Syntax

```
LTRIM(<expC>)
```

Usage This function returns the specified character expression with all leading blanks removed.

See Also ALLTRIM( ), RTRIM( ), TRIM( )

▸ The MAX( ) Function

Syntax

```
MAX(<expr1>, <expr2> [,<expr3> . . .])
```

Usage This function returns the expression in the list that has the largest value. All expressions must have the same data type.

See Also BETWEEN( ), MIN( )

▸ The MD ¦ MKDIR Command

Syntax

```
MD <path> ¦ MKDIR <path>
```

Usage This command creates a new directory. The <path> may be specified as a full path name of a directory, including drive designator. If it does not include a drive designator, the new directory is created as a child directory of the current directory.

See Also CD ¦ CHDIR, RD ¦ RMDIR

▸ The MENU( ) Function

Syntax

```
MENU()
```

Usage This function tells you the name of the current menu bar. This is particularly useful in programming, when a particular program must carry out different tasks depending on the user's choice on the active menu. The PAD( ) and MENU( ) functions serve to convey the user's choice and the name of the menu from which the choice was made. The default value of MENU( ) is a null string.

See Also DEFINE MENU, PAD( )

The MIN( ) Function

Syntax

```
MIN(<expr1>, <expr2> [,<expr3> . . .])
```

Usage This function returns the expression in the list that has the smallest value. All expressions must have the same data type.

See Also BETWEEN( ), MAX( )

The MINUTE( ) Function

Syntax

```
MINUTE(<expT>
```

Usage This function returns the minute portion from the specified time expression.

See Also HOUR( ), SEC( )

The MOD( ) Function

Syntax

```
MOD(<expN1> <expN2>)
```

Usage This function divides the first expression by the second and returns the remainder.

See Also

The MODIFY COMMAND Command

Syntax

```
MODIFY COMMAND [<file name>]
      [NOEDIT]
      [NOWAIT]
      [RANGE <expN1>,<expN2>]
      [[WINDOW <window name1>]
      [IN [WINDOW] <window name2> ¦ IN SCREEN]]
      [SAVE]
      [SAME]
```

Usage This command opens an editing window to let you create a new program file or edit an existing one.

A program file is a plain ASCII text file. When MODIFY COMMAND is used, the text editor has the default preferences that are most convenient for creating program files; for example, automatic indenting is turned on and word wrap is turned off.

Options If you specify a file name, and a file of that name exists, Visual FoxPro displays the file in an editing window, assuming a PRG extension if you do not specify an extension. If you specify a file name, and a file of that does not exist (again, assuming a PRG extension if you do not specify one), Visual FoxPro displays an editing window for a new file of that name.

If you do not specify a file name, Visual FoxPro displays a file with a name such as Program1, which you can name by choosing File ¦ Save.

The NOEDIT option lets you view but not edit text that is displayed.

The NOWAIT option allows a program to continue running when MODIFY COMMAND is used within it. If this option is not included, the program waits for the user to close the Edit window before continuing.

The RANGE option lets you select a particular range of the memo when the editing window is opened; the range starts at the character position specified by <expN1> and continues until the character position specified by <expN2>.

The WINDOW <window name1> option lets you give the editing window the characteristics of another previously defined window you specify. The IN WINDOW <window name2> option lets you open the editing window within another window you indicate, although the editing window will not necessarily have the characteristics of this other window unless you also specify the WINDOW option. IN SCREEN opens the window in the Visual FoxPro main window and is the default.

The SAVE option lets you keep the editing window on the screen for future reference after you leave it.

The SAME option prevents the editing window from coming forward as the active window if a program, text, or Memo Editing window is already open.

See Also * ¦ NOTE ¦ &&, DO, MODIFY FILE

▶ The MODIFY CONNECTION Command

Syntax

```
MODIFY CONNECTION [<connection name> ¦ ?]
```

Usage This command lets you use the Connection Designer to modify a named connection.

Options The <connection name> option lets you specify the name of the connection you want to modify.

The ? option lets you use the Open dialog box to select the connection you want to modify.

See Also CREATE CONNECTION, DELETE CONNECTION, DISPLAY CONNECTIONS, LIST CONNECTIONS

The MODIFY DATABASE Command

Syntax

```
MODIFY DATABASE
      [NOWAIT]
```

Usage This command opens the Database Designer to let you modify the current database.

Options The NOWAIT option is used only in programming. With this option, the program continues after the Database Designer is opened. If this option is omitted, the program waits for the user to close the Database Designer before continuing.

See Also CREATE DATABASE, DELETE DATABASE, DISPLAY DATABASE, LIST DATABASE, OPEN DATABASE, PACK DATABASE

The MODIFY FILE Command

Syntax

```
MODIFY FILE [<file name>]
      [NOEDIT]
      [NOWAIT]
      [RANGE <expN1>,<expN2>]
      [[WINDOW <window name1>]
      [IN [WINDOW] <window name2> ¦ IN SCREEN]]
      [SAVE]
      [SAME]
```

Usage This command opens an editing window to let you create a new text file or modify an existing one. The text editor has the default preferences that are most convenient for creating text files; for example, automatic indenting is turned off and word wrap is turned on.

Options If you specify a file name, and a file of that name exists, Visual FoxPro displays the file in an editing window. If you specify a file name, and a file of that does not exist, Visual FoxPro displays an editing window for a new file of that name. If you do not specify a file name, Visual FoxPro displays a file with a name such as File1, which you can name by choosing File ➤ Save.

The NOEDIT option lets you view but not edit text that is called up.

The NOWAIT option allows a program to continue running when MODIFY FILE is used within it. If this option is not included, the program waits for the user to close the Edit window before continuing.

The RANGE option lets you select a particular range of the memo when the editing window is opened; the range starts at the character position specified by <expN1> and continues until the position specified by <expN2>.

The WINDOW <window name1> option lets you give the editing window the characteristics of another previously defined window you specify. The IN WINDOW <window name2> option lets you open the editing window within another window you indicate, although the editing window will not necessarily have the characteristics of this other window unless you also specify the WINDOW option. IN SCREEN opens the window in the Visual FoxPro main window and is the default.

The SAVE option lets you keep the editing window on the screen for future reference after you leave it.

The SAME option prevents the editing window from coming forward as the active window if a program, text, or Memo Editing window is already open.

See Also * ¦ NOTE ¦ &&, DO

▸ The MODIFY GENERAL Command

Syntax

```
MODIFY GENERAL <general field1> [,<general field2>
      ...]
     [NOMODIFY]
     [NOWAIT]
```

```
[WINDOW <window name 1>]
[IN WINDOW <window name 2> ¦ IN SCREEN
```

Usage This command allows you to add an object from another program to a General Field of a Visual FoxPro table. It opens an editing window for a General field in the current record of the table that is open in the current work area; you can then insert, modify, or delete objects, using object linking and embedding (OLE).

Options The NOMODIFY option lets you view the OLE object and copy it to the Clipboard but not to modify it.

The NOWAIT option allows a program to continue running when MODIFY GENERAL is used within it. If this option is omitted, the program waits until the user closes the General field window before continuing.

The WINDOW <window name1> option lets you give the General field the characteristics of another previously defined window you specify.

The IN WINDOW <window name2> option lets you open the editing window within another window whose name you indicate, although the editing window will not necessarily have the characteristics of this other window unless you also specify the WINDOW option.

The IN SCREEN option opens the window in the Visual FoxPro main window and is the default.

See Also APPEND GENERAL

The MODIFY LABEL Command

Syntax

```
MODIFY LABEL [<file name> ¦ ?]
     [[WINDOW <window name1>]
     [IN [WINDOW] <window name2> ¦ IN SCREEN]]
     [NOENVIRONMENT]
     [NOWAIT]
     [SAVE]
```

Usage This command lets you modify an existing label form or create a new one.

Options The <file name> option lets you specify the name of a form you want to modify. If the file exists, Visual FoxPro lets you modify it; if it does not exist, Visual FoxPro creates a new file with that name.

The ? option displays a dialog box that lets you select it from a scrollable list of existing label files.

The WINDOW option allows you to give the Label Designer window the characteristics of another window you specify.

The IN WINDOW option allows you to open the Label Designer window within a parent window you specify, although it will not necessarily have the characteristics of the parent window unless you also use a WINDOW clause. The default is IN SCREEN.

The NOENVIRONMENT option prevents MODIFY LABEL from automatically restoring the Visual FoxPro environment that was saved with the original label definition file.

The NOWAIT option allows any program containing a MODIFY LABEL command to keep running while the Label Designer window is open.

The SAVE option keeps the Label Designer window on the screen after you exit the window.

See Also CREATE LABEL, LABEL

▸ The MODIFY MEMO Command

Syntax

```
MODIFY MEMO <memo field1> [,<memo field2> ...]
     [NOEDIT]
     [NOMENU]
     [NOWAIT]
     [RANGE <expN1>,<expN2>]
     [[WINDOW <window name1>]
     [IN [WINDOW] <window name2> ¦ SCREEN]]
     [SAME]
     [SAVE]
```

Usage This command opens a Memo window to let you edit the Memo field of the current record of the table that is open in the current work area. If a record has more than one Memo field, you can specify the particular Memo field(s) to open. All Memo fields that are displayed at once must be from the same record.

Options The NOEDIT option allows you to view the text of the Memo field without being able to change it.

The NOMENU option removes the text menu from the menu bar, so the user cannot change font or other features of the typeface.

The RANGE option lets you select a particular range of the memo when the Memo Editing window is opened; the range starts at the character position specified by <expN1> and continues until it reaches the position specified by <expN2>.

The WINDOW option allows you to give the Memo Editing window the characteristics of another window you specify.

The IN WINDOW option allows you to open the Memo Editing window within a parent window you specify, although it will not necessarily have the characteristics of the parent window unless you also use a WINDOW clause. The default is IN SCREEN.

By default, when MODIFY MEMO is used in a program, the Memo window is opened and the program does not continue until the user closes the Memo window. The NOWAIT option continues running the program without waiting for the user to close the Memo window.

The SAME option displays the Memo Editing window but does not let the user make it the active window.

The SAVE option leaves the Memo Editing window on the screen after you have exited it and activated another window. This option only applies to programs, and it has no effect when it is used in the Command window.

See Also CLOSE

▶ The MODIFY MENU Command

Syntax

```
MODIFY MENU [<menu name> ¦ ?]
     [WINDOW <window name1>]
     [IN [WINDOW] <window name2> ¦ IN SCREEN]
     [NOWAIT]
     [SAVE]
```

Usage Like CREATE MENU, this command activates Visual FoxPro's menu builder utility, which you can use to create menus to go with programs you create. This interactive utility lets you define a menu system without typing a long list of individual commands such as DEFINE MENU, DEFINE PAD, DEFINE POPUP, DEFINE BAR, ON PAD, and ON SELECTION.

Options If you specify a <menu name>, the menu builder creates a menu table with that name, followed by the MNX extension. If you use the ? option, Visual FoxPro presents you with a dialog box listing existing menu file names.

The WINDOW option gives the Menu Designer window the characteristics of another window you specify.

The IN WINDOW option opens the Menu Designer window within another specified window, but it will not necessarily take on the characteristics of the parent window unless you also use the WINDOW option. The default IN SCREEN option displays the Menu Designer window on the screen.

The NOWAIT option allows programs to keep running after the Menu Designer window is opened.

The SAVE option keeps the Menu Designer window open if the user activates another window. This option only applies to programs, and it has no effect when it is used in the Command window.

See Also ACTIVATE MENU, CREATE MENU, DEFINE MENU

► The MODIFY PROJECT Command

Syntax

```
MODIFY PROJECT [<file name> | ?]
     [WINDOW <window name1>]
     [IN [WINDOW] <window name2> | IN SCREEN]
     [NOWAIT]
     [SAVE]
```

Usage This command opens the Project Manager window to let you modify a project or create a new one; a project allows you to keep track of all the files in an application and to compile them into a single APP or EXE file.

To modify an existing project, specify its name or use the ? option to display the Open File dialog box and choose one.

Options The WINDOW <window name1> option gives the Project Manager window the features of the window specified.

The IN [WINDOW] <window name2> option opens the Project Manager window in the window specified.

The IN SCREEN option explicitly opens the Project Manager window in the screen rather than in another window. The Project Manager window is also opened in the screen by default.

The NOWAIT option can be used in programs to allow program execution to continue without pausing for the Project Manager window to be closed. If it is not used, the program waits for the user to close the Project Manager window before continuing.

The SAVE option can be used in programs to keep the Project Manager window open after another window becomes active.

Neither of these last two options has any effect if it is used from the Command window.

▶ The MODIFY QUERY Command

Syntax

```
MODIFY QUERY [<file name> ¦ ?]
     [IN SCREEN]
     [NOWAIT]
     [AS <code page>]
```

Usage This command opens the Query Designer window, which lets you interactively modify an existing SQL (Structured Query Language) query or create a new one. SQL queries are a flexible, powerful way to retrieve information from tables. A single SQL query can take the place of many other individual Visual FoxPro commands.

A previous query command exists as a Visual FoxPro program file with a QPR extension. A query can be run again by entering DO plus the name of the program and the QPR extension. To modify an existing query, just enter MODIFY QUERY <file name>; you do not have to include the extension.

Options The ? option after MODIFY QUERY displays a list of existing query files from which you can choose.

The IN SCREEN option explicitly opens the Project Manager window in the Visual FoxPro main window.

The NOWAIT option allows any program containing a MODIFY QUERY command to keep running while the Query Designer window is open. If this option is not included, the program waits until the user closes the window before continuing.

The AS <code page> option lets you specify the code page of the new file created by this command.

See Also CREATE QUERY, SELECT—SQL, CREATE VIEW, MODIFY VIEW

▶ The MODIFY REPORT Command

Syntax

```
MODIFY REPORT [<file name> ¦ ?]
      [[WINDOW <window name1>]
      [IN [WINDOW] <window name2> ¦ SCREEN]]
      [NOENVIRONMENT]
      [NOWAIT]
      [SAVE]
```

Usage This command lets you modify an existing report form. You can specify its name or use the ? option to display a dialog box that lets you select it from a scrollable list of existing report files.

Options You can use the WINDOW option to give the Report Designer window the characteristics of another window you specify. Likewise, you can use the IN WINDOW option to open the Report Designer window within another specified window, although this layout window will not necessarily take on the characteristics of the parent window unless you also use the WINDOW option. The default IN SCREEN option displays the Report Designer window on the screen.

The NOENVIRONMENT option prevents MODIFY REPORT from automatically restoring the Visual FoxPro environment that was saved with the original report definition file.

The NOWAIT option allows any program containing a MODIFY REPORT command to keep running while the Report Designer window is open.

The SAVE option keeps the Report Designer window on the screen after you exit the window.

See Also CREATE REPORT

▶ The MODIFY SCREEN Command

Syntax

```
MODIFY SCREEN [ <file name> ¦ ? ]
```

```
[WINDOW <window name1> ]
[IN [WINDOW] <window name2> ¦ IN SCREEN]
[NOENVIRONMENT]
[NOWAIT]
[SAVE]
```

Usage This command lets you change an existing screen file. You can specify the file name or use the ? option to display a dialog box that lets you select the desired screen from a scrollable list of existing screen files.

Options The WINDOW option gives the Screen Designer window the attributes of <window name1>.

The IN WINDOW option allows you to open the Screen Designer window inside <window name2> but does not give it the attributes of <window name2> unless you also use the WINDOW option. The default is IN SCREEN.

The NOENVIRONMENT option prevents the environment of the screen file—open tables, index files, and table relationships that may have been saved along with the screen file—from being restored when you modify the screen file.

The NOWAIT option is available only when the MODIFY SCREEN command is used within a program. It continues program execution while the Screen Designer window is open.

The SAVE option preserves the Screen Designer window on the screen after you finish MODIFY SCREEN.

See Also CREATE SCREEN

The MODIFY STRUCTURE Command

Syntax

```
MODIFY STRUCTURE
```

Usage This command lets you modify the structure of the table that is open in the currently selected work area. It displays the Structure dialog box, which specifies the current structure of the table. You can change the structure of the table by adding, deleting, or changing the length of fields.

Because this can lead to a loss of data, Visual FoxPro automatically backs up a table when you modify its structure. The backup for the

DBF file has the same name and the extension BAK. The backup for the memo file has the same name and the extension TBK.

See Also ALTER TABLE, CREATE, CREATE TABLE

The MODIFY VIEW Command

Syntax

```
MODIFY VIEW <name>
     [REMOTE]
```

Usage This command displays the View Designer, so you can modify the SQL view whose name is specified. The database that contains this view must be open when you use this command.

Options You must use the REMOTE option to modify a view that includes remote tables.

See Also CREATE SQL VIEW, DELETE VIEW, DISPLAY VIEWS, LIST VIEWS

The MODIFY WINDOW Command

Syntax

```
MODIFY WINDOW <window name> ¦ SCREEN
     FROM <row1>,<column1> TO <row2>,<column2>
     ¦ AT <row3>,<column3> SIZE <row4>,<column4>
     [FONT <expC1> [,<expN1>]] [STYLE <expC2>]
     [TITLE <expC3>]
     [HALFHEIGHT]
     [DOUBLE ¦ PANEL ¦ NONE ¦ SYSTEM]
     [CLOSE ¦ NOCLOSE]
     [FLOAT ¦ NOFLOAT]
     [GROW ¦ NOGROW]
     [MINIMIZE ¦ NOMINIMIZE]
     [SHADOW ¦ NOSHADOW]
     [ZOOM ¦ NOZOOM]
     [ICON FILE <file name 1>]
     [FILL FILE <file name 2>]
     [COLOR SCHEME <expN2> ¦ COLOR <color pair list>
```

Usage This command allows you to modify a screen window that you have previously defined with DEFINE WINDOW.

You can change the upper-left and lower-right corners of the window by changing FROM and TO coordinates. Likewise, you can use an AT clause to specify a new upper-left corner location for the window. If AT is used in conjunction with the SIZE option, Visual FoxPro adjusts the size of the window to accommodate the font and amount of text in the window.

After a window has been modified, you can activate it for use with ACTIVATE WINDOW <window name list>, or you can display it without letting it be used with SHOW WINDOW <window name list>. The command HIDE WINDOW <window name list> lets you stop displaying one or more windows without deactivating them, while DEACTIVATE WINDOW <window name list> lets you deactivate them. SAVE WINDOW lets you save your window definitions to a disk file or a Memo field. Finally, you can clear windows from the screen and from memory by means of the command CLEAR WINDOWS or RELEASE WINDOWS <window name list>.

Options The SCREEN option lets you modify the main Visual FoxPro window. To change this window back to its original form, simply type MODIFY WINDOW SCREEN.

The FONT <expC> [,<expN] [STYLE <expC> option lets you specify the typeface, size, and style of the font used. <expC> and <expN> should be the name and size of an available font; if the font you specify is not available, Visual FoxPro tries to substitute a similar font. If you omit the FONT clause, the main Visual FoxPro window font is used, and if you include the clause but omit the size option, a 10-point font is used. The STYLE clause may be followed by one of the following codes:

- B: boldface
- I: italic
- N: normal
- O: outline
- Q: opaque
- S: shadow
- -: strikeout

- T: transparent
- U: underline

If this clause is omitted, normal style will be used.

The TITLE option lets you modify any title you may have placed at the top of the window.

The HALFHEIGHT option lets you create windows with half-height title bars. This is used to make the title bars in Visual FoxPro for Windows the same size as title bars in FoxPro for DOS.

The DOUBLE ¦ PANEL ¦ NONE ¦ SYSTEM ¦ <border string> options let you define the border around the window with a double line, a wide solid panel, no line, or the window border currently used by the system. The default is a single line. You can customize your windows with the <border string> option.

The CLOSE option makes it possible for a user to remove the window from memory later on by using the File menu. The default option is NOCLOSE, which requires an activated window to be closed by means of a DEACTIVATE WINDOW, CLEAR WINDOWS, HIDE WINDOW, or RELEASE WINDOWS command.

The FLOAT option allows later users to move a window to other locations on the screen by using the File menu, pressing Ctrl+F7, or clicking the mouse on the window's top border and moving the window while holding down the mouse button. The default is NOFLOAT, which does not allow windows to be moved.

The GROW option allows later users to change the size of a window by using the Window menu, pressing Ctrl+F8, or clicking the mouse on the window's lower-right corner and adjusting the size while holding down the mouse button. The default is NOGROW, which does not allow the window's size to be adjusted.

The MINIMIZE option lets the user reduce a window to an icon. The default NOMINIMIZE option prevents the user from doing this.

The SHADOW option displays the window with a shadow behind it. NOSHADOW is the default.

The ZOOM option lets you maximize a window to cover the entire Visual FoxPro main window (or a document window) and restore it to its original size.

The ICON FILE option lets you specify the icon displayed when the window is minimized.

The FILL FILE option allows you to select a "wallpaper" as a background for the window by specifying the name of a BMP file.

The COLOR option allows you to specify the color attributes of the Browse window. You can do this by means of a color pair list (for example, COLOR 'B/R'), or a COLOR SCHEME (a number between 1 and 24 that lets you choose any of 24 preset color schemes) clause.

See Also ACTIVATE WINDOW, CLEAR WINDOWS, DEACTIVATE WINDOW, DEFINE WINDOW, HIDE WINDOW, RELEASE WINDOWS, SAVE WINDOW, SHOW WINDOW

The MONTH( ) Function

Syntax

```
MONTH(<expD> ¦ <expT>)
```

Usage This function returns the month of the date from the date or datetime expression in numeric form. For example, **MONTH({01/01/94})** returns 1.

See Also CMONTH( )

The MOVE POPUP Command

Syntax

```
MOVE POPUP <popup name>
TO <row>,<col> ¦ BY <expN1>,<expN2>
```

Usage This command lets you move a menu popup that you previously created with the DEFINE POPUP command to a new location on the screen or within a window. You can either specify the new row and column address or tell Visual FoxPro to move the popup menu by a certain number of rows or columns in any direction.

See Also ACTIVATE POPUP, DEFINE POPUP

The MOVE WINDOW Command

Syntax

```
MOVE WINDOW <window name>
     TO <row>,<col> ¦ BY <expN1>,<expN2> ¦ CENTER
```

Usage This command lets you move a window to a new location on the screen or within another window. You can either specify the new row and column address or tell Visual FoxPro to move the window by a certain amount in any direction. You must have first defined the window with a DEFINE WINDOW command.

Options The CENTER option lets you center the window within the main Visual FoxPro window or its parent window.

See Also ACTIVATE WINDOW, DEFINE WINDOW

▸ The MTON Function

Syntax

```
MTON(<curr exp>)
```

Usage This function returns a currency expression in the numeric data type.

See Also NTOM( )

▸ The NOT LIKE Operator

Syntax

```
<search_in exp> NOT LIKE <search_for exp>
```

Usage This operator returns .T. if <search_in exp> (the expression being searched in) is not equal to <search_for exp>.

See Also !=, #, $, <, <=, <>, =, ==, >, >=, EXACTLY LIKE, GREATER THAN, GREATER THAN OR EQUAL TO, LESS THAN, LESS THAN OR EQUAL TO, LIKE

▸ The NOTE Command

Syntax

```
NOTE | *
      <text>
```

Usage This command allows you to place comments in a program file to help others understand what the program is doing by looking at the program code. NOTE or * may be used at the beginning of a line to tell Visual FoxPro that everything on that line is a note and should be ignored when the program runs.

See Also *, &&

The NTOM Function

Syntax

```
NTOM(<expN>)
```

Usage This function returns a numeric expression in the currency data type.

See Also MTON()

The OCCURS( ) Function

Syntax

```
OCCURS(<expC1>, <expC2>)
```

Usage This function returns the number of times that the first character expression occurs within the second character expression.

See Also $

The ON BAR Command

Syntax

```
ON BAR <expN> of <popup name1>
     [ACTIVATE POPUP <popup name2>
     | ACTIVATE MENU <menu name>]
```

Usage This command, used in programming, activates another menu whenever the user chooses a particular bar on a menu popup. By using this command you can create a nested series of menu popups within your program.

ON BAR is very similar to the ON SELECTION BAR command; however, the former is used to present additional menus to the user, while the latter is used to run programs or procedures based on the user's choice.

See Also CREATE MENU, DEFINE BAR, DEFINE POPUP, ON SELECTION BAR

► The ON PAD Command

Syntax

```
ON PAD <pad name> of <menu name1>
     [ACTIVATE POPUP <popup name>
     ¦ ACTIVATE MENU <menu name2>]
```

Usage This command, used in programming, activates another menu whenever the user chooses a particular pad on a previous menu. By using this command you can create a nested series of menus within your program.

ON PAD is very similar to the ON SELECTION PAD command; however, the former is used to present additional menus to the user, while the latter is used to run programs or procedures based on the user's choice.

See Also CREATE MENU, DEFINE MENU, DEFINE PAD, ON SELECTION PAD

► The ON SELECTION BAR Command

Syntax

```
ON SELECTION BAR <expN> OF <popup name> [<command>]
```

Usage This command, used in programming, carries out a particular command (for example, a DO command to run another program) if the user chooses a specified bar from your popup.

See Also DEFINE BAR, DEFINE MENU, DEFINE PAD, DEFINE POPUP, ON BAR, ON PAD, ON SELECTION MENU, ON SELECTION PAD, ON SELECTION POPUP

► The ON SELECTION MENU Command

Syntax

```
ON SELECTION MENU <menu name> ¦ ALL [<command>]
```

Usage This command, used in programming, executes the specified command if the user chooses any option from the designated menu bar. For example, this command might be used to run another program or procedure, which will then perform different functions based on the values of BAR( ) or PAD( ) that are passed along to it to convey the user's choice.

See Also DEFINE BAR, DEFINE MENU, DEFINE PAD, DEFINE POPUP, ON BAR, ON PAD, ON SELECTION BAR, ON SELECTION PAD, ON SELECTION POPUP

▶ The ON SELECTION PAD Command

Syntax

```
ON SELECTION PAD <pad name> OF <menu name> [<command>]
```

Usage This command, used in programming, carries out the specified command if the user chooses a particular pad from a menu bar you have created.

See Also DEFINE BAR, DEFINE MENU, DEFINE PAD, DEFINE POPUP, ON BAR, ON PAD, ON SELECTION BAR, ON SELECTION MENU, ON SELECTION POPUP

▶ The ON SELECTION POPUP Command

Syntax

```
ON SELECTION POPUP <popup name> ¦ ALL [<command>]
```

Usage This command, used in programming, executes the specified command if the user chooses any option from the designated popup. For example, this command might be used to run another program or procedure, which will then perform different functions based on the values of PAD( ) that are passed along to it to convey the user's choice.

See Also DEFINE BAR, DEFINE MENU, DEFINE PAD, DEFINE POPUP, ON BAR, ON PAD, ON SELECTION BAR, ON SELECTION MENU, ON SELECTION PAD, PAD( )

▶ The OPEN DATABASE Command

Syntax

```
OPEN DATABASE
    [<file name> ¦ ?]
    [EXCLUSIVE ¦ SHARED]
    [NOUPDATE]
    [VALIDATE]
```

Usage This command opens a database, making it the current database.

Options The <file name> option lets you specify the name of the database to be opened.

The ? option lets you use the Open dialog box to select the database to be opened.

The EXCLUSIVE option opens the database in exclusive mode, so other users cannot access or open it.

The SHARED option opens the database in shared mode, so other users can access it.

The NOUPDATE option opens the database in read-only mode, so that it cannot be modified. This clause affects only the database, not the tables in it.

The VALIDATE option makes Visual FoxPro check to see that all the database's tables, index tags, and fields referenced in index tags exist.

See Also CREATE DATABASE, DELETE DATABASE, DISPLAY DATABASE, LIST DATABASE, MODIFY DATABASE, PACK DATABASE

▸ The PACK Command

Syntax

```
PACK
        [MEMO] [DBF]
```

Usage This command permanently removes all records marked as deleted from the currently selected table and reduces the size of Memo fields associated with the table.

Use this command with caution! Data will be permanently removed from the file.

If index files are in use when you pack a table, those indexes will be automatically rebuilt. If you pack a file without updating an index, that index will no longer work properly.

Options The MEMO option reduces the size of Memo fields without packing the table itself.

Likewise, the DBF option packs the table without touching the Memo fields.

See Also DELETE, RECALL, ZAP

The PACK DATABASE Command

Syntax

```
PACK DATABASE
```

Usage This command removes records that are marked for deletion in the table used to store the database. It does not pack the tables in the database, but permanently removes references in the database to tables that have been removed from it.

See Also CREATE DATABASE, DELETE DATABASE, DISPLAY DATABASE, LIST DATABASE, MODIFY DATABASE, OPEN DATABASE

The PAD( ) Function

Syntax

```
PAD()
```

Usage This function contains the name of the last option chosen on a menu bar. It is particularly useful when a program must carry out different functions depending on the user's choice on a previous menu.

See Also DEFINE MENU, DEFINE PAD, ON PAD, ON SELECTION

The _PAGENO System Variable

Syntax

```
_PAGENO
```

Usage This system variable specifies the current page number and is automatically incremented to number pages sequentially.

The PARAMETERS Command

Syntax

```
PARAMETERS <parameter list>
```

Usage This command lets a program or procedure receive the values of variables from the command line or from a calling program.

It must be the first line of code (excluding comments) in the program or procedure where it is used. The parameter list is a list of memory variables separated by commas. These memory variables can be assigned values by using a DO WITH <parameter list> command that was used to call the program or procedure or, if they are in a user-defined function, by putting the parameter list in the parentheses following the command that calls it. In either case, the expressions in the parameter list of the calling command or function are assigned to the variables in the parameter list following the command PARAMETERS. If there are more memory variables in the list of the PARAMETERS command than in the list of the DO WITH command, extras are initialized with the value of .F.

See Also DO

► The Payment( ) Function

Syntax

```
PAYMENT(expN1, expN2, expN3)
```

Usage This function returns the amount of the periodic payment needed to pay off a loan in a fixed amount of time. It assumes that the interest rate remains constant and that the payment is made at the end of each period. expN1 represents the amount of the principal of the loan, expN2 represents the interest rate, and expN3 represents the number of periods in which the loan must be paid off.

► The PCOL( ) Function

Syntax

```
PCOL()
```

Usage This function returns the current column position of the printer's print head relative to the left margin. This function can be used in combination with SET DEVICE and @ … SAY … GET to direct printer output to a position that is expressed as an offset from the current column position of the print head.

See Also @ … SAY … GET, COL( ), PROW( ), ROW( ), SCOLS( ), SET DEVICE, SROWS( ), WCOLS( ), WROWS( )

► The PI( ) Function

Syntax

```
PI()
```

Usage This function returns the constant Pi (3.1416), the ratio of the diameter to the circumference of a circle.

See Also SET DECIMALS

▶ The PLAY MACRO Command

Syntax

```
PLAY MACRO <macro name>
     [TIME <expN>]
```

Usage This command lets you play back the keystrokes that were saved in the macro whose name is specified. If it is used in a program, the macro is not played back until there is an opportunity to use the keystrokes as input. If more than one PLAY MACRO command has been used in a program without there being an opportunity for input, so that several are waiting to execute, they are used in reverse order; the last command that was issued is the first macro that is played.

Options The TIME option lets you specify a time delay (between 0 and 10 seconds) between the replay of each keystroke from a keyboard macro.

See Also CLEAR MACROS, RESTORE MACROS, SAVE MACROS

▶ The POPUP( ) Function

Syntax

```
POPUP()
```

Usage This function tells you the name of the current popup. This is useful when a program must carry out different functions depending on the user's choice on a previous menu bar or popup. Both the choice and the popup name are often passed along to subsequent programs using BAR( ) and POPUP( ). The default value of POPUP( ) is a null string.

See Also BAR( ), DEFINE BAR, DEFINE POPUP, ON BAR, ON SELECTION

▶ The PRIMARY( ) Function

Syntax

```
PRIMARY([<index number>]
     [, <work area num> ¦ <table alias>
```

Usage This function returns .T. if the index tag specified is a primary index. By default, it applies to the index currently used as the controlling index.

Options Use the <index number> argument to specify the index, with all open indexes numbered as follows. All single-file indexes are numbered first, in the order that they were opened. All tags in the structural compound index file are numbered next, in the order in which they were created. All tags in open independent compound index files are numbered next, in the order in which the files were opened, and in the order in which the tags were created within each file.

If you specify a number larger than all open indexes, the function returns the empty string.

The <work area num> option specifies the number of the work area in which the table is open; and the <table alias> option specifies the name or alias of the table. If neither option is used, the function applies to the current table.

See Also ALTER TABLE, CANDIDATE, CREATE TABLE, INDEX

▸ The PRIVATE Command

Syntax

```
PRIVATE <memvar list>
      ¦ ALL [LIKE <skeleton> ¦ EXCEPT <skeleton>]
```

Usage This command allows you to create memory variables that are accessible only to the program or procedure where they are defined, so more than one program or procedure can have memory variables of the same name. PRIVATE can be used only in programs and has no effect if used from the Command window.

If a memory variable is defined as PRIVATE, any memory variables from other programs or procedures that have the same name are temporarily hidden while the program or procedure where they are defined is executed; after it is done, they become active again.

You can use PRIVATE with a list of all the memory variables that you want to be private or use ALL to make all memory variables private. If ALL is followed by LIKE <skeleton>, all variables that match the skeleton will be private. If ALL is followed by EXCEPT <skeleton>, all variables that do not match the skeleton will be private. Skeletons may be created using literals and the wildcard characters, ? and *.

See Also PUBLIC

▶ The PROCEDURE Command

Syntax

```
PROCEDURE <name>
```

Usage This command is used within a program or a procedure file to mark the beginning of a procedure or a user-defined function. If it is in a program file, the program may call it by using the DO command followed by its name. If it is in a procedure file, you may call it by using the DO command from a program or from the Command window by using the SET PROCEDURE command before using the DO command or by using the IN <file name> option of the DO command. It can receive parameters from the DO command that calls it; for more information, see PARAMETERS.

After all the code in a procedure is executed, control returns to the line following the line that called it (or to the Command window). Alternately, control can be returned to that point by using the command RETURN. A user-defined function must use RETURN followed by an expression to return a value.

The command PROCEDURE is identical to the command FUNCTION, but stylistically it is best to use FUNCTION for user-defined functions and PROCEDURE for procedures that do not explicitly return a value. A program file may contain up to 1170 procedures and functions.

See Also DO, FUNCTION

▶ The PROPER( ) Function

Syntax

```
PROPER(<expC>)
```

Usage This function returns the specified character expression with the initial letter of each word converted to uppercase and the other letters converted to lowercase. It does not affect nonalphabetic characters.

See Also LOWER( ), UPPER( )

▶ The PROW( ) Function

Syntax

```
PROW()
```

Usage This function returns the current row position of the printer's print head relative to the top margin. This function can be used in combination with SET DEVICE and @ ... SAY ... GET to direct printer output to a position that is expressed as an offset from the current row position of the print head.

See Also @ ... SAY ... GET, COL( ), PCOL( ), ROW( ), SCOLS( ), SROWS( ),WCOLS( ), WROWS( )

▸ The PUBLIC Command

Syntax

```
PUBLIC [ARRAY] <memvar list>
```

Usage This command lets memory variables be used by any program or procedure. This sort of variable is called a global variable.

A memory variable must be declared as PUBLIC before it is assigned a value. When it is first created by the PUBLIC command itself, the variable is assigned the temporary value of .F.

See Also PRIVATE

▸ The QUIT Command

Syntax

```
QUIT
```

Usage This command terminates Visual FoxPro and returns the user to the operating system. It can be used in programs as well as from the Command window. To avoid possible loss of data, always use this command before turning off the computer.

▸ The RAT( ) Function

Syntax

```
RAT(<search_for exp>, <search_in exp>)
        [, <occurrence>]
```

Usage This function returns the position of a character expression within another character expression or memo field as a number, counting from the end of the string you are searching in. This function is similar to AT( ), but it counts from the right rather than the left to indicate the expression's position. For example **AT("a","axe")** would return 3, and **AT("x" "axe")** would return 2.

Options By default, this function returns the location of the first occurrence of the string counting from its right. Enter a numeric expression as the <occurrence> option to search for a later occurrence. For example, use 2 to search for the second occurrence of the string counting from the right.

See Also AT( ), ATCLINE( ), ATLINE( ), LEFT( ), RATLINE( ), RIGHT( ), SUBSTR( )

▶ The RATLINE( ) Function

Syntax

```
RATLINE(<search_for exp>, <search_in exp>)
```

Usage This function returns the line number of the first occurrence of a character expression within another character expression or memo field, counting from the end of the string you are searching in. This function is similar to RAT( ), but it returns the line number of the expression, rather than its position.

See Also AT( ), ATCLINE( ), ATLINE( ), LEFT( ), RIGHT( ), SUBSTR( )

▶ The RD ¦ RMDIR Command

Syntax

```
RD <path> ¦ RMDIR <path>
```

Usage This command deletes the specified directory. The <path> may be specified as a full path name of a directory or as a child directory of the current directory. You may not remove a directory that has files in it.

See Also MD ¦ MKDIR

▶ The READ Command

Syntax

```
READ
      [CYCLE]
      [ACTIVATE <expL1>]
      [DEACTIVATE <expL2>]
      [MODAL]
      [WITH <window title list>]
      [SHOW <expL3>]
```

```
[VALID <expL4 | expN1>]
[WHEN <expL5>]
[OBJECT <expN2>]
[TIMEOUT <expN3>]
[SAVE]
[NOMOUSE]
[LOCK | NOLOCK]
[COLOR <color pair list> | COLOR SCHEME <expN4>]
```

Usage This command lets the user edit the variables of all active @ ... GET commands. It is used in programming to allow the user to enter data into a data entry screen that you design.

Options The CYCLE option prevents the READ from being ended when you finish the last GET. Instead, the cursor cycles back to the first GET, until you press Esc, Ctrl+W, or other terminating keys.

The ACTIVATE <expL1> option can be used when your READ command activates GETs in multiple windows. As the user moves from window to window, the READ is activated for the current window only if the logical expression <expL1> evaluates as a logical true.

The DEACTIVATE <expL2> option is likewise used when a READ activates GETs in multiple windows. It allows the user to leave the current window only if the logical expression <expL2> evaluates as a logical true. This function is similar to the VALID clause, which applies to all windows in a READ, and is a useful error-checking device.

The MODAL option prevents all windows from being activated except for the windows involved in the READ.

The WITH <window title list> option specifies a list of windows involved in the READ. This clause automatically creates a MODAL READ; it is not necessary also to use the MODAL clause.

The SHOW <expL3> option works in conjunction with the SHOW GETS command. SHOW GETS refreshes the information displayed on the screen by previous READs; if a SHOW clause is present, the routine <expL3> is executed by SHOW GETS, giving you additional control over what gets redisplayed.

The VALID option can be used to help you error-check the data entered in a READ; the user is allowed to exit the READ only if the logical expression you specify evaluates to a logical true.

The WHEN option activates the READ command only if a logical expression that you specify evaluates to a logical true.

The OBJECT <expN2> option allows you to specify which GET object will be selected first by specifying the sequential number of that GET. (The first GET is 1, the second is 2, and so on.)

The TIMEOUT <expN3> option lets you specify how many seconds the READ command will remain active without the user entering any input.

The SAVE option saves GET statements after a READ is completed so they can be activated again by another READ. Normally, GET statements are cleared once the READ is finished, or when a CLEAR, CLEAR GETS, or CLEAR ALL command is executed.

The NOMOUSE option requires the user to use the keyboard for most cursor movement operations.

The LOCK ¦ NOLOCK option specifies whether or not the records that contain the data are locked during the READ. If LOCK is used, Visual FoxPro attempts to lock all records used by the objects, and allows you to edit them only if the lock is successful. NOLOCK displays the objects in read-only form, so they cannot be modified. These options only apply to networks.

The COLOR option allows you to specify the color attributes of the Browse window. You can do this by means of a color pair list (for example, COLOR 'B/R'), or a COLOR SCHEME clause (a number between 1 and 24 that lets you choose any of 24 preset color schemes) .

See Also CLEAR GETS, @ ... SAY ... GET

The READ EVENTS Command

Syntax

```
READ EVENTS
```

Usage This command stops the execution of a program and instead waits for events such as mouse clicks and keystrokes. This command is used in combination with CLEAR EVENTS, which continues the execution of the program on the next line after the READ EVENTS command.

Before READ EVENTS can be used, the menu system or dialog boxes must be set up so that one or more choices issue the CLEAR EVENTS command. For example, after running a menu program, a program could include the command READ EVENTS, which makes the program wait for the user's menu choices. If the user chooses File ➤Exit, it would execute the command CLEAR EVENTS.

See Also CLEAR EVENTS

▸ The RECALL Command

Syntax

```
RECALL
      [<scope>]
      [FOR <expL1>]
      [WHILE <expL2>]
      [NOOPTIMIZE]
```

Usage This command unmarks a record that has been marked for deletion. In its simplest form, it unmarks only the current record (the record where the pointer is in the table open in the current work area).

Options If an optional scope, FOR, or WHILE clause is used, all the records included in the specified scope or all the records for which the logical expression following the FOR or WHILE is evaluated as true are unmarked. For more information on how these clauses work, see Chapter 11.

The NOOPTIMIZE option for this command disables the Rushmore technology, which normally speeds up data access when you use a FOR statement containing fields in existing indexes. You can disable Rushmore with the NOOPTIMIZE option on a number of Visual FoxPro commands, but in this case there is little reason to do so.

See Also DELETE, PACK, SET DELETED

▸ The RECCOUNT( ) Function

Syntax

```
RECCOUNT([<expN> ¦ <expC>])
```

Usage This function tells you how many records are contained in the table currently in use. You can also specify an alias name or work area number to determine the record count of a table in another work area.

See Also COUNT

▶ The RECNO( ) Function

Syntax

```
RECNO([<alias> ¦ <exp>])
```

Usage This function returns the record number of the current record (the record where the pointer is located).

By default, this function applies to the table open in the currently selected work area, but the <alias> ¦ <exp> option lets you specify another work area; use the alias of an open file or the letter or number of its work area.

If the table has no records in it or if you attempt to place the pointer before the first record, RECNO( ) returns 1. You can distinguish the first from a file where the pointer is on record number 1 because EOF( ) returns .T., and you can distinguish the second from a file where the pointer is on record number 1 because BOF( ) returns .T.

The option RECNO(0) can be used in combination with a SEEK command. If the SEEK is unsuccessful, RECNO(0) returns the number of the record that comes closest to matching or, if no record comes close to matching, returns 0.

See Also GO, SKIP

▶ The REINDEX Command

Syntax

```
REINDEX
    [COMPACT]
```

Usage This command rebuilds all index files that are open in the current work area. It is necessary only if an index file has not been updated to reflect changes in the file because it was not open when its file was being modified.

Options The COMPACT option allows you to convert regular IDX index files to compact IDX files, which take up much less disk space.

See Also INDEX, SET INDEX, USE

▶ The RELEASE BAR Command

Syntax

```
RELEASE [BAR [<expN> ¦ ALL] OF <popup name>]
```

Usage This command removes a menu item in a user-defined menu from memory.

Options BAR <expN> is used to specify the number of the bar on the specified popup to remove from memory.

ALL removes all bars on the specified popup from memory.

See Also CLEAR, DEFINE BAR, DEFINE POPUP

▶ The RELEASE Command

Syntax

```
RELEASE [<memory variable list> ¦ ALL [LIKE
<skeleton> ¦ EXCEPT <skeleton>]
```

Usage This command removes memory variables and arrays from memory.

Options The <memory variable list> option specifies the memory variables and arrays to be released from memory.

The ALL option releases all memory variables and arrays from memory.

If ALL is used with the LIKE <skeleton> option, it releases all memory variables that match a skeleton that uses the wildcard character **?** to represent any character or * to represent any series of characters. Likewise, if it is used with EXCEPT <skeleton>, it releases all memory variables except those that match the skeleton.

See Also CLEAR

▶ The RELEASE MENUS Command

Syntax

```
RELEASE MENUS <menu list> [EXTENDED]
```

Usage This command removes a user-defined menu bar from memory.

Options The EXTENDED option releases not just the menus on the list but also all submenus and associated ON SELECTION BAR, ON SELECTION MENU, ON SELECTION PAD, and ON SELECTION POPUP commands.

See Also CLEAR, DEFINE MENU

The RELEASE PAD Command

Syntax

```
RELEASE PAD [<pad name> ¦ ALL] OF <menu name>
```

Usage This command removes a pad of a user-defined menu from memory.

Options The <pad name> option to specify the menu pad to remove from memory.

The ALL option removes all pads on the specified menu from memory.

See Also CLEAR, DEFINE PAD

The RELEASE POPUPS Command

Syntax

```
RELEASE POPUPS [<popup list> [EXTENDED]]
```

Usage This command removes a popup menu of a user-defined menu or of the Visual FoxPro System menu from memory.

Options If the command is used without a popup list, all user-defined menus are removed from memory.

The <popup list> option specifies menu popups to remove from memory. You may use the internal names of the FoxPro system menu popups (such as _MFILE) or the names of user-defined menu popups.

The EXTENDED option releases not just the menus on the list but also all submenus and associated ON SELECTION BAR, ON SELECTION MENU, ON SELECTION PAD, and ON SELECTION POPUP commands.

See Also CLEAR, DEFINE POPUP

The RELEASE WINDOWS Command

Syntax

```
RELEASE WINDOWS [<window list>]
```

Usage This command removes user-defined windows or Visual FoxPro system windows from memory.

Options If the command is used without a window list, the currently active user-defined window is removed from memory.

The <window list> option specifies menu popups to remove from memory.

See Also CLEAR, DEFINE WINDOW

▸ The REMOVE TABLE Command

Syntax

```
REMOVE TABLE <table name> ¦ ?
     [DELETE]
```

Usage This command removes a table from the current database, either making it a free table or deleting it from the disk.

Options The <table name> option lets you specify the name of the table to remove from the database.

The ? option lets you use the Remove dialog box to select the table to remove from the database.

The DELETE option deletes the table from the disk. If this option is omitted, the table becomes a free table.

See Also ADD TABLE, ALTER TABLE, CLOSE, CREATE, CREATE TABLE, DISPLAY TABLES, FREE TABLE, LIST TABLES, MODIFY STRUCTURE, USE

▸ The RENAME Command

Syntax

```
RENAME <file name 1> TO <file name 2>
```

Usage This command gives a new name to a disk file. The file that had been named <file name 1> is named <file name 2> instead. The full path name of files may be used.

When this command is used, there must already be a file named <file name1> and it must not be open. There must not be a file named <file name2>.

This command is similar to the DOS command RENAME.

See Also COPY FILE

The REPLACE Command

Syntax

```
REPLACE [<scope>] <field1> WITH <exp1>
     [ADDITIVE]
     [<field2> WITH <exp2> [ADDITIVE] ...]
     [FOR <expL1>]
     [WHILE <expL2>]
     [NOOPTIMIZE]
```

Usage In its simplest form, this command puts new data into one field of the current record. The current data in the field is replaced with <exp1>.

The command can also be used with additional fields and expressions to replace the data in all of the fields that are listed.

Options If an optional scope, FOR, or WHILE clause is used, all the records included in the specified scope or all the records for which the logical expression following the FOR or WHILE is evaluated as true have the specified fields replaced with the specified expressions. For more information on how these clauses work, see Chapter 11. REPLACE cannot be used with these options on the key field of an active index; if it is, the replacement may not occur in all the fields specified.

The ADDITIVE option can be used only with Memo fields. If it is used, the data currently in the Memo field remains there, and the data specified in the expression is added to the end of the Memo field.

The <field2> WITH <exp2> [ADDITIVE] ... option indicates that you can include a list of fields and of expressions to replace the data in each. An ADDITIVE clause can be used for each field in the list.

The NOOPTIMIZE option for this command disables the Rushmore technology, which normally speeds up data access when you use a FOR statement containing fields in existing indexes. You can disable Rushmore with the NOOPTIMIZE option on a number of Visual FoxPro for Windows commands. The only time you need to do this is when your command changes data in the field(s) that make up the index key, since the version of the file used by Rushmore may then become outdated, and incorrect answers may result.

See Also APPEND, INSERT

▶ The REPLICATE( ) Function

Syntax

```
REPLICATE(<expC>,<expN>)
```

Usage This function repeats a particular character string a specified number of times. For example, REPLICATE("_",60) returns an underline 60 characters long.

▶ The REPORT Command

Syntax

```
REPORT FORM <file name 1> | ?
     [ENVIRONMENT]
     [<scope>]
     [WHILE <expL1>]
     [FOR <expL2>]
     [PLAIN | HEADING <expC>]
     [NOEJECT]
     [NOCONSOLE]
     [PREVIEW]
     [SUMMARY]
     [TO PRINTER [PROMPT] | TO FILE <file name 2>]
     [NOOPTIMIZE]
```

Usage This command produces reports using report layouts (report forms) that have been designed earlier. If CONSOLE has not been SET OFF, the reports are displayed on the screen. They can also be sent to the printer or to a text file.

Before this command is used, the report form must have been created and saved in a file. The command CREATE REPORT lets you design these report forms using the Report Designer window. The default extension for these files is FRX.

Options An existing form can be specified as <file name 1> of the command, or if the ? option is used, Visual FoxPro displays a scrollable list allowing you to choose among available report forms.

The ENVIRONMENT option can be used if the environment was saved when the report form was created. It automatically uses the same environment—including, for example, an index file to set the order in which reports are printed.

By default, reports are produced for all records in the table. A scope clause makes the command produce reports only for the records that fall in the specified scope. A FOR or WHILE clause makes the command produce reports only for the records that meet some logical criterion. See Chapter 11 for more discussion of how these clauses work.

The PLAIN option suppresses the printing of the heading at the top of each page.

The HEADING option prints the specified character expression as the heading at the top of each page.

The NOEJECT option prevents the printer from ejecting a page before it prints the report. By default, this command sends a form-feed to the printer before beginning its first page.

The NOCONSOLE option prevents reports from being shown on the screen while printing or being sent to a disk file.

The PREVIEW option displays a preview of the report on the screen. You must then enter another REPORT command without the PREVIEW option to generate the full report.

The SUMMARY option prints only totals and subtotals, rather than detailed line printing.

The TO PRINTER and TO FILE options let you send the reports to the printer or to the text file whose name is specified. If the PROMPT option is included, Visual FoxPro will display the Print dialog box before printing. This option must come immediately after the TO PRINTER option.

The NOOPTIMIZE option for this command disables the Rushmore technology, which normally speeds up data access when you use a FOR statement containing fields in existing indexes. You can disable Rushmore with the NOOPTIMIZE option on a number of Visual FoxPro commands, but in this case there is little reason to do so.

See Also CREATE REPORT, MODIFY REPORT

▶ The RESTORE FROM Command

Syntax

```
RESTORE FROM <file name> ¦ FROM MEMO <memo field>
     [ADDITIVE]
```

Usage This command restores memory variables that you previously saved to a disk file or Memo field with the SAVE TO command. It is often used in programming.

Options The ADDITIVE option preserves any current memory variables while adding additional ones from a disk file or Memo field. Otherwise, current memory variables are erased when you restore a specified set of variables.

See Also SAVE TO

▸ The RESTORE MACROS Command

Syntax

```
RESTORE MACROS FROM <file name> ¦
     [FROM MEMO <memo field name>]
```

Usage This command restores a set of keyboard macros that was saved previously or restores the default macros.

Options If the command is used without a file or memo field name, it clears all macros from memory and restores the default macros.

FROM <file name> restores macros that were saved in a file with an FKY extension.

FROM MEMO <memo field name> restores macros that were saved to a memo field. The table that includes this field must be open.

See Also PLAY MACRO, SAVE MACROS

▸ The RESTORE WINDOW Command

Syntax

```
RESTORE WINDOW <window list> ¦ ALL
     FROM <file name> ¦ FROM MEMO <memo field>
```

Usage This command restores windows to memory from window definition files stored on disk or in a table Memo field. Used in programming, it avoids the necessity of issuing a new DEFINE WINDOWS command whenever a particular window is needed.

Options The ALL option restores all windows that were previously defined with the DEFINE WINDOW command and saved with the SAVE WINDOW command.

See Also ACTIVATE WINDOW, CLEAR WINDOWS, DEACTIVATE WINDOW, DEFINE WINDOW, HIDE WINDOW, RELEASE WINDOWS, SAVE WINDOW, SHOW WINDOW

▶ The RESUME Command

Syntax

```
RESUME
```

Usage This command resumes execution of a suspended program. You can use this if you include SUSPEND in a program to help with debugging. When a program is interrupted because of a bug or because you have pressed Esc, Visual FoxPro displays a dialog box with the options Cancel, Suspend, and Ignore. If you use the SUSPEND command or select Suspend from this dialog box, memory variables, window and menu definitions, and other aspects of the programming environment are preserved, and you can continue running the program from the point where it left off by entering the command RESUME.

See Also CANCEL, SUSPEND

▶ The RETURN Command

Syntax

```
RETURN [TO MASTER ¦ <exp> ¦ TO <procedure name>]
```

Usage This command returns program control from the current program or procedure to the program or procedure that called it (or to the Command window or operating system, if it was called from there).

RETURN is optional at the end of a program or procedure; control returns to the calling program or procedure automatically.

Options The TO MASTER option returns control to the highest level calling program or procedure instead of to the program or procedure that called the current one. The TO <procedure name> option returns control to the procedure that is named instead of to the program or procedure that called the current one.

RETURN may be followed by the <exp> option when it is used in a user-defined function. It then returns the value specified by the expression to the calling program or procedure.

See Also CANCEL, QUIT

► The RIGHT( ) Function

Syntax

```
RIGHT(<expC>, <expN>)
```

Usage This function returns the number of characters specified from the rightmost characters of the character expression. For example, **RIGHT("abcdefg", 3)** would return **efg**.

See Also AT( ), ATCLINE( ), ATLINE( ), LEFT( ), RAT( ), RATLINE( ), SUBSTR( )

► The RLOCK( ) Function

Syntax

```
RLOCK([<work area num> | <table alias>]
     | [<record num list>, <work area num> | <table
          alias>])
```

Usage This function attempts to lock a record or multiple records in the specified table. It returns .T. if it succeeds in locking all records specified, and .F. if it fails.

Options By default, this function attempts to lock the current record in the table in the current work area.

If you use a numeric expression as the <work area num>, it attempts to lock the current record in the table open in the work area you specify. If you use a character expression as the <table alias>, it attempts to lock the current record in the table whose name or alias you specify.

If you use a <record num list> followed by either a <work area num> or a <table alias>, it attempts to lock all the records specified in the table specified.

See Also FLOCK( ), LOCK, SET REPROCESS

► The ROUND( ) Function

Syntax

```
ROUND(<expN>)
```

Usage This function returns the integer that is closest in value to the numeric expression that is specified.

See Also CEILING( ), FLOOR( ), INT( )

▶ The ROW( ) Function

Syntax

```
ROW()
```

Usage This function returns the row number of the current position of the cursor. This function can be used in combination with @ ... SAY ... GET to direct screen output to a position that is expressed as an offset from the current row position of the cursor.

See Also @ ... SAY ... GET, COL( ), PCOL( ), PROWS( ), SCOLS( ), SROWS( ), WCOLS( ), WROWS( )

▶ The RTOD( ) Function

Syntax

```
RTOD(<expN>)
```

Usage Converts radians to degrees. The numeric expression represents the size of an angle in radians, and the function returns a numeric expression that represents the size of the same angle in degrees.

See Also ACOS( ), ASIN( ), ATAN( ), COS( ), DTOR( ), SIN( ), TAN( )

▶ The RTRIM( ) Function

Syntax

```
RTRIM(<expC>)
```

Usage This function removes spaces following a character expression or field that you specify. For example, if two fields, Lastname and Firstname, are both 12 characters long, the expression **? FIRSTNAME+LASTNAME** will return an answer like `Janet        Jones`. But you can use the RTRIM( ) function to remove the trailing blanks from Janet's first name. By typing **? RTRIM(FIRSTNAME)+" "+LASTNAME**, you will get the answer `Janet Jones`.

The RTRIM( ) function is identical to TRIM( ).

See Also ALLTRIM( ), LTRIM( ), TRIM( )

► The RUN Command

Syntax

```
RUN <command> ¦ ! <command>
```

Usage This command lets you run a DOS command or any external command that can be used at the DOS prompt from the Visual FoxPro Command window.

► The SAVE MACROS Command

Syntax

```
SAVE MACROS TO <file name> ¦ TO MEMO <memo field name>
```

Usage This command saves the current set of keyboard macros.

Options You must use one of the two options.

TO <file name> saves the macros to the file you specify, which Visual FoxPro automatically gives an FKY extension.

TO MEMO <memo field name> specifies a memo field to which the macros are saved. The table that includes this field must be open.

See Also PLAY MACRO, RESTORE MACROS

► The SAVE TO Command

Syntax

```
SAVE TO <file name> ¦ TO MEMO <memo field>
     [ALL LIKE ¦ EXCEPT <skel>]
```

Usage This command saves memory variables to a disk file or Memo field. They can later be retrieved with the RESTORE FROM command. These commands are generally used in programming.

Options The ALL LIKE option allows you to save only a certain set of memory variables; for example, ALL LIKE m* saves all variables beginning with the letter m.

The ALL EXCEPT option allows you to save all variables except a certain specified group.

See Also RESTORE FROM

The SAVE WINDOW Command

Syntax

```
SAVE WINDOW <window list> ¦ ALL
     TO <file name> ¦ TO MEMO <memo field>
```

Usage This command saves windows that you have defined with the DEFINE WINDOWS command to a disk file or a Memo field associated with a table. (The windows' names must be listed with commas between them.) You can then retrieve the window definitions for future use with the RESTORE WINDOW command.

A default extension of WIN is assigned to window files unless you specifically assign another extension.

Options The ALL option saves all currently defined windows. If it is used, the list of window names is omitted.

See Also ACTIVATE WINDOW, CLEAR WINDOWS, DEACTIVATE WINDOW, DEFINE WINDOW, HIDE WINDOW, RELEASE WINDOWS, RESTORE WINDOW, SHOW WINDOW

The SCAN Command

Syntax

```
SCAN [<scope>] [FOR <expL1>] [WHILE <expL2>]
     [NOOPTIMIZE]
     [LOOP]
     [EXIT]
     ...
ENDSCAN
```

Usage This command creates a loop that is something like a DO WHILE loop, except that it is used for going through all the records in a table and performing the statements between SCAN and ENDSCAN on all of them. You do not have to use the SKIP command within the loop when you use this command, as you would if you used a DO WHILE loop to read the file; it reads through the file automatically.

By default, the statements are performed for all the records.

Options A scope clause makes the statements apply only to the records that fall in the specified scope. A FOR or WHILE clause makes the statements apply only to the records that meet some logical criterion. See Chapter 11 for more discussion of how these clauses work.

The command EXIT or LOOP can be used at any point within the SCAN … ENDSCAN command. EXIT causes the program to proceed with the next line following ENDSCAN. LOOP causes the program to return immediately to the SCAN statement.

The NOOPTIMIZE option for this command disables the Rushmore technology, which normally speeds up data access when you use a FOR statement containing fields in existing indexes. You can disable Rushmore with the NOOPTIMIZE option on a number of Visual FoxPro for Windows commands. The only time you need to do this is when your SCAN loop changes data in the field(s) that make up the index key, since the version of the file used by Rushmore may then become outdated.

See Also DO WHILE, FOR

▶ The SCOLS( ) Function

Syntax

```
SCOLS()
```

Usage This function returns the number of columns available in the main Visual FoxPro window. This function can be used in combination with @ … SAY … GET to ensure that the location of screen output is in the main window.

See Also @ … SAY … GET, COL( ), PCOL( ), PROW( ), ROW( ), SROWS( ), WCOLS( ), WROWS( )

▶ The SEC( ) Function

Syntax

```
SEC(<expT>
```

Usage This function returns the seconds portion from the specified time expression.

See Also HOUR( ), MINUTE( )

▶ The SECONDS( ) Function

Syntax

```
SECONDS()
```

Usage This function returns the number of seconds between midnight and the current time, as a decimal number with a precision of .001 second.

See Also TIME( )

▶ The SEEK Command

Syntax

```
SEEK(<exp>)
```

Usage This command searches an indexed table for a record that matches an expression you specify. For example, if a mailing list table is indexed on the last name field, you might type **SEEK "Jones"**.

If a match is found, the pointer will be positioned at the first matching record, the RECNO( ) function will contain that record number, the FOUND( ) function will return a logical true (.T.), and the EOF( ) function will return a logical false (.F.).

If no match is found, the pointer will be positioned at the end of the table, the FOUND( ) function will return .F., and the EOF( ) function will return .T.

See Also FIND, LOCATE

▶ The SELECT Command

Syntax

```
SELECT <work area>
```

Usage This command lets you choose the current work area.

Visual FoxPro lets you open tables in up to 225 work areas. By default, commands apply to the file in the current work area. You begin in Work Area 1 but can change the work area by using this command.

When you are using this command, you can refer to the work area using one of three names:

- The name of the file that is open in it, if any
- A number from 1 through 225
- A letter from *A* through *J* (Letters can be used only for work areas 1 to 10.)

You can also refer to work area 0, and Visual FoxPro automatically interprets the number to mean the lowest numbered work area in which no table is currently open.

▸ The SELECT—SQL Command

Syntax

```
SELECT [ALL ¦ DISTINCT] [<alias1>] <select item>
     [,[<alias>,] <select item> ...]
     FROM <table> [<alias2>][,<table> [alias3>] ...]
     [[INTO ARRAY <name> ¦ INTO CURSOR <name> ¦ INTO
          TABLE ¦ DBF <name>}
     ¦ [TO FILE <file name> [ADDITIVE] ¦ TO PRINTER ]]
     [NOCONSOLE]
     [PLAIN]
     [NOWAIT]
     [WHERE <join condition> [AND <join condition>
          ...]
          [AND ¦ OR <filter condition> [AND ¦ OR
               <filter condition> ...]]]
     [GROUP BY <group column> [,<group column> ...]]
     [HAVING <filter condition>]
     [UNION [ALL] <SELECT command>]
     [ORDER BY <order item> [ASC ¦ DESC]
          [,<order item> [ASC ¦ DESC] ...]]
```

Usage This powerful SQL command allows you to retrieve data from one or more tables and to direct the output into a new table or other location of your choosing. A relatively recent addition to Visual FoxPro and other Xbase languages, Structured Query Language (SQL) commands give experienced users great power and flexibility in performing operations on files.

At a minimum, you must specify an item to be selected and one or more tables from which to select it. The item can be a field, a constant, or an expression.

Options The default ALL option displays all records satisfying the conditions of the query, while the DISTINCT option eliminates duplicates.

The INTO option directs query results into an array of memory variables, a temporary table called a cursor (which will be deleted once you close it), or a permanent table.

The TO FILE and TO PRINTER options direct output into a text file or to the printer, as well as to the screen. The TO FILE <file name>

ADDITIVE option appends the new data to any existing data in the specified file.

If all of the INTO and TO options are omitted, the output is displayed in a Browse window.

The NOCONSOLE option keeps output from being displayed on the screen, while the PLAIN option prevents column headings from appearing.

The NOWAIT option eliminates the usual pause when the screen becomes full while displaying data. The query results will continue to scroll across the screen until completed.

The WHERE option helps you retrieve data from multiple tables by allowing you to specify conditions that link the files and by allowing you to filter out unwanted records. Each "join condition" statement compares one field from one table with one field from another table—for example, field1 = field2. Each "filter condition" statement likewise compares two fields or compares one field with other variables or constants.

The GROUP BY option allows you to group records from your query according to values in one or more fields. The HAVING option includes groups in the query as long as they meet a certain specified condition.

The ORDER BY option allows you to sort the query results according to data in one or more fields. You can add ASC or DESC to the ORDER BY option to specify whether the result is sorted in ascending or descending order; if neither is specified, the data is sorted in ascending order by default.

The UNION option allows you to combine the results of one SELECT query with those of another SELECT query. Duplicate records are eliminated unless you add the keyword ALL.

See Also CREATE QUERY, INSERT

▶ The SET ALTERNATE Command

Syntax

```
SET ALTERNATE ON ¦ OFF
```

Usage Used with ON, this command saves unformatted screen output in a text file. Used with OFF, it stops sending screen output to the text file. Before this command is used, the text file must be designated using the command SET ALTERNATE TO <file name>.

The default setting is OFF, so after the file is designated, SET ALTERNATE ON must be entered before output is sent to it.

See Also SET ALTERNATE TO, SET PRINTER

▸ The SET ALTERNATE TO Command

Syntax

```
SET ALTERNATE TO [ <file name> [ADDITIVE] ]
```

Usage If it is used with a file name, this command designates a text file to which you can send screen output by using the command SET ALTERNATE ON.

If it is used without any file name, it cancels a previous designation of this sort of file, so you can no longer save screen output in a text file.

Options The ADDITIVE option adds screen output to any text that is currently in this file. By default, the SET ALTERNATE TO command overwrites any text in the file, if it already exists —but using SET ALTERNATE ON ¦ OFF repeatedly afterward will continue to add text to the designated file and not overwrite what is in it.

See Also SET ALTERNATE

▸ The SET BELL Command

Syntax

```
SET BELL ON ¦ OFF
```

Usage Used with OFF, this command prevents Visual FoxPro from beeping during data entry when you reach the end of a field or enter invalid data. Used with ON, it causes Visual FoxPro to beep again. The default setting is ON.

See Also SET BELL TO

▸ The SET BELL TO Command

Syntax

```
SET BELL TO [<frequency>,<duration>]
```

Usage This command lets you change the pitch and duration of the beep that occurs during data entry. The number that designates the frequency can be between 19 and 10,000 hertz. The number that controls how long the beep lasts can be between 1 and 19. Used without these optional numbers, the command returns the beep to the default settings, which are 512 hertz and a duration of 2.

See Also SET BELL

▶ The SET CARRY Command

Syntax

```
SET CARRY ON ¦ OFF
```

Usage Used with ON, this command carries forward the data that is entered in each record while you are appending data, so it appears as the default entry in the next record. Used with OFF, it disables this feature. This command is useful if you must do repetitive data entry.

The default setting for CARRY is OFF.

See Also SET CARRY TO

▶ The SET CARRY TO Command

Syntax

```
SET CARRY TO [ <field list> [ADDITIVE] ]
```

Usage Used with a field list, this command determines which fields will be carried forward when SET CARRY ON is used. Only the listed fields will appear in the next record as default entries.

Used without a field list, this command returns to the default setting, in which all fields are carried forward if a SET CARRY ON is entered.

Options The ADDITIVE option adds the fields that are listed to the fields listed in a previous SET CARRY TO command that is still active. Without this option, only the fields listed in the most recent SET CARRY TO command are carried forward.

See Also SET CARRY

▶ The SET CENTURY Command

Syntax

```
SET CENTURY ON ¦ OFF
```

Usage Used with ON, this command makes dates appear with all four digits of the year displayed. SET CENTURY OFF makes dates appear with only the last two digits of the year displayed. The default setting for CENTURY is OFF.

► The SET COLLATE TO Command

Syntax

```
SET COLLATE TO <collation sequence name>
```

Usage This command determines how character fields will be sorted in newly created indexes, but does not affect indexes that were created earlier and are opened after the SET COLLATE command is used.

Options The <collation sequence name> can be one of many collation sequences available in Visual FoxPro. The most important are:

- MACHINE: sorts in ASCII order, which considers all uppercase letters to come before all lowercase letters.
- GENERAL: sorts in alphabetical order for English, French, German, Modern Spanish, and Portuguese.

MACHINE is the default, but it is best to use SET COLLATE TO "GENERAL" for most indexes.

The following options are also available: CZECH, DUTCH, GREEK, HUNGARY, ICELAND, NORDAN (Norwegian or Danish), POLISH, RUSSIAN, SLOVAK, SPANISH (Traditional Spanish), SWEFIN (Swedish or Finnish), UNIQWT (Unique Weight). These options allow names in various languages to be sorted with letters that have accent marks in their proper location, rather than their ASCII location.

See Also INDEX

► The SET COLOR Command

Syntax

```
SET COLOR TO [[<standard>][,[<enhanced>]
     [,[<border>]]]]
SET COLOR OF NORMAL ¦ MESSAGES ¦ TITLES ¦ BOX
     ¦ HIGHLIGHT ¦ INFORMATION ¦ FIELDS TO
        [<standard>]
SET COLOR OF SCHEME <expN1> TO
     [[<color pair list] ¦ [SCHEME <expN2>]]
SET COLOR SET TO [<color set name>]
```

Usage These commands let you specify the colors of a number of elements of the screen. There are several common ways to define screen colors with a SET COLOR command. You may specify a color pair list, which is a list of between 1 and 10 color pairs separated by commas. These pairs determine foreground and background colors that appear in different circumstances—for example, W/B, R/B, W+/BG, R+/B. Possible color codes are as follows:

- N (Black)
- X (Blank)
- B (Blue)
- GR (Brown)
- BG (Dyan)
- G (Green)
- RB (Magenta)
- R (Red)
- W (White)
- GR+ (Yellow)

A plus sign specifies high intensity, while an asterisk denotes bright or blinking color.

Alternately, you can specify a preset color set (designated by a number between 1 and 24 that lets you choose any of 24 preset color schemes) or a color scheme.
The RGB( ) option lets you precisely define color pairs by specifying a list of six numeric values between 0 and 255. The first three numbers determine the red, green, and blue values of the foreground color; the second three determine the RGB values of the background color (for example, RGB(255,0,0,255,255,255)).

The SET CONFIRM Command

Syntax

```
SET CONFIRM ON ¦ OFF
```

Usage This command determines whether you must press Enter to move to the next field when entering data using @ … GET … READ statements.

If CONFIRM is OFF, the cursor jumps immediately to the next field when you reach the last character in the previous field. If CONFIRM is ON, you must press a terminating key such as Enter, Tab, and so on, to end data input in that field.

CONFIRM also affects the operation of popups and menu bars. With CONFIRM set OFF, you can simply press the first letter of the option to make a menu choice; with the ON option, you must also press a terminating key such as Enter.

The default setting is OFF.

▸ The SET CONSOLE Command

Syntax

```
SET CONSOLE ON ¦ OFF
```

Usage Used with OFF, this command stops output to the screen. Used with ON, it makes output appear on the screen. The default setting for CONSOLE is ON.

▸ The SET DATE Command

Syntax

```
SET DATE [TO] AMERICAN ¦ ANSI ¦ BRITISH ¦ FRENCH
    ¦ GERMAN ¦ ITALIAN ¦ JAPAN ¦ USA ¦ MDY ¦ DMY ¦
    YMD
```

Usage This command allows you to change the way dates are displayed. You can determine the relative order of month, day, and year, as well as the characters that are used to separate these categories. The options are

Option	**Format**
AMERICAN	mm/dd/yy
ANSI	yy.mm.dd
BRITISH/FRENCH	dd/mm/yy
GERMAN	dd.mm.yy
ITALIAN	dd-mm-yy
JAPAN	yy/mm/dd

USA	mm-dd-yy
MDY	mm/dd/yy
DMY	dd/mm/yy
YMD	yy/mm/dd

See Also SET CENTURY

The SET DECIMALS Command

Syntax

```
SET DECIMALS TO <expN>
```

Usage This command specifies how many decimal places are used to display the results of division, multiplication, and mathematical functions.

The SET DEFAULT Command

Syntax

```
SET DEFAULT TO <path name>
```

Usage This command lets you change the current drive or directory, where Visual FoxPro looks for files by default. The path name used is a disk drive designation (a letter followed by a colon). It may be a disk drive and DOS path name (a letter followed by a colon, followed by a backslash and a subdirectory name or names separated by backslashes). Or it may consist just of subdirectories separated by backslashes, if the path is on the current drive.

The SET DELETED Command

Syntax

```
SET DELETED ON ¦ OFF
```

Usage This command determines whether Visual FoxPro commands disregard records that are marked for deletion. Used with ON, it makes commands ignore records marked for deletion. The default for DELETED is OFF; by default, commands use records that are marked for deletion.

This setting does not affect the commands INDEX and REINDEX, which always act on all records, regardless of whether they are marked for deletion.

▶ The SET DEVICE Command

Syntax

```
SET DEVICE TO
      SCREEN ¦ PRINTER ¦ FILE <file name>
```

Usage This command controls where Visual FoxPro sends the output of @ … SAY commands.

The default is SCREEN, which displays the output on the monitor. This command can be used to send the output to the printer or the text file whose name is specified.

The output of @ … SAY commands cannot be redirected using SET CONSOLE, SET PRINT, or SET ALTERNATE. Thus, SET DEVICE makes up for this deficiency of these commands.

▶ The SET ECHO Command

Syntax

```
SET ECHO ON ¦ OFF
```

Usage This command controls the Trace window, which is useful for debugging programs. When it is used with ON, the source code for your program is displayed in the Trace window as it runs, and the line that is currently being executed is highlighted. The default setting is OFF.

▶ The SET ESCAPE Command

Syntax

```
SET ESCAPE ON ¦ OFF
```

Usage This command controls whether the Esc key can be used to interrupt the program. If it is used with OFF, the Esc key has no effect and the program continues to execute. If ESCAPE is ON, pressing the Esc key makes Visual FoxPro display a dialog box with the choices Cancel (which stops program execution), Suspend (which stops program execution temporarily, until the command RESUME is used), and Ignore (which continues program execution as if Esc had not been pressed).

The default setting is ON. It is best not to add the command SET ESCAPE OFF until a program is thoroughly tested and debugged.

▶ The SET EXACT Command

Syntax

```
SET EXACT ON ¦ OFF
```

Usage This command determines whether strings that are compared using the = operator must be identical for there to be a match. If EXACT is ON, there will be a match only if the strings are the same length and have the same characters. If EXACT is OFF, there can be a match as long as all characters are identical up to the point where one string comes to an end.

The default setting is OFF.

▶ The SET FIELDS Command

Syntax

```
SET FIELDS ON ¦ OFF

SET FIELDS LOCAL ¦ GLOBAL
```

Usage SET FIELDS ON ¦ OFF determines whether the fields list in a previously used SET FIELDS TO command will determine which fields of the table are accessible. If it is used with OFF, all fields are displayed. If it is used with ON, only fields listed in the SET FIELDS TO command are displayed.

The default setting is OFF, but when the command SET FIELDS TO is used, the setting is automatically changed to ON, so a separate SET FIELDS ON command does not have to be used.

SET FIELDS LOCAL ¦ GLOBAL determines whether fields from all tables of a relational database created using the SET RELATION command that are included in a previously used SET FIELDS TO command are accessible. If it is used with LOCAL, only fields from the current table are displayed. If it is used with GLOBAL, fields from all related tables are displayed. LOCAL is the default.

See Also SET FIELDS TO

▶ The SET FIELDS TO Command

Syntax

```
SET FIELDS TO [<field list> ¦ ALL]
```

Usage If this command is used with a field list, only the fields that are listed will be accessible to the user or to other commands. For example, if the user opens a Browse/Edit window, it will include only these fields.

When it is used with a field list, this command is additive. If it is used a second time, the fields that are listed are added to the fields that are already accessible because they were listed in the first SET FIELDS TO command.

When it is used with ALL, the command makes all fields accessible once again.

Using SET FIELDS TO without a field list or ALL cancels the fields that have been listed by earlier uses of this command, so a new SET FIELDS TO <field list> can then be used without being additive.

The command SET FIELDS OFF temporarily disables the restrictions imposed by this command, and the command SET FIELDS ON enables them again. When SET FIELDS TO is executed, FIELDS also is automatically set ON.

See Also SET FIELDS

► The SET FILTER TO Command

Syntax

```
SET FILTER TO [<expL>]
```

Usage After this command is used with a logical expression, only the records of the currently selected table for which the logical expression is evaluated as true are accessible.

Using it without a logical expression removes the filter, so that all records are accessible again.

► The SET HELP Command

Syntax

```
SET HELP ON ¦ OFF
```

Usage This command lets you activate or deactivate Visual FoxPro's online Help utility or another help table that you set up with custom-designed help messages. SET HELP OFF deactivates the online Help utility. The default is SET HELP ON.

See Also HELP, SET HELP TO

▶ The SET HELP TO Command

Syntax

```
SET HELP TO [<file name>]
```

Usage The SET HELP TO command allows you to designate a custom-created Help file to provide the user with online help information.

If you type SET HELP TO without naming a user-created Help file, Visual FoxPro looks for a table named FOXHELP.DBF or FOXHELP.HLP. If you create your own help table, the first field must be a Character field and the second a Memo field.

With Visual FoxPro for Windows, you can select either Windows-style help or DBF-style help by typing SET HELP TO FOXHELP.HLP or SET HELP TO FOXHELP.DBF.

See Also HELP, SET HELP

▶ The SET HOURS Command

Syntax

```
SET HOURS TO [12¦24]
```

Usage This function sets the system clock to 12-hour format, with times from 1 to 12 AM and PM, or to a 24-hour format.

Options With no argument, this command returns the clock to the default 12-hour format.

The 12 option also sets the clock to the 12-hour format.

The 24 option sets the clock to the 24-hour format.

See Also HOUR( )

▶ The SET INDEX Command

Syntax

```
SET INDEX TO [<index file list> ¦ ?]
    [ORDER <expN> ¦ <.IDX index file> ¦ [TAG] <tag
    name> [OF <.CDX file>]]
     [ASCENDING ¦ DESCENDING]
     [ADDITIVE]
```

Appendices

▶▶

Usage This command opens one or more index files. The files must already have been created for the table that is active in the current work area.

If you include a list of index files, the first index in the list is the controlling index (or master index) that sets the order of the file's records.

If you use the ? option, Visual FoxPro displays a dialog box that lets you choose from a scrollable list of available index files.

If SET INDEX TO is used alone, any indexes that are open in the current work area are closed.

This command does not affect the structural compound index file, which is always open.

Options The ORDER option lets you specify which index is to be the current controlling index (or master index). It can be used in three ways:

- If you use the ORDER <expN> option, the indexes are numbered according to their position in the index list you specified. For example, ORDER 3 refers to the third index.
- Use the ORDER <.IDX index file> option to use an index in a separate IDX file as the controlling index.
- The ORDER TAG option lets you specify that a particular tag within a compound index file is to be the current controlling index.

The ASCENDING ¦ DESCENDING option determines whether records are displayed in ascending or descending order. The default is ASCENDING.

The ADDITIVE option keeps previously opened index files open for the current table.

See Also CLOSE, INDEX, SET ORDER, USE

▸ The SET KEYCOMP Command

Syntax

```
SET KEYCOMP TO DOS ¦ WINDOWS
```

Usage This command allows you to use either the keystroke combinations of Visual FoxPro for DOS or else Windows-style keystrokes for moving through menus and other screen controls.

▶ The SET MESSAGE Command

Syntax

```
SET MESSAGE TO [<expC>]
SET MESSAGE TO [<expN>] [LEFT ¦ CENTER ¦ RIGHT]
```

Usage The first version of this command lets you display a message <expC> in the status bar. For the message to appear, you must first use SET STATUS ON.

The second version lets you specify the location where messages will appear later on within menus and popups you create. <expN> is the screen row where the messages will appear.

See Also DEFINE MENU, SET STATUS

▶ The SET NEAR Command

Syntax

```
SET NEAR ON ¦ OFF
```

Usage This command determines where the pointer is after an unsuccessful indexed search using the SEEK or FIND command.

If the command is used with ON, the pointer is left at the record nearest to a match if the search is unsuccessful, so the user can browse through nearby records. If NEAR is OFF, the pointer is left at the end of the table if the search is unsuccessful. The default for NEAR is OFF.

If NEAR is ON and a search fails, FOUND( ) returns .F. to indicate that the search was unsuccessful, just as it does when NEAR is OFF. However, EOF( ) does not return .T., as it does when NEAR is OFF, because the pointer is not at the end of the file.

See Also EOF( ), FOUND( ), SET EXACT

▶ The SET ODOMETER Command

Syntax

```
SET ODOMETER TO [<expN>]
```

Usage This command allows you to change the reporting interval for commands that update you on their progress while they are processing records in a file. For example, COPY keeps you informed of how many records have been copied from one file to another. SET TALK must be ON for this screen updating to occur.

The default value for SET ODOMETER TO is 100.

► The SET OPTIMIZE Command

Syntax

```
SET OPTIMIZE ON ¦ OFF
```

Usage This command lets you disable a technique called Rushmore, which optimizes data retrieval for certain commands such as AVERAGE, BROWSE, COPY TO, COUNT, DELETE, DISPLAY, EDIT, LOCATE, SORT, and TOTAL. In rare cases in which a command that uses Rushmore alters data in fields being used by the relevant index, the version of the file being used by Rushmore may become outdated, and incorrect answers may result. In these cases you can manually disable Rushmore by typing SET OPTIMIZE OFF. You can also make use of a NOOPTIMIZE option on many commands to serve the same purpose.

The commands that use Rushmore are all those that support a FOR clause.

► The SET ORDER Command

Syntax

```
SET ORDER TO
      [<expN> ¦ <.IDX index file>
      ¦ [TAG] <tag name> [OF <.CDX file>]
      [IN <expN2> ¦ <expC>]
      [ASCENDING ¦ DESCENDING]]
```

Usage This command can be used to change the index that is the controlling index (or master index) that determines the order of the records if a table is in use with a number of indexes active.

The numeric expression refers to the order the indexes were in when they were first opened with a USE command or a SET INDEX command. The first index listed in any of these commands is made the controlling index. But the SET ORDER command makes the index whose position in the list is specified by the numeric expression into the controlling index instead.

If SET ORDER is used with no numeric expression or with the number 0, the indexes remain open but none sets the order of the records. The records are displayed in the actual order in which they appear in the file.

Options The TAG option lets you specify that a particular tag within a compound index file is to be the current controlling index.

The IN option lets you specify the controlling index for tables open in other work areas.

The ASCENDING ¦ DESCENDING option determines whether records are displayed in actual or reverse order. The default is ASCENDING, which arranges the records in index order. DESCENDING arranges the records in the reverse of index order.

See Also INDEX, SET INDEX

▶ The SET PATH Command

Syntax

```
SET PATH TO [<path list>]
```

Usage This command allows you to tell Visual FoxPro to search a list of disk directories for files that are not found in the current directory. Its usage is identical in function to the PATH command in DOS, although you can set a Visual FoxPro path that is different from the DOS path. Use commas or semicolons to separate the directories in <path list>.

▶ The SET PRINTER Command

Syntax

```
SET PRINTER ON ¦ OFF
```

Usage When it is used with ON, this command sends unformatted screen output to the printer. The default is OFF. This command does not work with screen output that is formatted using the @ … SAY command. To send that output to the printer, see SET DEVICE.

See Also SET DEVICE

▶ The SET PROCEDURE Command

Syntax

```
SET PROCEDURE TO [<file name>]
```

Usage When it is used with a file name, this command activates the procedure file that is specified, so procedures and user-defined functions in it can be used. If the file name does not include an extension, Visual FoxPro assumes the extension PRG.

Used without a file name, this command closes an open procedure file.

See Also PROCEDURE

► The SET RELATION Command

Syntax

```
SET RELATION TO [<exp1> INTO <alias1>]
      [,<exp2> INTO <alias2>]
      [ ... ]
      [ADDITIVE]
```

Usage This command lets you relate two files, and its most important use is in creating relational databases.

To create a relational database, <exp1> must be a field expression based on the table that is open in the currently selected work area. <alias1> must refer to an indexed file that is open in another work area by its name, by the letter or number of its work area, or by an alias you gave it when you opened the file. When the command is used in this way, Visual FoxPro looks for the record in the second file whose index key expression matches <exp1>; as you move the pointer in the first file, it automatically moves the pointer to the corresponding field in the second file. Thus, you can set up a database based on a one-to-one or one-to-many relation between two files.

This command can also be used with an unindexed <alias1> file. In this case, <exp1> must be a numeric expression. As you move the pointer through this file, the pointer automatically moves to the record in the alias file whose record number is equal to the value of this expression. For example, this version of the command can be used with the function RECNO( ) as <exp1>, so the pointer will move to the record in the alias file that has the same record number as the current record in the first file.

In either case, if there is no corresponding record in the second file, the pointer moves to the end-of-file and the function EOF( ) becomes true; thus, you can use this function for error trapping when you are programming a relational database.

The optional second <exp2> INTO <alias2> and … indicate that you can set more than one relation between the two files with a single command.

Options The ADDITIVE option adds the relations you are creating to any current relations that exist. By default, the relations you create replace any existing ones.

SET RELATION used by itself removes any existing relations for the currently selected table.

See Also INDEX, SET RELATION OFF, SET SKIP

The SET RELATION OFF Command

Syntax

```
SET RELATION OFF INTO <expN> ¦ <expC>
```

Usage This command allows you to eliminate a relation previously established between two tables with the SET RELATION command. You must currently be in the work area of the parent table; the second table is designated by its alias or work area number.

See Also SET RELATION

The SET REPROCESS Command

Syntax

```
SET REPROCESS TO
    <expN1> ¦ <expN2> SECONDS ¦ AUTOMATIC
```

Usage This command specifies how Visual FoxPro continues to attempt locking a record or file if an attempt at locking fails.

Options The <expN1> option specifies how many times Visual FoxPro attempts to lock the record or file. The default is 0 and the maximum is 32,000.

If you use the <expN2> SECONDS option, Visual FoxPro continuously repeats attempting to unlock the record or file for the number of seconds you specify.

If you use the AUTOMATIC option, Visual FoxPro attempts to lock the record or file for an indefinite amount of time, displaying a system message that says "Attempting to lock. Press Escape to Cancel."

See Also FLOCK( ), LOCK( ), RLOCK( )

▶ The SET SAFETY Command

Syntax

```
SET SAFETY ON ¦ OFF
```

Usage This command determines whether you will be warned before overwriting any files.

When you are working with Visual FoxPro, you will probably want to keep the safety setting ON. The SET SAFETY OFF command is useful in programming if you do not want future users of your programs to be interrupted by unnecessary warning messages.

The default setting is ON.

See Also SET TALK

▶ The SET SKIP Command

Syntax

```
SET SKIP TO [<alias1> [,<alias2>] ...]
```

Usage This command is used after SET RELATION TO to help set up a relation between two tables in which one (the child table) has many records corresponding to each record in the other (the parent table). When you use this command, the <alias1>,<alias2> ... names represent child tables related to the parent table in your current work area.

As you move record-by-record through the parent table, the system skips through all corresponding records in the child table.

If you type SET SKIP TO with no additional options, the one-to-many relation will be ended.

See Also SET RELATION

▶ The SET SKIP OF Command

Syntax

```
SET SKIP OF MENU <menu name> <expL>
...
SET SKIP OF PAD <pad name> OF <menu name> <expL>
...
SET SKIP OF POPUP <popup name> <expL>
...
```

```
SET SKIP OF BAR <expN>
    ¦ <System option name> OF <popup name> <expL>
```

Usage This command lets you disable or enable menus, menu pads, menu popups, or menu bars (the individual options on popups). If the logical expression evaluates as .T., the menu item is disabled. If it evaluates as .F., the item is enabled once again. By default, items are enabled.

Options Menu bars (the options on menu popups) can be referred to either by name or by number; for example, BAR 1 OF DATAPOP would refer to the first option on a popup that you named DATAPOP.

See Also DEFINE BAR, DEFINE MENU, DEFINE PAD, DEFINE POPUP

▶ The SET STATUS BAR Command

Syntax

```
SET STATUS BAR ON ¦ OFF
```

Usage This command determines whether the Windows-style status bar, showing information about the active table and the current keyboard status, is shown at the bottom of the screen. By default, this status bar is ON in Visual FoxPro for Windows.

Both FoxPro for Windows and FoxPro for DOS also let you use a character-based status bar, controlled by the command SET STATUS ON ¦ OFF.

See Also SET STATUS

▶ The SET STATUS Command

Syntax

```
SET STATUS ON ¦ OFF
```

Usage This command determines whether the character-based status bar, showing information about the active table and the current keyboard status, is shown at the bottom of the screen. By default, the character-based status bar is ON in FoxPro for DOS, but in FoxPro for Windows a Windows-style status bar is used instead.

You can use the character-based status bar in FoxPro for Windows by entering the command SET STATUS BAR OFF to remove the Windows-style status bar and by entering the command SET STATUS ON to add the character-based status bar.

See Also SET STATUS BAR

▶ The SET STEP Command

Syntax

```
SET STEP ON ¦ OFF
```

Usage Used with ON, this command lets you execute a program one line of code at a time to make debugging easier. When you use this command, the Trace window is automatically opened and displays the program with each line of code highlighted as it is run. You can select Resume to execute the next line of code or Cancel to stop executing the program.

The default setting for STEP is OFF.

See Also SET ECHO

▶ The SET SYSMENU Command

Syntax

```
SET SYSMENU ON ¦ OFF ¦ AUTOMATIC
        ¦ TO [<system menu popup list> ¦ <pad list>]
        ¦ TO [DEFAULT]
```

Usage This command determines whether a user can access the System menu bar while a program is running. The OFF option prevents the user from doing this. The default setting is ON.

Options The AUTOMATIC option sets the System menu on and automatically makes the menu and individual pads accessible and inaccessible as appropriate while a program is running.

The TO <system menu popup list> ¦ <pad list> options allow you to display only certain system popups and pads during program execution. The TO DEFAULT option restores the full set of popups and pads.

▶ The SET TALK Command

Syntax

```
SET TALK ON ¦ OFF
```

Usage Used with OFF, this command lets you disable the Visual FoxPro talk messages that scroll on the screen (behind any open windows that happen to be in the way) when you perform many different functions. The default setting for TALK is ON. It is best not to SET TALK

OFF when you are using Visual FoxPro. The command is useful in programs, where you do not want the end user to be confused by the talk.

The SET TYPEAHEAD Command

Syntax

```
SET TYPEAHEAD TO <expN>
```

Usage This command controls how many characters are stored in the keyboard buffer. If you type more quickly than Visual FoxPro can react, it stores, by default, 20 keystrokes in a part of memory called the keyboard buffer. As soon as Visual FoxPro has reacted to earlier commands and is ready for more keystrokes, it will use the keystrokes stored in the buffer as if you had just typed them.

You can use this command to set the keyboard buffer so it stores up to 128 characters. This is useful if you are a good typist and have a slow computer, causing your typing to get ahead of the program.

Visual FoxPro uses a very brief beep when the keyboard buffer is full to let you know that the keystrokes you are entering will not be stored and used.

The SET VIEW Command

Syntax

```
SET VIEW ON ¦ OFF
```

Usage This command opens and closes the View window to let you set up a working environment. Entering SET VIEW ON is equivalent to choosing Window ➤ View; entering SET VIEW OFF is equivalent to closing the window by pressing Esc or clicking the close box.

See Also CREATE VIEW, SET VIEW TO

The SET VIEW TO Command

Syntax

```
SET VIEW TO <file name> ¦ ?
```

Usage This command lets you use a working environment (or view) that you have previously saved in a VUE file. You can specify the file name or use the ? option to select it from a scrollable list of available VUE files.

See Also CREATE VIEW, SET VIEW

▸ The SHOW GETS Command

Syntax

```
SHOW GETS
     [ENABLE | DISABLE]
     [LEVEL <expN1>]
     [OFF | ONLY]
     [WINDOW <window name>]
     [LOCK]
     [COLOR <color pair list> | COLOR SCHEME <expN2>]
```

Usage This command, used mainly in programming, refreshes all GET fields and controls on the screen with new data—for example, as your program moves from one record of a table to the next.

Options The default ENABLE option redisplays all GET fields, boxes, and other objects, while the DISABLE option shows these objects without allowing them to be changed by the user.

The LEVEL option is used in relatively advanced programming in which the program includes several levels of nested READ statements. By specifying LEVEL <expN1>, you can direct the SHOW GETS command to update the GETs on a different level (1, 2, 3, 4, and so on) than the current one.

The OFF option redisplays the previous @ … SAY statements, without refreshing the GETs. Conversely, the ONLY option refreshes the GETs only, without updating the SAYS.

The WINDOW <window name> option lets you redisplay only those GETs that appear in a certain window you specify.

The LOCK specifies that the SHOW GETS attempts to lock the records. This can override a READ NOLOCK command. These options only apply to networks.

The COLOR option allows you to specify the color attributes of the Browse window. You can do this by means of a color pair list (for example, COLOR 'B/R'), or a COLOR SCHEME (a number between 1 and 24 that lets you choose any of 24 preset color schemes) clause.

See Also @ … SAY … GET, CLEAR, READ

The SHOW MENU Command

Syntax

```
SHOW MENU <menu name1> [,<menu name2> ...] ¦ ALL
     [PAD <pad name>]
     [SAVE]
```

Usage This command displays one or more menus without activating them. You must previously have defined the menus with the DEFINE MENU command, as part of a system of programs you have created.

Options The ALL option displays all currently defined menus on the screen.

The PAD option allows you to highlight a particular pad on the menu bar as though this is the desired menu choice.

The SAVE option saves an image of the specified menu bars on the screen during subsequent program operation. This image can later be removed with the CLEAR command.

See Also ACTIVATE MENU, CLEAR MENUS, CREATE MENU, DEACTIVATE MENU, DEFINE MENU, HIDE MENU, MODIFY MENU

The SHOW POPUP Command

Syntax

```
SHOW POPUP <popup name1> [, <popup name2> ...] ¦ ALL
     [SAVE]
```

Usage This command displays one or more popup menus without activating them. You must previously have defined the popups with the DEFINE POPUP command, as part of a system of programs you have created.

Options The ALL option displays all currently defined popups on the screen.

The SAVE option saves an image of the specified popup on the screen during subsequent program operation. This image can later be removed with the CLEAR command.

See Also ACTIVATE POPUP, CLEAR POPUPS, CREATE POPUP, DEACTIVATE POPUP, DEFINE POPUP, HIDE POPUP

▸ The SHOW WINDOW Command

Syntax

```
SHOW WINDOW <window name1> [,<window name2> ...] ¦
ALL
      [IN [WINDOW] <window name> ¦ IN SCREEN]
      [TOP ¦ BOTTOM ¦ SAME]
      [SAVE]
```

Usage This command displays one or more windows. If the windows have not been activated previously, this command displays them without activating them. The window must have been previously defined with the DEFINE WINDOW command.

Options The ALL option displays all currently defined windows on the screen.

The IN [WINDOW] <window name> option displays the specified window(s) within a parent window.

The IN SCREEN option specifically places the new window(s) in the main Visual FoxPro window. This is the default setting.

The TOP option places the new window(s) on top of other previously displayed windows, while the BOTTOM option puts them behind these other windows.

The SAME option puts a window that has been deactivated with the DEACTIVATE WINDOW command back on the screen in the same place that it was before it was deactivated.

The SAVE option saves an image of a window on the screen after the window is overwritten or hidden. The image can later be removed with the CLEAR command.

See Also ACTIVATE WINDOW, CLEAR WINDOWS, DEACTIVATE WINDOW, DEFINE WINDOW, HIDE WINDOW, RELEASE WINDOWS, RESTORE WINDOW, SAVE WINDOW

▸ The SIGN( ) Function

Syntax

```
SIGN(<expN>)
```

Usage This function returns 1 if the numeric expression is positive, −1 if the numeric expression is negative, or 0 if the numeric expression is zero.

See Also ABS( )

The SIN( ) Function

Syntax

```
SIN(<expN>)
```

Usage This function returns the sine of an angle. The numeric expression represents the size of the angle in radians. You can use the DTOR( ) function to convert angles from degrees to radians.

See Also ACOS( ), ASIN( ), ATAN, COS( ), DTOR( ), RTOD( ), TAN( )

The SKIP Command

Syntax

```
SKIP [<expN1>] [IN <alias> ¦ <expN2>]
```

Usage This command moves the pointer in a table, changing the record that is the current record. Used by itself, SKIP moves the pointer of the table that is open in the current work area to the next record; that is, it moves the pointer forward one record.

Options The optional numeric expression <expN1> can be used to move the pointer forward the number of records that is specified. If a negative number is used, the pointer moves back that number of records; for example, SKIP -1 would move the pointer to the previous record.

If you try to use this command to move the pointer to a location that is beyond the last record, the function EOF( ) is given the value .T. If you use it to move to a location that is before the first record, the function BOF( ) is given the value .T.

The IN <alias> ¦ <expN2> option can be used to move a record in a file that is open in a work area that is not currently selected. Specify the file's name or the number of its work area.

See Also GO, SET SKIP

The SORT Command

Syntax

```
SORT TO <file name> ON <field1>
     [/A] [/C] [/D]
     [,<field2> [/A] [/C] [/D] ...]
     [ASCENDING ¦ DESCENDING]
     [<scope>]
     [FOR <expL1>]
     [WHILE <expL2>]
     [FIELDS <field list>]
     [NOOPTIMIZE]
```

Usage In its simplest form, this command sorts the file that is open in the current work area, based on the field that is specified, in ascending order, and it puts the result in the file that is specified.

In practice, the SORT command is rarely used since index files provide a far more versatile way to make a table appear sorted and to find and retrieve data. Index files are far quicker to create than sorted copies of a table and take up much less disk space.

The SORT command uses temporary work files as well as creating a new output file, so it uses up to three times as much disk space as the space occupied by the original file. If this disk space is not available, Visual FoxPro can terminate abnormally, causing a loss of data.

Options The option [/A] lets you specify ascending order explicitly, although it is done by default if it is not specified.

The option [/D] lets you sort in descending order. The option [/C] makes the sort ignore the case of a Character field; if it is not included, the sort will be in ASCII order, with uppercase before lowercase letters.

If you specify more than one field to sort on, subsequent fields will be used as tie-breakers, in case the values in the first field are identical. You can use the [/A], [/C], or [/D] option separately for any of the fields.

The ASCENDING and DESCENDING options apply only to fields that do not include the [/A] or [/D] options and determine whether these fields will be sorted in ascending or descending order.

By default, all the records in the currently open file are sorted into a new file. If a scope clause is used, only the records that fall in the specified scope are sorted into the new file. If a FOR or WHILE clause is used, only the records that meet some logical criterion are sorted into the new file. If a FIELDS clause is used, only the fields that are listed are included in the new file. See Chapter 11 for more discussion of how these clauses work.

The NOOPTIMIZE option for this command disables the Rushmore technology, which normally speeds up data access when you use a FOR statement containing fields in existing indexes. You can disable Rushmore with the NOOPTIMIZE option on a number of Visual FoxPro for Windows commands. The only time you need to do this is when your command changes data in the field(s) that make up the index key, since the version of the file used by Rushmore may then become outdated.

See Also COPY TO, INDEX

▶ The SOUNDEX( ) Function

Syntax

```
SOUNDEX(<expC>)
```

Usage This function returns a four-character string that is a phonetic representation of the character expression. By comparing the SOUNDEX( ) of a character expression that the user enters to the SOUNDEX( ) of the contents of your table, you can find data that sounds similar to what the user enters, even if the spelling is totally different. The user can enter a name beginning with a *K*, for example, and still find the record for a person whose name begins with *Q*. For faster searches, you can index on the SOUNDEX( ) of some field and then SEEK the SOUNDEX( ) of the user's entry.

▶ The SPACE( ) Function

Syntax

```
SPACE(<expN>)
```

Usage This function returns a character string made up of a number of blank spaces equal to the numeric expression specified.

▶ The _SPELLCHECK System Variable

Syntax

```
_SPELLCHECK = <expC>
```

Usage This system variable specifies the name of the program that will be used as the spell checker by Visual FoxPro. By default, it uses SPELLCHK.APP, the spell checker that comes with Visual FoxPro.

► The SQRT( ) Function

Syntax

```
SQRT(<expN>)
```

Usage This function returns the square root of the numeric expression that is specified.

See Also **, ^

► The SROWS( ) Function

Syntax

```
SROWS()
```

Usage This function returns the number of rows available in the main Visual FoxPro window. This function can be used in combination with @ … SAY … GET to ensure that the location of screen output is in the main window.

See Also @ … SAY … GET, COL( ), PCOL( ), PROW( ), SCOLS( ), ROW( ), WCOLS( ), WROWS( )

► The STORE Command

Syntax

```
STORE <exp> TO <memvar1> [,memvar2 ...]
¦ <memvar> = <exp>
```

Usage If the memory variable it specifies does not yet exist, this command creates it and assigns it the specified value. If the memory variable that it specifies does exist, it replaces its current value with the specified value.

If you use STORE, you can assign values to (and, if necessary, create) a list of memory variables with a single command. If you use =, you can assign a value to (and create) only one memory variable at a time (unless you are working with an array).

See Also DECLARE, DIMENSION

▶ The STR( ) Function

Syntax

```
STR(<expN1> [,<expN2> [,<expN3>]])
```

Usage This function returns the value of the specified numeric expression as a character string.

Options The optional <expN2> specifies the length of the string that is returned. If the length you specify is longer than you need, the string is padded with leading spaces. If the length is shorter than you need to hold the integer value, the function returns a series of asterisks to indicate an error.

The optional <expN3> specifies the number of decimal places that will be included. Any decimal places beyond the number specified are simply truncated.

See Also VAL( )

▶ The SUBSTR( ) Function

Syntax

```
SUBSTR(<expC>,<expN1>[,<expN2>]
```

Usage This function returns a substring of the specified character expression that begins with the character indicated by the first numeric expression. If the optional second numeric expression is included, it determines the length of the substring; if it is not included, the substring continues to the end of the original string.

▶ The SUM Command

Syntax

```
SUM
        [<exp list>]
        [<scope>]
        [TO <memvar list> ¦ TO ARRAY <array name>]
        [FOR <expL1>]
        [WHILE <expL2>]
        [NOOPTIMIZE]
```


▶▶

Usage In its simplest form, this command adds the values in all Numeric fields of all records in the table that is open in the currently selected work area.

Options The optional <exp list> lets you specify fields (or field expressions) to be totaled, rather than adding all numeric fields.

The option TO <memvar list> ¦ TO ARRAY <array name> lets you store the results in memory variables. Visual FoxPro creates the memory variables specified if they do not already exist. The array must be declared with the DIMENSION or DECLARE command before this command is used. The order in which values are assigned to the memory variable list or to the elements in the array depends on the order in which the Numeric fields appear in the table.

By default, all the records in the currently open file are added. If a scope clause is used, only the records that fall in the specified scope are added. If a FOR or WHILE clause is used, only the records that meet some logical criterion are added.

The NOOPTIMIZE option for this command disables the Rushmore technology, which normally speeds up data access when you use a FOR statement containing fields in existing indexes. You can disable Rushmore with the NOOPTIMIZE option on a number of Visual FoxPro for Windows commands, but in this case there is little reason to do so.

See Also AVERAGE, CALCULATE, COUNT, TOTAL

► The SUSPEND Command

Syntax

```
SUSPEND
```

Usage This command temporarily suspends execution of a program but preserves memory variables, window and menu definitions, and other aspects of the programming environment, to help with debugging. When a program is interrupted because of a bug or because you have pressed Esc, Visual FoxPro displays a dialog box with the options Cancel, Suspend, and Ignore; selecting Suspend from this dialog box is equivalent to using the SUSPEND command. You can continue running the program from the point where it left off by entering the command RESUME.

See Also CANCEL, RESUME

The _TALLY System Variable

Syntax

```
_TALLY
```

Usage This system variable contains the number of records processed by the most recently used table command.

The TAN( ) Function

Syntax

```
TAN(<expN>)
```

Usage This function returns the tangent of an angle. The numeric expression represents the size of the angle in radians. You can use the DTOR( ) function to convert angles from degrees to radians.

See Also ACOS( ), ASIN( ), ATAN( ), COS( ), DTOR( ), RTOD( ), SIN( )

The TIME( ) Function

Syntax

```
TIME([<expN>])
```

Usage This function returns the current time as stored by your computer's internal clock, in a 24-hour format. (For example, 3 P.M. becomes 15:00:00.)

Options If you include any number <expN> within the TIME( ) function, time will be returned using a figure that includes hundredths of a second, but actually this function is accurate only to about 1⁄18 of a second. A more accurate function is SECONDS( ), which returns time to the nearest thousandth of a second.

See Also DATE( )

The TOTAL Command

Syntax

```
TOTAL TO <file name> ON <key field>
     [<scope>]
     [FIELDS <field list>]
     [FOR <expL1>]
```

```
[WHILE <expL2>]
[NOOPTIMIZE]
```

Usage This command lets you create a new table that contains totals of the Numeric fields of the table that is open in the currently active work area.

By default, the totals are given for all records that have the same value in the key field that is specified. For example, assuming there is a State field in the table, if you TOTAL ON STATE, the new file you create will have a record for each state in the original file, and that record will include the totals of all the Numeric fields in the original file's records from that state.

For this command to work properly, the file must be sorted on the key field or must be indexed on the key field and have that index specified as the controlling index that determines the order of the records.

Options If a scope clause is used, only the records that fall in the specified scope are included in the totals. If a FOR or WHILE clause is used, only the records that meet some logical criterion are included in the totals.

By default, all numeric fields are totaled, but if you include the FIELDS <field list> clause, only the fields you specify will be totaled.

The NOOPTIMIZE option for this command disables the Rushmore technology, which normally speeds up data access when you use a FOR statement containing fields in existing indexes. You can disable Rushmore with the NOOPTIMIZE option on a number of Visual FoxPro for Windows commands, but in this case there is little reason to do so.

See Also AVERAGE, CALCULATE, SUM

▸ The TRIM( ) Function

Syntax

```
TRIM(<expC>)
```

Usage This function returns the specified character expression with trailing blanks removed, something that is often necessary for labels or reports. For example, if two fields, Lastname and Firstname, are both 12 characters long, the expression **? FIRSTNAME+LASTNAME** will return an answer like `Janet       Jones`. You can use the TRIM( ) function to remove the trailing blanks from Janet's first name. The expression **? TRIM(FIRSTNAME)+" "+LASTNAME** will display `Janet Jones`.

The TRIM( ) function is identical to RTRIM( ).

See Also ALLTRIM( ), LTRIM( ), RTRIM( )

▶ The TTOC( ) Function

Syntax

```
TTOC(<expT> [,1] )
```

Usage This function returns a datetime expression in the character data type. It can be used in expressions that concatenate datetime values with values of other data types.

Options If the 1 option is used, the character expression is returned in a form that is appropriate for indexing: yyyy:mm:dd:hh:mm:ss.

See Also CTOD( ), TTOD( )

▶ The TTOD( ) Function

Syntax

```
TTOD(<expT>)
```

Usage This function returns the date of a datetime expression in the date data type. If the datetime expression includes only a time, it returns the date 12/20/1899.

See Also CTOT( ), TTOC( )

▶ The TYPE Command

Syntax

```
TYPE <file name 1>
     [AUTO]
     [WRAP]
     [TO PRINT [PROMPT] ¦ TO FILE <file name 2>]
     [NUMBER]
```

Usage This command displays the contents of a text file on the screen or in the front output window. The file's full name, including its extension, must be used.

Options The AUTO option turns on automatic indentation. If you also include the WRAP option, all wrapped text in a paragraph is indented by the same amount as the first line of the paragraph.

Using the TO PRINT option sends the contents of the file to the printer, and using the TO FILE <file name 2> option sends it to the file whose name is specified. If the PROMPT option is included, Visual FoxPro will display the Print dialog box before printing. This option must come immediately after the TO PRINTER option.

The NUMBER option adds a line number at the beginning of each line of the output. By using it in combination with TO FILE <file name 2>, you can create a second file that is identical to the first except that its lines are numbered.

This command is similar to the DOS command TYPE.

▶ The TYPE( ) Function

Syntax

```
TYPE(<expC>)
```

Usage This function evaluates a character expression that is the name of a field or variable and returns its data type. It uses the following one-character codes to represent data types:

- C: Character
- N: Numeric, Float, Double, or Integer
- Y: Currency
- D: Date
- T: DateTime
- L: Logical
- M: Memo
- O: Object
- G: General
- U: Undefined

See Also EVALUATE( )

▶ The UPDATE Command

Syntax

```
UPDATE ON <field name 1> FROM <table name>
     REPLACE <field name 2> WITH <expr 1>
```

```
[, <field name 3> WITH <expr 2>]
[...]
[RANDOM]
```

Usage This command updates the table that is open in the currently selected work area by replacing the contents of specified fields with data from another table that is open in another work area.

Options ON <field name 1> specifies a common field used to indicate which records in the current table are equivalent to which records in the table you are updating from. The two tables must have a single common field, and the current table must be indexed or sorted in ascending order on this field.

FROM <table name> specifies the name of the table you are updating from. This must be open in another work area

REPLACE <field name 2> WITH <expr 1> specifies the field in the current table whose values are being changed and expression that its current values are being replaced with. This expression is usually the name of a field from the other table or is based on a field from the other table.

The <field name 3> WITH <expr 2> ... option indicates that multiple fields can be updated with a single command. Include a list of all the fields to be updated and all the expressions to update them with, separated by commas.

The RANDOM option must be used if the update table is not indexes or sorted in ascending order on the common field. Performance is faster if the update table is indexed or sorted. If the update table is not indexed or sorted and the RANDOM option is omitted, the update may give incorrect results.

The UPPER( ) Function

Syntax

```
UPPER(<expC>)
```

Usage This function returns the specified character expression with all alphabetic characters capitalized. It does not affect any nonalphabetic characters in the character expression.

See Also LOWER( ), PROPER( )

► The USE Command

Syntax

```
USE [<table> | ?]
     [IN <expN>]
     [AGAIN]
     [INDEX <index file list> | ?]
     [ORDER [<expN> | <.IDX index file> | [TAG] <tag
         name>
          [OF <.CDX file>]
     [ASCENDING | DESCENDING]]]
     [ALIAS <alias>]
     [EXCLUSIVE]
     [SHARED]
     [NOUPDATE]
```

Usage In its basic form, this command opens the specified table in the current work area. If another file is open in that work area already, that file is closed.

If it is used with a ? instead of with a file name, this command displays a scrollable list to let the user choose among available tables.

The command USE by itself simply closes any table that is already open in the current work area without opening a new one.

Options The IN <expN> option opens the table in the work area whose number is specified instead of in the current work area, closing any file that is already open in that work area. You can also use the clause IN 0 to open the file in the lowest-numbered work area that does not have a file already opened in it.

The AGAIN option lets you open the same table simultaneously in several work areas.

The INDEX option opens the specified index files as well as the table. These index files must have been created previously. The first index file in the list is the main index, which sets the order of the records, and all index files in the list are updated to reflect changes made in the table.

The ORDER option lets you designate a controlling index (master index) file or tag using either individual (IDX) or compound (DDX) index files.

The ASCENDING | DESCENDING options allow you to specify whether indexed records will appear in ascending or descending order. The default is ASCENDING.

The ALIAS option lets you give the file a second name. If it has an alias name, the file can be referred to by this alias as well as by its name or by the letter or number of its work area.

The EXCLUSIVE option opens a table for exclusive use on a network. The SHARED option opens a table for shared use on a network.

The NOUPDATE option prevents the user from making any changes to the table.

See Also CREATE, MODIFY STRUCTURE

▶ The VAL( ) Function

Syntax

```
VAL(<expC>)
```

Usage This function returns the specified character expression in the Numeric data type, so it can be used in calculations. It reads the character expression from left to right, ignoring leading blanks, and continues to read it until it reaches a character that is not numeric; thus, it returns the value of the number to the left of any nonnumeric character in the expression. If the first character of the expression, apart from leading blanks, is nonnumeric, it returns 0.

See Also STR( )

▶ The WAIT Command

Syntax

```
WAIT [<expC>] [TO <memvar>]
     [WINDOW [NOWAIT]]
     [TIMEOUT <expN>]
```

Usage Used by itself, the command WAIT displays the message `Press any key to continue...` and causes program execution to pause until the user presses a key.

Options If the optional character expression is included, it is used as a prompt instead of the default message mentioned above.

If the TO option is used, the key the user presses is stored in the memory variable that is specified. Thus, the user can input a keystroke without having to press Enter afterward. For example, the command "WAIT 'Enter your answer now:' TO answer" displays the prompt `Enter your answer now` and accepts the user's choice to a variable called "answer".

If the specified memory variable does not already exist, Visual FoxPro creates it. If the user presses ↵ or a nonprintable character, the memory variable is assigned the NULL character (ASCII character 0).

The WINDOW option displays the WAIT message in the System message window in the upper right of the screen.

The NOWAIT option, used in conjunction with the WINDOW option, allows you to create a WAIT WINDOW message resembling Visual FoxPro system messages.

The TIMEOUT option lets you specify how long the WAIT message will remain on the screen without any response from the user.

See Also ACCEPT, INPUT

► The WCOLS( ) Function

Syntax

```
WCOLS([<window name>])
```

Usage This function returns the number of columns available in the currently active window. This function can be used in combination with @ ... SAY ... GET to ensure that the location of screen output is in the active window.

Options If the optional <window name> is included, the function returns the number of columns in the window that is specified.

See Also @ ... SAY ... GET, COL( ), PCOL( ), PROW( ), ROW( ), SCOLS( ), SROWS( ), WROWS( )

► The _WIZARD System Variable

Syntax

```
_WIZARD = <expC>
```

Usage This system variable specifies the name of the program that is used when you run Visual FoxPro Wizards. By default, its value is WIZARD.APP, the Wizard program that comes with Visual FoxPro. Change it if you create a custom Wizard program.

See Also CREATE MENU

The WROWS( ) Function

Syntax

```
WROWS([<window name>])
```

Usage This function returns the number of rows available in the currently active window. This function can be used in combination with @ ... SAY ... GET to ensure that the location of screen output is in the active window.

Options If the optional <window name> is included, the function returns the number of rows in the window that is specified.

See Also @ ... SAY ... GET, COL( ), PCOL( ), PROW( ), ROW( ), SCOLS( ), SROWS( ), WCOLS( )

The YEAR( ) Function

Syntax

```
YEAR(<expD ¦ expT>)
```

Usage This function returns the year of the specified date or datetime expression.

See Also DAY( ), MONTH( )

The ZAP Command

Syntax

```
ZAP
```

Usage This command removes all records from a table, leaving only the table structure; this data cannot be recovered. It is equivalent to entering the command DELETE ALL and then the command PACK, except that it works more quickly. If SAFETY is SET OFF, it will not warn you before deleting all your data permanently.

Needless to say, it should be used with great caution. It is useful primarily in programming to eliminate data from temporary files after it has been added to a permanent file.

See Also DELETE, PACK

APPENDIX C

The Visual FoxPro Desktop Utilities

▶▶ *Visual FoxPro* comes with a number of built-in utilities, including a Calendar/Diary, a Calculator, and a file management utility. These features are not accessible through the menu system, but you can use them through the Command window. They are very handy if you are developing applications or customizing the menu system, since you can add a menu option with just a single line of code to let the user access one of these utilities—a very easy way to make your applications more impressive.

You display the calculator or calendar by using variations on the ACTIVATE WINDOW <window name> command, and you display the file management utility by using the command FILER.

▶▶ The Calculator

Use the command **ACTIVATE WINDOW CALCULATOR** to call up the Calculator, shown in Figure C.1.

The Calculator is used like many pocket calculators, so it is easy to learn. If you are using the mouse, you simply click the numbers or operators you want to use, just as you would press the buttons of a calculator. If you are using the keyboard, you just press the key of any number or operator that is represented on your keyboard; for functions that are not represented by a single key on the keyboard, use the keys shown in Table C.1.

The functions of the calculator keys may be familiar to you.

The number keys and the decimal point are, of course, used to enter numbers. Simply type the number, and it appears on the display panel at the top of the Calculator.

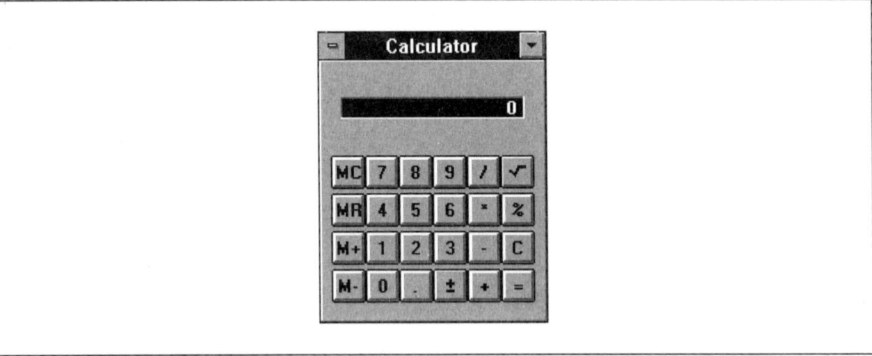

FIGURE C.1

The Visual FoxPro Calculator

TABLE C.1: *Special Keys for Using the FoxPro Calculator with the Keyboard*

Key	Function	Calculator Equivalent
Q	Square root	√
N	Plus/minus	±
A	Add to memory value	M+
S	Subtract from memory value	M–
R	Recall value from memory	MR
Z	Clear menory	MC

The arithmetic operator keys +, –, *, and / are used to indicate addition, subtraction, multiplication, and division. To perform these operations, type the first number, then type the operator (when you type the operator, the first number you type is highlighted in the display panel to indicate that it is fully entered, and the operator you type appears to its right), and then type the second number. Once the second number is on the display panel, type = to complete the calculation.

To find a square root, first type the number. When it is displayed correctly, use the square root operator. The result is displayed immediately in the display panel.

The percent operator lets you perform operations that use some percentage of the number in the display panel. For example, to find a number 10 percent larger than a given number, first type the given number, and when it is in the display panel, type +, then type 10, and then use %. A number 10 percent larger than the original number is displayed.

The ± *(plus/minus)* operator changes the sign of the number that is displayed; it is equivalent to multiplying the number by –1. Just use this operator, and the sign of the value that is displayed changes instantly.

C clears the value from the display area. If you have pressed an operator key and there is an operator displayed to the right of the value, then you must use C twice to remove the operator as well as the number.

The MC, MR, M+ and M– buttons let you temporarily store values in the Calculator's memory and work with those values. When a value is stored in memory, an *M* appears to the left of the display panel.

To store the value that is currently displayed in the display panel, simply use M+. An *M* appears to the left of the display panel to indicate that there is a number stored in memory. To recall the number from memory, use MR. The value in memory appears in the display panel, overwriting any value that is currently displayed. To clear the value that is in memory, use MC. The value is cleared and the *M* to the left of the display panel disappears.

The M+ and M– keys are used to add or subtract from the number that is in memory. For example, if you want to subtract 10 from the value in memory, enter 10, and then use M–.

►► The Calendar/Diary

Use the command ACTIVATE WINDOW CALENDAR to call up the Calendar/Diary window and add the Diary menu to the menu system, as shown in Figure C.2.

Whenever you select the Calendar/Diary, the calendar is displayed by default with the current date highlighted, and any entry for that date in the diary is shown in the Diary panel (the right half of the window). Selecting dates on the calendar lets you see existing diary entries and make entries in the diary for those dates. The diary entry is thus associated with the calendar date and is displayed when that date is selected.

FIGURE C.2

The Calendar/Diary window and the Diary menu

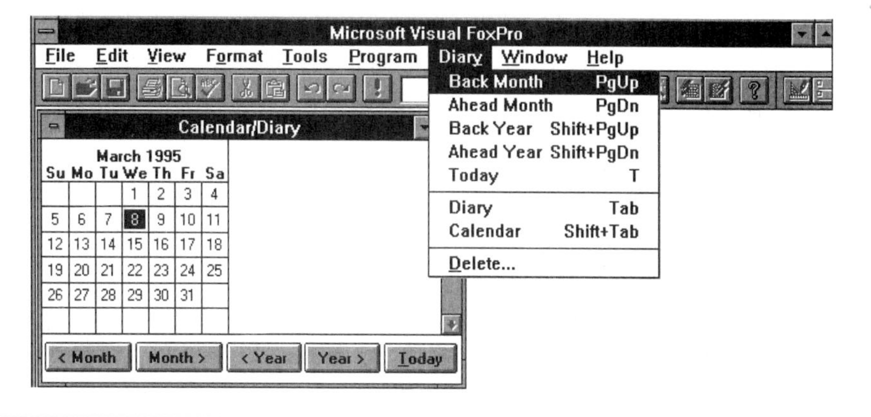

If there is an entry for a given day, that date appears on the calendar in enhanced display.

TIP

You can control which date is displayed when you open the calendar by changing the value of the _DIARY system variable. For more information, see the entry on that variable in Appendix B.

When you begin, the Calendar is selected. The name of the month is highlighted in the Calendar panel when the Calendar is active, and the cursor appears in the Diary panel when the Diary is active. You can move between the two in the following ways:

- Press Tab to move to the Diary panel and press Shift+Tab to move to the Calendar panel.
- Choose Diary ➤ Diary to move to the Diary panel and choose Diary ➤ Calendar to move to the Calendar panel.
- Using the mouse, simply click the panel you want to move to.

When the Diary panel is active, use the usual editing techniques to make diary entries. They may be of any length, and you can scroll through them in the usual ways or resize the Calendar/Diary window to see more of an entry.

► Moving among Dates

When the Calendar panel is active, move among the days of the current month by using the arrow keys or simply by clicking the day you want. To move to a different month, use the buttons at the bottom of the Calendar panel, the corresponding options on the Diary menu, or the hot keys, as follows:

- The < Month button, the menu option Diary ➤ Back Month, or the PgUp key moves you back a month.
- The Month > button, the menu option Diary ➤ Ahead Month, or the PgDn key moves you forward a month.
- The < Year button, the menu option Diary ➤ Back Year, or the Shift+PgUp key combination moves you back a year.
- The Year > button, the menu option Diary ➤ Ahead Year, or the Shift+PgDn key combination moves you forward a year.

In addition, the Today button, the menu option Diary ➤ Today, or the T key moves you back to the current date, no matter where you are in the calendar when you select it.

► Deleting Entries

The Diary ➤ Delete option lets you delete *all entries* in the Diary *prior to* the date selected on the calendar. It presents you with a warning before deleting this data to avoid deleting data by mistake.

Use conventional Windows editing techniques to delete the entry for a single day.

►► Puzzle

You can use the command ACTIVATE WINDOW PUZZLE to display the puzzle shown in Figure C.3.

FIGURE C.3

The Puzzle window

As you can see, this puzzle is similar to those you work by hand by sliding numbered tiles to rearrange them in numeric order. The difficulty is that there is only one empty space to slide the tiles in, so only the tiles immediately adjacent to this space can be moved.

Select the Shuffle button to rearrange the numbers in random order. Click any tile that is adjacent to an empty space to slide it into that space. Alternatively, use an arrow key to move the tiles adjacent to the empty space; for example, press ↓ to move the arrow above the empty space into the space. You can unshuffle the numbers immediately by pressing the "instant winner" key, Ctrl+End.

►► The Filer

The Filer is a file management utility that can perform most of the functions of the Windows or DOS operating systems. It has some capabilities that are greater than those of the Windows File Manager.

The Filer has two windows, named Files and Tree. The Files window lets you work with individual files, and the Tree window lets you work with the entire subdirectory system to manipulate all the files in a directory or a group of directories. You can view only one window at a time, and when either is displayed, a button in the lower-right corner (labeled either Files or Tree) lets you toggle to the other.

Start the Filer by entering FILER in the Command window. When you first start the Filer, the Files Window appears.

▸ The Files Window

The Files window, shown in Figure C.4, is the default window of the Filer.

FIGURE C.4 ▸

The Files window

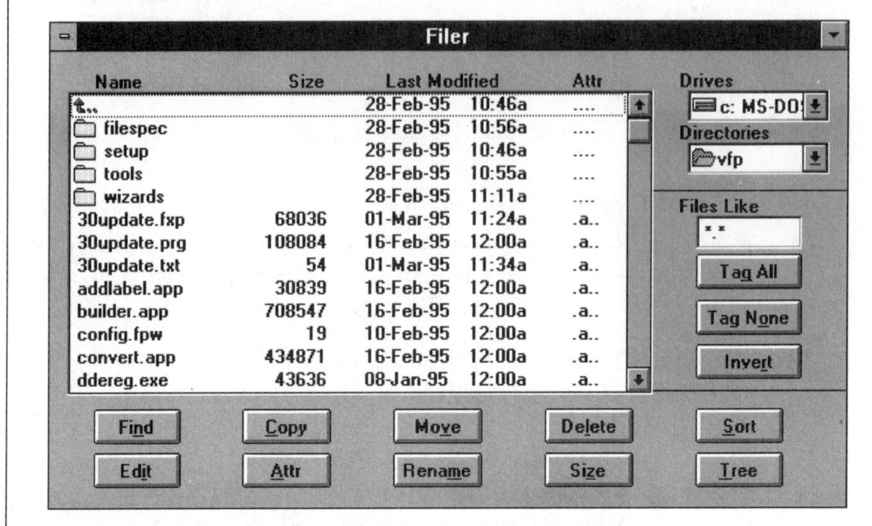

Moving among Directories and Files

The Files window contains a scrollable list of files and Drives and Directories drop-down controls that are very similar to the ones you have seen elsewhere in Visual FoxPro—for example, in the Open and Save As dialog boxes.

As in these other dialog boxes, the scrollable list of files in the Filer includes, in addition to the names of the files in the current directory, the names of all the child directories that are under the current directory. A File Folder icon is displayed to the left of the child directories, and two dots with an arrow to their left at the top of the list represent the parent directory of the current directory. By selecting parent or child directories, you can move up and down through the entire directory system.

This scrollable list also contains other details about the file, which are not included in similar file lists you have seen in Visual FoxPro. In addition to a file's name and extension, the Filer's scrollable list includes the file's size (in bytes) and the date and time it was last modified. Finally, in the column at its far right, the Filer's scrollable list includes the files' attributes; these determine such things as whether a file can be written to or is read-only. You can change attributes using the Attr button. Attributes are discussed later in this appendix.

The two drop-down controls in the Filer also work like the drop-down controls you have seen in the Open and Save As dialog boxes. The Drives control lets you change the drive; for example, you can select A: to make floppy disk drive A the current drive. The Dir drop-down control lets you move quickly through a directory structure that is many levels deep.

The text box labeled Files Like (under the Dir drop-down control) lets you display only those files in the current directory that match a filename pattern or extension you specify. The default setting for Files Like is *.*, which displays all files, but you can specify files to be displayed by using literal characters in combination with the following two wildcard characters:

- * represents any series of characters
- ? represents any single character

The file name and extension are two different words, so *.* represents any name followed by any extension. If you wanted to list only your Visual FoxPro database files, you could enter ***.DBF** in this text box, so that files with any name followed by the DBF extension would be listed. If you have a group of files whose names begin with J, you could list them all by entering **J??????.*** or **J*.*** in this text box.

You can combine more than one specification in this box if you separate them with semicolons. For example, you could enter the specification ***.DBF;*.DBT;*.FPT** to list all database files and any associated memo files (including both Visual FoxPro and the older Xbase-compatible memo files). Do not leave a space after the semicolon.

Tagging Files

The process of tagging files is the key to using the Filer. *Tagging* a file simply means selecting a file in such a way as to highlight it permanently—or until you explicitly remove the tag. Most buttons or menu selections in the Filer work only on files that are tagged. If no file is tagged when you select such an option, it simply displays an error message.

Tagging Files Using the Keyboard To tag an individual file using the keyboard, move the highlight to it and press the spacebar.

Since you generally want to perform commands on a single file, tagging one file normally eliminates any tag you previously put on another file. If you want to tag more than one file while selecting files individually, press Ctrl plus the spacebar to create a new tag, and the tags you created previously will not be eliminated.

To tag multiple files in Visual FoxPro for Windows, first tag the file at one end of the series of files you want tagged. Then move the highlight to the file at the other end of the series of files and press Shift plus the spacebar. All the files between the two will be tagged.

If a file is already tagged, moving the highlight to it and pressing Ctrl plus the spacebar eliminates the tag.

Tagging Files Using the Mouse To tag an individual file using the mouse, just point to the file and click. To tag more than one file, hold down the Ctrl key when you select later files. To tag consecutive files, tag the file at one end of the series and hold down Shift while you click the file at the other end.

To untag a file using the mouse, press Ctrl and click the file. If it is already tagged, the tag disappears.

Tagging Groups of Files The Filer also contains three buttons that let you tag and untag groups of files:

- **Tag All:** Tags all the files that are displayed in the scrollable list. This option is most useful in combination with the Files Like text box. For example, enter ***.DBF** in the Files Like text box so that your database files are displayed; then select Tag All to tag all the database files.

- **Tag None:** Removes tags from all files in all directories. Unlike Tag All, Tag None does not work only on displayed files; it works on all files in all directories. Use it to make sure you do not have any files tagged that you do not know about.

- **Invert:** Removes tags from all tagged files, and tags all untagged files in the current directory. For example, if you want to delete all except the database files in the current directory, you can tag the database files and then select Invert. The database files will be untagged and all the other files will be tagged, at which point you can select Delete.

You can also tag more than one file at a time by selecting the Find button, described in the next section.

Find

Selecting the Find button calls up the Find Files dialog box, shown in Figure C.5.

FIGURE C.5

The Find Files dialog box

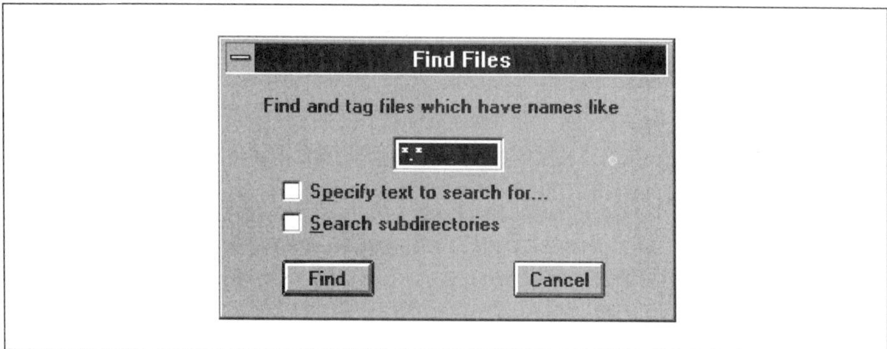

The Find Files dialog box lets you tag files based on either name or content. It can search in just the current directory or in a number of directories.

The simplest way to use Find is to fill in the text box in the same way you do the Files Like text box of the Filer dialog box. As you can see in Figure C.5, this box contains *.* by default, which means it matches all files unless you instruct it to do otherwise. You can fill it out with the wildcard characters (* and ?) and literal characters just as with the Files Like text box.

But the Find Files dialog box does more than the Files Like text box; you can select its Search Subdirectories check box to find matching files in all subdirectories under the current directory. To search all the directories in the current drive, just make the root directory the current directory before beginning the search. For example, if you make the root directory the current directory, enter ***.DBF** in the text box, and check the Search Subdirectories check box, you can tag all the database files in all the directories of the current disk drive.

You can also use Find to search text files. It will tag those that contain text you specify. If you select the Specify Text To Search For check box, you will call up the dialog box shown in Figure C.6.

FIGURE C.6

Tagging files based on content

There are three text boxes under the words *of the following strings* where you can fill in the character strings you want to search for. The Any and All radio buttons are useful if you fill in more than one of these text boxes; they let you specify whether the file or files should be tagged if they contain any of the strings you specified or only if they contain all the strings you specified.

The Ignore Case check box lets you determine whether the search will tag a file if the capitalization of the characters in the file is different from the capitalization in the string you specified. As you can see, the search ignores capitalization by default.

Checking the Match Words check box makes the search tag a file only if the string that matches your specification is a separate word, not embedded in some larger word. If you were looking for the word *id,* for example, you would want to check this check box so the program does not tag files that contain words such as *slid, idiom,* and *widget.*

Consider an example that combines several capacities of Find—tagging all the Visual FoxPro PRG programs in your hard disk that contain the name of the Emplist table. First, you can move to the root directory of your hard disk. Then select Find to call up the Find Files dialog box, and enter ***.PRG** in its text box. Check the Search Subdirectories check box, check the Specify Text to Search For check box to call up the second dialog box, and enter Emplist in its text box as the string to search for, and select OK to return to the Find Files dialog box. Finally, select Find to tag the matching files.

As you will see, you can use the Filer to perform operations on all of these files after they are tagged. For example, you can delete, copy, or even edit all of them at once.

Copy

If there are any files tagged, you can select the Copy button to call up the Copy Files dialog box, shown in Figure C.7.

FIGURE C.7

The Copy Files dialog box

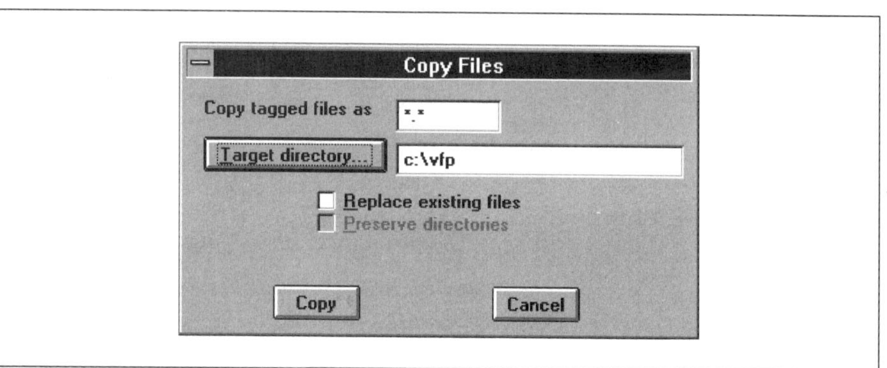

This dialog box lets you copy tagged files. Copying a file preserves the original file and creates a duplicate of it that either has another name or is in another location. Remember that the files you plan to copy must be tagged before you call up the Copy Files dialog box.

The Copy Tagged Files As text box, at the top of this dialog box, lets you specify the name of the new file. The default, *.*, keeps the original name of the file. You can change the name by adding literals instead of the wildcard characters. For example, if you want to make backups of tagged files, you can enter ***.BAK** in this text box; all the tagged files will be copied to files with the same name and the BAK extension.

The Target Directory button and text box let you specify the directory in which to store the copies. Selecting this button calls up the Target Directory dialog box, where you can select the target directory just as you do when you use the familiar Open or Save As dialog box.

You can see in Figure C.7 that the default directory is the current directory and the default entry for the files' names is *.*, which gives the new files the same names as the originals. You must change one of these defaults. You can copy files to another directory or disk while keeping their current names, or you can copy files in the current directory with different names, but you cannot have two files with the same name in the same directory.

If you check the Replace Existing Files check box of this dialog box, the files produced by the COPY command overwrite existing files of the same names without giving you any warning. If you do not check this check box, the command displays an alert before it overwrites a file. After you select Yes or No to determine whether that file will be overwritten, the command copies the rest of the tagged files. You can also select Cancel to cancel the copying.

If you check the Preserve Directories check box, the command copies the directory structure as well as the files that are tagged. If this check box is not checked, tagged files from various subdirectories are all copied into a single subdirectory. This feature, which lets you work with multiple directories, as explained in the section "The Tree Window" later in this appendix.

Move

Selecting the Move button calls up the Move Files dialog box, shown in Figure C.8.

FIGURE C.8

The Move Files dialog box

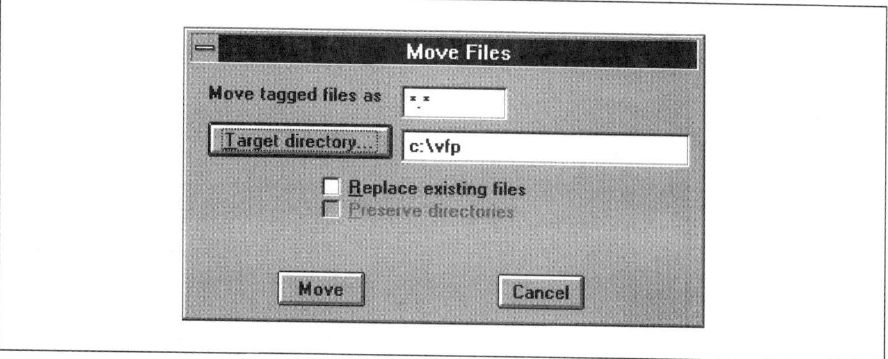

Move is like Copy, and the features of its dialog box function in the same way, except for one point. Copy creates a copy of the file and preserves the original; Move creates a copy of the file and eliminates the original. The effect is that the file is moved from its current location to the specified location; it is not just copied there.

Delete

Selecting the Delete button calls up the Delete Files dialog box, shown in Figure C.9.

FIGURE C.9

The Delete Files dialog box

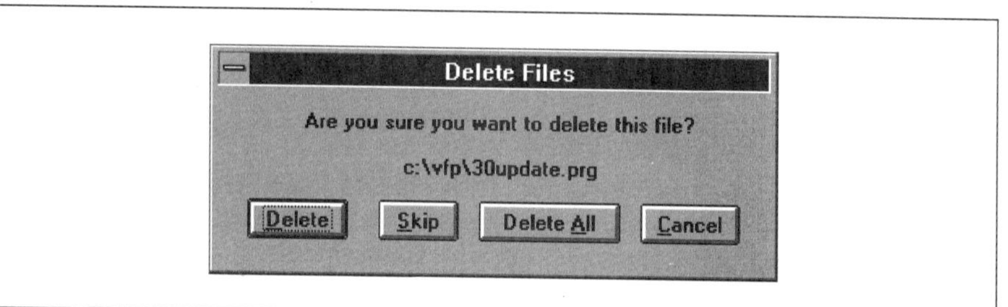

This dialog box asks you to confirm that you want to delete each of the tagged files. Select Delete to delete the file whose name is displayed. Select Skip to retain the file whose name is displayed; the dialog box then asks you about deleting any other tagged files. Select Delete All to avoid this file-by-file confirmation process and delete all tagged files immediately. You can also select Cancel to cancel the command.

Sort

Selecting the Sort button calls up the Sort Files dialog box, shown in Figure C.10.

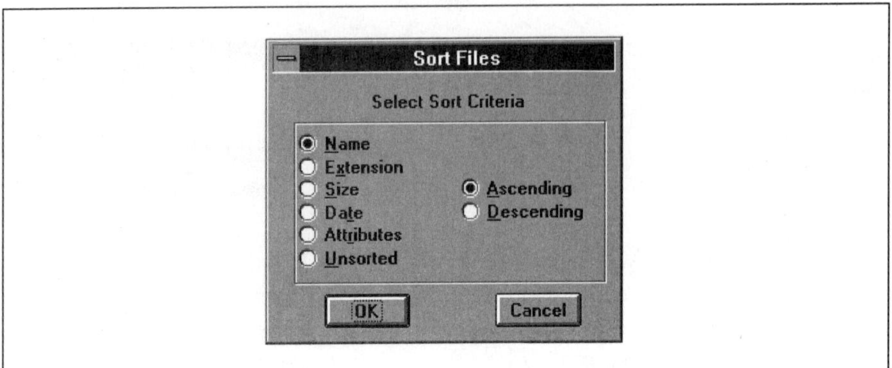

FIGURE C.10
The Sort Files dialog box

This dialog box lets you change the order in which files are displayed in the Filer's scrollable list. As you can see, the radio buttons Name and Ascending are selected by default, and so the files are displayed alphabetically by name.

You can also select radio buttons to display the files in the order determined by their extension, size, date, or attributes. (Attributes are discussed later in this appendix.) The most useful of these is Extension; it is often handy to sort by extension so that files of the same type (database files, index files, program files, and so on) are grouped together.

The other two radio buttons let you choose ascending or descending order. You might want to choose Descending in order to have the files with the most recent dates come first, for example.

Edit

Selecting Edit opens edit windows for all tagged files. You might find this useful, for example, if you want to open edit windows for all your program files. You could enter ***.PRG** in the Files Like text box and then select Tag All to tag all program files, and then simply select Edit to open edit windows for all these files. The edit windows will appear to be stacked, and you can call any one forward to work on it.

Attr

Selecting the Attr button calls up the Attributes dialog box, shown in Figure C.11.

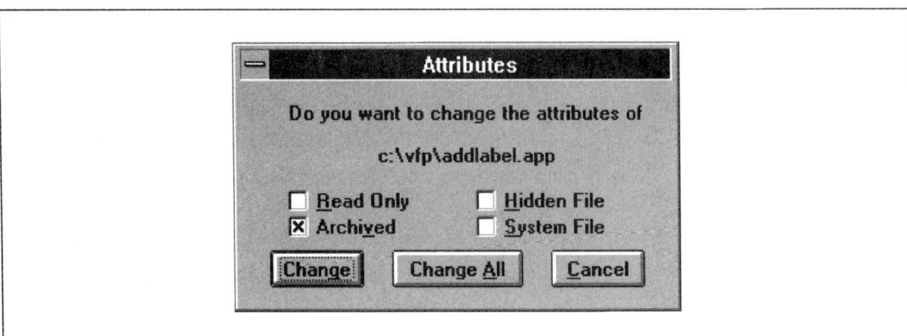

FIGURE C.11

The Attributes dialog box

These attributes are represented by letters in the Attr column of the file list, as follows:

- An *r* in this column means the file is read-only; a user can read the file but cannot delete, edit, or otherwise modify it.
- An *a* in this column means the file is newly created or has been modified since it was last backed up. Most backup programs back up only files that have this attribute and switch this attribute off so they do not copy them again the next time they do a backup. The attribute is switched on again if the file is modified.
- An *h* in this column identifies a hidden file, which does not appear in an ordinary DOS directory. For example, DOS includes two hidden files in the root directory; you cannot see these by using the DOS command DIR or the Windows File Manager, but you can see them, with the *h* attribute, if you use the Filer to look at your root directory.
- An *s* in this column means the file is a system file. There are several key DOS files that are protected with this attribute because they must have a specific location on the disk. The Filer does not let you move, delete, rename, or overwrite a file with this attribute.

You can alter any of these attributes by selecting the appropriate check box. Then, if you select the Change button, Visual FoxPro asks you to confirm that you want to make this change to each of the tagged files. If you select Change All, Visual FoxPro changes all tagged files without this confirmation process.

►► **WARNING**

Changing the system or the hidden attribute can cause later errors that prevent your operating system from working.

Rename

Selecting the Rename button calls up the Rename Files dialog box, shown in Figure C.12.

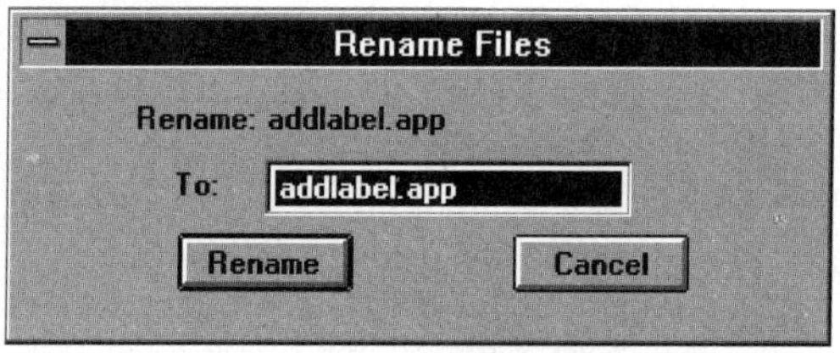

FIGURE C.12

The Rename Files dialog box

To rename a file using this dialog box, simply fill in the new name in the text box and select Rename. The current file name appears in the dialog box by default, in case you want to give the new file a similar name. The dialog box lets you rename all of the tagged files in turn.

If another file already has the new name you want to give to a file, an alert appears, saying you have made an error: You cannot use Rename to give a file a name that is already used. The alert asks you to choose Yes to continue renaming other tagged files or No to cancel the process and return to the Files window.

Size

Selecting the Size button calls up the Size dialog box, shown in Figure C.13.

FIGURE C.13

The Size dialog box

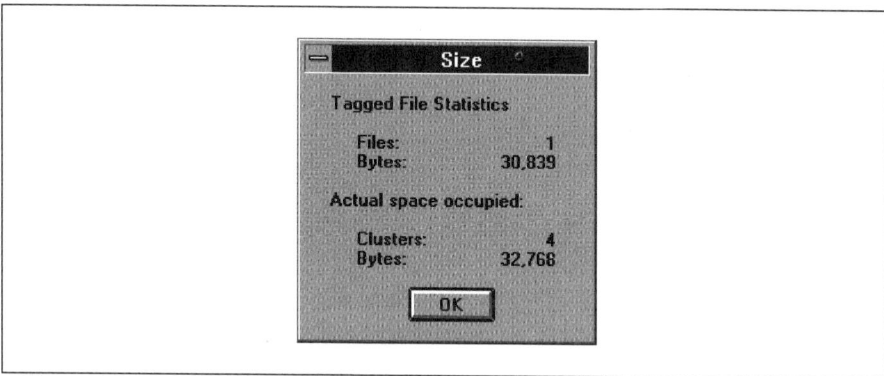

This dialog box simply displays information about tagged files, including the number of files currently tagged, their total size in bytes, and the amount of space they occupy on the disk in clusters and bytes.

The number of bytes the files occupy on the disk is greater than the number of bytes in the files themselves. This is because disk space is broken up into clusters, and files must be allocated some whole number of clusters. You can see in Figure C.13 that although the file itself is only 30,839 bytes in size, it has been allocated four clusters, so it actually takes up 32,768 bytes of space on the disk.

The Tree Window

Selecting Tree, the final button on the lower right of the Files window, displays the Tree window, shown in Figure C.14.

First, Visual FoxPro takes a moment to scan your entire directory structure because it uses this window to work with entire subdirectories and all the files they contain (rather than just with files in the current subdirectory, as the Files window does).

As you can see, this window displays a graphical representation of the directory structure. The C: (or other letter) at the top represents the

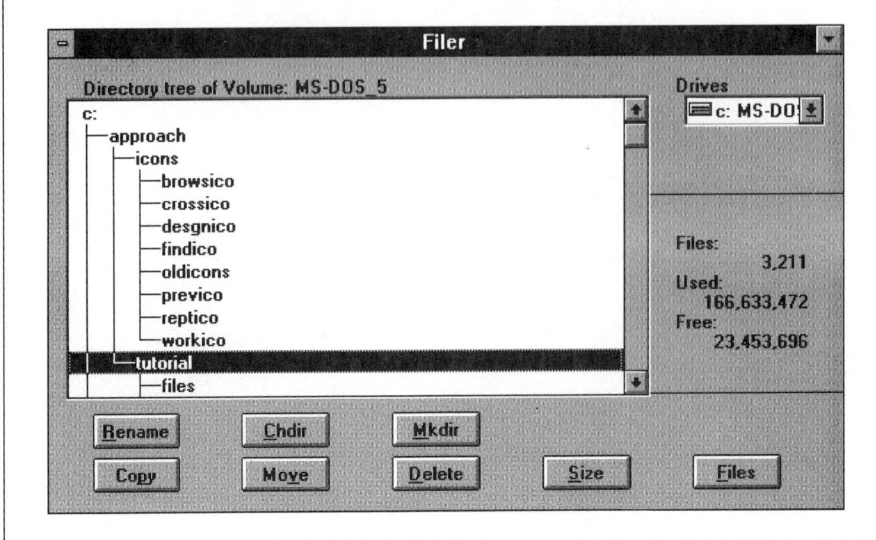

FIGURE C.14

The Tree window

root directory. All of the subdirectories connected directly with it by lines are directly under the root, and their subdirectories are connected to them by lines.

All these directories are in a scrollable list, and you can move the highlight among them as you do in any scrollable list. This window also has a drop-down control that lets you select the drive, and it displays some basic data on the number of files on the disk, the amount of space they use, and the amount of space free.

Tagging Directories

You tag the directories you manipulate with the Tree window using the same techniques as for tagging files in the Files window, as discussed earlier in this appendix.

Rename

Selecting the Rename button calls up the Rename Directory dialog box, shown in Figure C.15.

This dialog box renames the tagged directories and works just like the Rename dialog box in the Files window. Fill in the new name in its text box; the current name appears as the default, in case you want to use a

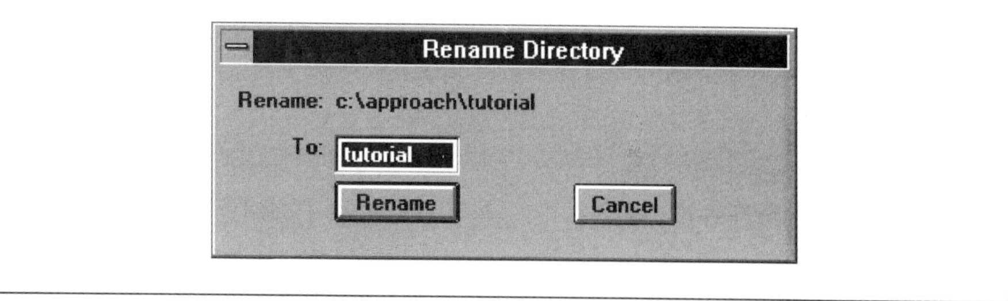

FIGURE C.15

The Rename Directory dialog box

similar name. If multiple subdirectories are tagged, the Filer lets you rename them all in sequence.

Chdir

Selecting the Chdir button lets you change the current directory. Simply tag the directory you want as the current directory, and make this selection. The arrowhead that shows which directory is current moves to indicate the change.

Mkdir

Selecting the Mkdir button calls up the Make Directory dialog box, shown in Figure C.16.

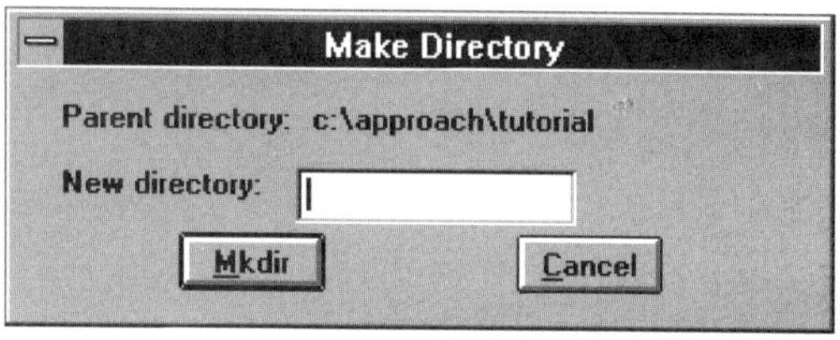

Make Directory
Parent directory: c:\approach\tutorial
New directory:
Mkdir
Cancel

FIGURE C.16

The Make Directory dialog box

To create a new subdirectory under the current directory, simply enter the name you want to give it and select Mkdir.

Copy

Selecting the Copy button calls up the Copy Directory dialog box, shown in Figure C.17.

FIGURE C.17

The Copy Directory dialog box

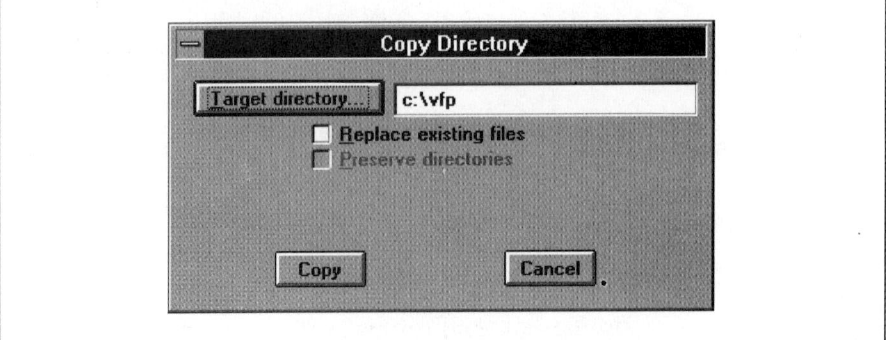

This dialog box is like the one you use to copy files, and it is used the same way, except that it copies all the files of the *directories* that are tagged when you use it from the Tree window.

The Preserve Directories check box becomes useful in this window. If you do not check it, all the files in tagged directories are copied into a single target directory. If you do check it, the Filer reproduces, under the target directory, the structure of tagged subdirectories under the highest tagged directory. The files in the highest tagged directory are copied into the target directory, but files in the subdirectories under it are copied into separate, newly created subdirectories with the same names as their original directories.

Move

Selecting the Move button calls up the Move Directory dialog box, shown in Figure C.18.

FIGURE C.18

The Move Directory dialog box

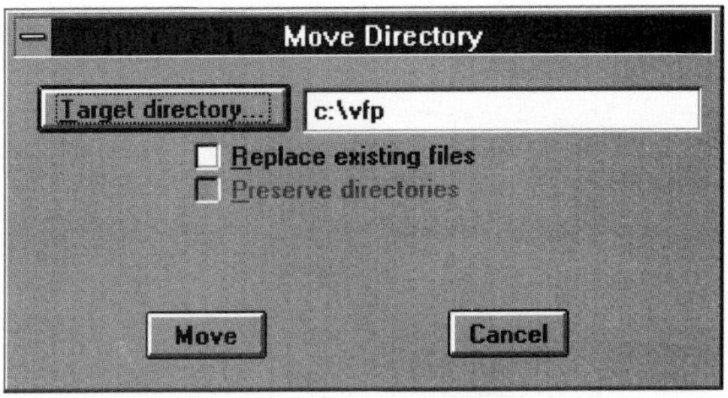

As in the Files window, the Move option of the Tree window is identical to the Copy option, except that the original files are deleted and only the copies in the new locations are left.

Delete

Selecting the Delete button calls up the Delete Directory dialog box, shown in Figure C.19.

FIGURE C.19

The Delete Directory dialog box

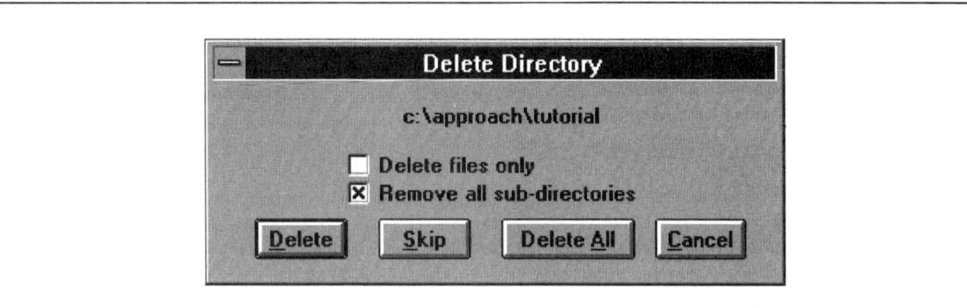

WARNING

Use this feature with extreme caution, as you cannot see the names of the individual files in the directories you are deleting.

This dialog box looks like the one the Files window uses to delete files, but there is one vital difference. The one in the Files window lets you confirm the deletion of each file that is tagged; here you confirm the deletion of each *directory* that is tagged. You can select Delete to confirm the deletion of the directory, or select Skip to skip it and make the Filer continue with the next directory.

You can also delete all tagged directories without confirmation by selecting Delete All.

If the Delete Files Only check box is checked, the files in the specified directories are deleted, but the directories themselves remain (although, of course, they will be empty). By default, the Delete Files Only check box is *not* checked; unless you check it, the files will be deleted *and* the directories themselves removed.

If the Remove All Subdirectories check box is checked, not only the tagged directory but all the subdirectories under it are deleted. You do not need to tag the subdirectories individually; just tag the single directory at the top of the group you want to delete and use this check box.

►► **WARNING**

The fact that this check box is checked by default makes it very dangerous. If you mistakenly tag your root directory and then select Delete All without changing the default setting of the check boxes, the Filer can delete every file and every directory of your hard disk.

Size

Selecting the Size button calls up the Size dialog box, shown in Figure C.20.

FIGURE C.20 ►

The Size dialog box

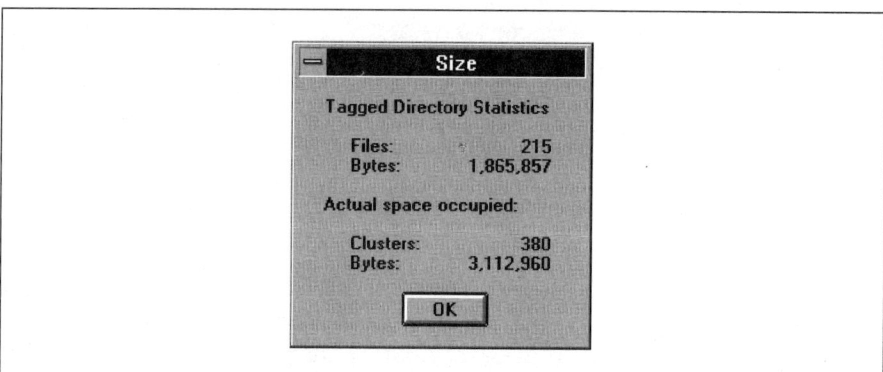

As you can see, this dialog box gives you basic statistics about the number of files in the tagged directories, their total size, and the number of clusters and actual disk space they occupy, just like the dialog box that appears when you select Size from the Files window.

Files

Selecting the Files button on the lower right, or selecting Files Window from the Filer menu, brings you back to the Files window.

▸▸ Index

Note:

Main entries are in **boldface** text. **Boldfaced** numbers indicate pages where you will find the principal discussion of a topic or the definition of a term. *Italic* numbers indicate pages where topics are illustrated in figures.

▸ Numbers and Symbols

B

C

D

E

▶ G

 **H**

I

J

K

L

M

▶ N

O

Q

S

▶ T

U

V

▶ W

X

Y

Z

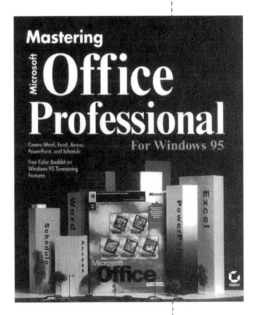

Comprehensive, Organized, and Complete

This completely revised edition reveals new and overlooked ways to reduce work, improve performance, and achieve better results. You'll find highlighted coverage of new features; new chapters on charting, pivot tables, and macros; loads of insider information; and a comprehensive function reference. Includes a pull-out color guide on Windows 95, revealing all the new time-saving features.

1,050 pages
ISBN: 1785-6

SYBEX Inc. • 2021 Challenger Drive • Alameda, CA 94501 • 800-227-2346 • 510-523-8233

PINT-SIZED, BUT PACKED WITH ALL THE RIGHT STUFF

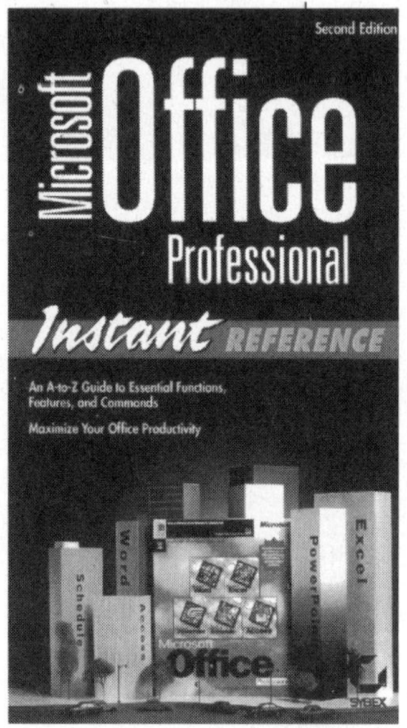

What a find! A compact, yet comprehensive command reference that covers the latest versions of Word, Excel, PowerPoint, Access, and Mail/Schedule. Part one offers a brief overview of each program; part two supplies an alphabetical reference to every command, feature, and function. With notes, tips, and troubleshooting help.

544 pages
ISBN: 1776-7

SYBEX Inc., • 2021 Challenger Drive • Alameda, CA 94501 • 800-227-2346 • 510-523-8233

For Every Computer Question, There Is a Sybex Book That Has the Answer

Each computer user learns in a different way. Some need thorough, methodical explanations, while others are too busy for details. At Sybex we bring nearly 20 years of experience to developing the book that's right for you. Whatever your needs, we can help you get the most from your software and hardware, at a pace that's comfortable for you.

We start beginners out right. You will learn by seeing and doing with our **Quick & Easy** series: friendly, colorful guidebooks with screen-by-screen illustrations. For hardware novices, the **Your First** series offers valuable purchasing advice and installation support.

Often recognized for excellence in national book reviews, our **Mastering** titles are designed for the intermediate to advanced user, without leaving the beginner behind. A **Mastering** book provides the most detailed reference available. Add our pocket-sized **Instant Reference** titles for a complete guidance system. Programmers will find that the new **Developer's Handbook** series provides a more advanced perspective on developing innovative and original code.

With the breathtaking advances common in computing today comes an ever increasing demand to remain technologically up-to-date. In many of our books, we provide the added value of software, on disks or CDs. Sybex remains your source for information on software development, operating systems, networking, and every kind of desktop application. We even have books for kids. Sybex can help smooth your travels on the **Internet** and provide **Strategies and Secrets** to your favorite computer games.

As you read this book, take note of its quality. Sybex publishes books written by experts—authors chosen for their extensive topical knowledge. In fact, many are professionals working in the computer soft-ware field. In addition, each manuscript is thoroughly reviewed by our technical, editorial, and production personnel for accuracy and ease-of-use before you ever see it—our guarantee that you'll buy a quality Sybex book every time.

To manage your hardware headaches and optimize your software potential, ask for a Sybex book.

For More Information, Please Contact:

Sybex Inc.
2021 Challenger Drive
Alameda, CA 94501
Tel: (510) 523-8233 • (800) 227-2346
Fax: (510) 523-2373

Sybex is committed to using natural resources wisely to preserve and improve our environment. As a leader in the computer books publishing industry, we are aware that over 40% of America's solid waste is paper. This is why we have been printing our books on recycled paper since 1982.

This year our use of recycled paper will result in the saving of more than 153,000 trees. We will lower air pollution effluents by 54,000 pounds, save 6,300,000 gallons of water, and reduce landfill by 27,000 cubic yards.

In choosing a Sybex book you are not only making a choice for the best in skills and information, you are also choosing to enhance the quality of life for all of us.

[1647] Mastering Visual FoxPro® 3 Special Edition

GET A FREE CATALOG JUST FOR EXPRESSING YOUR OPINION.

Help us improve our books and get a ***FREE*** full-color catalog in the bargain. Please complete this form, pull out this page and send it in today. The address is on the reverse side.

Name ______________________________ **Company** ______________________

Address ______________________________ **City** __________ **State** ___ **Zip** ______

Phone (   ) ______________

1. How would you rate the overall quality of this book?

- ❑ Excellent
- ❑ Very Good
- ❑ Good
- ❑ Fair
- ❑ Below Average
- ❑ Poor

2. What were the things you liked most about the book? (Check all that apply)

- ❑ Pace
- ❑ Format
- ❑ Writing Style
- ❑ Examples
- ❑ Table of Contents
- ❑ Index
- ❑ Price
- ❑ Illustrations
- ❑ Type Style
- ❑ Cover
- ❑ Depth of Coverage
- ❑ Fast Track Notes

3. What were the things you liked *least* about the book? (Check all that apply)

- ❑ Pace
- ❑ Format
- ❑ Writing Style
- ❑ Examples
- ❑ Table of Contents
- ❑ Index
- ❑ Price
- ❑ Illustrations
- ❑ Type Style
- ❑ Cover
- ❑ Depth of Coverage
- ❑ Fast Track Notes

4. Where did you buy this book?

- ❑ Bookstore chain
- ❑ Small independent bookstore
- ❑ Computer store
- ❑ Wholesale club
- ❑ College bookstore
- ❑ Technical bookstore
- ❑ Other ______________

5. How did you decide to buy this particular book?

- ❑ Recommended by friend
- ❑ Recommended by store personnel
- ❑ Author's reputation
- ❑ Sybex's reputation
- ❑ Read book review in ________
- ❑ Other ______________

6. How did you pay for this book?

- ❑ Used own funds
- ❑ Reimbursed by company
- ❑ Received book as a gift

7. What is your level of experience with the subject covered in this book?

- ❑ Beginner
- ❑ Intermediate
- ❑ Advanced

8. How long have you been using a computer?

years ______________

months ______________

9. Where do you most often use your computer?

- ❑ Home
- ❑ Work
- ❑ Both
- ❑ Other ______________

10. What kind of computer equipment do you have? (Check all that apply)

- ❑ PC Compatible Desktop Computer
- ❑ PC Compatible Laptop Computer
- ❑ Apple/Mac Computer
- ❑ Apple/Mac Laptop Computer
- ❑ CD ROM
- ❑ Fax Modem
- ❑ Data Modem
- ❑ Scanner
- ❑ Sound Card
- ❑ Other ______________

11. What other kinds of software packages do you ordinarily use?

- ❑ Accounting
- ❑ Databases
- ❑ Networks
- ❑ Apple/Mac
- ❑ Desktop Publishing
- ❑ Spreadsheets
- ❑ CAD
- ❑ Games
- ❑ Word Processing
- ❑ Communications
- ❑ Money Management
- ❑ Other ______________

12. What operating systems do you ordinarily use?

- ❑ DOS
- ❑ OS/2
- ❑ Windows
- ❑ Apple/Mac
- ❑ Windows NT
- ❑ Other ______________

13. **On what computer-related subject(s) would you like to see more books?**

14. **Do you have any other comments about this book? (Please feel free to use a separate piece of paper if you need more room)**

PLEASE FOLD, SEAL, AND MAIL TO SYBEX

SYBEX INC.
Department M
2021 Challenger Drive
Alameda, CA
94501

►► Relational Databases

As you'll learn in Part III (Chapters 12–16), Visual FoxPro gives you several ways to work with relational databases. Use the Wizards to create data entry forms, queries, and reports easily, use the View window to open and relate the tables, or use the Query Designer or View Designer to relate the tables visually and generate SQL programming code that you can view and copy into your own programs.

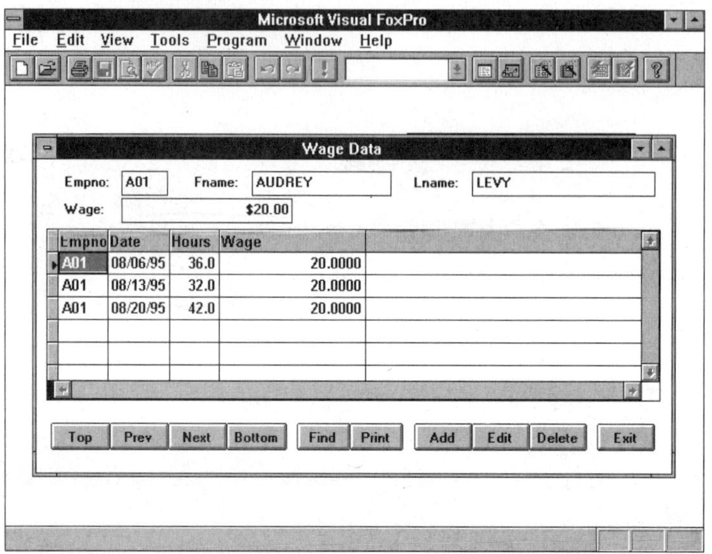

A form created by the One-to-Many Wizard

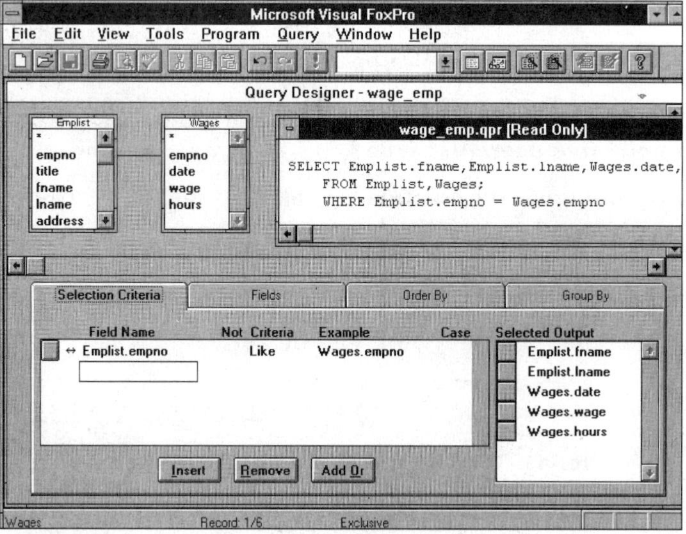

The Query Designer and the SQL code it generates